C000027425

The Southern African Gender Protocol Alliance's vision is an inclusive, equal and just society in the public and private space in accordance with the SADC Protocol on Gender and Development. The Alliance campaigned for the adoption, implementation and review of the SADC Protocol on Gender and Development. The Alliance is now advocating for action and results in the implementation of the Protocol which is aligned to the Sustainable Development Goals (SDGs), Beijing Plus Twenty and the African Union Agenda 2063. The Gender Protocol is the only SADC Protocol with a Monitoring, Evaluation and Results Framework.

Gender Links coordinates the work of the Alliance.

© Copyright 2018
Southern Africa Gender Protocol Alliance
ISBN 978-0-620-80662-6

Gender Links
9 Derrick Avenue
Cyrildene, 2198
Johannesburg, South Africa
Phone: 27 (11) 029 0006
or 27 (11) 028 2410
Email: alliance@genderlinks.org.za
Websites: www.genderlinks.org.za
Twitter: @GenderProtocol
@GenderLinks
FaceBook: Gender Links
Instagram: GenderLinks

Editors: Colleen Lowe Morna,
Lucia Makamure and Danny Glenwright

Design/Layout: Debi Lee

Sponsors: Diakonia, Commonwealth Foundation, Southern Africa Trust, Hivos, AmplifyChange, African Women's Development Fund

Alliance partners
Coordinator
Gender Links
Constitutional and legal rights
Women and Law Southern Africa (WLSA)
Governance
Women in Politics Support Unit (WIPSU)
Sexual and Reproductive Health and Rights
Southern Africa HIV and AIDS Information Dissemination Service (SAfAIDS)
Care work
Voluntary Services Overseas - Regional Aids Initiative South Africa
Climate Change
Gender CCSA
Economic Justice
Zimbabwe Women's Resource Centre Network (ZWRCN)
Angola
Plataforma Mulheres em Acção (PMA)
Botswana
Botswana Council of NGO (BOCONGO)
DRC
Union Congolaise des Femmes des Medias (UCOFEM)
Lesotho
Women and Law in Southern Africa (WLSA-Lesotho)
Madagascar
FPFE Federation Pour la Promotion Feminine et Enfantine
Malawi
NGO Gender Coordinating Network (NGOGCN)
Mauritius
Media Watch Organisation
Mozambique
Forum Mulher
Namibia
Namibia Association of Non-Governmental Organisations Trust
Seychelles
GEMPLUS
South Africa
South African Women in Dialogue SAWID
eSwatini
Coordinating Assembly of Non-Governmental Organizations (CANGO)
Tanzania
Tanzania Gender Network Programme
Zambia
Women and Law in Southern Africa – Zambia
Zimbabwe
Women's Coalition of Zimbabwe
Faith Based Organisations
Norwegian Church AID Southern Africa Office
Men's Groups
Sonke Gender Justice

CONTENTS

ACCORD	Africa Centre for the Constructive Resolution of Disputes	**CRPD**	Convention on the Rights of Persons with Disabilities
ADFD	Abu Dhabi Fund for Development	**DCS**	Domestic Violence, Child Protection and Sexual Offenses
AFCP	Association des Femmes Comoriennes de la Presse	**DFID**	Department for International Development
AfDB	African Development Bank	**DFJ**	Dynamique des Femmes Juristes
AIDS	Acquired Immune Deficiency Syndrome	**DHS**	Demographic and Health Survey
AMCEN	African Ministerial Conference on the Environment	**DIRCO**	Department of International Relations and Cooperation
ANC	African National Congress	**DPP**	Democratic Progressive Party
ANDCH	Africa Nationally Determined Contributions Hub	**DREAMS**	Determined, Resilient, Empowered, AIDS Free, Motivated and Supported
ART	Anti-Retroviral Treatment	**DSD**	Differences of Sexual Development
ARVs	Anti-Retroviral	**DSW**	Department of Social Welfare
AU	African Union	**EAC**	East African Community
AUC	African Union Commission	**EAD**	Department of Energy Affairs
BCP	Botswana Congress Party	**ECA**	Economic Commission for Africa
BDF	Botswana Defence Force	**ECOWAS**	Economic Commission for West Africa States
BDP	Botswana Democratic Party	**ECZ**	Electoral Commission of Zambia
BDPA	Beijing Declaration and Platform for Action	**EIMC**	Early Infant Medical Circumcision
BEAM	Basic Education Assistance Module	**EMBs**	Election Management Bodies
BIUST	Botswana International University of Science and Technology	**ERA**	Employment Rights Act
BNF	Botswana National Front	**EUC**	European Union Commission
BPC	Botswana Power Corporation	**FAO**	Food and Agriculture Organisation
CAP	Capable Partners	**FARDC**	Armed Forces of the Democratic Republic of the Congo
CATS	Community Adolescent Treatment Supporters	**FGM**	Female Genital Mutilation
CCA	Climate Change Adaptation	**FIB**	Force Intervention Brigade
CEDAW	Convention on the Elimination of all forms of Discrimination against Women	**FODSWA**	Federation Organization of the Disabled People in eSwatini
CEO	Chief Executive Officer	**FPTP**	First Past the Post
CGPU	Child and Gender Protection Unit	**GAMAG**	Global Alliance on Media and Gender
COEs	Centres of Excellence	**GAP**	Gender Action Plan
COMESA	Common Market for Eastern and Southern Africa	**GBV**	Gender Based Violence
COPs	Conferences of the Parties	**GBVI**	Gender-based Violence Initiative
CPS	Cash Paymaster Services	**GDP**	Gross Domestic Product
CSA	Climate Smart Agriculture	**GeAD**	Gender Affairs Department
CSC	Citizen Score Card	**GEM**	Gender Equitable Men
CSOs	Civil Society Organisations	**GEMI**	Global Expanded Monitoring Initiative
CSTL	Care and Support for Teaching and Learning	**GGCA**	Global Gender and Climate Alliance
CSW	Commission on the Status of Women	**GHG**	Greenhouse Gas
CTDO	Community Technology Development Organisation	**GW**	Gigawatt
		GIME	Gender in Media Education
CWGL	Centre for Women's Global Leadership	**GL**	Gender Links
CGE	Commission for Gender Equality	**GLM**	Gender Links Mauritius
		GMBS	Gender and Media Baseline Study
		GMC	Gender and Media Connect

GMMP	Global Media Monitoring Project	MDGs	Millennium Development Goals
GMPS	Gender and Media Progress Study	MER	Monitoring, Evaluation and Reporting
GNU	Government of National Unity	MERF	Monitoring, Evaluation and Reporting Framework
GPI	Global Peace Index		
GSIM	Gender-Sensitive Indicators for Media	MHD	Medium Human Development
HIV	Human Immunodeficiency Virus	MK	Mkhonto We Sizwe
HPTN	HIV Prevention Trials Network	MMEWR	Ministry of Minerals, Energy and Water
HPV	Human papilloma virus	MMR	Maternal Mortality Ratio
IAAF	International Association of Athletics Federation	MoU	Memorandum of Understanding
		MP	Member of Parliament
ICBT	Informal Cross Border Trade	MPAs	Marine Protected Areas
ICCPR	International Covenant on Civil and Political Rights	MRG	Mediation Reference Group
		NAP	National Adaptation Plan
ICM	International Confederation of Midwives	NAPAs	National Adaptation Plans of Action
		NAPs	National Action Plans
ICPD	International Conference on Population and Development	NATO	North Atlantic Treaty Organisation
		NCCC	National Climate Change Committee
ICT	Information and Communication Technology	NCCSAP	National Climate Change Policy and Strategy and Action Plan
IDPs	Internally Displaced Persons	NDCs	Nationally Determined Contributions
IEC	Independent Electoral Commission	NDF	Namibia Defence Force
IFASIC	Faculty Institute of Information and Communication Sciences	NDP	Nations Development Programme
		NEPAD	New Partnership for Africa's Development
IFFs	Illicit Financial Flows		
IIED	International Institute for Environment and Development	NGO	Non-Governmental Organisation
		NGP	National Gender Policy
INDC	Intended Nationally Determined Contribution	NSOs	National Statistical Offices
		NSP	National Strategy Plan
IPU	Inter-Parliamentary Union	OAU	Organisation for African Unity
IPV	Intimate Partner Violence	PEI	Planet Earth Institute
IT	Information Technology	PEPFAR	President's Emergency Plan for AIDS Relief
IUDs	Intra-Uterine Devices		
IWMF	International Women's Media Foundation	PGCDs	Police Gender and Children Desks
		PIE	Promoting Inclusive Education
IWRM	Integrated Water Resources Management	PISA	Participatory Initiative for Social Accountability
JMP	Joint Monitoring Programme	PMCT	Prevention of mother-to-child transmission
LAD	Legal Aid Directorate		
LEGABIBO	Lesbians, Gays & Bisexuals of Botswana	PNC	Post Natal Care
LePHIA	Lesotho Population Based HIV Impact Assessment	PR	Proportional Representation
		PrEP	Pre Exposure Prophylaxis
LGBTI	Lesbian, Gay, Bisexual, Transsexual and Intersexual	RC	Regional Commissioner
		REIPPPP	Renewable Energy Independent Power Producer Procurement Programme
LHPP	Lesotho Highlands Power Project		
LSES	Lesotho Solar Energy Society	RG	Registrar General
LUSLM	Lower Usuthu Sustainable Land Management	RISDP	Regional Indicative Strategic Development Plan
MDC	Movement for Democratic Change	RNA	Radio National de Angola
MDC-T	Movement for Democratic Change Tsvangirai	RWPC	Regional Women's Parliamentary Caucus

SABC	South African Broadcasting Corporation	UNPF	United Nations Population Fund
SACMEQ	Southern and Eastern Africa Consortium for Monitoring Educational Quality	UNSCR	United Nations Security Council Resolution
SADC	Southern Africa Development Community	UNWOMEN	United Nations Entity for Gender Equality and the Empowerment of Women
SADC-PF	Southern African Development Community Parliamentary Forum	VAC	Violence against Children
SALRC	South African Law Reform Commission	VAM	Violence against Men
SANDF	South African National Defence Force	VAW	Violence against Women
SAPMIL	SADC Preventive Mission in the Kingdom of Lesotho	VAWG	Violence against Women and Girls
		VAWIE	Violence against Women in Elections
SAPS	South African Police Services	VFR	Victim Friendly Rooms
SAPS	South African Police Services	VMMC	Voluntary Medical Male Circumcision
SARPCCO	Southern African Regional Police Chiefs Cooperation Organisation	WACC	World Association for Christian Communication
SBI	Subsidiary Body for Implementation	WACC	World Association of Christian Communicators
SBSTA	Subsidiary Body for Scientific and Technological Advice	WANIFRA	World Association of Newspapers and News Publisher
SCA	Supreme Court of Appeal	WASH	Water, Sanitation and Hygiene
SDGI	SADC Gender and Development Index	WCoZ	Women's Coalition of Zimbabwe
SDGs	Sustainable Development Goals	WGC	Women and Gender Constituency
SMEs	Small to Medium Enterprises	WHO	World Health Organisation
SRHR	Sexual and Reproductive Health and Rights	WiLGF	Women in Local Government Forum
		WIN	Women in News
STEM	Science, Technology, Engineering and Mathematics	WIPSU	Women in Politics Support Unit
		WISETO	Women in Science, Engineering and Technology Organisation
STIs	Sexually Transmitted Infections		
SWAGGA	eSwatini Action Group against Abuse	WISPI	World Internal Security and Police Index
SWIFT	Sisters Working in Film and Television	WomEng	Women in Engineering
TDF	Tanzania's Defence Force	WPS	Women, Peace and Security
TIP	Trafficking in Persons	WWF	World Wide Fund for Nature
TPA	Televisão Publica de Angola	YONECO	Youth Net and Counselling
TPF Net	Tanzania Police Female Network	ZAMEC	Zambia Media Council
TVPA	Trafficking Victims Protection Act	ZANIS	Zambia News and Information Services
UN	United Nations	ZANU-PF	Zimbabwe African National Union-Patriotic Front
UNDP	United Nations Development Programme		
UNECA	United Nations Economic Commission for Africa	ZCEA	Zambia Civic Education Association
		ZDF	Zimbabwe Defence Forces
UNEP	United Nations Environment Programme	ZGC	Zimbabwe Gender Commission
		ZNASP	Zimbabwe National HIV and AIDS Strategic Plan
UNESCO	United Nations Educational, Scientific and Cultural Organisation		
		ZWRCN	Zimbabwe Women Resource Centre Network
UNFCCC	United Nations Framework Convention on Climate Change		
UNODC	United Nations Office on Drugs and Crime		

CONTRIBUTORS

Colleen Lowe Morna *(South Africa)* is CEO of Gender Links. A South African born in Zimbabwe, Colleen began her career as a journalist specialising in economic and development reporting including as Africa Editor of the New Delhi-based Women's Feature Service. She joined the Commonwealth Secretariat as a senior researcher on the Africa desk in 1991, and later served as Chief Programme Officer of the Commonwealth Observer Mission to South Africa. Colleen subsequently served as founding CEO of the South African Commission on Gender Equality. A trainer, researcher and writer, Colleen has written extensively on gender issues in Southern Africa. She holds a BA degree in International Relations from Princeton University; Masters in Journalism from Columbia University and certificate in executive management from the London Business School. She has received awards from the Woodrow Wilson School of International Relations; the Newswomen's Club of New York and the Mail and Guardian newspaper in South Africa. In 2007, South Africa's Media Magazine named Colleen runner up in the Media Woman of the Year Award. In 2013, CEO magazine named Colleen the "most influential woman" in South Africa and Africa as a whole in the civil society category. A year later the University of Johannesburg awarded Colleen honorary membership of the Golden Key Association that recognises excellence in academia and public service. Colleen has served as editor-in-chief of all ten Barometers.

Lucia Makamure *(Zimbabwe)* is the Alliance and Partnerships Manager at Gender Links. She is a journalist with more than 10 years of experience working on human rights and public policy issues in Southern Africa. Lucia is a 2016 Commonwealth Scholar currently finalising her Master's in Public Policy and Management with the University of York. Lucia managed the authors and design team responsible for producing the 2018 Barometer. She authored the Economic Justice and Data Chapters. She also served as sub-editor and proof reader of several chapters of the Barometer.

Danny Glenwright *(Canada)* is the executive director of Action Against Hunger Canada, an international humanitarian and development organisation specialised in fighting hunger and its underlying causes. He is also the managing editor of *The Philanthropist*, an online journal for practitioners, academics, supporters, and others engaged in the non-profit sector in Canada. A journalist by training, Danny has more than 15 years of experience in the non-profit and media sectors in Canada and internationally - and his work has taken him to more than 55 countries. This includes a stint as Communications Manager at Gender Links in Johannesburg, a role with the United Nations in Palestine, and media training experience in Sierra Leone, Namibia, and Rwanda. Danny holds a Master's degree in international development from Italy's Pavia University. He has written extensively about gender issues, media literacy, and LGBT rights. Glenwright served as co-editor of the 2018 Barometer.

Debbie Budlender *(South Africa)* is an Independent Consultant. Between 1988 and June 2012 she worked as a specialist researcher with the Community Agency for Social Enquiry (CASE): a South African non-governmental organisation working on social policy research. Between April 1997 and March 2002 Debbie was on a long-term part-time secondment to Statistics South Africa, the country's national statistical bureau where she worked on gender, employment, poverty and children's issues. She was also in charge of planning and running the country's first national time use study. Debbie served as the overall coordinator of South Africa's Women's Budget Initiative when it started in 1995. In subsequent years, she has served as consultant on gender-responsive budgeting to non-governmental organisations, governments, parliamentarians and donors in more than thirty-five countries. In this project, Debbie computed the SADC Gender and Development Index (SGDI).

Kubi Rama *(South Africa)* has 25 years-experience working in non-governmental organisations (NGOs) and institutions of higher learning. In that time her main focus has been on media, communication, education, research, training and gender. In her time at Gender Links from 2003 to 2014, Kubi contributed to growing the organisation from four to 60 people with offices in ten countries. In the last three years Rama has spent time understanding and developing monitoring and evaluation systems that move beyond the numbers to measuring change. Rama has contributed to several Barometers as the author of the Gender Based Violence and Constitutional and Legal Rights chapters. Rama is the author of the Education and Training chapter of the 2018 Barometer.

Mukayi Makaya Magarangoma *(Zimbabwe)* joined GL in December 2008. She is currently serving as GL Training and Services Manager. Makaya Magarangoma has over 10 years' experience working in the development and non-governmental sector. A strong feminist passionate about women's rights and empowerment, Makaya Magarangoma is currently studying towards an Honours Degree in Gender Studies with the University of South Africa. She holds a Bachelors in Business Admini-stration degree. Prior to joining Gender Links, Makaya Magarangoma served at the Southern African Research and Documentation Centre (SARDC) in Zimbabwe for over five years. In this barometer she co-authored the Governance chapter and was part of the Editorial team.

Makanatsa Makonese *(Zimbabwe)* holds a PhD in Law from the University of Zimbabwe with a focus on women's law and rights, land law and international human rights law. She is an experienced and highly skilled human rights lawyer who has worked in various countries in the Southern African Development Community (SADC) Region and internationally. Her passion lies in using the law, national constitutions and international human rights frameworks to promote human rights, the rule of law, equality, access to justice and good governance. She has worked as the Executive Secretary/Chief Executive Officer of the SADC Lawyers Association (Botswana and South Africa), a Senior Environmental Lawyer

and Gender Programme Coordinator for the Zimbabwe Environmental Law Association, an Advocacy Officer for the Child Protection Society in Zimbabwe and as a Magistrate in Zimbabwe. She is currently the Executive Secretary/ Chief Executive Officer of the Zimbabwe Human Rights Commission, the National Human Rights Institution for the Republic of Zimbabwe.

Linda Musariri-Chipatiso *(Zimbabwe)* joined GL in 2013 as the GBV Indicators Research Officer. As a Hewlett Fellow, Musariri-Chipatiso holds a Master of Arts degree in Demography and Population Studies from the University of Witwatersrand. She holds a BA Honours degree in Theatre Arts from the University of Zimbabwe. Linda is currently studying for her PHD degree at the University of Amsterdam. She has contributed to five of the seven GBV Indicators Studies conducted by GL and partner organisations and governments. Linda wrote the Gender Based Violence chapter.

Lynette Mudekunye *(Zimbabwe/ South Africa)* is public health professional who is an Advisor with REPSSI, a regional organisation providing technical support to psychosocial support for children and youth in 13 countries of East and Southern Africa. She has worked in the Health, HIV and AIDS sectors in Zimbabwe, South Africa and in the region. She wrote the Health, HIV and AIDS chapters, under the guidance of SAfAIDS.

SAfAIDS (SADC) is a regional non-profit organisation whose vision is to ensure that all people in Africa realise their sexual and reproductive health rights (SRHR) and are free from the burden of HIV, TB and other related developmental health issues. In recognition of the role that stigma and discrimination, gender inequality and related social structures and norms play in driving the epidemic and creating barriers to access to services in southern Africa, the organisation works to address gender equality and the rights of women, girls and key population groups, to access sexual reproductive health services and rights by confronting complex issues like culture, human rights and stigma. SAfAIDS, which leads the SRHR cluster of the Alliance, oversaw the Health, and HIV and AIDS chapters.

Tarisai Nyamweda *(Zimbabwe)* is the Media Manager at Gender Links. She is responsible for the gender and media projects undertaken by the organisation. She joined Gender Links as Media Policy and Research intern in January 2010. This is where she became involved in gender and media monitoring through the Gender and Media Progress Study (GMPS) in 2010. She coordinated research teams on the recently completed GMPS 2015 study and the South Africa Global Media Monitoring Project (GMMP) study. She wrote the Media, Information, and Communication chapter of the Barometer.

Dorah Marema *(South Africa)* has worked with a wide range of NGOs in different sectors in both rural and urban settings since 1997. She has been involved in issues of sustainability since 2000 and worked with multi-stakeholder participatory initiatives involving communities, NGOs, government and other institutions in various sectors including small-scale agriculture, environment, climate change, renewable energy, gender and land-rights at local, national and international levels. She helped establish an NGO called "Green House Project" - an Environmental Sustainability Demonstration Centre in inner-city Johannesburg, which she also managed for five years. Dorah founded Gender Climate Change-Southern Africa (GenderCC-SA) as a NPO organisation. GenderCC coordinates NGOs, community-based groups and individuals who are lobbying and advocating around gender and climate change in the region and internationally. Through this organisation, she implemented a gender and climate change capacity building project in South Africa which provided information about climate change. She is the Current President of GenderCC International. Marema updated the Climate Change chapter of the Barometer.

Sifisosami Dube *(Zimbabwe)* is the Head of Programmes at Gender Links. Sifisosami has been with the organisation since September 2012 when she joined as the Gender and Governance Manager, and subsequently served as the Southern Africa Gender Protocol Alliance manager. Sifisosami holds a BCOM in Entrepreneurship and a Master's in Public Administration and Development Management. She undertook Gender Studies at the University of Pretoria and African Thought Leadership at the

Thabo Mbeki African Leadership Institute (TMALI). She is currently studying towards a BA in Law degree with the University of South Africa. Prior to joining Gender Links, Sifisosami worked at CIVICUS, a global civil society network where she led a gender mainstreaming programme. Sifisosami updated the Implementation chapter of the Barometer.

Fanuel Hadzizi *(Zimbabwe)* holds an Honours Degree in Sociology from the University of Zimbabwe. He is a dynamic professional with extensive strategic analytical skills in Monitoring, Evaluation and Learning. His core expertise is in data analysis, research, report writing, knowledge management, donor financial budgeting, website management, training and events coordination. Fanuel has a passion for writing and vast experience in results based management. At Gender Links he has been key in linking people to systems that provide them with MEL resources, services and opportunities, learning and contributing to development and improvement of institutional knowledge. He oversaw the gathering and analysis of the SADC Protocol @Work case studies; knowledge quiz and Citizen Score Card.

Thandokuhle Dlamini *(Swaziland)*, GL Communications Officer, served as photo editor for the Barometer. Thando formerly served as GL programme officer in Swaziland. He is a keen photographer and videographer.

Sandiswa Manana *(South Africa)* is the Alliance and Partnerships Intern at Gender Links since April 2018. Sandiswa holds a Bachelor's degree in Geography and Environmental Management and an Honours in Gender Studies from the University of KwaZulu. Sandiswa provided support to the editorial team with data collection and editorial support.

Yolanda Dyantyi *(South Africa)* joined Gender Links in April 2018 as the Alliance and Partnerships Intern. She acted as an assistant to the editorial team. Yolanda is a former University of Rhodes student pursing a Bachelor of Arts, double majoring in Political Science and Drama Studies.

EXPERT PEER REVIEW GROUPS IN EACH COUNTRY

The following expert groups carried out the Gender Responsive Assessment (GRA) of the Constitutional and Legal Sector Score of the SADC Gender and Development Index (SGDI).

COUNTRY CO-ORDINATING NETWORK	EXPERT	DESIGNATION	ORGANISATION
Angola Platforma da Mulheres Accao (PMA)	Veronica Sapalo	Executive Director	Women Platform in Action
	Victoria Francisco Correia da Conceiçao	Ministry of Social Action, Family and Women Promotion	Ministry of Women Affairs
	Pedro Castelo Joao	Director of the Minister's office	Ministry of Women Affairs
	Joana Cortez	Gender Department	Ministry of Women Affairs
	Judith Caluassi	Focal Point Icolo e Bengo	Women Platform in Action
	Antonio Rogerio Carlos	Manager	Women Platform in Action
Botswana Botswana Council of NGOs (BOCONGO)	Lorato Moalusi	Chief Executive Officer	Kagiso Society Women's Shelter
	Kentse Mollentze	Vice President Women's League	Botswana National Front
	Tapologo Mokoka	Member Women's League	Botswana Democratic Party
	Rhoda Sekgororoane	Women's League President	Botswana Movement for Democcracy
	Daisy Bathusi	Women's League President	Botswana Congress Party
	Idah Mokereitane	Executive Director	Emang Basadi
	Bonang Modise	Youth Activist	Alliance/Botswana Council of NGOs
	Agang K Ditlhogo	Volunteer	UN Women
	Mmaotho Segotso	Women's League member	Alliance for Progressives
	Gaofenngwe Kabubi	Chairperson	Women In Peace
	Lydia Mafhoko-Ditsa	Gender Activist	Independent Consultant
	Chigedza V Chinyepi	Gender Activist	Alliance Bocongo
	Valenciah Mogegeh	Director	Gender Perspectives
	Gomolemo Rasesigo	Country Manager	Gender Links
	Keletso Metsing	Officer	Gender Links
Democratic Republic of Congo Union Congolaise des Femmes des Medias (UCOFEM)	Jeanne Kabvo	Member	Solidarité Féminine pour la Paix et le Développement Intégral (SOFEPADI)
	Serge Ndongo	Chargé de programme	Coalition des Femmes pour la Paix et le Développement, CFPD
	Christiane Munoki Ekambo	Directrice générale	Journaldesnations.net
	Marceline Kisita	Coordinatrice/SGE	Réseau des Organisations des Droits de l'Homme et Education civique, RODHECIC
	Christine Feza Nyembo	Membre	Association des Journalistes de la Presse Féminine, AJPF
	Me Jacques Mwanangongo	Secrétaire Général	Association pour la Promotion des droits de l'Enfant et de la Femme, APRODEF
	Aimée Kilembe	Point Focal	Genre Ministère de l'Intérieur
	Béatrice Makaya Samba	Chef de section	Institut Supérieur Pédagogique, ISP/Gombe
	Felly Diego	Directrice	Association Africaine pour les Droits de l'Homme, ASADHO
	Charlotte Makulo Toytely	Chef de division et Point Focal Genre	Ministère de la Justice
	Anicette Ebamba	Point Focal Genre	Ministère du Genre de la Famille et de l'Enfant
	Laetitia Mvuemba	membre/ Journaliste	L'Union Congolaise des Femmes des Médias
	Mampuya Anselme	Membre	Association pour la Santé Intégrale de la Fille et de la Femme, ASIFF
	Bampengesha Maraviya	Membre/ Journaliste	L'Union Congolaise des Femmes des Médias
	Elodie Musafiri	Vice présidente du CA	Fonds de la Femme Congolaise, FFC
	Jeanne Kavuo	Membre du CA	Solidarité Féminine pour la Paix et le Développement Intégral, SOFEPADI
	Blandine Nzovo	Membre/ Journaliste	L'Union Congolaise des Femmes des Médias
	Anna Mayimona Ngemba	Directrice	L'Union Congolaise des Femmes des Médias
	Mimy Mopunga	Membre	Cadre de Concertation de la Femme Congolaise, CAFCO
Lesotho Women and Law in Southern Africa (WLSA)	Lerato Molise	Advocacy Officer	Catholic Commission for Justice and Peace (CCJP)
	Lineo Rakaibe	Officer	Ministry of Gender, Youth, Sports and Recreation
	Ndabe Rasethuntsa	Legal Officer	Women and Law in Southern Africa (WLSA)
	Molapo Matelile	Programme Officer	SHE-HIVE

	Mamolibeli Ngakane	Officer	Ministry of Gender, Youth, Sports and Recreation
	Masentle Selikane	Officer	Young Women Christian Association(YWCA)
	Peter Buyundo	Manager	Skillshare
	Mpho Marathane	Gender Activist	Marathane Consulting Agency
	Lintle Ramatla	Journalist	Bokamoso FM
	Lydia Muso	Officer	Lesotho Child Counselling Unit
	Liemiso Koetlisi	Intern	Gender Links (GL)
	Manteboheleng Mabetha	Manager	Gender Links (GL)
	Ntolo Lekau	Officer	Gender Links (GL)
Madagascar FEDERATION POUR LA PROMOTION FEMININE ET ENFINTINE (FPFE)	Razafindramboho Samoelà Héredia	Vice Coordinator FPFE	Cluster droit constitutionnel
	Vaohita Barthélémi	University Teacher Psycho Pédagogue	Université DEGS Antananarivo
	Rakotoarimanana Estella	Jurist	La Cellule d'écoute et de Conseils juridiques CECJ
	Céline Marie Yolande	Assistant Public Prosecutor	Legal Magistrate
	Rajaovelo Rivonarinjaka	Executive Director	Le Projet Imagine
	Razafindrakoto Gaby	Focal Point	Federation pour la promotion feminine et enfintine (FPFE)
	Lydia rakotonjatovo	Parliamentary Officer	National Parliament
	Rakotonjanahary Mahefa Freddy	Deputy Chair	Federation pour la promotion feminine et enfintine (FPFE)Youth Association.
	Ravelojaona Hajaharimanana	General Direction of the Protection of woman	Ministry of Population, Social Protection and the Promotion of women
Malawi NGO Gender Coordinating Network	Barbra Banja	National assistant of women	National Association of Business Women (NABW)
	Florence Khonyongwa	M & E officer	Malawi Health Equity Network
	Andrew Mkandawire	Centre coordinator	Malawi Institute of Journalism
	Elizabeth Chambakata	Network coordinator	Malawi Police
	Ruth Mthekwana	Program officer	Council for Non-Governmental Organizations (CMD)
	Aubrey Chapuzika	M & E officer	NGO Gender Coordinating Network (NGOGCN)
	Victor Nyirenda	Assistant communications officer	NGO Gender Coordinating Network (NGOGCN)
	Chimwemwe Sakunda	Program officer	NGO Gender Coordinating Network (NGOGCN)
	Loveness Nkuniva	Student intern	Malawi Human Rights Resource Centre (MHRRC)
	Ellen Howa	Project officer	Civil Society Network on Climate Change (CISONECC)
	Martha Mtenje	Deputy director	Department of Human Resource Management & Development (DHRMD)
	Alfred Chauwa	Journalist	Nyasa Times
	Amon Lukhehe	Director	Outreach Scout Foundation (OSF)
	Eddah Chavula	Assistant chief	Law Commission
	Thandizo Mphwiyo	Civic education coordinator	Centre for Human Rights and Rehabilitation (CHRR)
	Michael Nhlema	Finance officer	Malawi Human Rights Resource Centre (MHRRC)
	Chimwemwe Lufupfu	Finance intern	Malawi Human Rights Resource Centre (MHRRC)
	Chikondi Kamphinda	Accountant assistance	NGO Gender Coordinating Network (NGOGCN)
	Loyce Mulaga	Administration assistant	Malawi Human Rights Resource Centre (MHRRC)
	Emma Kaliya	Chairperson	SADC Gender Protocol Alliance
Mauritius Media Watch Organisation	Sivakoura Ramen	Member	Media Watch Organisation
	Florent Didier Marcel	Member	Rotary Club Tamarin
	Mary Coopan	Treasurer	Media Watch Organisation
	Sheistah Bundhoo	Program and finance officer	Gender Links (GL)
	Anushka Virahsawmy	Country manager	Gender Links (GL)
	Invulnerable Mireille	Auditor	Young Queer Alliance
	Yashvind Kumar Poteeram	Counselor	Ministry of Infrastructure
	Meethilesh Nashib	Director / Jurist	Forescue
	Sarah Belle	Chemistry student	University of France
	Zeim Gopee	Psychology	University of France
	Steffi Honiss	LLB student	University of France - Paris
	Azegen Mootoocurpen	Auditor	Media Watch Organisation
	Nesha Ramen	Alliance focal person	Media Watch Organisation
	Toshni Dabysing	Law student	University of London

Mozambique Forum Mulher	Sheila Haudlhate	Coordinator	Forum Mulher member
	Rebeca Gomes	Coordinator	Mozambican Forum of Rural Women (FOMMUR)
	Aida Nhaveto	Getoa Decom	Forum Mulher member
	Mangia Mauacca	Activist	Forum Mulher member
	Osvalda Amelia Chichava	Activist	Forum Mulher member
	Dalila Moiceoine	Gender Coordinator	Associacao Socio - Cultural Horizonte
	Ivesa Diolene	Communications officer	Associacao Socio - Cultural Horizonte
	Fatima Nabime	Coordinator	Association of Widows and Single Mothers (AVIMAS)
	Maria Salome	Activist	Mwoti
	Abdulfatahe Ijo	Facilitator	Mozambican association supporting Sex workers with children (AMORA)
	Milagne Olaimbe	Activist	Forum Mulher member
	Aloimoladilo	Activist	Forum Mulher member
	Julie Nfuno	Coordinator	Forum Mulher member
	Ednizinda Nhaule	Official de campo	Kutenga
Namibia Namibia University of Science and Technology	Emily Brown	Namibia University of Science and Technology	Senior Lecturer
	Jordanian Andima	Namibia University of Science and Technology	Lecturer
	Tinana Matjila	Office of the Judiciary	Director Judicial Commissions Secretariat
	Charlemaine Husselmann	Lifeline/Childline	Programme Manager: Gender
	Elizabeth M'ule	Editors Forum of Namibia	Coordinator
	Naita Hishoono	Namibia Institute for Democracy	Director
	Chisom Okafor	Law Reform and Development Commission	Senior Legal Officer
	Gerson Kamatuka	Namibia Broadcasting Corporation	Human Resources Manager
	Umbi Karuaihe- Upi	Namibia Broadcasting Corporation	Senior Manager
	Salatiel Shinedima	Women's Action for Development	Chief Executive Officer
	Wanja Njuguna	Namibia University of Science and Technology	Lecturer
	Nadia Meding	Namibia University of Science and Technology	Projects Officer
	Rosalia Nghikagwa	Ministry of Gender Equality and Child Welfare	Officer
	Ndapwa Alweendo	Institute for Public Policy Research	Senior Researcher
	James Itana	Regain Trust	Programmes Manager
	Ngamami Karuaihe- Upi	Independent	Gender and Media Consultant
	Nashitati Tuafeni	Hans Seidel Foundation	Intern
Seychelles Gender and Media Plus Association of Seychelles (GEM Plus)	Brena Mein	Programme Officer	Ministry of Health
	Beryl Dookly	Teacher	Ministry of Education
	Dalanda Bah	Entreprenuership	Perseverance an Mouvman
	Ben Viel	Gender Consultant	Independent Consultant
	Sharon Ernesta	Senior Jouranlist	Gem Plus
	Marie Annette Ernesta	Political and Economic Assistant	Gem Plus
	Daniel Leurence	Gender Activist	Gay Rights Association
	Salfa Karapehyan	Journalist	Gem Plus
South Africa South African Women in Dialogue	Lubelihle Banda	Chairperson	South African Women in Dialogue (SAWID)
	Susan Nkoro	Researcher	South African Women in Dialogue (SAWID)
	Liegollo Pheho	Senior Research Fellow	South African Women in Dialogue (SAWID)
	Marthe Muller	Chief of Operations	South African Women in Dialogue (SAWID)
	Jody-Lee Fredericks	Attorney	Jody Fredericks Attorneys
	Beverley Cortse	President	First Nation's Women's Commission
	Audrey Jaftha	Funding Member	First Nation's Women's Commission
	Coleen Losper	Funding Member	First Nation's Women's Commission
	Ruche Daniels	CEO	Entrepreneur
	Noziwe Routledge	Executive director	Embrace Dignity
	Faadilah Gierdien	CEO	Reconnect Foundation
	Thozi Theko-Oum	Project Manager	Noralis Ubuntu Institute
	Philip Molekoa	Advocacy & Researcher	South African Human Rights Commission (SAHRC)
eSwatini Coordinating Assembly of Non-Govermental Organisations (CANGO)	Sisana Nxumalo	eSwatini Diabetes	Psychologist
	Nqobile Motsa	eSwatini Diabetes	Public Relations Officer
	Katie Hope	Communications	eSwatini Action Group Against Abuse

	Maleigh Austin	Advocacy Officer	Family Life Association of Swaziland
	Slindelo Nkosi	Communications Officer	Swaziland Action Group Against Abuse
	Goodman Simelane	Programme officer	Swaziland Association for Crime Prevention & Rehabilitation of Offenders
	Dumsani Dlamini	Legal officer	Women and Law
	Lucky Simelane	Public Relations Officer	Autism eSwatini
	Tenele DuPont	Information Officer	Woman Farmer Foundation
	Lungile Mnisi	Advocacy Officer	Coordinating Assembly for NGO's
	Nkosingphile Myeni	Communications Officer	Coordinating Assembly for NGO's
	Lobesuthu Mncina	Public Relations Officer	Autism eSwatini
	Racheal Manzini	Counsellor	Autism eSwatini
	Lomcebo Dlamini	Consultant	Women's Rights Organisation
	Ncane Maziya	Country facilitator	Gender Links
	Zethu Shongwe Thring	Intern	Gender Links
Tanzania Tanzania Gender Network Programme	Catherine Mhina	Legal officer	Tanzania Gender Network Programme (TGNP)
	Winifrida Magah	Legal officer	ZSALMARK Advocate
	Marcela Lungu	Executive director	Transformative and integrative build out for All
	William Kahale	Legal officer	Legal and Human Rights Centre (LHRC)
	Geofrey Gham	Gender Analyst	Independent Consultant
	Jackson Malongaliza	Budget and Policy analyst	Tanzania Gender Network Programme (TGNP)
	Mariam Ousleododa	Co-ordinating trainings	Tanzania Gender Network Programme (TGNP)
	Hellen Un'o	Co-ordinating trainings	Tanzania Gender Network Programme (TGNP)
	Speratus Kyanizi	APO Librarian	Tanzania Gender Network Programme (TGNP)
	Elain Godson	Media monitor	Tanzania Gender Network Programme (TGNP)
	Maureen Mbolca	Research and Analyses officer	Tanzania Gender Network Programme (TGNP)
	Irene Musokwa	Advocate	Tanganyika Law Society
	Mwanahaus Auray	Legal officer	FK Law Chambers
	Nollie Deogratius	Legal officer	FK Law Chambers
	Edna Maponda	Legal officer	Univesity of Dar es salam School of Law
Zambia Women and Law in Southern Africa - Zambia	Salome Nakazwe	Programe Cordinator	Women for Change
	Nathan Mungo	Programe Officer	Young Women Christian Association
	Mary Katimbe	Board Member	Women and Law in Southern Africa
	Chileshe Nsama	Program Officer	Foundation for Democratic Process (FODEP)
	Priscilla Chileshe	Chairperson	Women and Law in Southern Africa
	Namatama Chinyama	Gender Analyst	Ministry of Gender
	Simon Kapilima	Assistant Director	Ministry of Gender
Women & Law in Southern Africa - Zambia	Mwenya Nshitima	Programe Officer	Forum for African Women Educationalists of Zambia (FAWEZA)
	Faggy Chibanga	Project Cordinator	Zambia National Women's Lobby Group (ZNWLG)
	Rudo Mooba	Programe Officer	Women and Law in Southern Africa (WLSA)
	Matrine Hazyondo	Project Assistant	Women and Law in Southern Africa (WLSA)
	Sangulukani Zulu	Research and Development Officer	Local Government Association of Zambia
	Monica Munachonga	Gender Consultant	Women and Law in Southern Africa (WLSA)
	Khuta Hangoma	Women Participation Cordinator	Women and Law in Development in Africa
	Maube Siyanga	Head of communications	Non-Governmental Organizations Coordinating Council (NGOCC)
	Febby Maambo	Adminstration Officer	Zambia Association for Research and Development
	Cathrine Muwaya	Communication Officer	Women and Law in Southern Africa (WLSA)
	Themba Mazyopa	Research and Documentation	Human Rights Commission
Zimbabwe Women's Coalition of Zimbabwe	Edinah Masiyiwa	Executive director	Womens Action Group
	Lydia Madyirapanze	National coordinator	Forum for African Women Educationalists Zimbabwe (FAWEZI)
	Vimbai Ndonde	Legal Intern	Women and Law in Southern Africa (WLSA)
	Rebecca Musimwa	Program manager	Law Society of Zimbabwe
	Karen Mukwasi	Program officer	Women's Coalition of Zimbabwe (WCoZ)
	Kudzai Mushangahande	Intern	Women's Coalition of Zimbabwe (WCoZ)
	Sally Ncube	National coordinator	Women's Coalition of Zimbabwe (WCoZ)
	Violah Chidemo	Program assistant	Women's Coalition of Zimbabwe (WCoZ)

#SheDecidesSouthernAfrica #TheTimeIsNow!
By Lois Chingandu and Colleen Lowe Morna

Lois Chingandu,
Executive Director,
SAFAIDS

Colleen Lowe
Morna, GL CEO

Around the globe, 2017 will be remembered for the groundswell of women's rights activism that began with spontaneous Women's Marches as President Donald Trump took office in the USA, and gained momentum with the #MeToo, #TimesUp and #SheDecides campaigns. In a world where information moves with the speed of light, Southern Africa had its own variants to these campaigns - like the #MenAreTrash, #NotInMyName, #JusticeForKarabo #IWearWhatILike and #TotalShutDown, to name a few.

In March 2018, the virtual #SheDecides campaign came to Southern Africa, with a meeting in Pretoria that attracted several ministers, MPs and high profile personalities from the region; from progressive European countries as well as the Executive Director of UN Women, Dr Phumzile Mlambo-Ngcuka. Like the Sixteen Days of Activism that began as the brainchild of a few activists but has since mutated into a global campaign, #SheDecides is an idea whose time has come, and whose principles need to be customised by every region.

In this edition of the Barometer, we launch #SheDecidesSouthernAfrica by putting a spotlight on Sexual and Reproductive Health and Rights (SRHR). The 2018 Barometer abounds with evidence on the need for bold action on this front. The graphic illustrates how SRHR is a key cross-cutting theme. While the core chapters for this theme are health, HIV and AIDS and Gender Based Violence (GBV), issues of bodily integrity feature in the constitutional and legal, education, economic and governance chapters, to name a few.

As the tenth edition of the Alliance's flagship publication went to press, Zimbabweans prepared to go to the polls after campaigns that served as a stark reminder that politics is still an unwelcome space for women. Four women presidential candidates were variously derided for their marital status; referred to as witches and "hures", a derogatory Shona word for prostitutes. While women are not likely to make significant gains in the polls, the elections will be remembered for women finding their voice and claiming their space amid the misogyny, with one outspoken opposition MP donning a T shirt marked "Hure!" and at the back #MeToo!

Women's lack of voice, choice and control in SRHR reflects in the high rates of GBV and HIV in the region. Violence Against Women Baseline studies conducted by GL in seven SADC countries show lifetime prevalence rates ranging from 25% in Mauritius to 86% in Lesotho. Southern Africa has the highest rates of HIV and AIDS in the world. Sexual violence against women and girls remains one of the major causes of HIV infection. Marital rape is pervasive and contributes to the HIV and AIDS pandemic. For every two people enrolled in HIV treatment, five become newly infected. Women account for 59% of those living with HIV in Southern Africa, while men account for 53% of AIDS-related deaths.

The 2018 Barometer reveals that contraceptive usage in the region among women ranges from 12% in Mozambique to 76% in Mauritius. The Barometer reports that only South Africa and Mozambique give women the choice to terminate pregnancy. Unsafe abortion contributes to high rates of maternal mortality across the region. While maternal mortality ratios are declining in other regions, in SADC they increased between 1990 and 2010 mainly as a result of HIV.

Key SRHR concerns relating to youth include significant percentages of sexually active adolescents below the age of 16; multiple concurrent sexual relations; increasing trends of inter-generational sexual relations; low levels of consistent condom usage during sex; high levels of maternal mortality amongst young mothers; compromised quality of antenatal care to young mothers compared to older mothers; high levels of HIV and AIDS among young people, especially young women, and high levels of GBV.

Punitive policies and restrictive laws against vulnerable groups create barriers to their access to SRHR services. Only four SADC countries have decriminalised homosexuality - South Africa, DRC, Mozambique and Seychelles, but recent high court rulings in Botswana suggest the ground is thawing in other countries. South Africa is the only country in the world whose Constitution recognises sexual orientation. No SADC country has decriminalised sex work, although the ruling African National Congress (ANC) in South Africa voted at its December 2017 congress in favour of doing so.

Local action for SRHR in Southern Africa | Action locale pour SRHR en Afrique australe | Na luta contra VBG e Promoção da SSR

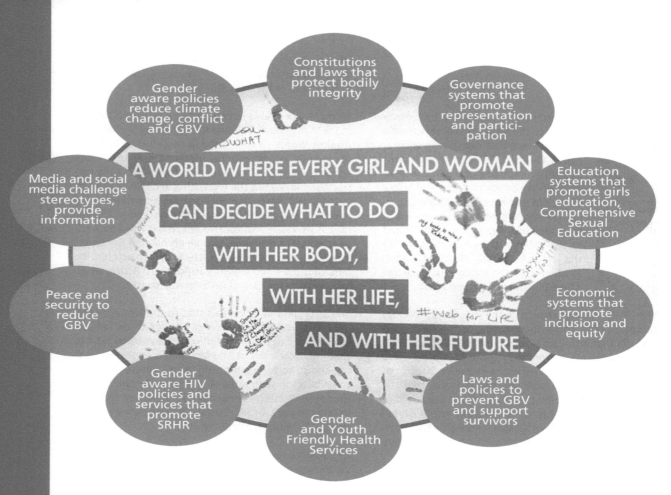

A WORLD WHERE EVERY GIRL AND WOMAN CAN DECIDE WHAT TO DO WITH HER BODY, WITH HER LIFE, AND WITH HER FUTURE.

Since 2016, the Alliance has succeeded in lobbying for the inclusion of SRHR in the Post 2015 Protocol; established an SRHR cluster; undertook training of members on SRHR led by cluster lead Southern Africa HIV and AIDS Information Dissemination Service (SAfAIDS) and on LGBTI led by Gender Links (GL). The Alliance also strengthened tracking of SRHR in the annual Barometer; identified key campaigns; established a Young Women's Network; gathered and analysed over 300 Good Practices on SRHR at the annual SADC Protocol@Work summits. SAfAIDS has launched an ambitious regional programme called *Transforming Lives* with a focus on sexual-based gender violence (SGBV), teenage pregnancy, unsafe abortion, and promotion of social accountability for youth.

Key inter-linked campaigns identified by the Alliance include resurgence of HIV and AIDS among young women; menstrual health; teenage pregnancies, unsafe abortion; child marriages; Comprehensive Sexual Education in Schools; and decriminalisation of homosexuality. These will be accompanied by:
✓ Building the organisational capacity of small network members (one in each country); further work on the LGBTI sub-group in the SRHR cluster, and inclusion of Faith Based Organisations through our partnership with the ACT Alliance.
✓ Strengthening advocacy through a Gender Responsive Budgeting (GRB) tracking initiative for SRHR; this will also complement the policy work in the strategic grant.

✓ Working with the media.
✓ A strong Community of Practise that includes discussion groups, training and advocacy resources; and access to dynamic data bases.
✓ Creating strong linkages between national networks and the Centres of Excellence for Gender in Local Government.
✓ Strengthening the Young Women's Alliance to include a Network of Young Women Junior Councillors.
✓ Developing model SRHR policies at national level and cascading these to the local level.
✓ Gathering evidence, peer learning and sharing through the SADC Protocol@Work summits; tracking progress through the Barometer.

As the lead cluster on SRHR and Coordinator of the Alliance respectively, SAfAIDS and GL commit to further analysis for a pull out SRHR Barometer to be launched during the Sixteen Days of Activism, which stretches from 25 November (International Day of No Violence Against Women) to 10 December (Human Rights Day). The launch of the 2018 Barometer in Johannesburg on the eve of Women's Day (9 August); in Windhoek (host of the 2018 SADC Heads of State Summit) and in all countries in the region will be accompanied by year-long campaigns to give women voice, choice and control of their lives. #TheTimeIsNow!

A region of possibilities: Ezulwini Market, eSwatini.

"In 2017 we saw an unprecedented upsurge of movements for women's rights, equality, safety and justice. The tireless work of activists has been central to this global drive, and women all over the world continue to demonstrate the power of many voices speaking as one. Together, we are calling for opportunity and accountability, drawing momentum from grass-roots networks and forging coalitions that stretch right up to the leaders of governments, businesses and civic institutions."- *Phumzile Mlambo-Ngcuka, Executive Director, UN Women in the foreword to The Time is Now! UNWomen, 2018 Annual Report.*

2018 is the tenth anniversary of the SADC Protocol on Gender and Development, as well as the Barometer produced annually by the Southern African Gender Protocol Alliance. It is also the year in which, incensed by the stream of sexual harassment allegations against businessman-turned-US President Donald Trump and other celebrities, high profile women have found their voice in the #MeToo, #TimesUp and many other social media campaigns that are putting gender equality squarely on the global agenda.

Breaking with the usual tradition of its Person (usually man) of the Year in 2017, Time Magazine named the "Silence Breakers" as the Persons of the Year. In South Africa, the murder of Karobo Mokwena by her partner, also much amplified by social media, gave rise to the black dresses and red lipstick #CountMeIn campaign; the #MenAreTrash debate, and #NotInMyName response by progressive men.

Globally, the #SheDecides movement has drawn renewed focus to the imperative of enabling women, and particularly young women, to have control over their own sexual and reproductive health and wellbeing. The movement is galvanising support across the globe to Stand Up, Speak Out, Change the Rules and Unlock Resources.

This year, the Southern Africa Gender Protocol Alliance launches the #SheDecidesSouthernAfrica campaign, with our spotlight on SRHR, and a pull out Barometer to be launched during the Sixteen Days of Activism. Welcome to 2018, and to a world in which women and girls finally exercise voice, choice and control over their bodies! Welcome also to a world and region in which for every step forwards for gender equality, there seem to be two steps backwards.

	Target 2030	Baseline 2009	Progress 2018	Variance (Progress minus 2030 target)
CONSTITUTIONAL AND LEGAL RIGHTS				
15 Constitutions provide for the promotion of gender equality		7	13	2 (Botswana and Seychelles)
15 Constitutions have no claw back clauses		7	10	5 (Botswana, Lesotho, Malawi, Mauritius and eSwatini)
15 Constitutions provide for special measures to promote gender equality		9	13	2 (Angola, Botswana)
15 countries decriminalise homosexuality		1	4 (DRC, Mozambique, South Africa and Seychelles)	11
Marriage age for girls and boys is a minimum of 18 in 15 countries		8	14	1 (Mauritius)
GOVERNANCE				
50% women in parliament (regional average)		25%	26%	-24%
Highest % women in parliament		South Africa (42%)	South Africa (41%)	-9%
Lowest % women in parliament		DRC (8%)	DRC (8%)	-42%
50% women in cabinet		21%	20%	-30%
Highest % women in parliament		South Africa (42%)	South Africa (50%)	-0%
Lowest % women in parliament		Mauritius (10%)	Lesotho, DRC (10%)	-40%
50% women in local government (regional average)		23%	23%	-27%
Highest % women in local government		Lesotho (58%)	Namibia (48%)	-1%
Lowest % women in local government		Mauritius (6%)	DRC (6%)	-44%
EDUCATION				
Equal number of girls and boys enrolled in primary school in 15 countries		5	13	2 (Angola and Malawi)
Equal number of girls and boys enrolled in secondary school in all 15 countries		7	8	8 (Botswana, DRC, Lesotho, Namibia, Seychelles, Swaziland, Tanzania and Zambia)
Equal number of women and men enrolled in tertiary school in all 15 countries		7	11	5 (Botswana, DRC, Mauritius, Seychelles and South Africa)
Girls and boys have access to quality early childhood development in all 15 countries		N/A	11	4 (Angola, Seychelles, Tanzania and Zambia[2])
ECONOMY				
15 countries with a Human Development Index[4] of more than 0.7		2 (Mauritius and Seychelles)	2 (Mauritius and Seychelles)	13
50% women in economic decision-making		18%	20%	-30%
Highest % women in economic decision-making		44% (Botswana)	44% (Botswana)	-6%
Lowest % women in economic decision-making		13% (Madagascar)	None (Mauritius)	-50%
Lowest % difference in earnings between women and men		12% (Namibia)	12% (Botswana)	12%
Highest % difference in earnings between women and men		58% (Mauritius)	54% (eSwatini)	54%
GBV				
Laws on domestic violence in 15 countries		9	12	3 with no laws (DRC, Lesotho and Tanzania)
Laws on sexual assault in 15 countries		7	13	2 with no laws (Angola and Seychelles)
15 countries have specialised facilities, including places of shelter and safety		3	14	1 With no specialised facilities (Seychelles).
Comprehensive treatment, including post-exposure prophylaxis (PEP) in 15 countries		3	15	0
National action plans in 15 countries		7	15	0
GBV or VAW baseline data study in 15 countries		None	7	8 no baseline studies (Angola, DRC, Madagascar, Malawi, Mozambique, Namibia, Swaziland and Tanzania)
HEALTH				
Highest % contraceptive use among sexually active women		South Africa (65%)	Mauritius (76%)	-24%
Lowest % contraceptive use among sexually active women		Angola (6%)	Mozambique (12%)	-88%
Highest maternal mortality per 100 000 births		Angola (1400)	DRC (693)	
Lowest maternal mortality per 100 000 births		Mauritius (13)	Seychelles (0)	
Highest % births attended by skilled personnel		Mauritius (100%)	Mauritius, Seychelles (100%)	0
Lowest % births attended by skilled personnel		Angola/Tanzania (46%)	Madagascar (44%)	-56%
Highest % who say a woman should be able to choose to terminate pregnancy in first three months			Angola (52%)	-48%

---

[1] Select indicators from the Barometer.
[2] No statistics available.

Target 2030	Baseline 2009	Progress 2018	Variance (Progress minus 2030 target)
Lowest % who say a woman should be able to choose to terminate pregnancy in first three months		Madagascar (13%)	
Highest % sanitation coverage	Mauritius/ Seychelles (100%)	Seychelles (98%)	-2%
Lowest % sanitation coverage	Madagascar (14%)	Madagascar (12%)	-38%
HIV and AIDS			
Highest percentage of women living with HIV	Namibia (68%)	Tanzania (61%)	-11%
Lowest percentage of women living with HIV	Mauritius (15%)	Mauritius (28%)	+32%
Highest coverage of PMCTC	Seychelles (99%)	Seychelles 100%	0
Lowest coverage of PCTC	Madagascar (3%)	Madagascar (11%)	-89%
Highest % of those on ARV	Namibia 68%	eSwatini (85%)	-15%
Lowest % of those on ARV	Madagascar (3%)	Madagascar (7%)	-93%
Highest % of women with comprehensive knowledge of HIV	South Africa (95%)	Seychelles (100%)	0
Lowest % of women with comprehensive knowledge of HIV	Angola (7%)	DRC (17%)	-83%
PEACE AND SECURITY			
15 countries with UNSCR National Action Plans	1	3 (DRC, Angola Namibia)	12
15 countries with sex disaggregated data on defence	5	14	1 (Madagascar)
Highest % women in defence	South Africa (24%)	South Africa (30%)	-20%
Lowest % women in defence	DRC (3%)	DRC (3%)	-47%
15 countries with sex disaggregated data on the police force	6 countries	15	0
Highest % women in police force	South Africa (21%)	Seychelles (39%)	-11%
Lowest % women in police force	Mozambique (7%)	DRC (6%)	-44%
15 countries include women in peacekeeping forces	7	8	7 (Angola, DRC, Lesotho, Mauritius, Mozambique, Seychelles and eSwatini)
Highest % women in peacekeeping	Namibia (46%)	Zimbabwe (35%)	-15%
Lowest % women in peacekeeping	Tanzania (6%)	DRC (none)	-50%
MEDIA			
% women sources (regional)	19%	20%	-30%
Highest % women sources	1 Lesotho (32%)	2 Botswana and Seychelles (28%)	-32%
Lowest % women sources	2 Mozambique and Zambia (14%)	1 DRC (6%)	-44%
% women in management	27%	34%	-16%
Highest % women in management	1 Lesotho (52%)	1 Lesotho (53%)	+3 %
Lowest % women in management	DRC (10%)	DRC (17%)	-23%
CLIMATE CHANGE			
50% women in decision-making bodies that address climate change	24%	25%	-25%
Highest Representation	Zambia (60%)	50% Zimbabwe	0
Lowest Representation	Seychelles (0)	DRC, Tanzania (0)	-50%
% women sources on climate change	27%	27%	-23%
15 countries ratify the global climate change treaty (Paris Agreement)	13 countries	14 countries	1 country (Tanzania)
15 countries have gender-sensitive climate change adaptation and mitigation measures (MERF)	Not measured this period	Sporadic evidence	15 countries
IMPLEMENTATION			
Signing and ratifying of the Post 2015 SADC Gender Protocol			
15 countries that have signed the Protocol and the amended Protocol	13 countries (Protocol)	9 countries[3] (amended Protocol)	-6 countries (Malawi Mauritius, Namibia, Seychelles, South Africa and Zambia)
Knowledge of the Protocol (regional)	49%	48%	-1%
Highest knowledge of the Protocol	70% (Swaziland)	58% (Swaziland, Lesotho)	-42%
Lowest knowledge of the Protocol	35% (Zimbabwe, Mauritius)	37%(Angola)	-63%
Gender Progress Score- GPS (attitudes - regional average)	53%	61%	8%
Highest GPS	Mauritius (65%)	76% (Seychelles)	-24%
Lowest GPS	Mozambique (49%)	51% (Mozambique and Angola)	-49%

---

[3] 0 = no human development; 1 = optimal human development
[4] Based on: Life expectancy at birth; Mean years of schooling; Expected years of schooling; and Gross national income per capita
SARDC (June 2017) SANF 17 no 23 available at https://www.sardc.net/en/southern-african-news-features/sadc-gender-ministers-to-review-progress-on-regional-gender-development/ (Accessed 25 July 2017)

Southern Africa is rich in commitment and in activism. In 2005, gender activists began a campaign that led to the adoption in 2008 of the SADC Protocol on Gender and Development: the only sub-regional instrument in the world that brings together existing African and global commitments to gender equality and enhances this through a legally binding Protocol, with initial targets aligned the 2015 Millennium Development Goals. The Southern African Gender Protocol Alliance, comprising women's rights networks in all the 15 SADC countries as well as cross-cutting theme NGOs, has produced the Barometer annually since then.

In 2014, the Alliance launched a campaign for the updating of the Protocol in line with the Sustainable Development Goals (SDGs), African Agenda 2063, and Beijing Plus Twenty. The SADC Gender Protocol is one of only two SADC Protocols (there are 27 altogether) that have been amended and the only one to be accompanied by a Monitoring Evaluation and Results Framework (MERF).

As reported in Chapter Eleven on Implementation, all of the 15 existing SADC Member States[5] except Mauritius have signed the SADC Protocol on Gender and Development, but only ten have signed the amendment. One more country needs to do so for the amendment to go into force. This means that two years after the adoption of the updated SADC Gender Protocol in 2016, it has not gone into force.

As incoming chair of SADC, Namibia is expected to become the eleventh country to sign, so that the amended Protocol goes into force. By the time of the Gender Ministers meeting in June, only seven countries (Botswana, Madagascar, Mauritius, Mozambique, Namibia, Seychelles and Zimbabwe) had submitted their two yearly reports. The Secretariat cited late reports as a "recurring challenge".

At the local level 363 Centres of Excellence for Gender in Local Government councils are championing gender equality at the local level. Seven countries held SADC Protocol@work summits between November 2017 and June 2018, with Swaziland and South Africa holding a joint summit. These yielded 406 best practices on how the SADC Gender Protocol is being applied, especially at the local level.

The Barometer uses two measures of progress, both updated in 2016 in line with the amended Protocol. The SADC Gender and Development Index (SGDI) comprises 36 empirical indicators (such as women in parliament) weighted to a factor of 100. The Citizen Score Card (CSC) is derived from scoring of performance against target by nearly 10,000 women and men around the region. Reflecting the lacklustre performance, the SGDI in 2018 is at 59%, one percentage point lower than 2017. The CSC at 62%, three percentage points lower than last year. The following are key highlights of the red lights and green lights in the 2018 Barometer:

Each year the Alliance administers the Gender Progress Score (GPS) that measures gender attitudes in the region. The Alliance added five questions in 2016 on tough issues such as sex work and sexual orientation. In 2018, the region registered a score of 61%, eight percentage points higher than the 2016 score of 53%.

Responses to individual questions reflect the contradictions in Southern African society. For example, 55% of respondents said that people should be treated the same whether they are women or men, yet 56% said that a woman should obey her husband!

Thirty percent said that homosexuality is a disease. Considering the high levels of homophobia in the region it is heartening that 70% of respondents disagreed.

Only 32% said that a woman can choose to terminate her pregnancy in the first three months. This shows that there is still a lot of public education and awareness required on abortion.

While it is heartening that the lowest scores are on issues such as "if a man beats a woman in shows that he loves her" it is sobering that almost one fifth of respondents agreed or strongly agreed with this statement.

Overall, the results show that there is still a big lag between normative frameworks and the patriarchal attitudes that drive gender disparities.

---

[5] Comoros is set to become the 16th member in August

Constitutional and legal rights: Governments continue to send out mixed messages on women's rights. Over the last decade eleven countries in the region have undertaken Constitutional reviews. All but two (Botswana and Seychelles) now have specific references to promoting gender equality. But five countries (Botswana, Lesotho, Malawi, Mauritius and eSwatini) have "claw back clauses" giving precedents to customary provisions that may undermine equality. Mauritius still refuses to sign the Protocol because it disagrees with the minimum age of 18 for marriage of girls, citing religious provisions for earlier marriage, and despite the mounting pressure to eradicate child marriages. Around the region, domestication of the SADC Model Law on Eradicating Child Marriage and Protecting Children Already in Marriage has been slow.

While eSwatini passed laws on gender violence and political participation, the monarchy pronounced that widows in mourning would not be allowed to participate in the 2018 general elections due later in the year. Only widows who had been in mourning for at least two years and had been "cleansed" will be allowed to participate.

Homophobia continues to run high in the region. Despite boasting the only country in the world with a constitution that recognises sexual orientation (South Africa) only three other countries in the region (Mozambique, DRC and Seychelles) have decriminalised homosexuality. But in a progressive move by the judiciary, the Botswana High Court ordered the government to change the gender of a transgender woman on her identity documents. The government had initially refused to effect the change.

In another win for gender justice, the Lesotho High Court ruled that the Defence Forces could not dismiss female soldiers who get pregnant during the first five years of their engagement, as still stated in army regulations. This represents an important precedent given that many Defence Forces in the region have similar regulations.

Governance: Over the past year three countries held elections: Angola (national); eSwatini (local, urban) and Lesotho (local). In both Angola and Lesotho the proportion of women declined from 38% to 30%; and 49% to 40% respectively. Women's representation in parliament in SADC is at 26%, one percentage point lower at baseline in 2009, but two percentage points higher than the global and Sub-Saharan average of 24%. Women's representation in cabinet in the region is lower at 20%. This is also true in local government (23%).

Five more countries are due to hold elections in 2018: DRC (tripartite), Madagascar (tripartite), eSwatini (national), Mozambique (local), and Zimbabwe (tripartite). Five countries will hold elections in 2019: Mozambique (national); Malawi (national); Mauritius

(national); South Africa (national and provincial); Botswana (national and local); Namibia (national, regional and local). The coming period is therefore one in which maximum effort needs to be given to the Fifty Fifty campaign. "Special measures" and conducive electoral systems give the greatest assurance for increasing women's representation in politics at all levels.

As the 2018 Barometer went to press, all indications were that the Zimbabwe elections, with four women presidential candidates, will be remembered for women finding their voice, but failing to make any significant electoral headway. Elections marred by violence and misogyny did witness some promising new young candidates who answered hate speech with calm logic. Young women also broke new ground by demanding a 25% quota for young women.

> Blazing the trail for a new brand of young female leadership, independent candidate for Mount Pleasant suburb in Harare and Cambridge trained barrister Fadzayi Mahere fought back social media derision about her not being married with tweets like: " Marriage, though often a beautiful thing, is not an achievement. It does not qualify one for public office. It's an irrelevant factor when we assess whether one will or won't succeed. Individual character is the true test. Grace (Mugabe), after all, was married." A prominent member of the #ThisFlag Movement that galvanised public opinion against Mugabe, Mahere's strapline was that *"Africa's future is bright and it is young."* Challenging the old boys network through prolific use of social media, she is running a refreshingly modern campaign calling for clean governance under her hashtag #Bethechange.

Education: An encouraging development over the last decade is the narrowing of gender gaps in education. As reflected in the tracking table, out of the 15 SADC countries, 13 now have equal enrolment at primary school (compared to five at baseline); 8 at secondary school (compared to seven at baseline) and 11 at tertiary (compared to 7 at baseline). Literacy levels are within an acceptable range for most countries in the region with a few exceptions (women in Angola, Malawi and Mozambique, and women and men 65 and older across the region).

But child labour is keeping young people out of school. More than 20% of children between ages seven and 14 spend their days working instead of studying in nine SADC countries. Teenage pregnancy, violence in schools, child labour and inadequate physical infrastructure continue to impact learning, enrolment, performance and completion rates. Teaching is also a critical challenge in the region. There are low levels of trained teachers at secondary level - and in some countries at primary level.

The Barometer calls for inclusivity in education as evidence shows that member countries in the region have failed to create enabling environments for all children, including those with disabilities.

Economic Justice: Over the decade women's representation in economic decision-making has increased by a mere two percentage points from 19% to 20%. Botswana (44%) has the highest proportion of women in economic decision-making, while Mauritius has no women in the economic decision-making positions measured in the Barometer.[6]

On the other hand, Mauritius and Seychelles are the only countries in the region with a Human Development Index of over 0.7 (with 1 indicating optimal development of life expectancy at birth; mean years of schooling and Gross National Income per capita). This is the same as ten years ago, showing that the economic growth being experienced in many countries is not translating into development; a worrying signal for gender equality. Tax justice issues have started gaining traction in the SADC women's movement with SADC Gender Protocol Alliance joining forces with Femnet to bring attention to the effects of ilicit financial flows on women and

girls. Evidence on the ground shows that illicit financial flows undermine the possibility of closing financing gaps, which impedes the attainment of gender equality and women's and girl's rights.

GBV: Over the decade considerable progress has been made in passing progressive laws. Of the 15 countries, 13 have sexual assault legislation (compared to seven at baseline, with eSwatini the most recent) and 12 on domestic violence (compared to 9 at baseline). All SADC countries now have National Action Plans to End GBV (compared to seven at baseline).

Seven countries have undertaken Violence against Women (VAW) Baseline studies. Botswana and Seychelles studied both violence against women (VAW) and violence against men (VAM), allowing for an informed and gender-specific response to GBV. These studies show that at least one in three women in the region have experienced GBV in their lifetime. Emotional abuse, the most prevalent form of GBV, is the type of GBV least likely to be reported to the police. Sexual and physical abuse are grossly under-reported. There is little or no government support for prevention and places of safety.

Innovative work at community level through the Centres of Excellence for Gender in Local Government shows promising signs of ending violence community by community. These councils are supporting the Sunrise Campaign - entrepreneurship training for survivors of GBV, making the link between economic empowerment and sustainable solutions to GBV. But political will and leadership are key to tacking this human rights abuse that has become so normalised that it hardly features in political discourse.

Sexual Reproductive Health and Rights: The region has recorded slow progress on health over the past year. Maternal mortality across most of SADC, with the exception of Mauritius and Seychelles, is unacceptably high and declining too slowly to meet even the SDG target of 70 per 100 000. The quality of services that are available for women, including the levels of skill and motivation of service providers are receiving increased attention.

Only South Africa and Mozambique have legislation that allows abortion on request. In late 2017 Madagascar passed the Reproductive Health and Family Planning Law after a clause that would have legalised abortion had been removed and Angola has withdrawn a bill that was passed in early 2018 that would have made abortion illegal after women marched in the streets against it.

March against ritual killings in Swaziland. Photo: Zethu Shongwe

---

[6] Minister, deputy minister and permanent secretaries of the ministries of finance, economic planning, trade and industry, as well as governors and deputy governors of the reserve banks.

In the past year there has been significant focus on menstrual health and hygiene is as a key SRHR issue. This is particularly focused on young women but there is acknowledgement that there are also issues for older women and in menopause that need to be addressed. As reported last year, the Botswana parliament voted to provide free sanitary ware in schools.

Tanzania has removed taxes on sanitary ware. But the Tanzanian government sparked an outcry when in a public address in June 2017, President John Magufuli reinforced a ban on teenage pregnancies. Magufuli challenged human rights groups to open schools for young parents, stating that the government provides free education for students "who have really wanted to study."

HIV and AIDS: SADC remain at the epicentre of the HIV epidemic. Though rates of new infections are declining, at the current rate of decline the region will still have at least 570,000 new infections annually (more than double the target). Gender inequality is still a strong driver of the pandemic: 59% of new infections in Southern Africa are women, but 53% of AIDS related deaths are men. Young women 15 to 24 years old are only 10% of the total population but 26% of new HIV infections.

Considerable effort is being invested in many aspects of prevention including comprehensive sexuality education, voluntary medical male circumcision, services for Key Populations such as harm reduction, condoms, PrEP and continued PMTCT. While most countries in the region are making progress on UNAIDS 90- 90- 90 goals[7], Madagascar, Angola and DRC still require support and resources.

There is greater focus on adolescents especially the girls as the rate of infection is generally three times higher than that of adolescent boys. A number of studies have shown that small cash transfers combined with adult care and regular attendance to secondary school is associated with lower incidence of HIV as well as improved treatment adherence for adolescent girls and boys. The rising number of people on treatment requires a much greater focus on differentiated care within the community, from community caregivers who need training, support, supplies, remuneration and recognition.

Peace and Security: While Southern Africa is now a much more peaceful region than a decade ago, security concerns emerged in DRC, Madagascar and Zimbabwe.

Botswana police marching against GBV.   Photo: Keletso Metsing

The DRC failed to hold elections in 2017. It remains in a tenuous state with elections now scheduled for December 2018. Violent protests re-emerged in Madagascar over its new electoral laws leading to a postponement of elections. In Zimbabwe, former deputy president Emmerson Mnangagwa ousted Robert Mugabe as president after a 38 year reign that brought the country to its knees, and paved the way for credible elections.

The SADC Secretariat adopted a Regional Framework for Mainstreaming Gender into the SADC Organ. It calls on all countries in SADC to adopt Women, Peace and Security (WPS) National Action Plans (NAPs). However progress has been very slow in this area. Only the DRC and Angola have adopted UNSCR 1325 NAPs while Namibia is validating its NAP.

Fourteen countries, compared to five at baseline, now have publicly accessible data on women in the security sector. South Africa (30%) has the highest proportion of women in defence, up from 24% a decade ago. DRC (3%) has ranked lowest over the decade. Women in the police services range from 6% in DRC to 39% in Seychelles (39%).

Media: The sixty-second session of the Commission on the Status of Women review theme focused on women's participation and access to media. It recognised the role the media can play in the achievement of gender equality and the empowerment of women and girls.

The proportion of women sources is the single most important measure of women's voice. The Gender and Media Progress Study (GMPS) reports that women sources have increased by a mere three percentage points: from 17% in 2003 to 20% in 2015.

The region has seen an encouraging increase in the proportion of women in media management, from 27%

---

[7] The UNAIDS programme to diagnose 90% of all HIV-positive persons; provide Anti-Retroviral Therapy (ART) for 90% of those diagnosed and achieve viral suppression for 90% of those treated by 2020

to 34%. The #MeToo and #TimesUp campaigns have re-energised discussions about gender discrimination and sexual harassment in the media and film industries.

Climate Change: The addition of gender and climate change to the Protocol in 2015 is a key Extreme weather events, such as droughts and floods, pose an increasing threat to the population and, according to climate scenarios, their frequency and intensity will continue to increase. Women and girls constitute the majority of those impacted by the effects of climate change and environmental degradation, yet they remain less likely to have access to environmental resources.

Along with the projected reduction in rainfall and increase in temperatures across large parts of the region, experts expect climate change will significantly affect productivity in the agricultural sector.[8] In SADC, 77% of the population rely on this sector for income and employment. Climate change therefore presents a serious

threat to food security and livelihoods, particularly among poor segments of the population in rural areas. However women can be powerful agents for change in the transition to, and promotion of, sustainable energy. Whilst women own less than 10% of the land they are key managers of the environment.

Looking ahead: Effective implementation of the amended SADC Gender Protocol requires systematic engagement by SADC, Member States and Non State Actors. Strengthening gender programmes at a local level has the potential to reignite movement building and amplify the voice of women. Collecting the right data to monitor progress is critical to sustaining momentum. Ten years since the historic adoption of the SADC Gender Protocol, the Alliance demand for action and results remains as important as ever.

Members of the Southern Africa Gender Protocol Alliance at the 2017 Annual strategy meeting.   *Photo: Thandokuhle Dhlamini*

---

[8] https://www.giz.de/en/worldwide/53743.html

Women in eSwatini are using the SADC Gender Protocol to hold their governments accountable on gender equality.

Photo: Zethu Shongwe

Data is vital for tracking progress on development. It also increases citizens' ability to make more effective[9] decisions in their daily lives, entrepreneurs to create new business opportunities and institutions to make the governing process more efficient, responsive, inclusive and transparent.[10]

Data collection and curation is a key feature of the annual SADC Gender Protocol Alliance Barometer. Each year Gender Links, working with Alliance partners, uses the latest harmonised data across the ten themes of the SADC Gender Protocol to assess the region's performance in achieving an equal society as per the regional, continental and global developmental agendas.

The analysis, and advocacy campaigns shaped by the analysis, plays a critical role in helping to shape the gender agenda in Southern Africa. The data collected is computed into the SADC Gender and Development Index (SGDI) which together with the Citizen Score Card (CSC) are used to track progress in attaining gender equality. Both of these measures were updated in 2017, in line with the updated SADC Gender Protocol. The details of this are contained in the 2017 Barometer. Below is a summary of these two measures.

---

9 Atlanta Declaration for the Advancement of Women's Right of Access to Information.
10 Africa Data Revolution Report 2016.

How the CSC and SGDI work

The **Citizen Score Card (CSC)** gives ordinary men and women the opportunity to hold their government accountable. It also ensures that women and men engage critically with the provisions of the Protocol. It comprises 40 key provisions of the Protocol. Women and men score their governments on a scale of one to ten. This is converted to a percentage. Chapter 11, which details the different M and E tools administered by the Alliance, shows that members throughout the region distributed 9188 Citizen Score Cards in 2018, 63% of the target number, but still a sizeable sample (especially considering the very low budget on which this is done) and a valuable educational tool.

The challenge is to couple perception measures (qualitative) with empirical measures (quantitative). As detailed in **Annex Two**, there have been several attempts globally and in Africa to develop indexes for measuring progress towards attaining gender equality. Each of these is fraught with challenges. Running through all these challenges is the difficulty of obtaining a wide enough variety of indicators to capture the many facets of gender equality or the lack of it.

The updated **SADC Gender and Development Index (SGDI)** is innovative on several fronts. The previous SGDI, like other gender related indexes, drew heavily on political participation, education, health and labour-related indicators because the data is easily available. However such indicators did not adequately capture the more rights-based issues, such as voice; agency; the right to make decisions about one's body; safety and security.

In July 2017, the Alliance adopted a new SGDI which is a mix of empirical data and gender attitude scores, drawn from the **Gender Progress Score (GPS)** one of the M and E Tools administered by the Alliance. This was a recommendation from an expert group meeting where participants highlighted the need to adopt a new index that would result in 'better data for better decisions" to close all gender gaps by 2030. Another innovation in the 2017 SGDI is the inclusion of the **Gender Responsive Assessment (GRA)** of Constitutions and Laws. While this area is difficult to assess empirically, it is crucial to measuring gender equality. The Alliance set up expert groups in each country (see list of contributors) to assess and score these provisions of the Protocol, using a detailed questionnaire, so that the Constitutional and Legal sector could be included in the SGDI.

As a result, the SGDI has 36 indicators across nine sectors of the Protocol, excluding only the Peace and Security sector for which there are still too many data gaps across countries to compute a composite score. The indicators for GBV are all based on the attitude questionnaire, ie they are all proxy indicators, given the paucity of reliable data on the extent of GBV. As such they are not commented on as a separate sector in this section. The same applies to climate change which has just two indicators. Due to several data gaps, a composite index could not be computed for Angola; this should be resolved by 2019. Despite these limitations, the composite SGDI provides a reliable measure of voice, choice and control at both country and regional level.

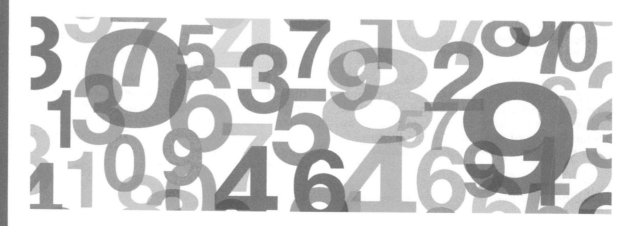

Table I: Key Indicators															
Indicator	ANGOLA	BOTSWANA	DRC	LESOTHO	MADAGASCAR	MALAWI	MAURITIUS	MOZAMBIQUE	NAMIBIA	SEYCHELLES	SOUTH AFRICA	eSWATINI	TANZANIA	ZAMBIA	ZIMBABWE
Constitutional and legal															
GRA of Constitutions and Laws	59	69	54	55	67	77	72	47	72	52	64	49	55	58	62
Governance															
% women in parliament	31	10	8	23	20	17	12	40	36	21	41	15	37	18	36
% women in local government	n/a	19	6	40	8	12	27	36	48	n/a	41	14	34	9	16
% women in top party posts	0	0	0	0	0	33	17	17	17	0	17	0	0	17	0
% women in electoral bodies	24	14	31	40	14	30	53	13	40	20	20	25	43	22	40
% women in cabinet	33	17	10	10	17	19	12	21	17	36	50	21	19	25	14
% women judges	31	24	20	33	12	26	48	30	21	15	36	23	43	54	50
% women sources on political topics	n/a	17	5	7	13	26	8	20	19	13	17	18	23	11	14
Education															
Secondary school enrolment rates for girls	11	52	36	45	32	36	86	19	58	81	88	41	48	43	45
Secondary school enrolment rates for boys	14	48	54	29	31	37	81	18	45	76	88	32	52	47	44
Secondary school completion rates girls	35	49	54	29	31	37	81	18	55	76	88	34	34	47	44
Secondary school completion rates boys	15	87	34	50	37	n/a	90	21	63	100	n/a	50	32	51	67
% women in tertiary education	8	28	4	12	5	1	42	5	10	20	23	6	3	3	8
% men in tertiary education	10	19	10	8	5	1	32	7	8	9	16	5	5	5	9
% women teachers in secondary schools	48	53	12	56	44	31	62	21	50	58	55	49	28	0	46
% women in STEM subjects in tertiary education	3	12	2	3	3	0	9	3	9	2	9	0	3	0	6
Economic justice															
% women in economic decision-making	24	44	14	21	16	18	0	25	25	31	23	40	21	23	23
Length of maternity leave (weeks)	12	12	12	12	14	18	12	12	14	10	12	12	12	12	14
% women sources on economic topics	n/a	5	8	28	16	18	9	18	18	22	17	20	20	15	19
% who agree or strongly agree that men should share the work around the house with women such as doing dishes, cleaning	67	37	80	45	85	69	39	45	40	75	44	46	49	24	36
GBV															
% who say if a woman works she should give her money to her husband	45	15	68	26	14	13	1	29	10	6	28	29	19	25	25
% who say if a wife does something wrong her husband has the right to punish her	53	26	16	23	33	18	3	41	16	8	17	32	18	14	15
% who say if a man beats a woman it shows that he loves her	29	23	13	24	10	7	1	45	9	6	14	22	8	14	16
% who say if a woman wears a short skirt she is asking to be raped	44	29	8	26	22	20	2	44	18	5	21	26	26	19	19
SRHR															
Maternal Mortality Ratio (per 100,000)	447	129	693	542	353	634	53	489	265	0	138	389	398	224	443
Skilled attendance at birth (per 100)	50	100	80	78	44	90	100	54	88	99	94	88	64	63	78
Contraceptive coverage	18	53	20	60	40	59	76	12	56	41	60	65	34	49	67
% who say a woman should be able to choose to terminate a pregnancy in the first three months of her pregnancy	52	44	15	45	13	30	30	43	14	46	36	38	15	25	21
% coverage with improved sanitation	52	63	30	30	12	41	93	21	34	100	66	57	18	44	37
HIV and AIDS															
Women who are HIV positive as a % of total	59	55	59	59	46	59	28	58	60	42	60	58	61	52	58
PMTCT coverage	34	90	59	90	11	92	100	86	95	100	95	90	85	92	95
Comprehensive knowledge of HIV and AIDS	14	97	27	81	3	73	96	66	90	100	87	95	71	86	82
% of those living with AIDS who are on ARV treatment	26	84	55	74	7	71	67	54	84	61	61	85	66	75	84
% who say a woman has the right to insist on a man using a condom.	75	43	31	42	66	71	34	46	46	72	58	55	43	33	61
Media															
% women media management positions	n/a	32	17	53	34	39	43	31	40	24	35	44	24	37	10
% women sources	n/a	28	6	21	21	21	10	25	19	28	20	18	22	19	24
% women images	n/a	34	15	21	29	26	30	24	27	50	27	28	10	25	30
Sustainable development and climate change															
% women in climate change decision-making	30	9	0	11	14	0	10	0	20	50	33	40	11	15	43
% women sources on gender and climate change	30	9	21	38	23	14	20	30	10	55	41	22	23	30	39

Progress against the SGDI and CSC

Table I presents the 2018 data for the 36 indicators of the SGDI across the 15 countries of SADC where this data is available. These figures are statistically converted to a factor of 100 in each case to give percentage progress by country, sector and overall in nine sectors (constitutional and legal rights, governance, education and training , the economy, gender based violence, health, HIV and AIDS, and the media and climate change).

The Citizen Score Card (CSC), administered to a representative sample across the region, measures perceptions of women and men on the change that is taking place around them against all 40 targets from the SADC Gender Protocol, in ten sectors. Unlike the SGDI, the CSC captures nuances that are not incorporated in the empirical data. For example, while the SGDI records enrolment levels for boys and girls, the CSC includes qualitative aspects like safety in schools and gender biases in curriculum. The CSC covers (in addition to the nine SGDI sectors) Peace and Security for which there is no SGDI scores because of the unavailability of data. Like all indicators, both the SGDI and the CSC have limitations. However, read together, they provide a fair reflection of the progress and challenges.

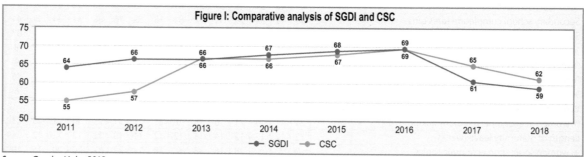

Source: Gender Links, 2018.

Figure I shows that in 2018, the SGDI stood at 59%, one percentage point lower than 2017, and the CSC at 62%, three percentage points lower than last year. These lower scores reflect regression in several areas over the last year, including gender based violence, women's participation in politics, provision of health services, economic and productive opportunities. In the year of the #MeToo, #TimesUp and various other campaigns, the scores for 2018 are a sobering reminder that despite the higher profile of gender issues, the journey to equality is fraught with many ups and downs.

Comparative analysis of SGDI and CSC

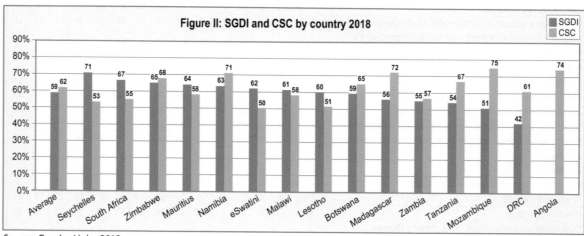

Source: Gender Links, 2018.

Figure II compares the SGDI and CSC for 2018 overall and by country. The graph shows that with an SGDI of 71%, Seychelles comes first, followed by South Africa (67%), Zimbabwe (65%), Mauritius (64%) and Namibia (63%). Mozambique (51%) and DRC (42%) score lowest. At least six countries (Seychelles, South Africa, Mauritius, eSwatini, Malawi and Lesotho) recorded an SGDI score higher than the CSC score. Citizens in those countries are more sceptical than what the numbers suggest. Mozambique (75%) has the highest CSC. The country also recorded the largest gap between the CSC and SGDI, i.e. citizens are much more optimistic than what the numbers suggest, possibly a reflection of the buoyant economy and general optimism. At 42%, DRC is the only country in the region with an SGDI score below 50%. As media monitoring did not take place in Angola in 2015 due to financial constraints, this excludes six indicators for the country, making it impossible to award an SGDI score in 2018. The Alliance is working to rectify this. Angola scored 74% in the CSC.

Women and men's perceptions on government commitment

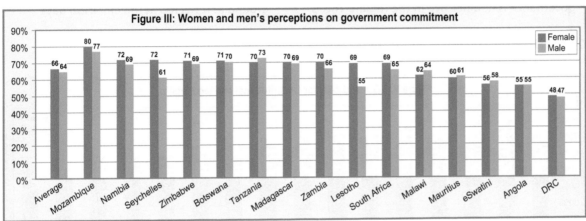

Source: Gender Links, 2018.

Figure III provides sex disaggregated data on the CSC. It shows that overall there is no significant gap in the scores of women (66%) and men (64%). Women's greater optimism reflects the perception that their voices are beginning to be heard. Women scored their governments higher than men in Mozambique, Namibia, Seychelles, Zimbabwe, Botswana, Madagascar, Zambia, Lesotho, South Africa, and Angola. The opposite is true in Tanzania, Malawi, Mauritius and eSwatini and Mauritius.

Sector scores

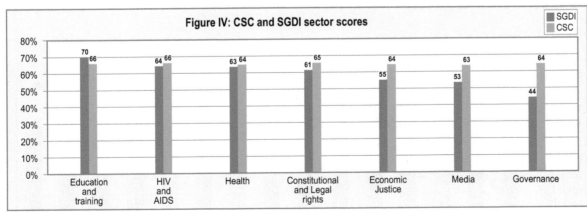

Source: Gender Links, 2018.

Figure IV compares the SGDI (empirical scores) and CSC (perception) scores in the seven sectors from which the SGDI can be disaggregated by sector (as mentioned earlier GBV and climate change do not have a sufficient variety of indicators to be broken down by sector). While the scores are constructed in different ways, the trends are interesting, as they reflect the extent to which perceptions and reality either converge or diverge. The graph is sorted in descending order according to SGDI scores. It shows that:

- For both indices, education and training, HIV and AIDS score highest. This is consistent with the positive developments in these sectors reported on in respective chapters of the Barometer.
- The biggest gap between the two scores is for the governance sector. The SGDI ranks governance last (44%) while at 64% the CSC score for governance is number five in the region. This is

a stark reminder of the need to consider both quantitative and qualitative evidence in assessing progress. While there has been much hype over the 50/50 campaign, creating a mirage of progress, Chapter three underscores the regression taking place in all areas of decision-making at the very moment when we should be stepping it up for gender equality.

- The second largest gap is the media sector (63% for the CSC and 53% for the SGDI). Again, this is an area of increased advocacy but limited delivery on gender equality.
- Scores for HIV and AIDS, Health and Constitutional and Legal Rights show that citizen's perceptions are not far off the reality on the ground as reflected in the empirical data.

Constitutional and legal rights

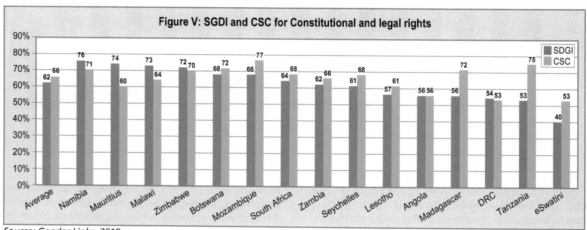

Figure V: SGDI and CSC for Constitutional and legal rights

Source: Gender Links, 2018.

Figure V compares the SGDI and CSC scores for Constitutional and Legal Rights for 2018. It shows that overall, at 62% for the SGDI and 66% for the CSC, these scores are quite close. Mauritius has the highest positive variance (i.e. people who are more

sceptical than what the numbers tell us). Tanzania and Madagascar had the highest negative variances, i.e. where citizens are more optimistic than what the facts on the ground tell us.

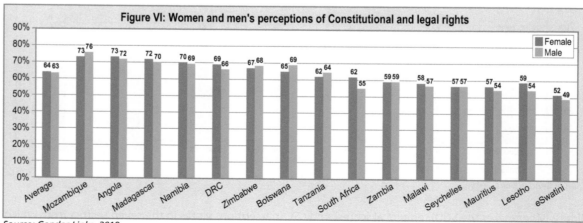

Figure VI: Women and men's perceptions of Constitutional and legal rights

Source: Gender Links, 2018.

Figure VI provides sex disaggregated data on the CSC for the sector for 2018. On average women (64%) had slightly higher scores than men (63%). Since this is the sector that determines the policy and legal framework for gender equality, it is a positive sign that women are overall even more optimistic than men about the progress achieved.

This is especially so in South Africa, Mauritius and eSwatini and Lesotho which have slightly higher variances between women and men. In Botswana and Mozambique, women are slightly less optimistic than men. The same is true in Tanzania and Zimbabwe.

Governance

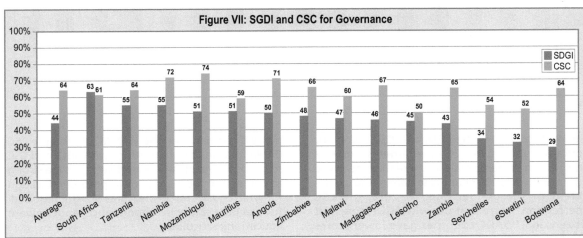

Figure VII: SGDI and CSC for Governance

Source: Gender Links, 2018.

Figure VII shows that overall at 44% for the SGDI and 64% for the CSC, there is quite a wide divergence between these scores - wider than in any other sector. The CSC was higher than the SGDI

in all countries. This is likely due to the high visibility of 50/50 campaigns and women taking up a few high public office positions while in reality there is regression in this sector across the region.

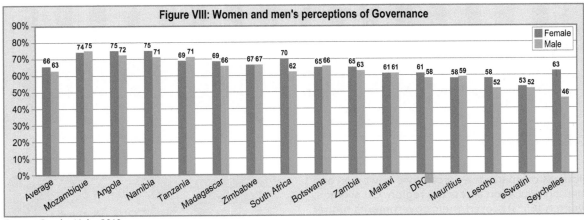

Figure VIII: Women and men's perceptions of Governance

Source: Gender Links, 2018.

Figure VIII compares the CSC for women and men. This shows that overall at 66% women score their governments higher than men at 63%. Generally women are more optimistic about women's repre-

sentation in public office as compared to men which is worrying considering the low representation of women in this sector.

Education and training

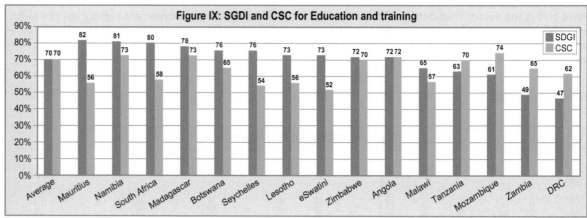

Figure IX: SGDI and CSC for Education and training

Source: Gender Links, 2018.

Figure IX compares the SGDI and CSC scores for Education and Training. As the target is women's and girls' equal participation, where this is achieved a country scores 100% and less depending on the extent of the gender gap. At 70%, the CSC "perception" score is at par with SGDI score. But citizens in 11 SADC countries gave lower scores compared to the SGDI. Mauritius recorded the highest gap between the SGDI (82%) and the CSC (56%) followed by South Africa with SGDI and CSC scores of 80% and 58% respectively. This is a strong reminder that there are many aspects of education for which quantitative measures are still required: for example safety in schools, and gender aware education curriculum.

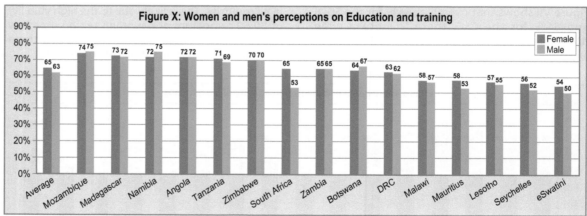

Figure X: Women and men's perceptions on Education and training

Source: Gender Links, 2018.

Figure X compares the perceptions of women and men on education across the region. On average, women (65%) scored their governments higher than men (63%). Women in nine countries (Madagascar, Tanzania, South Africa, DRC, Malawi, Mauritius, Lesotho, Seychelles and eSwatini) scored their governments higher than men while in three countries (Angola, Zambia and Zimbabwe) men and women gave the same score. In Mozambique, Namibia and Botswana women scored government performance in education lower than men.

Education is power!   *Photo: Adapt*

Economic justice

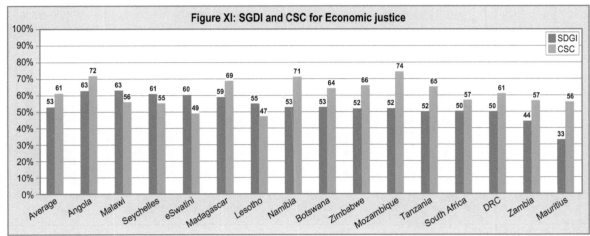

Figure XI: SGDI and CSC for Economic justice

Source: Gender Links, 2018.

Figure XI shows that the gap between the regional average SGDI (53%) and the CSC (61%) is eight percentage points. The SGDI scores are lower than the CSC in 11 countries. Mozambique (22 percentage points) and Mauritius (23 percentage points) have the greatest differences between the actual performance and the citizen perceptions. Only four countries (Malawi, Seychelles, eSwatini and Lesotho) have SGDI scores higher than the CSC scores. This shows that citizens are generally more optimistic about the economic outlook than the actual figures suggest. This is consistent with economic growth in many countries and the adoption of policies that promise a better future for women and girls.

In SADC, women still have limited access to land ownership and control. *Photo: Informative newspaper*

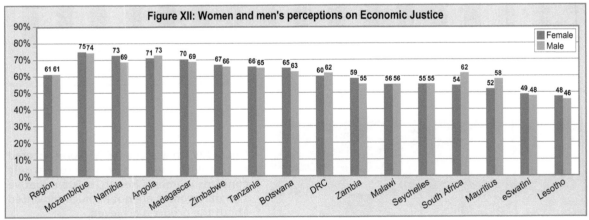

Figure XII: Women and men's perceptions on Economic Justice

Source: Gender Links, 2018.

Figure XII disaggregates women and men's perceptions of economic justice by sex. Both men and women scored their governments 61%. Mozambique had the highest score (75% for women and 74% for men).Women and men in eSwatini and Lesotho gave scores less than 50%.

The variations in scores reflect the economic challenges being faced by most countries in the region as a result of the high level of unemployment, the widening economic gaps and rising cost of living.

Sexual and Reproductive Health

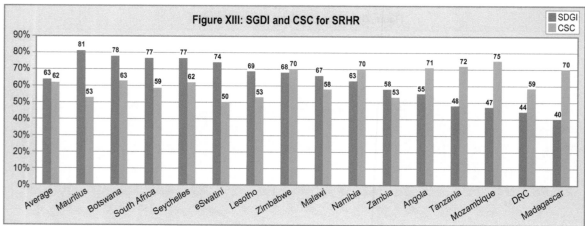

Figure XIII: SGDI and CSC for SRHR

Legend: SDGI, CSC

Average: 63, 62
Mauritius: 81, 53
Botswana: 78, 63
South Africa: 77, 59
Seychelles: 77, 62
eSwatini: 74, 50
Lesotho: 69, 53
Zimbabwe: 68, 70
Malawi: 67, 58
Namibia: 63, 70
Zambia: 58, 53
Angola: 55, 71
Tanzania: 48, 72
Mozambique: 47, 75
DRC: 44, 59
Madagascar: 40, 70

Source: Gender Links, 2018.

Figure XIII shows that with an SGDI of 63% and CSC of 62%, the scores for SRHR are quite close. Mauritius, Botswana and South Africa have the highest positive variances (i.e. people who are more skeptical than what the numbers tell us).

Mozambique, DRC and Madagascar have the highest negative variances, i.e. where citizens are more optimistic than what the facts on the ground tell us.

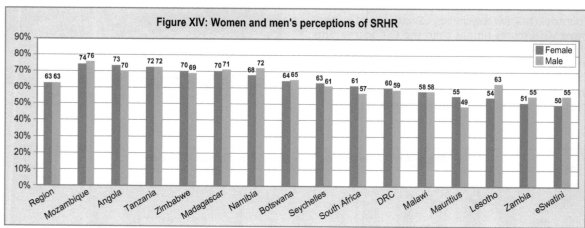

Figure XIV: Women and men's perceptions of SRHR

Legend: Female, Male

Region: 63, 63
Mozambique: 74, 76
Angola: 73, 70
Tanzania: 72, 72
Zimbabwe: 70, 69
Madagascar: 70, 71
Namibia: 68, 72
Botswana: 64, 65
Seychelles: 63, 61
South Africa: 61, 57
DRC: 60, 59
Malawi: 58, 58
Mauritius: 55, 49
Lesotho: 54, 63
Zambia: 51, 55
eSwatini: 50, 55

Source: Gender Links, 2018.

Promoting safe sex at the Zimbabwe Summit Awards Night in Zimbabwe.
Photo: Gender Links

Figure XIV On average (66%) women scored at par with men. As this sector largely concerns women's health, it is a negative sign that women are not as much convinced about the progress achieved.

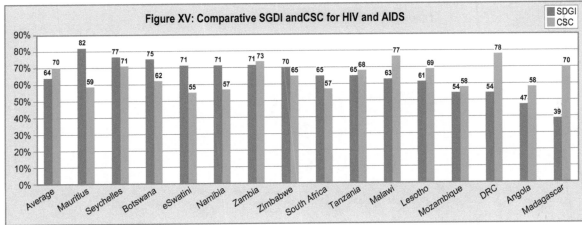

Figure XV: Comparative SGDI andCSC for HIV and AIDS

Source: Gender Links, 2018.

Figure XV shows that the SGDI of 64 for HIV and AIDS is much lower than the CSC at 70%. Seychelles and Mauritius have the highest positive variances (i.e. people who are more sceptical than what the numbers tell us). Angola and Madagascar have the highest negative variances, i.e. where citizens are more optimistic than what the empirical data suggests. Governments in the region have become much more proactive in the fight against HIV and AIDS. These measures are yielding positive results.

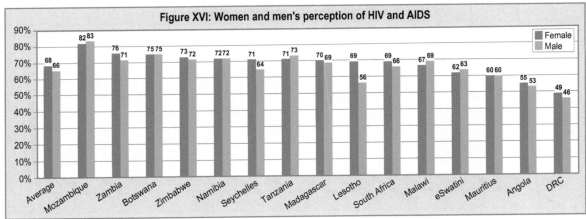

Figure XVI: Women and men's perception of HIV and AIDS

Source: Gender Links, 2017.

On average women (68%) had slightly higher scores than men (66%). As women are dispropor-tionately affected by HIV and AIDS, it is a positive sign that women are overall even more optimistic than men about the progress achieved. This is especially so in Lesotho, which has the highest variance between women and men. In other countries the perceptions of women and men are very similar. In Mozambique, Tanzania, Malawi and eSwatini women are slightly less optimistic than men.

Children in Arandis, Namibia, join the march against GBV, HIV and AIDS.   *Photo: Gender Links*

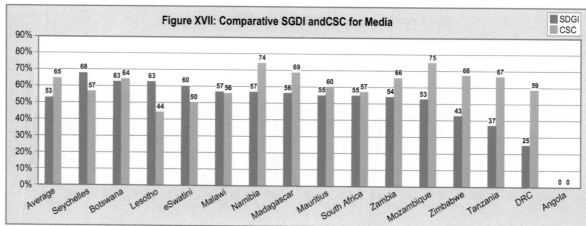

Figure XVII: Comparative SGDI andCSC for Media

Source: Gender Links, 2018.

Figure XVII illustrates the media SGDI and CSC scores for media. At 65% the media CSC score is twelve percentage points higher than the SGDI. In all countries except eSwatini, Seychelles and Lesotho, citizens believe that their countries are doing better than they actually are. This is reflective of a troubling reality - that most citizens are blind to the gender gaps and biases in the media, which play a large role in shaping public perceptions of gender issues.

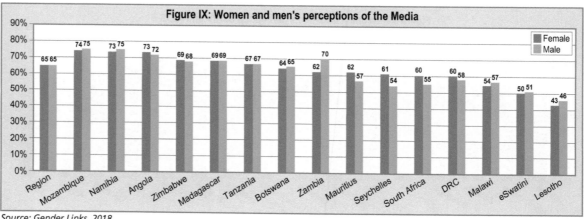

Figure IX: Women and men's perceptions of the Media

Source: Gender Links, 2018.

Figure IX shows sex disaggregated data on the CSC for the media sector for 2018. On average, women and men gave the same score (65%). Women in Mozambique are most optimistic about the media they consume while women in Lesotho (43%) are the least optimistic. The highest variance between women and men is in Zambia at eight percentage points.

- **2005:** Audit of achievements against the SADC Declaration on Gender and Development leads to a paper - "Rationale for the Elevation of the SADC Declaration on Gender and Development to a Protocol" - the most legally binding of SADC instruments. Civil society organisations for the Southern African Gender Protocol Alliance.
- **2005-2008:** Alliance members form part of a Task Team constituted by the SADC Gender Unit to prepare drafting notes for a legal team, comment on and canvass seven drafts of the Protocol before its final presentation to Heads of State.
- **August 2008:** 13 out of 15 HOS Sign the SADC Gender Protocol, a unique sub regional instrument that brings together and enhances existing commitments to gender equality through 28, time bound targets aligned to the 2015 deadline for MDG 3. Alliance members launch a campaign to get Mauritius and Botswana to sign.
- **August 2009:** The Alliance launches the SADC Gender Protocol Baseline Barometer - a key tracking tool assessing progress of 15 countries against the 28 targets of the Protocol
  - http://www.genderlinks.org.za/page/sadc-research.
- **August 2009:** Alliance launches the "Roadmap to Equality" - strategies and lessons learned in the campaign; key provisions of the Protocol in 23 languages; radio spots; a DVD; knowledge and attitude quiz; village level meetings to popularise the Protocol that have since reached 15,000 citizens directly and thousands more indirectly.
- **2009/2010:** Alliance devises a Citizen Score Card that is used to gauge citizen perceptions of government progress and is administered at village meetings.
- **August 2010:** Progress Barometer and Alliance annual meeting. Alliance gets better organised into country and theme clusters, each leading on a key issue, e.g. GBV, economic justice.
- **August 2011:** SADC Gender Protocol goes into force with South Africa becoming the ninth country to ratify the Protocol giving the two thirds critical mass required. With data from 15 countries on 23 indicators, the 2011 Barometer introduces the SADC Gender and Development Index - see http://www. genderlinks.org.za/page/sadc-sgdi. Alliance forms a Think Tank to guide the work of the Alliance in between annual meetings.
- **2011/2012:** Alliance networks in-country identify champions for the 28 targets of the Protocol, begin to collect case studies of the Protocol@Work - see http://www.genderlinks. org.za/ page/protocol-work.
- **September 2011:** The Alliance collaborates with the SADC Gender Unit on a tool and process for aligning national gender action plans to the targets of the SADC Gender Protocol, and costing their implementation.

Namibia pilots this process - see http://www.genderlinks. org.za/page/ implementation.
- **November 2011:** Intense lobbying for an Addendum to the Protocol on Gender and Climate Change linked to COP17.
- **February 2013:** Gender ministers meeting in Maputo ahead of the 57th meeting of the Commission on the Status of Women (CSW) commit to take forward the Addendum. Alliance releases a progressive statement on gender justice concerns in the region. Mounts a presence at the CSW and produces a daily newsletter; generates debate on the post 2015 agenda.
- **March-April 2013:** Twelve country summits and a regional summit lead to 672 case studies being gathered on the SADC Protocol@Work from NGOs, CSO, Faith-Based Organisations.
- **By June 2013:** Lesotho, DRC, Malawi, Mozambique, Tan-zania, Zambia and Zimbabwe learn from Seychelles, Namibia, Zambia and eSwatini on aligning their policies and action plans to the SADC Protocol and costing implementation.
- **August 2013:** Alliance annual meeting ahead of the SADC Heads of State Summit in Malawi with a key focus on implementation, the 50/50 campaign, gender and climate change and Coalition Building. Round table meeting with the new Southern African head of UNWOMEN, Phumzile Mlambo-Ngcuka. Study visit to the Gauteng *Women Demand Action Now* Alliance networking meeting sparks ideas for strengthening country, provincial and district-level net-working.
- **August 2013:** Coalition building and networking at the regional level through the SADC Heads of state summit held in Malawi in August 2013. The regional barometer was officially launched then.
- Strengthening the alliance network through a strategy meeting held in August 2013 and a think tank meeting held alongside the SADC HOS summit.
- **August 2013:** Production of the fifth edition of the SADC Gender Protocol Regional Barometer, tracking progress against the 28 targets. The 2013 barometer had in-depth analysis of implementation of the SADC Gender protocol by the governments and civil society.
- **December 2013:** 12 country barometer reports; 9 launches. SADC Gender Protocol village level workshops in 10 countries through the country networks resulting in 72 meetings.
- **By October 2013:** Strengthening the country focal networks through mapping of country thematic clusters and championing resulting in 11 country level meetings and 82 signed up champions.
- **May 2014:** SADC Gender Protocol@Work summit preceded by 12 national summits with a special category on the Faith Based Organisations (FBOS).
- **March 2014:** Alliance participates in the 58th Commission on the Status of Women.

- **July 2014:** Gender ministers meeting in Malawi ahead of the 35thth HOS Summit in Harare in August, followed by the SADC CNGO civil society forum in Harare. Alliance makes the case for a strong post 2015 gender agenda.
- **August 2014:** 35th SADC Heads of State Summit in Victoria Falls; Alliance lobbies for review of the SADC Gender Protocol.
- **March 2015:** The Alliance participate at CSW 59 with a focus on the targets and indicators for the SDGs and the SADC Gender Protocol Post-2015.
- **March:** The Alliance's input on the Global SDGs consultations is acknowledged.
- **May 2015:** The SADC Executive Secretary requests the Alliance together with UN Women to work with the SADC Secretariat as technical partners in the review process.

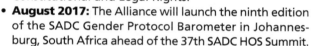

- **May-June 2015:** The Alliance holds 13 national SADC Protocol@Work summits.
- **August 2015:** The Alliance launched the sixth edition of the SADC Gender Protocol Barometer in Botswana on the eve of the 35th SADC HOS Summit in Gaborone at the SADC Protocol@Work summit.
- **October 2015:** The Alliance participates actively at the first review process of the Protocol together with UN Women, governments and the SADC secretariat.
- **March 2016:** The Alliance holds two side events on localising SDGs through the SADC Gender Protocol at the 60th session of the Commission on the Status of Women.
- **June 2016:** The Alliance participates at the SADC Gender Ministers meeting which adopted the reviewed Protocol.
- **June/July 2016:** The Alliance holds country level consultations on the Post 2015 Protocol reaching 1224 people.
- **August 2016:** The Alliance launches the eighth edition of the SADC Gender Protocol Barometer in eSwatini ahead of the 36th SADC HOS Summit.

- **November 2016:** The Alliance holds eight national SADC Gender Protocol Summits producing 737 case studies.
- **November 2016:** The Alliance reviews M and E tools for the SADC Gender Protocol.
- **December 2016:** The Alliance joins the social media platform, Twitter @GenderProtocol.
- **January 2017:** The Alliance joins the Women's March Global.
- **March 2017:** The Alliance participates at the 61st session of the Commission on the Status of Women.
- **May 2017:** The Alliance works with EASSI to produce the pilot East Africa Community Barometer.
- **July 2017:** The Alliance finalises the reviewed SGDI which has 36 empirical indicators.
- **June/July 2017:** The Alliance holds gender and rights scoring meetings in 15 countries giving a baseline score for the indicator on Constitutional and Legal Rights.
- **August 2017:** The Alliance will launch the ninth edition of the SADC Gender Protocol Barometer in Johannesburg, South Africa ahead of the 37th SADC HOS Summit.
- **October 2017:** Alliance attends the inaugural African Feminists Microeconomics Academy.
- **December 2017:** Alliance launches a Community of Practice and the Barometer Portal.
- **March 2018:** The Alliance participates at 62nd session of the Commission on the Status of Women.
- **May/June 2018:** The Alliance holds gender and rights scoring meetings in 15 countries giving a score for the indicator on Constitutional and Legal Rights.
- **July 2018:** Alliance participates in the West Africa Women's Dialogue to share experiences on the SADC Gender Protocol Barometer process.
- **August 2018:** The Alliance launches the ninth edition of the SADC Gender Protocol Barometer in Johannesburg, South Africa ahead of the 38th SADC HOS Summit in Namibia.
- **August 2018:** Alliance launches the Southern Africa #She Decides Southern Africa campaign.

CHAPTER 1

Constitutional and legal rights

Articles 4-11

Lesotho High Court.

Photo: Majara Molupe

Constitutional and legal rights are a **crucial** indicator of the **level** of **respect** for **human rights** in a country

KEY POINTS

- The South African High Court in Pretoria found the government's participation in signing regional legal instruments disbanding the original SADC Tribunal to be illegal and unconstitutional. This paves the way for the reconsideration of the role and position of the SADC Tribunal, including its role in disputes relating to the interpretation of the SADC Protocol on Gender and Development.

- The Government of eSwatini pronounced that widows in mourning would not be allowed to participate in the 2018 general elections due later in the year. Only widows who had been in mourning for at least two years and had been "cleansed" will be allowed to participate.

- In Lesotho, the High Court ruled that the Defence Forces could not dismiss female soldiers who get pregnant during the first five years of their engagement, as noted in the army regulations. This represents an important precedent given that many Defence Forces in the region have similar regulations.

- In Botswana, the High Court ordered the government to change the gender of a transgender woman on her identity documents. The government had initially refused to effect the change.

- In a landmark ruling in South Africa, the Supreme Court of Appeal recognised the responsibility of both parents to pay school fees for their children in cases of divorce or separation.

- The murder of people with albinism continued in the region. In South Africa, police found the bodies of a 13-year-old girl with albinism and a toddler - her killers had harvested body parts from the 13-year-old girl.

- In Zimbabwe, President Emmerson Mnangagwa said the country might need to develop a law to regulate commercial sex work.

Table 1.1: Trends in Constitutional and Legal Rights since 2009

	Target 2030	Baseline 2009	Progress 2018	Variance (Progress minus 2030 target)
GENDER AND RIGHTS ASSESSMENT OF CONSTITUTIONS AND LAWS				
Highest	100%		77%	-23%
Lowest	100%		47%	-53%
Number of countries that undertake constitutional reforms and review processes to align with the SADC Protocol on Gender and Development	15 countries	0	11 with 10 complete (Angola, DRC, Madagascar, Malawi, Mauritius, Mozambique, Namibia, Seychelles, Zambia and Zimbabwe) and one in process (Tanzania, although the process is currently stalled)	5 countries have yet to complete this process
Number of countries that provide for non-discrimination on the basis of sex and others	15 countries	14 (Angola, Botswana, DRC, Lesotho, Madagascar, Malawi, Mauritius,Mozambique, Namibia, South Africa, eSwatini, Tanzania, Zambia and Zimbabwe)	All SADC countries	All SADC countries have completed this process
Number of countries' Constitutions that provide for the promotion of gender equality	15 country Constitutions	7 (Angola, DRC, Lesotho, Malawi, Mozambique, South Africa and eSwatini)	13 (Angola, DRC, Lesotho, Madagascar, Malawi, Mauritius, Mozambique, Namibia, South Africa, eSwatini, Tanzania, Zambia and Zimbabwe)	2 remain without constitutions that provide for the promotion of gender equality (Botswana and Seychelles)
Number of countries that have no claw back clauses	15 countries	7 (Angola, DRC, Madagascar, Mozambique, Namibia, Seychelles and South Africa)	10 (Angola, DRC, Madagascar, Mozambique, Namibia, Seychelles, South Africa, Tanzania, Zambia and Zimbabwe)	5 countries (Botswana, Lesotho, Malawi, Mauritius and eSwatini)
Number of countries that address the contradictions between the constitution, laws and practices	15 countries	4 (Namibia, South Africa, eSwatini and Tanzania)	12 (Angola, Lesotho, Madagascar, Malawi, Mozambique, Namibia, Seychelles, South Africa, eSwatini, Tanzania, Zambia and Zimbabwe)	3 countries remaining (Botswana, DRC, Mauritius)
Number of countries that provide for special measures in their constitutions	15 countries	9 (DRC, Lesotho, Malawi, Namibia, Seychelles, South Africa, eSwatini, Tanzania and Zimbabwe)	13 (DRC, Lesotho, Madagascar, Malawi, Mauritius, Mozambique, Namibia, Seychelles, South Africa, eSwatini, Tanzania, Zambia and Zimbabwe)	2 countries (Angola, Botswana)
Number of countries that decriminalised LGBTI people	15 countries	None	4 (DRC, Mozambique, South Africa and Seychelles)	11 countries
Marriage age for girls and boys is a minimum of 18 in 15 countries	15 countries	8 (Angola, Botswana, Madagascar, Mauritius, Mozambique, Namibia, Seychelles and South Africa)	14 (Angola, Botswana, DRC, Madagascar, Malawi, Mozambique, Namibia, Seychelles, South Africa, Tanzania, Zambia and Zimbabwe)	Only Mauritius remains without this minimum
Marital rape is a crime in 15 countries	15 countries	None	9 (Angola, Lesotho, Malawi, Mozambique, Namibia, Seychelles, South Africa, eSwatini and Zimbabwe)	6 countries
15 countries decriminalise sex work	15 countries	None	None (although in May 2018 Zimbabwean President Mnangagwa signalled that the country might need a law to regulate commercial sex work)	All 15 countries
15 countries legalise abortion	15 countries	2 (South Africa and Zambia)	3 (Mozambique, South Africa and Zambia)	12 countries

Source: Gender Links, 2018.

Courts continue to **play** a **vital role** in upholding ⚢ rights

Table 1.1 shows that:
- In some areas, the region has seen limited progress since 2009. This is especially true for decriminalisation of sex work, decriminalisation of Lesbian, Gay, Bisexual, Transgender and Intersex (LGBTI) people, and legalisation of abortion.
- By 2018, only four countries had decriminalised homosexuality (DRC, Mozambique, Seychelles and South Africa). Seychelles is the latest addition.
- Marital rape criminalisation represents the most notable development, with three more countries adopting laws to criminalise marital rape (Angola, Mozambique and Seychelles).
- Most countries have begun or completed constitutional reforms and review processes to align with the SADC Protocol on Gender and Development.
- All constitutions now provide for non-discrimination on the basis of sex, and all countries except Botswana and Seychelles provide for the promotion of gender equality.
- Most countries also now address the contradictions between the constitution, laws and practices, with only Botswana, DRC and Mauritius yet to do so.

Background

Constitutional and legal rights are a crucial indicator of the level of respect for human rights in a country and they provide context in its developmental trajectory. Development cannot occur without human rights and protection of women's rights plays a significant role in any country's development process. This chapter highlights progress made in the last year based on the Post-2015 SADC Gender Protocol. With its improved rights language, stakeholders expected the 2015 Gender Protocol to stimulate positive advancements in women's rights protections. However, the region shows mixed progress, with countries stalled in certain instances. The courts have continued to play a vital role in upholding women's rights and compelling SADC Member States to do more to protect women's rights.

The fight to end child marriage continues, with policymakers making pronouncements on the need to end the scourge. Ending the practice, however, remains a challenge, with statistics indicating little or no change in many SADC countries. There region has also seen little movement in its domestication of the SADC Model Law on Eradicating Child Marriage and Protecting Children Already in Marriage despite parliaments and governments making the right noises about the issue.

The contentious issues of marital rape, commercial sex work, LGBTI rights and abortion remain contested. Open discussions around the issues are often difficult due to highly personalised views, which come up against conservative religious and cultural beliefs.

One ruling in South Africa has revived hope for the reopening of the original SADC Tribunal, which lawmakers disbanded in 2012 - or at least one that allows access to SADC citizens. In February 2018, the South African High Court in Pretoria found the South African government's participation in signing regional legal instruments disbanding the original SADC Tribunal to be illegal and unconstitutional. This ruling will play an important role in improving access to justice for all, including women and girls.

As one expert noted, "Much hope was vested in the court, whose mission was to effectively and efficiently ensure compliance and resolve disputes related to the interpretation and application of SADC treaty and subsidiary legal instruments. Through this mandate, the court also both directly and indirectly support[ed] sustainable and equitable economic growth and socio-economic development and promote deeper cooperation among SADC's 15 member countries."[1] The Government of South Africa has, however, appealed the decision, signalling that the fight to bring back the SADC Tribunal with its original powers will be long and drawn out.[2]

Activist Kumi Naidoo and a staff member from Earthlife Africa launch the Kilimanjaro Declaration on Africa Day in Johannesburg in 2017. The Declaration commits to expand space for civic and political action and fight for women's rights and freedoms. *Photo: Gender Links*

[1] https://www.brookings.edu/blog/africa-in-focus/2018/04/02/a-house-of-justice-for-africa-resurrecting-the-sadc-tribunal/
[2] Eye Witness News (2008), 'Afriforum: Presidency Files Notice to Appeal SADC Tribunal Ruling', available at: http://ewn.co.za/2018/03/23/afriforum-presidency-files-notice-to-appeal-sadc-tribunal-ruling (accessed 12 June 2018).

Most countries have begun or completed constitutional reforms and review processes to align with the SADC Gender Protocol

Gender and rights score card

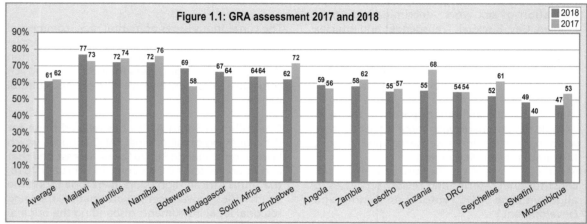

Figure 1.1: GRA assessment 2017 and 2018

	2018	2017
Average	61	62
Malawi	77	73
Mauritius	72	74
Namibia	72	76
Botswana	69	58
Madagascar	67	64
South Africa	64	64
Zimbabwe	62	72
Angola	59	56
Zambia	58	62
Lesotho	55	57
Tanzania	55	68
DRC	54	54
Seychelles	52	61
eSwatini	49	40
Mozambique	47	53

Source: GRA scorecard.

Figure 1.1 shows the scores of the Gender and Rights Assessment (GRA), determined by legal and gender experts in each SADC country - a tool introduced as part of the Barometer in 2017. The GRA covers Articles 4 to 11 of the SADC Gender Protocol, including special measures, domestic legislation, equality in accessing justice, marriage and family rights, persons with disabilities, widow and widowers' rights, the girl and the boy child. The average regional score is 61%, a slight drop from 62% in 2017. Malawi scored the highest (77%) while eSwatini scored lowest at 47%, although it posted a seven-percentage point increase from 2017. Fourteen SADC countries scored higher than 50%. This assessment indicates that the region has seen progress in legal and policy frameworks to promote gender equality. However, what is on paper does not always translate into reality. Only seven countries received a score higher than in 2017, while six received a lower ranking.

Group discussion during a SADC Gender and Rights Scorecard meeting.   *Photo: Gender Links*

Table 1.2: Analysis of gender equality clauses in Constitutions

Country	Provides for non-discrimination generally	Provides for non-discrimination based on sex specifically	Provides for non-discrimination on the basis of sex and others e.g. marital status, pregnancy	Provides for the promotion of gender equality	Has other provisions that relate to gender equality	Has claw back clauses	Addresses issues of contradictions between the Constitution, law and practices	Provides for special measures
Angola	Yes, Article 23	Yes, Article 21	Yes, Article 21	Yes, Article 21 and 35	Yes, Article 36 and 77	No	Yes, Article 239	No
Botswana	Yes, Section 15	Yes, Section 3	Yes, Section 15	No	No	Yes, Section 15	No	No
DRC	Yes, Articles 11, 12 and 13	Yes, Articles 14, 36 and 45	Yes, Articles 40	Yes, Article 14	Yes, Article 16	No	No	Yes, the national policy of gender mainstreaming, promotion of women, of the family and children
Lesotho	Yes, Chapter II, Section 1 and 18	Yes, Section 18	Yes, Section 18	Yes, Chapter III, Section 26 and 30	Yes, Section 26	Yes, Section 18	Yes, Section 18	Yes Article 18 and 26
Madagascar	Yes, Article 8	Yes	Yes, Article 8	Yes	Yes, Article 17	No	Yes, Article 160	Yes
Malawi	Yes, Section 20	Yes, Article 20	Yes, Section 13 and 20	Yes, Article 13	Yes, Section 19 and 18	Yes, Section 26	Yes, Article 5	Yes, Article 30
Mauritius	Yes, Article 3	Yes, Section 16	Yes, Section 16	Yes, Article 16	No	Yes, Section 16	No	Yes, Article 16 - to provide for gender neutral quota: 30% of either sex on party lists as candidates
Mozambique	Yes, Article 35	Yes, Article 36	Yes, Article 39	Yes, Article 120	Yes, decriminalisation of homosexuality and termination of pregnancy	No	Yes, Article 143	Yes
Namibia	Yes, Article 10	Yes, Article 10	Yes, Article 14	Yes, Article 95	Yes, Article 8	No	Yes, Article 19	Yes, Article 23
Seychelles	Yes, Article 27	No	Yes, Article 30	No	No	No	Yes, Article 5	Yes Article 27
South Africa	Yes, Chapter 1	Yes, Chapter 2, Section 9	Yes, section 9	Yes, Section 9	Yes, Section 12	No	Yes, Chapter 7, Section 15, 30	Yes, Section 9, Article 187
eSwatini	Yes, Section 20	Yes, Section 20	Yes, section 20 (2)	Yes, Section 28	Yes, Section 28	Yes, Section 20	Yes, Section 2 and Article 20	Yes, Section 20, Article 86
Tanzania	Yes, Article 13	Yes, Article 9	Yes, Article 16	Yes, Article 66	Yes, Article 13	No	Yes, Article 30	Yes, Article 78
Zambia	Yes, Article 23	Yes, Article 23	Yes, Article 23	Yes, Article 231 Gender equality and equity commission	Yes, Articles 45, 69, 231	Amended	Yes, Article1(1)	Yes
Zimbabwe	Equality and Non-Discrimination Section in the Declaration of Rights	Section 23, Declaration of Rights	Section 23, Declaration of Rights	Gender equality is listed among the Founding Values and Principles; Gender Balance is one of the Sections articulated in the National Objectives	The Declaration of Rights in the new Constitution has been expanded to include Equality and Non-Discrimination	The new constitution invalidates customary law and practices that infringe on women's rights	A law review and reform process has started to align the countries laws, policies and practices to the provisions of the new Constitution	Yes, Section 23

Source: Gender Links (2016), Updated 2018.

Table 1.2 illustrates the diversity of legislation linked to gender equality in SADC constitutions. Some countries, such as Lesotho, Madagascar and South Africa, have progressive constitutions with provisions linked to gender equality mainstreamed throughout. Botswana and Seychelles lag behind the others, with several gaps linked to gender equality in their Constitutions.

Constitutional rights

Article 4.1: State parties shall enshrine gender equality and equity in their Constitutions and ensure that any provisions, laws or practices do not compromise these.

In general, Constitutions of SADC Member States have strong gender provisions. The main challenges relate to aligning, repealing or amending existing contradictory and discriminatory laws and implementing the existing positive provisions. In addition, inherent discrimi-nation based on customary law remains a problem in some of the countries in the region.

 Due to **Namibia**'s gender equality laws and policies, the Common-wealth Secretariat in August 2017 expressed satisfaction with the country's gender parity in decision-making struc-tures. Commonwealth Secretary General Patricia Scotland urged the Namibian President to share Namibia's formula on gender equality with other Commonwealth countries.[3]

Zambia took a long time to estab-lish its Gender Equity and Equality Commission, citing resource con-straints.[4] The Commission, as provi-ded for in Article 231 of the Constitution, has a mandate to promote the attainment and main-streaming of gender equality. Legislators also expect the Commission to monitor, investigate, research, educate, advise and report on issues concerning gender equality; ensure institutions comply with legal requirements and other standards relating to gender equality; take steps to secure appropriate redress to complaints relating to gender inequality; and perform such other functions as prescribed. Its operationalisation is therefore a long overdue but important action for equality and equity in the country.

 In **Zimbabwe**, policymakers unveiled the revised National Gender Policy (NGP) on 6 July 2017, paving the way for policy direction in coordinating efforts to ensure gender equality and non-discrimination in the country. Similarly, the Zimbabwe Gender Commission (ZGC) held its inaugural National Forum, an annual event that the Zimbabwe Gender Commission Act: Chap-ter 10:31 provides for to ensure a constant and consistent national platform to discuss and promote gender equality and non-discrimination.

In **Tanzania**, finalisation of the con-stitutional review process remains stalled, even though a research survey has shown that 67% of Tanzanians want a new constitution.[5] This means that the positive provisions in the draft constitution will remain of little benefit in the promotion of women's rights and gender equality in the country. There are even fears that the government might discard the current draft and start a whole new process, and it has indicated that it has no intention of resuming the constitution-making process in the near future.[6] Meanwhile, repression in the country has reached alarming levels, with the Roman Catholic Church[7] and a local Government official[8] indicating that officials must arrest and prosecute teenage girls who get pregnant, along with their parents.[9] One researcher has, however, indicated that such drastic measures do not present a solution as such pregnancies often result from poverty and limited options for young girls, not bad behaviour.[10]

 In **Madagascar**, lawmakers imple-mented amendments to the Nation-ality Law in 2017, which will allow both men and women to pass on their nationality to their children. This will help address gender-based discrimination regarding parents' responsibility towards their children.

---

3 Namibian Broadcasting Corporation (2017), 'Commonwealth impressed with Namibia's Gender Equality in Decision-Making Structures' available at: https://www.nbc.na/news/commonwealth-impressed-namibias-gender-equality-decision-making-structures.10097 (accessed 27 March 2018).
4 Interview between the author and a Zambian senior female lawyer.
5 Twaweza (2017), Unfinished Business: Tanzanians' Views on the Stalled Constitutional Review Process, Sauti za Wananchi. Brief No. 44.
6 The Citizen, 14 March 2018.
7 Priest from the Roman Catholic Church, Rev Father Leonard Kasimila.
8 Mlele District Commissioner (DC), Ms Rachel Kasanda.
9 AllAfrica.com, 25 February 2018, Tanzania: Church Wants Girls, Parents Arrested to Curb Teenage Pregnancies.
10 Pincock K, (2018), 'Punishment won't stop teenage pregnancies in Tanzania because 'bad behaviour' isn't the cause', available at: https://theconversation.com/punishment-wont-stop-teenage-pregnancies-in-tanzania-because-bad-behaviour-isnt-the-cause-90187, (accessed on 9 June 2018).

Discrimi-nation based on customary law remains a **problem** in some countries in the region

In **Mauritius**, the government committed to pursue discussions and consultations with relevant stakeholders to work towards an electoral reform that would address inclusiveness and gender representation. Representatives noted this to the UN Human Rights Council in October 2017 as they presented the country's report on implementation of the provisions of the International Covenant on Civil and Political Rights.[11]

The Constitution of **Lesotho** guarantees the right to equality and non-discrimination on the basis of sex. However, it exempts customary laws from this guarantee. In addition, patriarchal and institutional practices and regulations often perpetuate discrimination against women. For example, army regulations in Lesotho allow for dismissal of women soldiers who fall pregnant within the first five years of joining.[12] Fortunately and to the relief of many women's rights advocates, the Lesotho High Court on 14 February 2018 ruled that the Lesotho Defence Force could not dismiss female soldiers for this reason.[13] The Court ruled that this practice is illegal and discriminatory: an important precedent-setting decision given that many defence forces in the region have similar regulations. In overturning the decision, the judge stated: "Although in form the case is about the legality of the decision of the commander of the Lesotho Defence Force to discharge pregnant soldiers, it is in substance a challenge to the culture of patriarchy in the military and an assertion of sexual and reproductive rights in military service. What is being contested is the idea that female soldiers are incapable to bear arms and babies at the same time and, on that account, are not fit for military purpose."[14]

In 2018, the Lesotho High Court ruled that the Lesotho Defence Force could not dismiss female soldiers who fall pregnant.
Photo: Lekau Mary Ntolo

Discriminatory legislation

Article 4:2: State parties shall develop and strengthen specific laws, policies and programmes to achieve gender equality and equity.
Article 4:3: State parties shall implement legislative and other measures to eliminate all practices which negatively affect the fundamental rights of women, men, girls and boys, such as their right to life, health, dignity, education and physical integrity.
Article 6: State parties shall review, amend or repeal all discriminatory laws and specifically abolish the minority status of women.

Several countries in the SADC region still have discriminatory laws on their statute books. These include laws that provide differentiated inheritance rights between men and women, boys and girls (Lesotho), laws that have limitations on maternity leave (in South Africa, a woman can go on four months' maternity leave but her employer is not obliged to pay her during that period),[15] laws that discriminate against and criminalise the LGBTI community. Five SADC countries (Botswana,

---

[11] CNBCAFRICA, 24 October 2017, "Human Rights Committee Considers the Report of Mauritius"
[12] Lesotho Defence Force (Regular Force) (Discharge Regulations 1998)
[13] Private Lieketso Mokhele and Ors v The Commander of the Lesotho Defence Force and Ors, CIV/APN/442/16
[14] Ibid.
[15] Even though the employer is not obliged to pay a woman during maternity leave, the woman can claim a maternity benefit from the Unemployment Insurance Fund (UIF) provided they she was contributing to the fund for at least four months before going on maternity leave. Whilst South Africa has a generous four months maternity leave, the non-compulsion for an employer to pay the woman whilst she is on maternity leave means that many women go without money at a time when they need it most.

In a **victory** for ⚧ **rights, Lesotho High Court** ruled Defence Forces could **not** dismiss female soldiers when they get **pregnant**

Lesotho, Malawi, Mauritius and eSwatini) have claw back clauses in constitutions that effectively allow for discrimination on the grounds of gender.

At the international level, there have been noteworthy positive shifts around the need to protect the rights of LGBTI people. One of the most notable came from British Prime Minister Theresa May when she addressed the Commonwealth Joint Forum Plenary on 17 April 2018, stating: "Across the world, discriminatory laws made many years ago continue to affect the lives of many people, criminalising same-sex relations and failing to protect women and girls. I am all too aware that these laws were often put in place by my own country. They were wrong then, and they are wrong now. As the UK's prime minister, I deeply regret both the fact that such laws were introduced, and the legacy of discrimination, violence and even death that persists today."[16]

In the same speech, May also reported that the Commonwealth had agreed to accredit the first organisation for LGBTI people. Whilst the colonial powers that introduced the discriminatory laws now note the injustices against the LGBTI community, their former colonies, including many in Southern Africa, continue to criminalise it. In the SADC region, homophobia runs high in most countries, as reflected in the attitude survey in 2016: 59% of men and 57% of women agreed or strongly agreed with the statement that "people who are attracted to the same sex should be outlawed."

 In **Madagascar**, it is legal for two persons of the same sex to have sexual intercourse if they are 21 years or older. The Penal Code prohibits same-sex intercourse for those younger than 21 and punishes perpetrators with two to five years of gaol time and a fine. Madagascar forbids marriage between two persons of the same sex.

In **South Africa**, violence against LGBTI people, and in particular lesbian women, continues, with many being raped and/or mur-

dered. Legislators have yet to enact the Prevention and Combating of Hate Crimes and Hate Speech Bill. If passed, the Bill would help in addressing hate crimes and hate speech against certain groups in society, including members of the LGBTI community.

 In **Tanzania**, the government has perpetrated a crackdown against the LGBTI community. It closed 40 private health centres accused of providing services to the community[17] and arrested and detained activists attending a workshop on access to health services for LGBTIs, including two South Africans, for 10 days in February 2017.[18] Officials later released them without a charge. However, Amnesty International has reported that threats against the LGBTI community continue, including by the Home Affairs Minister, who on 25 June 2017 threatened to deport foreign nationals and prosecute anyone working on LGBTI rights.[19]

Mozambique decriminalised homosexuality in its Penal Code in 2015, making it one of a handful of African countries to legalise same-sex relationships. Despite this development, the Human Rights World Report 2018 notes that the government has yet to register the country's biggest LGBT group, Lambda.

The **Namibia**n Constitution says that all persons must have equal rights under the law. It forbids discrimination on several grounds, including race and sex (Article 10). The Constitution also says that men and women must have equal rights in all aspects of marriage (Article 14). Although Namibia's Constitution has an inalienable Bill of Rights, it also still has a sodomy law in place, enacted under South African rule in 1927. There appears to be no immediate political move to rescind it. Organisations such as the Legal Assistance Centre and Sister Namibia advocate for the recognition of gay rights in the country.[20]

Botswana has seen progress thanks to a landmark Court of Appeal ruling allowing the registration of an LGBTI organisation in the country. The court ruled that Botswana has no legislation preventing citizens from being homosexual. In keeping with this approach, in another landmark ruling in 2017, the Botswana High Court ordered the government to change the sex of a transgender woman on her identity documents. The transgender woman's documents identified her as male at birth even though she had undergone gender reassignment surgery. The government refused to legally recognise her as a woman until the High Court intervened.

[16] United Kingdom Government (2018), 'PM speaks at the Commonwealth Joint Forum Plenary: 17 April 2018', available at: https://www.gov.uk/government/speeches/pm-speaks-at-the-commonwealth-joint-forum-plenary-17-april-2018 (accessed 11 June 2018)

[17] VOA, 17 February 2017, 'Tanzania Stops Private Health Centers From Offering AIDS Services'

[18] Green, A (2017), In an apparent crackdown, Tanzania government raids NGO meeting on reproductive rights', available at: https://www.devex.com/news/in-an-apparent-crackdown-tanzania-government-raids-ngo-meeting-on-reproductive-rights-89394, (accessed 11 June 2018)

[19] Amnesty International (2018), Amnesty International 2017/2018 Report, Amnesty International, London

[20] OSISA (2013), 'Tough times for LGBTI in Namibia too' available at: http://www.osisa.org/lgbti/blog/tough-times-lgbti-namibia-too (accessed on 17 March 2018).

Botswana High Court decision celebrated as landmark victory for trans rights

Tshepo Ricki Kgositau is a Motswana and the Director of the Cape Town-based organisation, Gender Dynamix, which works to advance transgender human rights. In 2011, she applied to the Botswana Civil and National Registration Office in Gaborone to have her sex as assigned at birth and as indicated on her identity documents changed because "her birth assigned gender [did] not correspond with her internal and individual experience of gender" (Mmegi 2017).

The government denied her request, so she approached the High Court for an order compelling the Registrar of National Registration and the Attorney General to change the sex marker on her identity documents. In December 2017, the High Court of Botswana ordered the Government of Botswana to legally recognise Kgositau as a woman and to change her identity documents from male to female. Following the High Court decision, Kgositau told the media that "she had identified as a woman from an early age and that being marked as male on official documents caused her emotional distress and made her vulnerable to abuse and violence."   *Source: UK Independent, 2017*

Tshepo Ricki Kgositau leads Gender Dynamix, a Cape Town-based organisation.
Photo courtesy of Gender Dynamix

 In a similar case, the Western Cape High Court in **South Africa** ruled that individuals had the right to change their sex descriptor, even in situations where they had been married as heterosexuals. The court made the ruling after three women and their spouses took the government to court when it refused to amend their identity documents.[21]

In the world of sport, the International Association of Athletics Federation (IAAF) proposed regulations in 2018 for female athletes with Differences of Sexual Development (DSD) to lower their testosterone levels if they planned to compete as females. Many saw the move as targeting South African athlete Caster Semenya, a dominant female runner on the international athletics scene. When the IAAF proposal went public, South African Minister of Sport Tokozile Xasa described it as "Caster Semenya Regulations" (The Guardian 2018). The reaction was entirely understandable, especially given that the IAAF has for many years been trying to get Semenya off the track. Semenya, who identifies as female, has often been called a man by fellow athletes and the IAAF Secretary General Pierre Weiss once stated that "she is woman, but maybe not 100%" (Longman 2016). The persecution that Semenya faced and continues to face reflects the persecution that the LGBTI community often faces from many angles.

The International Covenant on Civil and Political Rights (ICCPR) committee in 2017 questioned **eSwatini** on the legal and practical measures that it had put in place to protect LGBTI rights since signing the Covenant in 2004. The committee wanted eSwatini to give information on measures put in place "to protect persons from discrimination and violence based on sexual orientation and gender identity, including in housing and employment, and to promote tolerance."[22] However, despite these efforts, in the same year, the eSwatini Senate threw out a motion to debate access to health by the LGBTI community, arguing that such provisions would be "discriminatory" in favour of LGBTI people in the country. In the same vein, in 2018, parents at an unnamed school in the country called for the removal of a gay teacher.[23]

 The LGBTI rights situation in **Malawi** remains precarious, with Amnesty International[24] and Human Rights Watch[25] calling on authorities to address it. In January 2017, Kenneth Msonda, a senior political actor and spokesman for the People's Party, called gay people worse than dogs and stated that they must be killed. At the same time, the Malawi Human Rights Commission said it would undertake a public inquiry to determine whether the laws affecting the LGBTI community should be changed. However, many criticised the methodology of the public hearing for potentially exposing the LGBTI community in the country at a time when they faced heightened vulnerability to attacks.

21 Human Rights Watch (2018), World Report 2018, Human Rights Watch, New York
22 AllAfrica (2017), 'ESwatini: Kingdom Faces LGBTI Rights Review' available at http://allafrica.com/stories/201705010687.html (accessed 11 June 2017)
23 AllAfrica (2018), ESwatini: Parents Want 'Lesbian' Teacher Out' available at: http://allafrica.com/stories/201803280593.html (accessed 12 June 2018)
24 Amnesty International (2018), Amnesty International Report 2017/2018, Amnesty International, London
25 Human Rights Watch (2018), 'Malawi: Letter to Human Rights Commission re Public Inquiry into LGBTI Rights' available at: https://www.hrw.org/news/2017/08/21/malawi-letter-human-rights-commission-re-public-inquiry-lgbti-rights (accessed 1 April 2018)

Botswana High Court ordered the government to **change** the **sex** of a transgender ♀ on her identity documents

SA

Consti-

tution

and laws

on

affirma-

tive

action

not

always

applied

> **Zimbabwe: Gays Praise Mnangagwa**
>
> President Emmerson Mnangagwa has received rare praise from the lesbian, gay, bisexual, transgender and intersex (LGBTI) community for abandoning his predecessor Robert Mugabe's politics of discrimination, hatred and intolerance.
>
> Mugabe was a fervent critic of homosexuals, and was known for making homophobic statements over the years. He often described homosexuals as worse than pigs and dogs, with the LGBTI community also having its programmes disrupted by state security.
>
> In a first, authorities allowed the LGBTI community and sex workers to exhibit at this year's premier trade showcase, the Zimbabwe International Trade Fair (ZITF), held in Bulawayo in April. Under Mugabe, this was unthinkable as they were often denied permission.
>
> The LGBTI and sex workers exhibiting at the 2018 ZITF got support from organisations such as Women Against All Forms of Discrimination, Zimbabwe Aids Network, Sexual Rights Centre and the National Aids Council, among others.
>
> "The operating environment under President Mugabe was quite restrictive in terms of what people could say or do. It was quite limiting in that we were also not able to meet with stakeholders that we thought could be important to facilitate dialogue.
> *Source: Zimbabwe Standard - read the full article on http://allafrica.com/stories/201806170003.html*

Special measures

Article 5: State parties are to put in place special measures with particular reference to women in order to eliminate all barriers which prevent them from participating meaningfully in all spheres of life and to create a conducive environment for such participation.

 South Africa has implemented special measures with particular reference to women in order to eliminate all barriers that prevent them from participating meaningfully in all spheres of life as well as create a conducive environment for such participation. The Constitution and laws in South Africa allow for affirmative action. However, while the South African Constitution looks good on paper, legislators often struggle to implement its provisions in practice.

At the start of the monitoring, nine countries employed affirmative action (now referred to as special measures in the revised Protocol) provisions in their constitutions. This has since increased by four countries to 13. Angola and Botswana still do not have special measures provisions in their constitutions. Botswana, however, implements special measures strategies to improve the lives of its citizens. For example, the Botswana Revised Area Development Programme of 2009 provides broad strategies aimed at uplifting members of remote areas.

Elizabeth Gwaunza, Zimbabwe's first female deputy chief justice.
Photo courtesy of Google images

In 2018, the new president of **Zimbabwe** appointed women to key positions in various areas of governance. These included the chairperson of the Zimbabwe Electoral Commission (Priscilla Chigumba), Vimbai Nyemba as chairperson of the Procurement Regulatory Authority of Zimbabwe (PRAZ) and the deputy chief justice of the country (Elizabeth Gwaunza). The appointment of Gwaunza, however, came against the backdrop of a controversial constitutional amendment. It replaced an open interview-based selection process for all members of the higher courts with direct appointment by the president for the three most senior judicial positions (chief justice, deputy chief justice and judge president). The positive news is that this led to the appointment of the first female deputy chief justice in the country's history: a welcome development considering that the cabinet only has four women out of 22 posts.

 Lesotho's Law, Human Rights and Constitutional Affairs Minister Lebohang Hlaele appointed the country's first female Director of Public Prosecutions in 2017, Hlalefang Motinyane, albeit in an acting capacity (apanews, 2017).

Although the **Zambia**n government passed the Land Act in 1996, which guarantees women the ability

to own land, the legislation simultaneously allows for customary laws to dictate land ownership, which mainly confers land ownership to men. Under customary law, men dominate the allocation, inheritance and use of land. Women generally lack control over land but may have access and user rights to the land.

 In **Mozambique**, a 2017 World Resources Institute report concluded that commercialisation and large-scale land acquisition negatively affected women more than men. It also noted that community decision-making regarding large scale land acquisitions often side-lines women, who are not consulted and often do no participate. It noted that "women's social disadvantages, including their lack of formal land rights and generally subordinate position, make it difficult for them to voice their interests in the management and proposed allocation of community land to investors. While the development of community and civil society have pushed for standards and safeguard policies that promote the meaningful involvement of rural communities generally in land acquisitions and investments, strengthening the participation of women as a distinct stakeholder group requires specific attention."

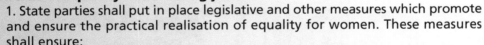

Article 7: Equality in accessing justice

1. State parties shall put in place legislative and other measures which promote and ensure the practical realisation of equality for women. These measures shall ensure:

(a) Equality in the treatment of women in judicial and quasi-judicial proceedings, or similar proceedings, including customary and traditional courts and national reconciliation processes;

(b) Equal legal status and capacity in civil and customary law; including, amongst other things, full contractual rights, the right to acquire and hold rights in property, the right to equal inheritance and the right to secure credit;

(c) The encouragement of all public and private institutions to enable women to exercise their legal capacity;

(d) Positive and practical measures to ensure equality for women as complainants in the criminal justice system;

(e) The provision of educational programmes to address gender bias and stereotypes and promote equality for women in the legal systems;

(f) That women have equitable representation on, and participation in, all courts, including traditional courts, alternative dispute resolution mechanisms and local community courts; and

(g) Accessible and affordable legal services for women.

[26] CEDAW reports.
[27] World Resources Institute (2018), 'Making Women's Voices Count in Community Decision-Making on Land Investments' available at: https://www.business-humanrights.org/en/tanzania-mozambique-poor-rural-women-discriminated-in-compensation-after-displacement-to-pave-way-for-agribusiness-says-report (accessed 11 June 2018).

Mozam-bique 2017 report found that largescale land acquisition affected more than

Accessing justice in Southern Africa, especially for women, remains a struggle. In most situations, lack of resources, the complexity of the formal justice system and the failure of the traditional/customary justice systems to accord women their rights represent the main hindrances to accessing justice. Legal aid organisations have often stepped in to provide free legal assistance for women as a way of ensuring they can access justice. Such organisations include the Women and Law in Southern Africa Research and Educational Trust, various women lawyers' associations and various judges' associations. Governments also step in once in a while, although such efforts are often ad hoc and insufficient.

For example, in **Tanzania**, the government called on all women who had been deserted by their partners to register for legal aid to get assistance in claiming maintenance from their children's fathers. The Dar es Salaam Regional Commissioner (RC) made this call on International Women's Day 2018. Many women turned out, indicating the need for legal aid as well as the fact that women often forego their legal rights and fail to access justice because of a lack of legal representation and legal. In total 480 women turned up at the RC's office, with only 61 receiving assistance. The RC later reported that it started the programme to compel men to take responsibility for their children.[28]

In **Zimbabwe**, the Legal Aid Directorate (LAD) now has offices in all ten provinces in the country and it is actively exploring establishment at the district level.[29] At the time of writing, stakeholders had almost competed launching it in the first district, Chikomba, giving hope for access to justice for citizens, including women, at the district level. The Policy Department of the Ministry of Justice, Legal and Parliamentary Affairs established LAD in 1982. It became a stand-alone directorate in 1996.[30] It is a concern that it has taken so long for government to decentralise it. Government needs to do more to ensure accessibility of the directorate.

In **Malawi**, women judges launched a programme to improve access to justice for poor urban and rural women, with the judiciary playing a leading role in providing legal clinics for the women. Justice Esme Chombo, president of the Women Judges Association of Malawi, said of the initiative: "We want to reach many vulnerable women and girls as much as possible through our outreach programs including legal clinics: and assured women that the Association would scale up its outreach programmes"[31]

Women gather outside the Dar es Salaam Regional Commissioner's office to register for legal assistance in claiming child support from their former partners.
Photo courtesy of All Africa

[28] AllAfrica (2018), 'Hundreds of 'abandoned mothers' flock Dar es Salaam RC office for legal assistance,' available at: http://allafrica.com/stories/201804100725.html, (accessed 11 June 2018).
[29] Interview with the Legal Aid Directorate Director, Mr Nyangombe on 12 June 2018.
[30] Ibid.
[31] The Maravi Post (2017), 'Malawi female judges commit on women rights protection; sign MoU, to provide legal clinics,' available at: http://www.maravipost.com/malawi-female-judges-commit-women-rights-protection-sign-mou-provide-legal-clinics/ (accessed 30 March 2018).

Marriage and family rights

Article 8: 1. State parties enact and adopt appropriate legislative, administrative and other measures to ensure that women and men enjoy equal rights in marriage and are regarded as equal partners in marriage.
2. Legislation on marriage shall therefore ensure that:
(a) No person under the age of 18 shall marry;
(b) Every marriage takes place with free and full consent of both parties;
(c) Every marriage including civil, religious, traditional or customary, is registered in accordance with national laws; and
(d) During the subsistence of their marriage the parties shall have reciprocal rights and duties towards their children with the best interest of the children always being paramount.
3. State parties shall enact and adopt appropriate legislative and other measures to ensure that where spouses separate, divorce or have their marriage annulled:
(a) They shall have reciprocal rights and duties towards their children with the best interest of the children always being paramount; and
(b) They shall, subject to the choice of any marriage regime or marriage contract, have equitable share of property acquired during their relationship.
4. States parties shall put in place legislative and other measures to ensure that parents honour their duty of care towards their children, and maintenance orders are enforced.
5. States parties shall put in place legislative provisions which ensure that married women and men have the right to choose whether to retain their nationality or acquire their spouse's nationality.

Table 1.3 overleaf shows that, in ten SADC countries, women have the right to decide whether to retain their nationality or to acquire their spouse's nationality. In the case of Lesotho, only men have the right to decide their nationality and a woman acquires the nationality of her husband upon marriage following an application. All SADC countries prohibit polygamy in civil marriages, but it remains permissible under customary law marriages.

In principle, marriages take place with a woman's consent in most countries: Under civil law in all countries except Tanzania, marriage can only take place with the woman's consent. In Tanzania, a woman's parents can decide on her behalf under the Law of Marriage Act. In some other Southern African countries, parents can "give away" their daughters' hand in marriage or in some instance sell them under customary law. The justice system allows, for example in the case of South Africa, a judge to permit the marriage of a minor. In most countries, except Lesotho, the legal age of marriage is 18 years and older, which makes it proper for young girls to continue with school until completion without fearing that their parents or community may force them into marriage.

In eSwatini, King Mswati III in 2017 told his subjects that they cannot divorce, stating that there is no word for divorce in siSwati. Given that the King's word holds a lot of weight, such pronouncements can lead to women staying in dysfunctional and violent marriages because they believe that divorce is wrong and illegal. The King's eighth wife reportedly died by suicide in April 2018, reportedly following banishment by the King and three years in isolation. At the time, and as part of the strategy to isolate her, the King had reportedly refused permission for the woman to attend her sister's funeral.[32] This report, which various media houses carried, signifies one of the worst forms of domestic violence, perpetrated by a national leader against his own wife.

Increasingly, men and women have reciprocal duties towards children in cases of divorce or annulment of marriage: In Zimbabwe, the Registrar General (RG) has, over the years, insisted on a practice (which is not in the law) compelling fathers who want to obtain birth certificates for their children to bring the mother of the child along. Yet mothers can obtain birth certificates for their children without the father being present at

---

[32] The Citizen (2018), 'King Mswati's 8th wife commits suicide following 'abuse', available at: https://citizen.co.za/news/news-africa/1880787/2king-mswatis-8th-wife-commits-suicide/ (accessed 10 June 2018).

In some countries, **parents** can **"give away"** their daughter or **sell them** under customary law

the RG's office. A father who did not get a birth certificate for his child because of this policy and due to non-cooperation by the mother of the child recently sued the RG and the Minister of Home Affairs, arguing that the practice is discriminatory and unconstitutional, in addition to violating the rights of the child to a birth certificate and a nationality.[33] The case is still before the courts. Meanwhile, in South Africa, the Supreme Court of Appeal (SCA), decided a landmark ruling in which it recognised the responsibility of both parents to pay school fees for their children in cases of divorce or separation.[34] The SCA ruled that, in applying the rules for school fee exemptions, education authorities must make an assessment based on the personal circumstances of the parent applying for the exemption in situations where the other parent is unavailable or unwilling to provide information on his or her financial situation. The refusal to assess based on the financial situation of one parent has typically affected mothers, who often must take full responsibility for their children after a divorce or separation.

Table 1.3: Marriage and family laws

Country	No person under the age of 18 shall marry	Every marriage shall take place with the full consent of both parties	Every marriage, including civil, religious or customary is registered	Parties have reciprocal rights and duties towards their children, including when spouses separate, divorces or have the marriage annulled	Law to enforce maintenance orders	Married women and men have the right to decide whether to retain their nationality or acquire spouses nationality
Angola	Yes, Although legal age of marriage is 18, with exception boys can marry at 16 and girls at 15 with the consent of the person with legal control over them	Yes	No	Yes	No	Yes
Botswana	Yes, the minimum age for marriage is 18	Yes	No	Yes	Yes	Yes
DRC	Minimum age for marriage increased from 14 for girls and 18 for boys to 18 for both in 2009.	Yes	No	Yes	No	Yes
Lesotho	No, legal age for marriage is 21, but girls can legally marry at 16 and at 18 for boys with the consent of the Minister of Justice. Under customary law, girls and boys can marry after puberty	Yes	No	Yes	No	No
Madagascar	Yes, the legal age for civil marriage is 18 but under customary law there is no fixed age requirement	Yes	No	Yes	No	No
Malawi	Yes, the legal age for marriage for girls and boys is 18, A Feb 2017 Constitutional amendment has reinforced this position	Yes	Yes	Yes	Yes	Yes
Mauritius	No, the official age for marriage is 18 for boys and girls but girls can get married from 16 with parental consent	Yes	Yes	Yes	Yes	Yes
Mozambique	Yes, the minimum age for marriage is 18	Yes	Yes	Yes	Yes	Yes
Namibia	Yes, the age for civil marriage is 21	Yes	No	Yes	Yes	No
Seychelles	No, the legal age for marriage is 18 but girls can get married from 15 with parental consent	Yes	Yes	Yes	Yes	Yes
South Africa	Yes, the minimum age for marriage is 18	Yes	Yes	Yes	Yes	Yes
eSwatini	Legal age of marriage is 18, but girls can civilly marry from 16 with the consent of the Minister of Justice. Under customary law, marriages can take place from puberty	Yes	No	No	Yes	Yes
Tanzania	No, girls can marry from 15 and boys from 18	No	No	No	No	No
Zambia	No, the legal age to marry is 21 but at 16 boys and girls can marry with parental consent. Under customary law marriage can take place from puberty	Yes	No	Yes	Yes	Yes
Zimbabwe	A landmark court case has set the age of marriage at 18.	Yes	No	Yes	Yes	No

Source: Gender Links.

[33] Pindula (2018), 'Mudede sued for not allowing men to acquire birth certificates for their children' available at: https://news.pindula.co.zw/2018/04/05/mudede-sued-for-not-allowing-men-to-acquire-birth-certificates-for-their-children/ (accessed 10 June 2018).
[34] Head of Department: Western Cape Education Department & another v S (Women's Legal Centre as Amicus Curiae) (1209/2016) [2017] ZASCA 187 (13 December 2017).

Child marriages

Table 1.4: Incidence of child marriages in SADC		
Countries and areas[35]	**Child marriage (%) 2010-2017***	
	Married by 18	**Married by 15**
Angola	30	8
Botswana		
Malawi	42	9
Mozambique	48	14
Zambia	31	6
Madagascar	41	12
DRC	37	10
Tanzania	31	5
Zimbabwe	32	4
Lesotho	17	1
Mauritius		
Namibia	7	2
Seychelles		
eSwatini	5	1
South Africa	6	1

Source: UNICEF (https://data.unicef.org/topic/child-protection/child-marriage/) No data available for Botswana, Mauritius and Seychelles.
*The statistics in the table 1.4 record the percentage of girls married before the age of 15 or 18 in a sample of respondents between ages 20 - 24 in 2017.

Table 1.4 shows that child marriage remains common in the region despite efforts to tackle the issue, which have yet to translate into tangible results on the ground. In Mozambique, almost half of women marry before they turn 18, while 14% marry before 15. Several other countries have high numbers of women marrying before age 18, including Malawi (42%), Madagascar (41%) and DRC (37%). Experts believe that child marriages contribute to the high number of maternal deaths in the region, with 13% of these caused by unsafe abortions.[36]

 Zambia's incidents of child marriage have significantly reduced from a high of 42% in 2013 to 31% in 2017. Despite this, the rate remains one of the highest in the world (Zambia is ranked 16th globally amongst countries with the highest incidents of child marriage). In the Eastern Region of the country, incidences of child marriage are as high as 60%, with Lusaka having the lowest rate at 28% (UNFPA 2018). The government has implemented important measures to fight child marriages in the country including what it calls "a civil society coalition against child marriage," which is a ten-member ministerial committee led by the Ministry of Gender, as well as "a draft policy on ending child marriage, and a National Strategy on Ending Child Marriage for the period 2016-21."[37]

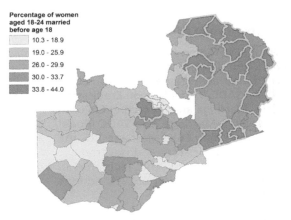

Percentage of women aged 18-24 married before age 18
- 10.3 - 18.9
- 19.0 - 25.9
- 26.0 - 29.9
- 30.0 - 33.7
- 33.8 - 44.0

In Zambia, 31% of girls are married before their 18th birthday, making it one of the countries with the highest rates of child marriage in the world. *Courtesy of UNFPA*

In 2017, Zambian President Edgar Lungu urged traditional leaders to take the lead in ending child marriages. Harmonising the marriage laws and definitions of "child" in legislation, with the provisions of the 2016 amended constitution, will go a long way in addressing legal paradoxes, especially in terms of customary law. In January 2018, the president acknowledged that the country had experienced a 10% drop in cases of child marriages.[38]

In **South Africa**, despite having the second lowest rates of child marriages in the region, the national statistical agency (Stats SA) in 2017 reported that the country saw an increase in child marriages, especially in the three provinces of KwaZulu-Natal, Gauteng and the Eastern Cape. The Commission for Gender Equality (CGE) expressed concern over the situation and outlined new efforts and strategies to address the issue.[39]

---

[35] UNICEF (2018) 'Child Marriage' available at: http://www.unicef.org/search/search.php?q_en=child+marriage&go.x=0&go.y=0 (accessed 12 June 2018).
[36] UNICEF (2016).
[37] Population Council (2017), 'Child Marriage in Zambia' available at: http://www.popcouncil.org/uploads/pdfs/2017RH_ChildMarriageZambia_brief.pdf (accessed 15 April 2018).
[38] African Leadership (2018), 'Zambia Progresses on ending Child Marriage_ Records 10% Decline' available at: http://africanleadership.co.uk/zambia-progresses-ending-child-marriage%E2%94%80-records-10-decline/ (accessed 12 June 2018).
[39] Commission for Gender Equality (2017), 'Gender Commission Supports COSATU and SACCAWU Strike at Shoprite' available at: http://www.cge.org.za/category/press-statement/page/2/ (accessed 18 April 2018).

Child marriage remains common

 In terms of the minimum legal age of marriage, the **Mauritius** Civil Code provides that a person can get married at the age of 18 years. However, a person aged 16 years can get married with the consent of their parents, or with the consent of one of the parents exercising parental authority, or, in the absence of the consent of parents, by the Judge in Chambers if the latter considers that it would be in the interests of the minor to get married. During the negotiations on the Post-2015 Protocol, Mauritius legislators voiced concerns about rigidly setting the legal age of marriage at 18, stating that certain religious groups in the country allow for marriage before the age of 18.

Bringing child brides back to the classroom

The SADC region has recently taken a bold and determined approach to end child marriages. The adoption, in 2016, of the SADC Model Law on Eradicating Child Marriage and Protecting Children Already in Marriage (the SADC Model Law on Ending Child Marriages) by the SADC heads of state and government presents a clear sign that legislators in the region want to effectively address the issue.

Research has shown that Malawi is one of the countries most affected by child marriages in the region (and the world over), in many instances occupying the pole position in this regard. Because of this, lawmakers in the country have taken measures to end child marriages and to protect those children already in marriages.

Girl children in Malawi help with family chores. Child marriage affects almost half of all girls in the country. *Photo: Colleen Lowe Morna*

In April 2018, it started a collaboration with many independent organisations to bring child brides back to school. Organisations such as Youth Net and Counselling (Yoneco), Save the Children and Malawi Girl Guides Association have played a significant role in rescuing children from marriages and helping them to go back to school. In rolling out the project, one stakeholder noted that "The problem with our society is patriarchy... Girls are convinced they were meant for marriage and not (to be) bread-winners." Taking girls back to school is a way of removing them from a "marriage rut," and ensuring that they can fend for themselves and their children.

The Department of Child Affairs in the Ministry of Gender, Children, Disability and Social Welfare acknowledged the impact of the project, indicating that it had so far rescued more than 5000 children from child marriage in 2017. However, few of them ended up staying in school.

Many challenges remain, including lack of societal support and the fact that the implementing organisations did not have adequate resources to pay school fees for the affected children. This provides an opportunity for the state to step in to ensure that the affected children receive emotional and material support so that they can enrol and stay in school. Education is one of the surest ways of ensuring that children affected by early marriages can have a brighter future.

Malawi and other SADC countries should implement sustainable programmes to end child marriages and ensure that children already in marriage can go back to school. Stakeholders can replicate the above programme, not only in Malawi but in other SADC countries. Parents, guardians, schools and communities must all play their part to supported, implement, replicate and sustain such programmes.

Source: Relief Web
https://reliefweb.int/report/malawi/out-wedlock-and-back-school-educating-malawis-underage-brides

Nine SADC countries have now established the legal age for marriage at 18 or older: Namibia is amongst the most progressive in SADC, with the age of marriage at 21 for boys and girls. In Botswana, the Marriage Act (amended in 2001) sets the legal age of marriage at 18 for both sexes, conditional on parental consent. Without parental consent, the legal age is 21. This age limit does not apply to marriages conducted under customary or religious law, which have no age limits. The marriage age for girls in Lesotho, Tanzania, and Zambia is between 15 and 16. In these countries the marriage age for boys is 18.

 In **Zimbabwe**, more than two years after the landmark ruling wherein the constitutional court outlawed child marriages, legislators have yet to revise relevant national legislation - the Customary Marriages Act: Chapter 5:07 and the Marriages Act: Chapter 5:11 - to align with the judgment and the Constitution. Whilst some have argued that the lack of alignment of the laws does not stop the implementation of the judgment and the provisions of the Constitution, at a practical level such alignment makes implementation easier and improves certainty.

 In **Malawi**, government reported in April 2018 that the country had reduced the rate of child marriage in just two years from 50% to 42% (2015-2017). Jean Kalilani, Minister of Gender, Children, Disability and Social Welfare, attributed this to the legal framework that government had created to reduce child marriages. Some of the legal frameworks included the harmonisation of the marriage laws, the constitutional amendment to set the age of marriage at 18 and the 2017 National Strategy on Ending Child Marriages. The country also implemented a National Action Plan to Combat GBV (2016-2021). A particularly innovative approach used by legislators in Malawi involved the adoption of local by-laws to end child marriages by local chiefs. Through these, local chiefs increased the age of marriage to 21 in their

Marriage age for **girls** in Lesotho, Tanzania, and Zambia is between **15** **&** **16**

villages and supported penalties for men who married underage girls through imposition of fines paid in goats, chickens and even land.[40]

 In **Mozambique**, research has shown that social and economic stresses have reversed gains made in promoting gender equality, including reducing child marriages. The drought that hit Southern Africa in 2016/2017 hit Mozambique particularly hard. Aid agencies such as CARE International noted that, as the drought hit, families turned back to traditional gender roles to survive. Families also handed over their daughters in marriage to get resources such as food and cattle.[41]

In **Lesotho**, Princess Senate, the daughter of King Letsie III, took up her first public role in April 2018 as the "national champion to end child marriage." At 16, she urged her peers to concentrate on their studies, indicating that education would give them a happy and healthy adulthood. Stating that marriage is not for children, she launched the #endchildmarriagenow campaign.

In 2017, the Lesotho Ministry of Education and Training reported that it was finalising a Gender-Based Violence Policy for presentation before Cabinet. Reports noted that the policy would "serve as a guideline on reproductive health, early marriages, unintended pregnancies and gender-based violence."[42] Legislators have not yet adopted it.

Governments across Southern Africa still need to prioritise the harmonisation of Policies and Legislation to bring an end to child marriage: At the international level, the AU Agenda 2063 and the SDGs promote the end of child marriages. Meanwhile, SADC has enacted Provisions to guard against child and forced marriages in the form of the SADC Protocol on Gender and Development and the SADC Model Law to end Child Marriages. The region has seen increased collaboration between government, civil society, traditional leaders, international development agencies and religious leaders in the fight to end child marriages. Such collaboration has had tremendous results and stakeholders should continue it going forward.

The SADC Model Law on child marriages gets the region one step closer to ending child marriage in Southern Africa: Since the passing of the Model Law, Parliaments in the region have debated its domestication into national law, but no country has yet domesticated it.

Choice of termination of pregnancy

Most SADC countries outlaw abortion. Only three countries have legislation in place legalising abortion (South Africa and most recently Mozambique). Following the 1996 Choice on Termination of Pregnancy Act, South Africa is the only country in SADC in which abortion is available upon request. In several other countries, including Angola, DRC, Lesotho, Madagascar, Malawi and Namibia abortion is permissible only to save a woman's life. Zimbabwe permits abortion to save a woman's life or if the pregnancy is as a result of rape or incest.

In **Madagascar**, parliament recently rejected efforts by the Ministry of Public Health to make amendments to the family planning law to allow for therapeutic abortion. As a result, abortion remains illegal in Madagascar under all circumstances, even when the mother's life is in danger. In rejecting the amendments which the House of Deputies had adopted, one senator stated that "Abortion is not consistent with Malagasy culture.

Members of Madagascar's Constitutional High Court gather in Antananarivo. *Photo: Zoto Razanadratefa*

Only South Africa and Mozambique **have legalised abortion**

[40] RiseUp (Undated), 'Ending Child Marriage in Malawi' available at: http://www.riseuptogether.org/wp-content/uploads/2016/09/Malawi-Case-Study-FINAL.pdf (accessed 18 April 2018).
[41] NewsDeeply (2017), 'Drought Threatens to Undo Mozambique's Gender Equality Progress' available at: https://www.newsdeeply.com/womenandgirls/articles/2017/01/19/drought-threatens-undo-mozambiques-gender-equality-progress (accessed 18 April 2018)
[42] AllAfrica (2017), 'Lesotho: Ministry Finalises Gender-Based Violence Policy', available at: http://allafrica.com/stories/201708250190.html (accessed 21 March 2018).

Our blessings encourage even young married women to give birth to seven girls and seven boys. If abortion was permitted, it would change young people."[43] As a result, health professionals who perform abortion would be liable to imprisonment and loss of their professional practice.

 Namibia's Abortion and Sterilisation Act makes it a crime for a woman to seek an abortion, or to terminate her own pregnancy, except in very specific circumstances. Namibia permits abortion to save a woman's life or in the event of rape or incest or due to foetal impairment. It is not permitted for social or economic reasons.

In **Lesotho**, government acknowledges the devastating effects of illegal backyard abortions on girls and women but still will not relent to make abortion legal in the country. Instead, it surreptitiously advises women to go across the border into South Africa where abortion is legal. The irony is not lost on human rights lawyer Lineo Tsikoane, who has said of the Ministry of Health "They know abortion is illegal, but they're telling us to advise girls to go elsewhere, and [yet] won't change our own law."[44]

 In **Angola**, in March 2017, lawmakers set in motion a law to make abortion an offence in all circum-stances. The current law allows abortion in narrow circumstances, including to safeguard the health of the mother, in cases of foetal deformity or where the pregnancy is because of rape. Parliamentary debate on the amendment stalled following a public outcry over it, leading to the ruling party proposing a revised version of the legal amendment. The revised version retained the legality of abortion in cases of rape or maternal health risk.[45]

Increasingly women have turned to social media, in particular Facebook, to look for illegal abortion services. This can lead to serious complications and death if they receive the service from unqualified people and in unhygienic conditions (CNN 2018).

Public opinion on abortion remains deeply divided: In the Southern African attitudes survey, less than half (36% women and 28% men) said they agreed or strongly agreed that a woman had a right to terminate her pregnancy within the first trimester. Even in South Africa, with its strong pro-abortion laws, access to the service remains a challenge, with only 7% of the country's health facilities providing abortions.[46] Research shows that many health workers refuse to perform the procedure, with government unable to do anything about it. At the same time, information about where and how to acquire the service remains limited.[47]

Persons with disabilities

 Article 9: State parties shall, in accordance with the SADC Protocol on Health and other regional and international instruments relating to the protection and welfare of people with disabilities to which Member States are party, adopt legislation and related measures to protect persons with disabilities that take into account their particular vulnerabilities.

Article 9 remained unchanged in the Post-2015 Gender Protocol. However, SADC adopted a code on social security that includes social allowances for persons with disabilities with reference to Article 5 of the SADC Treaty.[48] Women with disabilities often face combined discrimination because of their sex and their disability. As the SDGs call for "leaving no one behind" in development, organisations such as the Southern Africa Federation of the Disabled have called on Member States to mainstream disability in all development activities and develop a stand-alone protocol on disability.

[43] International Campaign for Women's Right to safe Abortion (2018), 'MADAGASCAR - Attempt to legalise therapeutic abortion sabotaged' available at: http://www.safeabortionwomensright.org/madagascar-attempt-to-legalise-therapeutic-abortion-sabotaged/ (accessed 11 April 2018).
[44] Warren S (2018), 'In Lesotho, Women say they are Finding their Abortion on Facebook' available at: https://edition.cnn.com/2018/03/07/health/lesotho-abortions-asequals-intl/index.html, accessed 12 June 2018.
[45] The Citizen (2017), 'Angola Backs Down on Total Abortion Ban' available at https://citizen.co.za/news/news-africa/1542075/angola-backs-total-abortion-ban/ (accessed 1 April 2018).
[46] Skosana, I (2017), 'Less than 7% of health facilities nationwide offer abortions - Amnesty International', available at: http://bhekisisa.org/article/2017-02-14-00-only-260-health-facilities-nationwide-offer-abortions-amnesty-international/ (accessed 11 June 2018).
[47] Amnesty International (2018), Amnesty International Report 2017/2018, Amnesty International, London.
[48] Code on Social Security in SADC.

Less than half agree or strongly agree that a ♀ has a **right** to terminate her pregnancy within the 1st trimester

Seven SDG targets specifically mention persons with disabilities (education, accessible schools, employment, accessible public spaces and transport, empowerment and inclusion, and data disaggregation). The UN Statistics Division explored development of SDG indicators that can be disaggregated by disability and sex, particularly for the targets on poverty, social protection, child mortality, health coverage, violence against women, sexual and reproductive health, access to water and sanitation and birth registration.[49] The SADC Monitoring, Evaluation and Reporting (MER) Framework for the Protocol includes two indicators for persons with disabilities: evidence of legislation to protect persons living with disabilities and evidence of targeted programmes for women with disabilities. These programmes will contain, among others, measures to ensure the full development, advancement and empowerment of women, for the purpose of guaranteeing them the exercise and enjoyment of the human rights and fundamental freedoms set out in the UN Convention on the Rights of Persons with Disabilities (CRPD).

The UN Committee on the Rights of Persons with Disabilities recognised **Seychelles** as a leading country in the promotion of women's rights and urged the country to do the same in relation to the rights of persons with disabilities, including women. It stated this in Geneva when representatives from Seychelles presented their initial report on the country's implementation of the CRPD.[50]

South Africa's pre-1994 negotiation process that disabled people must have the right to speak for themselves in all matters affecting their lives. The country has also mainstreamed disability across government machinery.[51] Its 1997 Integrated National Disability Strategy proved to be a historical milestone in the fight to promote the rights of people with disabilities by guiding the formulation of policies and programmes aimed at advancing their rights. It supports services ranging from free health care to social assistance and inclusive education that targets both adults and children with disabilities and provides access to opportunities. In 2009, President Jacob Zuma announced that the government would establish a new department for people with disabilities.

However, in 2017, the South African Human Rights Commission expressed concern over the barriers children with disabilities face in accessing education. The Commission stated that more than half a million children with disabilities cannot access education.[52]

A recent report noted that women make up 58% of **eSwatini**'s total population with disabilities.[53] eSwatini signed the CRPD in 2007 and ratified the Convention on 24 September 2012. The Kingdom's Constitution Section 14, a clause on the fundamental rights and freedoms of the individual, provides for disability in 14(1)(e) and 14(3). The Provisions prohibit discrimination based on disability. Similarly, Section 20 provides for equality before the law. Section 30 provides for the rights of persons with disabilities. Subsequent to ratification of the CRPD, lawmakers developed a National Policy on Disability, aimed at promoting the mainstreaming of disability issues across all government development programs. The Federation Organisation of the Disabled People in eSwatini (FODSWA) strives to promote gender sensitivity amongst its affiliates. In 2018, the Government of eSwatini began developing a Disability Bill with the hope that Parliament would pass it into law. FODSWA emphasised the importance of the Bill in promoting the rights of people with disabilities, including women, and indicated that the Bill should compel government to pay school fees for children with disabilities. Similarly, the government indicated that the National Strategic Plan for 2017-2022 gave special attention to disabled people, especially at the Inkundla level.[54]

Nomcebo Mbamali, Sonia Ntimane and Fezile Dlamini take part in a discussion about women living with disabilities in 2018 at Bethel Court, eZulwini, in eSwatini.

Photo courtesy of Zethu Shongwe

[49] United Nations Secretariat of The Convention on The Rights of Persons with Disabilities.

[50] CNBCAfrica (2018), 'Committee on the Rights of Persons with Disabilities Reviews the Initial Report of the Seychelles' available at: http://www.cnbcafrica.com/apo/2018/02/28/committee-on-the-rights-of-persons-with-disabilities-reviews-the-initial-report-of-the-seychelles/ (accessed 12 June 2018).

[51] Vukuzenzele (2014), 'Women, people with disabilities empowered' available at https://www.vukuzenzele.gov.za/women-people-disabilities-empowered (accessed 10 June 2018).

[52] Human Rights Watch (2017), 'South Africa Events of 2017' available at https://www.hrw.org/world-report/2018/country-chapters/south-africa (accessed 10 June 2018).

[53] University of Pretoria (2015), African Disability Rights Year Book (2015) Volume 3, Pretoria.

[54] Swazi Observer (2018), 'FODSWA President calls for Tertiary Education for the Disabled' available at https://www.pressreader.com/eSwatini/swazi-observer/20180329/281719795135548 (accessed 10 June 2018).

Living with albinism in Southern Africa

Earline Chimoyo, a student at The Polytechnic in Malawi, interviews Alex Machila of the Association of People with Albinism.
Photo courtesy of Maclan Kanyangwa

Over the past few years, people with albinism have increasingly made the news in Southern Africa related to stories of abuse against them, as well as murder. This is common in Malawi, Tanzania, Mozambique and South Africa, where people with albinism live at risk that they may be hunted for their body parts for ritual purposes. Reports indicate that at least 20 Malawians with albinism have been murdered since 2014, whilst more than 75 have been killed in Tanzania since 2000. In South Africa the story of the abduction and murder of two children, including a 13-year-old girl with albinism, raised the alarm about the growing issue. When police located the bodies of the two, relatives reported that the killers had removed several body parts from the 13-year-old.

Deprose Muchena, Amnesty International's regional director for Southern Africa, noted that: "Deep-seated cultural traditions persist, including a belief in mythical powers of people with albinism and a conviction that their body parts could change lives, bringing fabulous wealth, power or good fortune. Some believe that albinos are not human, that their only value is monetary and that they have gold in their bones."

Governments in Southern Africa must pay closer attention to the rights of people with albinism and treat this issue as a regional crisis. They should implement measures to protect them through education and ensuring that the justice system appropriately punished perpetrators of abuse.

Source: Dr Makanatsa Mokonese[55]

Widow and widower rights

Article 10: 1. State parties shall enact and enforce legislation to ensure that widows and widowers:
  (a) Are not subjected to inhuman, humiliating or degrading treatment;
  (b) Automatically become the guardians and custodians of their children when their husband/wife dies unless otherwise determined by a competent court of law;
(c) Have the right to an equitable share in the inheritance of the property of their spouses;
(d) Have the right to remarry any person of their choice; and
(e) Have protection against all forms of violence and discrimination based on their status.

The Protocol guards against inhuman treatment of widows. At the insistence of Botswana policymakers, the Post-2015 SADC Gender Protocol refers to both widows and widowers, although the issues of inheritance, remarrying, custody of children, violence and discrimination primarily pertain to widows. The Post-2015 Protocol also removed the reference to a widow having "the right to employment and other opportunities to enable her to make a meaningful contribution to society" on the grounds that governments cannot guarantee employment for widows.

The **Botswana** Abolition of Marital Power Act provides women equal rights regarding decision-making about family property management, including upon the death of a husband although this does not apply to customary or religious marriages where the eldest son assumes the role

[55] https://www.amnesty.org/en/latest/news/2018/06/malawi-impunity-fuels-killings-of-people-with-albinism-for-their-body-parts/
https://citizen.co.za/news/south-africa/1809083/kidnap-of-two-kids-one-an-albino-may-be-related-to-superstition-mayor/

The Post-2015 SADC Gender Protocol refers to both **widows** and widowers as head of the household. In Botswana, if a spouse dies intestate (without a will) customary rules allow for the estate devolvement.

 In **Angola**, the inheritance rights of widows and divorced women remain particularly precarious. Although divorced women or widows may inherit land, this is commonly only in trust for their children. A study conducted by the Rural Development Institute in 2008 found that only 23% of widows use the land left by their deceased husbands and many women lack knowledge of their land and inheritance rights.

The **DRC** Family Code gives preferential treatment to the children of the deceased and does not discriminate between women and men within the second category of heirs, although in practice women are not often full recipients of inheritance.[56] Article 758, paragraph 3, of the Family Code stipulates that women have the right to inherit their husband's property.

 In 2011, the **Malawi** Parliament passed the Deceased Estates (Wills, Inheritance and Protection Act) Act, which provides widows and daughters equal inheritance rights and addresses the issue of widows being denied their inheritance upon the death of a spouse.[57]

Following a 2009 Constitutional Court decision in **South Africa**, the government introduced the Reform of Customary Law of Succession and Regulation of Related Matters Act 11 of 2009 so that the Intestate Succession Act, which also recognises polygamous marriages, now governs the rights of women to inherit property under customary law. The Recognition of Customary Marriages Act provided many headaches for courts in the administration of estates. It recognised polygamous marriages and noted that inheritance in such marriages did not apply to polygamous marriages that occurred before 15 November 2000, when the Act became operative. The Limpopo High Court ruled in 2017 that the Provisions should apply in retrospect and that failure to do so negatively affected the proprietary rights of women in older polygamous marriages, thereby discriminating based on gender, race, ethnicity and social origin, which is unconstitutional. The court also urged Parliament to enact legislation to clearly address the proprietary and inheritance rights of women in older customary law marriages.[58]

 In **eSwatini**, in April 2018, the King ordered all widows to take off their mourning clothes to participate in celebrating his 50th birthday and the country's 50th anniversary of Independence. Government scheduled the celebrations for 19 April 2018. Ordinarily in eSwatini, traditional culture limits widows' participation in public life. For example, earlier in 2018 the government stated that widows would not be allowed to participate in the 2018 elections. A Senior Government Official stated that widows would "not be allowed to contest the election until they had been in mourning for two years and gone through a cleansing ceremony" (AllAfrica 2018).

Legislators amended the **Zimbabwe** Administration of Estates Act to make the surviving spouse and the children of a  deceased person as his or her major beneficiaries, as opposed to the eldest son. The Act also provides that the matrimonial home, whatever the system of tenure under which the family holds it, and wherever it is situated, remains with the surviving spouse. However, a 2017 Human Rights Watch research report concluded that, despite the existence of progressive legislative provisions, the relatives of deceased husbands routinely deprive widows of their property - and widows have little reference or recourse to the courts and the justice delivery system in general.[59] Widows often suffer in silence due to lack of information, traditional and cultural imperatives and difficulties accessing justice. The case of Elizabeth Macheka, the widow of the late Morgan Tsvangirai, former Prime Minister, is one example. Macheka faced public humiliation from her late husband's relatives following the death of Tsvangirai on 14 February 2018. The family reportedly disowned Macheka, with Tsvangirai's mother threatening to commit suicide if Macheka attended her husband's funeral.[60] Jacob Mudenda, the Speaker of Parliament, castigated the Tsvangirai family for their behaviour, urging his colleagues to protect widows and their inheritance.[61]

[56] Chronic Poverty Research Centre (2011).
[57] Women's Inheritance Now (2012).
[58] Ramuhovhi and Others v President of the Republic of South Africa and Others (CCT194/16) [2017] ZACC 41; 2018 (2) BCLR 217 (CC); 2018 (2) SA 1 (CC) (30 November 2017).
[59] Human Rights Watch (2017), You will get Nothing: Violation of Property and Inheritance Rights of Widows in Zimbabwe, Human Rights Watch, New York.
[60] Pindula News (2018), 'Updated: Tsvangirai Family Disowns Elizabeth, Planning To Grab Entire Inheritance', available at: https://news.pindula.co.zw/2018/02/19/tsvangirai-family-disowns-elizabeth-planning-grab-entire-inheritance/ (accessed 11 June 2018).
[61] Newsday (2018), 'Speaker blasts Tsvangirai family', available at: https://www.newsday.co.zw/2018/03/speaker-blasts-tsvangirai-family/ (accessed 11 June 2018).

Widows often suffer in silence

Zimbabwe Council helping women claim their property rights

Beneficiaries in Kadoma meet to discuss how to acquire property deeds.
Photo courtesy of Kadoma Municipality

Zimbabwe's Kadoma Council has noted an increase in court cases about property ownership. In one week, it recorded at least four cases about disputes between a widow and her deceased spouse's relatives. In many cases, women and children become destitute following divorce or the death of a spouse.

Because most women do not know of the procedures needed to acquire ownership of a property, the Council, in association with the police and the Ministry of Gender and Women Affairs, facilitates procedures to ensure joint ownership of properties by divorced spouses, or property transfer to widows or divorcees.

The Council notes that its initiative has helped decrease gender-based violence. Women now also have the confidence to go to court to claim their property rights. Women who took part in the initiative have shared the knowledge and information they gained with other women, which means more women claim their property rights.

Source: SADC Protocol@Work summit, Zimbabwe, 2018

The girl and boy child

Article 10: 1. State parties shall adopt laws, policies and programmes to ensure the development and protection of the girl and the boy child by:
(a) Eliminating all forms of discrimination against them in the family, community, institutions and at state levels;
(b) Ensuring that they have equal access to education and health care, and are not subjected to any treatment which causes them to develop a negative self-image;
(c) Ensuring that they enjoy the same rights and are protected from harmful cultural attitudes and practices in accordance with the United Nations Convention on the Rights of the Child and the African Charter on the Rights and Welfare of the Child;
(d) Protecting them from economic exploitation, trafficking and all forms of violence including sexual abuse; and
(e) Ensuring that they have equal access to information, education, services and facilities on sexual and reproductive health and rights
2. State parties shall develop concrete measures to prevent and eliminate violence, harmful practises, child marriages, forced marriages, teenage pregnancies, genital mutilation and child labour as well as mitigate their impacts on girls' and boys' health, wellbeing, education, future opportunities and earnings.

The updated SADC Gender Protocol highlighted that boys also need protection. The escalation of child labour due to economic hardships in the region has forced many boys and girls out of school as they seek additional income for their families. SADC has also seen an increase in child-headed households due to HIV and AIDS pandemic and migration of parents looking for better economic opportunities. This leaves young girls and boys vulnerable to sexual abuse, drug abuse, economic exploitation and trafficking, and with limited access to education and health opportunities. It also increases the multiple roles of girls.

 A 2018 Human Rights Watch Research Report urged the Government of **Zimbabwe** to protect children from child labour on the country's tobacco farms. The Report indicated that children as young as 11 work on tobacco farms, exposing them to toxic chemicals. The Report, Bitter Harvest, showed that families often force children to work in these conditions to increase family income and raise school fees, thereby exposing the inadequacies of Government policies meant to provide school fees for disadvantaged children. The country's Basic Education Assistance Module (BEAM), which seeks to provide school fees and other school essentials for such children, has not received adequate budgetary allocations for many years.

 Meanwhile, in **eSwatini**, the Children's Protection and Welfare Act bans sexual activity with underage females and penalises parents who arrange early marriages with prison sentences of up to 20 years.

Governments often deny girls their fundamental right to education, especially where poverty persists. Due to stigmatisation of teenage pregnancies, girl usually drop out of school when they become pregnant. Many face ridicule from staff at health centres when seeking access to ante-natal care, which has contributed to increases in HIV infections in the region.

In 2017, a United Nations Population Fund report noted that **Zimbabwe** had the highest teenage pregnancy rates in sub-Saharan Africa. The report revealed that 10% of girls aged 15-19 fell pregnant every year, often signalling an end to their educational ambitions. The report attributed teenage pregnancy in the country to cultural and religious practices and beliefs as well as child marriage. At Policy level, government allows a pregnant girl to go on maternity leave for three months and then come back to school (Ncube and Mdau 2017). However, stigma, unsupportive school environments and the responsibilities of motherhood, amongst others, make the return impossible or difficult.

Girls take part in an IT course in Mauritius. Legislators in the region have taken steps to ensure more girls learn about the STEM subjects. *Photo: Colleen Lowe Morna*

Schools often neglect the girl child in Science, Technology, Engineering and Mathematics (STEM) subjects: This has led to a lower proportion of girls graduating at tertiary level in these subjects. However, SADC Member States have embarked on a drive to increase the number of girls studying STEM subjects. In July 2017, the SADC Ministers of Justice and Attorneys General adopted the Draft SADC Charter on Women in Science, Engineering and Technology Organisation. This will go a long way in operationalising the SADC Gender Protocol Provisions on STEM and in ensuring national level policies and programmes to support STEM for girls and women.

Next steps

The adoption of the revised SADC Gender Protocol in 2016 represents a step in the right direction for the region concerning the promotion of women's rights and gender equality and equity. As such, the next steps should focus on implementation of the Protocol at both regional and national levels.

- Governments must make tangible efforts that go beyond words and political expressions to ensure national-level domestication and implementation of the SADC Model Law on Child Marriage.
- Stakeholders must create and maintain platforms for dialogue on difficult but critical issues such as termination of pregnancy, LGBTI rights and marital rape.
- Legislators should improve equal access to justice to all through effective legal centres, by increasing the number of judicial officers and police per 100 000 people and through public education on equal rights.
- Abolish harmful traditional practices such as female genital mutilation and forced marriages by working with traditional and religious leaders.
- Improve resource mobilisation to ensure a rights-based approach in localising the SDGs and implementing the Revised Protocol.
- Ensure effective measurement and tracking linked to progress in gender responsive laws.
- Build partnerships with civil society, the private sector and development partners around the Post-2015 Protocol implementation and SDG localisation.
- Encourage the courts to continue giving guidance through positive and progressive interpretation of laws that address the SADC Gender Protocol targets.
- Lobby parliaments to enact the necessary laws that address the SADC Gender Protocol targets using precedents from the courts.

CHAPTER 2

Gender and governance

Articles 12-13

Matau Futo Letsatsi, Director of Lesotho Ministry of Gender Youth, Sports and Recreation (centre), is a tireless champion of the Fifty Fifty Campaign.   *Photo: Ntolo Lekau*

Quotas and the PR electoral system **deliver results**

KEY POINTS

- Three countries held elections in SADC from August 2017 to June 2018: Angola (national); eSwatini (local, urban) and Lesotho (local). In both Angola and Lesotho the proportion of women declined from 38% to 30%; and 49% to 40% respectively.

- In eSwatini, the proportion of women in urban councils dropped to 12%, and the overall representation of women in local government dropped from 15% to 14%. Things could change in eSwatini following local rural and national elections in September 2018, following the passing of a new law to give effect to the 30% constitutional quota.

- Women's representation in Parliament in SADC is at 26%, one percentage point lower than last year, but two percentage points higher than the global and Sub-Saharan average of 24%.

- Women's representation in Cabinet in the region is lower at 20%. This is also true in Local Government (23%).

- Five more countries are due to hold elections in 2018: DRC (tripartite), Madagascar (tripartite), eSwatini [national and local (rural)], Mozambique (local), and Zimbabwe (tripartite). Five countries will hold elections in 2019: Mozambique (national); Malawi (national); Mauritius (national); South Africa (national and provincial); Botswana (national and local); Namibia (national, regional and local). The coming period is therefore one in which maximum effort needs to be given to the Fifty Fifty campaign.

- "Special measures" and conducive electoral systems give the greatest assurance for increasing women's representation in politics at all levels.

- With an average of 38% women, countries with a PR system and quotas in parliament have almost three times the percentage of women compared to 13% in the First Past the Post (FPTP) system (with no quota).

in all areas of political decision-making

Table 2.1: Trends in Governance since 2009			
	Baseline 2009	Progress 2018	Variance (Progress minus 2030 target)
WOMEN IN PARLIAMENT			
The average proportion of women in parliament reaches 50%	25%	26%	-24%
No. of countries that have achieved over 30% women in Parliament	5 (Angola, Mozambique, Namibia, South Africa, Tanzania)	6 (Angola, Mozambique, Namibia, South Africa, Tanzania, Zimbabwe)	9 (Botswana, DRC Lesotho, Malawi, Madagascar, Mauritius, Seychelles, eSwatini, Zambia)
Highest (country/%)	South Africa (42%)	South Africa (41%)	-9%
Lowest (country, %)	DRC - 8%	DRC (8%)	-42%
WOMEN IN CABINET			
Average proportion of women in cabinet reaches 50%	21%	25%	-25%
No. of countries that have achieved over 30% women in Cabinet	1 (South Africa)	3 (South Africa, Seychelles, Angola)	12 (Botswana, Democratic Republic of Congo - DRC, Lesotho, Madagascar, Malawi, Mauritius, Mozambique, Namibia, eSwatini, Tanzania, Zambia, Zimbabwe)
Highest (country/%)	South Africa (42%)	South Africa (50%)	-0%
Lowest (country/%)	Mauritius (10%)	DRC, Lesotho (10%)	-40%
WOMEN IN LOCAL GOVERNMENT			
Average proportion of women in local government reaches 50%	23%	23%	-27%
No. of countries that have achieved over 30% women in Local Government	5 (Lesotho, Mozambique, Namibia, South Africa, Tanzania)	5 (Lesotho, Mozambique, Namibia, South Africa, Tanzania)	10 (Angola, Botswana, DRC, Malawi, Madagascar, Mauritius, Seychelles, eSwatini, Zambia, Zimbabwe)
Highest (country/%)	Lesotho (58%)	Namibia (48%)	-1%
Lowest (country/%)	Mauritius (6%)	DRC (6%)	-44%
WOMEN IN TOP POLITICAL PARTY POSTS			
Average proportion women in top political party posts reached 50%		10%	-39%
No. of countries that have achieved over 50% women in top political party posts		None	15 (Angola, Botswana, DRC, Lesotho, Malawi, Madagascar, Tanzania, South Africa, Mozambique, Mauritius, Namibia, Seychelles, eSwatini, Zambia, Zimbabwe)
Highest (country/%)		Malawi, Mauritius, Mozambique, Namibia, South Africa, Zambia, Zimbabwe (33%)	-23%
Lowest (country/%)		Angola, Botswana, DRC, Lesotho, Seychelles, eSwatini, Tanzania (0%)	-50%
WOMEN IN ELECTORAL BODIES			
Average proportion women in Electoral Bodies reached 50%		30%	-20%
No. of countries that have achieved over 50% women in Electoral Bodies		2 (Mauritius and Zimbabwe)	13 (Angola, Botswana, DRC, Lesotho, Malawi, Madagascar, Tanzania, South Africa, Mozambique, Namibia, Seychelles, eSwatini, Zambia)
Highest (country/%)		Mauritius (53%)	Exceeded target (Needs to set new country target)
Lowest (country/%)		Mozambique (13%)	37%
WOMEN JUDGES			
Average proportion women Judges reached 50%		28%	-22%
No. of countries that have achieved over 50% women Judges in SADC		2 (Madagascar and Mauritius)	13 (Angola, Botswana, DRC, Malawi, Tanzania, South Africa, Mozambique, Mauritius, Namibia, Seychelles, eSwatini, Zambia, Zimbabwe)
Highest (country/%)		Madagascar (88%)	Exceeded target (Needs to set new country target)
Lowest (country/%)		DRC (6%)	-44%
WOMEN SOURCES IN POLITICAL TOPICS			
Average proportion women sources in political parties reached 50%		15%	-35%
Highest (country/%)		Malawi (26%)	-24%
Lowest (country/%)		DRC (5%)	-45%

Source: Gender Links, 2018.

Table 2.1 shows that:
- There are wide variations in women's represen-tation in all levels of governance. Countries need to adopt different timeframes and realistic targets for achieving gender parity, with 2030 the outside deadline.
- Women's representation in Parliament increased by two percentage point from 25% in 2009 to 27% in 2015. This slipped down to 26% in 2017 because of the decline in women's representation in Angola from 38% to 30%. No country has reached the 50% target. At 42%, South Africa has the highest proportion of women in Parlia-ment. Since 2015, Seychelles has dropped out of the group of countries close to achieving the 50% target having dropped from 44% women in parliament in 2015 to 21% women in parlia-ment after the September 2016 national elections. DRC has the lowest proportion of women in Parliament at 8%.
- Women's representation in Cabinet (Ministers only) dropped by one percentage point from 21% in 2009 to 20% in 2018. Cabinet appoint-ments that are at the sole discretion of the head of state. They provide the ideal opportunity for leaders to "walk the talk". This has not been the case as women are least represented in most SADC countries. Following President Cyril Rama-phosa's cabinet reshuffle in February, South Africa is the only country in the region to have achieved 50% women in cabinet. Only three countries have more than 30% women in cabinet.
- Five countries in the region (Namibia, South Africa, Lesotho, Tanzania and Zimbabwe) have deputy ministers. The average percentage of women deputy ministers is 40%. Namibia (55% women deputy ministers) leads the way, with South Africa following (50%). A question that arises is why the progress at the deputy level is not being replicated at the cabinet level.
- The proportion of women in Local Government increased by one percentage point from 23% in 2009 to 24% in 2015, but dropped again to 23% in 2017 as a result of the proportion of women in Lesotho declining from 49% to 40% in the September 2017 elections. Only five countries have achieved over 30% women in Local Govern-ment. Namibia (48%); South Africa (41%) and Lesotho (40%) are the only three countries with over 40% women in Local Government.
- Since 2017, the Barometer has been measuring women in the top three party posts of the ruling party and the main opposition party. At a regional average of 10%, few political parties have "special" or "affirmative" measures to promote women's representation and participation in their own ranks. Most countries have no women in political party leadership.
- Women comprise 30% of Commissioners in independent electoral commissions in the region. This ranges from 13% in Mozambique to 53%

in Mauritius. Zimbabwe broke new ground with the appointment of a women chair of its Election Commission.
- Madagascar (88%) and Mauritius (50%) have made outstanding gains by reaching the 50% target of women judges. But more needs to be done in the region, where overall women judges comprise 28% of the total.
- At 15% news sources in the political topic category, women still lack a voice in this critical area of participation. This ranges from 5% in DRC to 26% in Malawi.

Background

A strong and vibrant democracy is only possible when all levels of government and leadership are fully inclusive of the people they represent. No public or private office is inclusive unless it has the **full participation of women**. This is not just about women's right to equality and their contri-bution to the conduct of public affairs, but also about using women's resources and potential to determine political and development priorities that benefit societies and the global community. Women have proven abilities as leaders and agents of change, and their right to participate equally governance is essential for a healthy democracy and sustainable development.

Women face several obstacles to participating in political life. Structural barriers through discrimi-natory laws and institutions still limit women's options to run for office. Capacity gaps mean women are less likely than men to have the educa-tion, contacts and resources needed to become effective leaders. Individual women have overcome these obstacles with great acclaim, and often to the benefit of society at large. But for women as a whole, the playing field needs to be level, opening opportunities for all.[1]

Women's leadership, inclusivity at all levels of decision-making and representation is central to achieving human development and promoting human rights. When women are marginalised in politics, issues that concern them, children and youth tend to be compromised at the political decision-making levels.[2] When women are equal partners in decision-making, their experience consi-dered, and voices heard, national and develop-ment policies are more inclusive and have a broader influence and impact.

---

[1] UNWOMEN Thematic Brief on Women's Leadership and Political Participation. See http://www.unwomen.org/-/media/headquarters/attachments/sections/library/publication s/2013/12/un%20womenlgthembriefuswebrev2%20pdf.pdf. Retrieved 28 July 2017.
[2] African Woman and Child Feature service, 2010. "Beyond Numbers: Narrating the Impact of Women's Leadership in Africa."
[3] OSCE report.

NO countries achieved over **50%** ♀ in top political party posts

Representation

Article 12.1: State parties shall ensure equal and effective representation of women in decision-making positions in the political, public and private sectors including through the use of special measures as provided for in Article 5.
12.2 State parties shall ensure that all legislative and other measures are accompanied by public awareness campaigns which demonstrate the vital link between the equal representation and participation of women and men in decision-making positions, democracy, governance and citizen participation.

represen-
tation
in
politics
begins
with
political
parties

Women in political party leadership

Political parties are often referred to as the gate-keepers of democracy and have multiple functions within the electoral process. They are first and foremost organisations that serve as the representatives of their membership, citizens of their countries. They also mirror the democratic soundness of their nations.

Internally, political parties facilitate political recruitment and play a crucial role in candidate selection in the nomination process. Through their party structures, they provide support, financial and professional, to potential candidates that inevitably form legislative bodies as elected members of parliament and in some cases, the executive branch of government[3]. Political parties and their support for women within their party structures and candidates are crucial to enhancing and sustaining women's representation in the electoral process and in decision-making process as a whole.

When parties fail to ensure that women assume leadership posts, this raises questions about their commitment to advancing gender equality more broadly. At a practical level, having women in decision-making within parties' plays an important role in pushing for, and implementing special measures like quotas for women.

Zimbabwe: Women leaders fight backlash

As Zimbabwe prepared for elections on 30 July 2018, the leadership wrangle in the main opposition Movement for Democratic Change (MDC) underscored the hostile environment towards women's participation in decision-making.

The dispute between Nelson Chamisa and Thokozani Khupe following the death of MDC founding president Morgan Tsvangirayi ended with Khupe forming her own faction of the MDC-T. Khupe will stand as Presidential candidate for MDC-T while Nelson Chamisa is the MDC Alliance Presidential candidate.

Social media was awash with hate speech towards Khupe's defiant stance in taking over the leadership of the MDC-T, with people calling her all sorts of names including "hure" (Shona slang for "prostitute"). MP for Matebeleland South Priscilla Misihairambwi-Mushonga protested against such language by wearing a T-shirt inscribed "HURE, ME TOO!" This says that women in politics are no longer afraid of standing their ground.

Priscilla Misihairabwi, Chief Election Agent for Thokozani Khupe wore a #Metoomovement jumper written "HURE" at the back.
Photo courtesy of Twitter, Violet Gonda

Table 2.2: Women in political party leadership 2018

Country	Party	Leader	M	F	Secretary General	M	F	DSG	M	F	Total M	Total F	Overall Total	M	Other positions held in parties
Angola															
Ruling party	People's Movement for the Liberation of Angola	José Eduardo dos Santos	1		Paulo Kassoma	1		n/a			2	0	2	0%	
Main opposition	National Union for the Total Independence of Angola	Isaias Samakuva	1		Vitorino Nhany	1		Rafaeel Massanga Savimbi	1		3	0	3	0%	
Botswana															
Ruling party	Botswana Democratic Party	Mokgweetsi Masisi	1		Mpho Balopi	1		n/a			2	0	2	0%	
Main opposition	Umbrella for Democratic Change	Duma Gideon Boko	1		Moeti Mohwasa	1		n/a			3	0	3	0%	
DRC															
Ruling party	People's Party for Reconstruction and Democracy	Henri Mova Sakanyi	1		Henri Mova Sakanyi	1		n/a			3	0	3	0%	
Main opposition	Union for Democracy and Social Progress	Félix Tshisekedi	1		Étienne Tshisekedi	1		n/a			3	0	3	0%	
Lesotho															
Ruling party	All Basotho Convention	Tom Thabane	1		Samonyane Ntsekele	1		Lebohang Hlaele	1		2	0	2	0%	
Main opposition	Democratic Congress	Pakalitha Mosisili	1		Ralechate Mokose	1		Semano Sekatle	1		3	0	3	0%	
Madagascar															
Ruling party	Hery Vaovao ho an'i Madagasikara - HVM	Rivo Rakotovao	1		Henri Rabary Njaka	1		Paul Rabary	1		3	0	3	0%	
Main opposition	Tiako i Madagasikara - TIM	Marc Ravalomanana	1		Ivohasina Razafimahefa	1		Olivier Donat Andriamahefaparany	1		3	0	3	0%	
Malawi															
Ruling party	Democratic Progressive	Peter Mutharika	1		Grezelder Jeffrey wa Jeffrey		1	Francis Mphepo	1		2	1	3	33%	Administrative secretary
Main opposition	Malawi Congress Party	Lazarus Chakwera	1		Jessie Kabwila		1	Eisenhower Mkaka	1		2	1	3	33%	
Mauritius															
Ruling party	Militant Socialist Movement	Pravind Jugnauth	1		Nando Bodha	1		Leela Devi Dookhun - vice president		1	2	1	3	33%	
Main opposition	Muvman Liberater	Ivan Collendavelloo	1		Rajesh Bhagwan	1		Jaya Krishna	1		3	0	3	0%	
Mozambique															
Ruling party	FRELIMO	Filipe Nyusi	1		Esperança Bias		1	Eliseu Machava	1		2	1	3	33%	
Main opposition	Mozambican National Resistance	Afonso Dhlakama	1		Manuel Zeca Bissopo	1		Jose Manteigas	1		3	0	3	0%	
Namibia															
Ruling party	South West Africa People's Organization	Hage Geingob	1		Nangolo Mbumba	1		Laura Mcleod		1	2	1	3	33%	
Main opposition	Democratic Turnhalle	Henry Venaani	1		Martin G Dentlinger	1		Jan J. van Wyk.	1		3	0	3	0%	
South Africa															
Ruling party	African National Congress	Cyril Ramaphosa	1		Gwede Mantashe	1		Jessie Duarte		1	2	1	3	33%	
Main opposition	Democratic Alliance	Mmusi Maimane	1		Athol Trollip - Chairperson	1		Ivan Meyer/Refiloe Nt'sekhe/ Desiree Vander Walt - Deputy Chairperson		1	2	1	3	33%	
Seychelles															
Ruling party	Linyon Demokratik Seselwa	Roger Mancienne	1		Clifford André	1		Roy Fonseka *	1		3	0	3	0%	Treasurer
Main opposition	Seychelles Peoples Party	Vincent Meriton	1		n/a			n/a			1	0	1	0%	
Tanzania															
Ruling party	Chama Cha Mapinduzi	John Magufuli	1		Abdulrahman Kinana	1		Abdalla Juma	1		3	0	3	0%	
Main opposition	Chadema	Edward Lowassa	1		Vincent Mashinji	1		Salum Mwalimu	1		3	0	3	0%	Chairperson
eSwatini															
Ruling party											0	0	0		Banned
Main opposition											0	0	0		Banned
Zambia															
Ruling party	Patriotic Front (PF)	Edgar Lungu	1		Davies Mwila	1		Mumbi Phiri		1	2	1	3	33%	
Main opposition	United Party For National	Hakainde Hichilema	1		Freeman Mbowe	1		Brian Mwiinga	1		3	0	3	0%	
Zimbabwe															
Ruling party	Zimbabwe African National Union (ZANU)	Emmerson Munangagwa	1		Constantino Chiwenga	1		Kembo Mohadi	1		3	0	3	0%	
Main opposition	Movement for Democratic Change	Nelson Chamisa	1		Douglas Mwonzora	1					2	0	2	0%	
Totals			28	0		24	3		19	5	71	8	79	10%	

Source: Gender Links and political party websites accessed July 2018.

Table 2.2 shows that
- Women constituted only 8 of the 79 top three functionaries in political parties and main opposition parties in SADC in 2018 (10% of the total).
- No woman leads a ruling or main opposition party in the region. It follows that there is no women President or Head of State in the region.
- Three out of 27 (11%) of the Secretary General positions in ruling and main opposition parties are held by women.

- Women comprise five out of 26 (20%) Deputy Secretary Generals in main and opposition parties.
- Despite their stated commitment to gender equality, political parties have not "walked the talk" of gender equality in their own ranks. Most are reluctant to adopt special measures through quotas and policy reforms in their manifestos.

Country	Last elections		Elections planned 2018-2019	
	Local	National	Local	National
eSwatini	2017	Monarchy	2023	2018
Zimbabwe	2013	2013	2018	2018
DRC	2012	2011	2018	2018
Madagascar	2015	2013	2020	2018
Mozambique	2014	2014	2018	2019
Malawi	2014	2014	2019	2019
Mauritius	2015	2014	2020	2019
South Africa	2016	2014	2021	2019
Botswana	2014	2014	2019	2019
Namibia	2014	2014	2019	2019
Seychelles	2011	2016 (National Assembly)	N/A - Local authorities by government appointment	2020
Tanzania	2015	2015	2020	2020
Zambia	2016	2016	2021	2021
Lesotho	October 2017	June 2017	2023	2022
Angola	N/A	2018	N/A	2023

Table 2.3 Elections in SADC past and future

Table 2.3 shows elections held in SADC in 2017 and early 2018 and upcoming elections in 2018/2019. Between August 2017 and mid-2018 Angola (national); Lesotho (local) and eSwatini (local) held elections. In 2018, Zimbabwe, DRC and Madagascar will hold tripartite elections and Mozambique local elections. In 2019 Mozambique (national); Malawi (national); Mauritius (national); South Africa (national and provincial) and Botswana (national and local) and Namibia (national, regional and local) will hold elections.

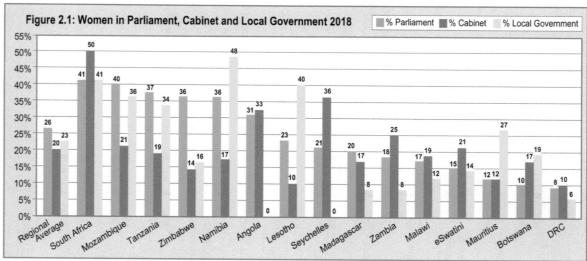

Figure 2.1: Women in Parliament, Cabinet and Local Government 2018

Source: Gender Links 2018, SADC Gender Protocol Country reports and IPU last accessed 18 June 2018.
Angola local government figures not available. Seychelles does not have elected local government.

Political parties are NOT walking the talk of gender equality

Figure 2.1 shows that:
- Performance continues to be mixed in different areas of political decision-making.
- Only South Africa achieved over 40% women in Parliament, Cabinet and Local Government.
- Only eight countries have exceeded the 30% mark in one or more areas including South Africa (Parliament, Cabinet and Local Government); Mozambique (Parliament, Cabinet and Local Government); Tanzania (Parliament, Cabinet and Local Government); Angola (Parliament); Namibia (Parliament, Cabinet and Local Government); Zimbabwe (Parliament), Lesotho (Local Government) and Seychelles (Cabinet).
- All perform better on women in Parliament than Cabinet and Local Government except for South Africa where women comprise 50% of Cabinet compared to Parliament (42%) and Local Government (41%).
- Madagascar, eSwatini, Mauritius, Malawi, Zambia, DRC and Botswana still have a long way to go to achieve gender parity across all categories.
- Namibia, Mozambique and Tanzania have over 30% women in Parliament and Local Government.

- Generally there are much lower proportions of women in Cabinet than in Parliament and Local Government. As Heads of State appoint Cabinets and can therefore make rapid changes in this area, the relatively low level of women in Cabinet reflects weak political will at leadership level.

Parliament

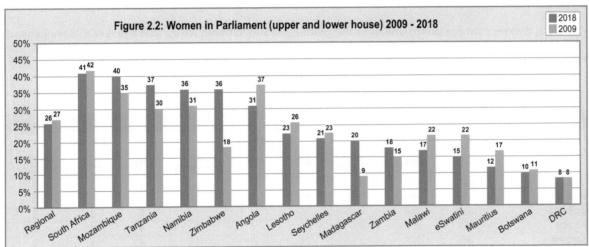

Figure 2.2: Women in Parliament (upper and lower house) 2009 - 2018

Source: Gender Links and IPU http://www.ipu.org/wmn-e/world.htm - accessed 18 June 2018.

Fig 2.2 shows that in the ten years of the SADC Gender Protocol:
- No SADC country has attained the 50% target of women in Parliament[4].
- Two SADC countries (South Africa and Mozambique) have 40% or more women in Parliament.
- Six countries have passed the 30% mark, compared to seven in 2015 due to Seychelles dropping from 44% 21% women in Parliament.
- Nine countries have less than 30% women's representation in Parliament. Of the nine, seven have below 20% women's representations with the lowest being Botswana (10%) and DRC (8%).

- In the ten years of tracking, the overall average of women in Parliament in SADC has dropped by one percentage point, from 27% to 26%. Eight countries have experienced a reduction in the proportion of women in parliament; six have experienced an increase and one has remained constant. The biggest increase took place in Zimbabwe, where the proportion of women in Parliament doubled in the 2013 elections, from 18% to 36%, due to the introduction on a constitutional quota.

in parlia-ment

27%
in 2009

26%
in 2018

---

[4] In countries where there is an upper and lower house, the two have been combined.

Table 2.4: Global comparison of women in parliament by region			
Ranking	Average % of women in parliament (single/lower house)	2017	2018
1	Nordic countries	42%	41%
2	Americas	28%	29%
3	SADC	27%	26%
4	Europe-OSCE member countries including Nordic	27%	28%
5	Europe-OSCE member countries excluding Nordic	25%	26%
6	Sub-Saharan Africa	24%	24%
7	Asia	20%	20%
8	Arab States	18%	18%
9	Pacific	15%	16%
	Global % of Women in Parliament	25%	24%

Source: www.ipu.org, 18 June 2018.

Table 2.4 shows that:
- The average representation of women in global Parliaments decreased from 25% in 2017 to 24% in 2018.
- SADC is two percentage points ahead of the global and Sub-Saharan Africa average. SADC is well ahead of Asia, the Arab States and the Pacific.
- As a region SADC now ranks third in the world (after the Nordic countries and the Americas).

Table 2.5: Regional and Global ranking of Women in Parliament									
Country	Representation			Global rank			SADC rank		
	2017	2018	Variance (2018-2017)	2017	2018	Variance (2018-2017)	2017	2018	Variance (2018-2017)
South Africa	42%	41%	-1%	10	10	0	1	1	0
Mozambique	40%	40%	0%	12	14	2	2	2	0
Zimbabwe	33%	37%	4%	35	36	1	6	3	3
Namibia	36%	36%	0%	11	5	-6	4	4	0
Tanzania	36%	36%	0%	24	25	1	4	4	0
Angola	38%	30%	-8%	18	47	29	3	6	-3
Lesotho	23%	23%	0%	70	83	13	7	7	0
Seychelles	21%	21%	0%	87	90	3	8	8	0
Madagascar	19%	19%	0%	102	103	1	9	9	0
Zambia	18%	18%	0%	111	111	0	10	10	0
Malawi	17%	17%	0%	119	120	1	11	11	0
eSwatini	6%	15%	9%	176	176	0	15	12	3
Mauritius	12%	12%	0%	150	148	-2	12	13	-1
Botswana	10%	10%	0%	162	163	1	13	14	-1
DRC	9%	8%	-1%	167	167	0	14	15	-1

Source: www.ipu.org, 18 June 2018 and Gender Links.

Table 2.5. illustrates where SADC countries rank globally and relative to each other against 193 countries listed by the Inter-Parliamentary Union (IPU). The table shows that:
- SADC countries range from 10th to 167th in the global ranking. At 41% women in Parliament, South Africa is the only country in the region in the global top 10. No SADC country is in the global top five. What this shows is that countries elsewhere in the world are moving up the global scales as SADC countries move down.
- Over the last year, two SADC countries improved their global raking; three remained the same and ten dropped in the global ranking.
- Within SADC rankings, Angola fell by two places as a result of the decline in women's representation in the last elections.

Women mayors in Madagascar march for equality.

Photo: Zoto Razanadratefa

Table 2.6 overleaf tracks the performance of all SADC countries with regard to women's representation in national elections and provides projections to 2020. The information is sorted in descending order according to 2020 projections. The explanations for these projections are in the last column. Those shaded green are countries that have or are likely to achieve 40% or more women in Parliament. Those shaded amber have or are likely to achieve 30% or more women in Parliament. Those shaded red are in the danger zone of not having achieved, and not likely to achieve 30% women in Parliament. Projections, based on an assessment of electoral systems, quotas, and past trends (see comments in the predictions table) show that:

- At best the region will achieve an average of 36% women in parliament by 2020. However, this is highly dependent on the performance of countries having elections in 2018 and 2019; and on a concerted Fifty-Fifty campaign being mounted.
- With Seychelles dropping out of the lead and the regression that took place in Angola in the 2017 elections, only four countries (Tanzania; Mozambique; Namibia and South Africa) will likely come close to achieving the 50% target,

especially if they strengthen their existing voluntary and legislated/constitutional quotas and review special measures in party manifestos before their next elections by 2020.

- Three countries - Zimbabwe (which has a Constitutional quota for women in Parliament), Angola (which has had elections and just held the 30% line) and eSwatini (which has passed a law to strengthen constitutional provisions for 30% women in politics)- will achieve or exceed the 30% target if they stay the course.
- Eight countries are likely to remain below 30%. Lesotho, Seychelles and Zambia are below 30% and they do not have elections before 2020. Malawi, Mauritius, Madagascar, Botswana and DRC have elections, but they are all FPTP countries with no quota. The chance of substantial increases in women's representation in Parliament in elections in these countries is slim.
- Given the wide variations between countries - from 8% women in parliament in DRC and 10% in Botswana, to South Africa currently the SADC leader at 42% - countries need to adopt different timeframes for achieving gender parity in parliament, with 2030 the outside deadline for doing so.

Women in Parliament in SADC 2018										
	Structure	Date of last election	Total members in lower/ single house	Women in lower/ single house	Lower house	Total members in upper/ senate house	Women in upper/ senate house	Upper house	Upper and lower	Total number of women	% Women in parliament
Regional Average			1495	422	28%	258	88	34%	2539	807	32%
Tanzania	Unicameral	Sep-15	390	145	37%				390	145	37%
Mozambique	Unicameral	Oct-14	250	99	40%				250	99	40%
Namibia	Bicameral	Nov-14	104	48	46%	41	10	24%	146	53	36%
South Africa	Unicameral	May-14	393	165	42%	54	19	35%	447	184	41%
Zimbabwe	Bicameral	Jul-13	250	83	33%	79	38	48%	329	121	37%
eSwatini	Bicameral	Aug-13	65	4	6%	30	10	33%	95	14	15%
Angola	Unicameral	Aug-17	220	67	30%				220	67	30%
Malawi	Unicameral	May-14	192	32	17%				192	32	17%
Mauritius	Unicameral	Jul-14	69	8	12%				69	8	12%
Madagascar	Bicameral	Jul-13	151	29	19%	63	13	21%	214	42	20%
Lesotho	Bicameral	Jun-17	122	27	22%	32	8	25%	154	35	23%
Seychelles	Unicameral	Sep-16	33	7	21%				33	7	21%
Botswana	Unicameral	Oct-14	63	6	10%				63	6	10%
DRC	Bicameral	Nov-11	492	44	9%	108	5	5%	600	49	8%
Zambia	Unicameral	Aug-16	167	30	18%				167	30	18%

Source: Gender Links, 2018.

Local government

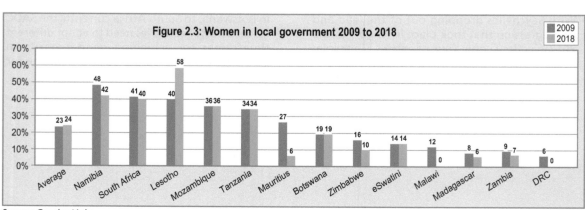

Source: Gender Links.

Women in parliament by 2020 - prediction table

Date of next election	Total members in lower/single house	Women in lower/single house	Lower house	Total members in upper/senate house	Women in upper/senate house	Upper house	Upper and lower	Total number of women	% Women in parliament	Assumptions
	1520	492	32%	260	93	36%	2511	915	36%	36% by 2020 but still short of the 50% target.
Oct-20	350	150	43%				350	150	43%	Efforts to increase the current constitutional provision of 30% women in decision-making to 50% in the reviewed constitution has not materialised as the new Constitution is yet to be adopted.
Oct-19	250	120	48%				250	120	48%	Has had steady growth over last two elections and 50/50 campaign underway.
Nov-19	104	50	48%	26	10	38%	130	60	46%	SWAPO has voluntary 50% quota, move towards legislated quota.
May-19	400	180	45%	54	20		454	200	44%	Only the ruling ANC has a zebra style quota; the proportion of women is thus closely linked to the fortunes of the ANC.The outlook for the ANC has improved following the resignation on Jacob Zuma.
Jul-18	270	90	33%	80	40	50%	350	130	37%	Next election in 2018.
Oct-18	65	22	34%	30	10	33%	95	32	34%	Law passed by parliament in 2018 should ensure at least 30% women in accordance with the Constitution.
Aug-23	220	67	30%				220	67	30%	Relapse in the 2017 elections. No elections before 2020.
May-19	192	50	26%				192	50	26%	Opposed to quotas but pressure political pressure is mounting.
Dec-19	69	17	25%				69	17	25%	Enough time for local quota to be escalated to national.
Nov-18	151	32	21%	63	15	24%	214	47	22%	No quotas adopted. Still have FPTP system. Unlikely to be many changes.
Oct-22	120	27	23%	33	8	24%	153	35	23%	No elections before 2020.
Sep-22	33	7	21%				33	7	21%	No elections before 2020.
Oct-19	63	13	21%				63	13	21%	Opposed to quotas but political pressure is mounting.
Dec-18	482	100	21%	108	19	18%	590	119	20%	Opposed to quotas but political pressure is mounting.
Sep-21	167	30	18%				167	30	18%	No elections before 2020.

Figure 2.3 shows women's representation in local government in Southern Africa from 2009 to 2018, where comparative figures are available. Malawi held local elections for the first time in 2014. Salient facts include:

- The average representation of women in local government has declined from 24% to 23% over the ten years. This is largely due to the decline of the proportion of women in local government in Lesotho from 58% to 40% over this period (see case study in a later section of this chapter).
- Key gains have been made in Mauritius (from 6% to 27%) as a result of the adoption of a gender neutral quota there; and Namibia (from 42% to 48%). Namibia currently leads the way with regard to women's representation in local government.
- Only five countries have exceeded 30% women in local government (Tanzania, Mozambique, Lesotho, South Africa and Namibia).
- Seven SADC countries (Botswana, Zimbabwe, eSwatini, Malawi, Madagascar, Zambia and DRC) have less than 20% women in local government. DRC (6%) has the lowest representation of women in local government.

Table 2.7: Women's representation in Local Government 2017 to 2018

Country	2018	2017	Variance 2018-2017	Progress to target 50%
Average	**23**	**24**	**-1**	**-27**
Namibia	48	48	0	-2
South Africa	41	41	0	-9
Lesotho	40	49	-9	-10
Mozambique	36	36	0	-14
Tanzania	34	34	0	-16
Mauritius	27	27	0	-23
Botswana	19	19	0	-31
Zimbabwe	16	16	0	-34
eSwatini	15	12	-3	-35
Malawi	12	12	0	-38
Madagascar	8	8	0	-42
Zambia	9	9	0	-41
DRC	6	6	0	-44

Source: Gender Links, 2018.

Table 2.7 compares performance over the last year with regard to women's representation in Local Government and progress towards achieving the target of 50%.
- All 13 SADC countries with elected Local Government failed to reach the 50% target. Only one country (Namibia) is close to reaching the target.
- Two countries held Local Government elections in the year under review - Lesotho and eSwatini (urban). Lesotho regressed by nine percentage points from 49% to 40%. Women constitute 12% of Councilors in eSwatini urban councils. When this is combined with women in the rural councils, the proportion of women in Local Government in eSwatini is 14%, down from 15% before the urban elections. Following the passing of a law to give effect to the Constitutional quota of

30%, the proportion of rural women is set to increase in the September 2018 elections. This could result in women's representation at the local level increasing after the local (rural) and national elections.

Table 2.8 tracks the performance of all SADC countries with regard to women's representation in local elections and provides projections to 2020. The information is sorted in descending order according to 2020 projections from the highest to lowest. The explanations for these projections are in the last column. Those shaded green are countries that are likely to achieve 40% or more women in Local Government. Those shaded amber have or are likely to achieve 30% or more women in Local Government. Those shaded red are in the danger zone of not having achieved, or not likely to achieve 30% women in Local Government. Projections, based on an assessment of electoral systems, quotas, and past trends (see comments in the predictions table) show that:
- At best the region will achieve an average of 29% women in Local Government by 2020.
- Four countries (Lesotho, Namibia, South Africa and Tanzania) have reached or are highly likely to reach or come close to the 50% target by 2020 especially if political parties adopt special measures for increasing women's representation and participation with their manifestos, effectively implement the policies and strengthen their existing voluntary and legislated/constitutional quotas.

SWOT analysis of gender and local government in Mozambique.

Photo: Raul Manhica

- Two countries (Mozambique and Mauritius) have or will achieve the 30% target if they stay the course and leverage off their quotas as well as fifty-fifty campaigns at community and party levels.
- eSwatini could improve its performance in the Rural Local Government elections in September 2018, thanks to the law that has been passed to give effect to the Constitutional quota of 30%.

- Six countries (Madagascar, Malawi, Botswana, Zambia, DRC and Zimbabwe) will remain below 30% as they have already had elections or have failed to implement special measures that would alter this scenario.
- GL could not obtain data of local government in Angola. Seychelles does not have elected local government.

	Table 2.8: Women in local government in SADC in 2018 and projections to 2020								
	Women in Local gvt 2018				**Women in local gvt projected 2020**				**Assumptions**
	Date of election	Total LG councillors	Women in LG	% Women in LG	Next election	Total LG councillors	Women in LG	% Women in LG	
Regional Average		36989	8652	23%		34125	9784	29%	
Namibia	Nov-15	230	110	48%	Nov-20	323	160	50%	SWAPO has a voluntary 50% quota; legislated 30% quota.
Lesotho	2011	1394	555	40%	Mar-22	1394	555	40%	Elections in October 2017 resulted in a step backwards.No new elections before 2020.
Tanzania	2015	3477	1190	34%	Oct-20	3477	1500	43%	Possibility of a constitutional 50/50 quota being adopted by the 2020 elections.
South Africa	Aug-16	10235	4219	41%	Jul-21	10235	4219	41%	Election in 2021; only ruling party has quota but subtle pressure on other parties.
Mozambique	2014	1196	431	36%	2018	1196	450	38%	Mozambique has made steady progress in increasing women's representation, national figure is 40%.
Mauritius	Dec-15	1290	346	27%	Dec-20	1614	500	31%	Have a legislated quota of 30%.
Botswana	Oct-14	605	117	19%	Oct-19	605	150	25%	Opposed to quotas, but lots of work on the ground. Have signed SADC Protocol on Gender and Development.
eSwatini	Sep-17	485	67	14%	Sep-23	485	120	25%	Efforts underway to gain ground after losses in urban elections.
Zimbabwe	2013	1962	318	16%	Jul-18	1962	350	18%	No legislated quota in place for the 2018 elections.
Madagascar	Jul-15	12677	1019	8%	Jul-20	9608	1500	16%	Constitution encourages but does not prescribe women's increased representation; too late for quota.
Malawi	May-14	467	54	12%	May-19	462	70	15%	Next election is in 2019; likely to resist quota but some time for lobbying.
Zambia	Sep-16	1589	127	8%	Sep-21	1382	120	9%	Elections in 2021; no quota in the constitution.
DRC		1382	85	6%	Dec-18	1382	90	6%	No special measures in place.
Angola									Data unavailable about the number of councillors.
Seychelles					N/A				No elected local government.

Source: Gender Links, Inter Parliamentary Union website, EISA website, 20 July 2017.

Electoral systems and quotas

Despite the provisions in the Post 2015 SADC Gender Protocol for "special measures" the extent to which these have been taken on board in different SADC countries varies widely. Unfortunately, in the negotiations for the updating of the Protocol, Ministers decided to drop the reference to reviewing and amending electoral systems that have a key bearing on women's political representation.

By way of background there are two main types of electoral systems:

- In the **Proportional Representation (PR)**, or "list system," citizens vote for parties that are allocated seats in parliament according to the percentage of vote they receive. Individual candidates get in according to where they sit on the list. In an open list system, voters determine where candidates sit on the list. In a closed list system, the party determines where candidates sit on the list, although this is usually based on democratic nomination processes within the party.

- In the constituency, or **"First Past the Post" (FPTP)** system, citizens vote not just for the party, but also for the candidate who represents the party in a geographically defined constituency. Thus, a party can garner a significant percentage of the votes, but still have no representative in parliament, because in this system "the winner takes all."

There is overwhelming evidence internationally to suggest that women stand a better chance of being elected under the PR (and especially the closed list PR system) as opposed to the constituency electoral system.[5] In a PR system voters choose based on the party and its policies, rather than on a particular individual. This works in favour of women - at least as far as getting their foot in the door - because of socialised prejudices against women in politics.[6] The chance of women being elected is even higher when the PR system works in concert with a quota.

Table 2.9: Political parties and quotas 2018		
Country	**Ruling party**	**Quota and Nature/None**
Angola	Movement for the Liberation of Angola (MPLA)	30% quota of women
Botswana	Botswana Democratic Party (BDP)	None
DRC	The People's Party for Reconstruction and Democracy (PPRD) (Parti du Peuple pour la Reconstruction et la Démocratie (PPRD)	30% quota of women
Lesotho	Coalition government - All Basotho Convention (ABC), Alliance of Democrats (AD), Basotho National Party (BNP) and Reformed Congress of Lesotho (RCL)	ABC - None AD - None BNP - None RCL - None
Madagascar	New Forces for Madagascar (Hery Vaovao ho an'i Madagasikara) (HVM)	None
Malawi	Democratic Progressive Party (DPP)	None
Mauritius	Mauritius Labour Party (MLP)	None
Mozambique	Frente de Libertação de Moçambique; Mozambique Liberation Front (FRELIMO)	40% quota of women
Namibia	Southwest Africa People's Organisation (SWAPO)	50% quota for women
Seychelles	Coalition government - Linyon Demokratik Seselwa (LDS)	None
South Africa	African National Congress (ANC)	50% quota for women
eSwatini		Political parties do not contest seats in Parliament
Tanzania	Chama Cha Mapinduzi (CCM)	None
Zambia	The Patriotic Front (PF)	40 %
Zimbabwe	Zimbabwe African National Union - Patriotic Front (ZANU-PF)	30%
	Movement for Democratic Change (MDC)- Alliance adopted a fifty percent quota for women, but then stated that less than half these seats were taken up	50%

Source: Gender Links 2018.

Table 2.9 shows that ruling parties in seven countries have adopted quotas of one kind or another. In two instances (South Africa's African National Council (ANC) and SWAPO of Namibia) these quotas are in line with the Protocol parity targets. The opposition MDC Alliance in Zimbabwe declared a 50% quota but fell short of meeting it when nominations opened. The ruling Frelimo party in Mozambique and Patriotic Front in Zambia have

a 40% quota. However, while these quotas exist on paper they have failed to translate into women's representation in party structures and within government itself. Lesotho has a coalition government and none of the political parties have special measures for increasing women's representation in political leadership and this is also seen in the two percentage drop of women in the coalition government.

---

[5] For more information on the comparative global data on quotas for women in politics see www.idea.int/quota.
[6] Lowe-Morna, 1996.

Table 2.10: Electoral systems, quotas and women's political participation in SADC					
Country	Electoral system - national	Quota - National	Electoral system - local	Quota - local	% women national	% women local
South Africa	PR	Voluntary party	Mixed	Voluntary party	41%	41%
Mozambique	PR	Voluntary party	PR	Voluntary party	40%	36%
Tanzania	Mixed	Constitutional - 30%	Mixed	Constitutional - 30%	37%	34%
Zimbabwe	Mixed	Constitutional - 30%	FPTP	No	37%	16%
Namibia	PR	Voluntary party	PR	Law - 30%	36%	48%
Angola	PR	Voluntary party	PR	Voluntary party	30%	NA
Lesotho	Mixed	Law - 30% PR seats	Mixed	Law - 30%	23%	40%
Seychelles	FPTP	No	FPTP	No	21%	N/A
Madagascar	FPTP	No	FPTP	No	20%	8%
Zambia	FPTP	Voluntary party	FPTP	Voluntary party	18%	9%
Malawi	FPTP	No	FPTP	No	17%	12%
eSwatini	FPTP	Yes - Constitutional[7]	FPTP	Yes - Constitutional	15%	14%
Mauritius	FPTP	No	FPTP	Law - 30%	12%	27%
Botswana	FPTP	No	FPTP	No	10%	19%
DRC	FPTP	No	FPTP	No	8%	NA

Source: Gender Links, 2018.

Table 2.10 plots electoral systems and quotas at local and national levels against women's political representation in each country. The countries are shaded according to the electoral system at national level: PR, mixed and FPTP (South Africa has a mixed system at local and PR system at national). Within each colour band, countries are sorted according to the levels of political representation at the national level. Overall, the chart demonstrates the strong correlation between electoral systems, quotas and women's political representation. Specific observations include:

- *Nine out of the 15 SADC countries have either a Constitutional or legislated quota,* or voluntary party quota, in place. All of these except one (Mauritius local government, and ESwatini) have a PR system.
- *All countries except one that have over 36% women in local government and parliament have a PR (or in the case of local government in South Africa, mixed) electoral system.* In all four countries (South Africa, Mozambique, Namibia and Angola) ruling parties have adopted voluntary party quotas. In Namibia, the electoral law also prescribes a 30% quota for women in local government.
- *Countries with a mixed system coupled with Constitutional or legislated quotas come after those with a PR system in terms of performance.* Lesotho has always had a mixed system at the national level. The country adopted a mixed system at the local level so that 30% of seats can be reserved for women and distributed on a PR basis (in addition to the seats contested

on FPTP basis). Lesotho now has a quota for PR seats at the national level, but these are not reserved solely for women. The Lesotho formula at local level drew on the experience of Tanzania that has now also been emulated at the national level in Zimbabwe. In all these examples, countries have adopted a mixed system to get around the rigidities of the FPTP system when it comes to increasing women's political representation. The difference between women's representation at the local level in Zimbabwe (16%) where there is a FPTP system and no quota, and national (32%) where there is a mixed system and quota is a stark reminder of the key role played by electoral systems and quotas in determining women's political representation.

- *Constitutional or legislated quotas in a FPTP system do not work well unless accompanied by enforcement mechanisms:* The reason for this is that unless women are fielded in seats where they are likely to win, the numbers make little difference. The classic example of this

---
[7] A law was passed in eSwatini in June 2018 to give effect to the Constitutional quota.

9 SADC countries have a Constitutional or Legislated Quota

is eSwatini, where despite the 30% Constitutional quota, women's representation at local and national level has remained lower than 20%. A new law passed in May 2018 aims to give effect to the Constitutional quota. Mauritius managed to increase the proportion of women in Local Government from 6% to 27% in the 2015 elections through a strong advocacy campaign that accompanied the adoption of a gender neutral quota.

- **The lowest representation of women is in the eight countries with a FPTP system.** Within this category, Madagascar comes after Seychelles, following the increase in women's political representation from 6% to 21% in the recent elections. These elections showed that it is possible to increase women's representation in FPTP countries through strategic Fifty/Fifty campaigns, but still a challenge to go beyond around 20% without a quota.

Table 2.11: Electoral systems and women's representation in SADC parliaments			
Electoral system	Overall - % women	With quota - % women	Without quota - % women
FPTP	13%	15%	13%
PR	38%	38%	36%
MIXED	34%	37%	23%
OVERALL	26%	38%	16%

Source: Gender Links 2018.

Table 2.11 summarises the importance of electoral systems and quotas for women's political participation in the SADC region. Green denotes higher than 30%; red lower than 30%. The table shows that:

- At 38%, countries with quotas have a far higher representation of women than those without quotas (16%).
- Consistent with global trends, countries with the PR system (38%) have a much higher representation of women than the FPTP (16%).
- Women's representation in the mixed system (34%) is more than double the FPTP system.
- Quotas used in combination with the PR system (38%) and mixed system (37%) result in the highest representation of women.
- Women comprise 37% of parliamentarians in countries with a mixed system and quota, compared to 23% in countries with a mixed system and no quota.

The examples that follow show the relationship between quotas and electoral systems in determining women's political participation.

Making quotas work - eSwatini

 eSwatini has a 30% Constitutional quota for women in politics, but up to now this has not been observed. The passing of *The Election of Women Members to the House of Assembly Bill* ahead of the local (rural) and national elections on 21 September 2018 is timely. Nominations are set for 28-29 July, Primary Elections on 18 August and campaigning officially opens on 19 August 2018.

eSwatini is the smallest Southern African nation and is one of the world's few remaining absolute monarchies. In eSwatini the Westminster electoral model was replaced by the *tinkhundla* system to facilitate the practice of both traditional and the western styles of government in 1978. Political parties are not allowed to contest. Instead, individuals are elected to parliament from 55 constituencies known as "Tinkhundla."

The constituencies are sub-divided into about 350 chiefdoms in the four regions nationwide. In the primary elections voters choose candidates from their chiefdoms who then contest the secondary elections and compete against other candidates in their constituency for a seat in parliament.

The Constitution of eSwatini (2006) provides that if after a general election the female membership does not meet the required 30%, the house shall elect not more than four additional women by region. This provision has not been observed.

The Women's Caucus in Parliament set out to draft a Bill that would ensure that the Constitutional provisions are observed in the 2018 elections. *The Election of Women Members in the House of Assembly Bill* was finally passed by Senators on 31 May 2018, and now awaits signing by the King. The Bill provides for "the election of the women members to the House of Assembly where, after any general election, it appears that the female members of Parliament will not constitute less thirty percent of the total membership of Parliament." This gives effect to section 86 (1) in the ESwatini Constitution which states that: *"Where at the first meeting of the house after any general election it appears that female members of Parliament will not constitute at least 30 per cent of the total membership of Parliament, then, and only then, the provision of this section shall apply."*

Councillor Sibongile Mazibuko advocates for women's equal representation in politics in eSwatini. *Photo: Gender Links*

The debate on the Bill reflected the strong resistance that still exists to women's political participation. Mbabane West Member of Parliament (MP) Johane Shongwe said that wives should not stand for election unless they had the permission of their husbands: "It is difficult for women to nominate one another in chiefdoms. Therefore, it is advisable for them to get permission from their husbands. I was nominated by a woman to be where I am right now, to show that most women would rather nominate a man than another woman." The MP added that women MPs would sometimes attend workshops at places far away from their homes. This would mean they would have to go for days without sleeping next to their husbands at home. The local media reported that "traditionalists do not support a constitutional change to ensure 30 percent of members of the House of Assembly are women."[8]

FPTP politics is still hostile for women at the local level in Zambia[9]

Zambia is one of the eight countries in SADC that has a FPTP system with no quotas, resulting in low levels of women's representation at both national and local level. Recent local by-elections monitored by the Zambia National Women's Lobby (ZNWL) reflect the challenges faced by women in the cut-throat competition of FPTP politics, especially at the local level.

The by-elections in the 16 wards were as a result of convictions, resignations and deaths of incumbent councillors. The Electoral Commission of Zambia (ECZ) set Tuesday 24 April 2018 as the day for the by-elections in Luapula, Kansuswa, Chiweza, Chiwuyu, Ntumbachushi, Munwa, Nampundwe, Mikunku, Kalebe, Kakoma, Kanongo, Mushima, Kalilele, Mudyanyama, Mwanza East and Lealui Lower.

Only 7% female candidates participated in the by-elections compared to 93% male. Out of the 57 candidates who participated in the 16 councillor by-elections only one out of four female candidates won. The total number of female councillors in Zambia has increased from 126 to 127 (7.8%). This is a slight improvement on the 2011 General Elections when only 85 women won (5.9%).

The ZNWL commented: "Radical measures have to be put in place to ensure that the country's leadership truly reflects the population it represents. To let the country change its attitude towards women's representation on its own is not an option as this can take several years to achieve."[10]

FPTP and no quota -Gearing up for elections in Botswana

Ahead of the 2019 general election, the women's movement has launched a 50/50 campaign to promote the equal and effective participation of Batswana women in political decision-making. **Botswana**, which celebrated its fiftieth anniversary in 2016, has had a FPTP electoral system since independence. The only quotas in the country are voluntary political party quotas that for the most part have not been observed.

At 20% women's representation, the ruling Botswana Democratic Party (BDP) is far from reaching the target. Though the Botswana National Front (BNF) has a 30% quota, it has not actively implemented it. The Botswana Congress Party (BCP)

Only **7%** ♀ candidates in Zambia local bi-elections

---

8 http://allafrica.com/stories/201805250765.html
9 https://womeninleadership.hivos.org/an-analysis-of-zambias-sixteen-councillor-by-elections-in-2018/
10 Ibid.

has a quota of 30% and this has contributed to 44% women's representation within the party leadership. Other parties like the Botswana Movement for Democracy mention gender equality but have not made efforts to ensure women are equally represented in central committees.

The all-time highest female representation in Parliament stood at 18% following the 1999 elections. Since then, it has been a downwards spiral with women's representation in Parliament decreasing from 11% in 2009 to 10% in the 2014 general elections. Local Government representation went slightly up from 18% in 2009 to 19% in 2014. Botswana has never come even half way to achieving the gender parity target at local or national levels.

The general public perceptions of women in politics are that women are not confident to stand for leadership positions especially in politics. There is very limited voter education to mobilise the population to vote for women. Political education is still very weak especially for ordinary Batswana.

Women prepare for the 2019 elections.   *Photo: Keletso Metsing*

A recent 50/50 meeting convened by Gender Links and attended by all the main parties, made the following recommendations:
- Promote the effective implementation of the SDGs and Agenda 2030 SADC Gender Protocol to achieve 50% women's representation in all areas of decision-making ahead of the 2019 general elections.
- Lobby for permanent electoral systems reform from the FPTP to a PR system that is more inclusive and conducive to women's participation. At worst, there should be a constitutional quota to facilitate more women gaining access to political leadership.
- Political parties transform policies in party manifestos to include quotas and the proportional representation system.
- Remove structural barriers and perceptions rooted in culture, customs, religion and tradition; and invest in efforts that build strong political will and leadership by all to effect change. There is

a crucial need for more civic education about women and men's equal participation in politics and decision making in public service especially ahead of 2019 elections.
- Work with media houses to make sure "every voice counts" pre, during and post the 2019 general elections. Use the media as a critical platform and tool to effect change.

Lessons from Local Government in the countdown to 2019 in Mauritius

Mauritius is the only SADC country that has not signed the SADC Gender Protocol. One of the island's objections to the Protocol is Article 5 - affirmative action, now referred to as "special measures" in the Post 2015 Protocol in an effort to be more inclusive. Ironically, in 2015, Mauritius adopted a gender neutral quota for Local Government that led to the level of women's representation increasing four fold, to 27%. Although all elections in Mauritius are held primarily on a FPTP basis, public education and awareness helped to ensure that women candidates fielded in the elections won.

Pressure is mounting for a radical change from the FPTP electoral System to a PR system and at the least, for the quota system adopted at local level to be implemented at national level. A political dialogue organised by Gender Links Mauritius (GLM) and the Mauritius Council for Social Service as part of 50 years of independence celebrations at MACOSS in Ebène, heard that Mauritius seems no closer to breaking new ground at the national level as the 2019 elections draw closer. Analysis done by GLM shows that no political party has/nor implements voluntary quotas for women. The chances of a substantial increase in women's representation in the 2019 elections remain bleak.

Mixed systems and mixed blessings at the local level in Lesotho

Following the decline in women's representation in Local Government from 58% in 2005 to 49% in 2011, the proportion of women councillors in Lesotho decreased by a further nine percentage points to 40% in September 2011. **Lesotho** local government has become a textbook case study of the possibilities and challenges created by quotas.

During the first local elections in 2005, the country adopted a system of reserving one third seats in a FPTP system for women, i.e. only women could contest these seats. In addition to the reserved seats, women won 28% of the openly contested seats, bringing the total to 58%. However, following a challenge in the High Court, Lesotho opted for the "Tanzania model" (later adopted also in Zimbabwe at the national level). In this mixed system, 30% of council seats are allocated to women only in proportion to the percentage of the vote won by the parties in the elections, i.e. on a PR basis. In 2011, in addition to these PR seats women won 19% of the FPTP seats; a lower percentage than before, possibly because the first system had been so unpopular.

Local Government elections due in October 2016 were postponed to September 2017 as the date clashed with Lesotho's 50 years of independence. The elections were held in one municipal council,

Local Government elections, Malumeng Primary School, Lesotho.
Photocourtesy of Limpho Sello, Lesotho Times

11 urban councils and 64 community councils in all the ten districts of the country. In total there are 76 local authorities in Lesotho.

	Table 2.12: 2017 Lesotho Local Government Election Results									
	Total number of Councillors by sex and by %				FPTP Results for Men and Women Councillors			Women reserved seats		
	Women	Men	All Councillors	% of women	Women	Men	Total	% of women	Women	% of women
Party	510	735	1245	41%	196	735	931	21%	314	33%
ELECTED CHIEFS	45	104	149	30%	-	-	-	-	-	-
Total	555	839	1394	40%	196	735	931	21%	314	33%

Source: Gender Links.

Table 2.12 shows that women won 196 out of the 931 FPTP seats, giving them 21% of these seats (slightly higher than the 19% in 2011). The 314 additional seats reserved for women on a PR basis is one third of the number of FPTP seats.

Chiefs are not elected by ordinary members of Lesotho society. They are nominated by their peers and voted for by fellow traditional leaders. Women constituted only 30% of this category.

In all, 1394 Councillors were elected in the September 2017 polls (FPTP seats, special PR seats for women and elected chiefs). Of these 555 were women: 40% of the total.

Despite the setback in the 2017 elections, the reserved PR seats have been key to increasing women's representation at the local level. At national level, as reported last year, Lesotho has a mixed system with a bias towards FPTP and a quota applicable only to the PR seats. In the last national elections, Lesotho slipped backwards from 23% to 21%.

Key recommendations include:
- Lobby for electoral reform from the FPTP to the constitutional adoption of the PR system only. The PR system is more conducive for women's participation especially at local government.
- Ensure the effective implementation of the PR and quota at local government by decentralizing powers and giving local councils executive powers.

- Work with political parties to adopt the PR system and include a 50% quota to ensure women's equal opportunities and representation in political leadership at local and national levels. There is a tendency of having men standing for the FPTP and then women resorting to be put on the PR lists because of the legislated quota that exists. Political parties need to embed gender parity in all their policies and practices.
- There should be a quota for the chiefs that are elected to the council as more men are always elected. In the 2017 Local Chieftaincy Councils, women constitute only 30% of the total.

Missing the mark in the July elections?

Zimbabwe Women's Election Charter & Women's Manifesto.
Photo: Tapiwa Zvaraya

representation set to ⬇ in Zimbabwe

Despite the spirited 50/50 campaign launched by civil society partners ahead of the July 2018 elections in **Zimbabwe**, the outlook for women's increased representation, especially at the local level, is bleak. The quota at national level has not been extended to the local level, and the quota at national level is due to expire in 2023. Parties have failed to live up to their own voluntary quotas. Women's political participation has been marred by sexist mud-slinging, a reminder of the Violence Against Women in Elections (VAWIE) that undermines democracy and women's rights.The 2013 Zimbabwe Constitution brought with it renewed hope for all Zimbabweans, especially women who had been calling for a legislated quota.

Article 17 of the Constitution guarantees gender equality in all areas of decision-making, but the Constitution only spells out a quota for women in parliament, not in any other area, including local government. As a result the proportion of women in parliament increased from 18% to 35% in 2013, but that for women in local government dropped from 18% to 16%.

The Government of Zimbabwe (Ministry of Local Government; Ministry of Justice and Parliamentary and Legal Affairs), Zimbabwe Electoral Commission as well as UNWOMEN and Gender Links) embarked on a study visit to Mauritius to learn how the government of Mauritius had managed to institute a quota at the local level in the hope that these lessons would put pressure on government to also institute a quota at the local level but nothing came to fruition. The Women in Local Government

Forum (WiLGF) wrote to the Clerk of Parliament seeking the assistance of the legislature in extending the quota at national level to local level. NGOs led by the Women's Coalition of Zimbabwe (WCoZ), including Gender Links Zimbabwe, Women in Politics Support Unit (WIPSU), Hivos, working together with the United Nations Entity for Gender Equality and the Empowerment of Women (UNWOMEN) and the Women's Parliamentary Caucus embarked on a lobbying and advocacy drive for a 50/50 quota at the local level.

The resignation of former President Robert Mugabe as President of Zimbabwe on 21 November 2017 brought new hope to democracy in Zimbabwe. In March 2018, the Zimbabwe Women's Parliamentary Caucus in partnership with civil society launched the women's manifesto with five priority areas: women and economic development, women and social services, transport and infrastructure, access to justice and equal benefit of the law and women's representation in governance. Women from all walks of life converged to share their issues and concerns. An extension of the quota at national level beyond 2023 became the major focus, with WLGF calling for the quota to be extended to local government.[11]

In May 2018, Zimbabwean women from all walks of life got the chance to meet President Emmerson Mnangagwa on challenges they face. Women's representation especially in Local Government took centre stage. Mnangagwa reiterated the government's commitment to the African Union Charter which requires that member states have equal representation of women across the board.

As in Tanzania, and Lesotho (local) the constitutional quota in Zimbabwe allocates 30% seats to parties on a PR basis for women. This will guarantee 30% women in Parliament in the 2018 elections (though this clause expires in 2023). The question in 2018 is whether women will edge any closer to improving their performance in the FPTP seats.

Analysis of party lists by the Women in Politics Support Unit (WiPSU) show that neither the ruling Zimbabwe African National Union Patriotic Front (ZANU/PF), that has a 30% quota for women, nor the main opposition MDC Alliance, that boasted a 50% quota for women, have lived up to their manifestos. According to the local NGO watchdog, in the National Assembly 47 political candidates fielded candidates; 20 of these did not field any women candidates at all and two parties fielded only one woman each. Women comprise a mere 15% of candidates. 84 out of 210 Constituencies will be contested by men only. In the dog-eat-dog

---

[11] see http://www.parlzim.gov.zw/live/2018/03/06/5050-advocacy-campaign-and-womens-manifesto-launch-6-march-2018/)

contests where women are standing, there is no guarantee of them winning. "We are deeply concerned," WiPSU said in a statement before the elections, "that at this point it appears that the only women that will be in Parliament are the 91 that are required by law. This brazen disregard for the basic tenets of democracy is deplorable 38 years after Independence."

According to the WiPU analysis, 40 political parties fielded candidates for the Local Authority Elections. Of these, 12 fielded men only. Women constitute a mere 17% of the 6796 candidates. As the chances of all these women winning their seats are slim, the likelihood of women's representation slipping even below the 2013 figure of 16% is high.

As mentioned elsewhere in this chapter, the elections have been marred by sexist mudslinging, with Dr Thokozani Khupe of the MDC-T being referred to as "hure" (prostitute) and Dr Joice Mujuru once branded a witch by political rivals.

If nothing else, the 2018 elections in Zimbabwe will go down in history as ones in which women were determined to make their voice count. MDC-T's Priscilla Misihairabwi-Mushonga vowed to resist threats by the party's top leadership to recall her from Parliament owing to allegations of her supporting expelled Dr Thokozani Khupe's break-away faction.

"I am chairperson of the Parliamentary Committee on Gender and Youth Affairs and, therefore, cannot be persecuted for attending a solidarity tea for a woman who is basically under siege from male chauvinists. I am a women's activist and that defines who Priscilla Misihairabwi-Mushonga is. Nobody will take that away from me and not even a party can do that," she said.[12]

Young women have also found their voice, and are demanding a 25% quota for young women in politics:

Decrying the likely backtracking for women in the coming elections, the Institute for Young Women Development aired their frustration with stifling patriarchal norms in an open letter to political leaders.

"We believe that more young women in leadership especially at local government level will promote gender responsive service delivery because young women are primary consumers of these services," the young women declared.[13] Their clarion call - "nothing for us without us", building a society inclusive of women and youth - will be one of Zimbabwe's biggest challenges long after the election results are announced.

Setbacks even in the PR system in Angola

As all the figures presented earlier show, the PR system is by far the most conducive to women's political participation; especially when this is accompanied by a legislated quota, or well observed voluntary party quotas. The 2017 **Angola**n elections showed just how fragile even these gains are. The eight percentage point decline in the 2017 elections continued an almost 10-year trend: 39% in 2008, 35% in 2012, and 30% in 2017.[14]

The 220 members of the National Assembly are elected in two ways: 130 are elected by closed list proportional representation in a single nationwide constituency, with seats allocated proportionally. 90 are elected in 18 five-seat constituencies, using the d'Hondt method[15]. According to the Inter Parliamentary Union (IPU), in the 2012 elections, "a majority of parties respected the legislative quota of 30% women candidates on electoral lists, with the ruling party nominating women to 46% of its list. In 2017, the cumulative effect of fewer parties running for elections, and parties nominating fewer women, led Angola to slip further down the IPU ranking."[16]

[12] https://www.timeslive.co.za/news/africa/2018-05-24-analysis-witch-prostitute-women-to-face-sexism-in-zimbabwe-elections/
[13] https://www.newsday.co.zw/2018/06/making-a-case-for-25-young-womens-quota-in-zimbabwe/
[14] https://www.ipu.org/resources/publications/reports/2018-03/women-in-parliament-in-2017-year-in-review
[15] The D'Hondt method[a] or the Jefferson method is a highest averages method for allocating seats, and is thus a type of party-list proportional representation.
[16] https://www.ipu.org/resources/publications/reports/2018-03/women-in-parliament-in-2017-year-in-review

in Parliament in Angola
38%
in 2009

30%
in 2018

Table 2.13: Comparative data on the Angola National Elections in 2012 and 2017

PARTY	AUGUST 2012		AUGUST 2017	
	# seats	% seats	# seats	% seats
MPLA	175	72%	150	61%
UNITA	32	19%	51	27%
CASA-CE	8	6.%	16	9%
Social Renewal Party	3	2%	2	1.35%
National Liberation Front of Angola	2	1%	1	1%
National Patriotic Alliance			0	0.5%
% Women in Parliament	34%		30%	

Source: Gender Links.

Table 2.13 presents results by party. A further explanation for the reduction in women's representation is the decline in the ruling Movimento Popular de Libertação de Angola proportion of the vote, from 72% to 61%. In all post-conflict Southern African countries that have adopted the PR system (Namibia, South Africa, Mozambique) ruling parties have implemented their own quotas for women's political participation. The down side is that as their popularity reduces, so does the representation of women in parliament, as illustrated in the case of the 2017 Angola elections. This is why enforced legislated quotas are also required in PR systems. So far only Namibia (local) has a well enforced legislated quota in a PR system, resulting in 48% women's representation.

Table 2.14: Women in ambassadorial positions

	Total No.	No.of women	% women
Angola	17	13	76%
Botswana	21	5	24%
DRC	31	7	23%
Lesotho	16	8	50%
Madagascar	15	7	47%
Malawi	20	5	25%
Mauritius	16	1	6%
Mozambique	29	7	24%
Seychelles	12	4	33%
South Africa	125	35	28%
eSwatini	13	3	23%
Zimbabwe	41	10	24%
Total	**356**	**105**	**29%**

Source: SADC Gender and Development Monitor 2016.

Table 2.14 shows that:
• The regional average for women in the foreign service in the twelve countries that provided data is 29%. Although this is still far short of the 50% target, this represents a substantial change and achievement over time, as this is one of the most male dominated and hostile areas for women in decision-making.
• There are considerable variations between countries: from 6% in Mauritius to 76% in Angola. Four countries have above 30% women

in the foreign service - Madagascar, Lesotho, Seychelles and Angola.

Table 2.15: Women in top management in the Public Service

Member States	Permanent/Principal Secretaries/DG's		
	Total	Women	% of women
Angola	30	10	33%
Botswana	16	5	31%
DRC	238	23	10%
Lesotho	50	12	24%
Madagascar	30	4	13%
Malawi	66	18	27%
Mozambique	21	7	33%
Namibia	35	10	27%
Seychelles	26	11	42%
South Africa	68	16	24%
Zambia	53	15	28%
Zimbabwe	30	9	30%
Total	**579**	**113**	**20%**

Source: SADC Gender and development Monitor 2016.

Table 2.15 shows that for the ten countries in SADC that submitted information on women administrative heads of government ministries (permanent secretaries, DGs etc), the overall proportion of women in top management in the civil service is 20%. Seychelles leads at 42%, followed by Mozambique and Angola both at 33%. Other countries at 30% and above are Botswana (31%) and Zimbabwe (30%).

Woman voting duirng the June 2017 Lesotho elections.
Photo courtesy of Africa Research Institute

Legis-lated quota in PR System at Local level in Namibia

48% women

Table 2.16: Summary of 50/50 Campaign Strategy

COUNTRY	CABINET	PARLIAMENT				LOCAL GOVERNMENT			STRATEGY
	% Women	% Women	Next election	Electoral System & Quota	% Women	Next election	Electoral System & Quota		
Angola	33%	30%	2017	PR/ Legistlated 30%		2017			Work with Ministry of Gender and Alliance Focal Point/Women's umbrella organisation to enforce the 30% quota.
Botswana	17%	10%	October 2019	FPTP/ Voluntary party quota	19%	October 2019	FPTP No Quota		Advocate for legislated quota at local and national level through amendments to the Constitution and Electoral Act.
DRC	10%	8%	December 2018	FPTP/ 30%	0%	December 2018	FPTP		Advocate for legislated quotas at national and local level.
Lesotho	15%	23%	2020	Mixed Quota only for PR seats	40%	October 2022	Mixed 30% Quota		Escalate the quota at local level to national level. Monitor progress on 50/50 campaign. Review parties' manifestos and encourage quotas. Sensitise communities about 50/50 campaign.
Madagascar	17%	20%	July 2018	FPTP/ No Quota	8%	July 2020	FPTP No Quota		Use the Mauritius example to advocate for quotas at local level in the forthcoming elections.
Malawi	19%	17%	2019	FPTP/ No Quota	12%	2019	FPTP No Quota		Advocate for legislated quotas at national, local level using the Gender Equality Bill; Zimbabwe and Mauritius models in the 2019 elections. Train women on how to effectively engage with the media.
Mauritius	12%	12%	2019	Mixed/ No quota	27%	2020	FPTP Legislated quota		Use the White Paper on Electoral reform to advocate for the quota at local level to be extended to national level; build on momentum at local level.
Mozambique	21%	40%	October 2019	PR/ Voluntary party quota	36%	October 2019	PR Voluntary party quota		Advocate for all parties to adopt quotas and/or legislated quota. Increase efforts to mobilise women's participation in local government.
Namibia	36%	36%	November 2020	PR/ Voluntary party	48%	November 2019	PR Legislated quota		Work with the Ministry of Gender to table motion in Parliament for adoption; to put motion on the agendas of the local authorities. GL and Civil society organisations to popularise and domesticate at local level and increase efforts and women in politics trainings.
Seychelles	36%	21%	2016 (National Assembly); 2020 (Presidential)	Mixed No Quota	N/A	N/A	N/A		Document Seychelles' loss as a result of not having quotas or special measures for women's representation and participation.
South Africa	47%	41%	May 2019	PR/ Voluntary party	41%	August 2021	Mixed With Quota		Advocate for legislated quotas at local and national levels using the Equality Act and for all parties to follow the ANC's 50/50 lead. Name and shame political parties with no voluntary quotas.
eSwatini	21%	15%	2018 (National Assembly)	FPTP/ Legislated 30%	14%	2022	FPTP No Quota		Lobby for legislated quotas at local and national level, and for four seats to be reserved for women in parliament in the 2018 elections.
Tanzania	29%	37%	October 2020	FPTP Constitutional 30%	34%	October 2020	FPTP With Constitutional 30%		Advocate for the adoption of the 50% Constitutional quota.
Zambia	25%	18%	September 2021	FPTP No Quota	9%	September 2021	FPTP No Quota		Have space in the media to name and shame Boards and committees who do not have 50/50 representation on their Boards. Lobby for legislated quota and policy reforms in political parties and government.
Zimbabwe	15%	31%	July 2018	FPTP Legislated 30% on PR basis at National level	16%	July 2018	FPTP No Quota		Take stock of losses and gains in 2013, lobby for quota to be extended to local government and not to expire in 2023.

Source: Gender Links, Inter Parliamentary Union Website and EISA - http://www.content.eisa.org.za/node/279 , accessed and collated 18 June 2018.

Table 2.17: Women in Judiciary in SADC 2017

Member states	Registrars			President of Courts			Judges			Magistrates		
	Total	No. of women	% of women	Total	No. of women	% of women	Total	No. of women	% of women	Total	No. of women	% of women
Angola									31%			17%
Botswana	17	12	71%	2	0	0%	34	8	24%	89	55	62%
DRC				157	16	10%	678	136	20%	502	34	7%
Lesotho				1	0	0%			33%			42%
Madagascar				52	16	31%	50	6	12%	901	446	50%
Malawi	1	0	0%	1	0	0%	31	8	26%	198	63	32%
Mauritius				1	0	0%			48%			50%
Mozambique	152	56	37%	1	0	0%	464	140	30%	7	2	29%
Namibia			75%	1	0	0%	19	4	21%	99	50	51%
Seychelles	1	1	100%	1	0	0%	18	3	15%	6	3	50%
South Africa				15	2	13%	238	86	36%	1568	645	41%
eSwatini	2	1	50%	1	0	0%	10	2	23%	24	8	33%
Tanzania				5	3	60%			43%			29%
Zambia	10	2	20%				55	30	54%	207	62	30%
Zimbabwe	4	2	50%				54	27	50%			
Total	**188**	**75**	**40%**	**238**	**37**	**16%**	**1651**	**450**	**27%**	**3601**	**1368**	**38%**

Source: SADC Gender and Development Monitor 2016. Meeting of SADC Ministers Responsible for Gender and Women's Affairs, July 2018.

Table 2.17 illustrates that in the judiciary, the SADC region has failed to meet the 50% target on several fronts, but there is considerable variation.

- Overall, where data is available, women's representation is highest as registrars (40%) but this varies from 0% to 100% in Namibia and Seychelles.
- Women are least represented as court Presidents (16%). Madagascar (31%) has the highest representation of women as court presidents. Eight of the 12 countries with data have no women as court Presidents.
- With 65% women judges, Lesotho is the only SADC country to have more women than men judges. Four countries; Zimbabwe (48%), Zambia (49%), and Mauritius (49%), Tanzania (43%) are just a single digit shy of reaching the 50% mark

in the women judges' audit. Eight countries have over 30% women judges. Unfortunately many countries only provided percentages rather than the actual number of judges needed to calculate the regional average, which stands at 28% based on available data. It is important to obtain more actual figures in 2017 to calculate this more accurately.

- Women comprise 38% of magistrates based on available data (that again is patchy). Botswana has the highest representation at 62% followed by four countries: Namibia at 51%, Seychelles, Madagascar and Mauritius all at 50%. Five countries have more than 30% to 40% women's representation: Lesotho (42%), Malawi (32%), and South Africa (41%) eSwatini (41%) and Zambia (30%).

Election management

Article 13.1: State Parties shall adopt specific legislative measures and other strategies to enable women to have equal opportunities with men to participate in all electoral processes including the administration of elections and voting.

Election Management Bodies

Election Management Bodies (EMBs) ensure that the environment in which elections take place is conducive to the conduct credible elections.[17] EMBs are responsible for the management and conduct of elections and play a crucial role in ensuring that fair elections are held and in the end accepted.[18]

---

[17] SADC Gender and Development Monitor 2016.
[18] Commonwealth Secretariat (2016) Election Management: A Compendium, of Commonwealth Good Practice.

EMBs need to begin, "in their own institutions, by ensuring that women are given positions of responsibility and that the policies and practices of the institution work to improve the status of women in society. This might involve creating incentives for women to become election administrators; training all members of staff to be sensitive to gender issues; and collecting gender-disaggregated statistics in order to evaluate women's participation; and, identifying aspects of the democratic process that can be improved."[19]

Table 2.18 shows that election bodies have a long way to "practice what they preach" in ensuring women's equal representation in EMB's leadership and senior management. The table shows that:

- Overall women constitute 30% of EMBs in SADC according to data provided by the SADC Gender and Development Monitor in all 15 SADC countries.
- At 53%, Mauritius exceeded the target of women's equal representation in its Independent Electoral Commission (IEC).
- Four member states (Zimbabwe, Tanzania, Lesotho and Namibia) have 40% or above women's representation in EMBs yet still fall short in achieving the 50% target. Zimbabwe has a woman EMB chair, Justice Priscilla Chigumba.
- DRC (31%) and Malawi (30%) have exceeded the 30% women's representation in their EMBs, yet have a long way to go in achieving the post-2015 50% target.
- Eight countries (eSwatini, Angola, Zambia, Seychelles, South Africa, Botswana, Madagascar and Mozambique) have less than 30% women in EMBs.
- eSwatini, Seychelles, South Africa, Botswana and Mozambique only have one woman represented in their respective EMBs.

Table 2.18: Women in Election Management Bodies in SADC 2018			
	Total 2018	Women	% women
Regional Average	**233**	**70**	**30**
Mauritius	17	9	53
Tanzania	7	3	43
Lesotho	5	2	40
Namibia	5	2	40
Zimbabwe	9	4	40
DRC	105	33	31
Malawi	10	3	30
eSwatini	4	1	25
Angola	17	4	24
Zambia	9	2	22
Seychelles	5	1	20
South Africa	5	1	20
Botswana	7	1	14
Madagascar	21	3	14
Mozambique	8	1	13

Source: Gender Links 2018; SADC Gender and Development Monitor 2016.

Developing gender policies: Having a stand-alone policy gender policy helps to ensure that gender mainstreaming outlives particular individuals who may champion gender causes within the organisation. Ideally these gender policies should be reflected in the vision and mission of the EMBs (is these should move from being gender blind or gender neutral, to being gender aware).

Namibia has been proactive: "As an Electoral Management Body the importance of gender mainstreaming has been uppermost on our own strategic agenda and therefor efforts have been put in place with the assistance of International IDEA to develop a Gender Policy to ensure that we inculcate the principles of gender mainstreaming in our own institution. As an EMB we have been facilitators in conjunction with various organizations to provide platforms for political parties to consider the importance of introducing strategies towards increasing women representation in the political arena. The EMB also needs to include measures which may be encompassed in a Gender Policy which ECN has done as an institution."
Interview with Advocate Notemba Tjipueja on the Progress of Women's Political Participation in Namibia[20]

30%
of
EMBs

---

[19] Commonwealth Compendium of Good Election Management Practice.
[20] Lowe-Morna, C, 50/50 by 2030: A Handbook for Gender Inclusive Elections in Commonwealth Africa; Commonwealth Secretariat (2017).

Participation

Article 13.2: State parties shall ensure the equal participation of women and men in decision-making by putting in place policies, strategies and programmes for:
(a) Building the capacity of women to participate effectively through leadership and gender sensitivity training and mentoring;
(b) Providing support structures for women in decision-making positions;
(c) The establishment and strengthening of structures to enhance gender mainstreaming; and
(d) Changing discriminatory attitudes and norms of decision-making structures and procedures.

One of the first awakenings for women in decision-making is that simply getting into the institution and being able to function is not good enough. For them to be agents of change, they need to be able to function in all areas and at all levels of the institution. Where women sit within decision-making bodies thus becomes both a prerequisite for, and a target of, transformation.

Gender structures in legislatures

All politicians face dilemmas at one time or the other over divergences between political party positions and their own convictions. Women in politics often feel these tensions more acutely because of the expectation that they "represent women".

The dilemmas for women politicians over allegiance to party versus their commitment as women arise in all political systems, and cut across countries with high and low proportions of women in politics. Interviewees stressed that if a member takes a different line to that of her party, she stands a risk of being regarded as challenging the leader and might face disciplinary proceedings.

Women MPs, aware of divisions across party lines, are addressing them in the newly formed parliamentary caucuses where they share strategies to support each other on issues that are common to them as women. They further mentioned that the women's parliamentary caucus is a good opportunity to bring all women together and to extend solidarity on all issues affecting them.

Table 2.19: Gender structures in Parliament		
Country	**Women's caucus**	**Gender specific portfolio committee**
Lesotho	Yes	No
Mozambique	No	Social affairs, Gender and environment
Namibia	Parliamentary Women's Group	Human Resources and Gender Equality
Seychelles	Seychelles Women Parliamentarians	No
South Africa	Parliamentary Women's Group	Joint Monitoring Committee on the Improvement of the Quality of Life and Status of Women (JCIQSW)
Zambia	Yes	No
Tanzania	Tanzania Women's Parliamentary Group	Committee on Community Development, Youth, Gender and Labour

Source: Gender Links.

As illustrated in Table 2.19, there are two kinds of structures generally associated with women in parliament: informal caucusing networks for women MPs and formal parliamentary structures for advancing gender equality.

The SADC PF Regional Women's Parliamentary Caucus (RWPC) is a product of women's recognition of the need for supportive structures. This regional body has helped to form several women's caucuses at country level, for example in Zambia, Lesotho and Zimbabwe. Mozambique still does not have such an organisation and feels that it needs one.

Capacity building programmes focusing specifically on women decision-makers may be at national or regional level. At regional level, the SADC Gender Unit has developed a Gender Tool Kit for SADC Decision Makers that comprises basic concepts, tools and exercises on mainstreaming gender into legislation. This has been used for training trainers as well as women MPs from around the region.

Where women are placed within mainstream structures

Women tend to be more predominant in the "soft" committees of parliament and councils, and to be offered these kinds of portfolio in cabinet, than in the hard areas like finance, economics, security and defence. There is a debate on the implications of this gender division of labour across the different sectors of governance.

One view is that it is important to have women in the "hard" areas. Others argue that the distinction itself cannot be justified. Norwegian analysts have made the point that describing the areas in which women predominate as "soft" devalues these important areas, like education, health and social expenditure that in fact account for the bulk of expenditure.[21]

A key factor with regard to women's effective participation is the extent to which they occupy senior positions within decision-making bodies. Two examples are as presidents or speakers of parliament; and cabinet.

Municipality of Chinhoyi, Zimbabwe campaigns for 50/50

Training women for leadership.
Photo courtesy of Municipality of Chinhoyi

Currently all the decision-making positions at the Municipality of Chinhoyi is filled by men. To address this challenge the Municipality embarked on a campaign to increase the proportion of women in decision-making.

The campaign included three main activities:
- Community education and awareness
- Stakeholder sensitisation
- Build women's capacity in life and leadership skills

Key messages in the campaign focused on raising men's awareness of the importance of gender balance in decision making, boosting women's confidence to participate in decision making positions, to identify gender stereotypes and cultural barriers. Role models and facilitators implemented different components of the campaign.

As a result of the campaign several councillors have requested gender awareness workshops. Male councillors are advocating for gender equality in decision-making. Female councillors' confidence has grown and they are participating in decision-making processes.
Source: Zimbabwe SADC Protocola@Work Summit 2018

Women Presidents of Parliament

The President of the National Assembly is elected as guided by Constitutions of member states. The President's mandate is twofold. It is constitutional and institutional. This mandate is furthermore dual at the National Assembly and Parliamentary level. In both situations, it involves interacting with the global community at international, continental, regional and national levels. The President is the leader of the National Assembly.

The National Assembly has authority to legislate on behalf of the state including amending the Constitution, entering into bilateral agreements, treaties and signing international Human Rights Instruments. As a leader of the House, the President has to ensure that these processes are in accordance with Constitution. The President has to ensure that the members of the public participate in Legislation making and ensure that the house oversees and monitors the performance of the executive arm for effective implementation of legislation already passed by the House. The President also has the responsibility to provide political leadership and strategic direction to the House and exercise impartiality at all times in pursuance of these duties. In some SADC member states, the President is referred to as the Speaker of Parliament.

---

21 Lovenduski,J. and Karam,A. (1998) "Women in parliament: Making a Difference" in "Beyond Numbers:Women in Parliament." International IDEAS: p 136.

Table 2.20: Women presidents of parliaments in SADC 2018

Women as speakers of parliaments in SADC 2018

Country	Chamber	Structure of parliament	M	F	President
ANGOLA	National Assembly	Unicameral	1		Fernando da Piedade Dias dos Santos
BOTSWANA	National Assembly	Unicameral		1	Gladys Kokorwe
DEMOCRATIC REPUBLIC OF THE CONGO	Senate	Bicameral	1		Léon Kengo wa Dondo
DEMOCRATIC REPUBLIC OF THE CONGO	National Assembly	Bicameral	1		Aubin Minaku
LESOTHO	National Assembly	Bicameral	1		Sephiri Enoch Motanyane
LESOTHO	Senate	Bicameral	1		Morena Seeiso Bereng Seeiso
MADAGASCAR	National Assembly	Bicameral	1		Jean Max Rakotomamonjy
MADAGASCAR	Senate	Bicameral	1		Honoré Rakotomanana
MALAWI	National Assembly	Unicameral	1		Richard Msowoya
MAURITIUS	National Assembly	Unicameral		1	Santi Bai Hanoomanjee
MOZAMBIQUE	Assembly of the Republic	Unicameral		1	Verónica Nataniel Macamo Dlovo
NAMIBIA	National Council	Bicameral		1	Margaret Mensah-Williams
NAMIBIA	National Assembly	Bicameral	1		Peter Katjavivi
SEYCHELLES	National Assembly	Unicameral			Patrick Pillay
SOUTH AFRICA	National Assembly	Bicameral		1	Baleka Mbete
SOUTH AFRICA	National Council of Provinces	Bicameral		1	Thandi Modise
eSWATINI	Senate	Bicameral		1	Chief Gelane Zwane
eSWATINI	House of Assembly	Bicameral	1		Themba Msibi
ZAMBIA	National Assembly	Unicameral	1		Patrick Matibini
ZIMBABWE	National Assembly	Bicameral	1		Jacob F. Mudenda
ZIMBABWE	Senate	Bicameral		1	Edna Madzongwe
Totals			**12**	**8**	
Total presidents				**20**	
% Women				**40%**	

Source: www.ipu.org, 18 July 2018 and Gender Links.

Table 2.20 shows that:
- All 15 SADC countries have Presidents of Parliament. In some countries like in South Africa the leader is referred to as Speaker of Parliament.
- 8 of the 20 (40%) of the Presidents of Parliament are women.

Table 2.21: Top women leaders in SADC governments

Country	Head of Government / Vice President	Title
PRESENT		
United Republic of Tanzania	Samia Hassan Suluhu (2015-)	Vice President
Zambia	Inonge Mutukwa Wina (2015-)	Vice President
Namibia	Saara Kuugongelwa-Amadhila (2015-)	Prime Minister
PAST		
Mauritius	Ameerah Gurib-Fakim (2015-2018 March)	President
Malawi	Joyce Banda (2012-2014)	President
Malawi	Joyce Banda (2009-2012)	Vice President
Mauritius	Agnès Monique Ohsan Bellepeau (2010-2016)	Vice President
Mozambique	Luisa Diogo, (2004-2010)	Prime Minister
South Africa	Baleka Mbete, (2008-2009)	Deputy President
South Africa	Phumzile Mlambo-Ngcuka, (2005-2008)	Deputy President

Source: Gender Links 2018.

40%
of the
Presidents
of
Parliament

Table 2.21 shows that:
- Presently SADC has two women vice presidents (Tanzania and Zambia) and a woman prime minister (Namibia).
- SADC has had five women deputy/vice presidents; one prime minister and one president in the past.
- In 2009, Joyce Banda was elected as first female vice-president to President Mutharika of the Democratic Progressive Party (DPP) of Malawi.

She assumed the presidency after he died of heart attack in 2012 becoming the first female president in Malawi's history. This was relatively short lived (two years from 2012 to 2014).
- Mauritius is the only country in SADC to have had two women Presidents. Unfortunately the last woman president had to resign under pressure.

Mauritian President resigns in a cloud of controversy

Mauritian President Ameenah Gurib-Fakim's term as president of Mauritius ended abruptly in March 2018 after she resigned in a spat of controversy over expenditures on an NGO credit card. This unfortunate turn of events has been a major set-back for women's political participation in Mauritius, where women struggle against enormous odds.

Before she became president, Gurib-Fakim worked as a world-renowned biologist, winning several awards for her work and her importance as a woman in the scientific field. The former president was accused of buying jewellery and clothing using a credit card provided by an NGO, Planet Earth Institute (PEI), founded by an Angolan, Alvaro Sobrinho, who was interested in doing business in Mauritius. The PEI was supposed to give scholarships to Mauritian students to British Universities but only got a scholarship to study in South Africa.

The president joined the London-based Planet Earth Institute (PEI) in 2015 in an effort to further develop the scientific field in Africa. In 2016, she received a credit card from PEI to pay for travel and other expenses related to her work for the organisation.

Gurib-Fakim, 58, allegedly used the credit card to buy items worth $26,000 not related to her work for PEI. Gurib-Fakim claimed the use of the NGO credit card for these expenses was purely accidental, saying she used the PEI credit card because she also owned a personal credit card from the same bank.

This allegedly led her to accidentally mix up the two cards. Gurib-Fakim said she paid back any money she owed PEI and any other logistical expenses linked to her role. That claim was confirmed by PEI in a public statement, in which the organisation also said Gurib-Fakim had resigned from PEI.

However, it was not just the expenses but Gurib-Fakim's general involvement with PEI that raised eyebrows in Mauritius. PEI was founded by Alvaro Sobrinho, an Angolan businessman whose efforts to set up enterprises in Mauritius have come under scrutiny. Sobrinho is being investigated in Switzerland and Portugal for alleged fraud.

The post of president in Mauritius is ceremonial. Initially when the Prime Minister Pravind Jugnauth advised her to resign Gurib-Fakim refused saying that she would clear her name. But she finally resigned under public pressure on 23 March 2018.

Replying to a Private Notice Question in Parliament on 27 March, the Prime Minister said that resigning from the post of President of the Republic was the best decision that Gurib Fakim has taken for the country. The Prime Minister went further and said that he has asked for a Commission of Enquiry and put the matter into the hands of the Independent Commission Against Corruption (IAC). The ICAC enquiry is still on.

GL Board Member and Mauritian gender activist Loga Virasawmy commented: "on the eve of the celebration of the 50th Anniversary of the Independence of Mauritius, you are not only hurting women but the whole Mauritian nation and women in the SADC region at large. Political parties must file more women candidates in the next general and local elections and see to it that a woman of substance who has all the qualities to bring changes and do us proud be appointed President of the Republic of Mauritius."

Mauritian President **resigned** amidst controversy

Record number of women presidential candidates in Zimbabwe

Perhaps the highlight of the 2018 Zimbabwe elections is the Presidential election which has witnessed a record 23 candidates contesting the Presidential seat. Of these, four (17%) are women - the largest number of women who have ever competed for the highest office in the land. These are: Melbah Dzapasi (#1980 freedom movement Zimbabwe); Thokozani Khupe (MDC-T); Violet Mariyacha (Untied Democratic Movement) and Joice Mujuru (People's Rainbow Coalition).

Khupe and Mujuru are household names in Zimbabwe. Mujuru will bank on her contacts and experience as a former ZANU-PF legislator and possibly steal some votes from ZANU-PF as well as garner support from other portions of Zimbabwe, though she has not been so visible on the campaign trail.

Thokozani Khupe.   *Photo courtesy of MDC-T*

Khupe has her following from the MDC factions which will also have a bearing on the road to the State House.

Bets at the time of writing are for a runoff between the top two candidates, Emmerson Mnangagwa and Nelson Chamisa (MDC Alliance) or the formation of a Government of National Unity (GNU). Is Zimbabwe ready for a female President? Only the ballot will tell. What is evident is that the 50-50 advocacy campaign must not stop, even after the elections. *(Excerpt from an article by Tapiwa Zvaraya, GL News Service)*

Cabinet

Cabinet is one area in which governments should make rapid progress as members are appointed rather than elected. The regional average of only 20% women in Cabinet positions raises serious concerns regarding the political will of SADC heads of state to increase women's representation in decision-making.

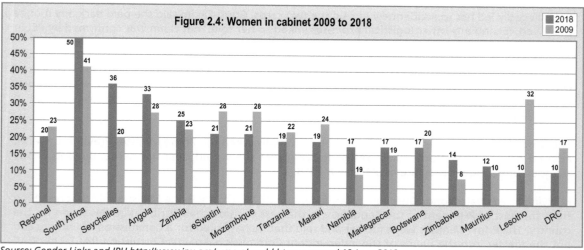

Figure 2.4: Women in cabinet 2009 to 2018

Source: Gender Links and IPU http://www.ipu.org/wmn-e/world.htm - accessed 18 June 2018.

Figure 2.4 reflects disappointing results in this area over the last ten years:
- Overall, women's representation in cabinet has dropped from 23% to 20%.
- Only four countries (South Africa, Seychelles, Angola and Zambia) have experienced an increase.

- Eleven countries have regressed. Lesotho experienced the largest decline, from 32% to 10% women in cabinet.
- Only one country, South Africa, has achieved gender balance in its cabinet, although NGOs remained sceptical about some of the choices made.

South Africa: Beyond numbers in Cabinet

While President Cyril Ramaphosa's new cabinet has taken South Africa to gender parity at the executive level it has failed to inspire a new vision for gender equality, according to an analysis conducted by Gender Links (GL).

According to the GL analysis, the emphasis continues to be on reshuffling rather than renewal. The most glaring switch is the shift of Bathabile Dlamini from social development to the women's ministry, formerly headed by Susan Shabangu, now minister of social development.

Dlamini came under fire for failing to usher in a new social grants distributor when the Cash Paymaster Services (CPS) contract ended. These grants play a crucial role in supporting women and families who remain on the fringes of the mainstream economy.

It took the intervention of the Constitutional Court, which permitted the extension of the contract with CPS for another 12 months, to provide a way forward concerning the payment of millions of beneficiaries on 1 April 2017. Dlamini's role in the social grants crisis will be determined by a commission of inquiry, which began work on 22 January. She also oversaw the disastrous handling the Life Healthcare Esidimeni Scandal involved the deaths of 143 people at psychiatric facilities in Gauteng from causes including starvation and neglect.

Ironically as Chair of the ANC Women's League, Dlamini led the march for Ramaphosa's rival, Nkosozana Dlamini Zuma to become South Africa's first woman president. Sadly this only followed Zuma's endorsement of her, and excluded other women who vied for the job.

At least four cabinet posts can be counted as gender benders - non- traditional posts that have gone to women. These include science and technology, sports and recreation, state security, defence and military veterans. The appointment of the well respected former minister of Science and Technology Naledi Pandor to the ministry of higher education is also a gain. However, she had been touted as Deputy President, a post that has gone to David Mabuza, resulting again in two men at the top.

Source: Gender Links News Service

Table 2.22: Women's representation in Cabinet 2017 to 2018				
Country	2018	2017	Variance (2018-2017)	50%
Regional average	**20%**	**23%**	**-3%**	**-30%**
South Africa	50%	41%	9%	0%
Seychelles	36%	43%	-7%	-14%
Angola	33%	21%	12%	-17%
Zambia	25%	26%	-1%	-25%
eSwatini	21%	25%	-4%	-29%
Mozambique	21%	23%	-2%	-29%
Tanzania	19%	20%	-1%	-31%
Malawi	19%	15%	4%	-31%
Namibia	17%	22%	-5%	-33%
Madagascar	17%	20%	-3%	-33%
Botswana	17%	17%	0%	-33%
Zimbabwe	14%	15%	-1%	-36%
Mauritius	12%	13%	-1%	-38%
Lesotho	10%	22%	-12%	-40%
DRC	10%	8%	2%	-40%

Source: Gender Links.

Table 2.22 shows that:
- The regional average of women's representation in Cabinet (Ministers only) has dropped to 20%. The region missed the Protocol target of 50% women in cabinet by 30 percentage points.
- The highest proportion of women in cabinet is in South Africa.

- There are only two countries with more than 40% women as Ministers: Seychelles (43%) and South Africa (41%) during the year under review.
- Only three countries experienced increases in the last year: South Africa, Angola and Malawi. Twelve countries regressed, at the very moment when heads of state should be demonstrating

their commitment to gender equality through cabinet appointments.

- Botswana remained constant following the appointment of a new President ahead of the 2019 elections. However, the appointment of a young woman to a key Economic Ministry had social media abuzz in the first half of 2018.

Young women lead the way in Botswana

Botswana's new President Mokgweetsi Masisi missed the opportunity to make good on Botswana's commitment to gender equality in his recent new cabinet, but had social media agog with his appointment of a young woman to the post of Investment Trade and Industry.

Masisi is Botswana's fifth President. The women's movement had hoped for the appointment of a woman Vice President. That did not happen, and the representation of women in Cabinet increased by a mere one percentage point to 18%.

Botswana remains one of the countries in Southern Africa with a low representation of women in Parliament and Cabinet. According to the SADC Gender Protocol Barometer 2017, women comprise 10% of Parliamentarians and 19% in local councils.

Cabinet is a test of political commitment because the President has the latitude to choose, although in Botswana cabinet ministers must also be Members of Parliament.

Previously four of the five women Parliamentarians were in Cabinet. The incoming President allocated Cabinet seats to all the women in Parliament. The women elected into Cabinet lead the Ministry of Local Government and Rural Development as both Minister and Deputy, one as a Minister the other Assistant Minister; Ministry of Nationality Immigration and Gender Affairs; Ministry of Investment, Trade and Industry and the Ministry of Infrastructure and Development. Four are full Ministers; the fifth is an Assistant Minister.

The ground breaking appointment by the new President is Bogolo Kenewendo, a 31 year old woman appointed as the Minister of Investment Trade and Industry. The women's rights movement welcomes the appointment. She is the youngest MP in the Botswana National Assembly. She completed her BA in Economics at the University of Botswana and holds MSc in International Economics from the University of Sussex in the United Kingdom and was a recipient of a prestigious Chevening Scholarship in 2012.

Bogolo Kenewendo.

Her areas of expertise include: Macroeconomic Policy, public debt management, trade policy, export development, trade in services, regulatory frameworks, trade related issues, trade and investment policy, industrial development policy, institutional frameworks for policy formulation, poverty alleviation, financial sector development,

She brings a new and youthful energy to the Botswana Cabinet having had come in as a specially elected member of Parliament under the former President Seretse Khama Ian Khama. Her appointment to the Ministry that contributes most to the economy underscores a new era for this diamond-rich country.

Dorcas Malesu is now the Minister of Nationality, Immigration and Gender Affairs becoming the first woman in over 10 years to lead the Ministry. Botswana, whose previous President Khama was not married, had been without a first lady for 10 years. Neo Masisi will now fill that role. She is passionate about women's empowerment.

As Botswana prepares to go to elections in 2019 it is necessary to step up efforts to break the cycle of women's low political participation. In the coming week Gender Links will engage in dialogues with political leaders for possible solutions such as the implementation of the quota system at party level and training of women candidates among others.

Source: Article by Gomolemo Rasesigo, ender Links Botswana Country Manager, GL news and blogs service

Table 2.23: Women as deputy ministers

Member States	Deputy Ministers		
	Total No.	No. of total Women	% of women
SADC Average	87	36	41%
Lesotho	5	2	40%
Namibia	33	18	55%
South Africa	11	5	45%
Tanzania	21	8	20%
Zimbabwe	17	3	18%

Source: www.ipu.org, 18 June 2018 and Gender Links.

Table 2.23 provides information on women Deputy Ministers, in the five countries that have Deputy Ministers. Overall, women constitute 41% of Deputy Ministers. Namibia has a higher proportion (55%) of women Deputy Ministers than men. A question that arises is if deputy ministerial posts are a training ground for Cabinet, why women in the region are not progressing from these posts to Cabinet.

 **Next steps**

This chapter continues to expand the scope for measuring women's representation and partici-pation in Public State Institutions by tracking women in Political Parties and Election Manage-ment Bodies; Parliament; the Public Service, and Judiciary; in addition to the usual yardsticks: women in Parliament, Cabinet and Local Government. The Private Sector remains a gap yet to be tackled through better data capture and analysis. Some key priorities going forward include:

- **Fire-up the 50/50 campaign post 2015:** Involve other stakeholders such as the private sector in the 50/50 campaign to encourage management to ensure that the target is integrated in all spheres and not just political decision-making bodies. Lobby the relevant structures for more women in government.
- **Holding Governments accountable:** Govern-ments made a commitment to achieving 50% representation of women in all areas of decision-making aligned to the SDGs. Inconsistent efforts have been made with some Governments adopting PR systems and systems in Zimbabwe, Lesotho, South Africa and Mauritius; and others fully opposed to doing so. Further inconsistencies at national and local levels have resulted in further variations in women's representation in political decision making and Public Service. Adopting special measures is a prerogative now more than ever before for an achievable post-2015 gender agenda.

- **Political parties transform policies in party manifestos to include quotas, the "Zebra System" and proportional representation system:** This chapter shows, through the examples of Angola and Lesotho, how easy it is to backslide because political parties do not have these special measures in their party manifestos and even when they do, these are not always effectively implemented. It is critical to ensure special measures are adopted and implemented for 50/50 to be achieved by 2030.
- **Remove major cultural and structural barriers rooted in culture, customs, religion, tradition, perceptions of women in society; and invest in efforts that build strong political will and leadership by all to effect change.** Civic education, voter education, targeting influential community and national leaders are pathways to influence change. There is a crucial need for more civic education about women and men's equal participation in politics and decision making in public service especially now, ahead of 2030.
- **Strengthen and adopt new approaches:** In many cases needs assessments have not preceded training for women in politics. Such training needs to be holistic in its approach. In addition to gender analysis skills, it should include an understanding of the nature and exercise of power, confidence and assertiveness skills, leadership training and communication skills, including debating, use of the internet and social media, accessing the main-stream media and integrating gender issues into political campaigns. While there is a place for empowerment strategies that specifically target women decision-makers, it is also important to design strategies that include the "new" men in politics. Gender equality activists need to actively engage political parties to strengthen and sustain any transformation towards gender-responsive democracy and governance. There should be a continuous sensitisation and awareness raising training and support for women to attain political positions. Promote and build capacity of men and boys in civil society to become more active and participate in the gender movement and deve-loping gender programmes and campaigns.
- **Revamp and upscale capacity building for women in politics and leadership:** Initiatives to strengthen the knowledge, information and gender analysis capacities of women members of Parliament and councillors should be scaled up in order to give women the confidence to retain their seats and inspire other women to participate in elections. Research on women's experience and participation in governance and political processes is required as well as a detailed analysis of the amount of funding that has been dedicated by government, civil society and donors to programmes to increase women's partici-pation, and for civic education across SADC.

The 50/50 Campaign needs to be **fired up!**

- **Research, monitoring and evaluation are key:** Research, advocacy and lobbying have been critical to achievements made to date. Structures and mechanisms should be found for strengthening collaboration between civil society and women in decision-making. Research, monitoring and evaluation remain key for qualitative and qualitative gains in the 50/50 campaign. Stakeholders should use this to strengthen collaboration between civil society, government, the private sector and women in decision-making.
- **The media as a platform and tool to effect change:** Gender, elections and media training shows that the media has a key role to play in changing mind-sets and promoting women candidates. These partnerships should be built and extended in all countries having elections

between now and 2020 as an opportunity to start anew. Increase involvement with the media, including an increased use of social media, to lobby for increasing the number of women in decision-making positions. The media must work to increase coverage of women and their various roles in order to change mind-sets and thus encourage more women to contest for political positions.
- **Involving young women:** The chapter reported on breaking new ground in Zimbabwe, with young women demanding a 25% quota in the coming elections. A new generation of young women are demanding a say in the matters that affect their lives. Working with junior councillors is one way to "start young" with political participation.

Starting young in Chinhoyi

The Municipality of Chinhoyi is situated in the Mashonaland West Province of Zimbabwe. Tariro Ngwanya , an active member of the municipality founded a Junior Council as part of the Gender Links Centres of Excellence for Gender in Local Government. The council forms part of local government and aims to promote economic justice through including education, training and economic developmental projects for its members and the communities it works in.

Empowering junior councillors on customer care in Chinhoyi.
Photo: Olivia Masongorera

According to Ngwanya, the junior council was started to "create a better Chinhoyi Municipality through youth participation." This project brought together youth from different walks of life from primary and secondary levels.

Youth make policy suggestions to the senior council for implementation. The junior council serves as a platform for youth to become active citizens in combating socio-economic injustices by placing them at the forefront of their issues, as leaders. The Junior Council is not a political organisation but an advocacy body for children and youth-related issues.

The council remains relevant as issues of teenage pregnancy, HIV and SRHR affect the girl child the most in the municipality of Chinhoyi. The junior council works and communicates with the youth from various parts of the community with the aim of bringing to light the various problems they face and alternative approaches to tackling those issues.

Sasha Vamba served as the first female junior council mayor in 2017. She led 15 young councillors in the municipality. "I feel honoured to be the first girl Junior Mayor for Municipality of Chinhoyi," she says. The junior council has served as a source of empowerment: women feel empowered by seeing a girl Junior Mayor leading the council and making representation within the community. The senior council appreciates the efforts made by the junior council and take their recommendations and implement them into resolutions. Ngwanya says that youth "are realising that they can be leaders and be in decision-making positions and produce results. The junior council continues to prove that children can bring a positive change in the community and schools. Children can also come up with brilliant ideas acceptable by the senior council."

Source: SADC Protocol@Work summit, Zimbabwe 2018

CHAPTER 3

Education and training

Article 14

"Bring a girl child to work" campaign in South Africa makes the links between girls education and economic prosperity.
Photo: Colleen Lowe Morna

KEY POINTS

- Most Grade 6 learners have only basic levels of literacy instead of the mathematical and reading skills commensurate with their level of schooling.
- More girls and boys need to attend and complete secondary school so they can enter institutions of higher learning. Thirteen SADC countries have low enrolment in secondary school - between 11% and 58%.
- Women predominate in the stereotypical "women's" careers as opposed to agriculture, science, engineering and construction. Most women study social sciences, business and law in tertiary institutions.
- Learners experience high levels of violence in school, including sexual violence, bullying and corporal punishment.
- Education needs to become more inclusive. States have failed to create enabling environments for all children, including those with disabilities.
- Access to water and sanitation at school remains low in many areas.
- Child labour is keeping young people out of school. More than 20% of children between ages seven and 14 spend their days working instead of studying in nine SADC countries.
- Ongoing teacher training and support is crucial given that many secondary school teachers do not have formal training.
- Enrolment in tertiary education remains low across SADC, for both young women and men.

More than **20%** of children between ages **7 - 14** spend their days working instead of studying in nine SADC countries

Target 2030	Baseline 2009	Progress 2018	Variance (Progress minus 2030 target)
Equal number of girls and boys enrolled in primary school in all 16 countries	5 countries (Lesotho, Namibia, Malawi, Seychelles and Tanzania)	14 countries have almost equal numbers of girls and boys enrolled in primary school - with a three or less percentage point difference (Botswana, Comoros, DRC, Lesotho, Madagascar, Malawi, Mauritius, Mozambique, Namibia, Seychelles, South Africa, eSwatini, Tanzania, Zambia and Zimbabwe)	2 countries with more than three percentage point difference in enrolment numbers for girls and boys - (Angola and Malawi)
Equal number of girls and boys enrolled in secondary school in all 16 countries	7 countries (Botswana, Lesotho, Mauritius, Namibia, Seychelles, South Africa and eSwatini)	8 countries have almost equal numbers of girls and boys enrolled in secondary school - with a three or less percentage point difference (Angola, Comoros, Madagascar, Malawi, Mauritius, Mozambique, South Africa, Zimbabwe)	8 countries with more than three percentage point difference in enrolment numbers for girls and boys (Botswana, DRC, Lesotho, Namibia, Seychelles, eSwatini, Tanzania and Zambia)
Equal number of women and men enrolled in tertiary school in all 16 countries	7 countries (Botswana, Mauritius, Namibia, Seychelles, South Africa, Zambia and eSwatini)	11 countries have almost equal numbers of women and men enrolled in tertiary education - with a three or less percentage point difference (Angola, Comoros, Lesotho, Madagascar, Malawi, Mozambique, Namibia, eSwatini, Tanzania, Zambia and Zimbabwe)	5 countries with more than three percentage point difference in enrolment (Botswana, DRC, Mauritius, Seychelles and South Africa)
Ensure that all girls and boys have access to quality early childhood development, care and pre-primary school in all 16 countries		12 countries have almost equal numbers of girls and boys in pre-primary education - with a three or less percentage point difference (Botswana, DRC, Lesotho, Madagascar, Malawi, Mauritius, Mozambique, Namibia, Seychelles, South Africa, eSwatini and Zimbabwe)	4 countries with more than three percentage point difference in enrolment (Angola, Seychelles, Tanzania and Zambia[2])

Table 3.1: Trends in Education since 2009[1]

Background

"Schooling is not the same as learning. Worldwide, hundreds of millions of children reach young adulthood without even the most basic life skills. This learning crisis is a moral crisis. When delivered well, education cures a host of societal ills."[3]

This quote, from the World Bank's *World Development Report 2018*, recognises the need for urgent action to change and improve education globally. It explores four main themes: education's promise; the need to shine a light on learning; how to make schools work for learners; and how to make systems work for learning.

The report confirms that, while many more students now attend school, they often do not receive rele-

Young girls in Comoros stand while doing schoolwork. Inadequate physical infrastructure in schools is a challenge across SADC.
Photo courtesy of Wikimedia commons

1 https://www.weforum.org/reports/the-global-gender-gap-report-2017; http://uis.unesco.org/country/ZA Accessed April 2018.
2 No statistics available.
2 World Bank. 2018. World Development Report 2018: Learning to Realize Education's Promise. Washington, DC: World Bank. doi:10.1596/978-1-4648-1096-1. License: Creative Commons Attribution CC BY 3.0 IGO.

vant learning and skills development. This will affect the quality of the available work force adversely and impact economic growth for years to come.

The *2017 African Economic Outlook* also emphasises the need for investment in education and skills development for young people. Africa has a rapidly growing youth population that also represents a potential workforce. The amount its leaders invest in education for young people will help determine whether the continent can harness this demographic dividend rather than risk a demographic time bomb.[4]

This chapter highlights the gaps and challenges in the provision of quality education. Increasing enrolment in primary school is an encouraging sign and the region maintains high literacy levels, with some exceptions. These include women in Angola, Malawi and Mozambique, women and men in the Comoros, and women and men 65 and older across the region. However, it is time to move beyond the numbers. Most Grade 6 learners in 12 countries in the Southern African Development Community (SADC) have only basic mathematics and reading literacy.[5] Many students enter secondary school with massive skills gaps.

Table 3.2: Access and enrolment in education																															
	Angola		Botswana		Comoros		DRC		Lesotho		Madagascar		Malawi		Mauritius		Mozambique		Namibia		Seychelles		South Africa		eSwatini		Tanzania		Zambia		Zimbabwe	
%	F	M	F	M	F	M	F	M	F	M	F	M	F	M	F	M	F	M	F	M	F	M	F	M	F	M	F	M	F	M	F	M
Literacy	53	80	89	87	43	56	66	89	85	68	68	75	55	70	91	95	46	73	88	89	94	93	93	95	82	84	73	83	78	89	88	89
Enrolment																																
Pre-primary	71	48	17	17	14	13	5	4	25	24	13	12	82	81	96	94	0	0	21	20	82	76	78	77	18	18	31	18	0	0	26	25
Primary	73	96	92	90	78	81	85	88	82	79	71	68	95	90	97	95	87	91	91	89	96	94	97	97	79	80	81	80	88	87	87	85
Secondary	11	14	52	48	46	43	36	54	45	29	32	31	36	37	86	81	19	18	58	45	81	76	88	88	41	32	48	52	43	47	45	44
Tertiary	8	10	28	19	8	10	4	10	12	8	5	5	1	1	42	32	5	7	10	8	20	9	23	16	6	5	3	5	3	5	8	9
Vocational	0	0	0	0	0	0	47	53	32	68	35	65	30	70	0	0	0	0	59	41	57	43	25	75	47	53	0	0	0	0	0	0

Source: https://www.weforum.org/reports/the-global-gender-gap-report-2017; http://uis.unesco.org/country/ZA. Accessed April 2018.

Many learners will not progress into tertiary education or go on to higher level study in the important STEM subjects - Science, Technology, Engineering and Mathematics. These areas of study help drive growth industries in the economy.

Teenage pregnancy, violence in schools, child labour and inadequate physical infrastructure impact learning, enrolment, performance and completion rates. Teaching is also a critical challenge in the region. There are low levels of trained teachers at

secondary level - and in some countries at primary level. The United Nations Educational, Scientific and Cultural Organisation (UNESCO) states that the optimum learner teacher ratio to promote effective teaching and learning is 1:25.[6] Only three SADC countries (Botswana, Mauritius and Seychelles) meet this criterion. This impacts on the quality of education delivered in the classroom. To achieve universal primary and secondary education, UNESCO advises that sub-Saharan Africa must see substantial growth in the number of educators.

Table 3.3: Number of teachers required to deliver universal primary and secondary education by 2030[7]					
	As at 2014	By 2020	By 2025	By 2030	Total required
Primary	*2 247 000*	2 700 000	4 463 000	**6 288 000**	*4 041 000*
Secondary	*6 046 000*	8 988 000	12 934 000	**17 043 000**	*10 997 000*

---

[4] African Economic Outlook 2017, Entrepreneurship and Industrialisation.
[5] SACMEQ.
[6] UIS Fact sheet 39, The world needs almost 69 million new teachers to reach the 2030 education goals, UNESCO, October 2016.
[7] IBID.

Table 3.3 shows that sub-Saharan Africa will need to train an additional four million primary and 11 million secondary school teachers over the next 12 years. Government expenditure on education must increase and be optimally utilised if the region is to realise its educational goals.

Table 3.4: Government expenditure on education[8]					
Country	% GDP to education	% Government spending	% Primary spending	% Secondary education	% Tertiary education
Angola[9]	3	9	31	42	9
Botswana	10	20	18	33	42
Comoros	4	15	55	28	10
DRC	2	17	62	14	22
Lesotho	11	25	36	21	36
Madagascar	2	14	47	19	15
Malawi	6	22	44	28	24
Mauritius	5	19	21	64	7
Mozambique	6	19	49	31	14
Namibia	8	26	40	24	23
Seychelles	4	10	24	16	33
South Africa	6	19	39	31	12
eSwatini	7	17	51	34	13
Tanzania	3	17	49	18	21
Zambia	1	6	56	27	11
Zimbabwe	8	30	48	27	17

Source: World Bank Education Statistics. Updated on the 09/01/2018. Trading Economics, Angola. Accessed April 2018.

NEEDED: Urgent review of education spending $$$

Table 3.4 illustrates the range of spending on education in the region, from a low of 6% in Zambia as a percentage of all government spending, to a high of 30% in Zimbabwe. UNESCO recommends that at least 6% of a country's Gross Domestic Product (GDP) should be allocated to education.[10] Eight SADC countries (Botswana, Lesotho, Malawi, Mozambique, Namibia, South Africa, eSwatini and Zimbabwe) have met this target and allocate 6% or more of their GDP to education. Zambia, at only 1%, is the lowest in SADC.

On the surface, it is impressive that eight SADC countries have reached or exceeded the recommended level of spending for education. However, a review of their performance at different schooling levels and at tertiary level is not hugely different from those countries that spend less than 6% of their GDP on education. This raises two key points: the region needs 1) further investment in education, especially in those eight SADC countries currently underspending and 2) a review of current spending on education to identify wastage, misappropriation and misallocated funds.

The 2017 Barometer highlighted the *SADC Policy Framework on Care and Support for Teaching and Learning* (CSTL). It assists schools to improve the quality of education and learning. Its goal (2013-18) is for SADC children and youth to realise their rights to education, safety, protection, care and support through an expanded and strengthened education sector response.

Seven SADC countries (DRC, Malawi, Mozambique, South Africa, eSwatini, Zambia and Zimbabwe) have begun implementing the policy. It is imperative that all other countries adopt and implement the CSTL. The Mozambique Ministry of Education uses the CSTL policy framework to change the teaching and learning environment, which has improved the quality of education in Mozambique.

8 http://databank.worldbank.org/data/reports.aspx?source=Education%20Statistics#
9 https://tradingeconomics.com/angola/public-spending-on-education-total-percent-of-government-expenditure-wb-data.html
10 http://www.unesco.org/new/en/education/themes/leading-the-international-agenda/efareport/

New Policy Framework in Mozambique

Through its adoption of the Care and Support for Teaching and Learning programme (CSTL), the Mozambique Ministry of Education has improved the delivery of essential services and support for learners at the school level.

Psychosocial support

EPC Magoanine is one of many schools that has benefited. This large primary school educates nearly 4800 students (more than 2200 girls and 2500 boys). Before the introduction of CSTL, many of the learners were underperforming, mostly due to lack of psychosocial and other support services required to help vulnerable children overcome learning barriers.

Thanks to the multisectoral partnerships established at school level through CSTL, stakeholders created a new support structure that includes a dedicated room in which professionals provide psychosocial support to both students and teachers. When students have issues, they can see a teacher whose responsibility is to provide guidance and counselling. If necessary, this teacher can refer students to relevant external service providers for further support.

Since 2015, the school has seen a dramatic improvement in student outcomes: from a pass rate of 70.3% in 2014 to 80.8% in 2015 and 81.5% in 2016. The school director attributes this positive change to the CSTL programme.

Safety and protection

...and another way is to talk to parents during meetings to accompany their children on the way to school and back home...

Following the abduction of two school age children in Mozambique, parents now often accompany children to and from school.
Photo courtesy of Care and Support for Teaching and Learning

In Mozambique, schools liaise with parents and communities primarily through school boards. Through the CSTL programme, school board members in CSTL laboratory schools have received training on parenting skills. One module addressed how parents can support schools in ensuring the safety and security of their children.

Following the 2014 abduction of two Grade 2 children on their way to EPC1 De Junho school, many children became scared to walk to school, which resulted in a drop in attendance. Faced with this situation, the school's management and board drew on their training and implemented the following safety and security measures:

- They arranged fencing for the school and employed a security guard to monitor the gate and schoolyard;
- Parents organised themselves into small groups to take turns to accompany children to school; and
- They created a permanent link between police and the school to ensure a quick response to any incidents reported at the school.

The school board worked quickly to execute these strategies so that students could feel safe. Police eventually located the two abducted children, and both are now back at school and doing well in Grade 4.

Source: http://www.cstlsadc.com/stories-from-mozambique/

Access to education

Article 14.1: State Parties shall enact laws that promote equal access to retention and completion in early childhood education, primary, secondary, tertiary, vocational and non-formal education, including adult literacy, in accordance with the Protocol on Education and Training and the Sustainable Development Goals.

Years of compulsory education in SADC

The Incheon Declaration[11] commits UN Member States to ensure the "provision of 12 years of free, publicly funded, equitable quality primary and secondary education," of which at least nine years are compulsory, leading to relevant learning outcomes. It also encourages the provision of at least one year of free and compulsory quality pre-primary education and access to quality early childhood development, care and education. All SADC countries are members of the UN and adopted the Incheon Declaration in May 2015.

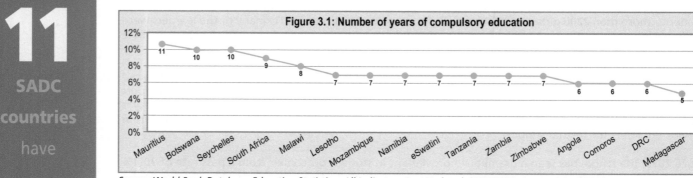

Figure 3.1: Number of years of compulsory education

Source: World Bank Database: Education Statistics - All Indicators. Last Updated: 09/01/2018. Accessed April 2018.

Figure 3.1 shows that SADC countries provide between five and 11 years of compulsory schooling. These figures have remained static for more than ten years. None of the countries have amended their compulsory schooling policies to meet the Incheon Declaration standard.

The *2017 Africa Outlook* report states: "Education - particularly post-primary education from the age of about 12 - is a critical dimension of human capital development and fundamental to harnessing the demographic dividend. Better educated and healthier people tend to earn higher wages. Research has proven that combining broad-based secondary education with universal primary schooling provides a significant boost to skills development and knowledge in poorer countries. The evidence suggests that an extra year of education raises economic growth by 1.2 percentage points per year."[12]

It is possible that girls and boys in Angola, Comoros, DRC and Madagascar, countries with between five and six years of compulsory schooling, leave school by the time they are 12 years old. This could severely impact their long-term ability to lead productive lives and contribute to their country's economic growth. All SADC countries should fulfil their commitments under the Incheon Declaration and amend their compulsory schooling requirement to 12 years.

Pre-primary

Pre-primary education creates momentum for early learning. Increasingly, compelling empirical evidence in all countries, both low and high income, supports this. In most cases, students with preschool experience demonstrate higher scores on literacy, vocabulary and mathematics. Good quality pre-primary education results in higher attendance and achievement, lower repetition and drop-out rates and less remedial and special education.[13]

---

[11] http://www.unesco.org/new/en/brasilia/about-this-office/single view/news/education_2030_incheon_declaration_and_and_framework_for_ac/
[12] http://www.africaneconomicoutlook.org/en/theme/Entrepreneurship-and-industrialisation
[13] https://www.globalpartnership.org/blog/can-pre-primary-education-help-solve-learning-crisis-africa

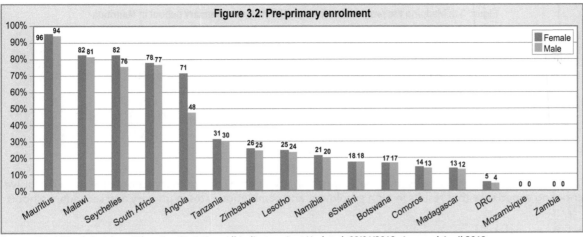

Figure 3.2: Pre-primary enrolment

Female / Male

Country	Female	Male
Mauritius	96	94
Malawi	82	81
Seychelles	82	76
South Africa	78	77
Angola	71	48
Tanzania	31	30
Zimbabwe	26	25
Lesotho	25	24
Namibia	21	20
eSwatini	18	18
Botswana	17	17
Comoros	14	13
Madagascar	13	12
DRC	5	4
Mozambique	0	0
Zambia	0	0

Source: World Bank Database Education Statistics - All Indicators. Last Updated: 09/01/2018. Accessed April 2018.

Figure 3.2 shows that high proportions of girls and boys attend pre-primary schools in Malawi, Mauritius, Seychelles and South Africa. Many more girls than boys attend pre-primary in Angola. Meanwhile, few pupils attend pre-primary in eight SADC countries (Botswana, Comoros, Lesotho, Madagascar, Namibia, eSwatini, Tanzania and Zimbabwe). The DRC has the lowest numbers of girls and boys in pre-primary schools. No data is available for Mozambique and Zambia.

Early childhood education prepares young children for school[14]

Pre-primary education is compulsory for children between ages three and five in Mauritius. *Photo courtesy of lileauxenfants*

Preschool programmes that target children ages three to six can foster foundational skills and boost children's ability to learn. Children who attend preschool also have higher attendance and better achievement in primary school. Moreover, they are less likely to repeat, drop out, or need remedial or special education, all of which benefit students and education systems.[15]

Across countries at all income levels, the most disadvantaged children benefit most from quality early child education programmes.[16]

For stakeholders to sustain early child education gains, they must integrate the content, budget and capacity of providers of preschool programmes into formal education systems. In addition, the quality of subsequent learning environments in primary school is an important determinant of the long-term effects of preschool programmes.[17]

---

[14] http://www.worldbank.org/en/publication/wdr2018
[15] Klees, Steven J. 2017. "Will We Achieve Education for All and the Education Sustainable Development Goal?" Comparative Education Review 61 (2): 425-40.
[16] Britto, Pia Rebello, Stephen J. Lye, Kerrie Proulx, Aisha K. Yousafzai, Stephen G. Matthews, Tyler Vaivada, Rafael Perez-Escamilla, et al. 2016. "Nurturing Care: Promoting Early Childhood Development." Lancet 389 (10064): 91-102.
[17] Johnson, Rucker C., and C. Kirabo Jackson. 2017. "Reducing Inequality through Dynamic Complementarity: Evidence from Head Start and Public-School Spending." NBER Working Paper 23489, National Bureau of Economic Research, Cambridge, MA.

Preschool programmes that **target** children ages **3-6** **foster** foundational skills children's **ability to learn**

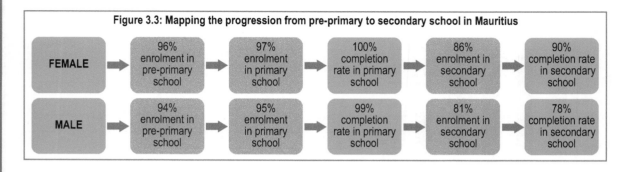

Figure 3.3: Mapping the progression from pre-primary to secondary school in Mauritius

FEMALE	96% enrolment in pre-primary school	97% enrolment in primary school	100% completion rate in primary school	86% enrolment in secondary school	90% completion rate in secondary school
MALE	94% enrolment in pre-primary school	95% enrolment in primary school	99% completion rate in primary school	81% enrolment in secondary school	78% completion rate in secondary school

The data in Figure 3.3 illustrates that the foundation provided by pre-primary school promotes a positive schooling experience that results in high enrolment and completion rates in primary and secondary schools.

Primary school

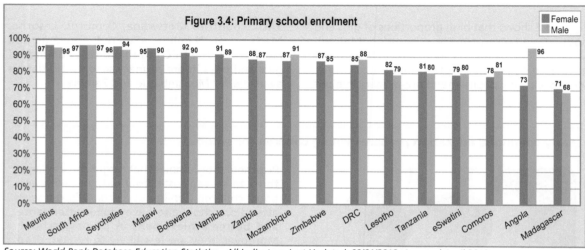

Figure 3.4: Primary school enrolment

Source: World Bank Database Education Statistics - All Indicators. Last Updated: 09/01/2018. Accessed April 2018.

Most SADC countries have achieved gender parity in primary schools: There is very little difference between girls' and boys' enrolment in primary school in SADC except in Angola, where boys' enrolment is 23 percentage points higher. However, the data may hide key issues related to learning in primary schools. As mentioned previously, most children leave primary school without the requisite mathematical and reading competencies. These skills are an important foundation.

Not all children attend school: Many children in SADC remain out of school. Out of primary school children refers to those learners who ought to be in school but for various reasons do not attend primary school.

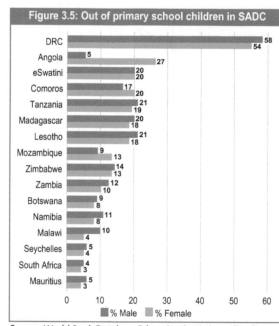

Figure 3.5: Out of primary school children in SADC

Source: World Bank Database Education Statistics - All Indicators. Last Updated: 09/01/2018. Accessed April 2018.

More than 50% of **girls and boys** of primary school age **out of school** in **DRC**

Figure 3.5 shows that more boys than girls do not attend school in 12 SADC countries (Botswana DRC, Lesotho, Madagascar, Malawi, Mauritius, Namibia, Seychelles, South Africa, Tanzania, Zambia and Zimbabwe). In four countries (Angola, Comoros, Mozambique and eSwatini) more girls remain out of school. Angola and the DRC are of concern, given the 22-percentage point difference between girls (22%) and boys (5%) out of primary school in Angola and the overall large number of girls and boys are out of primary school in the DRC.

The Norwegian Refugee Council says fighting in DRC continues to force hundreds of thousands of children to suspend their education, adding their names to the growing list of more than 7.4 million children who already do not attend school in the country.[18]

DRC tackles education challenges

While the DRC has made considerable progress in education, it remains one of the SADC countries with the largest number of out-of-school children.

Completion rates at primary level have increased, from 29% in 2002 to 70% in 2014. Yet an estimated 3.5 million (or 26.7%) of primary school age children remain out-of-school, of which 2.75 million live in rural areas.

To tackle this challenge, legislators in the DRC developed the Education Sector Plan for 2016-2025 with a focus on expanding access and equity, improving learning quality, and improving governance and management in the sector.

Displaced children at the Simba Mosala Site in Kikwit, DRC, do not attend school.
Photo courtesy of Badylon Kawanda Bakiman/IPS

The objectives include:
- Promote an equitable education system for growth and employment by: providing all children with free primary education, combined with specific measures for disadvantaged populations and children with special needs; preparing the gradual extension of basic education to eight years; and adapting learning to promote social integration of young people.
- Create an environment that boosts quality education systems by developing monitoring and quality assurance mechanisms.
- Develop an education environment conducive to quality learning which is enabled by the provision of learning materials and equipment for students and training for teachers.
- Improve transparency and efficiency of governance and management of the sector by: establishing standards and transparent mechanisms for the management of resources; enhancing efficient and equitable management at all levels through improved organisation of partnerships, decentralization and de-concentration, and community and civil society involvement in the sector; and increased public financing of education, from 9% of public expenditures in 2010 to 18% in 2014.

During the process of endorsing the new sector plan, the government committed to bringing the share of its budget allocated to education to 20% by 2018 and to maintain it at that level until 2025.
Source: https://www.globalpartnership.org/country/democratic-republic-congo

Severe gaps exist in Mathematics and reading skills amongst primary school students: The Southern and Eastern Africa Consortium for Monitoring Educational Quality (SACMEQ) comprises 16 Ministries of Education in both regions. It gathers data on the achievement levels of students and their teachers in Reading and Mathematics. SACMEQ has completed three rounds of data collection and is currently engaged in a fourth cycle. The third SACMEQ project involved data collection from around 61 000 learners, 8000 teachers and 2800 principals. The study included 12 SADC countries and three countries in East Africa. The results point to some major challenges.

[18] https://www.news24.com/Africa/News/drc-conflict-weak-education-leave-millions-out-of-school-20170911

Table 3.5: Mathematics competence of Grade 6 learners	Botswana	Lesotho	Malawi	Mauritius	Mozambique	Namibia	Seychelles	South Africa	eSwatini	Tanzania	Zambia	Zimbabwe
Level 1 - Pre-Numeracy %	1.5	3.5	8.6	1.1	5.1	5.4	1.9	5.5	0.2	0.7	13.7	3.6
Level 2 - Emergent Numeracy %	20.9	38.3	51.3	10.1	27.7	42.3	15.9	34.7	8.4	12.6	53.6	23.0
Level 3 - Basic Numeracy %	34.0	39.3	31.8	15.5	41.4	34.0	24.5	29.0	35.7	29.8	24.5	30.7
Level 4 - Beginning Numeracy %	27.2	13.6	6.6	17.9	20.9	12.2	26.4	15.4	37.0	25.5	6.5	22.6
Level 5 - Competent Numeracy %	9.2	3.4	1.3	12.8	3.9	3.4	14.4	7.1	12.9	19.3	1.5	9.8
Level 6 - Mathematically Skilled %	6.0	1.8	0.4	19.7	0.8	2.2	13.2	5.9	5.4	8.7	0.1	6.8
Level 7 - Concrete Problem Solving %	0.9	0.1	0.0	10.6	0.3	0.5	2.4	1.9	0.3	2.5	0.1	2.5
Level 8 - Abstract Problem Solving %	0.4	0.0	0.0	12.2	0.0	0.1	1.3	0.6	0.0	1.0	0.0	1.0

Source: SACMEQ.

While Grade 6 students should fall under Level 7 (concrete problem solving), Table 3.5 illustrates that most learners who participated the survey in 12 SADC countries measure well below this required mathematics skill level. Most sit in the basic numeracy and emergent numeracy categories. Very low proportions of learners in all 12 SADC countries reached the required level of competence.

Table 3.6: Reading competence of Grade 6 learners	Botswana	Lesotho	Malawi	Mauritius	Mozambique	Namibia	Seychelles	South Africa	eSwatini	Tanzania	Zambia	Zimbabwe
Level 1 - pre-reading %	2.9	4.4	9.7	3.7	6.7	2.8	4.4	9.9	0.2	1.4	15.8	6.0
Level 2 - emergent reading %	7.7	16.8	26.9	7.4	14.8	10.8	7.4	17.3	1.2	2.1	28.3	12.5
Level 3 - basic reading %	13.6	31.3	36.7	10.0	22.0	25.1	10.2	21.1	5.6	6.6	28.6	18.7
Level 4 - reading for meaning %	19.2	25.5	19.9	12.1	25.0	25.5	10.3	14.7	20.7	12.0	14.9	20.7
Level 5 - interpretive reading %	20.7	11.8	4.8	13.4	17.9	15.9	12.1	10.6	34.5	16.9	6.0	15.0
Level 6 - inferential reading %	16.5	6.3	1.4	15.7	10.7	10.5	18.0	9.6	25.7	28.0	3.7	11.0
Level 7 - analytical reading %	13.7	3.5	0.6	22.3	2.7	6.8	21.5	10.2	10.1	26.8	2.2	11.7
Level 8 - critical reading %	5.8	0.4	0.0	15.4	0.3	2.5	16.2	6.6	1.8	6.2	0.5	4.5

Source: SACMEQ.

Similarly, Grade 6 leaners should be at Level 7 (Analytical Reading). However, Table 3.6 illustrates that most students in the 12 SADC countries remain at the basic and emergent reading levels. As with Mathematics, the proportion of learners who meet the required level of reading is very low.

This data highlights major gaps in education quality, as well as the need to understand the underlying factors that produce them. Generally, Grade 6 is the penultimate year of primary schooling before learners move on to secondary. Thus, students will carry these skill deficits into secondary school, which will contribute to overall poor performance, particularly in the STEM subjects.

As learners move higher up in the school system, there is little time to work on these gaps in their knowledge and skills. As Nelson Mandela once said: "Education is the most powerful weapon we can use to change the world." SADC will only achieve education's promise if its leaders acknowledge these serious gaps and make new investments to address them.

Secondary school

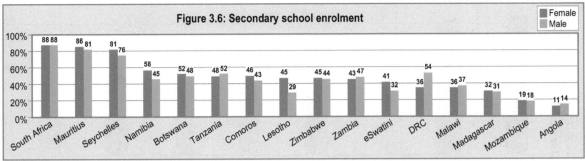

Figure 3.6: Secondary school enrolment

■ Female
■ Male

Source: World Bank Database Education Statistics - All Indicators. Last Updated: 09/01/2018 Accessed April 2018.

Most SADC countries have low levels of secondary school enrolment: As illustrated in Figure 3.6, many SADC countries have reached gender parity in enrolment at secondary school. However, enrolment remains low across the region, with only three countries (Mauritius, Seychelles and South Africa) able to claim that three-quarters of their youth attend secondary school. Fewer than than 20% of youth in Mozambique and Angola attend secondary school.

A 2018 report from the United Nations Development Programme (UNDP), titled Income Inequality Trends in sub-Saharan Africa: Divergence, Determinants and Consequences, identifies challenges preventing young people from progressing to secondary and tertiary education. Angela Lusigi, one of the authors, notes that, while Africa has made significant advances in closing the gap in primary-level enrolments, both secondary and tertiary enrolments lag.[19]

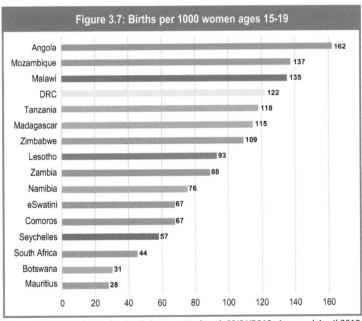

Figure 3.7: Births per 1000 women ages 15-19

Country	Births per 1000
Angola	162
Mozambique	137
Malawi	135
DRC	122
Tanzania	118
Madagascar	115
Zimbabwe	109
Lesotho	93
Zambia	88
Namibia	76
eSwatini	67
Comoros	67
Seychelles	57
South Africa	44
Botswana	31
Mauritius	28

Source: World Bank Gender Statistics. Last Updated: 09/01/2018. Accessed April 2018.

Teenage pregnancies prevent young girls from attending secondary school: As illustrated in Figure 3.7, more than 10% of girls between the ages of 15 and 19 have given birth in seven SADC countries (Angola, DRC, Mada-gascar, Malawi, Mozambique, Tanzania and Zimbabwe). While a little lower, the adolescent fertility rate in Lesotho, Namibia and Zambia remains high compared to global levels. Mauritius and Botswana have the lowest rates in the region.

Secondary enrolment

=

Tertiary enrolment

---

[19] https://southerntimesafrica.com/site/news/africa-grapples-with-huge-disparities-in-education-higher-enrolment-numbers-mask-exclusion-and-inefficiencies

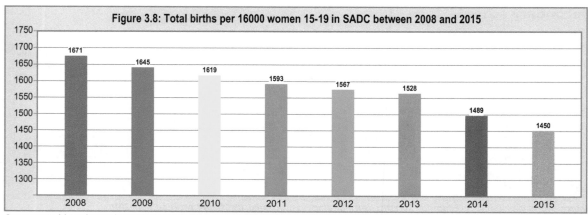

Figure 3.8: Total births per 16000 women 15-19 in SADC between 2008 and 2015

Year	Value
2008	1671
2009	1645
2010	1619
2011	1593
2012	1567
2013	1528
2014	1489
2015	1450

Source: World Bank Gender Statistics. Last Updated: 09/01/2018. Accessed April 2018.

Figure 3.8 shows the total of number of births amongst young girls between ages 15 and 19 in 16 SADC countries (births per 1000 women multiplied by all 16 SADC countries). It illustrates a decrease from 1671 to 1450 over the last seven years. This represents an average decrease of 32 births per year: slow progress. Concerted policy interventions and actions remain vital to support teenage mothers to re-enter the education system, as well as reduce teenage pregnancies.

Tanzanian lawmakers violate teenage mothers' right to education: The **Tanzania**n government has banned teenage mothers from continuing their education or returning to state-run schools following child birth. In a public address in June 2017, Tanzania's President John Magufuli reinforced the ban and added that the government should imprison men involved in teenage pregnancies. Magufuli challenged human rights groups to open schools for young parents, stating that the government provides free education for students "who have really wanted to study."

Tanzania: Teenage pregnancy shatters dream of becoming an accountant

Imani, a young woman from Tanzania who spoke with Human Rights Watch in 2017, had a dream to graduate from college and work as an accountant.

Her plans changed at age 16, when a private tutor, a secondary school teacher hired by her parents to teach her during the weekend, sexually abused her. When Imani discovered she was pregnant, she informed the tutor and he disappeared.

Teenage pregnancy is a major barrier to education for women in Tanzania.
Photo courtesy of The East African

At first, Imani skipped school on those days when the school nurse carried out monthly pregnancy tests on all girls at her school. But school officials eventually found out during the third month of her pregnancy. "My dream was shattered then," she told Human Rights Watch. "I was expelled from school. I was expelled from home too."

Like many adolescent girls in Tanzania, Imani tried to get back into education once she had her baby: "I tried to go back to school. I went to every preparatory programme, and I went to do the Form II national examination. I paid the examination fee to the teachers, they left with the money and did not register me. This was in 2015."

When Human Rights Watch interviewed her in January 2016, Imani had just started a computer literacy programme set up by a small non-governmental organisation in Mwanza to ensure more young women like her can find a way back into education.[20]

---

[20] https://www.hrw.org/report/2017/02/14/i-had-dream-finish-school/barriers-secondary-education-tanzania

Tertiary level

Students with poor-quality basic education often lack the preparation and foundation necessary to gain advanced skills from tertiary education or technical training.[21] Thus, countries with limited educational advances - such as low access to secondary and tertiary education - may have challenges in turning the youth demographic bulge into a net positive through skill and entrepreneurship development.[22]

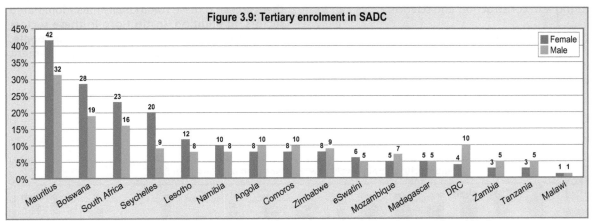

Figure 3.9: Tertiary enrolment in SADC

Source: World Bank Database Education Statistics - All Indicators. Last Updated: 09/01/2018. Accessed April 2018.

Tertiary enrolment in SADC is below the global average for women and men: The global average for women's tertiary enrolment is 38% and 36% for men. While women's enrolment in tertiary institutions in Mauritius exceeds the global average, Figure 3.9 illustrates that every other SADC country falls below the global average.

SADC countries must invest more in preparing young women and men at primary and secondary levels so they have the requisite knowledge and skills needed to enter, and complete, tertiary education.

Gender gaps persist in tertiary enrolment: More women attend tertiary institutions in most countries, including the top four performers, Botswana, Mauritius, Seychelles and South Africa.

Table 3.7: Breakdown of female students by area of study

	Science	Humanities and arts	Agriculture	Education	Health and welfare	Social sciences, business and law	Engineering, manufacturing and construction
Angola	3	2	0	17	16	54	7
Botswana	12	7	1	14	8	44	6
DRC	2	6	5	11	28	43	1
Lesotho	3	2	2	6	11	37	5
Madagascar	8	12	2	2	12	59	3
Mauritius	9	8	1	8	6	59	3
Mozambique	3	8	3	23	8	54	4
Namibia	9	15	2	22	8	42	1
Seychelles	2	8	1	6	9	71	1
South Africa	9	5	2	22	7	51	4
Tanzania	3	4	0	37	2	45	2
Zimbabwe	6	13	2	28	2	42	6

Source: World Bank Education Statistics. Updated on the 09/01/2018. Accessed April 2018.
No data available for the Comoros, Malawi, eSwatini and Zambia.

[21] http://www.worldbank.org/en/publication/wdr2018
[22] African Economic Outlook 2017, Entrepreneurship and Industrialisation

Encourage

to

choose

for

male-

dominated

sectors

Table 3.7 shows that, of the women surveyed by the World Bank in each country, the largest proportion in tertiary education - by a substantial margin and across 12 SADC countries - study in the fields of social science, business and law. Education, and health and welfare, with fewer women, have the second and third highest proportion of female students. The lowest proportions of women study agriculture, followed by engineering, manufacturing and construction and science.

The data shows that women continue to study in those fields traditionally referred to as "women's work." Meanwhile, the fields of agriculture, engineering, manufacturing and construction and science all represent important growth industries in the SADC region and Africa as a whole. So long as women do not take up study in these professions, they will remain marginalised from potential economic benefits and growth in these sectors.

Institutions of higher learning need to engage with secondary schools to ensure that they encourage young women to choose subjects that will give them access to these traditionally male-dominated sectors. In addition, institutions in these sectors should foster awareness amongst young people, particularly young women, about employment possibilities in these career areas.

Literacy

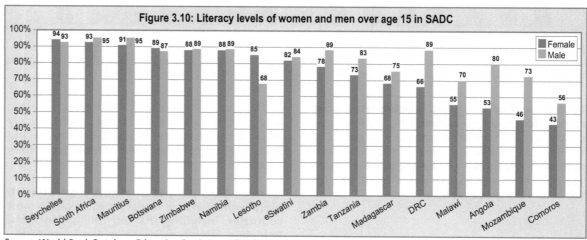

Figure 3.10: Literacy levels of women and men over age 15 in SADC

Country	Female	Male
Seychelles	94	93
South Africa	93	95
Mauritius	91	95
Botswana	89	87
Zimbabwe	88	89
Namibia	88	89
Lesotho	85	68
eSwatini	82	84
Zambia	78	89
Tanzania	73	83
Madagascar	68	75
DRC	66	89
Malawi	55	70
Angola	53	80
Mozambique	46	73
Comoros	43	56

Source: World Bank Database Education Statistics - All Indicators. Last Updated: 09/01/2018. Accessed April 2018.

St Catherins school children, St Famille, Mahamasina, Madagascar.
Photo: Zotonantenaina Razanandrateta

Figure 3.10 illustrates that literacy is high among women and men over age 15 in several countries in the region. In Lesotho, women over age 15 have a substantially higher literacy, while more men are literate in Angola, Comoros, DRC, Madagascar, Malawi, Mozambique and Tanzania. Literacy is lowest among women in the Comoros and Mozambique.

These numbers underscore the need for some SADC countries to provide opportunities for lifelong learning alongside the formal schooling system to assist older learners and out of school youth.

Lifelong learning for older learners and out of school youth

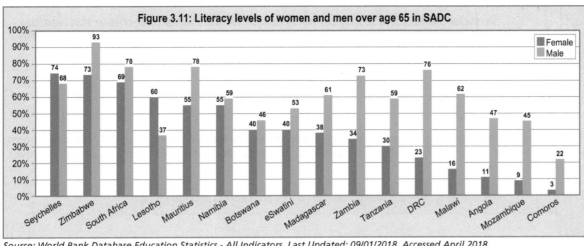

Figure 3.11: Literacy levels of women and men over age 65 in SADC

Legend: ■ Female ■ Male

Country	Female	Male
Seychelles	74	68
Zimbabwe	73	93
South Africa	69	78
Lesotho	60	37
Mauritius	55	78
Namibia	55	59
Botswana	40	46
eSwatini	40	53
Madagascar	38	61
Zambia	34	73
Tanzania	30	59
DRC	23	76
Malawi	16	62
Angola	11	47
Mozambique	9	45
Comoros	3	22

Source: World Bank Database Education Statistics - All Indicators. Last Updated: 09/01/2018. Accessed April 2018.

Figure 3.11 shows that women over age 65 have lower literacy levels than men in 14 SADC countries. Seychelles and Lesotho are the exception. The levels of literacy amongst women in this category are exceptionally low in Angola, Comoros, Malawi and Mozambique. Levels of literacy amongst box sexes in the Comoros is alarming, especially for women, at just 3%.

The Swiss non-govern-mental organisation *PartnerAid* is working in partnership with the Comoros Ministry of National Education to improve literacy levels.

Mother tongue literacy in the Comoros

The World Bank estimates that about half the population of the Comoros, mostly women, cannot read or write. In rural areas, estimates put the illiteracy rate even higher. PartnerAid has been working to address this issue in collaboration with local partners, including the Ministry of National Education.

Teachers educate students in the Comoros in French, which is a legacy of the colonial era, whereas the mother tongue of the Comorians is "Shikomori" (part of the KiSwahili family). In collaboration with a team of local specialists, PartnerAid created a new reading manual in the local language.

Women in the Comoros age 65 and older have very low levels of literacy. *Photo courtesy of Best-Country*

PartnerAid also supports an initiative that teaches children in their mother tongue. A child who reads in his or her mother tongue and understands the content will continue reading in adulthood - and will therefore be able to continue learning and studying.

Achievements of the programme so far include:
• Literacy textbooks in the local language (level one) and in French (levels two and three);
• Training literacy teachers for all three levels;
• Training of local supervisors;
• Organisation, implementation and supervision of 26 literacy classes (in three levels) in different villages, with a total of 700 students; and
• The launch of a new literacy manual in 2015/16 in the mother tongue for infant classes in 10 classes of the public school with about 500 children.

Source: https://partneraid.ch/en/about-us/

Article 14.2: State parties shall take special measures to increase the number of girls taking up Science, Technology, Engineering and Mathematics (STEM) subjects and ICT at the secondary, tertiary and higher levels.

STEM subjects

The earlier section on primary school enrolment covered the low levels of mathematical literacy amongst Grade 6 learners. This deficit affects young peoples' ability to study the STEM subjects at tertiary level.

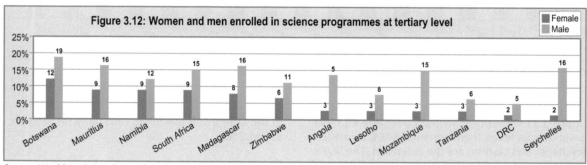

Source: World Bank Database Education Statistics - All Indicators. Last Updated: 09/01/2018. Accessed April 2018.

Enrolment of young Southern Africans in science programmes in 12 SADC countries is lower than 20%. Botswana has the highest numbers of women and men in science programmes at 12% and 19% respectively. The Seychelles and DRC have the lowest proportion of women in science programmes at 2%.

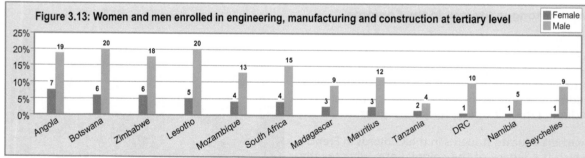

Source: World Bank Database Education Statistics - All Indicators. Last Updated: 09/01/2018. Accessed April 2018.

Figure 3.13 shows that enrolment in subjects related to engineering, manufacturing and construction is also low. The proportion of women in engineering, manufacturing and construction programmes is especially low, with only 1% of women enrolled to study these subject areas in DRC, Namibia and Seychelles.

Sidharth Oberoi, president of Zaniac, an organisation that provides STEM support in the United States, writes about the impact of inadequate STEM education on the US economy and job market. "STEM jobs alone have grown 17%, which is much faster than the nearly 10% growth rate in all other areas," he notes. "Yet the civic infrastructure is not there to support this growth. One of the most important factors that limits the United States' ability to stay ahead of the STEM curve is the lack of introduction to these educational areas at an early age."[23]

This underscores a recurring theme in this chapter: to address gaps in education, interventions must occur early as part of foundational learning. There is a need for curriculum reviews and redesigns to ensure that new entrants into the schooling system acquire the requisite mathematics knowledge and skills. Education stakeholders must implement a parallel system to address the current gaps in mathematical knowledge across the SADC region.

[23] https://www.ced.org/blog/entry/the-economic-impact-of-early-exposure-to-stem-education

Young women take to STEM subjects across the region

Botswana: To promote public interest in STEM and transform Botswana from a resource-based to a knowledge-based economy, the Botswana International University of Science and Technology (BIUST) hosts an annual STEM festival. Students and teachers from various primary, secondary and tertiary institutions attend the three-day festival. The programme includes exhibitions and displays, seminars, talk shows, symposia, demonstrations, and one-on-one interactions between inventors, interested members of the public and the media. The festival provides a platform for innovators and inventors, researchers and academics from all walks of life to showcase their inventions, concepts, blueprints or final products. Businesses and venture capitalists have also been known to invest in select products from the exhibition.[24]

Lesotho: To celebrate the International Day of the Girl Child on the 11 October 2017, the Lesotho National Commission for UNESCO hosted an intergenerational panel dialogue about women in STEM.

A group of young aspiring women leaders in the STEM sector met with established women in science to talk about difficulties girls and women face when pursuing a career in STEM or related studies. Science should become more important in schools, they stressed, noting that teachers should specifically encourage girls to consider STEM careers.

The panellists followed the dialogue with a coding training session for girls from Methodist High School. The training helped 30 girls to gain insight into the world of coding and computer science.[25]

Malawi: In a drive to coax more girls into Engineering, the organisation Women in Engineering (WomEng) plans to talk to girls in various secondary schools across Malawi. Susan Mponda, chair of the women's chapter of the Malawi Institute of Engineers, said she hopes the initiative will tackle the negative perception girls have about engineering.

Mponda spoke recently at St. Michael's Girls Secondary School to motivate students there to join the engineering profession. She tried to demystify fears associated with engineering, including that is a profession for men. Mponda said she hoped to open young girls' minds about the sciences because the world is changing and engineering can provide solutions to the country's challenges, such as water and electricity.

Student Vanessa Makina said the motivational talk came at the right time because her cohort is still making choices about their studies.[26]

eSwatini: The United States Embassy holds coding and robotics sessions with more than 400 young people from nearly 50 schools who have demonstrated an interest in engineering and technology. Programme leaders provide insights on how the skills learned in a coding workshop can help those who want to become chemical engineers. The workshops with have produced a robust cadre of students prepared to participate in the LEGO League National Robotics Competition. In preparation for this competition, students must identify and research a problem, formulate a possible solution, and present their work to a panel of judges.

The US Embassy in eSwatini encourages young women to study the STEM subjects through workshops that include lessons on coding. *Photo courtesy of US Embassy eSwatini*

Earlier this year, the US Embassy partnered with one of eSwatini's budding tech companies, eSwatini Action Group Against Abuse (SWAGAA), and schools from the Shiselweni region to begin developing a mobile application for girls to learn about gender-based violence. These young women learned about building codes and their confidence. During the 21 Days of Y'ello Care, a corporate social responsibility initiative of the MTN group, the young women provided two institutions - the School for the Deaf Primary and Kalamdladla High School - with digital offline databases to enhance their access to learning tools.[27]

[24] http://www.thepatriot.co.bw/news/item/5474-stem-festival-successful.html
[25] https://www.unesco.org.ls/single-post/2017/11/13/Lesotho-National-Commission-hosts-Intergenerational-Dialogue-of-women-in-STEM-on-the-11th-October-2017
[26] http://mwnation.com/female-engineers-want-girls-field/
[27] https://sz.usembassy.gov/remarks-ambassador-lisa-peterson-sadc-charter-women-science-engineering-technology-national-archives-lobamba/

Information and communication technologies

To evaluate school resources and their impact on achievement, UNESCO collected data on radio, television and computers in primary schools. It defined the target population as all pupils at Grade 6 level in 2007 who attended registered mainstream primary schools. Its researchers used a sample of schools covering all regions.[28]

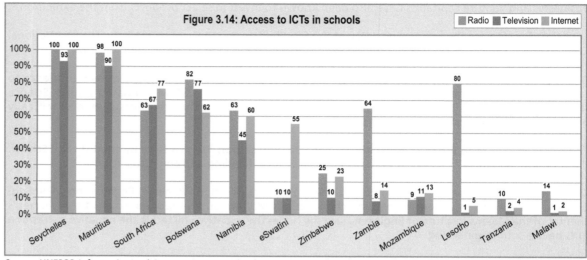

Figure 3.14: Access to ICTs in schools   Radio ■ Television ■ Internet

Country	Radio	Television	Internet
Seychelles	100	100	93
Mauritius	98	90	100
South Africa	63	67	77
Botswana	82	77	62
Namibia	63	45	60
eSwatini	10	10	55
Zimbabwe	25	10	23
Zambia	64	8	14
Mozambique	9	11	13
Lesotho	80	1	5
Tanzania	10	2	4
Malawi	14	1	2

Source: UNESCO Information and Communication Technology (ICT) in Education in Sub-Saharan Africa, A comparative analysis of basic e-readiness in school. No data for Angola, Comoros, DRC and Madagascar.

Figure 3.14 illustrates the highest access to the internet in descending order. It shows that educators in Seychelles and Mauritius have been harnessing ICTs to deliver education. The two countries use radio, television and the internet in teaching and learning. Botswana, Namibia and South Africa also utilise these tools but to a lesser degree.

eSwatini teachers use the internet much more than radio and television in classrooms, while educators in Lesotho and Zambia use radio as a key teaching tool. Malawi, Mozambique, Tanzania and Zimbabwe recorded low ICT usage in schools. Internet access remains spotty in many of these countries.

SADC countries should review ICT policies and frameworks to integrate education needs. They should also prioritise tracking implementation where policies already exist. The Seychelles, which launched an ICT Policy in 2007, has already seen increases in effective ICT usage in education.

Teachers play an integral role in improving the quality of education.
Photo courtesy of Voluntary Services Organisation (VSO) Ireland

---

[28] UNESCO Information and Communication Technology (ICT) in Education in sub-Saharan Africa, A comparative analysis of basic e-readiness in school.

Computers replace chalk and blackboards in Seychelles

Lawmakers developed an ICT policy for Seychelles after extensive consultations and discussions involving a wide range of participants from the public sector and civil society.

It sets out the national ICT policy objectives in five key focus areas:
- ICT infrastructure;
- Legal and regulatory framework;
- Human resources development;
- Industry; and
- Government.

Girls and boys use ICTs to enhance learning in Seychelles.
Photo courtesy of eduictseychellesblog

The policy includes specific policy goals in each of these focus areas, which collectively contribute to the overall vision. There is also a commitment to monitor the implementation of the policy through the use of appropriate indicators and review when necessary.

The policy has ensured that teachers receive training from experts and engineers to upgrade their technological skills so they can maintain equipment and create lessons using the computer software.

Intel Education Service Corps teamed up with the Ministry of Education's IT technical support unit to upgrade the Intel powered classmate PCs and provide support and training to primary schools and teachers. Linda Kenworthy, the team leader, said "The Seychelles primary school teachers are very engaged and want to improve their skills to become agents of change for 21st century schools and learning - their active participation in the classroom and during our visits to their computer rooms demonstrates their commitment."

This example shows that, through its ICT policy, the government recognises that accessible, affordable, high quality and well-regulated ICT facilities and services are critical to the realisation of its vision of a modern, ICT-enabled and knowledge-based information society. ICTs are a vital tool to promote sustainable development and improve the quality of life of people.

Source: http://eduictseychelles.blogspot.ca/

Challenging Stereotypes

Article 14.3: State parties shall adopt and implement gender sensitive educational, curriculum, policies and programmes addressing gender stereotypes in education and gender-based violence, amongst others.

Increasing gender-sensitive teacher training and the number of female teachers helps schools effectively challenge gender stereotypes and entrenched discriminatory social norms. In a learning environment, the content, processes and context of education should be free of gender bias and encourage and support equality and respect.[29]

Gender and education curriculum

Gender-sensitive curricula acknowledge and address issues of inclusion, promote gender equitable learning and help girls and boys challenge tradi-tional gender stereotypes. Gender reviews of curricula have helped raise awareness and support change towards more gender-responsive content and resources.

 In Tanzania, the national secondary school syllabuses, revised in 2010, contain gender-related topics. In civics, teachers devote nearly 25% of Form 2 lessons to gender, Form 4 includes gender in the study of culture, and the 2010 civics exam includes questions on gender inequality (Miske, 2013).[30]

---

[29] https://en.unesco.org/gem-report/report/2015/education-all-2000-2015-achievements-and-challenges
[30] IBID.

Quality of education

While the Protocol is interested in retention and enrolment, it also mentions education quality. Teacher's qualifications serve as one crucial factor to ensure quality education. Many countries in the region have struggled to employ well-trained educators. Further, many teachers receive quality training in one subject but lack a solid foundation in another. This is especially true of the STEM subjects, which the education system has traditionally not encouraged as a focus for female learners, many of whom become teachers. This can perpetuate a disparity that unqualified teachers pass down to future generations.

Gender gaps in the teaching profession

Table 3.8 provides an overview of the proportion of female teachers in SADC. In 11 countries, a higher proportion of women teach at primary level. Meanwhile, in Angola, Comoros, DRC, Malawi and Mozambique women hold fewer than 50% of teaching positions across primary, secondary and tertiary levels.

At secondary level, only six countries (Botswana, Lesotho, Mauritius, Namibia, Seychelles and South Africa) have 50% or more women teachers. Nine countries have fewer than 50% women teachers at secondary level. Out of the 13 countries for which data is available, only Lesotho has achieved gender parity for women teachers in tertiary education.

Table 3.8: Representation of women in the teaching profession			
	Primary	**Secondary**	**Tertiary**
Angola	37%	48%	35%
Botswana	74%	53%	37%
Comoros	43%	10%	9%
DRC	28%	12%	8%
Lesotho	76%	56%	50%
Madagascar	56%	44%	31%
Malawi	42%	31%	26%
Mauritius	75%	62%	N/A
Mozambique	43%	21%	26%
Namibia	68%	50%	41%
Seychelles	88%	58%	49%
South Africa	79%	55%	N/A
eSwatini	70%	49%	38%
Tanzania	51%	28%	30%
Zambia	53%	N/A	N/A
Zimbabwe	56%	46%	32%

Source: World Bank Database: Education Statistics - All Indicators. Last Updated: 09/01/2018 Accessed April 2018.

Teacher qualifications

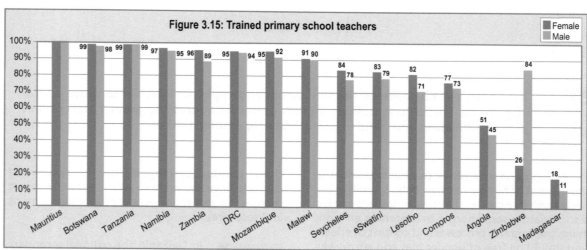

Source: World Bank Database: Education Statistics - All Indicators. Last Updated: 09/01/2018. Accessed April 2018.

No data for South Africa.

A high proportion of female and male primary school teachers in 12 SADC countries have received training, as noted in Figure 3.15. However, this is not the case in Angola, Madagascar and Zimbabwe. Only around half of primary school teachers in Angola have received training.

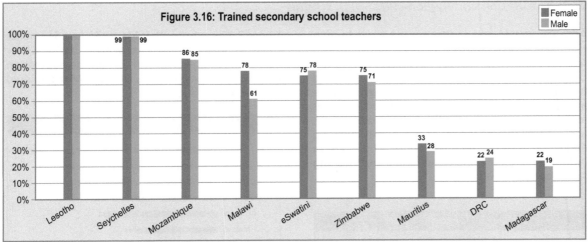

Figure 3.16: Trained secondary school teachers

Source: World Bank Database: Education Statistics - All Indicators. Last Updated: 09/01/2018. Accessed April 2018.
No data for Angola, Botswana, Comoros, Namibia, South Africa, Tanzania and Zambia.

Figure 3.16 shows that Lesotho (100%) and Seychelles (99%) have the most trained female and male secondary school teachers in the region. While Malawi, Mozambique, eSwatini and Zimbabwe have high proportions of trained teachers in secondary schools, DRC, Madagascar and Mauritius, have a worrying lack of trained educators. This points to a need for on-the-job training to recognise educators' existing knowledge and build their skills. SADC stakeholders are developing a set of regional standards for teaching and learning to guide educator capacity building.

Teacher qualifications

UNESCO recommends one teacher for every 25 learners.

As is evident from Table 3.9, only three SADC countries (Malawi, Mauritius and Seychelles) have achieved the UNESCO target, with eSwatini and the Comoros not far off. In 11 SADC countries classes have more than 30 learners per teacher, and Malawi and Mozambique have remarkably high learner teacher ratios at 70 and 55 respectively.

Effective teaching and learning suffers when teachers must manage large classrooms.

Table 3.9: Learner teacher ratio in SADC

Country	Learner to teacher ratio
Malawi	70
Mozambique	55
Zambia	48
Angola	43
Tanzania	43
Madagascar	41
Zimbabwe	36
Lesotho	34
DRC	33
Namibia	30
South Africa	30
Comoros	28
eSwatini	27
Botswana	23
Mauritius	18
Seychelles	14

Source: UNESCO Information Services, https://tellmaps.com/uis/ teachers/#!/tellmap/873758989. Accessed April 2018.

Regional standards for **teaching** and **learning** to **guide** teacher training

---

SADC task force developing regional teacher standards

Teacher Standards are one of nine key dimensions that experts consider crucial to any comprehensive teacher policy. Several SADC countries are developing professional standards for teachers. This contributes to the overall aim of improving education quality and learner outcomes.

Teacher standards refer to expectations about teachers' knowledge, competencies and attributes, and desirable level of performance. Standards should describe clearly and concisely what constitutes quality education in a particular context, and what teachers need to know and be able to do to implement it.

Stakeholders in SADC have created a task force to develop a SADC framework for teacher standards and competencies. So far, they have completed a draft framework.
Source: Report of the Southern Africa Regional Meeting on Teacher Standards and Competencies

Water, sanitation and hygiene (WASH) in schools

Access to water and sanitation is a basic human right, yet many children in SADC must attend schools where they do not have access to either. UNICEF notes that good water, sanitation and hygiene (WASH) services in schools lessens disease and can help reduce the 272 million school days missed every year due to diarrhoea. Additionally, access to WASH at school protects girls' right to education as girls often drop out of school due to lack of private, safe and clean toilets and washing facilities.[31]

Figure 3.17 illustrates that Mauritius and Seychelles have extensive access to water, while other countries struggle. Fewer than half the population in three countries (Angola, DRC and Mozambique) have access to water.

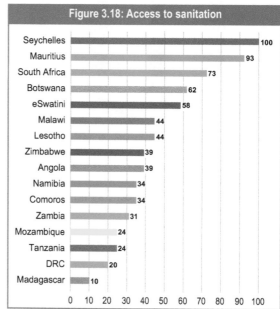

Figure 3.18: Access to sanitation

Country	Value
Seychelles	100
Mauritius	93
South Africa	73
Botswana	62
eSwatini	58
Malawi	44
Lesotho	44
Zimbabwe	39
Angola	39
Namibia	34
Comoros	34
Zambia	31
Mozambique	24
Tanzania	24
DRC	20
Madagascar	10

Source: Progress on Drinking Water, Sanitation and Hygiene: 2017 Update and SDG Baselines.

Figure 3.18 shows that even fewer people in SADC have access to sanitation. At 10%, access to sanitation in Madagascar is alarmingly low. Lack of sanitation at school means many girls do not attend classes while menstruating, which affects their right to education.

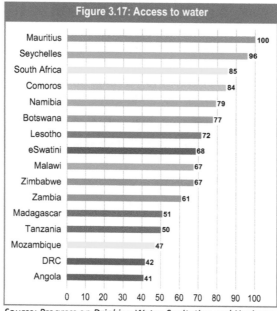

Figure 3.17: Access to water

Country	Value
Mauritius	100
Seychelles	96
South Africa	85
Comoros	84
Namibia	79
Botswana	77
Lesotho	72
eSwatini	68
Malawi	67
Zimbabwe	67
Zambia	61
Madagascar	51
Tanzania	50
Mozambique	47
DRC	42
Angola	41

Source: Progress on Drinking Water, Sanitation and Hygiene: 2017 Update and SDG Baselines.

Girl's pit toilet death reveals sad state of school sanitation in South Africa

Dilapidated toilets remain in use at a school in the Eastern Cape, South Africa.
Photo courtesy of The Big Issue South Africa

In 2018, South African media reported on the death of 5-year-old Lumka Mketwa, who died in a school pit toilet. Her body lay in the toilet overnight at Luna Primary School in Bizana while the community looked for her. The incident was similar to another at a school outside Polokwane in 2014, where 5-year-old Michael Komape also drowned in a pit toilet.

Komape's family, represented by the advocacy group Section 27, went to court to claim damages and compel the government to provide decent sanitation.

While legislation prohibits schools from using plain pit and bucket latrines, as of January 2018, 4 358 schools across South Africa continued to use only plain pit latrines as toilets. Meanwhile, 37 schools in the Eastern Cape had no ablution facilities.

---

[31] https://www.unicef.org/media/media_53234.html

Gender violence in schools

Gender violence in school can have a physical impact, cause psychological distress, permanent physical disability and long-term physical or mental ill-health. Physical impacts are the most obvious and may include mild or serious wounds, bruises, fractures, and deaths by homicide or suicide. Sexual assault may lead to unwanted and early pregnancy and sexually transmitted infections, including HIV and AIDS. The psychological impacts may include immediate impairment of emotional development and long-term mental distress and ill-health, which can also contribute to physical ill-health.[32]

Child rights clubs empower Zambia's schoolchildren: The Zambia Civic Education Association (ZCEA) works to promote and pro-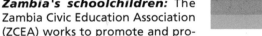tect children's rights through education. Through its child participation programme, it supports child rights clubs that empower children by raising their awareness of their rights under the United Nations Convention on the Rights of the Child, the African Charter on the Rights and Welfare of the Child, and other instruments. Zambia now has at least 300 child rights clubs in primary and secondary schools.[33]

---

eSwatini: Children experience violence at home and in school

Children in eSwatini face alarming rates of violence, according to UNICEF, including at the hands of teachers.
Photo courtesy of Google images

UNICEF estimates that nine in ten children in eSwatini suffer "violent discipline." In one example, a father tied his 11-year-old daughter to a house pillar and thrashed her with a pipe until she lost consciousness.

The 2017 UNICEF report revealed that sexual violence and bullying affects 38% and 32% of children in eSwatini, respectively. Another staggering statistic revealed that for every girl child who reports sexual violence, an estimated 400 girls have never received assis-tance after experiencing sexual violence.

UNICEF notes that Swazi culture is one of the main drivers of violence against children, especially its emphasis on family and community loyalty over the individual. Despite these findings, in a debate in the Swazi Parliament in March 2017 Members of Parliament called for schools to bring back caning as a form of punishment. They argued that teachers struggle to deal with wayward pupils.

eSwatini legislators banned corporal punishment in 2015, but caning continues. Reports from across eSwatini regularly cite examples of pupils beaten by their teachers.
Source: http://allafrica.com/stories/201804240741.html

Sexual assault

Little or no data exists on the prevalence of sexual abuse in SADC schools. Anecdotal evidence suggests that it is a problem, particularly amongst young women. Stakeholders must base strategies to address sexual violence in schools on evidence, there is need to collect baseline data on violence in school across all SADC countries.

High levels of sexual violence prevalent in South African schools: In May 2016, the UBS Optimus Foundation,[34] in partnership with the Centre for Justice and Crime Preven-tion, University of Cape Town and the Gender Health and Justice Research Unit launched a technical report entitled *Sexual Victimisation of Children in South Africa*. It covered urban and rural schools and included a total of 9717 respondents between the ages of 15 and 17. Researchers accessed 4086 of these in a school setting and 5631 in their households with self- or interviewer-administered questionnaires.

The findings of the study provide South African stakeholders with important baseline data to develop a roadmap for the prevention of violence against children.

---

[32] https://www.unicef.org/violencestudy/reports.html
[33] Ibid.
[34] UBS Optimus Foundation is a philanthropic organisation based in the United States, United Kingdom and Switzerland that is committed to delivering measurable, long-term benefits to the world's most vulnerable children.

Table 3.10: Abuse at school (inside, in school yard, or on a bus)		
Questions posed to the study participants	% Female	% Male
Sexual abuse by a known adult (Known adult ever touch your private parts when they should not have or made you touch their private parts or force you to have sex)	4.3	11.5
Sexual abuse by an unknown adult (Unknown adult ever touch your private parts when they shouldn't have or made you touch their private parts or force you to have sex)		16.7
Sexual abuse by a child or adolescent (Any child or teen ever made you do sexual things against your will)	26.5	30.2
Forced sexual intercourse (Anyone ever try to force you to have sexual intercourse of any kind, even if it did not happen)	10.8	12.1
Sexual exposure abuse (Anyone ever make you look at their private parts by force or surprise, force you to watch them masturbate, view nude pictures or pornographic videos or by flashing you)	4.5	36.6
Sexual harassment - verbal or written (Anyone ever hurt your feelings by saying or writing something sexual about you or your body)	44.4	60
Other sexual experience with an adult (Any sexual abuse)	0.6	2.4

Source: 2016 Sexual victimisation of children in South Africa.

Table 3.10 shows the prevalence of sexual violence in school, including in the school yard and on buses going to from school. These results come from the questionnaires administered by interviewers at school. Notably, the prevalence of sexual violence and abuse experienced by boys is higher than girls in all categories.

These results show that young people experience prominent levels of sexual violence in the school setting. It is incumbent on the South African government to urgently address this issue.

Bullying

Bullying affects both girls and boys. While girls often face psychological bullying, boys are more likely to be subjected to physical violence and threats.[35] Young people with a non-traditional sexual orientation and/or gender identity are especially vulnerable to targeted acts of violence.[36]

In addition to experiencing violence at the hands of educators, children face bullying from their peers. A global UNICEF *Violence against children* study included children aged 11, 13 and 15 from five SADC countries.

The findings, illustrated in Figure 3.19, are alarming. Over a two-month period, high proportions of young people said they experienced bullying at least once. In Zambia, more than 50% of girls and

boys had faced bullying. In Botswana, Namibia, eSwatini and Zimbabwe more boys reported bullying than girls. As always in these types of studies, it is possible that more girls experienced bullying but did not report it.

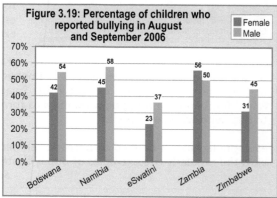

Figure 3.19: Percentage of children who reported bullying in August and September 2006

Source: UNICEF Violence against children, Violence against children in schools and educational settings.

Disability and education

Little will change in the lives of children with disabilities until attitudes among communities, professionals, media and governments begin to change. Disabled children remain marginalised and silenced due to ignorance about the nature and causes of impairments, serious underestimation of their potential and capacities, and other impediments to equal opportunity and treatment.[37]

---

[35] https://www.ncbi.nlm.nih.gov/pmc/articles/PMC1461415/
[36] Ibid.
[37] https://www.unicef.org/publications/files/SWCR2013_ENG_Lo_res_24_Apr_2013.pdf

Disability group lobbies for inclusive education

Pulane Makatisi, a 12-year-old Lesotho student, struggled to find a school willing to enrol her because she is wheelchair-bound. The government stepped in to help after the story broke in Lesotho's media. *Photo courtesy of Sunday Express*

Governments need to build inclusive education and training systems that create environments that enable every child to develop to their full potential. The Africa Disability Alliance created the Promoting Inclusive Education (PIE) programme to help governments with this process as well as ensure that African children with disabilities can realise their right to education.

This project seeks to address the following issues, with an initial focus in Southern Africa in collaboration with SADC, national government ministries of education and civil society organisations:

- ***Lack of a guiding strategy for implementing inclusive education:*** Although international, regional and national commitments about the right to education for children with disabilities exist, there is no accompanying framework to guide their implementation.
- ***Dearth of data:*** There is inadequate, out-dated and/or unreliable data across the region, which severely restricts interventions in this area of work.

- ***Inadequate teacher capacity:*** There are very few trained teachers with the skills and knowledge to work with children with different abilities in the region. Other challenges that adversely affect education services for learners with disabilities include lack of an adapted and diversified curriculum; lack of learning, teaching and support materials; inadequately prepared teachers; and lack of psychosocial support.

Source: www.africadisabilityalliance.org/index.php/programmes

Child labour

Large numbers of young people do not attend school in SADC. Many need to work instead to contribute to their household income. The ILO notes that progress to eliminate child labour has stalled in many parts of sub-Saharan Africa. Indeed, it found that child labour increased between 2012 and 2016 due to economic and demographic changes as well as crisis and state fragility. Most children work in the agricultural sector, often for members of their own family.[38]

Table 3.11 shows that high proportions of children between ages seven and 14 work in SADC. Malawi has the highest proportion, followed by DRC and Zambia. Between 21% and 35% of children work in six other countries - Angola, Comoros, Lesotho, Madagascar, Mozambique and Tanzania.

Table 3.11: Proportion of children between ages 7 and 14 who work		
	Female	**Male**
Malawi	44	51
DRC	44	39
Zambia	40	35
Tanzania	34	35
Mozambique	28	27
Comoros	28	26
Madagascar	27	29
Angola	25	22
Lesotho	21	25
Zimbabwe	14	12
Namibia	12	15
eSwatini	9	15
Botswana	7	11

Source: http://databank.worldbank.org/data/reports.aspx?source =gender-statistics# Updated April 2018. Accessed April 2018. Data not available for Mauritius, Seychelles and South Africa.

---

[38] http://www.ilo.org/ipec/Regionsandcountries/Africa/WCMS_618949/lang--en/index.htm

Child labour increased due to economic and demographic changes as well as crisis and state fragility

Next steps

Needed: basics & budgets

SADC member states and civil society partners need to:
- Develop a strategy and action plan to address the gaps in reading and mathematics for existing students and review the curriculum to eliminate these gaps for future learners.
- Campaign to change attitudes and curb violence and bullying in schools. School administrators must deal with educators' perpetrating violence in a speedy and efficient manner.
- Finalise and implement the SADC Teacher Standards.
- Implement a non-formal complementary education system to assist the elderly and older learners with literacy and skills development.

- Ensure all schools have the basic infrastructure and budgets they need to create an enabling environment for teaching, learning and promotion of inclusivity.
- Foster closer collaborations between all levels of education to raise awareness and strengthen skills in the STEM subjects.
- Invest in early childhood education with a concerted roll out plan. These foundational skills are crucial to success in subsequent years.
- Regularly measure the quality and delivery of teaching and learning.
- Administer a comprehensive situational analysis to establish why young people are out of school and then use the findings to develop a clear plan of action.

---

[39] https://www.hrw.org/report/2018/04/05/bitter-harvest/child-labor-and-human-rights-abuses-tobacco-farms-zimbabwe

CHAPTER 4

Productive resources and employment, economic empowerment

Articles 15-19

Gender equality and women's empowerment took centre stage at the SADC Industrialisation Week, held ahead of the 2017 SADC Heads of State Summit in Pretoria, South Africa.
Photo courtesy of Melody Kandare

KEY POINTS

- Women's economic equality and empowerment is central to the realisation of gender equality and women's rights in Southern Africa.

- Women make up just more than 50% of SADC's growing population, which is why legislators should address their under-representation in economic spheres if the region is to leverage the promise and potential their full participation holds.

- Men continue to dominate in key economic decision-making roles in the region.

- Women's participation in the formal economy in the SADC region remains undervalued.

- Many women and girls live in poverty and must contend with low-paid and poor-quality jobs. They also tend to be more dependent on state provisions and hold the burden of unpaid care work.

- Illicit financial flows undermine the possibility of closing financing gaps, which impedes the attainment of gender equality and women's and girl's' rights.

- SADC has adopted a Charter on Women in Science, Engineering and Technology Organisation as a way of increasing the number of women with access to STEM.

- In 2018, the Reserve Bank of Zimbabwe licenced the country's first ever women's bank to help more women access capital and other financial services.

- All SADC countries now provide for some maternity leave. The most common is a period of 12 weeks: four weeks before and six weeks after birth.

economic equality & empowerment is **central** to gender equality

Table 4.1: Trends in Economic justice since 2009

	Target 2030	Baseline 2009	Progress 2018	Variance (Progress minus 2030 target)
HUMAN DEVELOPMENT IN SOUTHERN AFRICA				
High (more than 0.7)	15 countries with the score of 1 or more. 0 = no human development	2 countries (Mauritius and Seychelles)	2 countries (Mauritius and Seychelles)	13 countries have not reached a target of more than 0.7 (Angola, Botswana, DRC, Lesotho, Madagascar, Malawi, Mozambique, Namibia, South Africa, eSwatini, Tanzania, Zambia and Zimbabwe)
Medium (between 0.55 and 0.7)	1 = optimal human development Based on: • Life expectancy at birth; • Mean years of schooling; • Expected years of schooling; and • Gross national income per capita	8 countries (Angola, Botswana, Lesotho, Madagascar, Namibia, South Africa, eSwatini and Tanzania)	4 countries (Botswana, Namibia, South Africa and Zambia)	
Low (less than 0.55)		4 countries (DRC, Malawi, Mozambique and Zambia)	9 countries (Angola, DRC, Lesotho, Madagascar, Malawi, Mozambique, eSwatini, Tanzania and Zimbabwe)	
WOMEN IN ECONOMIC DECISION-MAKING				
Proportion of women in decision-making (region)	15 countries have 50% women in positions of economic decision-making	18%	20%	No SADC country has reached this target
Highest proportion		44% (Botswana)	44% (Botswana)	
Lowest proportion		13% (Madagascar)	None (Mauritius)	
LABOUR FORCE PARTICIPATION				
Highest proportion of women	100% of women between the ages 15 and 64 are active in the labour force in 15 SADC countries	89% (Tanzania)	84% (Madagascar)	No SADC country has reached this target
Lowest proportion of women		45% (Mauritius)	43% (eSwatini)	
EARNINGS				
Lowest difference between women's and men's average earnings	Women earn on average the same as men in all 15 SADC countries	12% less than men (Namibia)	12% less than men (Botswana)	No SADC country has reached this target
Largest difference between women's and men's average earnings		58% less than men (Mauritius) Unemployment	54% less than men (eSwatini)	
UNEMPLOYMENT				
Lowest proportion of unemployed women	15 SADC countries have no unemployed women	4% (Madagascar)	2% (Madagascar)	No countries have reached this target
Highest proportion of unemployed women		26% (South Africa)	30% (Lesotho)	

Source: Gender Gap 2017, World Bank Economy data, Human Development country reports, Gender Links.

Lesotho has the **highest** proportion of unemployed

Table 4.1 shows that women still lag on all the key economic indicators in the commercial sector, highlighting the urgent need for more inclusive economies in the region. Women's participation in economic decision-making has improved only slightly, moving from 18% to 20% in the period under review. Botswana (44%) has the highest proportion of women in economic decision-making, while Mauritius has no women in economic decision-making positions. This underscores the need for Member States to fully implement Article 5 of the SADC Protocol on Gender and Development to close the existing economic justice gaps. It calls on them to implement special measures to enable women to participate equally with men in all spheres of life.

Labour force participation for both men and women continues to drop in line with the global labour market shrinkages.[1] Madagascar (84% women participation) remains the leader on this indicator despite a dip of two percentage points from last year, while eSwatini comes last in the region at 43%. In terms of unemployment, Lesotho (30%) has the highest proportion of unemployed women, while Madagascar (2%) has the lowest.

Labour force data shows that women's participation in non-traditional labour roles, such as forestry, remains limited.
Photo: Tapiwa Zvaray

---

[1] Oxfam 2018.

The key difference between the participation rate and unemployment rate is that the participation rate measures the percentage of people who work in the labour force, while the unemployment rate measures the percentage within the labour force who are currently without a job.

As highlighted in previous years, employers in all SADC states pay women less than men. The difference between women's and men's average earnings recorded in 2018 is in eSwatini, where the wage gap is 54% - almost double the global average. At 12%, Botswana has the lowest gap. An analysis of the Human Development Index also points to an increasing inequality gap. Table 4.1 shows that, while all 15 countries have not reached the target for optimal Human Development, the scores vary from a low of 0.418 in Mozambique to a high 0.781 in Mauritius. A score of one is considered optimal Human Development, taking into account life expectancy at birth; mean years of schooling; expected years of schooling; and gross national income per capita.

Of concern is the stagnation in the middle and low categories. An Africa Regional Report on the SDGs identified six key drivers of human development:
• Gender parity: women and youth empowerment;
• Access to social protection for vulnerable groups;
• Health for all, with special focus on women and child health;
• Empowerment of the elderly and disabled;
• Disaster risk reduction and management capacity and climate-adaptation initiatives; and
• Adequate shelter and access to water, sanitation and hygiene.[2]

This chapter provides an update on the progress made in closing economic justice gaps and transforming the lives of women in Southern Africa. The chapter will also discuss policy recommendations needed to achieve the economic justice-related targets of the SADC Gender Protocol. The Protocol aligns with the UN Sustainable Development Goals (SDGs) and the goals contained in Agenda 2063, a strategic framework for socio-economic transformation in Africa. The analysis will highlight key issues and challenges in achieving these targets.

Background

Despite some progress recorded over the past ten years in improving the economic status of women in the region, recent studies show that the gender gap is widening and contributing to the slow progress on human development in the region.[3] The Gender Inequality Index (GII) assesses disparities between the sexes in health, education, political participation and economic empowerment. It shows that, in countries with less inequality, such as Botswana, Mauritius, Namibia and South Africa, women obtain 96% of men's Human Development.[4] The same is not true in more unequal countries, where gender gaps persist in access to economic assets, workplace participation, entrepreneurship opportunities, and benefits from natural resources and the environment. According to United Nations Development Programme (UNDP) estimates, a 1% increase in gender inequality reduces overall Human Development by 0.75%.

A study by the World Bank found that increasing education increases the rate of economic growth for both poor and rich countries.[5] Most Grade 6 learners in 12 countries in the Southern African Development Community (SADC) have only basic mathematics and reading literacy. To achieve economic justice the region must improve the quality and nature of education on offer. Science, Technology, Engineering and Mathematics (STEM) subjects should be a major focus at all levels of education. Simultaneously, legislators must implement economic polices that ensure marginalised groups, including women, have equitable access to, and control of, productive resources and employment.

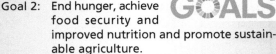

SDGs related to women's economic empowerment

Goal 1: End poverty in all its forms.
Goal 2: End hunger, achieve food security and improved nutrition and promote sustainable agriculture.
Goal 4: Ensure inclusive and equitable quality education and promote lifelong opportunities for all.
Goal 5: Achieve gender equality and empower all women and girls.
Goal 8: Promote sustainable, inclusive and sustainable economic growth full and productive employment and decent work for all.
Goal 9: Build resilient infrastructure, promote inclusive and sustainable industrialisation and foster innovation.
Goal 10: Reduce inequality within and among countries.

Most **Grade 6** learners have only **basic** mathematics and reading **literacy**

2 The 2016 Africa regional report on the sustainable development goals, United Nations Economic Commission for Africa, 2015 Addis Ababa, Ethiopia
3 Africa Economic Outlook 2016, African Development Bank, Organisation for Economic Co-operation and Development, United Nations Development Programme (2016).
4 African Economic Outlook 2017 Entrepreneurship and Industrialisation: Entrepreneurship and Industrialisation, African Development Bank, Organisation for Economic Co-operation and Development, United Nations Development Programme (2017).
5 Education Quality and Economic Growth, World Bank.

key
to
economic
growth

Agenda 2063: The Africa we want

A key lesson for Africa in the Millennium Development Goal (MDG) era proved to be the need to invest in women's economic empowerment to address the continent's main challenges.[6] Development stakeholders identified gender inequality as the driving force behind rising poverty levels, food insecurity, and gender-based violence (GBV). Thus, economic justice becomes a prerequisite to achieving the new Sustainable Development Agenda.

Agenda 2063 represents a strategic roadmap for the socio-economic transformation of Africa over 50 years. Its builds on, and seeks to hasten the enactment of, earlier and existing development frameworks for growth and development. Africa 2063 goals include the achievement of a high standard of living, quality of life and well-being for all citizens; modern agriculture for increased productivity and production; well educated citizens and a skills revolution underpinned by science, technology and innovation; transformed economies; engaged and empowered youth and children; and full gender equality in all spheres of life.

The SADC Industrialisation Strategy

This strategy, launched in 2015, notes that women and youth empowerment is critical to the future of the region and the achievement of sustainable development in it. A long-term strategy, it runs parallel to the AU Agenda 2063 and includes empowerment dimensions to widen the scope and quality of women and youth participation in the industrialisation process, notably through improved access to finance; skills development and small to medium enterprise (SMEs) support programmes; and livelihood skills of women and youth, particularly in high value-added industries.[7] This includes services, manufacturing, horticulture, transport, energy, agriculture and trade. SADC has also developed the Women's Economic Empowerment Framework, which is consistent with the SADC gender programme as stipulated by the Regional Indicative Strategic Development Plan (RISDP).[8]

Table 4.2: Economic growth and gender indicators

Country	GDP (US$ billion)	Average earning women (US$ annual)	Female population (%)	Women in economic decision- making (%)	Labour force, female (% of total labour force)	Female unemployment (%)
Angola	95.335	4789	51.0	24	75	8
Botswana	15.581	15 558	50.6	44	66	22
DRC	35.381		50.1	14	71	4
Lesotho	2.291	2258	51.5	21	59	30
Madagascar	10.001	1202	50.1	16	84	2
Malawi	5.433	1005	50.5	18	72	7
Mauritius	12.168	13 547	50.5	0	45	11
Mozambique	11.014	1122	51.2	25	82	27
Namibia	10.947	9915	51.4	25	58	25
Seychelles	1.42		50.6	31	n/a	n/a
South Africa	295.456	9938	50.9	23	48	29
Swaziland	3.720	5296	51.6	40	43	27
Tanzania	47.340	2337	50.6	21	79	3
Zambia	21.063		50.4	23	70	8
Zimbabwe	16.619	1617	51.3	23	78	4

Source: The Global Gender Gap Report, 2017, World Bank national accounts data, 2016, 2017 and OECD National Accounts data files.

Table 4.2 illustrates the economic justice disparities in the region. It shows that female unemployment rates remain high in many countries in the SADC region, with Lesotho recording the highest level at 30%. Madagascar has the lowest female unemployment rate at 2%. Madagascar also has the highest female labour force participation at 84%. Women's average income ranges from a high of $15 558 in Botswana to just $1005 in Malawi. Women comprise a majority in all countries, yet they also remain underrepresented as economic decision-makers in all SADC countries. Botswana, at 44%, comes closest to achieving parity on this indicator.

---

[6] Africa regional report on the sustainable development goals, Summary by the Economic Commission for Africa,2015.
[7] SADC Industrialisation strategy and roadmap 2015-2063,http://www.ilo.org/wcmsp5/groups/public/---africa/---ro-addis_ababa/---ilo-pretoria/documents/meetingdocument/wcms_391013.pdf
[8] www.sadc.int

Women and men in economic decision-making

Article 15.1: State parties shall ensure equal participation of women and men in policy formulation and implementation of economic policies.
Article 15.2: State parties shall ensure gender sensitive and responsive budgeting at the micro and macro levels, including tracking, monitoring and evaluation.

Since 2009, the Barometer has tracked the proportion of women in economic decision-making, which researchers define as minister, deputy minister and permanent secretaries of the Minister, Deputy Minister and Permanent Secretaries of the Ministries of Finance, Economic Planning, Trade and Industry, as well as Governors and Deputy Governors of the Reserve Banks.

Results for this indicator across all the SADC countries have consistently shown that men dominate in decision-making positions in the economic sector. The inclusion of Article 5 in the revised SADC Gender Protocol, which calls for the adoption of special measures to enable equal participation in all spheres, paves the way for a paradigm shift on appointments to key cabinet positions.

Economist Trudi Makhaya, the newly appointed economic advisor to South Africa's president. *Photo courtesy of Google images*

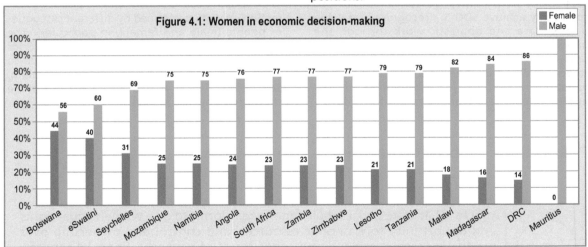

Figure 4.1: Women in economic decision-making

Source: Gender Links, 2018.

The country comparison in Figure 4.1 shows that Botswana (44%) leads the region in women in decision-making, while Mauritius had no woman representative in economic decision-making positions during the year under review. Only three countries have more than 30% of women in decision-making: Botswana, eSwatini and Seychelles.

Only **3** countries have more than **30%** in economic decision-making roles

Multiple roles of women

Article 16. 1: State parties shall:
a) Conduct time use studies and adopt policy measures to promote shared responsibility between men and women within the household and family to ease the burden of the multiple roles played by women.
b) Recognise and value unpaid cate and domestic work through the provision of public services, infrastructure and social protection policies.

WOMEN'S ECONOMIC EMPOWERMENT IN THE CHANGING WORLD OF WORK

At the 61st session of the UN Commission of the Status of Women (CSW 61) Member States adopted an agreement on the need to transform unpaid care work. It provides guidance on how to concretely achieve SDG-5: "recognise and value unpaid care and domestic work through the provision of public services, infrastructure and social protection policies, and the promotion of shared responsibility within the household and the family as nationally appropriate."[9] The Commission highlighted unpaid care work as caring for children,

the elderly, persons with disabilities and persons living with HIV and AIDS.

CSW 61 also recognised the uneven distribution of care responsibilities as a significant constraint on women's and girls' completion or progress in education; on women's entry and re-entry and advancement in the paid labour market; and on their economic opportunities and entrepreneurial activities.[10]

In SADC, only a handful of countries have conducted time use studies, sometimes called "time budget surveys," which aim to provide information on the activities people perform over a given time period. While the scope and purpose of such surveys differ enormously, the most common aim of these surveys in developing countries is to provide better information on work performed by different categories of people (male and female, in particular). The results of time-use studies provide entry points for quantifying and assigning a monetary value to work conducted by women. Malawi, Namibia, Seychelles, South Africa and Tanzania have conducted time use studies.

Productive resources and access to finance

Article 17.1: State parties shall undertake reforms to give women equal rights and opportunity to economic resources, and control and ownership over productive resources, land and other forms of property, financial services, inheritance and natural resources.
Article 17.2: State parties shall review their national trade and entrepreneurship policies to make them gender sensitive.
Article 17.3: State parties shall, in accordance with the provisions of special measures in Article 5, develop strategies to ensure that women benefit equally from economic opportunities, including those created through public procurement processes.

---

[9] Ibid.
[10] UN Women 217.

Only a handful of countries have conducted time use studies

Article 18.1: State parties shall review all policies and laws that determine access to, control of, and benefit from, productive resources by women in order to:
(a) End all discrimination against women and girls with regard to water rights and property such as land and tenure thereof;
(b) Ensure that women have equal access and rights to credit, capital, mortgages, security and training as men; and
(c) Ensure that women and men have access to modern, appropriate and affordable technology and support services.

Nearly all countries in the region have AU policies and legislation in place banning discrimination based on sex, as well as programmes to promote access to, and control over, productive resources such as land, livestock, markets, credit, modern technology and formal employment. However, according to research by the UN's Food and Agriculture Organisation (FAO), women own less than 10% of the land in most parts of Africa.[11] Young, disabled and migrant women remain the most disadvantaged in accessing land. Women's, especially young women's, "access, control and ownership of land" is a critical enabler of gender equality.[12]

Stringent credit facilities and customary practices hinder women's ownership of property: Women in SADC often lack ownership of property and resources. Immovable property such as housing usually requires a heavy investment, something most women do not have. Customary laws and practices, especially laws around inheritance, hinder widows and divorced women from owning property. In some countries, husbands must consent to wives' property ownership. The Protocol provides for protection of widows and equal access to resources.

Most landless workers in Mauritius sugarcane plantations are women.   *Photo: Sheistah Bundhoo*

Traditional systems largely govern communal land: Rural women often end up at the mercy of their deceased spouses' families when it comes to communal land ownership. Customary practices may strip a widow of the family land upon the death of her husband, under the auspices of preserving a family name. Customary laws skew ownership of assets such as cattle towards men due to inheritance practices. Where there are no sons to inherit the cattle, the male members of a husband's family may inherit the cattle. The harmful practice of widow inheritance disempowers women's economic decision making at the household level. National laws need to take into consideration the elimination of harmful customary practices to foster women's economic empowerment.

 The 1992 Land Act in **Angola** provides women and men equal land rights. However, Angola does not have a stand-alone, comprehensive land policy, and its 2004 Land Law (updating the 1992 law) does not include any statements on women's equal access to land.[13] Although women do have equal rights to property under the Civil Code and Family Code, it is unclear whether these rights extend to non-land assets, and how legislators implement such rights in practice. Regarding access to financial services, no laws exist to prevent women from opening bank accounts, from signing business contracts or from accessing property other than land.

The law in **Madagascar** upholds women's rights to ownership and Madagascar has no legal restrictions on women's access to land. Ordinance No. 60-146 of 1960 relating to land ownership gives men and women equal rights to become landowners. However, in practice, land acquisition is strongly dependent on customs which can, in some cases, infringe upon women's rights, particularly in the south of the country. Such rights denial occurs in the cases of inheritance and sharing

---

[11] Women in Agriculture Closing the gender gap for development
[12] Women and Land in Africa, A Common Position. Oxfam and Partners, 2017.
[13] OECD Gender Index, 2014

among spouses and is frequent given that most couples marry under customary practices rather than common law. Article 34 of the Constitution and Law no. 2007-002 guarantee women's access to non-land assets.

 Women in **South Africa** have entitlement to the same legal ownership rights as men, and the law guarantees them equality in the purchase, sale and management of the property. According to the Recognition of Customary Marriages Act of 1998, men and women have equal legal status regarding ownership of property (including land), with joint common ownership assumed in monogamous customary marriages unless a contract has been drawn up specifying an alternative arrangement. Laws like the Traditional Leadership and Governance Framework Act (2003) and Traditional Courts Bill (which lawmakers have proposed but not passed) marginalise women's voices, shifting the balance of power towards male household heads and traditional leaders.

Access to title deed land is also a challenge for women in **eSwatini**. While there is no specifically articulated discrimination against women, and the sole requirement is money to purchase the land, most women do not have sufficient funds - and securing bank credit is difficult. In 2012, the government issued a legal instrument amending the Deeds Registry Act, allowing women married in community of property to register and administer property (including land) in their own names.

Legislation allows women in **Zimbabwe** to have access to bank loans. The Immovable Property Prevention and Discrimination Act prohibits financial institutions from perpetuating discrimination on the grounds of sex, among other grounds, by refusing to grant loans or other financial assistance for the acquisition, hire, construction, maintenance or repair of any immovable property, to people of a particular sex.

Zimbabwe local council helps change attitudes about home ownership

Gender inequality is a key developmental issue for the city of Kadoma in Zimbabwe. In just one week, its City Council used to record as many as four court cases about property disputes linked to divorcing couples, or applications on disputed estates following a death.

The management team of the Kadoma City Council attend a gender responsive training meeting in 2016. Gender equality is a key priority for Kadoma City council. *Photo: Tapiwa Zvaraya*

Most women have no access to home ownership, especially widows and divorcees. As is common across the region, the deaths of husbands leave many women homeless after their deceased husband's relatives inherit the estate and prevent them from using it. Divorcees also suffer the same fate, as they lose the title to their properties, which authorities typically register in a man's name. Thus, many women and children became destitute or dependent on support from relatives after losing their home. To address these challenges, the City of Kadoma initiated a programme to teach women about property ownership. Most women there do not know the procedures necessary to obtain justice around property distribution. Following the training, women in Kadoma formed an association to assist themselves in this situation and help address property ownership disputes with the assistance of the Council, police and the Ministry of Gender and Women Affairs.

Council also encouraged women to facilitate joint ownership and certificate of ownership with their spouses, or to hasten change of ownership. The initiative has helped improve the livelihoods of many local women and decreased GBV in the city. Bill payments to the local authority also increased after identification and rectification of the actual tenants of the properties.

The activities have also helped build a stronger relationship between City Council and the Ministry of Women Affairs, Gender and Community Development as it has helped reduce the number of abused widows and divorcees.

Further, the campaign has increased the number of men approaching Council to include their wife and children's names as beneficiaries. More men now perceive their wives as the only legitimate inheritors of properties if they die. Men have also changed their attitudes around property ownership, increasingly consulting women when acquiring a property and ensuring joint ownership of it with their spouse.
Source: By Monica Monga for the SADC Protocol@Work Summit

Land ownership

Most African economies hinge on agriculture, which contributes an average of 30% to 40% of the GDP in the region. Smallholder women farmers make up nearly half of the labour force in Africa's agriculture sector. Subsistence and rain-fed agriculture make up the bulk of farming practices, and climate change has already significantly affected agriculture and food production. These changes hit smallholder women farmers especially hard due to their limited adaptive capacity and high levels of vulnerability. Insufficient access to justice, particularly for rural women, exacerbates the issue. Tackling the barriers that hold back agricultural production and productivity of smallholder women farmers could both enhance gender equality and usher in broader economic growth. Additionally, women and girls form the majority of those worst impacted by the effects of climate change and environmental degradation and are less likely to have access to environmental resources.[14] For women farmers to be more productive, they need equal access to environmentally and socially sustainable agricultural inputs, markets, and climate-resilient farming technologies and climate information.

Most SADC economies also remain predominantly agrarian.[15] A significant portion of those residing in rural areas survive on subsistence agriculture. These economies rely on the super-exploitation of peasant labour to subsidise labour reproduction for the formal sector. In turn, this exploitation becomes increasingly feminised as the formal sector absorbs male labour to the exclusion of female labour. The extreme inequality between men and women, urban and rural, and black and white in the colonial and post-colonial African economies reflects this exploitation.[16]

Subsistence farmers make up more than 61% of farmers in communal areas and at least 70% of agricultural produce in SADC. These women are the main providers of labour for farming and the primary managers of homes in communal areas since many men work as migrant workers in the cities or in other areas away from their homes.[17]

Women farmers show off their healthy gardens in Limpopo Province, South Africa. Women farmers thrive and improve local economies when they have access to sustainable agricultural inputs and markets.
Photo courtesy of GCC

Smallholder ♀ farmers make up nearly 1/2 of the **labour force** in the agriculture sector

---

[14] CARE International (2012) More Equal, More Resilient: Why CARE International is making gender equality and women's empowerment a priority for climate change adaptation. London: CARE International, available at: http://www.careclimatechange.org/files/CARE_Issue_Brief_010412_GenderFINAL.pdf
[15] ISSC, IDS and UNESCO (2016), World Social Science Report 2016, Challenging Inequalities: Pathways to a Just World, UNESCO Publishing, Paris.
[16] Ibid.
[17] FAO.

South Africa: Women must seize the moment

In South Africa, women make up 43% of the agricultural labour force. They are close to half of the workers on farms, in cellars, abattoirs, processing factories or markets. When it comes to small-scale farming, 69% of these farmers are women. They are the ones who complement the local market of food production in our communities.

Overall in Africa, according to the UN's Food and Agriculture Organisation, women produce up to 80% of food on the continent for personal use and to sell. Women play key roles as producers of food, managers of natural resources, income earners, and main caregivers of their families and communities.

A reality of the South African countryside is that female-headed households feature prominently as rural men historically migrate due to a lack of employment and other income-generating opportunities. This trend persists, and herein lies the initial tier of hope that the radical amendment to the property clause may portend - hope for the future of the household; a new dream to break the cycle of poverty for the daughters and sons in our rural communities; and land that can ensure we are food secure and properly sheltered, and which can stem this migration to urban centres.

But for many mothers and daughters, this dream will be shattered if they continue to have limited decision-making power and control over how to use the land or its outputs. As it is now, women rarely own the land they work, or have poor tenure security and rights to the land. Farmers Weekly magazine reports that female farmers in the country are, for the most part, "producing relatively small volumes of produce on relatively small plots of land."

While the Constitution and legal system may stipulate gender equality in access to land, customary legal arrangements and laws on marriage, divorce and inheritance can at times discriminate against women and daughters, preventing them from owning land.

This is part of the double-edged expropriation without compensation sword that black women have suffered since colonial invasion.

And it is not only about equitable ownership and access to land. Gender-based discrimination often stops rural women from attaining equitable access to education, productive resources, technologies, capital and support services, as well as the power to make decisions.

A South African woman displays her processed vegetables in Joubert Park, Johannesburg. Many women in South Africa work in the agricultural sector.
Photo: Albert Ngosa

Since 2015, the Rural Women's Assembly has championed the one woman, one hectare of land campaign the Commission for Gender Equality first proposed. It calls for the state to allocate one hectare of land for agricultural use to rural female-headed households since there is a direct link between women's right to land, economic empowerment, food security and poverty reduction. Where women have land, their families are generally better nourished, better educated and better able to break cycle of poverty.

As government's policy on land expropriation shifts, the Rural Women's Assembly calls for women in farming communities to be prioritised in the land restitution programme. At the same time, a more enabling environment should be created for women to participate in agricultural markets fully and more efficiently.

This must involve removing legal and cultural barriers to ownership and access to land, information and extension services, inputs and other resources.

Source: Farming Portal https://www.farmingportal.co.za/index. php/farminglifestyle/agri-woman/item/12598-women-must-seize-the-moment

While sex disaggregated data for land ownership in the region is scanty, the available data shows that men own most of the region's land. Given the studies showing the importance of including women in land ownership, SADC leaders should consider urgent measures to close the existing gaps.

♀ produce up to 80% of food on the continent

Table 4.3: Women land ownership in some SADC countries	
Country	% female land ownership
Malawi	37
Mozambique	13
DRC	8
Tanzania	8
Namibia	8
Zambia	7
Lesotho	6
Zimbabwe	4

Source: World Bank, 2011-2016 data.

Table 4.3 shows that, in the few SADC countries with sex disaggregated data for land ownership, Malawi ranked highest, with women owning 37% of its land followed by Mozambique at 13%. Zimbabwe (4%) takes the last position.

Mining

Despite rich mineral resource endowments in SADC, countries still have a high prevalence of poverty and inequality, even in Botswana, Namibia and South Africa, which the United Nations classifies as being in the Medium Human Development (MHD) category.[18]

Most women in the region remain excluded or marginalised from taking part in, or benefiting from, the vast mineral wealth of the region. They have limited access to mineral wealth in terms of ownership or equity participation and they are marginalised in terms of governance and management of the industry, as reflected in the tiny minority of women sitting on the boards of directors of mining companies and in senior management and supervisory positions. Women make up a very small proportion of employees in the sector. Benefits for women from corporate social responsibility expenditures of mining companies also remain limited.[19]

Women work under the most severe of the working conditions in the artisanal mining sub-sector. Increasing awareness will help to tackle the legal and institutional obstacles that reinforce discrimination against women. Strict regulations and high capital costs prevent women from owning mines and working in leadership positions in the sector. Women working in the sector face structural discrimination, violence and poor remuneration.

Women's views and voices are missing in mining; employers typically pay them less than their male counterparts, and without access or opportunities to gain technical skills, employers also often relegate them to some of the most dangerous jobs.[20] Stakeholders in the sector need to prioritise reducing violence against women as well as address women's sexual and reproductive health needs.

Women miners from South Africa take part in a media tour during the SADC Industrialisation Week. *Photo: Trevor Davies*

views and voices are missing in the mining sector

Zimbabwe: Women in mining demand protection

Women in mining experience a myriad of problems such as victimisation, dispossession of their mining claims, and gender-based violence.

Fanny Chirisa, representative of the sub-committee on women in mining in the Parliamentary Portfolio Committee on Mines and Energy, told NewsDay that women in areas such as Gwanda and Shamva pleaded with MPs to put in place a legal framework to protect them.

"Women in mining, particularly in the gold mining sector, are experiencing a number of challenges such as victimisation by male miners, dispossession of their claims, and various other forms of gender-based violence, resulting in many women fearing to venture into mining," she said.

"After the Parliamentary Portfolio Committee on Mines and Energy visited Shamva and Gwanda to speak to the affected women, it was recommended that there is need to appoint a gender focal person to address the gender-related issues in the mining sector."

---

[18] OSISA: Women and the Extractive Industry in Southern Africa.
[19] Ibid.
[20] Oxfam International (March 2017): Position Paper on Gender Justice and the Extractive Industries.

Women miners in Zimbabwe face discrimination at work and GBV.
Photo courtesy of Zimbabwe Herald

Chirisa said the mines ministry should also set up a department to specifically look at concerns of artisanal and small-scale miners in the country.

She said it is imperative to have more women in mining, which will economically empower them, as mining is one of the most lucrative sectors in the country.

"Government must invest more in women in mining and link them with strategic partners. There is also need to ensure mining laws resolve issues of gender discrepancies in the mining sector," Chirisa said, noting that women also need mining education so that they can understand mapping, the mining environment, and quality control so that they improve the quality and quantity of their mined products.

"Women in mining must be able to come up with plans and proposals that would attract investors, as well as look for partnerships which would assist their businesses to grow into big mining projects," Chirisa said.

Excerpt from an article by Veneranda Langa in NewsDay on 22 February 2018.

Access to finance

Support for women in business in SADC occurs through financing vehicles and affirmative action legislation. The region has seen the establishment of several women's banks that aim to support emerging women entrepreneurs. Recently, the Reserve Bank of Zimbabwe licenced the country's first ever women's bank.

First women's bank opens in Zimbabwe

The much-awaited women's bank opened its doors to the public in 2018, ending an anxious hiatus among prospective customers who had been waiting for the financial institution to start operating.

The opening of the Zimbabwe Women Microfinance Bank further consolidates the government's commitment towards ensuring women's participation in the mainstream economy.

Already, prospects are high that the Bank will cater for the financial needs of women, who had been struggling to get loans due to lack of collateral, among other factors.

By opening the Bank, Zimbabwe joins several countries, among them Tanzania, India and Pakistan, that have women's Banks as part of their efforts to ensure that women gain access to capital, one of the major hindrances towards their economic emancipation.

The Zimbabwe Women's Bank recently appointed Pamela Mhlanga, Zimbabwe Women's Coalition Chair and Alliance Steering Committee member, to its Board of Directors.
Photo courtesy of ZWRCN

A visit to the Bank revealed that customers, mainly women and a number of men, had begun utilising the customer care section to enquire on the basic requirements to open an account.

Rosemary Muradzi of Warren Park, who was among the first prospective customers to walk into the bank, applauded government's initiative to come up with a financial facility to cater for women.

"I am glad that the government has finally fulfilled its promise, and I believe we should be seeing the bank reaching out to all the women across the sectors, affording them an opportunity to deposit with them and also get loans in equal measure," she said.

Excerpted from an article by Ruth Butaumocho in The Herald on 14 June 2018

Despite these advancements, many barriers continue to hinder women's access to the economy in SADC. These include:

- A low level of education and business literacy among women; often relegating them to the informal economy;
- Inequalities in access to finance compared to their male counterparts that prevent women from "big business" start-ups. Most women use their own sources of income, often meagre, to raise capital for their business. This results in women owning the informal sector businesses compared to the formal sector business;
- Turn-around time to register formal businesses;
- Lack of affirmative action by firms to deliberately employ women;
- Women's needs for social protection such as maternity benefits, child care and the prevention of abuse;
- Lack of gender capacity-building in the private sector; and
- Non-enforcement of legislation and policies to include women in the private sector.

Employment

Article 19.1: State parties shall review, amend and enact laws and develop policies that ensure women and men have equal access to wage employment, to achieve full and productive employment, decent work including social protection and equal pay for work of equal value for all women and men in all sectors in line with the SADC Protocol on Employment and Labour.

Article 19.2: States parties shall review, adopt and implement legislative, administrative and other appropriate measures to ensure:
(a) Equal pay for equal work and equal remuneration for jobs of equal value for women and men;
(b) The eradication of occupational segregation and all forms of employment discrimination;
(c) The recognition of the economic value of, and protection of, persons engaged in agricultural and domestic work; and
(d) The appropriate minimum remuneration of persons engaged in agricultural and domestic work.

Article 19.3: State parties shall enact and enforce legislative measures prohibiting the dismissal or denial of recruitment on the grounds of pregnancy or maternity leave.

Article 19.4: State parties shall provide protection and benefits for women and men during maternity and paternity leave.

Article 19.5: State parties shall ensure that women and men receive equal employment benefits, irrespective of their marital status including on retirement.

In SADC, women constitute the highest proportion of the unemployed, while employed women typically work in the lowest paid positions. Most women work in the informal sector; in casual, part-time and non-permanent jobs. Most of the countries in the region do not meet the International Labour Organisation (ILO) standard of 14 weeks paid maternity leave.[21] The privatisation of essential services impacts opportunities for decent jobs for women as well as opportunities to reduce women's unpaid care responsibilities.

The SADC Protocol on Employment and Labour is amongst a number of gender aware Protocols in the region.[22] It reinforces the Provisions in the SADC Gender Protocol and provides for Laws and Policies to ensure that every person is equal and provided equal treatment and protection before the law. Governments must also undertake to promote equality of opportunity in employment and labour market policies and legislation as well as social security. Additionally, it obliges them to work to end all forms of direct or indirect discrimination on grounds such as sex, gender pregnancy, marital status, disability, age and HIV and AIDS status.

The Employment Protocol notes that Governments must take legislative, administrative and other appropriate measures to ensure equal pay for work of equal value, and equal remuneration for jobs of equal value for women and men. They must also eradicate occupational segregation and all forms of employment discrimination; adopt

---

[21] Ibid. South Africa, with 17 weeks paid maternity leave, had the highest.
[22] SADC Protocol on Employment and Labour.

Govern-ments must take **legislative** measures to

ensure

=

pay for work of

=

value

reasonable measures to enable men and women to reconcile occupational and family obligations; and create specific mechanisms for reporting and resolving cases of discrimination and intimidation of workers, particularly based on gender.

The Employment Protocol includes Provisions on preferential employment opportunities for youth, women and persons with disability; support structures to assist entrepreneurs in the establishment and development of small- and medium-sized enterprises; maternity and paternity rights; and gender sensitive training and skills development programmes. Taken together, these provisions offer a strong framework for promoting gender equality in employment in the SADC region.

Women increasingly find work in non-traditional jobs like serving as skippers in water vessels in Mauritius. *Photo: Loga Virahsawmy*

Unique products at Sandanezwe Invaders Craft and Lifestyle Centre, ESwatini

Sandanezwe Invader's Craft and Lifestyle Centre is a start-up, community-based social venture. The centre produces cloth buttons, clothes and blinds. Its craftspeople make the products using invasive alien plants such as Siam weed, paraffienbos and the organisation's titular Sandanezwe weeds.

As well as providing employment for disabled artists and their parents, who make all the products in the centre, the eco-friendly craft factory and store also helps save the indigenous flora and fauna from invasive weeds.

Thanks to the centre's success, the community now understands that people with disabilities, with the right support and access to equal opportunities, have the power to improve their livelihoods and address local challenges.

Labour force participation
Labour force participation measures the proportion of a specific population (such as women and older workers) considered to be either working or actively searching for a job. Researchers consider people of working age to be between the ages of 16 and 64. Students, homemakers and retired people younger than 64 do not count as part of the labour force. Labour force participation in this report also includes those working in the employment sector.

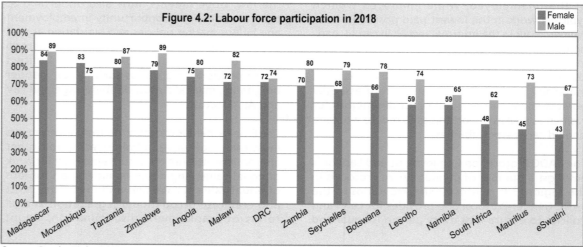

Figure 4.2: Labour force participation in 2018

Legend: Female, Male

Country	Female	Male
Madagascar	84	89
Mozambique	83	75
Tanzania	80	87
Zimbabwe	79	89
Angola	75	80
Malawi	72	82
DRC	72	74
Zambia	70	80
Seychelles	68	79
Botswana	66	78
Lesotho	59	74
Namibia	59	65
South Africa	48	62
Mauritius	45	73
eSwatini	43	67

Source: Gender Links, 2018.

Figure 4.2 shows that Madagascar has the highest proportion of women's participation in the labour force (84%) while eSwatini recorded the lowest at 43%. Tanzania (80 %) has slipped from pole position in 2016 to third place. Four countries (South Africa, Mauritius, ESwatini and the Comoros recorded a score less than 50%. Some countries show a slight gap between women and men, such as Madagascar and DRC, while others have a large disparity, such as Mauritius (with men at 73% and women at 45%).

Zimbabwe council provides training for staff with skill gaps

Chinhoyi Municipality in Zimbabwe has committed to efficiency and effective delivery of quality service to its stakeholders. For its employees to respond to trends more effectively and meet organisational demands, the council decided to train and development its staff.

The municipality has 369 employees and almost three quarters of them lack the necessary skills and qualifications, thereby causing a threat to quality service delivery. The council's training project thus set out to improve employee performance and impart knowledge and skills to develop staff capacity.

Council's first step in this process involved identifying skill gaps and then engaging the relevant employees. The council then began the employee training process.

In implementing the project, the municipality works with universities such as Zimbabwe Open University and Chinhoyi University. The campaign has resulted in change at the household level for many women, who have now become breadwinners. This empowers local women and fosters a redistribution of labour in the home: men now assist women with household chores.

Many women who received education through this project have also been promoted to key decision-making positions, including the chief town planner, Hilda Kabangure, who attained a master's degree in business administration.

The project also appraises employees to monitor their progress. Thanks to the initiative, men working for the municipality have become increasingly supportive of burgeoning women's leadership in the community.
Source: By Rumbidzai Kapesa for the SADC Protocol@Work Summit.

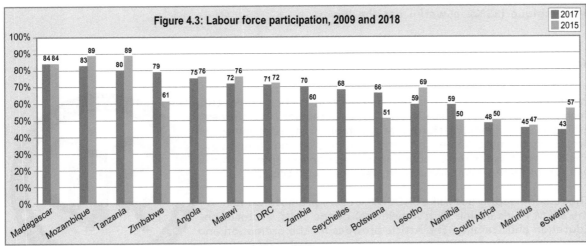

Figure 4.3: Labour force participation, 2009 and 2018

Source: Gender Gap 2016 and World bank 2017, accessed 13 June 2018.

Figure 4.3 shows that, over the period 2009 to 2018, women's participation in the labour force has decreased in nine countries (Mozambique, Tanzania, Angola, Malawi, DRC, Lesotho, South Africa, Mauritius and eSwatini). Four countries (Zimbabwe, Zambia, Botswana and Namibia) recorded increases, with Zimbabwe posting the biggest increase, from 61% to 79%.

In 2017, UN Women launched a campaign called #StoptheRobbery aimed at bringing attention to the gender pay gap.[23] According to the organisation, women across the world only make $0.77 for every dollar a man earns for work of equal value.

In Southern Africa, a gender division of labour exists in all 15 countries, with women predominating in lower paid areas traditionally associated with women, such as domestic work, teaching (at primary level), nursing, secretarial and clerical posts. Men dominate in higher paid professions such as engineering, construction, security, and in decision-making roles. The different value that society attaches to these kinds of work reflects in the average earnings of women and men.

Table 4.4: Average annual earnings in the SADC region			
	Women earnings (US$)	Men earnings (US$)	Women's earnings as a proportion of men's earnings (%)
Angola	4789	8277	58
Lesotho	2258	3847	59
South Africa	9938	16 635	60
Madagascar	1202	1812	66
Zimbabwe	1617	2417	67
Tanzania	2337	3247	72
Malawi	1005	1337	75
Mozambique	1122	1317	85
Mauritius	13 547	28 781	47
eSwatini	5296	11 586	46
Botswana	15 558	17 940	87
Namibia	9915	11 293	88

Source: The Global Gender Gap report 2016.

Table 4.4 shows the average earnings of women compared to men, highlighting that none of the SADC countries in which researchers can obtain data have achieved gender pay equity. Namibia has the closest to equitable earnings between women and men, with women earning 88% what men earn, followed by Botswana (87%) and Mozambique (85%). eSwatini has the lowest proportion of female to male earnings (46%) followed by Mauritius at 47%. Women in Malawi earn the least in the region, with an average wage of $1005, while women in Botswana earn the most with an average wage of $15 558. Men earn most in Mauritius ($28781) and least in Mozambique ($1317).

SADC adopts Charter on Women in Science, Engineering, and Technology

Policymakers adopted the Charter on Women in Science, Engineering and Technology Organisation (SADC WISETO) in December 2017, thus establishing a new regional platform that will implement programmes and projects to promote women in Science, Engineering and Technology. The Charter calls for the establishment of national chapters, which will constitute the membership of the regional SADC WISETO.

The region needs a body like SADC WISETO to promote women in the STEM fields in line with Article 3(e) of the SADC Protocol on Education and Training. The Article provides for the promotion and coordination in the formulation and implementation of policies, strategies and programmes for the promotion and application of science and technology, including modern information technology; and research and development in the region.

---

[23] UN Women, 2017.

Table 4.5: Conditions of employment across the SADC region				
Country	Maternity leave	Paternity leave	Retirement age and benefits for women and men	Sexual harassment provisions
Angola	**Yes** Three months paid.[24]	**No**	**No** Women at 55, men at 60. In public service, women can retire after 30 years, and men after 35 years, of service.	**No** While not illegal, some cases can be prosecuted under assault or defamation statutes.
Botswana	**Yes** Twelve weeks, six before, six after. Entitled to additional two weeks due to illness. Allowance of not less than 25% of the basic pay or 50 Thebe (US 5 cents) per day, whichever is greater.	**No**	**Yes** Same for women and men.	**Some** Recognised in the Public Service Act covering the public sector, but very few ministries mention this in their policies; some institutions have incorporated sexual harassment policies.
DRC	**Yes** Part of the Labour code. During maternity leave, a maternity allowance of 67% of the employee's basic pay.	**Yes** Part of the Labour code.	**Yes** Part of the Social Security Law.	**Yes** Part of the Labour code and the Sexual Violence Law.
Lesotho[25]	**Yes** Two weeks after one-year employment in the clothing, textile and leather industries. Six weeks in the private sector. Ninety days paid maternity leave to permanently employed female public servants. It remains at the discretion of the employer whether to pay full salary or part.	**No** There is a proposal for a Paternity Leave Bill to grant fathers a month's leave.	**Yes** Most employment sectors, including the public sector, are gender neutral on the issue.	**Yes** The 1992 Labour Code Order Sec. 200 prohibits sexual harassment in the workplace. "Any person who offers employment or who threatens dismissal [on the basis of] sexual favours or harasses workers sexually shall commit an unfair labour practice" (page 1350).
Madagascar	**Yes** Six weeks before, six weeks after for the private sector. Two months in the public sector.	**Yes** The Labour Act grants three days of paternity leave for the private sector, 15 days for the public sector.	**Yes, public service.** **No, private sector.** Sixty years for both sexes in public service. 55 for women and 60 for men in private sector.	**Yes** In general, the Labour Act guarantees respect for human dignity in all labour relations. Article 23 forbids sexual harassment.
Malawi	**Yes** Found in the Employment Act Sec 47.	**No** There is a public debate on the issue.	**Yes** 55 for women and 60 for men.	**Yes** Penal code criminalises sexual harassment. The Gender Equity Act (2013) addresses the same with clear provisions.

Lesotho lawmakers have drafted a **Paternity Leave Bill**

---

[24] However, there is no data on how many women benefit or know about this provision.
[25] Source: Labour Code 1992, Public Service Regulations 1969, Labour Code Wages (Amendment) Order 2007 and Interviews 2009.

Country	Maternity leave	Paternity leave	Retirement age and benefits for women and men	Sexual harassment provisions
Mauritius[26]	Yes[27] After one year of employment, 12 weeks, The Employment Rights Act (ERA) 2008.	Yes A male worker shall be entitled to five continuous working days.	Yes First Schedule of the Employment Rights Act up to the age of 65 years. A female officer recognising five years' service may retire on grounds of marriage irrespective of age.	Yes Sexual Harassment is provided in Part IV of the Discrimination Act 2002.
Mozambique[28]	Yes Sixty days, after which she can take up to an hour a day for breastfeeding, for a year unless otherwise prescribed by a clinician.	Yes This consists of two days consecutive or alternate leave during the 30 days from the date of birth of the child, every two years.	No 65 for men and 60 for women.	N/A
Namibia[29]	Yes 100% pay for the maternity leave period.	No	Yes 60 years for both women and men.	Yes A clause in the Labour Act, while difficult to define, condones sexual harassment.
Seychelles[30]	Yes Fourteen weeks paid leave, at least ten weeks to be taken after birth. Additionally provides for four weeks unpaid leave. A female worker cannot return to work before her paid leave is over.	No The Constitution and Employment acts make no reference to paternity leave or the roles of a working father. Order 102 of the Public Service Order (2011) makes provisions for sick leave for employees with a sick child, without being gender-specific.	Yes Compulsory at age 63. Retirement pay is equal for both, pension income depends on individual contributions, and social security benefits are equal.	Yes Employment Act protects all employees from any form of harassment in general and Public Officers' "Ethics Act" (2008), which is applicable to government, makes explicit reference to sexual harassment. Neither provides a clear definition. The Act is under review and efforts are being made to strengthen the law and bring it into compliance with International Labour Organisation (ILO) standards.
South Africa	Yes Four months; four weeks before, six after. The law also entitles a woman undergoing miscarriage in the third trimester of pregnancy or bearing a stillborn child to maternity leave.	Yes Three days.	No 65 for men and 60 for women.[31]	Yes The South African law prohibits sexual and other forms of harassment under the Employment Equity Act 1998 and the Equity Act. The country has issued a code of Good Practice on Sexual Harassment.

[26] 2008.
[27] For a miscarriage, two weeks leave on full pay. After a still-born child, a woman shall be entitled to a maximum of 12 weeks leave. A worker who is nursing is entitled every day at a time convenient to her at least two breaks of half an hour or one break of one hour for a period of six months.

Country	Maternity leave	Paternity leave	Retirement age and benefits for women and men	Sexual harassment provisions
eSwatini	**Yes** At least 12 weeks with two weeks fully paid after delivery. One-hour nursing breaks with pay per day for three months after maternity leave. Applicable if an employee has been in continuous employment with the same employer for 12 months, and only once after the lapse of 24 months from the previous maternity leave.	**No** There is no debate yet about providing it. Certain customs dictate that men should not be in close contact with new-born babies.	**Yes** 60 for women and 55 for men.	**No** The Employment Act is silent on the issue. The Sexual Offence and Domestic Violence Bill has a provision on sexual harassment.
Tanzania	**Yes** Eighty-four days paid maternity leave.	**Yes** Three days.	**Yes** The Employment and Labour Relations Act of 2004 states: Every employer shall ensure that he promotes an equal opportunity in employment and strives to eliminate discrimination.	**Yes** The Employment and Labour Relations Act of 2004 states: Harassment of an employee shall be a form of discrimination and shall be prohibited.
Zambia	**Yes** Employment and Industrial Relation Act: After two years of employment, a woman is entitled to 90 days. However, there is a campaign to increase the number of days to about 180 to encourage exclusive breastfeeding.	**No legal provision.** Some organisations allow a man to be on leave for a few days after the birth of a child. This is usually provided for in a collective agreement.	**Yes** Both men and women retire at the age of 55.	**No** Some organisations have in-house policies on sexual harassment. However, if reported, such cases would be dealt with under the Penal code.
Zimbabwe	**Yes** An amendment to the Labour Relations Act has increased maternity leave from 90 to 98 days in line with the ILO Convention No. 183 on Maternity Protection.	**No** Draft bill in place and yet to be presented in parliament	**No** The age of retirement in the private sector is provided for in the collective bargaining agreements for each sector in the private sector. In the public sector, the retirement age is 65 in terms of S17 of the Public Service Regulations.	**Yes** S8 of the Labour Act provides for the prohibition of sexual harassment as an unfair labour practice.

Both ♀ & ♂ retire at the age of **55** in Zambia

[28] 2009.
[29] Labour Act/Reviewed 2007/8 (2007).
[30] Source: Employment Act, 1991 revised 1995.
[31] A case was brought by one gentleman who argued that the differentiation in terms of retirement age was discriminatory towards men.

Table 4.5 shows several conditions of employment across SADC countries, including retirement age, maternity benefits and provisions for policies against sexual harassment.
It highlights that:

- All SADC countries provide for some maternity leave. The most common is a period of 12 weeks: four weeks before and six weeks after birth.
- Mozambique and Zambia have Provisions to encourage breastfeeding.
- The DRC, Madagascar and Tanzania have accommodated all the provisions in the table, with varying forms of maternity and paternity leave, equal retirement age, and sexual harassment clauses.
- Only six of the 15 countries provide for paternity leave. Those countries that do not should review their policies, considering that the 2014 SADC Protocol on Employment and Labour makes paternity leave mandatory.
- Nine of the 15 countries have equal retirement age benefits, with the others differing by an average of five years between women and men, mostly with women at 60 and men at 65.
- Ten of the 15 countries have measures in place to address sexual harassment in the workplace.

Formalising the informal sector

The informal economy, often characterised by either cross-border trade or vending, provides a livelihood for countless poor women in developing nations, especially in Africa, including Southern Africa. The informal economy acts as a safety net for unemployed people in the region, as outlined in a SADC Advocacy Strategy.[32]

The growth of informal cross border trade (ICBT) in Africa tends to align, in most cases, with increasing poverty and weak employment conditions.[33] ICBT is not only a common feature of expanding intra-Africa trade, it has also been incentivised over the years through dysfunctional policies that have resulted in shrinkage of the region's formal economic sector.[34] Further, the sole reason for women's engagement in ICBT is economic: that is, women have few other formal opportunities to earn income.[35]

Therefore, ICBT is not only a means of survival as formal sector job opportunities shrink, but a source of income and employment that plays a crucial role in household poverty reduction, thus complementing development objectives in African states. Most women work in ICBT as their main source of income and they tend to use the income earned from ICBT to meet the basic needs of their households: to buy food and pay for rent, school fees and healthcare services.

While women tend to be overrepresented in ICBT, gender dimensions also exist in the types of goods traded through the sector. There are clear differences between regions and countries. For instance, female informal cross border traders in Tanzania tend to dominate trade in industrial products while men in that country often trade agricultural products.[36]

Gofaone Ntwaetsile (left), a Gender Links Entrepreneurship Programme beneficiary from Ghanzi, Botswana selling food to a customer in her new restaurant.   *Photo: Keletso Metsing*

[32] OSISA: Women working in the informal economy: Challenges and Policy Considerations, 2015.
[33] Formalisation of informal trade in Africa: Trends, experiences and socioeconomic impacts, FAO, 2017.
[34] World Social Science Report 2016.
[35] Ibid.
[36] Ibid.

Regional summits highlight best practices linked to education and economic development

Gender Links (GL) works with all levels of government, organisations and communities to implement strategies and programmes to meet the targets set in the Revised SADC Protocol on Gender and Development. GL gathers good practices and analyses how they are contributing to the implementation of the targets set in the Protocol.

Regional stakeholders presented 64 good practices on education and economic development at summits between 2017 and 2018. Some of the main findings from the summits included:

- **STEM education is critical to economic growth:** Most growth industries require this knowledge and the region must increase the number people in these fields.
- **The economic agenda includes gender sensitive labour practices:** More than 60% of case studies covered the right to gender sensitive labour practices and the right to equal opportunities to economic resources, and control and ownership over productive resources, land and other forms of property, financial services, inheritance and natural resources.
- **Equal wages and fair labour practices are less of a priority:** Only 44% of the economic development case studies focused on fair labour practice while 38% focused on equal wages. The World Bank's report the, Unrealised Potential: The High Cost of Gender Inequality in Earnings, says that if women earned as much as men they would add $160 trillion to human capital worldwide.[37]
- **Recognition of unpaid care work and domestic work receives little attention:** Only 18% of case studies addressed unpaid care and domestic work.
- **There is an increased focus on entrepreneurship and employment:** Entrepreneurship and employment featured in more than 60% of case studies. Most initiatives take place at community level, ranging from catering and sewing to producing cayenne pepper.
- **Innovative employment intitiatives thrive at the local level:** For example, the Chegutu Young Men's Christian Association started a project employing women and men to manufacture sanitary pads to assist young women in the community who cannot afford the mass-produced commercial alternatives.
- **There is limited attention on land rights:** Only 27% of the case studies on economic development focused on land rights. Women have to secure land for agricultural purposes and food security, to guarantee shelter, to use for investment and to build a sustainable base for productive resources.

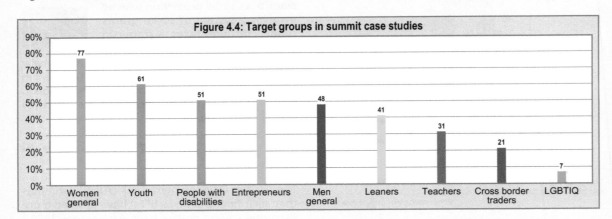

Figure 4.4: Target groups in summit case studies

Figure 4.4 shows that a high proportion of good practices target people with disabilities, while most of the economic justice entries target women. Less than half of the entries target men in general, learners and teachers, while only 21% of the case studies target cross border traders. As noted earlier, women cross border traders face many challenges, including high levels of GBV.

Almost equal numbers of NGOs and local government submitted economic and education good practices. Meanwhile, more than 75% of the good practices recorded changes in communities and society. Most of the good practices indicated a change of attitude and reduced stigma; greater public awareness; improved services and changes of behaviour. Unfortunately, a recurring theme is the lack of change in policy and regualtion, the only way to gaurantee sustainable change.

Source: GL Protocol@Work Summits

---

[37] http://www.worldbank.org/#a

Social protection

The area of social protection consists of policies and programmes designed to reduce poverty and vulnerability by promoting efficient labour markets, diminishing people's exposure to risks, and enhancing their capacity to manage economic and social risks, such as unemployment, exclusion, sickness, disability and old age. The SDGs and the June 2016 updated Protocol place a growing emphasis on social protection as a means of alleviating poverty and achieving gender equality. Existing social protection systems in SADC countries rarely address issues of care and decent work, except in the field of HIV and AIDS.

Women require social protection due to inadequately defined property rights linked to major productive assets such as land and cattle, while girls provide labour for various tasks, thus foregoing education. Challenges faced by SADC governments in effectively implementing social protection include making it more gender sensitive, administrative inefficiencies, inadequate funding, weak coordination of social protection initiatives and inadequate coverage of vulnerable groups.

SOUTH AFRICAN SOCIAL SECURITY AGENCY

The South African Social Security Agency runs the largest social security programme in Southern Africa.
Photo courtesy of Google images

In **Lesotho**, several social protection policies and programmes address specific aspects of poverty. Three strands that provide social protection include the Food Security Policy, social welfare programmes and disaster management interventions. The Ministry of Agriculture and Food Security adopted the Food Security Policy, which includes many social protection principles and programmes. These include public transfers and social safety nets, promotion of food production, mainstreaming HIV and AIDS, managing food aid and food stocks, and employment promotion. The Department of Social Welfare provides social assistance to targeted vulnerable groups.

In **Malawi**, some girls between the ages of 13 and 22 receive social protection cash transfers. Researchers found these girls spend more time in school and have a 60% lower HIV and AIDS prevalence rate than those in control groups. Social protection in Malawi focuses on education and health.

Mozambique adopted the Social Protection Law (4/2007) in 2007. In 2009, legislators also adopted the Regulation for Basic Social Security, while in 2010 they approved the National Strategy for Basic Social Security. Thus, Mozambique has made noteworthy progress in establishing a legal and policy framework for the implementation of social protection programmes. This framework is a step in the right direction towards setting up a social protection floor. The Social Protection Law organises the social protection system at three levels, namely, basic social security, obligatory social security and complementary social security. The systems assure universal access to primary health care and education by the most vulnerable. The law has no specific gender provisions.

Namibia's social protection scheme involves a system of social grants funded through taxes, a state-run contri-butory component and a privately-managed pension system for the formally employed in the private sector. Social transfers in Namibia play a role in reducing inequality, although this impact is less significant than the role they play in reducing poverty.

Gender dimensions of illicit financial flows

The African Development Bank (AfDB) estimates that illicit financial flows (IFFs) have drained more than one trillion dollars from Africa since 1980 - 5.5% of the GDP - exceeding Foreign Direct Investment (FDI) and Official Development Assistance (ODA). The AU estimates that 25% of GDP of African countries is lost to corruption every year.[39] This affects tax revenue and has a direct impact on the provision of social services, care services and social protection.[40] Institutionalised corruption continues to contribute to IFFs.

[38] UNDP: Social Protection in Africa, A Review of Potential Contribution and Impact on Poverty Reduction, March 2014.
[39] Africa Union.
[40] SADC Gender Protocol Barometer, 2017.

Where is the money?

On 31 May 2018, FEMNET hosted an hour-long webinar titled "Where is the Money?" with the intention to shine a spotlight on the issue of illicit financial flows and their gendered impact. The webinar sought to empower gender activists with the knowledge needed to amplify advocacy efforts to #StopTheBleeding in a way that will ultimately serve women and girls.

Liz Nelson, director of the Tax Justice Network, spoke about the feminisation of poverty, noting that women and girls remain disproportionately affected by the poverty that comes about as a result of IFFs. She said they suffer the extra burden of taking on a bulk of consumption taxes created to cushion governments against IFFs, as well as having to endure the experience of deteriorating public services.

Noting that tax justice issues are fundamental to respecting the rights of women, Nelson's presentation touched on the Bogota Declaration on Tax Justice for Women's Rights, launched in 2017, and its importance in pushing for tax justice and highlighting the impact of IFFS on women and girls. The declaration "sets out shared values and demands rights for women which can be realised through structural, systemic, cultural and fiscal policy changes."[41]

Caroline Othim, Policy and Campaigns Coordinator of the Global Alliance for Tax Justice (GATJ), spoke about the scale of the impact of IFFs and the amount of these illicit funds leaving the continent over the years ($100 billion USD annually). Stating that regressive consumption tax and privatisation will not help failing public systems, Othim advocated for coalition-building to push for tax justice. She also noted the need for gender and inequality assessments of all tax provisions and policy objectives. Othim ended her presentation with a call to all stakeholders to lend their voices in the fight to bring back Africa's money.

FEMNET continues to lead on macroeconomic policy in the women's rights space and recognises that IFFs exacerbate inequalities that only benefit male-dominated corporations. FEMNET believes that women's rights activists and tax-paying citizens can no longer remain on the margins of conversations on this emerging issue and the organisation plans to continue the conversation and the call for tax justice.

Source: Femnet

The digital divide

While there is scanty data about the digital divide in Southern Africa, studies from across the globe point to gender gaps in the use of information technology (IT). One paper on the digital divide (Robinson. L et al, 2010) highlights how usage of digital tools varies across countries, even within the developed world.[42]

Researchers point out that, while earlier research on gender and digital inequalities focused on identifying gaps and differences, recent studies have explored the mechanisms that underlie these gaps and the consequences for outcomes such as building social capital, employment opportunities and educational attainment. An important question is whether women use computers, the internet and mobile devices to the same extent as men.

Recent evidence suggests that digital inequalities intersect with gender in two main ways: through

Recent **evidence** suggests that **digital** inequalities **intersect** with **gender**

[41] https://www.taxjustice.net/2017/12/07/bogota-declaration-tax-justice-womens-rights/
[42] Laura Robinson, Shelia R. Cotten, Hiroshi Ono, Anabel Quan-Haase, Gustavo Mesch, Wenhong Chen, Jeremy Schulz, Timothy M. Hale & Michael J. Stern (2015) Digital inequalities and why they matter, Information, Communication & Society, 18:5, 569-582, DOI:10.1080/1369118X.2015.1012532.

the gendering of skills and content production patterns, and through gendered labour market processes associated with jobs involving technology. Both processes call for further investigation. Our behaviour online is an extension of broader social roles, interests, and expectations existent in society. We know that women are more likely to use the internet for communication and social support.

Deficiencies in online skills can have real consequences for online behaviour. Even though, in many cases, women adopt and use IT at the same rates as men, men still far outnumber women among IT developers and designers (and in corporate IT positions), a gap which only policy interventions can narrow.

Harnessing the demographic dividend

The 29th African Union Summit in 2017 declared "Harnessing the Demographic Dividend Through Investments in the Youth" as its theme. This connects to Agenda 2063 and offers a comprehensive development vision for the African continent. The youth of SADC will be the future of the region and they play a central in the implementation of the region's Sustainable Development Agenda. By 2030, Africa's youth population will increase by 42% from 226 million in 2015 and studies predict it will keep rising.[43] Thus, the Summit identified a vital entry point to empower and educate the leaders of tomorrow as they inherit an increasingly over-populated continent.

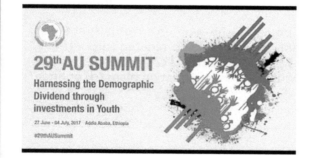

Achieving gender equality is another critical goal for SADC as it attempts to harness the demographic dividend. Young women remain absent in many discussions on youth development, with their voices considered peripheral and their bodies constructed as sites to be acted on through policy prescriptions developed by others for them.[44]

Next steps

The analysis in this chapter has shown how women's economic empowerment lies at the centre of achieving gender equality in the region. Recent findings and comparisons over the past ten years have shone the spotlight on the challenges that continue to hinder women in SADC from fully participating in the economic sphere. While the analysis has shown that regional stakeholders have successfully created policy frameworks on women's economic empowerment, implementation remains a challenge. In the coming year, SADC member states and other stakeholders in the sector should prioritise the following areas:

- Adopt special measures to increase the number of women in economic decision-making as provided for by the Protocol.
- Transform formal schooling and literacy programmes to ensure a well-educated future workforce.
- Close the wage gaps between women and men.
- Tackle the unequal share of unpaid care work and unequal distribution of domestic duties between women and men.
- Lobby for equal wages and the recognition of unpaid care and domestic work.
- Carry out time use surveys to better understand gender gaps in the sector.
- Invest in skill development in STEM areas for women.
- Implement new and existing Policies to improve access to productive resources for women.
- Improve the collection and availability of data, building capacity for national statistical offices, as data is crucial for tracking progress.
- Address the growth of informal cross border trade and develop policies to protect women in this sector.
- Prioritise funding for gender equality initiatives, especially in those areas, highlighted in this chapter, where countries have been lagging. This will also ensure accountability for commitments made by member states.

---

[43] African Union Roadmap on Harnessing the Demographic Dividend through Investments in Youth in response to AU Assembly decision (assembly/au/dec.601 (xxvi) on the 2017 theme of the year 2017.
[44] Young women and the demographic dividend, African Women's Development and Communication Network (FEMNET), June 2017.

CHAPTER 5

Gender Based Violence

Articles 20-25

Campaigners in Botswana call for an end to gender violence during the 16 Days of Activism.
Photo: Gender Links

Criminal justice system responses to GBV remain weak throughout the region

KEY POINTS

- Member States are vying for a regional approach to meet the goal of "eliminating" gender-based violence by 2030.
- Despite the fact that 12 out of the 15 countries now have Domestic Violence Legislation and 13 have Sexual Assault Legislation, criminal justice system responses to GBV remain weak throughout the region.
- Fourteen countries now have Legislation on sexual harassment.
- All countries have laws on human trafficking, but many lack the data to track victims.
- All countries offer some form of services to survivors of GBV, however under-resourced NGOs continue to do most of the work.
- All countries offer comprehensive treatment, including PEP, to survivors of violence.
- Seven countries have undertaken Violence Against Women (VAW) Baseline studies.
- Botswana and Seychelles studied both violence against women (VAW) and violence against men (VAM), allowing for an informed and gender-specific response to GBV.
- Throughout the region, social media has emerged as a strong tool for social mobilisation as well as for increasing the visibility of various forms of GBV.
- Member States acknowledge the urgent need for a comprehensive, reliable and coordinated instrument to collect data on GBV. There is need for all SADC countries to conduct GBV prevalence studies to track progress towards eliminating GBV.
- The European Union and the United Nations have invested 500 million euros towards the Spotlight Initiative, a global movement aimed at achieving significant improvements in the lives of women and girls. In Africa, the initiative targets harmful practices.

Table 5.1: Trends in GBV since 2009			
	Baseline 2009	**Progress 2018**	**Variance (Progress minus 2030 target)**
LEGISLATION			
Laws on domestic violence in 15 countries	9 (Botswana, Madagascar, Malawi, Mauritius, Mozambique, Namibia, Seychelles, South Africa, Zimbabwe)	12 (Angola, Botswana, Madagascar, Malawi, Mauritius, Mozambique, Namibia, Seychelles, South Africa, eSwatini, Zambia, Zimbabwe)	-3 (DRC, Lesotho, Tanzania)
Laws on sexual assault in 15 countries	7 (DRC, Lesotho, Madagascar, Mozambique, Namibia, South Africa, eSwatini)	13 (DRC, Lesotho, Madagascar, Mozambique, Namibia, South Africa, eSwatini, Mauritius, Zambia, Tanzania, Zimbabwe Botswana, Malawi)	-2 (Angola, Seychelles)
Human trafficking laws in 15 countries	3 (Madagascar, Mozambique, Zambia)	15 (Angola, DRC, Lesotho, Madagascar, Malawi, Mauritius, Mozambique, Namibia, South Africa, eSwatini, Tanzania, Botswana, Zambia, Zimbabwe, Seychelles)	0
Sexual harassment laws in 15 countries	2 (DRC, Madagascar)	14 (DRC, Lesotho, Madagascar, Malawi, Mauritius, South Africa, Zambia, Zimbabwe, Namibia, Seychelles, Botswana, Mozambique, eSwatini, Tanzania)	-1 (Angola)
GBV SERVICES			
Accessible, affordable and specialised services, including legal aid, to survivors of GBV in 15 countries	9 (Angola, Lesotho, Mauritius, Mozambique, Namibia, Seychelles, South Africa, Zambia, Zimbabwe)	12 (Angola, DRC, Lesotho, Malawi, Mauritius, Mozambique, Namibia, Seychelles, South Africa, Tanzania, Zambia, Zimbabwe)	0
Specialised facilities including places of shelter and safety in 15 countries	3 (Mauritius, South Africa, Botswana)	14 (Angola, DRC, Lesotho, Madagascar, Malawi, Mauritius, South Africa, Tanzania, Zimbabwe, Namibia, Zambia, Botswana, eSwatini, Mozambique)	-1 (Seychelles)
Comprehensive treatment, including post exposure prophylaxis (PEP) in 15 countries	2 (South Africa- Sexual Offences Act, Mozambique- HIV AIDS Act) Botswana since 2008(HIV Policy 2008)	15 (DRC, Lesotho, Madagascar, Malawi, South Africa, Zimbabwe, Tanzania, Seychelles, Botswana Namibia, Mauritius, eSwatini, Zambia, Angola, Mozambique)	0
COORDINATION, MONITORING AND EVALUATION			
Integrated Approaches: National Action Plans in 15 countries	7 (DRC, Mauritius, Namibia, Seychelles, South Africa, eSwatini, Tanzania)	15 (Angola, DRC, Lesotho, Madagascar, Malawi, Mauritius, Mozambique, Namibia, Seychelles, South Africa, eSwatini, Tanzania, Zambia, Zimbabwe, Botswana)	0
By 2030 construct a composite index for measuring GBV in 15 countries	None	9 (Botswana, DRC, Lesotho Mauritius, South Africa, Zambia, Zimbabwe, Angola, Seychelles)	6 (Malawi, Namibia, Mozambique, Madagascar, eSwatini)
By 2030 provide baseline data on GBV in 15 countries	None	7 (Botswana, Mauritius, four provinces of South Africa, four/ provinces of Zambia, Lesotho Zimbabwe, Tanzania)	8 (Angola, DRC, Malawi, Namibia, Mozambique, Madagascar, Tanzania, eSwatini)

Source: Gender Links, 2018.

Table 5.1 shows that 12 SADC countries (up from nine in 2009) have implemented Domestic Violence Legislation and 13 have Sexual Assault Legislation. Three countries (DRC, Lesotho and Tanzania) have yet to enact specific domestic violence laws. In 2009, two countries had laws on Sexual Harassment and three had legislation on human trafficking. Fourteen countries now have legislation on Sexual Harassment and all countries have laws on Human Trafficking. Despite the existence of relevant laws, enforcement remains a challenge due to limited resources as well as existing clashes between civil and traditional law in some settings, especially Lesotho and eSwatini (Musariri et al, 2015).[1]

The region has made significant strides on raising awareness around GBV laws and GBV in general. The growing use of social media as a campaign

[1] Musariri, L., Machisa M, T,. Nyambo, V. and Chiramba, K. (2014) The Gender based violence Indicators Study: Lesotho. Gender Links available at http://genderlinks.org.za/programme-web-menu/publications/gender-based-violence-indicators-study-lesotho-2015-02-27/

The region has made **significant** strides on GBV laws

tool accounts for much of this progress. Botswana provides a good case study: a comparison between the 2012 study and 2018 study show a notable increase in awareness of both GBV laws and campaigns in that country (Chiramba et al, 2018).[2]

Police officer Morongoe Makaliana addresses participants during a 2017 community dialogue on GBV in Mohales Hoek Lesotho.
Photo: Ntolo Lekau

Regarding GBV services, in 2009, nine countries offered accessible, affordable and specialised services, including legal aid, to survivors of GBV. Now all 15 countries offer some form of services to survivors of GBV. As previous Barometers highlighted, NGOs continue to carry the larger burden as service providers. Yet given funding for GBV services is increasingly limited, under-resourced NGOs struggle to deliver on their mandates. Services remain unevenly distributed, with rural areas largely disadvantaged. The number of countries that offer places of safety for GBV survivors has risen from only two countries in 2009 to 14 in 2018. However, the number and quality of services and resources available to survivors of GBV remains sub-standard. Again, small NGOs run most of the services (Lowe Morna et al, 2017).[3]

In 2009, only two countries provided PEP to survivors of sexual violence under statutory obligation.[4] Today, all 15 countries offer comprehensive treatment, including PEP, to survivors of violence. Having reached the quantitative target, there is need to devise new ways of measuring progress that focus on the quality of services rendered as well as the actual impact in the lives of ordinary people.

On coordination of GBV programmes, since the last reporting, only seven countries have undertaken GBV Baseline Studies (Botswana, Lesotho, Mauritius, Seychells, South Africa, Zambia and Zimbabwe) from a baseline of zero in 2009. Botswana has just finished its follow-up study, which is more comprehensive regarding sample and geographical coverage as well as scope.

Meanwhile, attitudes that fuel gender violence (used in 2017 as proxy indicators for gender violence) vary in the region. For example, 86% of women and men in Lesotho said that "if a woman works, she should give her money to her husband," compared to 23% in Namibia. While 15% of those interviewed in Mauritius said that "if a woman wears a short skirt she is asking to be raped," 75% of respondents in Tanzania agreed or strongly agreed with this statement.

Background

While notable efforts to address GBV have occurred across the region since the publication of the 2017 Barometer, at times progress seems invisible and unquantifiable. Globally, GBV awareness raising campaigns such as the 16 Days of Activism and One Billion Rising continue to draw attention to the scourge. Simultaneously, the NGO sector, government, academia and international development partners continue to emphasise the need for evidence-based and theoretically-grounded interventions.

> *"Violence against women and girls has nowhere to hide. We're coming for it, in all its forms and manifestations, and around the world."*
> Amina J. Mohammed, Deputy Secretary General of the United Nations

With the aim to direct focused attention to GBV, the European Union and the United Nations have invested more than US $500 million towards the Spotlight Initiative to eliminate violence against women and girls, with its mantra to "leave no one behind." The initiative targets those people that other programmes have not reached - women and girls in rural areas and conflict zones, the displaced and disabled, indigenous and minority populations, and especially the young and the old. If the global community is to make any progress in achieving gender equality or women's empowerment, as stipulated in the 2030 Agenda for Sustainable Development, it must address GBV.[5] In recent years, the UK government also contributed around £25 million to What Works to Prevent Violence, an evidence-generating global programme that has been engaging experts from across the globe to produce rigorous evidence on the most effective interventions to reduce rates of violence against women and girls (VAWG).

Only

7

countries

have

undertaken

GBV

Baseline

Studies

[2] Chiramba, K, Musariri, L. and Rasesigo, G. (unpublished). Botswana Relationship Study. Gender Links
[3] Lowe-Morna, C., Dube, S. Makamure, L.(2017) SADC Gender Protocol Barometer (online) available at http://genderlinks.org.za/shop/sadc-gender-protocol-barometer-2017/ (accessed 20 May 2018)
[4] Lowe-Morna, C and Walter, D. (2009). SADC Gender Protocol Barometer, Gender Links website, available at http://genderlinks.org.za/shop/sadc-gender-protocol-baseline-barometer-2009/ (accessed 12 June 2016)
[5] United Nations website available at http://www.un.org/en/spotlight-initiative/index.shtml (accessed 23 May 2018)

At regional level, some SADC countries have made progress in addressing GBV by implementing multisectoral approaches that include legislative and criminal justice responses, measuring incidence and costing of GBV, awareness-raising, women's empowerment programmes, community-based social norm programmes and health-based interventions (Lowe Morna et al, 2017). From 7-9 July 2017, United Nations Office on Drugs and Crime (UNODC) and SADC held a two-day workshop aimed at strengthening regional cooperation in addressing GBV from a criminal justice perspective.[6] Later, in March 2018, SADC representatives convened another two-day workshop to devise a harmonised way of collecting data on various forms of GBV across the region.

Women in Botswana take a stand against abuse as part of a local campaign, saying loudly and proudly: "I wear what I want!".
Photo courtesy of I wear what I want Facebook

The immense recognition and intense debate that GBV has generated through online platforms over the past year is perhaps the most notable recent advancement in this area. This has occurred in the form of campaigns such as the #MeToo, Not In My Name and Not Our Leaders, to name but a few. The momentum towards a change in thinking, from response to prevention, is intensifying as more voices speak out at different levels and platforms. The need to include men in the fight against GBV and gender inequality has been well communicated, as evidenced by a continued increase in initiatives that engage men and boys as allies (Aguayo et al., 2016).[7] Currently lacking, though,

is a broader recognition that men can also be victims, which contributes to their role as perpetrators.

Measuring GBV

Often referred to as the "silent epidemic," GBV has proven difficult to address because of a scarcity of reliable and adequate data. Serious under-reporting and the lack of universal indicators hinder effective collection of data. Socio-cultural factors such as fear of social stigma, attitudes and social pressures, prevent victims of violence from reporting cases of violence, particularly to institutional structures (such as police and health services), which are inherently patriarchal (Lowe Morna et al, 2017). This contributes to underreporting of violence, which is common across the region. However, several stakeholders, particularly gender ministries, have been making efforts to measure GBV in its various forms.

In some countries, researchers specifically design dedicated surveys with a module to measure GBV in all its different forms. These tend to be more in depth than other DHS modules, which fall into existing larger surveys measuring various health indicators.[8]

Table 5.2: Status of DHS Surveys in SADC countries				
Domestic violence module (most recent survey)		**No Domestic violence Module**		**No DHS**
Country	*Year*	*Country*	*Year*	
Angola	2015	Botswana	1988	Mauritius
DRC	2013-14	Lesotho	2014	Seychelles
Malawi	2015-16	Madagascar	2008-09	
Mozambique	2011	eSwatini	2006-07 FGM and child labour	
Namibia	2013			
South Africa	2016			
Tanzania	2015-16			
Zambia	2013-14			
Zimbabwe	2015			

Source: DHS Programme Website[9] in Regional Barometer 2016.

Table 5.2 shows that only nine SADC countries have adopted the domestic violence module; four countries have yet to adopt it. Mauritius and Seychelles have never conducted a DHS survey.[10] The fact that not all SADC countries have a DHS is a key reason that researchers could not use this as a measure in the SADC Gender and Development Index (SGDI).

---

6   UNODC Website at http://www.unodc.org/southernafrica/en/stories/unodc-continues-to-combat-gender-based-violence--meets-sadc-to-strengthen-cooperation-on-criminal-justice.html (accessed 1 June 2018).
7   Aguayo, F., Kimelman, P., Saavedra, J., Kato-Wallace. (2016). Engaging Men in Public Policies for the Prevention of Violence Against Women and Girls. Santiago: EME/CulturaSalud. Washington, D.C.: Promundo-US. Panama City: UN Women and UNFPA.
8   UN Expert Group (2007) available at http://www.un.org/womenwatch/daw/egm/IndicatorsVAW/IndicatorsVAW_EGM_report.pdf (accessed 10 June 2018).
9   DHS website available at http://dhsprogram.com/Where-We-Work/Country-Main.cfm?ctry_id=39&c=Tanzania&r=1 (cited in SADC Barometer 2017).
10 http://dhsprogram.com/topics/gender-Corner/index.cfm (cited in SADC Barometer 2017).

9

SADC

countries

have

adopted

the

domestic

violence

module

in DHS

Surveys

"What is not counted does not count:" harmonising statistics in Southern Africa

Uncoordinated data collection and lack of common indicators is making it difficult to measure progress to tackle GBV in the region, a group of stakeholders representing civil society and government noted at a recent workshop.

From 7-9 March 2018, the United Nations Economic Commission for Africa (UNECA) convened a group of regional stakeholders to discuss the harmonisation of GBV and Violence against Children (VAC) statistics. The workshop, which took place in Johannesburg, brought together SADC stakeholders working in institutions dealing with GBV statistics. Participants reviewed existing GBV data collection tools used in the different countries to devise a harmonised and standardised regional tool.

Representatives from Ministries of Gender and National Statistical Offices from several Southern African countries (Botswana, Lesotho, Malawi, Mauritius, Mozambique, Namibia, South Africa, eSwatini, Zambia, and Zimbabwe) attended. Gender links and the Zimbabwe Women Resource Centre Network (ZWRCN) represented civil society. UN agencies United Nations Population Fund (UNFPA) and UN Women also attended, while SADC and Common Market for Eastern and Southern Africa (COMESA) represented the regional economic communities. Organizers appointed these representatives to form a core team to spearhead the process, with UNECA as the Secretariat. Following country updates, the participants came up with recommendations to improve data collection.

Statistics play an integral role in putting a spotlight on GBV.
Photo courtesy of Google images

Recommendations from the workshop

Participants made recommendations in the following areas: harmonisation of data collection; resourcing GBV and VAC Machinery; cultural issues and GBV and VAC policies; strengthening GBV and VAC surveys; coordination of GBV and VAC issues at national and regional levels; creation of learning platforms on GBV and VAC; and the role of national statistical offices (NSOs) in GBV statistics.

There was a general consensus that there is a lack of comparable definitions, indicators and instruments, especially on the prevalence of different forms of violence. This makes it difficult to make comparisons across the region. The workshop participants, therefore, agreed that countries should continue using Demographic and Health Survey (DHS) data for comparability purposes but they urged each government to invest in dedicated and comprehensive GBV surveys. Participants also noted a need for a harmonised analytical methodology based on data and supported by evidence on the prevalence and incidence of GBV across the region.

Meanwhile, representatives of NSOs raised concerns about the problem of establishing a coherent and systematic sys¬tem of data collection on GBV, including in analysing GBV data from administrative records. Stakeholders have little or no access to administrative data across many countries in the region. Participants agreed that, even for administrative data, there is a need to develop standardised indicators that can measure the scope, prevalence, causes and consequences of the problem as well as the efforts undertaken to eradicate GBV.

The workshop highlighted that national statistical systems play a crucial role in providing and improving data. They can develop and maintain a sustainable statistical system able to produce and disseminate proper data on GBV in its various forms, on a regular basis. In addition to compiling and disseminating data from administrative sources, national statistical systems can also be involved with population-based surveys aimed at collecting more in-depth information on GBV and VAC.

The meeting came at an opportune time, during which stakeholders have been intensifying efforts to bring GBV into the spotlight. It is imperative for actors to harmonise and build from already existing instruments, such as the GBV Indicators project. In 2008, UNECA initiated a similar process that saw the development of the GBV Indicators project, which GL has spearheaded and implemented in seven countries. In these countries, GL has collaborated with national statistics offices and gender ministries, a key point that stakeholders raised in the meeting. In 2014, researchers revised the same data collection instrument following a critical thinking forum attended by representatives from several countries.

Source: Adapted from the workshop report[11]

[11] https://www.dropbox.com/home/Harmonizing%20on%20GBV%20statistics_workshop?preview=GBV+Workshop+Outcome+Statement+-+09+March+2018.pdf

Table 5.3: Difference between the DHS and VAW Baseline Studies

DHS	GBV Indicators
Scope	
30 questions	More than 150 indicators that seek to measure the prevalence, effects and drivers of violence.
Source	
	Several standard, globally accepted and tested measurement tools, including the WHO Multi-country Study on Women's Health and Domestic Violence, Gender Equitable Men (GEM) scale and the Harvard Trauma Questionnaire.
Measures	
Physical, emotional and sexual abuse in intimate relationships	Physical, sexual, psychological and economic intimate partner violence.
Physical abuse by stranger	The VAW/GBV Indicators only looked at physical abuse within intimate relationships not by strangers DHS has specific questions on physical abuse by someone who is not a partner.
Physical abuse in pregnancy	Physical, sexual, psychological and economic intimate partner violence in pregnancy.
Physical violence perpetration and alcohol	GBV violence perpetration and alcohol, child abuse, attitudes, demographic factors.
Rape by non-partner	
	Rape and sexual assault by a partner, stranger, acquaintance or family member, experienced by adults and in childhood.
Help seeking behaviour	Help seeking behaviour (medical, legal, police, shelter and family) and reporting and conviction patterns.
Witnessing domestic violence of parents	Witnessing domestic violence in the home and community.
	Sexual harassment in schools, workplace and public places.
	The study also has output indicators focusing on the response mechanisms and some of prevention strategies, such as campaigns.
	Effects, reproductive health (HIV, sexually-transmitted infections) mental (Post-traumatic stress disorder and Centre for Epidemiological Studies-Depression scales), physical and economic.

Source: GBV Indicators Questionnaire and DHS Domestic Violence Module

Table 5.3 compares the DHS studies with the GL GBV/VAW Baseline Studies, illustrating that the latter are far more comprehensive. The gaps in the DHS prompted the creation of the GL GBV/VAW Baseline Studies (2010-2016). The GL research uses a prevalence and attitude household survey; analysis of administrative data gathered from the criminal justice system (police, courts), health services, and shelters; qualitative research of first-hand accounts of women's and men's experiences of intimate partner violence, or "I" Stories; media monitoring; and political content analysis.

The flagship tool is the household prevalence and attitude survey, justified on the basis that statistics obtained from administrative data fall short as survivors do not report most incidents to police or service providers. Statistics from service providers also often cover physical and sexual assault but do not disaggregate GBV into other forms, such as marital rape, emotional and economic violence (Lowe Morna et al, 2017). In February 2013, SADC gender ministers, at a meeting in Maputo, urged all SADC member states to undertake GBV/VAW baseline studies to inform their action planning.[12]

Although they are costly, dedicated surveys provide the most reliable and comprehensive statistics on violence against women.[13] This is evident in the GBV/VAW Baseline studies undertaken in four provinces of South Africa; Botswana, Lesotho, Mauritius, Zambia and Zimbabwe. These pilot studies focused on women's experiences and men's perpetration of violence (Lowe Morna et al, 2017).

Adding Violence Against Men (VAM)
Following a plea from the governments of Botswana and Seychelles to include violence against men (VAM), GL convened a meeting in 2014 that brought together experts from various fields to strengthen the methodology. In 2016 the Ministry of Health and Social Affairs and Sports, the National Bureau of Statistics and GL piloted the new methodology in the Seychelles.

The revised questionnaire includes a module on VAM. Researchers administered the same questionnaire in Botswana in a follow-up study currently awaiting publication. It reached more than 7000 participants. The two questionnaires provide convincing evidence of the extent, causes, effects,

Dedicated **surveys** provide the most **reliable** statistics on GBV

[12] Lowe-Morna, C., Dube, S. Makamure, L., Robinson, K, (2014) SADC Gender Protocol Barometer (online) available at http://genderlinks.org.za/shop/sadc-gender-protocol-barometer-2016/ (accessed 12 July 2017).
[13] United Nations. (2007). Indicators to measure violence against women: Expert Group Meeting Report, United Nations , available at http://www.un.org/womenwatch/daw/egm/IndicatorsVAW/IndicatorsVAW_EGM_report.pdf (accessed June 2016).

response, support and prevention mechanisms in place in the countries where researchers have carried it out. Violence against men is not well recognised in many countries but evidence shows it cannot be ignored if the aim is to eradicate all violence (Ratele 2013), especially if we are operating in the spirit of "leaving no one behind."

Overall, as noted in Table 5.4, researchers interviewed 37 856 participants in seven countries: 1229 in Botswana; 3367 in Lesotho; 1357 in Mauritius; 1297 in the Zambia pilot study and 7602 in the Dimensions of Violence against Women in selected parts of Zambia study; 5621 in the South African provinces of Gauteng, Western Cape, KwaZulu-Natal and Limpopo; 8354 in Zimbabwe; 1109 in Seychelles; and most recently 7920 in the Botswana follow-up study. The sample breaks down into 52% women and 48% men.

Table 5.4: Participants in the GBV Indicators study

Country	Females	Males	Total
Botswana	639	590	1229
Lesotho	1777	1590	3367
Mauritius	679	678	1357
Zambia pilot study	578	719	1297
Zambia follow up study	3963	3639	7602
Four provinces of South Africa	2800	2821	5621
Zimbabwe	4507	3847	8354
Seychelles	578	531	1109
Botswana follow up study	4224	3696	7920
Total	19745	18111	37856

Source: VAW/GBV Baseline Studies 2010-2017, Gender Links.

Prevalence of GBV and intimate partner violence (IPV) in seven countries

Table 5.5: Proportions of women experiencing and men perpetrating GBV and IPV in lifetime

	Lifetime GBV			Lifetime IPV	
Country	Women experiencing	Men perpetrating	Country	Women experiencing	Men perpetrating
Lesotho	86%	41%	Selected provinces Zambia	79%	74%
Selected provinces Zambia	77%	66%	Zimbabwe	69%	41%
Zimbabwe	68%	46%	Lesotho	62%	37%
Seychelles	58%	43%	Seychelles	54%	42%
South Africa (4 provinces)	50%	39%	South Africa (4 provinces)	49%	40%
Botswana	37%	30%	Botswana	37%	28%
Mauritius	24%	23%	Mauritius	23%	22%

Source: GBV/VAW Baseline Studies, Gender Links.

Table 5.5 shows that lifetime experience of GBV among women ranges from a high of 86% in Lesotho to 24% in Mauritius. A higher proportion of women reported experiencing violence than the proportion of men that admitted to perpetrating violence in all seven countries. However, the extent to which men admit to such behaviour is high in all the countries and is almost equal in Mauritius.

The most predominant form of GBV experienced by women and perpetrated by men in the seven countries occurs within intimate partnerships. This ranges from 79% in Zambia to 23% in Mauritius. In all seven countries, the most common form of IPV is emotional violence - a form of violence usually not addressed in police statistics. Again, in all seven countries, a lower proportion of men admitted to perpetrating IPV.

Leaving no one behind: Botswana Relationship Study 2018

Young men make a statement during the 16 Days of Activism march in Maun, Botswana. *Photo: Gender Links*

Following the well-received 2012 National Baseline Study on GBV, in 2017 the Botswana's Gender Affairs Department (GeAD) commissioned GL to conduct a follow-up study: the Botswana Relationship Study. Building on the 2012 study, the Relationship Study adds VAM, which Seychelles successfully piloted in its GBV National Baseline Study in 2016. This study increased the sample size from 1229 (639 women and 590 men) in nine districts in 2012 to 7920 (4224 women and 3696 men) in all 16 districts in 2017, providing a much larger sample and therefore more accurate data.

Violence against men

In the spirit of "leaving no one behind," the study included findings from district level, such as vulnerable populations, including the disabled, and "hotspot" areas such the mining towns. It also explored men's experience of violence, a narrative that is critical in eradicating the scourge. The findings show that many men experience violence, though still fewer than women.

Table 5.6: Lifetime IPV experience and perpetration rates by women and men				
Country	Women experiencing	Men experiencing	Women experiencing	Men experiencing
IPV in lifetime	37%	18%	18%	27%
Emotional IPV	31%	14%	13%	17%
Physical IPV	21%	5%	7%	17%
Economic IPV	11%	6%	4%	4%
Sexual IPV	5%	2%	2%	3%
Abuse in pregnancy	15%	-	-	9%

Source: Botswana Relationship Study.

Table 5.6 shows that the most common form of IPV experienced by both women and men is emotional, followed by physical, economic and sexual. Basing on the experience rates, higher proportions of women reported experiencing IPV. Meanwhile, higher proportions of men reported perpetrating IPV. Among women, experience of IPV ranges from 31% of women experiencing emotional IPV to 5% of women experiencing sexual IPV. For men, rates range from 17% of men perpetrating emotional IPV to 3% of men perpetrating sexual IPV. Experience rates for men follow a similar trend, with 14% of men experiencing emotional IPV to 2% experiencing sexual IPV.

The study found men struggle to open up about IPV because of the stigma attached to the issue. When outsiders try to help, abused men often shut them out, as reflected in the "I" Story[14] excerpt. When interventions targeting men do not acknowledge this violence, they run the risk of receiving resistance from the men that they target. A qualitative study on masculinities and violence in South Africa by Musariri (2018, unpublished)[15] reveals that men feel that their lived experiences of violence tend to be watered down and their voices silenced. This contributes to the ambivalent attitude exhibited by some men towards gender equality initiatives, particularly those that target them with behavioural change projects. Thus, this study brings to light the complex position of both men and women as both victim and perpetrator. The study, therefore, provides significant insights and will strengthen efforts towards eradicating GBV.

> "My housemate's wife was very abusive to the man. Every month end the woman would demand the man's bank cards. She then withdraws all money from the account and spends most of the money on her relatives without buying food for the family. When the man tries to ask her why she does what she does, she beats the man up and insults him in front of their children. When this happens the children run away from home. I have tried on several occasions to intervene but the woman does not listen and she ends up hurling insults at me as well. I have tried to advise him to report the matter because of the emotional, physical and economic abuse but he refused, saying he is afraid of his wife. He also is not sure how the police will respond."
>
> - an excerpt from an "I" Story by Thabo*

---

14 * pseudonym used in the "I' story collected by GL as part of the GBV Relationship Study.
15 Musariri, L (2018) Fieldnotes: Masculinities and violence research project, Johannesburg. (Unpublished)

Cascading to district level

Increasing the sample made it possible to disaggregate data by district, allowing for more nuanced comparisons. GL has already been working at district level with the local government, developing local action plans to end GBV. The findings from this study will thus go a long way in strengthening these plans.

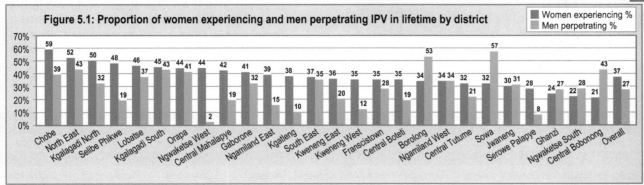

Source: Botswana Relationship Study.

Figure 5.1 shows that Chobe recorded the highest IPV experience rates by women at 59%, while Central Bobonong recorded the lowest (21%). Regarding perpetration rates by men, Sowa recorded the highest rate at 58% and Ngwaketse West recorded the lowest at 2%. This information is crucial as it allows stakeholders to develop localised action plans to address GBV. Edwin Jenamiso Batshu, minister of nationality, immigration and gender affairs, recommended that relevant stakeholders use these findings to review the National Strategy to End Gender Violence.

Source: Botswana Relationship Study, 2018

Different forms of violence
Femicide

Reports show that femicide and/or gender-related killings are on the rise across the globe.[16] Reasons include IPV, honour killings and witchcraft, to mention a few. The UNFPA estimates that, each year, 5000 women die at the hands of family members across the globe in honour killings.[17] According to the UNODC Global Study on Homicide (2013), an intimate partner or family member kills one of every two women victims of homicide.[18] Many countries have committed to respond to the high rates of femicide, for example South Africa held an anti-femicide imbizo (forum) in June 2017 in Soweto. Speaking at the event, Minister of Arts and Culture Nathi Mthethwa proposed introducing a "femicide watch" to enable detailed and accurate collection of data on the number of women murdered (South African Government Website).[19]

Hate crimes

Hate crimes include violence related to race, ethnicity, religion, gender or sexual orientation. Reports in the media have highlighted regular violence against Lesbian, Gay, Bisexual, Transgender and Intersex people (LGBTI). Yet many cases of violence against LGBTI people go unreported due to fear of secondary victimisation, which results in most survivors avoiding or delaying accessing healthcare, criminal justice services and psychosocial support (SIDA, 2015).[20] In 2018, South Africa became the first country in SADC to draft a Bill that seeks to provide protection for groups vulnerable to targeted crimes because of their race, sexual orientation or gender, national origin, occupation and disability. Legislators passed the Prevention and Combating of Hate Crimes and Hate Speech Bill in March 2018.[21]

---

[16] Laurent, C. (2013), The Killing of Women and Girls Around the World. Academic Council on the United Nations System (ACUNS) Vienna Liaison Office. Available at http://acuns.org/wp-content/uploads/2013/05/Claire-Laurent.pdf (accessed 3 August 2017)

[17] Laurent, C. (2013), The Killing of Women and Girls Around the World. Academic Council on the United Nations System (ACUNS) Vienna Liaison Office. Available at http://acuns.org/wp-content/uploads/2013/05/Claire-Laurent.pdf (accessed 3 August 2017)

[18] UNODC Global Study available at https://www.unodc.org/gsh/ (accessed 3 June 2018)

[19] South African Government website www.dac.gov.za/content/mrm-arts-and-culture-hosts-imbizo-anti-femicide-soweto (accessed 21 May 2018)

[20] Sida (2015). Preventing and Responding to Gender-Based Violence: Expressions and Strategies available at http://www.sida.se/contentassets/3a820dbd152f4fca98bacde8a8101e15/preventing-and-responding-to-gender-based-violence.pdf (accessed 3 July 2017)

[21] https://www.parliament.gov.za/storage/app/media/Docs/bill/9febb155-8582-4a15-bf12-5961db2828c2.pdf

5000 ♀ die at the hands of family members across the globe in honour killings

Women's rights groups protest against state-sponsored abuse against women in Zimbabwe. *Photo courtesy of Above Whispers*

Violence against women in politics

"While the influx of women into parliament is beneficial for representative democracy, it has tended to disrupt the established order, provoking some resistance," noted the Inter-Parliamentary Union in 2016.[22] Another study conducted in the UK in 2017 shows that more than half of British female MPs report having received physical threats.[23] In Zimbabwe, the think tank Research

Targets	Angola	Botswana	DRC	Lesotho	Madagascar	Malawi	Mauritius
LEGISLATION							
Laws on domestic violence	Domestic violence Act- July 2011	Domestic Violence Act 2008	VAW is covered in the Constitution	Domestic Violence Bill in progress. Covered by Legal Capacity of Married Persons Act 9 of 2006	Covered by Penal Code	Prevention of Domestic Violence Act 2006	Protection from Domestic Violence Act 2004
Laws on sexual assault	No	Sexual Offences Bill 2010, currently covered in the Penal code addresses defilement, incest, rape	Law Sexual Violence 2006	Sexual Offences Act 2003	Sexual Offences Act, 2000	Penal code, Gender Equality Act 2013 covers sexual harassment, no specific stand-alone act/law	Sex Discri-mination Act, Sexual Offences Bill
Comprehensive treatment, including PEP	Yes	Only policy	Yes	Yes	Yes	Yes	Only in policy
Specific legislative provisions to prevent human trafficking	1886 Penal Code was amended February 2014 to prohibit all forms of trafficking	Anti-Human Trafficking Act, 2014 (Act No. 32 of 2014)	Law on Human Trafficking especially women and girls 2008	Human Trafficking Act of 2011	Law on the fight Against Human Trafficking and Sex Tourism, 2007	Trafficking in Persons Act 2015	Combating of Trafficking in Persons Act of 2009

Table 5.7: Key baseline indicators on GBV against

---

[22] Inter-Parliamentary Union (2016). Sexism, harassment and violence against women parliamentarians.
[23] http://blogs.lse.ac.uk/europpblog/2017/08/12/violence-against-women-in-politics-is-rising-and-its-a-clear-threat-to-democracy/ (accessed 2 June 2018).

and Advocacy Unit and its various partner have been raising awareness around politically-motivated VAW even before the 2008 elections. In 2016, Musasa, in collaboration with the Royal Netherlands Embassy, HIVOS, and UN Women, organised the Women and Peace Conference, which brought forth strong commitments by government ministers, UN agencies, international NGOs and local women's organisations to stop political violence and other forms of VAW (RAU website).[24] While there are several recorded incidences of women in politics being attacked, the recent case of Thokozani Khupe, the Deputy President of the MDC-T, Zimbabwe's biggest opposition party, made the news following her rejection of Co-Vice President Nelson Chamisa as the party's interim leader. Khupe faced a number of attacks from members of her own party (All Africa website).[25]

the SADC Protocol on Gender and Development							
Mozambique	Namibia	Seychelles	South Africa	eSwatini	Tanzania	Zambia	Zimbabwe
Law on Domestic Violence Against Women 2009	Combating of Domestic Violence Act (No. 4, 2003)	(Family Violence Act)	Domestic Violence Act 2006	Sexual Offenses and Domestic Violence Act	Partly covered by Law Marriage Act 1976	Anti- Gender-Based Violence Act 2011	Domestic Violence Act 2006, Criminal codification and Reform Act, chapter nine
Penal code	Combating Rape Act 2000	No	Sexual Offences Act of 2009	The Crimes Act/1889, the Girls and Women's Protection Act/1920, the Criminal Procedure and Evidence Act No 67/1938 and common law crimes covering rape, incest, indecent assault	Included Penal code. Miscellaneous Act 2002 section 130 of penal code	Anti- Gender-Based Violence Act 2011	Included in Criminal codification and Reform Act. moved from Sexual Offences Act
Yes	Only in policy	The Ministry of Health has developed procedures on standardised response to GBV including sexual assault	Yes	There is provision within the national guidelines for antiretroviral treatment and Post Exposure Prophylaxis (PEP)	Gender Based Violence Policy and Management Guidelines, Ministry of Health	National guide-lines for the multi-disciplinary Management of survivors of GBV in Zambia- 2011	In Zimbabwe National HIV and AIDS Strategic Plan 2011 -2015
Law Against Human Trafficking particularly Women and Children, 2008	Trafficking in Person bill 14 of 2017	Prohibition of Trafficking in Persons Act 2014	Prevention and Combating of Trafficking in Persons Act 2013	People Trafficking and People Smuggling (Prohibition) Act, 2009 Human Trafficking Task Force and Human Trafficking Unit	Anti-Trafficking in Persons Act of 2008	Anti-Human Trafficking Act of 2008	Trafficking in Persons act 2014 previously Criminal Codification and Reform Act, Section 83

[24] Research and Advocacy Unit available at http://researchandadvocacyunit.org/blog/2017/07/07/politically-motivated-violence-against-women-zimbabwe (accessed 2 June 2018).
[25] All Africa News (18 February 2018) available http://allafrica.com/stories/201802210524.html (accessed 9 June 2018).

Targets	Angola	Botswana	DRC	Lesotho	Madagascar	Malawi	Mauritius
Sexual harassment	No	Legislation recommended as part of Employment Act, Public Service Act 2000	Sexual Offences Act	Sexual Offences Act	Penal Code amended by Acts	The Malawi Constitution (sect. 24 (2) (a). Gender Equality Act	Labour act; Sex Discrimination Act
SERVICES							
Accessible, affordable and specialised legal services, including legal aid, to survivors of GBV	Yes	None; NGOs provide this. Legal Aid Pilot Project under the Attorney General's Chambers	Yes, done with support of UN agencies	Ministry of Justice legal aid service stretched; NGOs step in	Yes	Through Legal Aid Dept. with limited funds and human resource. Few NGOs also try to provide this	Yes, 6 Family support bureaux's are in operation at the Ministry of Gender. Psychological counselling and legal advice are provided to survivors of GBV
Specialised facilities including places of shelter and safety	Yes	Minimal state support; mostly NGOs	Yes, but very limited because of funds	Yes, there are police specialised units, but only one state shelter in Maseru	Yes	Minimal state support; Victim Support Units under Malawi Police Service provide this few NGOs	The National Children's Council operating under the aegis of the Ministry runs one shelter. Two shelters run by an NGO and a Trust aid partly funded by the Ministry
COORDINATION, MONITORING AND EVALUATION							
Integrated approaches: National Action Plans	Presidential Decree 26/13 of May Executive Plan of Fight against Domestic Violence	National Strategy 2016 - 2020 on the elimination of GBV and action plan	National Strategy on Combating Gender Based Violence being updated (2018)[26]	To be updated	Action Plan to end GBV and Strategy	National Plan of Action to Combat Gender-Based Violence in Malawi 2014-2020	National Action Plan to end gender based Violence 2012-15
Construct a composite index for measuring gender based violence	Yes, Integrated Gender Indicators system	Yes, GBV Indicators	Yes, involved at African level to provide indicator	Yes, GBV Indicators	No	No	Yes, GBV Indicators
Provide baseline data on gender based violence	DHS 2015/16	GBV Indicators study	DHS 2013/14	GBV Indicators study	No	DHS 2015/2016	GBV Indicators study

---

[26] http://documents.worldbank.org/curated/en/481341525730456994/pdf/Project-Information-Document-Integrated-Safeguards-Data-Sheet-DRC-Gender-Based-Violence-Prevention-and-Response-Project-P166763.pdf

Mozambique	Namibia	Seychelles	South Africa	eSwatini	Tanzania	Zambia	Zimbabwe
Brief mention in labour law; Article 66 (2)	Labour Act 11 of 2007, partly addressed in the Combating of Domestic Violence Act 4 of 2003 and Combating of Rape Act 8 of 2000	Public Officers' Ethics Act of 2008 Section 16 Ministry of Education policy; Ombudsperson	Protection from Harassment Act, 2011	Crimes Act of 1889- "inappropriate sexual behaviour"; outdated! New progressive proposed provision in the sexual offences and domestic violence bill	Penal Code; The Sexual Offences Special Provisions Act 1998; Employment and Labour Relations Act, 2004	The Anti-Gender- Based- Violence Act, 2011, Amendment in Penal Section 137 (a)	Labour Relations Amendment Act, under "unfair labour practice"
Limited government support but services from Association of Women Lawyers	Yes and Legal Resources Centre	Yes	Yes, through the Legal Aid Board, plus NGO support, and Thuthuzelas- but not affordable to run	There is no specialised or affordable legal aid service to survivors of GBV. The limited services offered by NGOs are compromised by a lack of funds	Ministry of Home Affairs is in the process of establishing Gender and Children's desks - guidelines are being developed	The National guidelines for the Multi-disciplinary Management of Survivors of gender Based Violence in Zambia- 2011	Ministry of Justice Legal Aid, Musasa Project and WLSA
NGOs main provider of services but face resource constraint	Mainly NGOs	None	Yes, but mainly NGOs that depend on foreign funding	The amendment of the Criminal Procedure and Evidence Act (section 223) facilitated the formation of a children's court eSwatini launched a first of its kind, a one-stop centre in Mbabane	No places of safety - only police stations	The National guidelines for the Multi-disciplinary Management of Survivors of gender Based Violence in Zambia- 2011	Minimal state support; NGOs main provider of services but face resource constraints
Multi-sectoral plan and plan to end GBV	Expired in 2016 National Action Plan to End Gender Violence	Yes, but strategy only focuses on Domestic Violence	Shadow report National Strategic Plan (NSP) to end GBV	National Strategy to End Violence 2017 -2022	National Plan of Action to End Violence Against Women and Children (NPA-VAWC 2017/18 - 2021/22	National Action Plans National Action Plan to End Gender Violence in place	Zero Tolerance 365: National Programme On GBV Prevention And Response 2016-2020
No	No	Yes, GBV Indicators		Surveillance System on Violence 2009	No	Gender Based Violence Information Management System (GBVIMS)	National GBV Information System
DHS 2015	DHS 2013 2003 Multi-country Study on Women's Health and Domestic Violence against Women	GBV Indicators study	GBV Indicators study in four provinces	No	DHS 2015 2003 Multi-country Study on Women's Health and Domestic Violence against Women	Provide baseline data on gender based violence GBV Indicators study	GBV Indicators study

Table 5.7 shows that:
- Twelve out of the 15 countries have laws on domestic violence;
- Thirteen have sexual assault legislation;
- All SADC countries offer comprehensive treatment, including PEP, to survivors of violence, although no legislation exists;
- Fourteen countries have legislation on sexual harassment;
- All SADC countries have laws on human trafficking;
- All countries offer some form of accessible, affordable and specialised legal services, including legal aid, to survivors of GBV although a lot of this is offered by NGOs; and
- All but one country offer specialised facilities including places of shelter and safety.

While all countries have had NAP to end GBV, most of the NAPs have expired. Seven countries have updates NAPs. Meanwhile, as noted earlier, seven countries have undertaken the GBV Baseline Studies (Botswana, Lesotho, Mauritius, Seychelles, South Africa, Zambia and Zimbabwe) and six have conducted DHS studies with the GBV module (Angola, DRC, Malawi, Mozambique, Namibia and Tanzania). However, Madagascar and Tanzania still do not have any baseline data.

Response

Article 20.1: States parties shall:
(a) enact and enforce legislation prohibiting all forms of gender-based violence;
(b) develop strategies to prevent and eliminate all harmful social and cultural practices, such as child marriage, forced marriage, teenage pregnancies, slavery and female genital mutilation; violence, including domestic violence, rape, femicide, sexual harassment, female genital mutilation and all other forms of gender-based violence are tried by a court of competent jurisdiction.
Article 20.3: States parties shall, review, reform and strengthen their laws and procedures applicable to cases of sexual offences and gender-based violence to:
(a) eliminate gender bias; and
(b) ensure justice and fairness are accorded to survivors of gender-based violence in a manner that ensures dignity, protection and respect.

In line with Article 20.1(a), which calls for state parties to enact legislation prohibiting all forms of violence, 12 countries now have laws on domestic violence. However, DRC, Lesotho, and Tanzania have yet to enact Laws on Domestic Violence.

Further, 13 countries also now have laws on sexual assault including rape. This is commendable. The region is doing well regarding legally dealing with GBV, either through specific pieces of legislation or penal codes. However, a disjuncture between constitutional and customary law remains a problem across the region. The customary law is relevant in the African context and, while it has managed to coexist with competing systems of domestic constitutional law, statutory law, common law and international human rights treaties, in some cases it created a hindrance to the enforcement of the latter (Diala, 2018).[27] For instance, most countries have legislation criminalising rape, but countries like Botswana, DRC and Zambia do not address marital rape in their legislation. Even in the settings where Legislation exists, some men remain opposed to this concept as they believe that there can be no rape between spouses (eSwatini Civil Society Report, 2017).[28] This is made worse in scenarios in which a man feels entitled to have sexual intercourse with his wife if and when he so desires, particularly in cases where paying of bride price equates to purchasing a wife (Musariri et al 2015).

---

[27] Diala, A, (2018), "Legal integration of state laws and customary laws is inevitable" available at http://nai.uu.se/news/articles/2018/04/18/162652/index.xml (accessed 22 May 2018).
[28] Swaziland Joint Civil Society. (2017). Civil Society report on the Implementation of the Covenant on Civil and Political Rights 120th session of the Human Rights Committee -

Clashing legal systems perpetuate inequality in Lesotho and eSwatini*

eSwatini and Lesotho represent two of the four countries in SADC that do not have specific laws on domestic violence despite having adopted the SADC Protocol on Gender and Development in August 2016. Both countries also remain the only two monarchies in the SADC region. According to UNAIDS, the two also have the highest HIV prevalence rates in the world: eSwatini at 27% and Lesotho at 25%.[29] Women account for 56% of adults living with HIV in the region.[30] The link between HIV and GBV is well documented (Jewkes et al 2010).[31] The twin epidemics are rooted in gendered power inequalities embedded in the patriarchal society. Both countries, like many other African countries, have a dual legal system in which the Roman Dutch laws and customary laws operate side by side.

In eSwatini, the Swazi customary Law has an upper hand over the civil law. Through the Swazi law and custom the King has powers over the three organs of the government: judiciary, legislature and executive. At present, King Mswati III holds supreme executive power and controls the judiciary.[32] This has seen the King making decisions that many see as detrimental to the well-being of women, exposing them to considerable risk of experiencing violence and contracting HIV.

The eSwatini civil society report on the implementation of the Covenant on Civil and Political Rights, presented to the 120th session of the Human Rights Committee in July 2017, sheds some light on how customary law may clash with human rights treaties. According to the report, eSwatini has seen delays in passing the Sexual Offences and Domestic Violence Bill of 2015 into law because of the King's perceptions that, if passed into law, the provisions might encroach on some Swazi laws and customs. The report lists four clauses that are apparently a cause for concern to the King and the traditional authorities. These pertain to provisions on stalking, flashing, marital rape and child marriage:

a) Stalking - in terms of custom, a woman may be pursued for a relationship endlessly no matter how many times she may refuse the advances;

b) Flashing - the nature of traditional attire is such that there is much display of flesh, for example, during the reed dance, young maidens go around bare-chested and with short beaded skirts that show off their buttocks;

c) Marital rape - generally, there is lack of understanding on marital rape, with society struggling with the concept. This also includes women, who have been conditioned to the fact that they have no rights over their sexual reproductive functions and activities;

d) Child marriage - the Bill seeks to outlaw child marriages, whereas in terms of Swazi law and custom, the marriageable age is determined by puberty, regardless at what age a young girl may reach this milestone. For these reasons the bill is has not passed into a law.[33]

Meanwhile, Lesotho customary law, which exists side by side with civil law, contains the customs of the Basotho, written and codified in the Laws of Lerotholi (Musariri et al, 2015).[34] The customary law plays a significant role in regulating the Basotho people. GBV levels are high in Lesotho, with nine in ten women having experienced some form of abuse in their lifetime (Musariri et al 2015). Since 2000, legislators have failed to pass the Domestic Violence Bill into law. The absence of domestic violence legislation has created a major gap in addressing GBV in Lesotho. Despite having national legislation that criminalises some forms of abuse, notable gaps persist that pertain to discriminatory traditional and cultural laws and practices of early child marriage, inheritance and succession to chieftainship (Mabetha, 2018).

In May 2018, reports noted that Lesotho lawmakers had drafted a Domestic Violence Bill of 2018. Relevant stakeholders have discussed this bill, including the Ministry of Gender, representatives of police from the Child and Gender protection Unit (CGPU) and NGOs, including Gender Links (Mabetha, 2018 Gender Links Website[35]). If passed, the Bill will close the existing gap in the legislation as it will address some traditional and cultural laws that continue to promote the minority status of women and increase their vulnerability to GBV.

Case study written prior to law being passed

---

29 Avert website available at https://www.avert.org/professionals/hiv-around-world/sub-saharan-africa/Swaziland
30 UNAIDS/UNICEF (2016) 'All in to end adolescent AIDS: A progress report'[pdf
31 Jewkes, R., Dunkle, K., Nduna, M., Shai, N. 2010. Intimate partner violence, relationship power inequity, and incidence of HIV infection in young women in South Africa: a cohort study. Lancet 376(9734):41-8.
32 Human Rights Watch, 2018, https://www.hrw.org/sites/default/files/Swaziland_1.pdf
33 Swaziland Joint Civil Society. (2017). Civil Society report on the Implementation of the Covenant on Civil and Political Rights 120th session of the Human Rights Committee -
34 Musariri, L. Nyambo, V. Machisa, MT, and Chiramba, K. (2014) Lesotho GGBV Baseline Study. Gender Links.
35 Mabetha (2018) GL News Service http://genderlinks.org.za/news/lesotho-domestic-violence-bill-2018-beacon-hope-ending-gbv/ (accessed 25 May 2018).

Roman Dutch laws and customary laws operate side by side

Article 20.1b calls for states to develop strategies to prevent and eliminate all harmful social and cultural practices, such as child marriage, forced marriage, teenage pregnancies, slavery and female genital mutilation. To achieve this, it is imperative to engage the traditional leadership, who serve as the custodians of some of the social and cultural practices.

The 2017 Barometer highlighted some of the progress towards eliminating child marriages and forced marriages. Some of the efforts to address child marriage in the region include the four-year African Union Campaign to End Child Marriage, which started in 2014. It saw member states adopting the African Common Position on Ending Child Marriage, resulting in countries developing national strategies and action plans to address the issue. Nineteen African countries have launched the campaign to date. Of these, only three are from the SADC: DRC, Madagascar and Zimbabwe[36] (Girls Not Brides Website). Following a regional dialogue on child marriages convened in February 2015 in Johannesburg, SADC leaders committed to develop a SADC Model Law on Child Marriage. Subsequently, in June 2016, the 39th Plenary Assembly Session of the SADC Parliamentary Forum adopted the Model Law on eradicating child marriage and protecting those already in marriage.[37]

"End child marriage," shout campaigners in Zimbabwe at a 2016 march against child marriages.
Photo courtesy of ROOTS Africa Mutambadarius

The African Law Service provides an update on law reform in the SADC region:
• In January 2016, the Zimbabwe Constitutional Court struck down section 22(1) of the Marriage Act, which allowed children under the age of 18 to marry.

• In July 2016, the Tanzanian Constitutional Court ruled that marriage under the age of 18 is illegal and stated that sections 13 and 17 of the Marriage Act are unconstitutional.[38]
• In South Africa, the South African Law Reform Commission (SALRC) released publication of its *Revised Discussion Paper on Project 138: The Practice of Ukuthwala*. The paper contains a draft bill, tentatively titled the *Prohibition of Forced Marriages and Child Marriages Bill*.
• The Government of Zambia on 8 April 2016 adopted a national strategy to end child marriage.
• Mozambique adopted the National Strategy to Prevent and Combat Child Marriage.
• In 2015, Malawi's Parliament removed from its constitution a provision allowing children between the ages of 15 and 18 to marry with parental consent. It also increased the legal age for marriage to 18 years from 15 years (Marriage, Divorce and Family Relations Bill, 2015).
• One of the traditional rulers in Malawi, Chief Inkosi Kachindamoto, annulled more than 330 customary marriages in June 2015 - of which 175 comprised girl wives and 155 comprised boy fathers in the Central Region of Malawi.[39]
• In June 2018, senators and MPs in eSwatini passed the Sexual Offences and Domestic Violence Bill, which aligns with Section 151 of the Constitution.

While female genital mutilation (FGM) is not especially prevalent in the SADC region, it occurs in some parts of the DRC and Tanzania. In Tanzania, the Sexual Offences Special Provisions Act, a 1998 amendment to the Penal Code, prohibits FGM (Gender Links, 2011).[40] Similarly, DRC passed a law in 2006, introducing amendments to provisions on sexual violence in the Penal Code, including one against FGM (Lowe Morna et al, 2017).[41]

---

[36] Girls not Brides website available at https://www.girlsnotbrides.org/kenya-becomes-19th-country-launch-african-union-campaign-end-child-marriage/ (accessed 10 June 2018)
[37] http://www.riatt-esa.org/blog/2016/6/16/child-marriage-and-early-pregnancy (cited in SADC Barometer 2017)
[38] https://www.girlsnotbrides.org/child-marriage/tanzania/ (accessed 10 June 2018)
[39] https://www.girlsnotbrides.org/kenya-becomes-19th-country-launch-african-union-campaign-end-child-marriage/
[40] Gender Links, (2011). Zero tolerance to female genital mutilation (FGM). Available at http://genderlinks.org.za/barometer-newsletter/zero-tolerance-to-female-genital-mutilation-fgm-2011-02-01/ (accessed 30 July 2017)
[41] Lowe-Morna, C., Dube, S. Makamure, L., (2017) SADC Gender Protocol Barometer (online) available at http://genderlinks.org.za/shop/sadc-gender-protocol-barometer-2017/

> **Article 20.2:** State parties shall ensure that laws on gender-based violence provide for the comprehensive testing, treatment and care of survivors of sexual offences, which shall include:
> (a) emergency contraception;
> (b) ready access to post exposure prophylaxis at all health facilities to reduce the risk of contracting HIV; and
> (c) preventing the onset of sexually transmitted infections.

Despite lack of laws, the region has seen a huge improvement in the provision of PEP over the past several years. All countries now offer comprehensive treatment, including PEP, to survivors of violence. However, since PEP is not a statutory obligation in many countries and is often aid-dependent, its provision across the region varies depending on funding and level of government prioritisation (Lowe Morna et al, 2017).[42]

Trafficking in persons (TIP)

> **Article 20.5:** State parties shall:
> (a) Enact and adopt specific legislative provisions to prevent trafficking in persons and provide holistic services to the victims, with the aim of re-integrating them into society;
> (b) Put in place mechanisms by which all relevant law enforcement authorities and institutions should eradicate national, regional and international trafficking in persons' syndicates;
> (c) Put in place harmonised data collection mechanisms to improve research and reporting on the types and modes of trafficking to ensure effective programming and monitoring.
> (d) Establish bilateral and multilateral agreements to run joint actions against trafficking in persons among origin, transit and destination countries; and
> (e) Ensure capacity building, awareness raising and sensitisation campaigns on trafficking in persons are put in place for law enforcement officials.

Trafficking in persons continues to be a political priority. All SADC Member States have enacted laws against it. The 10 Year SADC Strategic Plan of Action on Combating Trafficking in Persons Especially Women and Children (2009-2019), which SADC Gender Ministers adopted in Gaborone in June 2016, remains in effect. Tracking and monitoring of victims of trafficking remains a challenge, however, making it an invisible crime. There is a need for nuanced research to further understand the scope of this crime.

Human trafficking: *the invisible crime*.   *Photo: Gender Links*

PEP is not a statutory obligation in many countries

---

42 Lowe-Morna, C., Dube, S. Makamure, L., (2017) SADC Gender Protocol Barometer (online) available at http://genderlinks.org.za/shop/sadc-gender-protocol-barometer-2017/

Zimbabwe gets tough on human traffickers

Zimbabwe struggles with the scourge of human trafficking, especially because of the serious economic challenges facing the country. Many Zimbabweans have been trafficked under the false promise of getting a better life in other countries; the dire economic situation makes them easy prey for traffickers.

Thankfully, Zimbabwe recently recorded its first successful prosecution and conviction in a high profile human trafficking case since it enacted the 2014 Trafficking in Persons Act: Chapter 9:25. In March 2018, the courts sentenced 31-year-old Norest Maruma to a combined 50 years' imprisonment for five counts of human trafficking. The case involved the trafficking of women to Kuwait by Maruma, the ringleader in a syndicate that involved a network of people in Zimbabwe and Kuwait. The case also involved allegations against some employees of the Embassy of the State of Kuwait in Zimbabwe, accused of involvement in the trafficking case. Zimbabwe repatriated about 120 women from Kuwait after the case came to light, whilst reports indicated that dozens more women may remain stuck in the Gulf country.

The successful prosecution, conviction and deterrent sentencing of the accused in this case is thanks to the government's enacting the Trafficking in Persons Act. This provides encouragement for other SADC governments looking to do the same. The justice system used to handle similar trafficking cases under Section 83 of the Criminal Law Codification and Reform Act, which merely prohibits leaving the country with another person with the intention of leading them into prostitution. As a result, although such a scenario would clearly present a case of human trafficking, the sentences handed down were often short and not a deterrent for traffickers because the legislation did not make specific reference to human trafficking.

Zimbabwean Ministers and Senior Government Officials, as well as officials from international organisations, launch the the National Plan of Action (NAPLAC) to operationalise the Trafficking in Persons Act in August 2016. *Photo courtesy of zimbabwe.iom.int/news/*

Article 20 (5) of the SADC Gender Protocol enjoins state parties to put in place measures to address the scourge of human trafficking. The envisaged measures include enacting relevant legislation, support for victims of human trafficking and education and awareness on human trafficking. The successful prosecution of cases like the Maruma example will act as a deterrent to other would-be traffickers and thus reduce cases of human trafficking.

Zimbabwe **repatriated** **120** ⚥ trafficked to Kuwait

The United States Department of State annually prepares a Global Tracking Report on Human Trafficking using information from various sources in all countries across the globe. In the report, the department places each country into one of four tiers, as mandated by the United States Congress Trafficking Victims Protection Act of 2000 (TVPA), which stipulates that governments should make serious efforts to prohibit and eliminate various forms of trafficking in persons and punish acts of such trafficking. Therefore, it bases the analyses on the extent of governments' efforts to reach compliance with the TVPA's minimum standards for the elimination of human trafficking, consistent with the Palermo Protocol (Department of State, 2016).[43] The report classified SADC countries as follows:

---

[43] Department of State, USA. (2016). Trafficking in persons 2016 report. (0nline) available at https://www.state.gov/documents/organization/258876.pdf (accessed 14 July 2017).

Tier	Characteristics	SADC countries 2015	SADC countries 2016	SADC countries 2017	Comment
1	Countries whose governments fully comply with the TVPA minimum standards.	None	None		
2	Countries whose governments do not fully comply with the TVPA's minimum standards, but are making significant efforts to bring themselves into compliance with those standards.	Angola, Malawi, Mozambique, Seychelles, South Africa and Zambia	Angola, Botswana, Lesotho, Madagascar Malawi, Mauritius Namibia, South Africa and Zambia	Angola, Botswana, Lesotho, Madagascar, Malawi, Mauritius, Namibia, Seychelles, South Africa, Tanzania	Seychelles and Tanzania moved from tier 2 watch list to tier 2
2 - Watch list	Countries whose governments do not fully comply with the TVPA's minimum standards, but are making significant efforts to bring themselves into compliance with those standards and: The absolute number of victims of severe forms of trafficking is very significant or is significantly increasing; There is a failure to provide evidence of increasing efforts to combat severe forms of trafficking in persons from the previous year; or the determination that a country is making significant effort to bring itself into compliance with minimum standards was based on commitments by the country to take additional future steps over the next year.	Botswana, DRC, Lesotho, Mauritius and Namibia	DRC, Mozambique, Seychelles, eSwatini, Tanzania Zimbabwe	DRC, Mozambique, eSwatini, Zambia, Zimbabwe	Zambia downgraded from tier 2 to tier 2 watch list. Zimbabwe upgraded from tier 3 to tier 2 watch list.
3	Countries whose governments do not fully comply with the minimum standards and are not making significant efforts to do so.	Zimbabwe[45]			No SADC country in tier 3.

Source: Department of State, USA. Trafficking in persons 2017 Report.

Table 5.8 shows that since 2015, no SADC country has ever sat in tier 1. However, SADC countries have been moving in the right direction: in 2016, nine countries ranked in tier 2 and in 2017 that number rose to ten countries with Seychelles and Tanzania moving from tier 2 watch list to tier 2.

In the past year, the Seychelles government initiated its first investigation and prosecution under the anti-trafficking law and allocated a budget for the national anti-trafficking committee. Meanwhile, the Zimbabwean government has made some progress by working with Kuwait to repatriate and refer to care 121 female trafficking victims. It also repatriated five victims from Sudan.[46]

Article 20.6: State parties shall ensure that cases of gender-based violence are conducted in a gender sensitive environment.
Article 20.7: State parties shall establish special counselling services, legal and police units to provide dedicated and sensitive services to survivors of gender violence.
Article 23.2: State parties shall ensure accessible, effective and responsive police, prosecutorial, health, social welfare and other services to redress cases of gender-based violence.

---

[44] Ibid.
[45] Department of State, USA. Trafficking in persons 2017 report.
[46] Department of State, USA. Trafficking in persons 2017 report. Available at https://www.state.gov/documents/organization/271345.pdf (accessed 25 May 2018).

14

countries

now

have

Sexual

Harassment

Laws

The police and health care providers often serve as the first point of contact for victims of GBV, thus underscoring the need for specialised training for those working in both sectors. Police departments in all SADC countries have created specialised units that aim to address domestic violence cases in sensitive ways.

As of 2015, the **Angola**n government had 27 domestic violence counselling centres, seven other shelters and various treatment centres throughout the country.[47] The ministry in charge maintained a program with the Angolan Bar Association to give free legal assistance to

abused women and established counselling centres to help families cope with domestic abuse.

In **Zambia**, the police have been trained to provide pregnancy prevention and HIV prevention services to victims, as well as to refer them to health providers for further care.[48] As noted in the 2016 Barometer, almost all governments have made efforts to address GBV cases in gender sensitive ways by establishing specialised courts and one stop centres (Lowe Morna et al 2016).[49] The 2017 Barometer also outlined some of the countries that have victim support centres within police stations (Lowe Morna et al, 2017).[50]

Sexual harassment

Article 22.1: State parties shall enact legislative provisions and adopt and implement policies, strategies and programmes which define and prohibit sexual harassment in all spheres, and provide deterrent sanctions for perpetrators of sexual harassment.
Article 22.2: State parties shall ensure equal representation of women and men in adjudicating bodies hearing sexual harassment cases.

Fourteen countries now have sexual harassment legislation: Of these, only a few have stand-alone sexual harassment laws; in most countries this is covered in the labour laws and penal codes (Lowe Morna et al, 2016). Despite having far-reaching impacts on victims, sexual harassment is rarely acknowledged, let alone reported. Sexual harassment has often been hidden and normalised. In many settings, people in positions of power trivialise sexual harassment, sadly this includes the victims themselves (Hinde, 2017).[51] Thus, having legislation is only one step towards eradicating harassment. Activists and legislators must place more emphasis on raising an alarm around its abnormality. Following the Harvey Weinstein sexual

harassment saga in the United States, the #MeToo campaign has created a platform for women across the globe to share their experiences of sexual abuse in all its forms (Hinde, 2017).[52]

Prevention

To meet the goal of eliminating all forms of GBV by 2030, there is need for collaborative, integrated and coordinated approaches that aim at both responding to and preventing GBV. These approaches should operate at all levels, including individual, relationship, community and societal. The prevention model illustrates how a multisectoral approach would work.

47 Angola Human Rights Report 2017 https://www.state.gov/documents/organization/265434.pdf
48 https://www.sida.se/English/press/current-topics-archive/2016/african-network-uses-information-to-fight-gender-based-violence/
49 Lowe Morna, C. Makamure, L, Dube S. (2016). SADC Gender Protocol Barometer 2016. SADC Gender Protocol Alliance (cited in SADC Barometer 2017).
50 Lowe Morna, C. Dube S and Makamure, L (2017). SADC Gender Protocol Barometer 2017. SADC Gender Protocol Alliance.
51 Hinde, 2017. #MeToo: All Sexual Harassment Experiences Are Worth Reporting, But Don't Feel Pressured To ShareOpinion piece https://www.huffingtonpost.co.uk/entry/sexual-harassment-experiences-me-too-hashtag-pressure-to-share stories_uk_ 59e5dbf1e4b0a2324d1d825e (accessed 1 June 2018).
52 Ibid.

Figure 5.2: Multisectoral GBV Prevention Model

NATIONAL ACTION PLAN TO END GBV

PREVENTION

Arenas for action	Communication for social change strategies			Measuring change
	Short term	**Medium term**	**Long term**	
Society at large				Behaviour change
Political leadership	Targeted messages	GBV mainstreamed into programmes	GBV a key political issue	
Criminal Justice System	Tough laws	Training for personnel	Concerned as much with prevention as response	
Media	Increased media coverage	More sensitive coverage	Prevention agenda	Attitudes
Sport	Individual sportspersons take up cause	Teams take up cause at big events	GBV mainstreamed in sports training	
Community				Awareness
Community	Mobilise community to create safe spaces	Public education & awareness campaigns	Zero tolerance for GBV in communities	
Traditional leadership	Training	Harmful practices	GBV a key local issue	
Schools	Increase security in schools	Challenging gender stereotypes	Behaviour change	Information
Religion	Spread the word	Review own practices	Lead the campaign	
Home				
Abusive men	Stop violence	Join the campaign	Lead the campaign	
Abused woman or child	Shelter and temporary life skills	Secondary housing	Economic Empowerment	

SUPPORT

RESPONSE

Figure 5.2 presents the GBV Prevention Model, which UNICEF South Africa commissioned in the hope that stakeholders can adapt it for any context. The model brings all sectors together in GBV prevention efforts and is premised on the observation that GBV interventions have been more reactive than proactive. It covers what is meant by prevention and the relationship between prevention; response and support; the need for an overarching framework; the arenas for action as well as short, medium and long-term actions to be taken; communication for social change theories that should underpin any action as well as measuring progress to advance from information to behaviour change (Gender Links, et 2008).[53]

Often there is a fine line between prevention and response. Each can enhance the effectiveness of the other. For example, strong laws and sanctions against GBV can have a preventive effect. Strong rehabilitation programmes for perpetrators of GBV can help to ensure that they do not become repeat offenders. Programmes of support for women that include economic empowerment can help to ensure that women do not become repeat victims. To date, stakeholders have mostly addressed GBV through reactive strategies. Prevention efforts, to the extent they have existed, have largely been driven by the women's movement. These have focused on changing social norms, building individual empowerment and addressing underlying structures that perpetuate VAW. The primary focus, however, has been at the level of response (Lowe Morna et al 2017).[54] Response efforts focus on developing crisis services, law enforcement interventions, and judicial sanctions. In contrast, primary prevention focuses on education and includes efforts to change individual attitudes and social norms - what a community regards as acceptable behaviour from its citizens.[55]

Fine line between prevention and response

53 South Africa Violence Prevention Model and Action Plan developed by Gender Links, UNICEF (2008). Available at https://www.unicef.org/southafrica/SAF_resources_violenceprevmodel.pdf
54 Lowe Morna, C. Dube S and Makamure, L (2017). SADC Gender Protocol Barometer 2017 Southern Africa. SADC Gender Protocol Alliance.
55 Oregon Violence Against Women Prevention Plan; Oregon Department of Human Services; Office of Disease Prevention Epidemiology.

South African universities forced to address GBV following national outcry

South African universities have been grappling with the scourge of GBV on campus for some time. A 2017 research paper by Youth and Policy concluded that South African universities lacked policy frameworks to effectively address the issue, which some worried could derail efforts in the country to improve female university enrolment. This fear is not far-fetched given that students at some of the major universities in the country have previously reported that they left school because they felt unsafe and unprotected from GBV on campus.

Over the past several years, several rapes of students occurred at the University of Cape Town. Additionally, in November 2016, a student was raped at the University of the Witwatersrand's Junction

Rhodes University students take part in the anti-rape protests in April 2016. *Photo courtesy of Mail & Guardian*

Residence and the university indicated that it planned to assist the student in line with its sexual harassment, sexual assault and rape policy. In April 2016, students at Rhodes University held protests following what they called the university's failure to adequately deal with cases of rape at the university. At the time of the protests, the Student Representative Council reported that at least 21 students had been raped since the beginning of the year. University of the Witwatersrand students held protests in solidarity with their peers at Rhodes university following these reports.

Given that GBV is one of the most gendered human rights violations, it is critical that leaders tackle the scourge with the seriousness that it deserves. Thus, a crucial step occurred in April 2018, when the Department of Higher Education and Training announced that the South African government would come up with a standardised framework to address GBV at universities, which universities across the country must implement.

This is a major step given that the issue became a national crisis that required the intervention of government as opposed to leaving individual universities to come up with their own frameworks. The national framework will soon guide universities across the country in coming up with their own institutional frameworks. The standardised approach will also assist those universities that do not currently have frameworks or those that have weak or difficult to implement frameworks. Other SADC governments should consider a similar approach to guide universities in creating policies to protect students from GBV.

Stakeholders can adopt three categories of prevention intervention,[56] namely:
- ***Primary prevention:*** interventions aimed at addressing GBV before it occurs, to prevent initial perpetration or victimisation, targeted action aimed at behavioural issues and risk producing environments.
- ***Secondary prevention***, which happens immediately after the violence has occurred to deal with the short-term consequences, e.g. treatment and counselling.

- ***Tertiary prevention*** focuses on long term interventions after the violence has occurred to address lasting consequences, including perpetrator counselling interventions.

The DRC Gender-based Violence Initiative (GBVI) provides a good case study of synergising response and prevention mechanisms, with the effort to eradicate GBV. The project operated at all the three levels of prevention identified above.

---

[56] Centres for Disease Control and Prevention. (2004). Sexual Violence Prevention: Beginning the Dialogue. Atlanta, GA p.3.

Primary prevention aims to address GBV **before** it occurs

Creating "space" to address GBV in Mozambique

In 2011, the US President's Emergency Plan for AIDS Relief (PEPFAR) launched the US$55 million, three-year, interagency Gender-Based Violence Initiative (GBVI) in three SADC countries: the DRC, Mozambique and Tanzania. The GBVI aimed to integrate GBV prevention and response into existing HIV prevention, care, and treatment programmes at health facility, community and policy levels.

The GBVI report.

Photo courtesy of Google images

In Mozambique, stakeholders designed the US$21 million, three-year GBVI to prevent cases of GBV by addressing the sociocultural norms that condone it and by offering comprehensive post-GBV care services for survivors. The GBVI was unique in Mozambique because it attempted to address GBV prevention and response using a multisectoral, multilevel approach that involved health and social services and legal and law enforcement at national, institutional/facility, and community levels.

Strategies
At that time, because several Civil Society Organisations (CSOs) were conducting HIV prevention projects across the country, the GBVI saw an opportunity to work through these CSOs. Through the Capable Partners (CAP) project, run by FHI360, GBVI identified six CSOs with which to partner. The CSOs developed activities targeting individuals, communities and leaders for community dialogues, media campaigns and other activities.

Successes
- The GBVI contributed to shaping and operationalising plans and strategies, including a multisectoral plan and the national GBV plan for the health sector. The GBVI supported the Ministry of Health, the Ministry of the Interior, and the Mozambican Armed Forces to develop GBV prevention and response pre-service curricula and modules and conducted mass media campaigns and broader GBV and HIV awareness-raising activities at all levels.
- At institutional level, the GBVI facilitated an integration of GBV prevention and response activities within existing HIV clinical services by building clinical and medico-legal capacity and establishing comprehensive post-GBV care services. Stakeholders designed activities to build the capacity of NGOs and CSOs to include GBV within HIV prevention and behaviour change communication activities.
- Acknowledging the role of media, the GBVI trained journalists, including military journalists, to report responsibly on GBV issues, including child sexual abuse and child protection.
- Building on existing HIV prevention initiatives, the GBVI supported community-level prevention activities. It employed participatory and gender-transformative approaches to conduct information, education, and communication; social and behaviour change; community engagement; and community-clinic linking activities. This entailed developing training manuals, communications packages, and audio-visual materials such as pamphlets, radio and TV spots.

A government representative in Mozambique noted: "Now everyone is on board, they are willing to open up a budget line to address prevention regarding GBV. Even the other day, someone from the Ministry of Culture said they want to do a radio soap opera on GBV. It wasn't like this before. There is space to address GBV now."

Source: adapted from an FHI360 report[57] and a PEPFAR report[58]

---

[57] FHI 360. Mozambique GBV integration available at https://www.fhi360.org/sites/default/files/media/documents/resource-spt-cap-mozambique-gbv-integration.pdf (Accessed 1 June 2018).
[58] AIDS Free. Lessons from GBVI in DRC. available at https://aidsfree.usaid.gov/sites/default/files/aidsfree.usaid.gov/sites/default/files/events/presentations/gbvi_5.10_gennari_moz_0.pdf (Accessed 1 June 2018).

Protocol@Work

Article 21.1: State parties shall take measures including legislation, where appropriate, to discourage traditional norms, including social, economic, cultural and political practices which legitimate and exacerbate the persistence and tolerance of gender-based violence with a view to eliminate them.

Mellish and Colleagues (2015) did a literature review of harmful traditional practices that perpetuate GBV in Malawi. The review brought forward an extensive list including forced marriage, child marriage, polygamy, paying of bride price, acceptance of extra-marital sex in men, ceremonial dances and rituals, property rights and wife inheritance, among others. However, they did not include practices such as witchcraft allegations in their list. But recent evidence shows that women continue to fall victim to this practice, as noted in the GBV Study in Limpopo, South Africa (Machisa et al 2014).[59]

Highlighting witchcraft allegations as a form of GBV

Witchcraft allegations constitute one of the most common cultural practices in sub-Saharan Africa, where the belief in witchcraft remains widespread. Ghorbani (2015) reports that, on average, 55% of the population believes in witchcraft with the rate varying from 15% in Uganda to 95% in Ivory Coast, with Ghana (77%), Democratic Republic of Congo (76%) and Tanzania (64%) in the top 10 countries with strong personal beliefs in witchcraft. Witchcraft is a criminal offence in all these countries. Women make up most people targeted by accusations of witchcraft, resulting in them experiencing abuse and other harmful practices.[60] According to the Angola 2016 Report on Human Rights Practices, several women and children faced abuse following accusations of witchcraft by their communities.[61] Similarly in DRC, one NGO reported receiving several

messages highlighting the practice of "witchcraft tests" on women suspected of witchcraft in the South Kivu province. This Province is known for high levels of violence against women. With the aim of bringing GBV to light in all its various forms, it is important to recognise such practices as infringements on women's rights.[62]

Witchcraft is widespread in sub-Saharan Africa - women are mostly accused, resulting in abuse and other harmful practices.
Photo courtesy of Google images

59 Machisa, M, T. and. Musariri L. (2013). Peace Begins at Home, the Gender Based Violence Indicators Study, Limpopo Province of South Africa. Gender Links.
60 Ghorbani, M. (2015) Witchcraft Accusations Perpetuate Women's Oppression in Sub-Saharan Africa available at https://www.awid.org/news-and-analysis/witchcraft-accusations-perpetuate-womens-oppression-sub-saharan-africa (accessed 29 May 2018).
61 USAID. (2016). Angola Human Rights Practices Report. Available at https://www.state.gov/documents/organization/265434.pdf (accessed 29 May 2018).
62 https://www.awid.org/news-and-analysis/witchcraft-accusations-perpetuate-womens-oppression-sub-saharan-africa (accessed 29 May 2018).

South Africa witchcraft accusations persist even as courts dispense harsh punishments

History is replete with cases of women, and in particular elderly women, being killed, assaulted or harassed on allegations of practising witchcraft. In Western Europe, more than 200 000 "witches" were tortured, hanged or burned between 1484 and 1750. Whilst the killing of "witches" has vanished in Western Europe, the issue persists in Africa, including in Southern Africa, and other regions of the world.

Five members of one family killed Catherine Nkovani in 2016 after accusing her of witchcraft.
Photo courtesy of Daily Sun

South Africa has recorded its fair share of witchcraft murders, violence and harassment, with many women targeted by communities and family members. The courts in the country have played an important role in punishing perpetrators of this violence and in the process protecting women from one of the worst forms of GBV. In 2016, the Limpopo High Court sentenced five members of the same family to between 16 years and life imprisonment for murdering 52-year old Catherine Nkovani, whom they accused of practising witchcraft. Nkovani's 18-year old grandson also died on the same day when the five villagers torched their hut.

In March 2018, the Willowvale Regional Court in the Eastern Cape sentenced a 29-year-old man to four life terms for, amongst other offences, killing an 80-year old grandmother and her two grandchildren after accusing the grandmother of witchcraft. Similarly, in April 2018, the Limpopo High Court sentenced 35-year old William Lebogo to life imprisonment for murdering his grandmother, whom he accused of witchcraft.

The pattern shows that courts have been handing down life sentences for murders linked to accusations of witchcraft. These sentences should be a deterrent, and they plan a vital role in protecting women, and in particular older women, from so-called witchcraft murders. It is important for courts in South Africa and in other SADC countries to continue playing this important role in protecting women from this dangerous form of GBV. The approach taken by the courts also acts as an awareness-raising approach to end the harassment, murder and torture of women on allegations of witchcraft.

Political commitment
The GBV/VAW Baseline studies measure political commitment at three levels:
- Short term, which looks at targeted messages made by the government officials;
- Medium term, including policy (re)formulation and (re)programming to mainstream GBV; and
- Long term commitments that include budget readjustment towards financial commitment for GBV policies and programming.

While it is easy to assess the targeted messages and policy-related progress, financial commitment is more difficult due to lack of explicit budgets ringfenced for GBV programming. Bureaucratic barriers make it even harder to access information on budgets and expenditure related to GBV. For the sake of accountability, as well as for monitoring and evaluation, governments should make this information available.

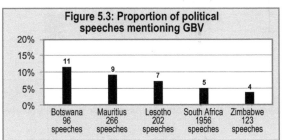

Figure 5.3: Proportion of political speeches mentioning GBV

	Botswana 96 speeches	Mauritius 266 speeches	Lesotho 202 speeches	South Africa 1956 speeches	Zimbabwe 123 speeches
	11	9	7	5	4

Source: GBV/VAW Baseline studies, Gender Links.

Figure 5.3 shows the extent to which GBV featured in high level speeches, ranging from 11% in Botswana, to 4% in Zimbabwe. In Botswana, only 6% of speeches featured GBV as the main topic. In South Africa, only 1% specifically focused on GBV, with 91% of these occurring during the 16 Days of Activism and on Women's Day (Lowe Morna et al 2017).[63]

GBV featured in **high level speeches**, ranging from **4%** in Zimbabwe to **11%** in Botswana

---
[63] Lowe Morna, C. Dube S and Makamure, L (2017). SADC Gender Protocol Barometer 2017 Southern Africa. SADC Gender Protocol Alliance.

are

more

aware

of the

16 Days

campaign

in all

countries

except

Botswana

Article 21.2: State parties shall in all sectors of society introduce and support gender sensitisation and public awareness programmes aimed at changing behaviour and eradicating gender-based violence.

Community mobilisation and campaigns

To date, all SADC countries have implemented prevention strategies to raise awareness and advocate for GBV prevention. These include coordinated campaigns, which, based on anecdotal evidence, remain the most common strategy across the region, especially during the 16 Days of Activism. While the 16 Days campaign has gained momentum across the region, many governments and civil society organisations want to turn the campaign into a 365-day campaign. GL has worked with ten countries to develop 365 Days NAPs to end GBV. However, lack of political commitment has resulted in many of these NAPs sitting on shelves.

16 Days of Activism

The 16 Days of Activism on VAW, which runs from 25 November through 10 December each year, continues to be one of the most publicised awareness-raising campaigns. Over the years, this period has occupied a significant place in the calendars of tens of thousands of civil society organisations, women's organisations, governments and activists who come together to raise awareness about VAW. However, the VAW/GBV Baseline Studies in the seven countries show that, on average, most women and men in all seven countries remain relatively unaware of this campaign.

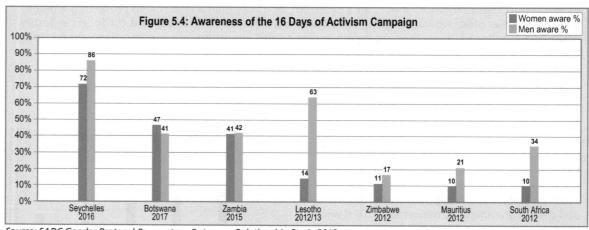

Figure 5.4: Awareness of the 16 Days of Activism Campaign

Source: SADC Gender Protocol Barometers, Botswana Relationship Study 2018.

Figure 5.4 shows that women's awareness of the 16 Days campaign ranges from 72% in Seychelles to 10% in Mauritius and South Africa. Men's awareness levels range from 86% in Seychelles to 17% in Zimbabwe. In all countries except Botswana - and most significantly in Lesotho, where 63% of the men interviewed, compared to 14% of women, said they knew about the campaign) - men appear more aware of the campaign. However, in interpreting these findings, it is important to note when researchers conducted the study because there has recently been a notable increase in awareness, as seen in the most recent study from Botswana. The Botswana Relationship Study of 2018 illustrated a distinct increase in the proportions of women and men knowledgeable about 16 Days since the 2012 study.

Table 5.9: Awareness of GBV campaigns

	Women		Men	
	2012 Study	2017 Study	2012 Study	2017 Study
Heard about 16 Days	16%	47%	18%	41%

Source: Botswana Relationship Study 2018.

As noted in Table 5.9, small numbers of men and women said they had heard about the 16 Days campaign when asked in the 2012 Baseline Study: 16% of women and 18% of men. Yet in the 2018 follow-up study, 47% of women and 41% of men knew of the same campaign. This significant rise in awareness may attest to the success of staying the course with awareness-raising campaigns on the part of both civil society and government.

However, the Executive Director of the Center for Women's Global Leadership (CWGL) notes that there is a need to transition "from Awareness to Eradication" of GBV for the next phase of 16 Days (Thompson 2017) activism.[64] It is important to also look at the impact of these campaigns. The Seychelles GBV study (2017) and Botswana Relationship Study (2018) assessed if the knowledge and awareness of campaigns translated to action. Both studies show that being knowledgeable about campaigns is significantly associated with intervening in domestic violence cases (Musariri and Chiramba, 2017; Chiramba et al 2018).[65]

Role of the media

Article 29.7: State parties shall take appropriate measures to encourage the media to play a constructive role in the eradication of gender-based violence by adopting guidelines which ensure gender sensitive coverage.

The Protocol urges the media to ensure gender equality in and through the media and to challenge gender stereotypes. The Protocol also discourages media from promoting pornography and violence against all persons, especially women and children.[66]

It is hard to dispute the role of the media as potential opinion-shapers and agenda-setters in the fight against GBV (Chiramba et al, 2018).[67] The media does this by covering stories that promote awareness and prevention and also counteracting myths and negative attitudes that may perpetuate violence. Drawing attention to positive stories of empowerment and resilience, for example, can assist in illustrating how survivors often act as advocates and agents of change (Lowe Morna et al, 2017).[68] In South Africa, the femicide case of Karabo Mokoena in March 2017 received extensive coverage, including daily coverage of the trial. The same is true of the 2013 femicide case of Reeva Steenkamp. Thus, it appears that the general news coverage of GBV cases has improved, even though many cases still go unreported.

Coverage
According to the *Gender and Media Progress Study* (GMPS) of 2015, which monitored news content in 14 SADC countries over one month, GBV coverage constituted 1% of the total stories covered: a significant drop from the 4% coverage in the similar study conducted in 2010. The study further reports that women's voices remain underrepresented in the media, particularly when it comes to reporting GBV (Chiramba et al, 2018).[69]

BTV covering Sixteen Days launch is Goshwe, Botswana.
Photo: Keletso Metsing

GBV

1%

of

all

stories

in 14 SADC

countries

---

[64] Thompson, C. (2017). A Life of Its Own: An Assessment of the 16 Days of Activism Against Gender-Based Violence Campaign, Center for Women's Global Leadership, New Jersey available at http://16dayscwgl.rutgers.edu/downloads/16-days-documents-general/1500-16-days-campaign-assessment-report/file (quoted in Barometer 2017)
[65] Musariri, L. and. Chiramba K, Dimensions of VAW in selected areas of Zambia, unpublished
[66] SADC Protocol on Gender and Development Article 29 (1-7).
[67] Chiramba, K. Musariri, L and Rasesigo G, (2018-unpublished). Botswana Relationship Study. Gender Links.
[68] Lowe Morna, C. Dube S and Makamure, L (2017) . SADC Gender Protocol Barometer 2017 Southern Africa. SADC Gender Protocol Alliance
[69] Chiramba, K. Musariri, L and Rasesigo G, (2018-unpublished). Botswana Relationship Study. Gender Links.

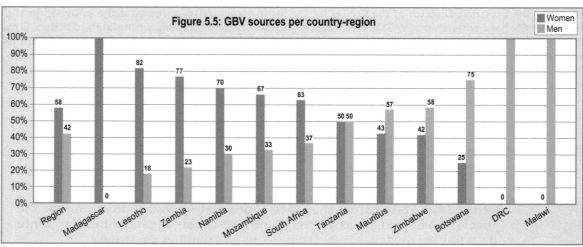

Source: Gender and Media Progress Study 2015.

Figure 5.5 shows that in some countries, only men speak to the media about GBV - DRC and Malawi, both at 100% - while in others, mostly women speak on the topic. Lesotho (82%), Zambia (77%), Namibia (70%), Mozambique (67%) and South Africa (63%) represent those countries in which more women serve as news sources in stories about GBV: a sign of progress in a region that long looked to men as experts on a subject that mostly affects women.

Sensitivity
The Global Media Monitoring Project (GMMP) 2015 conducted by the World Association of Christian Communicators (WACC), found that "Overall, women remain more than twice as likely as men to be portrayed as victims than they were a decade ago, at 16 and 8%, respectively." The VAW Baseline studies shows that, while GBV is one of the better-covered gender topics in the media, coverage is often gender biased. Men still make up most sources and most stories emanate from court reporting, where the cards remain heavily stacked against women. First-hand accounts of women seldom feature (Lowe Morna, 2017).[70]

Critical engagement
When it comes to covering GBV stories, media houses tend to sensationalise and trivialise the stories, inhibiting critical engagement by the public. "Often the media fails to move beyond the tragic headlines and into the reality of what gender violence is and how to address it in daily life to give context and more information for the betterment of their stories" (Chiramba et al, 2018).[71]

Social media
The intersection between social media and mainstream media is important. Mainstream media often picks and augments its story ideas from social media (Chiramba et al, 2018). The last 15 years have seen a growing use of the social media as a platform for discussing and debating GBV, creating opportunities for community mobilisation. Although there is no evidence that social communications alone can prevent violence, some assessments have shown significant changes in knowledge and use of services, attitudes towards gender, and acceptance of VAW as a major issue.[72] A study by Powell (2015), explores how communication technologies (such as social media campaigns) can be viewed as new mechanisms of informal justice outside of the state for GBV survivors. This is the case in the name and shame campaigns, which in some ways empower the survivors.[73]

more than twice as likely as to be portrayed as victims

[70] Lowe Morna, C. Dube S and Makamure, L (2017). SADC Gender Protocol Barometer 2017 Southern Africa. SADC Gender Protocol Alliance.
[71] Chiramba, K. Musariri, L and Rasesigo G, (2018-unpublished). Botswana Relationship Study. Gender Links.
[72] Thompson, C. (2017). A Life of Its Own: An Assessment of the 16 Days of Activism Against Gender-Based Violence Campaign, Center for Women's Global Leadership, New Jersey available at http://16dayscwgl.rutgers.edu/downloads/16-days-documents-general/1500-16-days-campaign-assessment-report/file (cited in Barometer 2017).
[73] Powell, A. (2015). Seeking rape justice: Formal and informal responses to sexual violence through technosocial counter-publics. Theoretical Criminology.

Social media for social activism

Social media tools such as Facebook, YouTube, Twitter and blogging sites have become part of the daily lives of millions of people across the globe (Chiramba et al 2018). Recently, social media has played a critical role in shedding light on some of the less-researched and difficult-to-detect forms of violence. Recent online campaigns have managed to break geographical and socio-economical barriers by collapsing the world and bringing people from diverse backgrounds together to talk about gender issues and share their experiences of GBV, thereby fostering solidarity (Chiramba et al, 2018).[74]

In 2017 in Botswana, protesters took part in a march under the slogan, "I wear what I want."
Photo courtesy of Thalefang Charles (The Monitor)

The #MeToo campaign, which began in the United States in October 2017,[75] brought a new category of people into the discussion: the elite. The campaign started with one Hollywood actress encouraging women to share their experiences of sexual abuse. Numerous sexual abuse allegations then emerged against film producer Harvey Weinstein. The now global campaign disrupted the Hollywood film industry and other sectors, with many women speaking out to expose the famous, powerful, rich and usually untouched perpetrators of sexual violence. These campaigns underscore that GBV has no social barriers: rich and powerful women share the same risk of experiencing violence at the hands of their male counterparts, possibly even a higher risk.

In South Africa, a group of activists with the mandate of highlighting GBV cases perpetrated by powerful political leaders, launched the #NotOurLeaders campaign during the 16 Days of Activism in 2017. Spearheaded by Women and Democracy Initiative, Lawyers for Human Rights and gender violence specialists, the campaign highlighted 20 cases of political leaders who have faced allegations of sexual misconduct. The nature of the misconduct included demanding sex for jobs or promotions, verbal and physical harassment, sexual assault and rape - including rape of children (Dullah Omar Institute Website).[76]

In 2016, the social media campaign #MenAreTrash emerged as a response to the femicide case of Karabo Mokeana and many other femicide cases in South Africa (Lowe Morna et al, 2017).[77] It generated much debate in South Africa and the world over, with many responding with a counter campaign #NotAllMenAreTrash. Some activists rejected the counter campaign as a tactic by men to silence women through refusing to take responsibility for their actions. The debate surrounding these campaigns serves as a mirror to reflect societal attitudes surrounding gender equality, particularly the rift between men and women activists.

The Botswana #IWearWhatIWant campaign also made waves recently and invoked much debate. It came in response to a sexual harassment incident in 2017 at a taxi rank in Botswana in which a woman said she faced harassment for wearing a mini skirt. Following this report, activists took to the streets in revealing outfits to send the message that women can dress as they like and feel safe from abuse and harassment. Conservative groups condemned the campaign as obscene. Again, the dialogue surrounding this campaign revealed the general attitudes in many communities (Chiramba et al 2018).[78]

The success of these campaigns provides evidence that activists can use social media as a tool for campaigning. At the opening of the 62nd Session of the Commission on the Status of Women (CSW62), UN Women Executive Director Phumzile Mlambo-Ngcuka applauded the #MeToo movement and women in Hollywood as having energised changes in attitudes about sexual harassment. "We want to continue to forge an alliance with women who are in that [Hollywood] space so that their victory will be everyone's victory."[79]

---

74 Chiramba, K. Musariri, L and Rasesigo G, (2018-unpublished). Botswana Relationship Study. Gender Links.
75 Although the MeToo campaign was popularised in 2017 via the hashtag campaign, it is said to have started in 2006.
76 Dullah Omar Website available at https://dullahomarinstitute.org.za/women-and-democracy/notourleaders accessed 30 May 2018.
77 Lowe Morna, C. Dube S and Makamure, L (2017). SADC Gender Protocol Barometer 2017 Southern Africa. SADC Gender Protocol Alliance.
78 Chiramba, K. Musariri, L and Rasesigo G, (2018-unpublished). Botswana Relationship Study. Gender Links.
79 UN Women website available on http://www.unwomen.org/en/news/stories/2018/3/press-release---eu-un-spotlight-initiative-urges-action-on-vaw (accessed 29 May 2018).

Growing use of social media to discuss and debate GBV

Engaging men and boys in the fight against GBV

If the goal is to eradicate GBV, there is a need to work with men and understand why they perpetrate it. The role of men, not only as aggressors, but also as potential allies, facilitators, and activists in the fight against GBV, has begun to be viewed as an indispensable element that requires specific policies and strategies (MenEngage, 2014 in Aguayo et al., 2016). There is also an emerging recognition of the need to involve male traditional and religious leaders. For many women around the world, community-based, customary justice mechanisms remain the only available method of redress.

As noted earlier, the Seychelles National Baseline Study (2016) and the Botswana Relationship Study 2018 brought key issues to light about violence against men that previously had not received much attention, despite being critical in the fight against GBV.

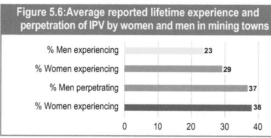

| Figure 5.6:Average reported lifetime experience and perpetration of IPV by women and men in mining towns | | |

Source: Botswana Relationship Study 2017.

Figure 5.6 shows that the average experience of IPV by women in mining towns is 38%, closely corroborated by 37% men reporting perpetration. At the same time, 23% of men reported experiencing, and 29% of women reported perpetrating, IPV in the mining towns of Botswana. This points to the need to target mining towns in prevention campaigns, and to pay attention to VAM.

Support

Women victims of GBV often experience life-long emotional distress, mental health problems and poor reproductive health, as well as being at higher risk of acquiring HIV and becoming intensive long-term users of health services.[80] This underscores the need for efficient support structures. Studies show that survivors of VAW seek support from formal and informal sources (Coker, 2000). Informal resources include family, friends and faith-based communities where survivors generally seek support before approaching formal support sources. Formal resources include health professionals, the criminal justice system and police services (Musariri et al 2015).[81] The region now has several good examples of support structures to help address and respond to GBV.

Shelter workers in Mauritius file information about GBV into their database.   *Photo: Loga Virahsawmy*

The **South African** Police Service (SAPS) has more than 800 Victim Friendly Rooms (VFR) at police stations across the country. 87 VFRs were placed at other locations such as airports, railway police stations.[82]

In **Tanzania**, the government established 417 Police Gender and Children Desks (PGCDs) to deal with cases of GBV.[83]

The **eSwatini** government established the Domestic Violence, Child Protection and Sexual Offenses (DCS) Unit in 2002 to provide services to survivors of violence particularly women and children. eSwatini now has child friendly units in 24 police stations[84].

---

80 Lowe-Morna, C., Makamure, L., Dube, S. (2016) SADC Gender Protocol Barometer (online) available at http://genderlinks.org.za/shop/sadc-gender-protocol-barometer-2016/ (accessed 12 July 2017).
81 Musariri L., Nyambo, V., Machisa, M, T., Chiramba, K. (2015). The Gender Based Violence Indicators Study, Lesotho. Gender Links.
82 Musariri L., Nyambo, V., Machisa, M, T., Chiramba, K. (2014). The Gender Based Violence Indicators Study, Western Cape. Gender Links. Available at http://genderlinks.org.za/wpcontent/uploads/imported/articles/attachments/19466_chp6_gbv_wc_pg89-pg108lr.pdf#page/10 (accessed 1 August 2017).
83 USAID. 2017. Police Action Planning Report available at https://aidsfree.usaid.gov/sites/default/files/2017.1.4_police-action-planning-report_v2.pdf (accessed 1 August 2017).
84 Observer website. Available at http://www.observer.org.sz/news/74803-cops-trained-on-gbv.html (accessed 1 August 2017).

As of 2013, **Malawi** had established Victim Support Units in 34 police stations as well as 200 support units in 300 Traditional Authority institutions.[85]

In **Botswana**, each police station has a police officer trained on GBV and other gender-related matters.

The GBV/Baseline Studies by Gender Links established that women prefer informal or traditional support to formal support. The excerpt below from Lerato's "I" Story (from the Botswana "I" Stories) shows how the traditional and civil support structures can work well together, underscoring the need to include informal support systems in the efforts to eradicate GBV.

*"The police then made me a piece of writing to go to the hospital with and we were asked to return to the police station for the matter once my eye had healed. Once my eye healed we were summoned to the police station and in the presence of the Chief, * Phokoje[86] was informed that his actions were against the law and he could go to jail for assault. Phokoje apologised to me, my family and the Chief for his actions and explained that he had never acted in that manner before. He was reprimanded and warned that if he repeated the offence we would end up in jail. Phokoje has since that occasion never laid a hand on me nor has he raised his voice towards me. We live happily together and my eye is completely healed and has no problems."*

Article 23.1: State parties shall provide accessible information on services available to survivors of gender-based violence.

Previous sections on awareness-raising touched on the progress of state parties in providing information to the public. The case study below touches specifically on how survivors of GBV receive information from an NGO in DRC.

Women lawyers donate their time to represent survivors in DRC

The DRC does not yet have a specific law to respond to its high levels of domestic violence. Legislators made some amendments in the new Family Code (2016) removing several discriminatory provisions in terms of access to land and resources for women as well as increasing the minimum age of marriage for girls from 15 to 18.[87] Meanwhile, the sexual offences act addresses some forms of domestic violence.

The DFJ comprises eight women lawyers who donate their time to represent women affected by violence. *Photo courtesy of DFJ website*

Despite a lack of strong laws to protect GBV survivors, some members of DRC civil society have taken responsibility for tackling this scourge. Dynamique des Femmes Juristes (DFJ) is a human rights organisation of female lawyers that works in eastern DRC to assist survivors of domestic violence. DFJ is dedicated to raising awareness about domestic violence and offering legal recourse to local women affected by GBV. Due to prolonged periods of war in the eastern part of DRC, many members of society have normalised violence, particularly rape. Thus, DFJ raises awareness by engaging communities in questioning the normality of violence. As lawyers, they have framed GBV as a human rights issue that requires legal recourse.

---

[85] United Nations. 2013. Statement by Malawi Minister available at http://www.un.org/womenwatch/daw/csw/csw57/generaldiscussion/memberstates/malawi.pdf (accessed 1 August 2017).
[86] Pseudonym used in the 'I" Story project conducted by GL.
[87] http://documents.worldbank.org/curated/en/481341525730456994/pdf/Project-Information-Document-Integrated-Safeguards-Data-Sheet-DRC-Gender-Based-Violence-Prevention-and-Response-Project-P166763.pdf

prefer informal or traditional support to formal support

The eight female attorneys who make up the organisation work hard to let women know that justice is not a luxury that society can choose to bestow upon women: it is a well-deserved right. They advocate for the rights of vulnerable women who cannot afford court costs and represent local women in their court cases. In their Kirumba field office, they help in around eight cases of rape and domestic violence each month.

In 2017, the organisation says it reached more than 100 000 people with campaigns about protecting women's rights. During the same period, they helped resolve around 24 cases, with perpetrators facing arrest or incarceration for abusing women. Apart from working directly with victimised women and the community at large, DFJ has also formed strategic partnerships with human rights defenders, men and local authorities. They also assist human rights defenders who have been threatened or who have proceedings initiated against them because of their work.

By witnessing perpetrators being arrested, communities can see that violence is wrong and the authorities will punish perpetrators. Simultaneously, it may encourage survivors to speak out and report cases of violence to the police if they feel assured of legal recourse. Despite being run by attorneys whose main role is to provide legal services, the DFJ also provides medical, psychological and financial services. The organisation also builds women's skills so they can take part in decision-making bodies in both the public and private sectors, developing the potential of women so that they engage in the promotion, protection and defence of their rights.[88]

Adapted from the Global Press Journal

 **Article 23.3:** State parties shall provide accessible, affordable and specialised legal services, including legal aid to survivors of gender-based violence.

All SADC countries now have accessible, affordable and specialised services for survivors of GBV. However, legal aid is still a challenge in most countries. The 2016 Global Study on Legal Aid by UNDOC shows that one third of 153 countries have not yet enacted specific legislation on legal aid and only half offered legal aid to GBV survivors. The study covered five countries from the SADC region: Angola, DRC, Mauritius, Seychelles and South Africa.[89] The VAW Baseline studies in the seven countries also showed that legal aid to survivors of violence remains limited. In most countries, NGOs provide these services, with many struggling due to inadequate funding.

 Article 23.4: State parties shall provide specialised facilities including support mechanisms for survivors of gender-based violence.

Specialised units for survivors of violence, known as one-stop centres, are now widespread in the region. Every SADC country has at least one form of these, including one-stop centres, rape crisis centres, victim support units and sexual offences courts. One stop centres provide multi-sectoral case

The Mauwa community one-stop centre in Malawai helps families deal with physical and sexual violence.
Photo: UNFPA Malawi / Henry Chimbali

---

88 Adopted from Global press Journal available at https://globalpressjournal.com/africa/democratic-republic-of-congo/drc-female-lawyers-take-domestic-violence/ and DFJ website http://www.dfj-rdc.org/forum-sur-le-leadership-feminin-en-action-au-nord-kivu/
89 UNODC Report (2016) available https://www.unodc.org/documents/justice-and-prison-reform/LegalAid/Global_Study_on_Legal_Aid_-_FINAL.pdf

management for survivors, including health, welfare, counselling and legal services in one location. Most countries link them to the police through referral pathway, usually locating crisis centres in health facilities, including the emergency departments of hospitals, or as stand-alone facilities near a collaborating hospital.[90] Many countries have rape crisis centres, which NGOs usually run, providing support to victims (e.g., counselling, telephone helpline) and information about the legal system.

Perpetrators of GBV

Article 20.4: Article 20.4: States parties shall put in place mechanisms for the social and psychological rehabilitation of perpetrators of gender-based violence.
Article 23.5: State parties shall provide effective rehabilitation and re-integration programmes for perpetrators of gender-based violence.

"Filling up prisons and detention centres is not the solution. The solution is education, structural inclusion and ending poverty and marginalisation."[91] (Tarcila Rivera, Indigenous Rights Activist from Peru)

Although not well documented, most countries provide some psychological rehabilitation to perpetrators of GBV. The departments of correctional services in most countries in the region also offer rehabilitation and re-integration services for perpetrators of GBV. To engage perpetrators of violence, South Africa has been employing a restorative justice approach that seeks to address the hurts and the needs of both victim and offender in a way that brings healing to both parties, including their families and or communities.[92] However, some have contested this approach because they believe it encourages a culture of impunity as it ignores the need for punishment (ISS Africa Website).[93] Organisations that work with men to end GBV have played a significant role in engaging perpetrators of GBV, including the MenEngage network, which has a presence in most SADC countries.[94] One example is Sonke Gender Justice, a member of MenEngage.

Training of service providers

Article 24: State parties shall introduce, promote and provide:
(a) Gender education and training to service providers involved in gender-based violence, including the police, the judiciary, health and social workers;
(b) Community sensitisation programmes regarding available services and resources for survivors of gender-based violence; and
(c) Training of all service providers to enable them to offer services to people with special needs.

The solution = education, structural inclusion and ending poverty

90 End VAW Now website http://www.endvawnow.org/en/articles/1564-one-stop-centres-osc.html accessed 2 June 2018)
91 Quote by Tarcila Rivera, Indigenous Rights Activist from Peru, Spotlight Initiative CSW 2018 http://www.unwomen.org/en/news/stories/2018/3/news-coverage-csw62-side-event-on-the-eu-un-spotlight-initiative (accessed 2 June 2018).
92 South Africa Department of Justice available at http://www.justice.gov.za/rj/rj.html (accessed 27 May 2018).
93 Batley M, Restorative Justice In The South African Contexthttps://oldsite.issafrica.org/uploads/111CHAP2.PDF
94 Minerson, Todd, H. Carolo, T. Dinner, C. Jones. (2011). Issue Brief: Engaging Men and Boys to Reduce and Prevent Gender-Based Violence. Status of Women Canada. Available at http://whiteribbon.ca/wp-content/uploads/2012/12/wrc_swc_issuebrief.pdf (accessed 29 July 2017).

Seeng Manko and Matumelo Seboko take part in a GBV training workshop at Mmelesi Lodge in Lesotho in 2018. *Photo: Ntolo Lekau*

The VAW Baseline studies show that the attitude of police officers toward GBV survivors discourage women from reporting such violence. The establishment of victim support units within police stations has resulted in increased training of police officers throughout the region (Lowe Morna, 2017).[95]

To date, all countries in SADC have conducted some form of training with GBV service providers, especially police officers. Most countries refer to the number of people trained rather than the impact of the training. There is a need to assess the quality of training to ensure it is effective, as well as to develop indicators for measuring the outcome of training.

Integrated approaches

Article 25: State parties shall adopt integrated approaches including institutional cross sector structures, with the aim of **eliminating** gender based violence.

At some point over the past decade, all SADC countries have created NAPs to end GBV. In some instances, stakeholders did not formally adopt the draft NAPS until they expired, although they implemented some of the actions. Implementing agencies cite resource constraints as a key limitation. This has led to the drive for stakeholders to financially cost all NAPs. Lesotho, Mauritius, Seychelles, eSwatini and Zimbabwe have developed fully-costed NAPS.

Another challenge in the implementation of NAPS links to the coordination of implementation and data management. Some countries have developed multi-sector structures with a mandate to track and evaluate implementation. Examples include the Mauritian Platform against GBV, Zambia Anti-GBV National Committee, the Zimbabwean Anti-Domestic Violence Council and the now-defunct SA GBV Council. These structures have also had limited impact because of a lack of funding for their operations.

Table 5.10: Trends Table - Number of National Action Plans to end GBV							
Angola	**Botswana**	**DRC**	**Malawi**	**eSwatini**	**Tanzania**	**Zimbabwe**	**Expired/status unknown**
Presidential Decree 26/13 of May Executive Plan of Fight against Domestic Violence	National Strategy 2016 - 2020 on the elimination of GBV and action plan	National Strategy on Combating Gender Based Violence being updated (2018)	National Plan of Action to Combat Gender-Based Violence in Malawi 2014-20	National Strategy to End Violence 2017 -2022	National Plan of Action to End Violence Against Women and Children (NPA-VAWC 2017/18 - 2021/22	Zero Tolerance 365: National Programme On GBV Prevention And Response 2016-2020	Seychelles (2011) Lesotho Madagascar Mauritius (2015) Mozambique Namibia (2016) Seychelles South Africa Zambia

Source: SADC Barometer (2017).

95 Lowe-Morna, C., Makamure, L., Dube, S. (2017) SADC Gender Protocol Barometer (online) available at http://genderlinks.org.za/shop/sadc-gender-protocol-barometer-2017/

Countries have conducted training with GBV service providers, especially police

As illustrated in Table 5.10, only seven countries currently have current NAPs. Nine countries have action plans that expired or that lawmakers need to update. In the countries in which GL conducted GBV baseline studies, GL worked with national and local governments to develop action plans to end GBV. In all these countries, GL has managed to work with local government to review local action plans to end GBV, aligning them to the findings from the study. To date, stakeholders have reviewed more than 50 GBV local action plans in the seven countries. GL is using the results from the GBV Baseline studies to lobby local governments to review and develop action plans that address economic justice at local level.

 The successful launch of the **Botswana** VAW Baseline study gave the Botswana government an impetus to develop a new costed NAP. Having just concluded the follow-up study, the government should be able to strengthen the local action plans using its findings.

Lesotho launched its VAW Baseline Report in April 2015, followed by a two and half day intensive work- shop to review the NAP to end GBV and to develop a national strategic communication plan. The workshop resulted in a comprehensive NAP to end GBV which the Ministry of Gender reviewed, costed and adopted in May 2015.

Similarly, in **Zimbabwe**, GL successfully launched the VAW Baseline study, for which stakeholders then drafted a 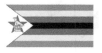 costed NAP. However, Zimbabwe has note yet fully implemented the NAP.

 South Africa has not adopted a NAP since the annulment of the SA GBV Council in 2014. Civil society has been mobilising the public and spear-heading a campaign demanding the government create a national strategy plan (NSP) to end GBV. In the process, activists drafted a shadow NSP that the national government has yet to adopt. GL continues to lobby the government to conduct a national Baseline GBV Study to inform the NSP.

During the launch of the **Mauritius** Baseline Study in 2012, the govern- ment also launched a now-expired, costed NAP. The NAP addressed some of the recommendations from the VAW Baseline study. Since inception, GL has been enga- ging the government on strengthening the updated NAP using findings from the baseline study.

GL Botswana staff displaying play cards on GBV.

Photo: Keletso Metsing

Next steps

Prioritise GBV data

- **Prioritise GBV data:** If the goal is to eliminate GBV, there is a need to understand the root causes (through comprehensive and reliable data) and to assess what is working in effectively addressing various forms of GBV across the region (through standardised monitoring and evaluation). The GBV/VAW Baseline studies, which researchers have so far conducted in seven countries, provide this comprehensive information. Botswana is the first country to undertake a follow-up GBV study, which is more comprehensive and covers violence against women and men. GL will continue lobbying other countries in the region to undertake GBV Baseline Studies and follow up studies in the six pilot countries.
- **Spotlight GBV:** There is a need to ride on the current wave of various campaigns, especially those targeting leadership e.g. #NotOurLeaders. A lack of political commitment has been hindering GBV response as some of these leaders are perpetrators themselves hide behind money and power. Once society holds these leaders accountable, the effects can trickle down to the whole society.
- **Prevention** needs to sit at the centre rather than at the end of the continuum for ending GBV. This entails addressing those factors that make individuals victims or perpetrators.
- **Legal:** There is a need for a comprehensive mapping exercise on the content of various laws.

Such an analysis will ensure that stakeholders can outline and address the current gaps and concerns in GBV-specific laws. This is particularly important in the context of conflicting customary law or norms. The customary law and traditional practices in general may hinder the enactment, enforcement or the general acceptance of civil law by the society. The region can achieve these through strengthening, adopting and reforming of laws; increased efforts to raise awareness on, implement, and enforce laws; improved women's access to justice; and continued efforts to adopt and improve national action plans.
- **Support:** Overall, many countries provide services to survivors and perpetrators of GBV. However, some of the services are of low quality. Indicators should cover quantity and quality. It is also important to consider including informal structures of support, such as faith leaders and communities at large, to ensure they provide proper, human rights-based support.
- **Integrated approaches:** Addressing the different forms GBV requires strengthening the multi-sectoral approach. This includes the justice and legal, security, health (including sexual and reproductive health), education, economic, social services, humanitarian, and development sectors. These approaches must work at the individual, family, community, local, national, and global levels.

Articles 26

A group of interns at work at a hospital in Antananarivo, Madagascar, in 2018.
Photo: Zotonantenaina Razanandrateta

Teenage pregnancy remains an **issue** in several countries in the region

KEY POINTS

- The SheDecides movement has drawn renewed focus to the imperative of enabling women, and particularly young women, to have control over their own sexual and reproductive health and wellbeing.

- Maternal mortality across most of SADC, except for Mauritius and Seychelles, remains unacceptably high and it is declining too slowly to meet even the SDG target of 70 per 100 000 live births.

- Only South Africa and Mozambique have legislation that allows abortions on request. In late 2017, Madagascar passed the Reproductive Health and Family Planning Law after a clause that would have legalised abortion had been removed, and Angola has withdrawn a bill that legislators there passed in early 2018 that would have made abortion illegal after women marched in the streets against it.

- Leaders in SADC must address the differentials in access to all sexual and reproductive health services and maternal health services between rural and urban and across wealth quintiles to achieve the goals of the SADC Protocol.

- Stakeholders have been focusing on menstrual health and hygiene for the first time, especially for young women. But there is an acknowledgement that these issues also affect older women.

- Though SADC has seen some progress in reducing child marriage (e.g. Malawi and Zambia), teenage pregnancy remains an issue in several countries in the region.

- There is an urgent need for massive investment in expanding access to improved water and sanitation services, especially in countries such as Madagascar, Tanzania, Mozambique, Angola and the DRC.

Key trends

Table 6.1: Trends in health since 2009[1]				
	Target 2030	Baseline 2009	Progress 2018	Variance (Progress minus 2030 target)
CONTRACEPTIVE USE AMONG SEXUALLY ACTIVE WOMEN				
Highest proportion of women	100%	South Africa (65%)	Mauritius (76%)	24%
Lowest proportion of women	100%	Angola (6%)	Mozambique (12%)	88%
CURRENT MATERNAL MORTALITY RATE (MATERNAL DEATHS PER 100 000 BIRTHS)				
Highest	0	Angola (1400)	DRC (693)	693
Lowest	0	Mauritius (13)	Seychelles (0)	0
BIRTHS ATTENDED BY SKILLED PERSONNEL				
Highest	100%	Mauritius (100%)	Mauritius Seychelles (100%)	0 46%
Lowest	100%	Angola Tanzania (46%)	Madagascar (44%)	
% WHO SAY A WOMAN SHOULD BE ABLE TO CHOOSE TO TERMINATE A PREGNANCY IN THE FIRST THREE MONTHS OF HER PREGNANCY				
Highest	100%		Angola (52%)	N/A
Lowest	100%		Madagascar (13%)	N/A
TOTAL COVERAGE OF SANITATION				
Highest coverage	100%	Mauritius Seychelles (100%)	Seychelles (98%)	2%
Lowest coverage	100%	Madagascar (14%)	Madagascar (12%)	88%

Source: Gender Links 2018.

Table 6.1 shows that:

- Mauritius has the highest prevalence of contraception use at 76%. South Africa held this top position in 2009 when researchers took the baseline, but coverage has declined slightly to 60%. Mozambique currently has the lowest coverage, which is an exceptionally low 12%. Angola, which held the last spot in 2009, has increased to 18%, which remains low.
- Seychelles has the lowest maternal mortality ratio in the region, with a negligible number of women dying because of pregnancy or child birth. Seychelles and Mauritius have consistently had the lowest ratios. DRC (693 per 100 000) has the highest maternal mortality. DRC has surpassed Angola, where the maternal mortality ratio over this period dropped from 1400 per 100 000 to 477 per 100 000. As countries affected by, and recovering from, conflict, DRC and Angola have consistently had the highest maternal mortality ratios.

- Skilled personnel attend all births in Mauritius and Seychelles, which represent the SADC countries leading on this indicator. The lowest level has shifted slightly from 46% in Tanzania and Angola at baseline to 44% in Madagascar now. A stricter definition of what constitutes "skilled" may result in lower coverage rates in the future.
- The Barometer has introduced a score on attitudes towards abortion for the first time. The trends table shows that Angola (52%) had the highest proportion of women and men agreeing or strongly agreeing that "a woman should be able to choose to terminate a pregnancy in the first three months of her pregnancy." Madagascar (13%) had the lowest proportion of women and men agreeing with this statement.
- Madagascar also remains in the worst spot for sanitation coverage, at just 12%, a decrease of two percentage points since 2009.

---

[1] Tracking of trends in health is compromised as new data is only available when researchers conduct new surveys, which is often only once every five years or so. Even then, researchers do not conduct surveys for all countries in the same year and therefore data is not always comparable. Although much routine health data is collected and reported it is not easy to compile into coverage as it does not indicate the denominator.

Table 6.2: Health Indicators

Indicator	Angola	Botswana	DRC	eSwatini	Lesotho	Madagascar	Malawi	Mauritius	Mozambique	Namibia	Seychelles	South Africa	Tanzania	Zambia	Zimbabwe
% Contraceptive use among sexually active women	18	53	20	65	60	40	59	76	12	56	n/a	60	34	49	67
Country policy on termination of pregnancy	Illegal except to save a woman's life	Permitted in first 16 weeks in case of rape, defilement, incest	Illegal except to save a woman's life	Illegal except to save a woman's life	Illegal except to save a woman's life or if the child is in danger of abnormalities	Illegal except to save a woman's life	Illegal except when necessary to preserve a woman's life	Illegal except to save a woman's life; if woman is in danger of permanent damage of if the child is in danger of abnormalities	Legal up to 12 weeks; if incest up to 16 weeks; if foetal anomalies up to 24 weeks	Illegal except if a threat to health of mother, or if the child is in danger of abnormalities, or conception was illegal	Illegal except to save a woman's life	Legal and women can choose to terminate pregnancy	Illegal except when necessary to preserve a woman's life	Legal in limited circumstances, but lack of awareness and stigma inhibit access	Illegal except to save a woman's life; child is at risk or conception was unlawful
Maternal mortality ratio (out of 100, 000 live births)	477	129	693	389	487	353	634	53	489	265	(no input)	138	398	224	443
% Births attended by skilled personnel	50	99	80	88	78	44	90	100	54	88	99	94	64	63	78
% Total coverage of sanitation facilities	52	63	29	57	30	12	41	93	21	34	98	66	16	44	37
% Urban coverage	89	79	37	63	37	18	47	94	42	54	97	70	31	56	49
% Rural coverage	22	43	29	56	28	9	40	93	10	17	97	61	8	36	31

Source: Gender Links, 2018.

Table 6.2 goes into further depth of the key indicators linked to sexual and reproductive health and rights in the SADC region in 2018. This includes details of each country's legislative stance on abortion. It also illustrates huge disparities throughout the region in several indicators, including sanitation coverage, which remains inadequate in most countries, especially in rural areas, yet is very good in Seychelles, with almost full coverage in both rural (97%) and urban areas (97%).

Background

The World Health Organisation (WHO) notes that "Healthy women, children and adolescents whose rights are protected are the very heart of sustainable development." The WHO constitution enshrines their inherent right to the highest attainable standard of health, as does international human rights law. WHO notes that when countries uphold this right to health, "their access to all other human rights is also enhanced, triggering a cascade of transformative change."

Survive, thrive and transform: that is the clarion call of the Global Strategy for Women's, Children's and Adolescents' Health (2016-2030). If leaders uphold rights to health and through health, delivery of the Sustainable Development Goals (SDGs) will indeed leave no one behind.[2]

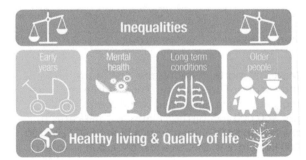

"Healthy children & adolescents whose **rights** are **protected** are the very **heart** of sustainable development"

---

2 WHO, 2017. Leading the realization of human rights to health and through health: report of the High-Level Working Group on the Health and Human Rights of Women, Children and Adolescents: Report of the High-Level Working Group on the Health and Human Rights of Women, Children and Adolescents. http://apps.who.int/iris/bitstream/handle/10665/255540/9789241512459-eng.pdf;j Accessed 16 June, 2017.

Maternal Mortality Ratio

Article 26 (a): State parties shall, in line with the SADC Protocol on Health and other regional and international commitments by member states on issues relating to health, adopt and implement legislative frameworks, policies, programmes and services to enhance gender sensitive, appropriate and affordable quality health care, in particular, to:

a) Eliminate maternal mortality; and

b) Develop and implement policies and programmes to address the mental, sexual and reproductive health needs of women and men in accordance with the Programme of Action of the International Conference on Population and Development (ICPD) and the Beijing Platform for Action.

The Maternal Mortality Ratio (MMR) represents the number of women of child-bearing age who die during pregnancy or within 42 days of termination of pregnancy, irrespective of the duration and site of the pregnancy; from any cause related to or aggravated by the pregnancy or its management (but not from accidental or incidental causes) per 100 000 live births.[3] The MMR represents the risk associated with each pregnancy and birth and reflects the ability of a country's healthcare system to provide safe care during pregnancy and childbirth. A live birth refers to any baby that is born and shows signs of life outside of the womb.

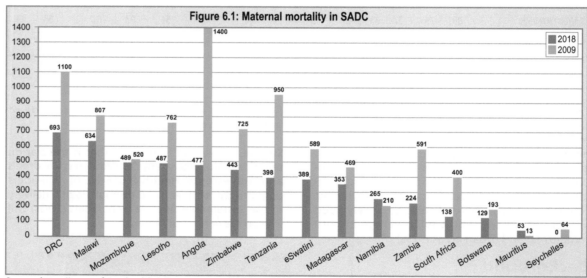

Figure 6.1: Maternal mortality in SADC

Source: https://www.africanhealthstats.org, accessed 14 June 2018, and Gender Links 2009.

Maternal mortality represents one of the sharpest indicators of inequality. Thus, while maternal mortality in the developed world stands at only 12 per 100 000 live births,[4] Figure 6.1 indicates that the rate in SADC varied from a high of 693 per 100 000 live births in DRC to a low of zero in Seychelles. It also shows progress in reducing the MMR in SADC member states from 2009 when Gender Links launched the first Barometer, to 2018. Angola had the greatest reduction (1400 to 477) followed by DRC (1100 to 693): both post-conflict countries with remarkably high levels in 2009. Both have also had lower HIV and AIDS prevalence compared to other SADC countries. High mortality related to HIV and AIDS has contributed to much slower rates of MMR reduction in much of SADC. Thus, maternal

---

[3] MMR definition.
[4] http://www.who.int/news-room/fact-sheets/detail/maternal-mortality accessed June 17, 2018

mortality increased slightly in Namibia (from 210 to 265), remained at almost the same level in Mozambique (520 to 489) and decreased very slowly in Botswana (193 to 129) and eSwatini (589 to 389).

Countries also have internal inequalities between younger and older women, rural and urban, poorer and wealthier. Achieving the SADC Protocol goal of eliminating maternal mortality will require commitment from families, local authorities, national governments and development partners.

Countdown to 2030

Mothers breastfeed their babies at a clinic in Mbare, a suburb of Harare, Zimbabwe's capital city. *Photo: Tapiwa Zvaraya*

The international community has established a multi-institutional body, Countdown to 2030, to track progress in implementation of Every Woman Every Child Global Strategy for Women's, Children's and Adolescents' Health (2016-2030). It tackles questions on improved achievement of reproductive, maternal, newborn, child and adolescent health. Countdown 2030 focuses on 81 countries that account for only 47% of the total global population and 64% of births but 90% of child deaths and 95% of maternal deaths:[5]
- Fifty-three countries with an under-five mortality rate or MMR higher than the SDG target fall among the countries that account for 95% of all under-five or maternal deaths. SADC members states included in this group include Angola, DRC, Madagascar, Malawi, Mozambique, South Africa, Tanzania, Zambia and Zimbabwe.
- The remaining 23 have an under-five mortality rate or MMR higher than the SDG but do not sit among the countries that account for 95% of all under-five or maternal deaths. These countries typically have small total populations and include

SADC member states Botswana, eSwatini, Lesotho and Namibia.

Because they have comparatively low under-five mortality rates and MMR, Countdown does not include Mauritius and Seychelles.

Countdown has developed a composite coverage index, which includes a set of indicators across the continuum of maternal and child care. Researchers calculated this index for those countries with available data. SADC member states exist in both the ten countries with the lowest coverage - Nepal, Afghanistan, Niger, **DRC, Angola,** Mali, Yemen, Guinea, Nigeria and Chad - as well as the ten countries with the highest coverage levels across the continuum of care: Turkmenistan, Dominican Republic, **eSwatini, Malawi, Namibia,** Algeria, Kyrgyzstan, **Lesotho,** Indonesia and **Zimbabwe.**

WHO estimated the major causes of maternal mortality in sub-Saharan Africa in 2013:

- Indirect (other conditions such as Malaria, HIV and AIDS, etc.)   29%
- Haemorrhage or severe bleeding (usually after delivery)   25%
- Hypertension during pregnancy   16%
- Sepsis because of infections (usually after delivery)   10%
- Unsafe abortion   10%

The Countdown report draws attention not only to access to services such as antenatal care, but to the quality of care that women can access. For instance, the range of interventions that is available for antenatal care (ANC) should include: tetanus immunisation; syphilis screening and treatment; HIV testing and access to anti-retroviral treatment (ART); intermittent therapy for malaria; hypertension screening and management; and iron supplementation. Many ANC services do not include this full range.

Access to health services

Most maternal mortality is preventable with access to good prenatal, delivery and post-natal care. This includes at least four ANC visits, with the first in the first trimester of pregnancy; deliveries in health facilities, attended by skilled health personnel; special support for younger and older mothers; adequate spacing between pregnancies; safe abortion and post-abortion services; and prevention and management of malaria and HIV and AIDS.

5   United Nations Children's Fund (UNICEF) and the World Health Organization (WHO), 2017. Tracking Progress towards Universal Coverage for Reproductive, Newborn and Child Health: The 2017 Report. Washington, DC: https://data.unicef.org/wp-content/uploads/2018/01/Countdown-2030.pdf   Accessed 17 June, 2018.

Maternal mortality is a telling indicator of inequality

Country	ANC (%)		Place of residence (%)		Household wealth quintile (% with ANC coverage)				
	At least one visit	At least 4 visits	Urban	Rural	1st	2nd	3rd	4th	5th
	2010-2015								
Angola	82	61	74	39	34	45	64	82	88
Botswana	94	73	76	70					
DRC	88	48	61	42	38	41	45	49	64
eSwatini	99	76	82	74	74	71	70	83	85
Lesotho	95	74	80	72	67	69	71	77	89
Madagascar	82	51	75	47					
Malawi	95	51	59	49	48	49	49	50	60
Mauritius	-	-							
Mozambique	91	51	60	47	37	42	50	54	64
Namibia	97	63	64	61	60	54	59	65	78
Seychelles	-	-							
South Africa	94	76	73	80	70	75	78	77	80
Tanzania	91	51	64	45					
Zambia	96	56	56	55	48	53	53	51	65
Zimbabwe	98	76	77	75					

Derived from Antenatal care coverage: at least one visit - Percentage and Antenatal care coverage: at least four visits - Percentage. https://data.unicef.org/topic/maternal-health/antenatal-care/ Last accessed 20 June 2018.

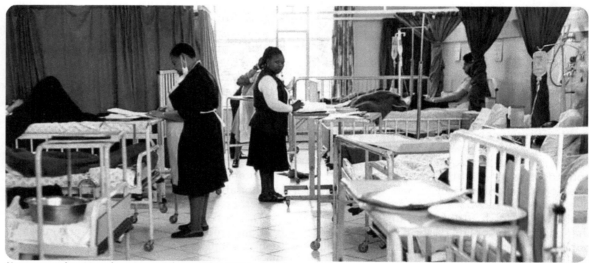

Nurses at work at Mamohato Memorial Hospital in Maseru, Lesotho.

Photo: Lesotho Times

Access to ANC is an important contributor to reduction in maternal mortality. Table 6.3 summarises the most recent data, showing that coverage of at least one ANC visit is high across the region, with the lowest levels at 82% in Angola and Madagascar and high levels up to 99% in eSwatini and 98% in Zimbabwe. However, coverage of the recommended four visits is much lower, as low as 48% in DRC and 51% in Madagascar, Malawi, Mozambique and Tanzania. Research shows the highest levels, at 76%, in South Africa, eSwatini and Zimbabwe.

Table 6.3 also highlights wide disparities between urban and rural ANC coverage in some countries. This includes Angola (74% urban compared to 39% rural) and Madagascar (75% urban compared to 47% rural), with much narrower differentials in countries such as Namibia, where the difference is 64% urban and 61% rural, and Zimbabwe at 77% urban and 75% rural. South Africa is unusual in having higher coverage in rural areas than urban, reflecting good rural coverage and poor health services in some urban areas, especially informal settlements. Table 6.3 also illustrates differentials according to wealth quintile, which separates households into five quintiles (lowest income through to highest income) to compare the influence of wealth on various population, health and nutrition indicators. The most pronounced differential is in Angola, with narrower differences in other countries, including South Africa and eSwatini.

W I D E
disparities
between
urban and
rural
antenatal
care

Table 6.4: Post-natal care coverage for mothers in SADC

Country	Year	National (%)	Residence (%)		Household wealth quintiles (% with PNC coverage)				
			Urban	Rural	1	2	3	4	5
Angola	2016	23	31	12	9	13	27	36	41
DRC	2014	44	57	38	35	36	42	48	63
eSwatini	2014	88	94	85	82	86	85	95	92
Lesotho	2014	62	70	59	46	54	68	68	80
Malawi	2016	42	52	41	39	39	42	47	48
Namibia	2013	69	69	69	61	74	73	69	66
South Africa	2016	84	85	81	81	80	87	85	87
Tanzania	2016	34	48	29	22	29	32	41	54
Zambia	2014	63	81	54	47	55	65	78	84
Zimbabwe	2015	57	67	53	47	52	56	64	69

Source: https://data.unicef.org/topic/maternal-health/ Post-natal check-up for mothers/ Last accessed 20 June, 2018.

Table 6.4 presents the most recent available data on post-natal care (PNC) for mothers, which is also a principal factor in maternal wellbeing because several conditions, such as sepsis, can result in maternal deaths after delivery. Coverage of PNC is lower than that of ANC, with the widest differential being in Angola (61% for four ANC visits compared to 23% for PNC). However, other countries such as South Africa, eSwatini, Namibia and Zambia have higher coverage of PNC than four ANC visits. The region has general differentials of access between urban and rural areas and across wealth quintiles. Only Namibia has the same level of access for urban and rural, but this is a relatively low 69%. eSwatini has the highest coverage at 88% overall.

Access to skilled health professionals

Access to skilled health professionals - such as doctors, nurses or midwives - who have access to transport for an emergency referral is a critical factor in reducing maternal mortality. Many conditions that result in maternal mortality can be managed or mitigated with timely medical assistance.

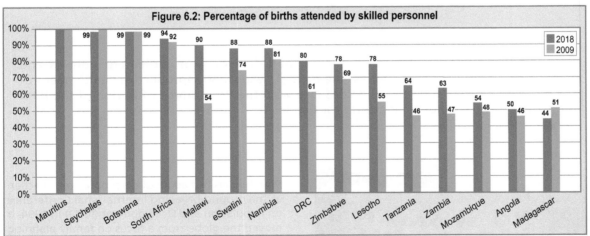

Figure 6.2: Percentage of births attended by skilled personnel

Source: UNICEF/WHO joint database on skilled attendance at birth https://data.unicef.org/topic/maternal-health/delivery-care/ accessed 16 June 2018 and Gender Links 2009.

Presence of skilled health professionals varies significantly: Figure 6.2 shows the percentage of births attended by skilled personnel in the region, comparing 2009 and 2018. It varies from a low of 44% in 2018 in Madagascar to a high of 100% in Mauritius. Five countries have more than 90% of births attended by a skilled health professional (Mauritius, Seychelles Botswana, South Africa and

Malawi) while only two still have 50% or fewer. Figure 6.2 also shows the progress countries have made in the decade since the Barometer has been tracking this indicator. This is marked for countries such as Malawi where the increase has been from 54 to 90%, Lesotho from 55 to 78% and slower for those which had high levels already in 2008 (Mauritius, Seychelles, Botswana and South Africa) or which were very low, such as Mozambique and Angola. Only one country, Madagascar, regressed, dropping from 51% of births attended by a skilled person to 44%. Overall, progress occurs thanks to political will and partnerships.

Throughout the MDG era, stakeholders paid attention to increasing the number of deliveries attended by a skilled health professional who could handle normal deliveries safely and recognise and refer complicated cases for emergency care. However, as increased coverage has not translated to marked reductions in maternal mortality, WHO, UNICEF and others convened a task force of experts to review the definition of skilled birth attendance. The revised definition is:

"Skilled health personnel, are competent maternal and newborn health (MNH) professionals educated, trained and regulated to national and international standards. They are competent to:
(i) Provide and promote evidence-based, human-rights based, quality, socioculturally sensitive and dignified care to women and newborns;

(ii) Facilitate physiological processes during labour and delivery to ensure a clean and positive childbirth experience; and

(iii)Identify and manage or refer women and/or newborns with complications.

Rusape Town Council members during a field visit in the council in north-eastern Zimbabwe.   *Photo: Tapiwa Zvaraya*

In addition, as part of an integrated team of MNH professionals (including midwives, nurses, obstetricians, paediatricians and anaesthetists), they perform all signal functions of emergency maternal and newborn care to optimise the health and well-being of women and newborns.

Within an enabling environment, midwives trained to International Confederation of Midwives (ICM) standards can provide nearly all of the essential care needed for women and newborns. (In different countries, these competencies are held by professionals with varying occupational titles.)"[6]

The new definition will bring greater focus to the issue of competence and motivation of health personnel, as well as support for health personnel to perform their life saving work.

Sexual and reproductive health and rights

Article 26 (b): State parties shall develop and implement policies and programmes to address the mental, sexual and reproductive health needs of women and men in accordance with the Programme of Action of the ICPD and the Beijing Platform for Action.

Photo: Boaki Fofana, All Africa.com

Stakeholders first adopted the programme of action at the ground-breaking International Conference on Population and Development (ICPD) in 1994. It moved the globe from a focus on family planning to reproductive and sexual health for women and men, girls and boys. The programme asserts that everyone counts, and that development policy must improve individual lives and address inequalities. In 2014, the UN General Assembly extended the programme of action indefinitely.

---

6 WHO. 2018. Definition of skilled health personnel providing care during childbirth: the 2018 joint statement by WHO, UNFPA, UNICEF, ICM, ICN, FIGO and IPA.

sexual,
reproductive
health and **rights**

"A state of physical, emotional, mental, and social well-being related to sexuality. It is not merely the absence of disease, dysfunction or infirmity. Sexual health requires a positive and respectful approach to sexuality and sexual relationships, as well as the possibility of having pleasurable and safe sexual experiences, free of coercion, discrimination and violence. For sexual health to be attained and maintained the sexual rights of all persons must be respected, protected and fulfilled."[7]

In line with the above WHO definition, reproductive healthcare is "the constellation of methods, techniques and services that contribute to reproductive health and well-being by preventing and solving reproductive health problems. It also includes sexual health, the purpose of which is the enhancement of life and personal relations, and not merely counselling and care related to reproductive and sexually transmitted disease."

Source: International Conference Population and Development report, para 7.2

SheDecides

Lilianne Ploumen, the Dutch minister for foreign trade and development cooperation, launched the SheDecides movement on 24 January 2017, a day after US President Donald Trump reinstated a rule blocking any US government funding to organisations that give women access to, or information about, safe abortion. Thirty-six champions lead the SheDecides movement - women and men, government ministers from developing and developed nations, activists from around the world - which urges all to "Stand up, speak out, change the rules and unlock resources" which can support education and information for girls and women about their bodies and their options, contraceptive methods and safe abortion.

WHEN SHE DECIDES

The world is better, stronger, safer.

She decides whether, when, and with whom.
To have sex.
To fall in love.
To marry.
To have children.

She has the right.
To information, to health care, to choose.

She is free.
To feel pleasure.
To use contraception.
To access abortion safely.
To decide.

Free from pressure.
Free from harm.
Free from judgement and fear.

Because when others decide for her, she faces violence, forced marriage, oppression.

She faces risks to her health, to her dignity, to her dreams, to her life.

When she does not decide, she cannot create the life she deserves, the family she wants, a prosperous future to call her own.

We – and you, and he, and they – are uniting. Standing together with her so she can make the decisions only she should make.

Political leadership and social momentum are coming together like never before.

But we can go further, and we can do more.

From today, we fight against the fear.
We right the wrongs.
We mobilise political and financial support.
We work to make laws and policies just.
We stand up for what is right.

Together, we create the world that is better, stronger, safer.

But only if. And only when.

She. Decides.

Activists marked the first SheDecides day on 2 March 2018, with events in 19 countries around the world. Youth representatives from Ethiopia, Kenya, Malawi, Mozambique, Namibia, Rwanda, Tanzania, Uganda, Zambia and Zimbabwe attended the main event in South Africa. Concrete actions

taken at the event included launching the Uganda and Tanzania SheDecides movements and a call from South African Health Minister Aaron Motsoaledi to SADC health ministers to adopt the SheDecides scorecard at their ministers' meeting in November.

Ten SADC countries have sexual and reproductive health policies:

- eSwatini - National Policy on Sexual and Reproductive Health, 2013;
- Lesotho - National Reproductive Health policy, 2008;
- Madagascar - Reproductive Health and Family Planning Law, 2017;
- Malawi - National Reproductive Health and Rights Policy, 2009;
- Mauritius - National Sexual and Reproductive Health Policy, 2007;
- Mozambique - National Sexual and Reproductive Health Policy, 2011;
- Namibia - National Policy for Reproductive Health, 2001;
- Seychelles - Reproductive Health Policy for Seychelles, 2012;
- South Africa - Sexual and Reproductive Health and Rights: Fulfilling our Commitments 2011-2021 and "National Adolescent Sexual and Reproductive Health and Rights Framework Strategy"; and
- Zambia - National Reproductive Health Policy, 2008.

Others have guidelines, such as:
- Botswana - policy guidelines and service standards for sexual and reproductive health, 2015; and
- Tanzania - SRHR guidelines and National Adolescent Reproductive Health Strategy, 2011 - 15.

Activists marked the 1st #SheDecides day on 2 March 2018

---

[7] World Health Organisation (2002). The world health report 2002 Reducing risks, promoting healthy life, World Health Organisation.

Local council in eSwatini provides SRHR education to younger adolescents, sex workers and adults

Even though eSwatini passed a National Policy on Sexual and Reproductive Health in 2013, access to SRH services in the country remains patchy. For this reason, the Pigg's Peak Council, in the north-west of the country, launched a programme to provide access to reproductive health services. It specialises in health education programmes for pregnant women and their partners, adolescents, sex workers and adults. It also provides capacity building and support for Council staff.

The Council works to meet the needs of adolescents in the community in a positive and responsible way. Initiatives include school retention and education programmes; sexuality education and life-skills training; health care training; and sensitisation on legal issues, such as age of consent and minimum age for marriage. Previously in the community, older adolescents, aged 15-19 years, traditionally received the lion's share of attention, while stakeholders have typically neglected the special needs and concerns of younger adolescents, those aged 10-14 years - some of whom are already sexually active.

Systematic data about the lives of young adolescents in developing countries remains scarce. Although researchers often collect data about school attendance and economic activities of 10-14-year-olds, they tend to only ask questions about sexual activity, condom and contraceptive use and knowledge of HIV and AIDS of respondents aged 15-19 years and older.

To serve younger adolescents, the Council partnered with Save The Children to provide sexual and reproductive information in a sensitive and age appropriate way. This includes through dialogues and discussions in communities. The programme also provides sex education to sex workers and adults to help them make healthy and informed sexual choices. It focuses on various themes, which include: combating HIV and AIDS infection in key populations such as sex workers, injecting drug users and men who have sex with men; SRHR and young people; and SRHR and young people in fragile states in Africa. This includes combating sexual violence against girls in conflict areas; female genital mutilation; teenage pregnancy; child marriage; and child prostitution.

So far, the project has served more than 600 people in the community. Bethulsile Mncina, one of the peer educators in the Council's youth department, noted "Each one of us can make a difference, and together we make change."

The Council has involved both women and men in the programme, pairing senior-level male staff with women to help build women's skills and prepare them to rise through the Council ranks. By making a conscientious effort to remove gender disparities and equalise the work environment, the Council's men

and women have increased support to each other, ensuring the entire organisation ends up better off as a result. "Many movies have strong female leads: brave, self-sufficient girls that don't think twice about fighting for what they believe with all their heart," said Sipho Shongwe, a former counsellor in the community. "They'll need a friend, or a supporter, but never a saviour. Any woman is just as capable of being a hero as any man."
Source: Protocol@Work Summit, 2018

Community members learn about SRHR during a 2018 training workshop in Pigg's Peak.   *Photo courtesy of Linda Chissano*

In December 2017, **Madagascar** passed the Reproductive Health and Family Planning Law after many years of advocacy to revoke colonial policy that prohibited promotion of contraception. The law recognises reproductive health and family planning as basic human rights for all, irrespective of age. It defines "counselling and family planning services for sexually active teens, married or unmarried" as one of the necessary reproductive health services. The law also provides for family planning education and outreach, community-based distribution of services, improved family planning technical capacity in health facilities, and availability of commodities, including emergency contraception."[8]

Girls at Mbizo High School, in Kwekwe, Zimbabwe in 2017 carry a petition against child prostitution.
Photo courtesy of Suzanne Hazel Madamombe

Adolescent SRHR

There is growing realisation that provision of sexual and reproductive health must begin in adolescence with a continuum of care.

Kwekwe City Council youth centres provide information to youth about SRHR

Gold mining areas that have attracted large numbers of informal miners surround the city of Kwekwe in central Zimbabwe. This commercial activity has led to an increasing number of children engaging in sex work. Girls from the peri urban and rural areas migrate to Kwekwe to take part in the trade. Other SRHR issues for adolescents in Kwekwe include:

• SRHR for adolescents living with HIV and AIDS: 730 adolescents live with HIV and AIDS, most of whom contracted HIV from mother to child transmission and are now in a sexually active age group.
• Risk of HIV infection for underprivileged girls who older men lure into sexual relationships.
• Boys' belief that they should be the dominant partner in a relationship with a girl, which can lead to sexual abuse.
• Use of technology for emotional abuse e.g. one girl committed suicide when a former partner posted a video of the couple engaging in sexual activity on social media.

The Kwekwe City Council has collaborated with NGOs such as Plan, Africaid and JF Kapnec Trust, as well as government ministries, to establish youth centres in clinics. At these clinics, adolescents meet with health staff to discuss SRHR and get access to SRH and HIV and AIDS services. The Zimbabwe National Family Planning Council (ZNFPC) also played a role by helping refurbish the youth centres. Additionally, the City Council contributed $5000 to support the project as well as $20 000 of in kind support.

The project aims to improve SRH decision-making skills for adolescent girls and boys and provide a space for them to discuss difficult issues such as rights to legal abortion and HIV testing; child sex work; sexual abuse; and gender-based violence (GBV). The project works with both girls and boys and has a focus on molding responsible men who will not abuse wome, who stand up against GBV and who will always practice safe sex. The youth centres also offer positive recreation for youth.

At the centres, NGOs and government ministries give workshops for the youth. The Ministry of Women's Affairs, for instance, has trained youth on entrepreneurial skills. NGOs have also conducted workshops for policymakers and the community on the SRH needs and rights of adolescents. The leadership of the centres created an adolescent SRH committee to oversee, implement and monitor the activities under the programme. So far, 1640 adolescents have benefitted directly and indirectly from the programme.

Before the programme, local adolescents living with HIV used to miss school to queue monthly for their medication. After some advocacy around the issue, the adolescents now receive enough medicine for a whole term. Stakeholders at the centres continue to advocate on other issues such as legalisation of termination of unwanted pregnancy and testing of children in schools.

One adolescent male in the programme instigated the Stop Child Prostitution campaign, noting that "Men are taking advantage of our sisters. The young girls in poverty end up doing sugar daddies and they get pregnant and die of HIV. It's now time to say 'No' to these sugar daddies."

---

8   https://medium.com/@FP2020Global_20685/madagascar-enacts-historic-family-planning-law-8ac7ab62e0ad. Accessed 20 June 2018.

Protocol@Work

One of the young women beneficiaries said: "I am a young girl whose parents have not been formally employed. I suffered sexual abuse at a young age and I was looked after by my grandmother. I got into child prostitution at 12 years after realisation that I had no hope in this life. My turning point happened when I contracted an STI and I got treatment at Al Davies Clinic and I got introduced to the adolescent SRHR programme. Since I started participating in the programme, I managed to get information that has given me hope. I am now out of prostitution."

In many places, communities cast out children involved in prostitution because they believe they are evil or did not listen to their parents. No one cares for these children. However, the community engagement provided by this project has helped shift attitudes. One woman assisted a girl after she noticed that the girl was walking strangely. The woman befriended the girl, who confided in her that she had contracted an STI but worried about seeking medical assistance. The woman took the girl to the clinic, where health professionals treated her.

In the past, the community had also held a negative attitude towards those who attended the youth centres, with many worrying the programme encouraged children to have sex. After a programme review, stakeholders decided that the programme could also train policymakers and community members. This sensitisation helped increase attendance to the centres.

Source: Protocol@Work Summit, 2018

Teenage pregnancy

There is a close relationship between teenage pregnancy and child marriage. In some instances, unintended pregnancy results in child marriage. In others, child marriage results in teenage pregnancy. Unintended pregnancy is often a result of poor or inaccurate knowledge about SRHR, with poor access to SRH services, especially contraception. Levels of access to contraceptives are much lower for adolescents than for older women.

Table 6.5: Rates of births by age 18	
Country	**Births by Age 18 (%)**
Mozambique	40
Madagascar	36
Malawi	31
Zambia	31
Lesotho	29
Tanzania	28
DRC	27
Zimbabwe	22
eSwatini	17
South Africa	15
Namibia	15

Source: UNICEF Global Database: Child Marriage. https://data.unicef.org/topic/child-protection/child-marriage/ and Births by 18. https://data.unicef.org/topic/maternal-health/adolescent-health/ Last accessed 29 June 2018.

Table 6.5 illustrates that high numbers of young girls in SADC continue to bear children before they turn 18 and become adults. This includes more than one-third of girls in Mozambique and Mada-gascar and more than a quarter of all young girls in Malawi, Zambia, Lesotho, Tanzania and DRC.

 In June 2018, **Zimbabwe** launched a school health policy that the ministries of health and child care and primary and secondary education jointly developed and will implement. The United Nations Population Fund (UNFPA) notes that some of the challenges facing adolescents in Zimbabwe include teenage pregnancy, sexually transmitted infections including HIV and AIDS, unsafe abortions, child marriage and lack of access to SRH information services.[9]

Menstrual health

There has been growing interest in the region around the subject of menstrual health or hygiene, particularly for adolescents. Menstruation begins with menarche, its first occurrence, usually by the age of 14. Some evidence suggests that improved health and nutritional status result in lower ages of menarche. Menstruation ends with menopause, usually around the age of 50. Menstruation signifies a woman's fertile age during which she can biologically become pregnant. Lack of preparation for menstruation, poor availability of menstrual hygiene products and pain result in menstruation often being associated with shame, fear and reduced participation by girls and women in social, cultural and educational endeavours. There has been recent interest in supporting girls to ensure participation in education, with several projects providing disposable or re-usable sanitary napkins and collaborating with schools to ensure they have adequate sanitation facilities.

---

[9] https://zimbabwe.unfpa.org/en/news/zimbabwe-school-health-policy-promote-sexual-and-reproductive-health-schools. Accessed June 30, 2018.

Teenage marriage & child marriage are **linked**

Women inspect sanitary napkins in Kadoma, Zimbabwe.
Photo: Tapiwa Zvaraya

Access to contraception

Access to contraception knowledge and commodities represents a critical step in promoting control over when and how often to have a child: being able to decide. Improved access, including availability of commodities when needed, for all women and men would result in much lower levels of unintended pregnancy, unsafe abortions and transmission of HIV from mothers to babies.

Contraceptive prevalence is the percentage of women currently using, or whose sexual partner currently uses, at least one method of contraception, regardless of the method. It is usually reported for married or in-union women aged 15 to 49. Contraceptive methods include clinic and supply (modern) methods and non-supply (traditional) methods. Clinic and supply methods include female and male sterilisation, intrauterine devices (IUDs), hormonal methods (oral pills, injectables, and hormone-releasing implants, skin patches and vaginal rings), condoms and vaginal barrier methods (diaphragm, cervical cap and spermicidal foams, jellies, creams and sponges). Traditional methods include rhythm, withdrawal, abstinence and lactational amenorrhoea.[11] As many women and their partners wish to become pregnant the target on this indicator is not 100%, but higher levels of prevalence represent more control over fertility.

There has been much less interest in menstrual health for older women, including the impact of menstruation on tertiary education or work, and little interest in issues of menstrual disorders such as dysmenorrhea (cramping) and menstrual irregularities. For women to embrace menstruation as a symbol of their power rather than something to be embarrassed about requires more research and investment in factors that promote menstrual health such as education and awareness about menstruation for girls and boys; availability and accessibility of menstrual products; and availability of adequate water and sanitation.[10]

Many **young girls** continue to **bear children** before they turn **18**

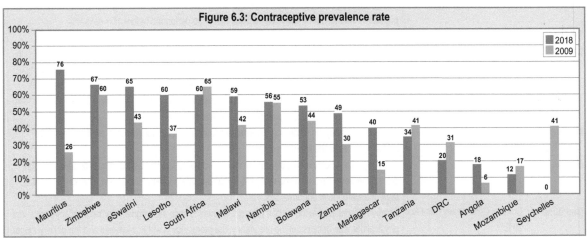

Source: https://www.africanhealthstats.org last accessed 15 June 2018, and GenderLinks 2009.

Contraceptive usage is improving: Figure 6.3 shows the contraceptive prevalence rate (CPR) in SADC, reflecting slow improvement in access to contraception in the decade that the Barometer has tracked this indicator. Mauritius has both the highest coverage at 76% and one of the greatest increases over the decade (from 26% to 76%). Other countries with significant increases in coverage over the decade include eSwatini, Lesotho, Malawi and Zambia. Mozambique still has very low coverage at 12%.

---

[10] UNFPA ESA. 2017. Menstrual Health Management in East and Southern Africa: a Review Paper. Johannesburg, South Africa.
[11] http://www.who.int/whosis/whostat2006ContraceptivePrevalenceRate.pdf

In July 2017, Family Planning 2020 (FP2020), a global partnership that "supports the rights of women and girls to decide, freely, and for themselves, whether, when, and how many children they want to have," convened a high-level meeting in London to reinvigorate efforts to expand access to contraceptives, especially for adolescents and women in humanitarian settings.[12] The meeting also considered how to finance this goal, including mobilisation of private sector contributions. FP2020 is focusing attention on 69 countries, including several SADC member states: DRC, Lesotho, Madagascar, Malawi, Mozambique, Tanzania, Zambia and Zimbabwe.

 In 2017, the **DRC** renewed its previous FP2020 commitments and committed to accelerate the achievement of 19% CPR and access to family planning services for 2.1 million additional women of reproductive age (15-49) by 2020. The DRC will: 1) support the implementation of the National Strategic Family Planning, 2014-2020; 2) from 2017, allocate domestic resources of at least

2.5 million dollars annually to "purchase of contraceptives;" 3) vote on the law on reproductive health and family planning, for all women of reproductive age, by December 2020; and 4) reform laws that protect adolescent girls from early marriage through education, awareness raising, social reintegration, and women's empowerment programs. Additionally, it will foster the support of the private sector for family planning and scale up community-based distribution of contraceptives.[13]

The right to choose

In 2006, the African Policy Framework on Sexual and Reproductive Health and Rights recommended in 2006 that policymakers needed to consider the issue of unsafe abortion in a dispassionate way. They called on them to view it as a public health issue because it results in elevated levels of morbidity and mortality in women, and particularly young women. However, in most SADC countries, the legislative environment remains unsupportive of safe abortion

Table 6.6: Legal status of abortion in SADC		
Country	Law	Main points
Angola	Penal Code 2014[14]	Termination only permissible to save the life of a woman.
Botswana	2. Penal Code (Amendment) Act, 1991 - Section 160	Abortion is only legal if: pregnancy is a result of rape; if the mother's life is at risk or may cause harm to her mentally (because of rape or incest) and physically; or the unborn child will suffer or later develop physical or mental abnormality. Termination has to be performed before 16 weeks.[15]
DRC	The constitution	Abortion is illegal except in cases where a woman's life is in danger.[16]
Lesotho	The Penal Code (2010)[17]	Abortion is not legal except to save the life of a pregnant woman (by a registered medical professional, with the written opinion of another registered medical professional); or to prevent the birth of a child who will be seriously physically or mentally handicapped, with the professional who performs the termination having obtained a certificate stating the handicap of the unborn child; termination can also be undertaken if the female is pregnant due to incest or rape.
Madagascar	Reproductive Health and Family Planning Law 2017	Abortion under any circumstance remains illegal. In Criminal Procedure law, an abortion can be performed to save the life of a woman.
Malawi	Penal Code	Currently, Malawi only allows abortion to save a woman's life. The Law Commission of Malawi has drafted the Termination of Pregnancy Bill to legalise safe abortion for women in the event of incest, rape or severe foetal abnormalities.[18]
Mauritius	Criminal Code Amendment Act 2012[19]	Abortion is legal to save the life of a pregnant woman; to save the pregnant woman from any permanent physical damage because of the pregnancy; the pregnancy is within 14 weeks and the girl is younger than the age of 16; and if the foetus may suffer severe malformation or abnormalities.

[12] http://www.familyplanning2020.org/
[13] http://www.familyplanning2020.org/entities/112   accessed June 23, 2018
[14] http://srhr.org/abortion-policies/documents/countries/01-Angola-Penal-Code-2014.pdf
[15] http://www.gov.bw/en/Citizens/Sub-Audiences/Women/Unsafe-Abortions/
https://www.hsph.harvard.edu/population/abortion/BOTSWANA.abo.htm   http://www.wipo.int/wipolex/en/text.jsp?file_id=238601
[16] https://www.google.co.za/#safe=off&q=abortion+bill+1991+democratic+republic+of+Congo (UN Publication)
[17] https://lesotholii.org/ls/legislation/num-act/6
[18] http://www.satregional.org/wp-content/uploads/2018/05/Age-of-consent-Malawi.pdf
[19] https://srhr.org/abortion-policies/documents/countries/02-Mauritius-Criminal-Code-Amendment-Act-2012.pdf
[20] https://www.womenonwaves.org/en/page/5009/abortion-law-mozambique

Mozambique has the region's **lowest** contra-ceptive prevalence

Country	Law	Main points
Mozambique	Penal Code	Abortion is legal to save the life of the pregnant woman and to safeguard her physical and mental wellness. Termination of pregnancy upon request is legal up to 12 weeks; in the case of incest, termination is legal up to 16 weeks; in the case of foetal anomalies, termination is legal up to 24 weeks. A certified practitioner must perform the termination at designated facilities.[20]
Namibia	Abortion and Sterilization Act 2 of 1975	Abortion is legal: (1) in the event that the pregnancy poses a threat to the physical and mental health of the pregnant woman - two medical practitioners must approve in writing that the pregnancy is a risk; (2) where the unborn child is at risk of a serious mental or physical deformity and handicap; (3) where two other medical practitioners confirm that the woman has been raped or is a victim of incest and (4) where a woman has been deemed to be an idiot or an imbecile as per the Immorality Act of 1957, which makes sex with her illegal.[21]
Seychelles	Termination of pregnancy Act, 2012	If three medical practitioners agree in good faith, termination can be undertaken at Victoria Hospital, Mahe, when a woman's life is deemed to be in danger or if the cost of carrying the foetus is greater than the pregnant woman's physical and mental health. Termination can be carried out if the child is at risk of serious mental and physical deformities.[22]
South Africa	Choice on Termination of Pregnancy Amendment Act No. 1 of 2008[23]	Specifies the kind of facility allowed to terminate, periods where women can terminate and the services available to any woman who wants to terminate out of choice, including counselling. It also specifies the right to terminate without consent of other parties apart from medical practitioners.
eSwatini	The Constitution	Only possible where the life of the pregnant woman is in danger.[24]
Tanzania	Penal Code[25]	Termination of pregnancy is only possible where the pregnant woman is at risk of death, or where the pregnancy threatens the mental and physical wellbeing of the pregnant woman.
Zambia	Termination of Pregnancy Act, 13 October 1972	Abortion is legal under certain conditions for social and economic reasons. Once three medical practitioners have agreed, a termination can be performed on a pregnant woman if the pregnancy will cause her death, or if the pregnancy will cause mental or physical damage to the woman, also in the event that the child is at risk of mental and physical deformities.[26]
Zimbabwe	Termination of Pregnancy Act of 1977, Chapter 15: 10[27]	Only under circumstances where the life of the mother is in danger, where the child will suffer from complications after birth or if conception is deemed unlawful (instances of rape). A magistrate must grant permission. In 2012, policy approved for women who undergo illegal abortions to receive medical post-abortion care without being referred to the police.

Source: Gender Links, 2018.

As illustrated in Table 6.6, abortion is only available on request in South Africa and Mozambique, while it is legal in Zambia under certain conditions. All other countries continue to criminalise most abortions with some exceptions, such as in circumstances where a woman's life is in danger or the pregnancy is a result of rape or incest.

 On 24 February 2018, **Angola**'s parliament approved an amendment to the abortion law, making all abortions, without exception, illegal and punish-able by between four to ten years' imprisonment. This is part of the process of replacing Angola's 1886 penal code. Parliament passed the first reading of the bill without public consultation, and activists accused parliamentarians of ignoring their views. Legislators later withdrew the bill pending further debate after women marched in the streets to support the right to abortion.[28]

SADC Protocol@Work case studies

A total of 75 good practices on Sexual and Reproductive Health and Rights (SRHR) were presented at Summits between 2017 and 2018. Of these 31 were on gender-based violence (GBV), 30 on health, and 14 on HIV and AIDS.

Abortion is **only** available on request in **SA** and **Mozambique**

[21] https://laws.parliament.na/cms_documents/abortion-and-sterilization-c5c7b99b28.pdf
[22] https://srhr.org/abortion-policies/documents/countries/01-Seychelles-Termination-of-Pregnancy-Act-2012.pdf
[23] http://www.parliament.gov.za/live/commonrepository/Processed/20140414/67169_1.pdf
[24] http://srhr.org/abortion-policies/country/swaziland/
[25] https://www.globalfinancingfacility.org/sites/gff_new/files/Tanzania_One_Plan_II.pdf
[26] https://www.hsph.harvard.edu/population/abortion/ZAMBIA.abo.htm
[27] http://cyber.law.harvard.edu/population/abortion/Zimbabwe.abo.html
[28] https://www.hrw.org/world-report/2018/country-chapters/angola accessed 15 June 2018.

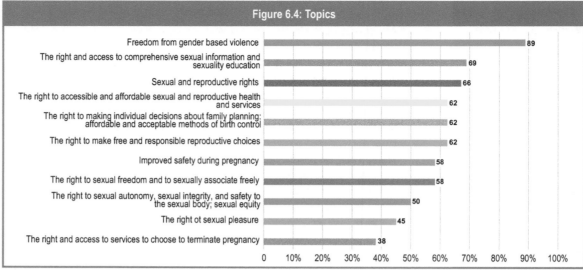

Figure 6.4: Topics

Source: Gender Links, 2018.

89%
of the
Summit
entries

on

freedom

from

GBV

Figure 6.4 shows that:
- A total of 89% of the Summit entries in the Sexual and Reproductive Health and Rights category included a focus on the freedom from GBV. This a positive sign given the scale of the GBV pandemic in the region.
- Of the 75 case studies 69% covered sexual information and sexuality education and 62% on sexual and reproductive rights.
- Of the total, 62% of the entries focus on the right to accessible and affordable sexual and reproductive health service. Similar proportions of case studies focused on decisions on family planning and reproductive choices. While more than 50% of the case studies focus on these topics it is not sufficient. Women need access to effective and high quality sexual and reproductive health services and contraception. There must an increased focus in these areas.
- Between 45 and 58% of the case studies conducted activities to promote safety in pregnancy, sexual freedom, sexual autonomy and sexual pleasure.
- In all SADC countries the right to termination of pregnancy is legal in a particular and limited set of circumstances except in South Africa where it is a fundamental human right for women. The right to abortion must become an inalienable right for all women across SADC. In the absence of the legal right to abortion women seek illegal abortions that have detrimental effects on their health and sometimes results in death.

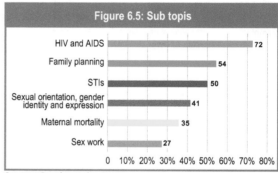

Figure 6.5: Sub topis

Source: Gender Links, 2018.

Figure 6.5 shows that:
- HIV and AIDS received extensive coverage in the case studies, 72% of the entries made reference to HIV and AIDS. The highest number of case studies covered the topic GBV. The intersection between GBV and HIV and AIDS may account for the large proportion of entries in that cover both areas. One of the 14 HIV and AIDS case studies focused on prevention and three on HIV and AIDS and sex work. The majority of the case studies focuses on care and treatment.
- Around half of the Summit entries focused on family planning and Sexually Transmitted Infections (STI's). This number is low given that many women are unable to negotiate safe sex and contract STIs and HIV and AIDS through unprotected sex.

- At 41%, the number of studies making reference to sexual orientation, gender identity and expression is on the rise. Homosexuality is still illegal in many SADC countries.
- Only 35% of the case studies referenced maternal mortality. Levels of maternal mortality in the SADC are high in several.
- Nine of the 16 SADC countries (DRC, Malawi, Mozambique, Lesotho, Angola, Zimbabwe, Tanzania, Swaziland and Madagascar) feature amongst the 35 countries with the highest mater-nal mortality rates worldwide. Health systems must provide improved safety and services for women during pregnancy.
- Only 27% of the case studies made reference to sex work. Sex workers are often experience marginalisation, stigmatisation and criminali-sation making preventing them from accessing healthcare, legal and social services. On average, sex workers are 10 times more likely to become infected with HIV than adults in the general population.[29]

Making care accessible to sex workers in Zimbabwe

Women accessing health care services in Kadoma.
Photo: Thomas Ferenando

Kadoma has many commercial sex workers who need access to health, treatment and care services. The Ministry set up a clinic at the Kadoma hospital to assist sex workers. The services include HIV therapy, treatment for STIs and counselling.

The clinic offers HIV prevention programs for sex workers, especially female sex workers. Given their marginalisation, concerted efforts must be made to ensure sex workers have equitable access to HIV prevention, care, and treatment services, as well as wider health services, particularly for STIs, mental health, and addictions.

Women in commercial sex work now have equal access to health, treatment and care services.
Source: SADC Protocol@Work summit, Zimbabwe 2018

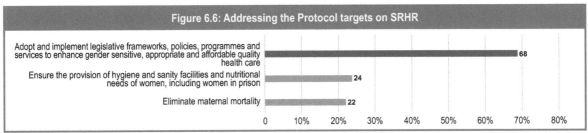

Figure 6.6: Addressing the Protocol targets on SRHR

Adopt and implement legislative frameworks, policies, programmes and services to enhance gender sensitive, appropriate and affordable quality health care	68
Ensure the provision of hygiene and sanity facilities and nutritional needs of women, including women in prison	24
Eliminate maternal mortality	22

Source: Gender Links, 2018.

Figure 6.6 show that:
- 68% of the case studies focused on the provision of gender sensitive, appropriate and affordable health care. While substantial there is a need for more interventions as the current health systems are providing inadequate treatment and care.
- About a quarter of all case studies focus on women's mental, sexual and reproductive health.

Only 24% of the submissions focused on the provision of the hygiene and sanitary facilities, and nutritional needs of women.
- The lowest proportion of case studies were on maternal mortality. As mentioned previously high levels of maternal mortality persist in SADC. The issue needs urgent attention.

---

[29] UNAIDS (2016) 'Prevention Gap Report'.

AMICAALL Swaziland promotes access to SRHR

The Alliance of Mayors and Municipal Leaders on HIV and AIDS in Africa (AMICAALL) creates access sexual and reproductive health services in Piggs Peak in the Hhohho district. UN agencies claim, sexual and reproductive health includes physical, as well as psycho-logical well-being vis-a-vis sexuality.

Reproductive health implies that people are able to have a responsible, satisfying and safer sex life and that they have the capability to reproduce and the freedom to decide if, when and how often to do so. Individuals face inequalities in reproductive health services. Inequalities vary based on socioeconomic status, education level, age, ethnicity, religion, and resources available in their environment.

AMICAALL Swaziland conducting a workshop on safe sex and contraception.
Photo courtesy of Linda Chissano

It is possible for example, that low income individuals lack the resources for appropriate health services and the knowledge to know what is appropriate for maintaining reproductive health. Women bear and usually nurture children, so their reproductive health is inseparable from gender equality. Denial of such rights also worsens poverty.

The organisation informs women and men about and have access to safe, effective, affordable and acceptable methods of birth control. Women are often unable to access maternal health services due to lack of knowledge about the existence of such services or lack of freedom of movement. The project provides access to health services particularly in areas with high levels of poverty.

AMICAALL Swaziland promotes positive sexuality. Sexual health requires a positive and respectful approach to sexuality and sexual relationships, as well as the possibility of having pleasurable and safe sexual experiences, free of coercion, discrimination and violence. For sexual health to be attained and maintained, the sexual rights of all persons must be respected, protected and fulfilled.

Source: SADC Protocol@Work summit, eSwatini 2018

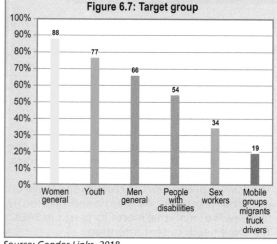

Source: Gender Links, 2018.

Figure 6.7 shows that:
- Women constitute 88% of the target group in the category sexual and reproductive health and rights. Lower proportions of youth (77%) and men (66%) are targeted.
- More than half (54%) the case studies targeted people with disabilities. This is an important development. Initiatives are targeting the unique needs of people with disabilities while at the same moving them from beng a "special population" to being an integral part of communities.
- Sex workers are afriad to access sexual and reproductive health services because of stigma and discrimination. They are particularly vulnerable to contracting HIV and to experiencing GBV. It is encouraging to note that 34% of the case studies specifically targeted sex workers.

- Less than a fifth of all case studies targeted mobile populations, drug users, LGBTIQ persons and prisoners: HIV and AIDS is one of SADC's most urgent challenges. Moblie populations, drug users and prisoners are vulnerable to contracting HIV. LGBTIQ persons sometimes need specialised sexual and reproductive health services and face discrimination when accessing such services. More targeted interventions are need to address the sexual and reproductive health and rights of these target groups.

Figure 6.8 shows that:
- Of the 75 case studies 86% created greater public awareness about sexual and reproductive health and rights, 81% and 80% resulted in changes in behaviour and attitudes respectively.
- Large proportion of the case studies contribute to better service delivery. The crisis in the provision of public health in most SADC countries has severely impacted sexual and reproductive health services. It is encouraging to note that 77% of the case studies focus on improved services.

- A recurring theme across all categories is the limited focus on policy and legislative change. This is true in the SRHR category with only 54% of the case studies recording changes in legislation and policy.

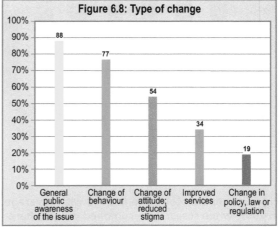

Figure 6.8: Type of change

Source: Gender Links, 2018.

Sanitation

Article 26 (c): Ensure the provision of hygiene and sanitary facilities and nutritional needs of women, including women in prison.

Availability of decent sanitation in easy reach of the home is fundamental for the health, safety and dignity of all, but particularly women and girls. Although providing hygiene and sanitation facilities are provisions of the Protocol, developments in the region in this area have been slow.

Focus on women's hygiene and nutritional needs is low.   *Photo: Gender Links*

HIV & AIDS is **1** of SADC's most **urgent** challenges

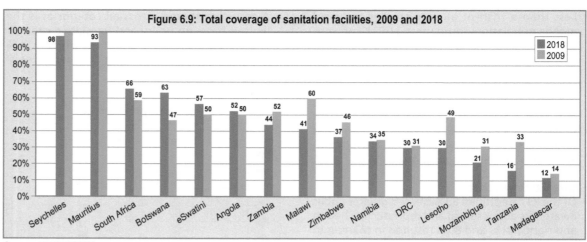

Figure 6.9: Total coverage of sanitation facilities, 2009 and 2018

Source: UNICEF 2017.

Fig 6.9 compares coverage in 2018 with coverage in 2009, when researchers compiled the first Barometer. Few countries have made significant improvements over this period, while coverage in most (Seychelles, Mauritius, Zambia, Malawi, Zimbabwe, Namibia, DRC, Lesotho, Mozambique, Tanzania and Madagascar) has declined. Rising populations require expanded investment just to maintain levels of coverage.

A recent WHO/UNICEF Joint Monitoring Programme for Water Supply, Sanitation and Hygiene (JMP) report, *Progress on drinking water, sanitation and hygiene: 2017 update and Sustainable Development Goal baselines*, presents the first global assessment of "safely managed" drinking water and sanitation services. The overriding conclusion is that too many people still lack access, particularly in rural areas.[29]

	NATIONAL				RURAL				URBAN			
Country	At least basic	Limited (shared)	Unimproved	Open defaecation	At least basic	Limited (shared)	Unimproved	Open defaecation	At least basic	Limited (shared)	Unimproved	Open defaecation
Seychelles	100	0	0	0	-	-	-	-	-	-	-	-
Mauritius	93	6	0	0	93	7	1	0	94	6	0	0
South Africa	73	17	8	2	69	10	17	5	76	20	4	1
Botswana	60	8	15	17	40	10	14	37	75	6	16	2
eSwatini	58	24	7	11	58	21	8	14	58	35	6	1
Malawi	44	23	27	7	43	20	30	7	49	38	12	2
Lesotho	44	17	9	30	43	7	10	40	46	44	7	4
Zimbabwe	39	24	11	27	31	15	15	39	54	42	4	0
Angola	39	15	13	33	21	6	17	56	62	27	8	3
Namibia	34	11	5	50	15	3	5	76	55	21	4	20
Zambia	31	12	42	15	19	7	50	25	49	20	30	1
Tanzania	24	13	52	11	17	4	63	16	37	34	27	2
Mozambique	24	5	36	36	12	3	38	47	47	9	32	13
DRC	20	21	47	12	18	13	51	18	23	32	42	4
Madagascar	10	15	32	44	6	9	29	55	16	24	37	23

Table 6.7: SADC sanitation in rural and urban areas

Derived from UNICEF Global Databases: Sanitation. https://data.unicef.org/topic/water-and-sanitation/drinking-water/ Accessed 20 June 2018.

[29] http://www.unwater.org/publication_categories/whounicef-joint-monitoring-programme-for-water-supply-sanitation-hygiene-jmp/

Table 6.7 shows the status of SADC countries regarding sanitation. Seychelles and Mauritius are clearly far ahead of the rest of SADC. Meanwhile, ten SADC countries do not have even 50% coverage of basic services nationally and, though urban coverage is much better, seven countries do not have 50% coverage of basic sanitation in urban areas. The extent of open defecation, especially in rural areas, is disturbing. Namibia (76%), Angola (56%) and Madagascar (55%) have more than 50% open defecation in rural areas. However, other countries, such as Malawi (7%) and South Africa (5%), have been able to make noteworthy progress in this regard and also have lower than 10% open defecation, even in rural areas.

Water provision is a critical issue for women's health and wellbeing. The JMP also monitors water-related SDG targets under the recently established Global Expanded Monitoring Initiative (GEMI). Improved drinking water sources are those which by nature of their design and construction have the potential to deliver safe water. The JMP classification of water sources for purposes of monitoring progress in meeting the SDG targets is:

- **Safely managed drinking water service:** improved source meeting three criteria:
  - Accessible on premises;
  - Water available when needed; and
  - Water should be free from contamination.
- **Basic drinking water service:** if the improved source does not meet any one of these criteria, but a round trip to collect water takes 30 minutes or less, including queuing.
- **A limited service:** if a round trip to collect water from an improved source exceeds 30 minutes, including queuing.

Fadzanayi Gamira collects water at a borehole in Ruwa, Zimbabwe. While men sometimes take responsibility for water collection, women primarily do this work in most SADC countries.   *Photo: Tapiwa Zvaraya*

The JMP classifies unimproved sources of water, which represent unsafe water which users must boil to be potable, as:

- **Unimproved:** Drinking water from an unprotected dug well or unprotected spring.
- **Surface water:** Drinking water directly from a river, dam, lake, pond, stream, canal or irrigation canal.

Previous JMP analysis has shown that collecting water that is either from unimproved sources or surface water is more likely to take more than 30 minutes. This represents a double burden.

Though globally 71% of the world's population is accessing water from a safely managed drinking water source, sub-Saharan Africa has the lowest coverage at 24%, with a further 34% accessing basic water services. This means that 42% of people in sub-Saharan Africa still only access limited or unimproved sources of water.[30]

[30] World Health Organization (WHO) and the United Nations Children's Fund (UNICEF), 2017. Progress on drinking water, sanitation and hygiene: 2017 update and SDG baselines. Geneva: Switzerland.

The
burden
of
collecting
water
falls
dispropor-
tionately
on

and **girls**

Table 6.8: SADC baseline drinking water status												
	NATIONAL				RURAL				URBAN			
Country	At least basic	Limited	Unimproved	Surface water	At least basic	Limited	Unimproved	Surface water	At least basic	Limited	Unimproved	Surface water
Mauritius	100	0	0	0	100	0	0	0	100	0	0	0
Seychelles	96	-	0	4	-	-	-	-	-	-	-	-
South Africa	85	10	2	3	63	24	5	9	97	3	0	0
Botswana	79	18	1	2	58	35	2	5	95	5	0	0
Namibia	79	6	5	10	63	11	7	19	97	1	2	0
Lesotho	72	12	16	1	66	13	21	1	87	8	4	0
ESwatini	68	8	10	15	60	9	12	19	95	2	2	2
Malawi	67	20	10	3	63	22	12	3	87	9	4	0
Zimbabwe	67	10	17	7	54	12	23	11	94	4	3	0
Zambia	61	6	21	12	44	7	29	19	86	4	9	1
Madagascar	51	3	31	16	34	2	41	23	82	4	12	2
Tanzania	50	13	24	13	37	15	31	18	79	9	9	3
Mozambique	47	14	24	14	32	17	32	19	79	9	8	3
DRC	42	12	36	10	21	11	53	16	70	14	14	2
Angola	41	16	19	24	23	13	22	42	63	19	15	3

Derived from UNICEF Global Databases: Drinking Water. https://data.unicef.org/topic/water-and-sanitation/drinking-water/ Accessed June 20, 2018.

Women collecting water in DRC.   *Photo: Gender Links*

Table 6.9 shows that Mauritius and Seychelles have already achieved almost universal coverage of at least basic safe water provision. Ten other countries have 50% or more basic coverage. Angola has the lowest coverage, at 41%, followed by DRC at 42%. There is wide disparity between rural and urban populations in the region, underscoring the fact that achieving SDG-6, to ensure "access to safe water and sanitation," will require a huge investment over the next 15 years.

Women in refugee camps and prisons

The DRC presents an ongoing and deepening refugee crisis in SADC. In early 2018 an estimated 740 000 refugees from DRC had fled to neighbouring countries, including Angola, Burundi, the Central African Republic, Rwanda, the Republic of Congo, South Sudan, Tanzania, Uganda, and Zambia, as well as Southern Africa and beyond.[31] Angola, Zambia and Uganda have received the greatest inflow of new refugees in 2018. The majority of refugees in Angola and Zambia are women and children under the age of 18. Immediate needs include: health (including maternal and child health, adolescent sexual and reproductive health); nutrition, food production, water and sanitation.

[31] UNHCR, 2018. The Democratic Republic of the Congo: Regional Refugee Response Plan, January - December 2018.

Mauritius & Seychelles have achieved almost universal coverage of basic safe water provision

Improved sanitation, hygiene and food preparation help address malnutrition in Zambia

The Tithandizane community-based programme in Zambia has set out to improve the health of infants and children through nutritional awareness and support. It provides knowledge and skills on food processing, utilisation and storage. The innovative project began out of a need to reduce malnutrition in the Katele District. Malnutrition impacts child development, especially for children younger than five years. The causes of malnutrition include poor feeding practices; inadequate food intake both in terms of quality and quantity; poor sanitation; and inadequate knowledge by mothers on food preparation.

The project, which began in 2009 in one area of Katete District in the Eastern Province, improves child health, growth and development through an increased focus on nutrition awareness to reduce child mortality and morbidity rates caused by elevated levels of malnutrition. This has been an issue in the area, especially due to poor feeding practices, culture and traditions, HIV and AIDS, poor maternal health, inadequate child care, low crop production causing food insecurity and poor food storage.

The programme has seen success by engaging the community in awareness and education programmes. In addition, the programme employs food processing demonstrations and health education to train community members. This has led to the establishment of nutrition clubs. The clubs align with local cooperatives that preserve vegetables and provide nutrition training. Stakeholders evaluate the programme at quarterly review meetings and through monitoring forms, questionnaires and in-field follow-ups.

The project has partnered with rural health centres, cooperatives, and the Ministry of Social Welfare. The project, which has been funded solely through community contributions, has so far reached 500 direct beneficiaries and indirectly benefitted approximately 5000 community members.

The community has been slow to adopt new cooking methods, which sometimes presents a challenge. Additionally, community members have inadequate knowledge of food processing, utilisation and storage, and poor sanitation and hygiene is common in the community.

Women have benefitted from the project through capacity building, dietary preparation, entrepreneurship skills, provision of inputs for conservation farming and through linkages to cooperatives. In addition to that, community members have seen changes in improved health, better food preparation and improved food security.

Community ownership is key in achieving good health, and volunteerism is important for planning, implementation and evaluation. The community feels confident that the programme will be sustainable in the long run.

Source: Zelipa Mwale, Katete District, Zambia SADC Protocol@Work 2018

Access to potable water is essential for the provision of women's sexual and reproductive health needs.
Photo: Tapiwa Zvaraya

Next steps

Key recommendations and next steps to ensure governments continue to improve the health of their populations are:

- Governments in SADC need to pay attention to the high levels of unsafe abortion, particularly amongst younger women, including through:
  - Increasing accessibility and availability of contraception to all to reduce the need for termination of pregnancy.
  - Reviewing legislation and provision of services to make safe abortions more readily available.

- Reduce inequities in the provision of SRHR services, maternal health services, water and sanitation between rural and urban areas and across wealth quintiles. This will require action at the local level in underserved areas.

- Provide and promote evidence-based, human-rights based, quality, socio-culturally sensitive and dignified care, especially to women and newborns.

- Improve the quality of services for all, including training and motivation of health care providers.

- Improve provision of SRHR services for adolescents, including information, menstrual health and access to contraceptives.

- Take action to end child marriage, including legislation and mobilisation of families and local leaders.

- Invest in programmes to bring safe drinking water and sanitation services to all, including rural and urban communities in all parts of the region.

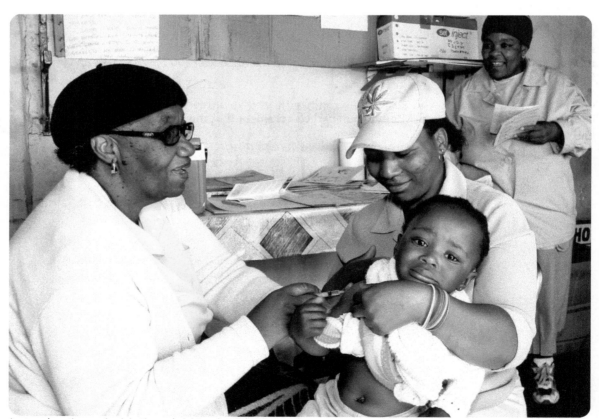

Immune boosting vaccine injections administered at a clinic in Lesotho.

Photo: Gender Links

High
levels
of
unsafe
abortion
NEED
attention!

CHAPTER 7

HIV and AIDS

Article 27

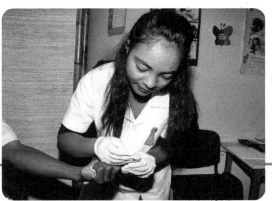

Blood testing for HIV in Antananarivo, Madagascar.
Photo: Zotonantenaina Razanatratefa

KEY POINTS

- Southern Africa Development Community (SADC) is still the epicentre of the HIV epidemic, accounting for 38% of new infections globally in 2017. South Africa accounts for 39% of new infections in SADC, Mozambique 15% and Tanzania 10%.
- Though rates of new infections are declining, at the current rate of decline the region will still have at least 570, 000 new infections annually in 2020, more than double the target of 230,000.
- Gender inequality is still a strong driver of the pandemic: 59% of new infections in Southern Africa are women, but 53% of AIDS related deaths are men.
- Young women 15 to 24 years old are only 10% of the total population but 26% of new HIV infections.
- Considerable effort is being invested in prevention including Comprehensive Sexuality Education (CSE), Voluntary Medical Male Circumcision (VMMC), services for key populations such as harm reduction, condoms, Pre-Exposure Prophylaxis (PrEP) and continued Prevention of Mother-to-Child Transmission (PMTCT). South Africa is set to become the first country in Southern Africa to decriminalise sex work.
- Progress is being made towards 90-90-90, the UNAIDS programme to diagnose 90% of all HIV-positive persons; provide Anti-Retroviral Therapy (ART) for 90% of those diagnosed and achieve viral suppression for 90% of those treated by 2020. Madagascar, Angola and DRC still require support and resources.
- All countries have made significant progress in PMCTC. Ten countries (Seychelles, Mauritius, Zimbabwe, Namibia, South Africa, Zambia, Malawi, Botswana, eSwatini and Lesotho) now have coverage of 90% or higher.
- Most countries in SADC have adopted Test and Treat which is rapidly increasing the number of people that are on ART.
- The rising number of people on treatment requires a much greater focus on differentiated care within the community, from community caregivers who need training, support, supplies, remuneration and recognition.

SADC is still the **epicentre** of the HIV epidemic

Table 7.1: Trends in HIV and AIDS since 2009				
	Target 2030	Baseline 2009	Progress 2018	Variance (progress minus 2030 target)
SHARE OF HIV INFECTION				
Highest percentage of women	50%	Namibia (68%)	Tanzania (61%)	11
Lowest percentage of women	50%	Mauritius (15%)	Mauritius (28%)	-32
HIV POSITIVE PREGNANT WOMEN RECEIVING PMTCT				
Country with highest coverage	100 %	Seychelles (99%)	Seychelles (100%)	0
Country with lowest coverage	100 %	Madagascar (3%)	Madagascar (11%)	-89
PERCENTAGE OF THOSE ELIGIBLE RECEIVING ARVS				
Country with the highest proportion	100 %	Namibia (68%)	eSwatini (85%)	-15
Country with lowest proportion	100%	Madagascar (3%)	Madagascar (7%)	-93
EXTENT OF COMPREHENSIVE KNOWLEDGE OF HIV AND AIDS				
Highest percentage of women	100 %	South Africa (95%)	Seychelles (100%)	0
Lowest percentage of women	100 %	Angola (7%)	DRC (17%)	-83

Source: Gender Links, 2018.

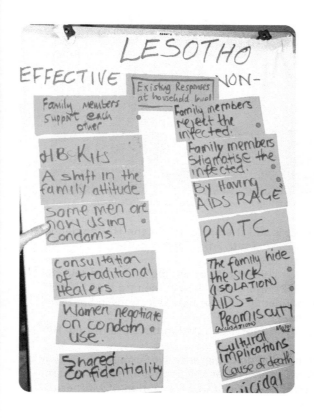

The trends table shows wide variations between SADC countries between the highest and lowest achievements. The most significant change has occurred in prevention of Prevention of Mother-to-child Transmission of HIV (PMTCT) where there are now at least ten countries (Seychelles, Mauritius, Zimbabwe, Namibia, South Africa, Zambia, Malawi, Botswana, eSwatini and Lesotho) that have achieved over 90% coverage. This is a major achievement for a country such as South Africa which has a large population that must be reached. The Post 2015 SADC Protocol on Gender and Development is set to support SADC's huge efforts to end AIDS by 2030. In East and Southern Africa (ESA), the populations requiring continued focus are: adolescent girls and young women and their partners; sex workers, older people, men who have sex with men, prisoners, migrants, injecting drug users and intimate partners.

Background

There has been remarkable progress on HIV and AIDS over the last decade with regard to increased access to treatment; much lower mother to child transmission; much reduced illness and death. However, SADC remains the epicentre of the epidemic. It is still home to at least 40% of all people that are living with HIV globally, though it accounts for less than 4% of the world's total population. Total number of AIDS-related deaths in SADC increased from 82,300 in 1990 (28% of the global total of 290,000), to 758,400 in 2003 (40% of the global total of 1.9 million). This figure has declined to 313,800 in 2017 or 33% of the global total of 940,000.[1]

The Post 2015 SADC Protocol supports huge efforts to **end** AIDS by 2030

---

[1]   Derived from UNAIDS: AIDS Info. AIDS Related Deaths. http://aidsinfo.unaids.org/ accessed 20 July, 2018.

Table 7.2: HIV Prevalence in Adults 15 - 49: 1990, 2008 and 2017				
Country	1990	2008	2017	Variance (2017 minus 2008)
eSwatini	1.9	27.2	27.4	0.2
Lesotho	1.3	22.8	23.8	1
Botswana	7.0	23.4	22.8	-0.6
South Africa	0.7	18.0	18.8	0.8
Zimbabwe	14.9	16.5	13.3	-3.2
Mozambique	1.8	14.1	12.5	-1.6
Namibia	1.6	14.3	12.1	-2.2
Zambia	8.1	12.7	11.5	-1.2
Malawi	9.1	11.5	9.6	-1.9
Tanzania	5.4	6.1	4.5	-1.6
Angola	0.2	1.6	1.9	0.3
DRC	1.7	1.4	0.7	-0.7
Madagascar	<0.1	0.2	0.3	0.1
Global	0.3	0.8	0.8	0

Source: UNAIDS: AIDS Info. HIV Prevalence. Adults 15 - 49. http://aidsinfo.unaids.org/ accessed 19 July, 2018.

Some improvement: Table 7.2 shows the adult HIV prevalence rates in SADC for 1990, 2008 (when the first Barometer was produced) and 2017. Data for Mauritius and Seychelles (which have very low prevalence rates) is not available. The table shows that the prevalence has stabilised in many countries and is beginning to decline in some such as Botswana, Zimbabwe, Mozambique, Namibia, Zambia, Tanzania, DRC and Malawi.

But SADC is home to three countries (eSwatini, Botswana and Lesotho) with the highest prevalence of HIV and AIDS in the world. All three have adult prevalence rates higher than 20%. South Africa, Zimbabwe, Namibia, Zambia and Mozambique have prevalence rates ranging from 10 to 19%[2]. Only DRC, Madagascar, Mauritius and Seychelles have HIV prevalence rates that are lower than the global average of 0.8%.

The pandemic is still distinctly gendered with a greater toll on young women and women than on men. However, this chapter underscores the fact that progress can only be made when women move with men. As we seek to "leave no one behind" governments must pay more attention to the most marginalised and ensure that appropriate services are available to all.

Southern Africa has for decades been a region of high mobility which increases the risk of HIV infection. The Lesotho Population-Based HIV Impact Assessment (LePHIA) found that HIV prevalence is 39.1% for women who have lived outside in comparison to 28.5% for women who have not lived outside and 27.5% for men who have lived outside compared to 17.8% for men who have not lived outside of Lesotho.[3] Female sex work is high along many of the transport routes in the region and the HIV prevalence rates are very high among female sex workers. Men who have sex with men, prisoners, other lesbian, gay, bisexual, and transgender and intersex (LGBQTI) populations, people living with disabilities and people affected by displacement and emergencies are all people at higher risk.

People who inject drugs remain vulnerable to HIV infection: Although the overall proportion of the SADC population that injects drugs is low, some countries with large numbers of drug users have high HIV prevalence in this group. For example, 44.3% of injecting drug users in Mauritius; 11.3% in DRC; 3.8% in Seychelles; 8% in Madagascar and 15.5% in Tanzania are HIV positive[4]. There is also evidence to suggest that women who inject drugs face violence from intimate partners, police and sex trade clients, which increases their vulnerability to HIV infection. Women who inject drugs remain less likely to access services, so if those living with HIV and AIDS become pregnant they are much less likely to access Prevention of Mother to Child Transmission (PMTCT) services.

SADC is home to 3 countries with the **highest** prevalence of HIV and AIDS in the **world**

---

[2] Prevalence of HIV, in Table 1 https://data.unicef.org/topic/hivaids/global-regional-trends/ Accessed 2 July, 2017.
[3] Lesotho Population Based HIV Impact Assessment. 2017. Summary Sheet Preliminary Results.
[4] Derived from People who inject drugs - HIV prevalence http://aidsinfo.unaids.org/#, last accessed July 20, 2016.

Policies

People who inject drugs remain vulnerable to HIV infection

Article 27.1: State Parties shall take every step necessary to adopt and implement gender sensitive policies and programmes, and enact legislation that will address prevention, treatment, care and support in accordance with, but not limited to, the Maseru Declaration on HIV and AIDS and the SADC Sponsored United Nations Commission on the Status of Women Resolution on Women, the Girl Child and HIV and AIDS and the Political Declaration on HIV and AIDS.
Article 27.2: State parties shall ensure that the policies and programmes referred to in sub-Article take account of the unequal status of women, the particular vulnerability of the girl child as well as harmful practices and biological factors that result in women constituting the majority of those infected and affected by HIV and AIDS.

Achieving the 90-90-90: The June 2016 high level meeting on HIV and AIDS adopted the Political Declaration on HIV and AIDS which endorses the UNAIDS strategy for 2016 to 2021: *On the Fast Track to End AIDS*[5]. Though the SDGs do not have specific targets for HIV and AIDS as the MDGs did, this strategy has specific targets that are linked to achievement of a number of SDGs. The **2016-2021 Strategic Agenda** is organised around five SDGs most relevant to the AIDS response: good health (SDG 3), reduce inequalities (SDG 10), achieve gender equality (SDG 5), promote just and inclusive societies (SDG 16) and revitalize global partnerships (SDG 17), while recognizing that other SDGs such as end poverty (1) and ensure quality education (4) are also important. It emphasises that all regions must analyse their own situations to ensure that no one is being left behind. In East and Southern Africa this requires much greater emphasis on adolescent girls and young women with focus also on sex workers, older people, men who have sex with men, prisoners, migrants, injecting drug users and intimate partners.

The vision of the strategy is **Zero new HIV infections, Zero discrimination and Zero AIDS-related deaths**. The strategy has three overall strategic directions:
• HIV prevention.
• Treatment, care and support.
• Human rights and gender equality for the HIV and AIDS response.

The ten targets of the five-year plan include:
1. 90% of people (children, adolescents and adults) living with HIV know their status, 90% of people living with HIV who know their status are receiving treatment and 90% of people on treatment have suppressed viral loads;
2. Zero new HIV infections among children, and mothers are alive and well;
3. 90% of young people are empowered with the skills, knowledge and capability to protect themselves from HIV;
4. 90% of women and men, especially young people and those in high-prevalence settings, have access to HIV combination prevention and sexual and reproductive health services;
5. 27 million additional men in high-prevalence settings are voluntarily medically circumcised, as part of integrated sexual and reproductive health services for men;
6. 90% of key populations, including sex workers, men who have sex with men, people who inject drugs, transgender people and prisoners, as well as migrants, have access to HIV combination prevention services;
7. 90% of women and girls live free from gender inequality and gender-based violence to mitigate the risk and impact of HIV;
8. 90% of people living with, at risk of and affected by HIV report no discrimination, especially in health, education and workplace settings;
9. Overall financial investments for the AIDS response in low- and middle-income countries reach at least US$ 30 billion, with continued increase from the current levels of domestic public sources;
10. 75% of people living with, at risk of and affected by HIV, who are in need, benefit from HIV-sensitive social protection.

---

[5] UNAIDS Strategy, 2016 - 2021. On the Fast Track to end AIDS http://www.unaids.org/en/resources/documents/2016/GlobalPlan2016 accessed 10 May, 2016.

All SADC member states have redoubled their efforts and designed new policies and programmes that are in line with the global call to halt the HIV epidemic by ensuring that 90% of all people living with HIV have been tested and know their status; that 90% of those that know that they are living with HIV are on antiretroviral treatment (ART) and that 90% of those that are on ART have reached viral suppression; coupled with a greater focus on primary prevention.

Some of the policies and plans are:
• Botswana National Policy on HIV and AIDS, Revised 2012.
• DRC National Strategic Plan 2015-2018.
• eSwatini National HIV Prevention Policy, 2012.
• Malawi National HIV and AIDS Strategic Plan, 2011- 2016.
• Mauritius National Strategic Framework on HIV and AIDS 2013 - 16.
• National Strategic Framework for HIV and AIDS Response in Namibia 2011- 16.
• Seychelles National AIDS Council ACT, 2013.
• South Africa National Strategic Plan for HIV, TB & STIs, 2017 - 2021.

• Tanzania Third National Multi-Sectoral Strategic Framework for HIV and AIDS (2013/14 - 2017/18)
• Zambia National HIV & AIDS Strategic Framework, 2017-2021.
• Zimbabwe National HIV and AIDS Strategic Plan (ZNASP III 2015-2018).

 Seychelles is preparing to develop a new HIV Strategic Plan. Some of the priorities that will be addressed in the plan include: injecting drug users, the LGBTQI community, sex workers and training of health workers.[6] The strategy will reflect advances in HIV care and knowledge to reach the whole nation and will acknowledge the role of NGOs in HIV care.

Botswana is implementing an HIV Testing Services Strategy, including self-testing, to increase testing yields. The HIV positive yield for HIV testing is around 5%. The strategy includes HIV testing in TB clinics, hospitals and Index testing.[7]

Table 7.3: Progress in achieving 90-90-90 in SADC 2015 and 2017						
	2015			**2017**		
	Percent of people living with HIV who know their status	Percent of people who know their status who are on ART	Percent of people on ART who achieve viral suppression	Percent of people living with HIV who know their status	Percent of people who know their status who are on ART	Percent of people on ART who achieve viral suppression
Angola	39	64		na	na	na
Botswana	76	>95		86	>95	>95
DRC	34	89	57	59	93	na
Eswatini				90	94	87
Lesotho	67	57	80	80	92	92
Madagascar	6	69	90	8	81	na
Malawi	65	90	>95	90	79	87
Mauritius				na	na	na
Mozambique	49	81	>95	59	92	na
Namibia	91	83	na	90	94	87
Seychelles			89			83
South Africa	86	60	78	90	68	78
Tanzania	62	85	na	na	na	73
Zambia	72	>95		na	na	na
Zimbabwe	70	>95	82	85	>95	na
Global	67	73	78	75	79	81

Source: UN AIDS: AIDSInfo. Progress towards 90 - 90 - 90. http://aidsinfo.unaids.org/ accessed 19 July, 2018.

6 Government of Botswana. 2018. Country Progress Report - Botswana. http://www.unaids.org/sites/default/files/country/documents/ BWA_2018_countryreport.pdf accessed 10 July, 2018.
7 http://www.nation.sc/article.html?id=256774 accessed 1 July, 2018.

SADC

▲

initiating
those
that test

+

on
treatment

Protocol@Work

Table 7.3 summarises available data on progress, between 2015 and 2017 in achieving the 90- 90- 90 goals that have been set for 2020. It shows that:

- **Percent of people living with HIV who know their status:** eSwatini, Malawi, Namibia and South Africa have achieved, or are very close to the 90% goal. Botswana and Zimbabwe made good progress between 2015 and 2017. Madagascar is still very low and a number of countries do not have data.

- **Percent of people who know their status who are on ART:** Overall SADC member states are doing well in initiating those that test positive on treatment. Botswana, DRC, eSwatini, Lesotho, Mozambique, Namibia and Zimbabwe have achieved over 90% coverage. South Africa is increasing coverage but was only at 68% which is below the global average, but represents a huge number of people on treatment.

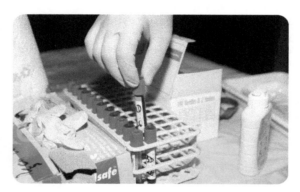

- **Percent of people on ART who achieve viral suppression:** Botswana and Lesotho have levels of viral suppression over 90% with other countries at least over 73%.

- **SADC Sponsored UN Resolution on Women, the Girl Child and HIV and AIDS:** In 2016 the CSW passed a SADC-sponsored resolution, put forward on behalf of SADC by Botswana: The SADC Sponsored United Nations Commission on the Status of Women Resolution on Women, the Girl Child and HIV and AIDS. Among others, the resolution calls on governments, the private sector and development partners to: give full attention to the high levels of new HIV infections among young women and adolescent girls and their root causes; attain gender equality and the empowerment of women and girls; eliminate all gender-based violence and discrimination against women and girls and harmful practices, such as child, early and forced marriage and female genital mutilation and trafficking in persons, and ensure the full engagement of men and boys to reduce women and girls' vulnerability to HIV.

In July 2017 women parliamentarians from SADC issued the Mahe Declaration committing to work for the domestication of the provisions of resolution CSW 60/2 and calling on their governments to accelerate implementation. The declaration makes specific mention of the much higher HIV prevalence in female sex workers.[8]

Women MPs back the SADC Gender and HIV Resolution

Women Members of Parliament from the Southern African Development Community (SADC) attending a two day conference organised by SADC Parliamentary Forum (PF) and other partners in Mahé, Seychelles from 5 to 6 July 2017, have made strong recommendations for greater parliamentary involvement in the ratification and domestication of relevant international and continental instruments relating to women, girls, HIV and Sexual and Reproductive Health Rights.

In a bold declaration dubbed the Mahé Declaration, the Parliamentarians resolved to implement and to advocate for the implementation of United Nations Commission on the Status of women (UNCSW) Resolution 60/2 entitled: "Women, the Girl Child and HIV and AIDS". This international instrument calls for attention to be paid to the high levels of new HIV infections among young women and adolescent girls and its root causes.

The Mahé Declaration was developed in the context of continued high prevalence of HIV, particularly among women and girls in the SADC Region, a situation which raises great public health and developmental concern. The Parliamentarians noted that HIV had the potential to undermine the SADC Region's attainment of Sustainable Development Goals (SDGs) whose end date is 2030.

As indicated in the declaration, Eastern and Southern Africa has less than 7% of the global population but it contributes close to 50% of new adult infections globally and it is home to more than 19 million people living with HIV, of which more than half are women. The prevalence of the epidemic continues to cause morbidity and mortality, as well as induce poverty and inequality both of which are an antithesis for sustainable development according to the Parliamentarians.

---

8 http://www.safaids.net/22-news/109-declaration-set-to-address-hiv-and-srhr-in-sadc Accessed 2 July, 2018.

SADC Parliamentarians step it up for gendered responses to HIV.
Photo courtesy of Seychelles News

The Mahé Declaration therefore contains extensive recommendations to address the root causes of HIV prevalence among women and girls. These include taking rapid actions to reduce poverty, ensuring access to quality integrated and adolescents and youth friendly health services, information and education opportunities with a special focus on comprehensive sexuality education for in- and out-of-school youth while eradicating child marriage as defined in the SADC Model law on Eradicating Child Marriage and Protecting those already in marriage.

Going forward, the Parliamentarians committed to acquainting themselves with the legal and policy environment in their respective countries with regards to HIV and sexual and reproductive health rights. They said enhanced knowledge of the legal and policy environment would be critical in making informed assessments of the effectiveness thereof and where necessary, enactment of laws aiming at protecting the sexual and reproductive health rights of all, with a specific focus on the most vulnerable.

A solid commitment was also made by the Parliamentarians to review, revise, amend or repeal all laws, regulations and policies including cultural and religious practises and customs that have a discriminatory impact on youths, especially girls and young women.

Economic inequality and unequal power relations; discrimination in society and in the workplace; all forms of violence; inhumane and degrading treatment; sexual exploitation; women and child trafficking and harmful practises and norms including some cultural practices, disempower women and girls and further expose them to substantial risks of contracting HIV, the lawmakers noted.

The Parliamentarians further noted that existing inequalities among certain key populations such as sex workers, people living with disabilities, migrants, girls living in poverty and transgender persons are disproportionately affected by HIV and AIDS.

Among the concerns highlighted in the Mahé Declaration, HIV among female sex workers in SADC is significantly higher than it is among the general adult population. This same population group also faces violence, stigma and discrimination at the hands of family members, in communities, at the workplace and in health-care settings. Often their rights to dignity, health and education are denied.

The Parliamentarians therefore lament that these persistent structural barriers as well as male chauvinism and patriarchy often work to reinforce women's unequal status in society and fuel HIV vulnerability among women and girls. Harmful social and cultural norms and practices also continually deny women and girls the opportunity to attend schools, further reinforce their vulnerability to violence and HIV while also denying them opportunities to economic independence.

The Mahé Declaration states that the prohibition of such practices and customs, can aptly be resolved by ensuring that provisions of domestic legislation conform more to international human rights laws and include protection from all harmful practices.

Additionally, the Parliamentarians pledged to enact laws aimed at improving inclusive access to education at all levels and provide for viable alternatives for the many young people. This would include paying particular attention to the participation of adolescent girls, who drop out of the formal education system, by facilitating re-entry, revamping informal education and training through standardized certification within and between African countries.

Various activities including the dissemination of information, training, sensitisation workshops and the development of Model Laws relating to the various issues of HIV and Sexual and Reproductive Health Rights are some of the ways through which SADC PF can come on board to assist parliaments enact national laws based on international and regional instruments.

SADC PF was supported in hosting of this conference by Sweden and Norway. It got additional financial and technical support from development partners that include UN Agencies, the United Nations Development Programme, UNFPA and UN Women as well as from regionally based Civil Society Partners, ARASA and SAFAIDS.
Source: Moses Magadza, SAFAIDS News Service

The Post
2015
SADC
Gender
Protocol

prevention

Article 27. 3: State Parties shall:
a) Develop gender sensitive strategies to prevent new infections.

The Post 2015 SADC Gender Protocol places a strong emphasis on gendered responses to prevention. The SADC-sponsored UN Resolution on women, girls, HIV and AIDS strengthens this through the following specific provisions:
- Achieve universal access to comprehensive HIV prevention, programmes, treatment, care and support to all women and girls and achieve universal health coverage.
- Enhance the capacity of low- and middle-income countries to provide affordable and effective HIV prevention and treatment products, diagnostics, medicines and commodities and other pharmaceutical products, as well as treatment for opportunistic infections and co-infections, and reduce costs of lifelong chronic care,
- Eliminate mother-to-child transmission and keep mothers alive.
- Provide combination prevention for women and girls for the prevention of new infections, to reverse the spread of HIV and reduce maternal mortality.
- Avail comprehensive data disaggregated by age and sex to inform a targeted response to the gender dimensions of HIV and AIDS.
- Build up national competence and capacity to provide an assessment of the drivers and impact of the epidemic.

- Support action-oriented research on gender and HIV and AIDS, including on female-controlled prevention commodities.

A Global HIV Partnership for Prevention: The June 2016 high level meeting on HIV and AIDS laid out an ambitious plan to reach epidemic control by 2030. The five elements of the prevention plan are:
1. Combination prevention, including comprehensive sexuality education, economic empowerment and access to sexual and reproductive health services for young women and adolescent girls and their male partners in high-prevalence locations.
2. Evidence-informed and human rights-based prevention programmes for key populations, including dedicated services and community mobilisation and empowerment.
3. Strengthened national condom programmes, including procurement, distribution, social marketing, private-sector sales and demand creation.
4. Voluntary medical male circumcision in priority countries that have high levels of HIV prevalence and low levels of male circumcision, as part of wider sexual and reproductive health service provision for boys and men.
5. Pre-exposure prophylaxis for population groups at higher risk of HIV infection.

In October 2017 the Global Partnership launched a specific campaign focused on 26 countries - including Angola, DRC, eSwatini, Lesotho, Malawi, Mozambique, Namibia, South Africa, Tanzania, Zambia and Zimbabwe. Countries in the partnership will report quarterly on progress and challenges.

Men's involvement is key: Men's sector in Botswana discussing HIV with former Minister of Labour and Home Affairs, Edwin Jenamiso Batshu. *Photo: Keletso Metsieng*

Table 7.4: New infections 2017 compared to maximum since 1990				
Country	Number of new infections, 2017	Maximum number of new infections in 1 year	Year in which maximum occurred	New infections 2017 as percent of the maximum number
Zimbabwe	41 000	230 000	1993	18
DRC	15 000	67 000	1996	22
Malawi	39 000	110 000	1992	35
Namibia	7 400	20 000	1996	37
Botswana	14 000	37 000	1995	38
Tanzania	65 000	170 000	1993	38
ESwatini	7 000	18 000	1995	39
Zambia	48 000	110 000	1992	44
Lesotho	15 000	32 000	1997	47
South Africa	270 000	530 000	1998	51
Mozambique	130 000	170 000	2001	76
Angola	27 000	28 000	2012	96
Madagascar	5 300			100
SADC Total	**683 700**			
Global	**1 800 000**			

Source: Derived from UNAIDS. AIDS Info. Number of new HIV Infections. http://aidsinfo.unaids.org/ accessed on 19 July, 2018.

Table 7.4 shows that:
- SADC is still a major source of new infections globally, accounting for 683,700 or 38% of new infections globally in 2017, compared to 35% in 1997 when the total number of new infections was at the highest level it has ever been, at 3.4 million with SADC accounting for 1,186,900 of these.
- South Africa accounts for 39% of new infections in SADC, Mozambique 15% and Tanzania 10%.
- Major progress in prevention has been achieved since as early as 1992 when some countries began to show decline in new infections. This is particularly true in countries such as Zimbabwe, DRC, Malawi, Namibia, Botswana, Tanzania and eSwatini where number of new infections are now less than 40% of the maximum number.

A Joint United Nations Programme on HIV/AIDS (UNAIDS) panel of experts has determined that an HIV incidence: prevalence ratio, which is the ratio of the number of new HIV infections to the number of people living with HIV within a population, of 0.03 is the level at which the epidemic will transition. The progress in reducing AIDS-related deaths and preventing new HIV infections has resulted in an incidence: prevalence ratio for eastern and southern Africa of 0.04. This is close to the transition level.[9]

Though rates of new infections are declining, at the current rate of decline the East and Southern

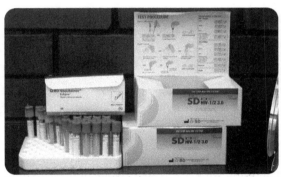

HIV and AIDS Test Ki t in Zimbabwe.   Photo: Tapiwa Zvaraya

African region will still have at least 570,000 new infections in 2020, compared to a target of 230,000. There is urgent need for continued focus on prevention in all member states. Countries have been categorised according to:
a. Those that need slight acceleration (up to 1.6 times the current rate of decline) which are Mozambique, Zimbabwe and eSwatini.
b. Those that need moderate acceleration (up to 2, 5 times the current rate of decline) which are Malawi, Botswana, South Africa and Tanzania.
c. Those that need acceleration up to 4 times the current rate of decline which include Zambia, Namibia, Lesotho, Angola.
d. Not on track - including Madagascar, where currently the prevalence rate is increasing and will need to be reversed and then rapidly decline.[10]

9   UNAIDS. Global AIDS Update, 2018. Miles to Go. Geneva, Switzerland.
10 UNAIDS. RSA ESA. 2017. Reinvigorating Prevention: Are we on Track? Presentation to the SADC meeting on Prevention, October, 2017. Johannesburg.

SADC accounted for 683,700 or **38%** of new infections globally in **2017**

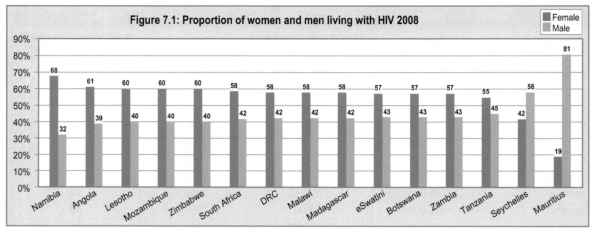

Figure 7.1: Proportion of women and men living with HIV 2008

Source: Gender Links 2018 and 2008, compiled from UNAIDS data.

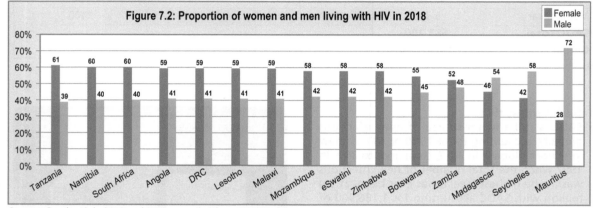

Figure 7.2: Proportion of women and men living with HIV in 2018

Source: Gender Links 2018 and 2008, compiled from UNAIDS data.

Figure 7.1 compares the proportion of women and men living with HIV in 2008, while figure 7.2 compares the proportion of women and men living with HIV in 2018. The proportions have not changed much. Most of SADC has a generalised epidemic that is largely driven by heterosexual sex. Key facts emerging are that:

- In general, prevalence in women is almost three times higher than in men in the 15 to 24 age range and prevalence in men begins to increase in the 30 to 40 age range.
- In these countries there are generally more women living with HIV than men, although maturing epidemics in Namibia, for instance, have resulted in a lower proportion of women (down from 68% in 2008 to 60% in 2018).
- At baseline in 2008, and in the 2018 statistics, Madagascar, Seychelles and Mauritius have much higher proportions of men, which is consistent with much smaller epidemics that are largely concentrated in two populations - injecting drug users who tend to be more male, and men who have sex with men.

While impressive gains are being made in the fight against HIV, the rates of new infections as well as mortality in young people are still cause for grave concern. In 2015, 300,000 of the 790,000 new infections in East and Southern Africa (ESA) were in young people 15 to 24 years old. Young women 15 to 24 years old are only 10% of the total population but constituted 26% of new HIV infections in 2017. The number and age of a young woman's sexual partners have a significant impact on her HIV status. While mortality is beginning to stabilise and decline, the rates are still high and are still increasing in adolescent boys and young men. Thus, while more adolescent girls are acquiring HIV more adolescent boys are dying of AIDS.[11] Globally, AIDS is one of the top ten causes of adolescent death.

---

[11] Govender, K et al. HIV Prevention in Adolescents and Young People in the Eastern and Southern African Region: A Review of Key Challenges Impeding Actions for an Effective Response. The Open AIDS Journal, 2018, 12, 3-00.

Gender inequality is still a strong driver of the pandemic: 59% of new infections in ESA are in women. The largest numbers of new infections are in young women. This occurs in 15 to 19 year olds in South Africa, Zambia, eSwatini, Madagascar; and in 20 - 24 year olds in Tanzania, Mozambique, Zimbabwe, Malawi, Lesotho, Angola, Namibia and Botswana. However, levels of knowledge of one's status are very low among young people.

Comprehensive, accurate knowledge of HIV and AIDS is fundamental to ensuring citizens use HIV services and engage in safe sexual behaviours. Yet, knowledge remains low among young women and men (aged 15-24) in SADC, with significant gaps in even basic knowledge about HIV and its transmission.

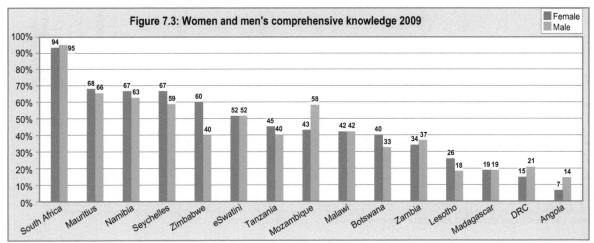

Figure 7.3: Women and men's comprehensive knowledge 2009

Source: 2009 Barometer.

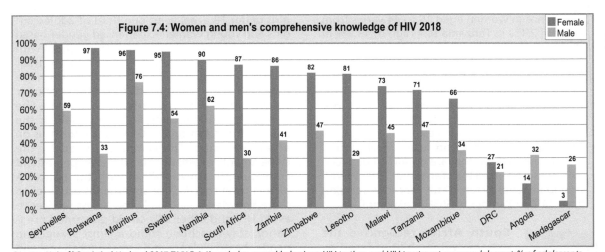

Figure 7.4: Women and men's comprehensive knowledge of HIV 2018

Source: Unicef | Statistical Update | 2017 TABLE 4: Knowledge, sexual behaviour, HIV testing, and HIV treatment among adolescents% of adolescents (aged 15-19) who have comprehensive knowledge of HIV, 2011-2016*
https://data.unicef.org/topic/hivaids/adolescents-young-people/ accessed 27 June, 2018.

Little change in levels of knowledge: Figure 7.3 and Figure 7.4 compare levels of HIV knowledge in young women and men in 2008 and 2018. The general picture is one of little change. Botswana, Mauritius and Seychelles, which all have relatively smaller populations have made the most progress in relation to women's knowledge, but there are no corresponding increases in men's knowledge. South Africa has shown a marked reduction as

have Mozambique and eSwatini. Only Mauritius, Madagascar, Lesotho and Angola show modest increases in knowledge in young men. Overall the levels of knowledge are too low for a region which needs such active engagement in prevention, testing, treatment and adherence. Ten countries still have knowledge levels of lower than 50% for both women and men.

59% of new infections in East and Southern Africa are

LOW rates of HIV testing in both young ♀ & ♂

In general, there are very low rates of testing in both young men and women: Table 7.5 presents data from six of the Population-Based HIV and AIDS Impact Assessment surveys that have been conducted in the last three years on HIV prevalence, self-reported awareness of HIV status, self-reported access to ART amongst those that know that they are HIV+, viral load suppression in those that report to be on ART and overall viral load suppression.

Table 7.5: HIV prevalence, knowledge of HIV status, ART access and VL Suppression in adolescent girls and young women

	Years survey conducted	HIV prevalence	Aware of HIV-positive status, %	Self-reported ART,* %	Viral load suppression among those self-reported on ART,† %	Viral load suppression among all HIV-positive,§ %
eSwatini	2016-2017	13.9	70.2	79.9	79.9	55.5
Lesotho	2016-2017	11.1	61.4	89.7	76.4	50.9
Zimbabwe	2015-2016	5.9	48.2	86.2	89.0	47.9
Zambia	2016	5.7	40.1	77.9	78.1	33.6
Malawi	2015-2016	3.4	55.3	84.8	79.6	49.7
Tanzania	2016-2017	2.1	46.3	88.2	90.6	47.1

Source: Derived from Brown, K. et al. Status of HIV Epidemic Control Among Adolescent Girls and Young Women Aged 15-24 Years - Seven African Countries, 2015-2017. MMWR / January 12, 2018 / Vol. 67 / No. 1.

Table 7.5 shows that:

- Prevalence in women aged 15 to 24 varies from a low of 2.1% in Tanzania to a high of 13.9% in eSwatini.
- Awareness of HIV status varies from a low of 40% in Zambia to a high of 70% in eSwatini, which is far short of the 90% target.
- The percentage of those that know their HIV status that are on ART is good, ranging from 78% in Zambia to 90% in Lesotho.
- There are relatively good levels of viral load suppression in those that are on ART of between 76% (Lesotho) to 91% (Tanzania), the overall viral load suppression is still very low (ranging from 34% in Zambia to 56% in eSwatini).

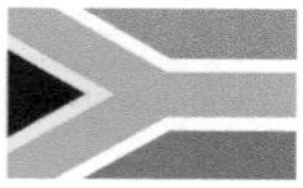

South Africa recognised the extreme vulnerabilities faced by adolescent girls and young women aged 15 to 24. In 2015, 1975 young women were being infected by HIV every week. This is now down to 1500 or 29% of all new infections. South Africa had 70,000 pregnancies in girls under 18 every year; one third of adolescent girls and young women experienced gender based violence and high dropout rate from school with 60% of young people failing to complete their matric (or secondary school) and high unemployment with few opportunities for economic activity. In 2016 South Africa launched the She Conquers national campaign, on behalf of the South African National AIDS Council, to focus on adolescent girls. The campaign is led by the Departments of Health, Social Development and Education, in collaboration with the police. A district level coordinator spearheads activities to share knowledge and skills and access services to avoid HIV and other STIs; avoid unwanted pregnancy; stay in school; stand against sexual and gender based violence and access educational and economic opportunities. Impact of the campaign is already being seen in reduced teen pregnancies in some schools which used to have very high rates of HIV and AIDS.[12]

[12] http://sheconquerssa.co.za/ and http://www.kznhealth.gov.za/mediarelease/2018/KZN-health-MEC-excited-about-the-impact-of%20%E2%80%93she-conquers-campaign-at-umgungundlovu27022018.htm accessed July 15, 2018.

Promoting HIV Education in schools in Chegutu, Zimbabwe

Sex education begins at an early age at Kaguvi Primary School in Chegutu. *Photo: Joseph Denga*

Kaguvi Primary School in Chegutu, in the Mashonaland West province of Zimbabwe has begun promoting health education through teaching grade 3 pupils in a once-a-week, after school club, about HIV and AIDS.

The club has sub groups: Girl Education Movement and Boy Education Movement. These are complementary and have a long term goal of equipping the learners with skills to help them become responsible citizens. The provision of information is facilitated through discussions, peer teaching, debate, simulation, drama, brainstorming and quizzes. The club aims to promote positive values, behaviour and attitudes that prevent the spread of HIV, STIs and other health concerns. The programme was inspired by the National AIDS Policy, which noted that the HIV pandemic requires a multi-sectoral approach, and the school is playing its part through education from a young age.

The broad goal of this is the promotion of responsible behaviour and positive values of Unhu/ Ubuntu. Other short term goals are:
- Appreciating the importance of good personal hygiene.
- Identifying or describing STIs and symptoms, prevention and treatment of STIs.
- Establishing the link between HIV and STIs.
- Distinguishing between useful and harmful effects of the Internet and social media.
- Understanding exploitation and victimisation.
- Understanding rights and responsibilities.
- Identifying ways in which communities deal with substance abuse, sexual abuse and sexual relationships.
- Challenging stigma and discrimination.
- Describing the economic, social, emotional challenges of living with HIV.
- Appreciating the importance of abstinence in HIV prevention.

The programme focuses on making sure the children know about freedom from gender based violence and access to comprehensive sexuality education, including about HIV, AIDS and STIs. Delivery methods include - peer teaching, drama, group discussions, brainstorming. In addition, written tests and quizzes were facilitated.

The project has worked and created synergies with the local schools, the local authority (Chegutu Municipality), the Ministry of Education, the police and clinic. The local National AIDS Council is also involved and the project sends them monthly reports.

So far the project has been allocated US$500 by the council to conduct their activities, resulting in 30 direct beneficiaries, and a total of 800 indirect beneficiaries. Time to meet all the club members remains a struggle, though the solution to this has been suggested as meeting on Friday afternoons, to allow members who cannot make previous sessions to catch up with others. The programme is monitored through feedback, which guides subsequent plans and sessions. The programme seems to benefit more girls as they note that most of the participants in the National AIDS Quiz are girls. The school team won a bronze medal at the National AIDS Quiz and their prize was a water tank. When community members come to fetch water from the tank, the children are very proud. Through this initiative, more and more parents are encouraging their children to join the AIDS Club.

Source: Joseph Denga, Chegutu. SADCProtocol@Work,2018

Protocol@Work

In **Zambia**, HIV testing uptake increased from 62% to 73% for girls and from 47% to 57% for their male peers when social cash transfers were provided with enhanced HIV treatment and prevention services for young people (aged 15-19 years). When health staff were trained and supported to provide adolescent-friendly services, and support through peer educators, theatre groups and youth-friendly gathering spaces, levels of condom use at last sex increased from 50% to 72% for girls and 48% to 61% for boys.[15]

Growing evidence is pointing to the protective value of social protection combined with parental care, education and caring health services for reducing the rate of new HIV infections in young women. These same interventions improve testing, access to treatment and adherence. In general, adolescents aged 15 to 19 are more likely to drop out of care than those 10 to 14 or adults, pointing to the need for different approaches for this age group. The evidence suggests that pregnant adolescents find it particularly difficult to stay in care.[13]

The US Government through President's Emergency Plan For AIDS Relief (PEPFAR) has supported the **DREAMS** (Determined, Resilient, Empowered, AIDS Free, Motivated and Supported) in ten countries that account for more than half of all infections in adolescent girls and young women globally, including Lesotho, Malawi, Mozambique, South Africa, eSwatini, Tanzania, Zambia, and Zimbabwe which are in SADC. In the 2018 report to Congress, PEPFAR reported that 41 of the 63 districts implementing the DREAMS programme achieved a decline of new HIV diagnoses of over 25% from 2015 to 2017. The decline was over 40% in 14 of the districts. In 2017 PEPFAR extended funding for programmes with adolescent girls, with a focus on reducing sexual violence amongst 9 to 14 year olds to five countries, including Botswana and Namibia in SADC.[14]

 In **South Africa**, only 18% adolescents aged 10-19 years who received food support, parental or caregivers support and participated in an HIV support group failed to adhere to anti-retroviral therapy, compared to 54% among adolescents who had none of these.

Voluntary Medical Male Circumcision (VMMC) is a cost-effective, once off intervention that provides lifelong partial protection for males. VMMC reduces female-to-male sexual transmission of HIV by 60%. WHO and UNAIDS recommend implementation of VMMC programmes in countries with a high HIV prevalence among the general population together with behavioural and structural strategies, as part of a comprehensive HIV prevention plan. It is important to note that VMMC alone does not provide complete protection for men. Men must also use condoms and desist from risky sexual behaviour. Available evidence suggests that circumcised men are not reducing condom usage or increasing other risky behaviour.

15 priority countries in eastern and southern Africa with high levels of HIV prevalence and low levels of male circumcision have been identified for intense effort to increase levels of VMMC. Ten of these are in SADC (Botswana, Lesotho, Malawi, Mozambique, Namibia, South Africa, eSwatini, Tanzania, Zambia and Zimbabwe). The new stra-

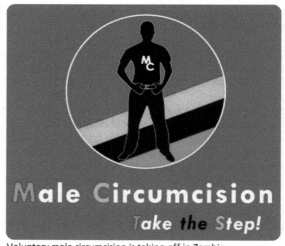

Voluntary male circumcision is taking off in Zambia .
Photo courtesy of Zambia VMMC

[13] UNAIDS. Global AIDS Update, 2018. Miles to Go. Geneva, Switzerland.
[14] PEPFAR. 2018. PEPFAR 2018 Report to Congress. Washington, DC. https://www.pepfar.gov/documents/organization/279889.pdf Accessed 9 July, 2018.
[15] UNAIDS. Global AIDS Update 2018. Miles to go. Geneva, Switzerland.

tegic plan aims to increase voluntary medical male circumcision (VMMC) in 10 to 29-year-old males in these priority countries to 90% by 2021.

One study used mathematical modelling to assess the likelihood of this target being achieved in eSwatini, Lesotho, Malawi, Mozambique, Namibia, South Africa, Tanzania, Uganda, and Zimbabwe, taking into account their historical VMMC progress and current implementation[16]. This study found that only Tanzania was likely to reach the target. The study concluded that it is necessary to rapidly increase the number of circumcisions conducted for 10 to 14 year olds and 15 to 29 year olds.

To do this requires a deeper understanding of the factors which motivate or discourage adolescent boys at different ages to be circumcised. Some evidence suggests that younger boys are influenced by others while older adolescents (15 to 19) are aware of the benefits in terms of reducing HIV risk. All adolescents are concerned about pain[17]. Further evidence suggests that support from female adolescent partners before and after the procedure is an important motivating factor[18] and that it is important to involve parents[19]. However, parents also need accurate information and motivation.

There is need for more awareness creation around other benefits of circumcision, including reduction of other sexually transmitted infections (STIs), penile cancer, and protection for women and girls from cervical cancer.

Lesotho: The VMMC programme which was launched in 2012 aims to circumcise 80 % of male adolescents aged 15 to 29 in five districts. The programme is integrating testing for HIV. 18 hospitals and over 100 health centres are providing VMMC and testing. In 2014 85,000 young men accessed VMMC, of whom 56% were also tested for HIV. Lesotho is also offering Early Infant Medical Circumcision (EIMC) but uptake has been slow as culturally boys are circumcised during initiation into adolescence.[20]

eSwatini VMMC was found to be highest in 15 to 19 year olds at 38,2% and decreases with age to a low coverage of 7,5% in men over 65.[21]

Preventing new HIV infections in children and keeping their mothers alive: UNAIDS developed a Global Plan for the elimination of new HIV infections among children by 2015 and keeping their mothers alive which focused on 22 high prevalence countries; 21 of which are in Africa and 12 in SADC (Angola, Botswana, DRC, Lesotho, Malawi, Mozambique, Namibia, South Africa, eSwatini, Tanzania, Zambia and Zimbabwe).

The Global Plan had four prongs:
• Preventing new HIV infections among women of childbearing age.
• Preventing unintended pregnancies among women living with HIV.
• Preventing HIV transmission from a woman living with HIV to her baby.
• Providing appropriate treatment, care and support to mothers living with HIV and their children and families.

All SADC member states have followed Malawi's introduction of Option B+ where all pregnant mothers living with HIV are immediately introduced to lifelong ART irrespective of CD4 count. This has led to rapid increase in the number of pregnant women on ART. In 2008 when the first barometer was developed, the guidelines indicated that women with a CD4 count lower than 200 should receive full ARVs. The majority were tested and given a single dose of nevaripine to take during delivery. South Africa added a short course of AZT in 2008. Figure 7.5 shows rapid expansion of PMTCT in many countries such as Zimbabwe, Namibia, South Africa, Zambia, Malawi, ESwatini, Lesotho, Mozambique, Tanzania (where the increase is from 10% coverage to 85%), DRC and Angola. In 2018, women are being initiated on to full ART immediately, with increased demands on the health system. Expanded coverage is accompanied by increased services.

[16] Njeuhmeli, E. et al. Scaling Up Voluntary Medical Male Circumcision for Human Immunodeficiency Virus Prevention for Adolescents and Young Adult Men: A Modeling Analysis of Implementation and Impact in Selected Countries. https://www.hivsharespace.net/resource/scaling-voluntary-medical-male-circumcision-human-immunodeficiency-virus-prevention accessed July 5, 2018.
[17] Motivations for Voluntary Medical Male Circumcision Among Adolescents in South Africa, Tanzania, and Zimbabwe. https://www.hivsharespace.net/resource/age-differences-perceptions-and-motivations-voluntary-medical-male-circumcision-among accessed July 5, 2018
[18] https://www.hivsharespace.net/resource/females-peer-influence-and-support-adolescent-males-receiving-voluntary-medical-male accessed July 5, 2018
[19] https://www.hivsharespace.net/resource/parental-communication-engagement-and-support-during-adolescent-voluntary-medical-male accessed July 5, 2018.
[20] https://www.avert.org/professionals/hiv-programming/prevention/voluntary male medical circumcision Last accessed 3 July, 2018.
[21] SHIMS2. 2017. Swaziland HIV incidence measurement survey2. A population based HIV Impact Assessment. Summary sheet.

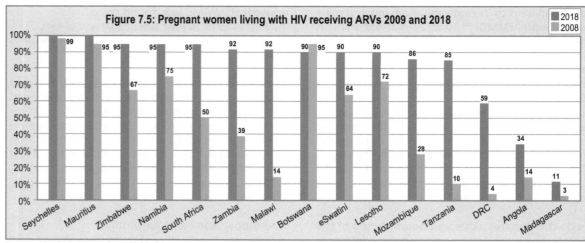

Figure 7.5: Pregnant women living with HIV receiving ARVs 2009 and 2018

Legend: 2018, 2008

Seychelles 99; Mauritius 95, 95; Zimbabwe 95, 67; Namibia 95, 75; South Africa 95, 50; Zambia 92, 39; Malawi 92, 14; Botswana 90, 95; eSwatini 90, 64; Lesotho 90, 72; Mozambique 86, 28; Tanzania 85, 10; DRC 59, 4; Angola 34, 14; Madagascar 11, 3

Source: PMTCT Coverage, http://aidsinfo.unaids.org/#, last accessed July 19, 2018 and Gender Links 2008.

Figure 7.5 shows that:
- All countries have made significant progress in increasing the coverage of pregnant women living with HIV receiving ARVs. Ten countries (Seychelles, Mauritius, Zimbabwe, Namibia, South Africa, Zambia, Malawi, Botswana, eSwatini and Lesotho) now have coverage of 90% or higher.
- This progress is especially significant in the case of Zimbabwe (75% to 95%); South Africa (50% to 95%); Zambia (39% to 92%); Malawi (14% to 92%); Mozambique (28% to 86%); Tanzania (10% to 85%); DRC (4% to 59%) and Angola (14% to 34%).
- DRC and Angola, with coverage of lower than 60%, remain a concern. Madagascar, at 11%, is of particular concern.

Despite the impressive progress there is little room for complacency. Many other targets have not been met and new knowledge raises fresh challenges. The Global Plan aimed to reduce the MTCT rate to less than 5% in breastfeeding women, and less than 2% in non-breastfeeding women. Overall, the 21 Global Plan countries reduced MTCT among breastfeeding women from 22.4% to 8.9% between 2009 and 2015. Four countries (South Africa, Uganda, eSwatini and Namibia), achieved the 5% or less. Botswana, the only non-breastfeeding Global Plan priority country, achieved an MTCT rate of 2.6% - just above the 2% target.[22]

The Global Plan aimed to reduce the number of new infections among women of reproductive age by 50%, but they only declined by 5% between 2009 and 2015. Lesotho and Malawi were amongst the five countries which reduced unintended pregnancies by more than 10% between 2000-2004 and 2010-2014. New evidence suggests that pregnant women have up to 3 times higher risk of acquiring HIV than other HIV- women. Women need to be encouraged to take more precautions to prevent infection during pregnancy and to be retested.

Factors influencing participation in continued access to PMTCT: Many women adhere to treatment during pregnancy but are lost to follow-up after the birth of their babies. Pregnant adolescents particularly struggle with adhering to lifelong treatment and need special attention.

1. ***Feeding options:*** WHO recommends that women in resource poor settings who are on ART should be encouraged to exclusively breast-feed.

 Malawi: A study reported that though the majority of mothers followed the advice to breastfeed, many reported mixed feeding in the first six months. Some of the reasons given for this were traditional feeding practices as well as a poor understanding of what exclusive breastfeeding involves or why women should exclusively breastfeed.

In **Tanzania**, a study comparing two hospitals: one which promoted exclusive breastfeeding as the only infant feeding option; and the other following Tanzanian PMTCT infant feeding guidelines which promote patient choice, found that women in the first were confident in exclusive breastfeeding while those in the second were unsure of what they should do.[23]

22 https://www.avert.org/professionals/hiv-programming/prevention/preventionmothertochildtransmission Last accessed 3 July, 2018.
23 Ibid.

2. **Stigma and discrimination:** A body of emerging evidence is showing the impact of stigma on access and adherence to ART for PMTCT. An HIV positive diagnosis often elicits shock, denial of disease, depression, or fear of handling side effects and a lifelong commitment to treatment. Pregnant women are often afraid of disclosing their status to their partners and other family members. Women often experience violence and desertion from partners. Women also experience stigma from health care providers, which reduces access to the very services which they need.

 Malawi: Stigma and fear of a partner's reaction has been found to inhibit women from accessing immediate treatment available under option B+.

3. **Limited health resources:** Patient overcrowding, poor treatment, limited availability of commodities all hinder uptake.

4. **Male involvement** has been found to have positive impact on PMTCT. Factors which reduce male involvement include fear of knowing their HIV status, unwelcoming health services. Men who already know their HIV status are more likely to participate in PMTCT. Being made to feel important in the process also encourages male involvement.

Key populations are people who inject drugs, men who have sex with men, transgender persons, sex workers and prisoners. Around the world, key populations face much higher rates of HIV and AIDS than the general population and are most at risk for contracting HIV[24].They face many hurdles which stop them from accessing services such as punitive laws and policies, police harassment and stigma and discrimination within health settings. Adolescent boys and young men who belong to key populations face heightened risks of HIV infection, but also demonstrate low knowledge, awareness and uptake of HIV services.

Female sex workers: There is increasing availability of data on sex workers - including prevalence which ranges from 4.6% in Seychelles to 71.9% in Lesotho; condom use with last partner (ranging from over 40% in the DRC to over 90% in Seychelles) and testing (ranging from about 20% in Seychelles to over 90% in Zimbabwe). Sex work is criminalised in almost all countries which hinders the provision of services.

 South Africa *is set to become the first Southern African country to decriminalise sex work:* The ruling African National Congress (ANC) party in South Africa resolved in December 2017 that sex work should be decriminalised. Parliament is debating decriminalisation. In March, 2018, the Commission for Gender Equality told parliament that the commission's position is that sex work should not be treated as a criminal activity. The Commission argued that decriminalisation would reduce the violence experienced by sex workers and increase access to services, including HIV prevention and treatment. Countries such as New Zealand which have fully decriminalised sex work have found that the numbers engaged in sex work have not changed significantly five years later.

Pre Exposure Prophylaxis (PrEP) is a daily course of Anti-RetroViral (ARV) drugs taken by HIV negative people who are at high risk of contracting HIV, such as sex workers, partners in sero- discordant couples and men who have sex with men. A number of studies in different settings have shown that if PrEP is taken correctly it can reduce the risk of HIV infection to almost zero. It has reduced infection rates from unprotected sex by 90% and from injecting drug use by 70%. However, for it to be effective there must be high levels of adherence. The 2016 declaration included a commitment to provide PrEP to three million people by 2020. Progress towards achieving this target is slow. PrEP at particular times of a person's life to prevent infection is more cost effective than long term ART to manage infection. There is demand for PrEP especially from men who have sex with men[25].

South Africa became the first African country to issue full regulatory approval for PrEP and to include it in the national HIV programme in December, 2015. The DREAMS programme, supported by PEPFAR, is supporting access to PrEP by adolescent girls and young women in Lesotho, Malawi, Mozambique, South Africa, eSwatini, Tanzania, Zambia and Zimbabwe who are at high risk of HIV.

 The SAPPHIRe project in **Zimbabwe** is trialling testing of sex workers with provision of ART for those that are positive and PrEP for those that are negative. Each woman belongs to a group which meets every month for support. She attends the group meetings with a "sister"

Sex work is criminalised in ALL countries

---

24 https://www.usaid.gov/what-we-do/global-health/hiv-and-aids/technical-areas/key-populations
25 https://www.avert.org/professionals/hiv-programming/prevention/pre-exposure-prophylaxis accessed 10 July, 2018.

and the pair supports each other to adhere to their treatment. Group members are reminded about meetings through sms. During the group sessions sex workers also receive legal advice and are encouraged to access their rights.

 In **Mauritius**, where the spread of HIV I has been largely due to injecting drug use, the focus is on **harm reduction**. From the beginning of the epidemic in 1987, to 2014, a total of 6090 cases of HIV were detected in Mauritius. The number of new cases rose very gradually to 98 in 2002 and then quite exponentially to 921 in 2005 and fell to 260 in 2013. 66.7% of all Mauritian HIV cases since 1987 have been people who inject drugs. This percentage increased from 7% in 2001 to 92% in 2005. Following the introduction of the Needle Exchange Programme and the Methadone Substi-

tution Therapy in 2006, it began to decrease to 34.7% in 2015 and 31.1% in the first six months of 2016[26].

An HIV Vaccine: Developing any new vaccine takes time as it must be tested rigorously. Developing a vaccine for HIV, which is found in a number of variants and which mutates, is very difficult. The 35-year quest for a vaccine is continuing and promising developments were reported in July 2018. A new 'mosaic' vaccine that Is made from pieces of different HIV viruses which are combined to elicit responses against a number of HIV strains was tested in a phase 1/2a clinical trial with positive results. This same vaccine will now be tested for safety and efficacy in a phase 2b trial in Southern Africa with 2600 women. This Is only the fifth HIV vaccine that has gone as far as efficacy trials in humans.

Treatment

 Article 27.3:
b) Ensure universal access to HIV and AIDS treatment for infected women, men, girls and boys; and

Major gains have been made: Most countries in SADC have now adopted the Test and Treat or Treat All approach, which is increasing the numbers of people on ART very quickly. In Botswana, for example, where Treat All was adopted in June 2016, the number of people on ART has increased by 37% since 2015.[27] In Zambia, which has also adopted the Treat All approach the number of

people living with HIV who have accessed ART increased from 530,702 in 2013 to 855,070 in 2017[28]. When it is considered that in 2008 those who were eligible for ART were only those with CD4 counts that were lower than 200 whereas in 2018 it is all people living with HIV, to be able to increase rates of coverage is a remarkable achievement.

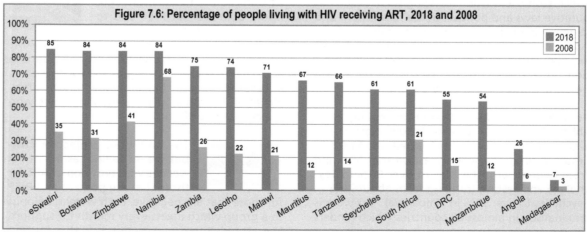

Figure 7.6: Percentage of people living with HIV receiving ART, 2018 and 2008

Source: Treatment coverage http://aidsinfo.unaids.org/#, last accessed July 19, 2018 and Gender Links.

---

[26] Republic of Mauritius Statistics on HIV/AIDS (as at end of June 2016).
[27] Government of Botswana. 2018. Country Progress Report - Botswana.
http://www.unaids.org/sites/default/files/country/documents/BWA_2018_countryreport.pdf accessed 10 July, 2018.
[28] Government of Zambia. 2018. Country Progress Report - Zambia.
http://www.unaids.org/sites/default/files/country/documents/ZMB_2018_countryreport.pdf accessed 10 July, 2018.

Figure 7.6 compares the situation with regard to treatment in 2008 with 2018. The graph shows that:
- By 2018, all countries had significantly improved their coverage compared to 2008.
- All countries have adopted a test and treat approach, which means providing ARVs for all people living with HIV, and increased their ART coverage and many have increased coverage significantly despite poor infrastructure for health and heavy HIV burdens.
- Four countries have achieved a reach of 80% or more. These are Namibia, Zimbabwe, Botswana and eSwatini.
- With coverage of only 26% and 7%, Angola and Madagascar remain a major concern.
- With its large population, South Africa has the largest number of people on ARV, but this only covers 61% of those needing to access.

 South Africa has the largest HIV treatment programme in the world with over 4 million people on treatment by the end of 2017. It is estimated that by the end of 2014, 2.7 million South African adults had died from AIDS. The number of deaths per year peaked in 2006, at about 231,000 adult AIDS deaths, which dropped to about 95,000 by 2014. This is approximately 75% lower than what would have been expected in the absence of ART. The ART programme was introduced in 2004 and rapidly expanded after 2008. It is estimated that the programme resulted in 1.72 million fewer adult deaths by the end of 2014, which corresponds to 6.15 million years of life saved[29].

Differentiated care: Health services across the region cannot give monthly care to such large numbers of people that are on ART. There is therefore a move to provide more care at community level for those that are stable and do not need to see a health professional every month. This is done through treatment clubs, community workers and various other methods. It is being suggested that treatment may be initiated at community level, especially for groups such as men, who are hesitant to access health facilities.

Adherence to treatment is enhanced when services are confidential and non-stigmatising; decentralised to minimise travel and waiting times; when there is a trusting relationship between clients and service provider and when clients recognize the value of treatment to their own lives and ability to care for and contribute to their families.

Drug Resistance: There are worrying reports of up to one in ten patients developing resistance to the most common first line ARVs[30]. This is particularly the case for those that have been exposed to ARVs before - either in previous PMTCT programmes with single dose nevirapine, or who discontinued treatment for other reasons. Detecting treatment failure requires interaction with health centres and viral load testing. Any patient who is failing on first line treatment should be rapidly considered for second line drugs, which are much more expensive.

HIV and cervical cancer: Cervical cancer is considered to be an AIDS Defining Cancer. Women living with HIV have increased risk for persistent HPV (Human Papilloma Virus) infection which is associated with progression to cervical cancer, and are at least 5 times more likely to develop cervical cancer as women who are HIV negative. Studies in Botswana have found that the survival rates for women who are living with HIV with cervical cancer are poor, even when the women are on ART.[31] There is great hope that expansion of HPV vaccination for girls before they reach sexual debut will provide greater protection for the next generation of women.[32]

Zimbabwe became the 8th African country to introduce HPV vaccination into its routine vaccination programme in May, 2018. HPV vaccination will be available to school girls aged 10 - 14. Zimbabwe has the fifth highest cervical cancer burden in the world[33]. Other countries in the region that are already offering HPV vaccination include Botswana, Namibia and South Africa.

Focus on Men: The UN AIDS December 2017 report, "Blind Spot"[34], brought attention to the need to engage with and plan for men's health. Even though there are consistently more women in SADC that are living with HIV than men, all over the world, men are less likely to access health care than women, to access testing, or treatment or to adhere. This behaviour is not peculiar to men that are living with HIV as many studies have shown that men generally visit health facilities less frequently than women, have fewer health check-

[29] Leigh Johnson, 17 December, 2017. South Africa's HIV treatment programme: a phoenix rising from the ashes? https://www.groundup.org.za/article/south-africas-hiv-treatment-programme-phoenix-rising-ashes/ Accessed 5 July, 2018.
[30] UNAIDS. Global AIDS Update 2018. Miles to go. Geneva, Switzerland.
[31] IAS Webinar, 25 Jan 2017. The Double Burden; HIV and Cervical Cancer.
[32] Melton, CL. How HIV affects cervical cancer risks and outcomes. https://www.infectiousdiseaseadvisor.com/hivaids/hiv-and-cervical-cancer-risk-outcomes/article/713414/ accessed 2 July, 2018.
[33] UNICEF Zimbabwe Media Centre. Cervical Cancer Vaccine Introduced in Zimbabwe. https://www.unicef.org/zimbabwe/media_21520.html accessed 5 July, 2018.
[34] UNAIDS. 2017. Blind Spot. Geneva, Switzerland.

SA largest HIV treatment programme in the world

25%
more
likely
than

to

die
from
AIDS-
related
causes

ups, ask fewer questions and are diagnosed for life threatening conditions at later stages than women.

Men are exposed to a number of risk factors such as higher rates of alcohol and smoking. There is evidence to suggest that higher alcohol use may be associated with risky sexual activity and acquisition of HIV. Alcohol use is also associated with progress of HIV infection to AIDS illness and is likely to influence poor adherence to treatment. Men are therefore more likely to die of AIDS related causes. In Sub Saharan Africa in 2016 41% of people living with HIV were men, but 53% of AIDS related deaths were in men.

 Botswana reported that adult males lag behind on all three 90-90-90 targets - 74% of men know their status compared to an overall 86%; 72% of men who knew their status accessed treatment compared to 84% overall and 70% of those on treatment were virally suppressed compared to 81% overall.[35]

In **South Africa** clinic data shows that men were 25% more likely than women to die from AIDS-related causes, even though  women were more likely to be living with HIV. 70% of the men who died from AIDS-related causes had never sought health care for HIV.

Youth activists from Lets Grow in Orange Farm, South Africa, offer care, support and public education on preventing new HIV infections.
Photo: Colleen Lowe Morna

 A UNAIDS and WHO review of national policies on health, HIV, sexual and reproductive health and mental health in 14 eastern and southern Africa countries found that only **eSwatini** had a policy which addresses the health of men and boys. eSwatini has a specific strategy to provide a male-tailored comprehensive service package that includes health risk reduction, regular screening for non-communicable diseases and a range of sexual and reproductive health and HIV services.[36]

Blind Spot recommends that more effort needs to be made by leaders at national and community level to engage with men, both to enhance their own health as well as to be positive factors in the health of women, recognising that men's and women's health are closely interlinked. Men should be encouraged to take more responsibility for their own health, to challenge negative notions of masculinity which prevent them from seeking care and to adopt more protective sexual behaviours that will benefit themselves and their partners. Providers of health and HIV services need to find innovative ways to reach men. Reaching men requires an understanding both of their work lives and their leisure and arranging services to fit with these. Sport offers a unique avenue for increasing engagement with men.

Review of the impact of the HPTN071 (PoPART) prevention package on HIV incidence in 21 communities across Zambia found that only 77% of men in **Zambia** knew their HIV status compared to 90% of women. The study team held focus group discussions with men to discuss alternative approaches to reaching men. These were the basis for a new campaign "Man up Now" which included weekend health events with a range of services including blood pressure readings, eye and dental check-ups, diabetes screening, voluntary medical male circumcision services and tests for tuberculosis, HIV and other sexually transmitted infections. Home visits were also conducted at times where men were more likely to be at home and workplace testing services were introduced. Later, self-testing was introduced, especially targeted to reach younger men.[37]

[35] Government of Botswana. 2018. Country Progress Report - Botswana. http://www.unaids.org/sites/default/files/country/documents/BWA_2018_countryreport.pdf accessed 10 July, 2018.
[36] Pascoe P. Addressing the Health Needs of Men and Boys: An Analysis of 14 Eastern & Southern African Countries' National Policies on Health, HIV, Sexual & Reproductive Health, &Mental Health. Commission by UNAIDS and WHO, 2017(unpublished).
[37] UNAIDS. 2017. Blind Spot. Geneva, Switzerland. See also https://www.hptn.org/research/studies/hptn071

Care work

Article 27.3

c) Develop and implement policies and programmes to ensure appropriate recognition of the work carried out by care givers, the majority of whom are women, the allocation of resources and the psychological support for care givers as well as support for care givers as well as support of people for people living with AIDS.

From the outset, the SADC Gender Protocol has been unique in its recognition of care work. This is reinforced in the SADC sponsored UN resolution on Women, Girls and HIV, which calls on governments to: "Recognise women's contribution to the economy and their active participation in caring for people living with HIV and AIDS and recognize, reduce, redistribute and value women's unpaid care and domestic work through the provision of public services, infrastructure."

The face of care work has changed dramatically in the decade since the Barometer began. In 2008, most care workers were older women, driven by passion for their communities, neighbours and orphaned children around them, to give tirelessly of their time and care to ill and often dying people that the health care system was unable to help. A decade later it is accepted that community-based HIV service delivery is critical to reach the numerous targets, and especially to be sure that no one is left behind. But the face of the community care worker has changed quite significantly.

In 2018 community care workers are mobilising communities for testing, treatment and adherence, and also:

- Reaching adolescent girls and boys and their families for improved access to services, including VMMC where prospective clients appreciate being able to ask questions in private;
- Reach men and promote positive masculinity, especially as men do not want to travel to health centres and prefer services which are closer to home and at times which are more convenient for them;
- Reaching key populations, including sex workers, men who have sex with men, injecting drug users;
- Supporting differentiated care models for different groups - adolescents, mothers on PMTCT, men and others, to reduce congestion

in the health system and supporting patients to adhere to treatment.

Many community outreach supporters are expert clients or patients who provide peer support. This ranges from young men who have been circumcised who encourage others to do the same and answer questions about the procedure, to mothers that have been through PMTCT, to adolescents living with HIV and adhering to their treatment who support other adolescents, to men who reach out to other men. In numerous settings, collaboration between the health system and communities has been found to reduce stigma and discrimination and help to deliver services to those in greatest need. However, the scale of the task of eliminating AIDS requires that such collaboration be institutionalized, rather than limited to a few pilot projects and dependent on volunteerism. This is especially true as more and more work related to even initiation of treatment is being shifted from health centres to community level. The lived experience alone of expert clients is not sufficient and there is need for continued investment in training, support and supervision of these new care workers. Policies which were developed to support care workers a decade ago are still relevant in the new era.

 In **Tanzania** early circumcision adopters who became voluntary community advocates contributed to a 500% increase in the number of circumcisions which were conducted.

In **Zambia**, the Government recognises the importance of investment in community care. Thus, the government of Zambia reports that it plans to double resources for community mobilization from 2016 to 2020. Further, spending on social enablers (including advocacy, political mobilization, law and policy reform and human rights) is expected to reach 8% of total AIDS expenditure by 2020[38].

---

[38] Government of the Republic of Zambia. 2018. Country Progress Report -Zambia. http://www.unaids.org/sites/default/files/country/documents/ZMB_2018_countryreport.pdf accessed 10 July, 2018.

Home based care offers solace in eSwatini

Umtfunti organisation is a home-based care project aimed at changing the lives of people living with HIV and AIDS. It was established due to the high AIDS mortality rate in the Lubombo region. Members were first trained as Lihlombe Lekukhalela (caregivers), under Siteki Alliance of Mayors and Municipal Leaders on HIV/AIDS in Africa (AMICAAL) and this is where the community work began.

Training included GBV, child care, PMTCT and women empowerment. Members do door-to-door visits in the communities, teaching households about PMTCT, HIV, AIDS, home based care and GBV, and in addition train community members and school pupils on the same topics.

The organisation was formed to assist family caregivers in providing AIDS-related care, as public health services could not cope with the increasing demand for treatment and care. Some home-based care services focus on providing social and psychological support, with some nutritional support and basic nursing care, others also dispense ARVs and treat opportunistic infections. These services, whether provided through NGOs, government health clinics, or community groups, are essential in supporting people living with HIV, as well as people who provide care and support within families.

Umtfunti Foundation teaches people about health and wellness, takes care of the people who are terminally ill in their homes and educates and empowers women to sustain themselves economically, and to improve their lives through teaching them about micro-business. There is always hope for donor funding as, at the current time, there has been no funding at all, nor any partnerships - there are 20 beneficiaries of the programme. Lack of transportation poses problems for both the volunteers and the trained staff, local clinics and hospitals do not have vehicles that can be assigned to the care givers to do their work. Consequently, patients who live in remote areas cannot be easily reached and caregivers find patients living under very bad conditions but there are not enough resources to help them. There is no formal monitoring or evaluation of this home based care programme - nurses use outpatient cards to document care.

As a next step, the foundation intends to conduct community education with men living with HIV, young men, community leaders and male opinion leaders on the importance of male involvement, providing concrete information to encourage them to assume caregiving roles.

Source: Gillian Zwane, Umtfunti Foundation. SADC Gender Protocol@Work 2018

Next steps

- *Focus more on prevention:* Although treatment has played an enormous role in reducing the impact of HIV and AIDS, experts agree that it is not possible to treat the epidemic away. Long term there must be much more emphasis on prevention, including prevention of gender based violence and access to services for the most marginalised including men who have sex with men, sex workers, those who inject drugs and prisoners. Criminalisation of sex work, homosexuality and injecting drugs as well as stigma and discrimination are major barriers to accessing services and therefore will continue to fuel the epidemic.
- *Invest more on prevention:* Currently only 20% of global funding for HIV is being focused on prevention.
- *Focus on adolescents and young people:* For prevention, treatment, care and support. One of the best vaccines for young people is to make sure that they are in schools which are safe, supportive and where they are learning skills that they can use in life. The epidemic in young girls and women must be tackled with specific approaches tailored to this age group and must also include boys and young men.
- *Renew the focus on co-infections*, especially TB and cervical cancer. Expand vaccination for HPV and strengthen screening for cervical cancer in women living with HIV.
- *Recognise the role of a range of community based caregivers:* Such caregivers need the same support as they have throughout the pandemic - training, remuneration, materials and psychosocial support. Increasingly tasks are being shifted from health care professionals to community cadres who require input in training, supervision and support to be able to work effectively.
- *Increase investment* in systems for health, including linkages between clinical facilities and community based services. This must include increased domestic funding.

Women officers in Namibia's Correctional Services take part in a Namibian Multi-Stakeholder Conference for the development of the Namibia National Action Plan on Women Peace and Security in Windhoek in July 2017.   *Photo: Cheryl Hendricks*

8
SADC countries deployed troops to **peacekeeping missions** in 2017

KEY POINTS

- The Southern Africa Development Community (SADC) Secretariat adopted a Regional Framework for Mainstreaming Gender into the SADC Organ. It calls on all countries in SADC to adopt Women, Peace and Security (WPS) National Action Plans (NAPs).

- The DRC and Angola have adopted UNSCR 1325 NAPs. Namibia is validating its NAP.

- The DRC failed to hold elections in 2017. It remains in a tenuous state with elections now scheduled for December 2018.

- In the run up to Madagascar's elections the country saw a re-emergence of violent protest over its new electoral laws.

- Zimbabwe saw the ousting of its long-time president, Robert Mugabe, in November 2017 and the inauguration of Emmerson Mnangagwa as president.

- Publicly accessible data on women in the security sector in Southern Africa remains a challenge to access. The Barometer annually produces much of the data that exists in the public domain. This makes it difficult to track progress. The situation is not consistent with global norms.

- Eight SADC countries deployed troops and support to peacekeeping missions in 2017.

- The number of peacekeepers deployed appears to be declining in many countries. Zimbabwe and Namibia continue to deploy the most female peacekeepers, while South Africa and Tanzania deploy the largest number of peacekeepers.

All
countries
now have
sex-
disaggre-
gated
police
data

Table 8.1: Trends in peace-building and conflict resolution since 2009			
	Baseline 2009	Progress 2018	Variance (Progress 2018-2030 - target)
COUNTRIES WITH UNSCR NATIONAL ACTION PLANS (NAPS)			
15 countries with UNSCR National Action Plans	1 country (DRC)	3: DRC is revising its NAP. Angola adopted its NAP in 2017 and Namibia is validating its NAP	12 countries (Botswana, Lesotho, Madagascar, Malawi, Mauritius, Mozambique, Seychelles, South Africa, eSwatini, Tanzania, Zambia and Zimbabwe)
COUNTRIES WITH SEX DISAGGREGATED DATA ON DEFENCE			
15 countries with sex disaggregated data on defence	5 countries (Botswana, Madagascar, Malawi, South Africa and Zimbabwe)	14 countries (Angola, DRC, Botswana, Lesotho, Malawi, Mauritius, Mozambique, Namibia, Seychelles, South Africa, eSwatini, Tanzania, Zambia and Zimbabwe)	Only Madagascar remains without
PROPORTION OF WOMEN IN DEFENCE (%)			
Highest	South Africa (24%)	South Africa (30%)	-20%
Lowest	DRC (3%)	DRC (3%)	-47%
COUNTRIES WITH SEX DISAGGREGATED DATA ON THE POLICE FORCE			
Fifteen countries with sex disaggregated data on the police force	Six countries (Botswana, Mauritius, Mozambique, Namibia, South Africa and Zambia)	All SADC countries now have sex disaggregated data	
WOMEN IN THE POLICE FORCE (%)			
Highest	South Africa (21%)	Seychelles (39%)	-11
Lowest	Mozambique (7%)	DRC (6%)	-44
COUNTRIES THAT INCLUDE WOMEN IN PEACE SUPPORT OPERATIONS			
15 countries include women in peacekeeping forces	7 countries (DRC, Malawi, Namibia, South Africa, Tanzania, Zimbabwe and Zambia)	8 countries (Botswana, Madagascar, Malawi, Namibia, South Africa, Tanzania, Zimbabwe and Zambia)	7 countries (Angola, DRC, Lesotho, Mauritius, Mozambique, Seychelles and eSwatini)
PROPORTION OF WOMEN IN PEACE SUPPORT INITIATIVES (%)			
Highest	Namibia (46%)	Zimbabwe (35%)	-50
Lowest	Tanzania (6%)	Tanzania (5%) and DRC (none)	

Source: Gender Links, 2018.

As illustrated in Table 8.1, South Africa is the only country to have reached 30% for women's representation in defence, still a long way from 50/50 representation. Other key trends include:

- Botswana now recruits female privates, which has increased the number of women in the Botswana Defence Force (BDF) from 1% to 5%.
- There is a need for SADC countries to make data publicly available to track the implementation of its own strategy on women, peace and security.
- Seychelles, at 39% for women's representation in the police, remains the highest in SADC on this indicator. Namibia has the second highest representation of women in the police in the region at 38%. Nine countries have reached or gone beyond the 20% mark.
- Experts rank the Botswana Police Force as the best in Africa.
- Sex disaggregated data is least available for correctional services, yet this is a sector that employs a high number of women. This report does not include findings on this indicator as it is difficult to access any data.

- SADC, despite all the training of women that has taken place in the region, is still not deploying many women as mediators in conflict situations.
- Only eight SADC countries deployed peace-keepers to UN missions in 2017: DRC, Madagascar, Malawi, Namibia South Africa, Tanzania, Zambia and Zimbabwe.

Background

In 2018, the African Union (AU) adopted the Continental Results Framework for Monitoring and Reporting on the Implementation of the Women, Peace and Security Agenda in Africa. It provides African countries with a set of indicators to track and monitor progress and challenges. State parties can use these for national self-assessment and dialogues on the state of Women in Peace and Security (WPS). This framework will go a long way in encouraging member states to adopt and imple-ment UN Security Council Resolution 1325 (UNSCR 1325), which affirms that peace and security efforts are more sustainable when women are equal partners in the prevention of violent conflict, the delivery of relief and recovery efforts and in the forging of lasting peace. The framework also standardises reporting mechanisms, complemented by the revised AU Gender Policy and Gender Strategy 2018-2027. Networks such as FemWise, which facilitates and supports women's participation in peace processes and preventative diplomacy, and the African Women's Leaders Network, also play key roles in progressing Africa's WPS agenda.

To date, 74 countries have adopted National Action Plans (NAPs) for the implementation of UNSCR 1325.[1] Of these, 22 are in Africa and two in Southern Africa (Angola and DRC). Namibia is preparing to adopt a NAP. Additionally, in 2017, SADC adopted a regional strategy for the implementation on WPS and validated a regional training manual on trafficking in persons. These frameworks call for the participation of women in peace and security structures and processes; the prevention of violence against women; and the protection of women during conflict. Since the adoption of UNSCR 1325, in 2000, stakeholders have developed frameworks but shows mixed progress in including women in, and transforming, the delivery of peace and security globally.

Bineta Diop, AU Special Envoy on Women Peace and Security, and Levinia Addae-Mensah from West Africa Network for Peacebuilding (WANEP), meet at the AU in October 2017 to discuss the Continental Results Framework.
Photo courtesy of Africa Union

There has, for example, been an increase in mentions of women in UN resolutions and in peace agreements. However, women's inclusion in peace-keeping activities has stagnated: they only represent 4.7% (of 91 058 UN peacekeepers) as of 31 March 2018.[2] Women in peace-making remain more at the level of observer status rather than as signatories, negotiators or mediators. Many challenges also remain around the protection of women in conflict situations and the prevention of violence against women.

Violence remains common in the DRC, which has hosted a UN peace support operation, the UN Organisation Stabilisation Mission (MONUSCO), for two decades. Additionally, the SADC-deployed Force Intervention Brigade (FIB) has operated in the DRC since 2013. Over the past year, however, the humanitarian crisis has deepened with continued deterioration of the security situation. DRC has recently seen the displacement of an estimated 1.9 million new people, while 120 000 have fled beyond its borders. Women comprise 78% of all displaced people and refugees from DRC.[3] This brings the total to approximately 4.49 million internally displaced persons (IDPs) and 630 000 refugees from DRC hosted in the region.[4] Displacement increases women's vulnerability and exposure to sexual and gender-based violence (GBV). The DRC has a NAP and the region has a strategy for WPS. Stakeholders now must translate these strategies into action to ensure improvement in the overall security situation and increased security for women.

SADC Organ on Politics Defence and Security

Lawmakers created the SADC Organ for Politics, Defence and Security (the Organ) in 1996, tasking it with maintaining peace and security in the region. The Organ focuses on six key areas: politics and diplomacy; defence; police; state security; public security; and regional peacekeeping.

A woman, Tanzania's Stergomena Tax, holds the position of SADC executive secretary. The SADC Organ operates on a Troika system whereby the SADC Summit and Organ Troika Summit are mutually exclusive; and the chairperson of the Organ does not simultaneously hold the chair of the Summit. The Protocol on Politics, Defence and Security Cooperation regulates the Organ structure. Like the Summit chair, the Organ chair rotates on an annual basis.[5]

1 Peacewomen.org [accessed on 20 May 2018].
2 "Summary of Troop Contributions to UN Peacekeeping Operations by Mission, Post and Gender." [accessed at peacekeeping.un.org].
3 UNHCR Congolese Situation: Responding to the Needs of Displaced Congolese and Refugees. Supplementary appeal January to December 2018. [accessed at reporting.unhcr.org on 19 May 2018].
4 See UNOCHA website.
5 https://www.sadc.int/about-sadc/sadc-institutions/org/

SADC is

home

to

7/10

most

peaceful

countries

in Africa

Angola currently chairs the Organ and Tanzania is the outgoing chair. Zambia is the incoming Chair (in August 2018). For 2017-2018, the Organ has been dealing with political conflict in the DRC, Lesotho, Madagascar and Zimbabwe. SADC lists its peace and security challenges as that of armed conflict, terrorism, HIV and AIDS, landmines, external aggression, reintegration of ex-combatants and rehabilitation of child soldiers, disaster relief, trafficking of small arms and light weapons, illegal migration, and maritime piracy.[6] The Organ has yet to integrate a gender perspective into its threat perceptions.

State of Peace and Security in Southern Africa

SADC saw dramatic changes in its political landscape in 2017/2018. In Angola, João Lourenço replaced long time President Jose Eduardo dos Santos. In Botswana, Mokgweetsi Masisi replaced President Ian Khama after Khama duly ended his two terms, and the people of Lesotho elected Tom Thabane as Prime Minister. Meanwhile, Cyril Ramaphosa replaced Jacob Zuma as president in South Africa and Emmerson Mnangagwa replaced long time Zimbabwe President Robert Mugabe. The military played a large role in Zimbabwe's "assisted transition."

TANZANIA

CABO DELGADO

MOZAMBIQUE

o Maputo

In 2018, terror attacks in Cabo Delgado in northern Mozambique had some in SADC worried about growing instability in the country.   *Photo courtesy of BBC News*

The 2018 Global Peace Index (GPI) indicates that SADC is home to seven of the ten most peaceful countries in Africa (Botswana, Madagascar, Malawi, Mauritius, Namibia, Tanzania and Zambia) - the same findings as in 2017. DRC saw the largest deterioration in the region, according to the GPI, caused by violent protests that erupted following an election delay. In April 2018, Madagascar also saw political violence in relation to proposed new electoral laws and hence had a decline in peacefulness. Moreover, incidents of terrorist activities

that left several people dead took place in June 2018 in Cabo Delgado in Northern Mozambique, which has regional experts worried about further instability in Mozambique. The 2017 Mo Ibrahim Index reveals a trend of some Southern African countries declining in terms of governance. These include Angola, Botswana, Mauritius, Lesotho, Zambia and Malawi. Meanwhile, the index put South Africa and Madagascar in a category of "slowing deterioration and bouncing back."[7] Governance deficits can create peace and security challenges. In SADC, governance challenges relate to corruption, credibility of elections, service delivery, authoritarianism and attempts to extend presidential term limits.

 Conflict in the oil rich Cabinda province continues to affect **Angola**. The region has recently seen clashes between separatist movements and the armed forces. In April 2018, President Lourenço sacked the chief of staff of the armed forces, the head of foreign intelligence and the son and daughter of former president Dos Santos, as he seeks to tackle the culture of corruption and nepotism and to assert his own authority in governing the country. Lourenço will have to deal with the country's declining economy and dependency on oil.

Botswana saw a peaceful handover of power in April 2018 with the inauguration of a new president, Mokgweetsi Masisi of the Botswana Democratic Party. Former President Khama represented one of the few presidents in Southern Africa who openly critiqued abuse of power, electoral irregularities and human rights violations in the region. Botswana remains one of Africa's most stable countries. It, however, continues to have one of the highest HIV and AIDS infection rates in the world.

 DRC has yet to hold national multiparty elections which were due in 2016. This has generated many ongoing protests in the country, with the belief that President Kabila is stalling on stepping down now that his term limit has expired. In December 2016, Catholic Church leaders mediated an agreement (the Saint Sylvester Agreement) between the government, opposition and civil society in which stakeholders agreed to hold elections before December 2017. The election date has once again been postponed to 23 December 2018. Meanwhile, the International Criminal Court acquitted former opposition leader Jean-Pierre

---

[6] SADC website.
[7] 2017 Ibrahim Index of African Governance [s.mo.ibrahim.foundation accessed on 20 May 2018].

Bemba Gombo on charges of war crimes and crimes against humanity in June 2018. This is likely to have an impact on the next presidential elections.

The DRC is once again facing dire humanitarian and human rights challenges and the conflict in its eastern region continues unabated. Police have violently cracked down on popular dissent. In addition, about 70 armed groups remain in the east of the country despite the longstanding presence of a peace mission and the deployment of the Force Intervention Brigade. The DRC is also currently experiencing an Ebola outbreak in the northwest; the ninth outbreak in the country. The early detection and administering of the vaccine will likely contain the spread of the virus.

 Lesotho legislators established a commission to conduct a national dialogue on the implementation of multi-sector reforms (constitutional, parliamentary, security, judicial and public service) prior to elections in 2017. They expressed dissent, however, over the proposed National Reform Commission Bill, with the opposition claiming that government had not consulted them on its draft and that any dialogue should happen before a bill's passage. Meanwhile, SADC leaders extended the mandate of the SADC Preventive Mission in the Kingdom of Lesotho (SAPMIL), a standby force to foster a conducive environment for the implementation of the above-noted reforms, by another six months to November 2018.

Protesters took to the streets in Madagascar last year in clashes that turned violent following political turmoil.
Photo: Zotonantenaina Razanandrateta

 Madagascar saw a re-emergence of violent protests in April 2018. New electoral laws, which opposition parties asserted would bar some presidential candidates from standing in elections

due in November 2018, sparked the violence. The Constitutional Court ordered the president to form a new government of national unity on 25 May 2018. Prime Minister Olivier Solonandrasanna willingly stepped down and leaders appointed the national unity government on 11 June 2018. It consists of 31 members, including eight women. The UN appointed Senegalese politician Abdoulaye Bathily as its special envoy to Madagascar to help settle the dispute, whilst the AU appointed Ramtane Lamamra of Algeria as its high representative. SADC also redeployed former president of Mozambique Joaquim Chissano to Madagascar to facilitate a national dialogue and to work on a common approach with the UN and the AU. The Independent National Electoral Commission and members of the government have yet to determine the new election dates.

 The **Mozambique** government may see an end to its longstanding civil war with Renamo, the Mozambican National Resistance, after the death of its leader, Alfonso Dhlakama. The ruling party, however, must address the grievances of economic marginalisation and over-centralisation of power that Renamo raised.[8] It will also have to undertake the demobilisation and reintegration of Renamo soldiers. Since October 2017, Mozambique has seen an increase in terrorist incidents carried out by a group calling itself Ahlu Sunna Wa -Jama in Cabo Delgado Province.[9] These incidents - attacks on police and military posts and beheadings of civilians, including women and children - have resulted in many people fleeing from the region. Many analysts note that this is another violent extremist group with possible links to other jihadist organisations.

In 2018, **South Africa** saw a recall by the governing African National Congress (ANC) of President Jacob Zuma and the inauguration of President Cyril Ramaphosa on 15 February 2018. Rampaphosa must deal with a divided ruling party, a struggling economy, major corruption in state enterprises, a resurgence of debates over land titles and high crime rates. The national cost of violence in South Africa is at 19% of its GDP.[10] The country averages around 18 500 murders per year and 50 000 sexual offences. Xenophobia, homophobia and sexism also remain a serious challenge in South Africa. As South Africa moves towards national elections in 2019, it needs to be vigilant about political killings. The Moerane Commission is investigating a spate of political killings in the KwaZulu-Natal region. The Independent Electoral Commis-

Xeno-phobia, homo-phobia & sexism remain a serious challenge in South Africa

---

8 Michael Aeby. 2018. *Peace and Security Challenges in Southern Africa: Governance Deficits and Lacklustre Regional Conflict Management.* Policy Note No.4. Nordiska Africa Institute.
9 Peter Fabricus. 2018. "Is another Boko Haram or al Shabaab erupting in Mozambique?" ISS Today 14 June
10 "What is the situation in South Africa? [Saferspaces.org accessed on the 2 June 2018]

sion (IEC) provincial electoral commissioner noted that, of its 391 councillor posts, 93 became vacant following the deaths of sitting elected representatives and, of the 111 ward councillors, 31 became vacant because of deaths of elected representatives. Since 2016, 19 councillors have died.[11] In areas of intense political risk, South Africa will likely see a decline in the number of women participating in elections.

 The **Zimbabwe**an military forced Robert Mugabe to step down in November 2017 after factionalism overwhelmed the Zimbabwe African National Union-Patriotic Front (ZANU-PF) ruling party. During the power struggle, Mugabe fired Emmerson Mnangagwa from his post as vice president and expelled Mnangagwa from ZANU-PF. The army stepped in on 15 November 2017 and took control of government, noting that "we wish to make it abundantly clear that this is not a military takeover of government. What the Zimbabwe Defence Forces (ZDF) is doing is to pacify

a degenerating political, social, and economic situation in our country which if not addressed may result in violent conflict."[12] This "military-assisted transition" ended 37 years of rule by Mugabe. Mnangagwa was sworn in as president, bringing the general who led the overthrow, Constantino Chiwenga, into his cabinet as vice president. This involvement of the military in politics sets an ominous precedent for civil military relations in Southern Africa. Lesotho and Madagascar have already have already seen similar military involvement. There is a pressing need for security sector reform. Zimbabwe's negotiation of the transition is crucial as it faces enormous challenges of institutionalising the rule of law, growing the economy, reducing corruption, and fostering national reconciliation.[13] Zimbabwe has scheduled national elections for July 2018. These will once again pit ZANU-PF against the Movement for Democratic Change (MDC), both with new leaders at the helm. It is likely to be a highly contested election. For the first time in 16 years, international electoral observers will oversee a Zimbabwean election.

Progress in implementation of UNSCR Resolution 1325

 Article 28: State parties shall put in place measures to ensure equal representation and participation in key decision-making positions in conflict resolution, peace building, peace-keeping in accordance to UN Security Council Resolution 1325 on Women, Peace and Security and other related resolutions.

In September 2015, the UN adopted Agenda 2030, the new framework guiding global development. This agenda has 17 goals and 169 targets, including Goal 5 on gender equality and Goal 16 on peaceful societies.[14] The 2030 Agenda provides a valuable tool for advancing the UNSC resolutions on WPS.

The UNSC has adopted eight resolutions that relate to WPS:
1) **UNSCR 1325 (2000)** is anchored on the pillars of participation, prevention, protection and relief and recovery;
2) **UNSCR 1820 (2008)** recognises sexual violence as a tactic of war;
3) **UNSCR 1888 (2009)** strengthens efforts to end sexual violence in conflict by calling for the position of a Special Representative of the Secretary-General;

4) **UNSCR 1889 (2009)** establishes indicators for the monitoring of resolution 1325 and calls for the Secretary-General to submit a report to the Security Council on women's participation and inclusion in peacebuilding;
5) **UNSCR 1960 (2010)** establishes a monitoring and reporting mechanism on sexual violence in conflict;
6) **UNSCR 2106 (2013)** focuses on accountability for perpetrators of sexual violence in conflict;
7) **UNSCR 2122 (2013)** addresses persistent gaps in implementing the WPS agenda; positions gender equality and women's empowerment as critical to international peace and security; recognises the differential impact of all violations in conflict on women and girls; and calls for consistent application of WPS across the Security Council's work; and

---

[11] "Due to political killings, KZN has had the most by elections in SA" [News 24.com accessed on 2 June 2018]
[12] Cited in Piers Pigou "The Zimbabwe Defense Forces have taken control of the country. What exactly happened? [accessed at crisisgroup.org on the 4 June 2018]
[13] International Crisis Group. "Zimbabwe's Military-Assisted Transition and Prospects for Recovery" Briefing No.134 December 2017.
[14] Loswick, A., Naidoo T., Smith R., Dhlamini M. and Mawowa S. (2016) "Gender, Peace and Security and the 2030 Agenda: A way forward for South Africa."

8) **UNSCR 2242 (2015)** establishes the Informal Experts Group (IEG); addresses persistent obstacles to implementation including financing and institutional reforms; focuses on emerging threats such as terrorism; and affirms the role of regional organisations and civil society in implementing the agenda.

Although SADC has seen some progress on the development of NAPs on WPS, it remains far too slow. Lawmakers adopted the DRC NAP in 2010 and are now revising it. Angola adopted its NAP in June 2017, for the period 2017-2020. The Ministry for Family and Promotion of Women and the Ministry of National Defence and Interior developed it. Legislators will validate the *Namibia Forward National Plan of Action on Women Peace and Security: Moving United Nations Security Council Resolution 1325 Forward* in July 2018; it covers the period 2018-2022. The Ministry of International Relations and Cooperation, Ministry of Defence and the Ministry of Gender Equality and Child Welfare with participation from other government ministries and Namibian civil society developed it. South Africa, Zimbabwe, Lesotho, Madagascar and Tanzania have all (to varying degrees) expressed an interest in developing a NAP but they have yet to either embark on, or complete, the processes.

The defence sector[15]

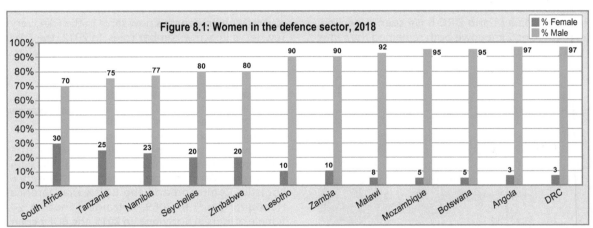

Figure 8.1: Women in the defence sector, 2018

Country	% Female	% Male
South Africa	30	70
Tanzania	25	75
Namibia	23	77
Seychelles	20	80
Zimbabwe	20	80
Lesotho	10	90
Zambia	10	90
Malawi	8	92
Mozambique	5	95
Botswana	5	95
Angola	3	97
DRC	3	97

Source: Cheryl Hendricks, collation of data 2018.

Figure 8.1 reflects the proportion of women in SADC defence forces in countries that provide data. Mauritius does not have a defence force. Madagascar has been removed because it has no reliable data at present (the previous Barometer statistic is now dated). South Africa (30%) ranks highest in the region, followed by Tanzania (25%). Seychelles and Zimbabwe have 20% women in their defence forces (though this, too, represents dated information). Women have increased in the Botswana Defence Force from fewer than 1% to around 5%. Lesotho has also seen an increase from 10% to 13%. The DRC's Defence Force, at 3%, and the Malawi Defence Force, at 8%, remain unchanged.

South Africa women in the Defense Forces.   *Photo: Source: GovernmentZA*

SA has **30%** ♀ in defence

---

[15] Represents all women in defence forces, civilian, non-combat and combat.

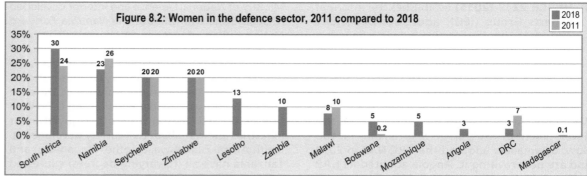

Figure 8.2: Women in the defence sector, 2011 compared to 2018

Legend: ■ 2018 ■ 2011

Country	2018	2011
South Africa	30	24
Namibia	23	26
Seychelles	20	20
Zimbabwe	20	20
Lesotho	13	
Zambia	10	
Malawi	8	10
Botswana	5	0.2
Mozambique	5	
Angola	3	
DRC	3	7
Madagascar	0.1	

Source: Cheryl Hendricks, collation of data 2010-2018.

Several countries

in

defence

Figure 8.2 reveals that mixed progress in the region in terms of increasing numbers of women in the defence sector. While South Africa has improved, going from 24% to 30%, other countries such as Namibia, Malawi and DRC have seen a decline. Seychelles and Zimbabwe both remained the same, at 20% in both 2011 and 2018.

In 2012, Angola promoted these four women from the Angolan Armed Forces (FAA) to the position of brigadier generals.
Photo courtesy of Kindala Manuel

 Angola policymakers estimate that the Angolan Armed Forces (FAA) have a total force strength of 175 500 (107 000 active and 68 500 reserve).[16] Global Fire Power ranked it Africa's fifth strongest military. Angola still has compulsory military service for two years for men and voluntary service for women. The country spends around 3% of its GDP on the FAA, down from 5% in 2014. There is still scanty sex-disaggregated data available for the FAA. Available data shows that women make up 2.6% of the armed forces. News reports note that women play a key role in the FAA. The head of the Combative Preparatory Division of the South Military Region recently noted a significant increase in the number of women in the FAA.[17]

Women mostly serve in social areas such as health and education as well as in operational areas. Luzia Inglez is the first woman to be promoted to the rank of general officer of the FAA.[18] Although several women generals now serve in the FAA, very few serve in active combat roles. In 2012, the FAA promoted four women military personnel to brigadier generals.[19]

Botswana first enlisted women into its defence force in 2007. In 2008, it sent 29 female officers for military training in Tanzania. They returned with the rank of second lieutenant and the BDF deployed them in units such as the Air Arm Command, Ground Forces Command, Defence Logistics Command and the Botswana Defence Headquarters.[20] In 2009, it trained another 24 female officers in Botswana. In 2015, the BDF began recruiting female privates (it accepted 382 females) and it noted that "there will be no separate training for females and males; they will train alongside each other."[21] In 2016, women made up "less than 10% and rank from as high as captain to the lowest rank of private."[22] The BDF has a total military personnel of 9000. Calculating a percentage based on the above figures means women comprise around 5% of the BDF, up from fewer than 1% indicated in previous years. Apelo Letsoma, one of the women among the first group of female officers

Lieutenant Apelo Letsomo is the only woman on the Botswana Defence Force's Firing Team. Her name appears among the BDF "top 10 crack shots."
Photo courtesy of Kutlwano

[16] See "2018 Angola Military Strength" [accessed at globalfirepower.com on 4 June2018].
[17] Mucuta, D. (2017) "Bravura das Mulheres nas fileiras das FAA".
http://jornaldeangola.sapo.ao/reportagem/bravura_das_mulheres__nas_fileiras_das_faa (Accessed 28/07/2017).
[18] Globo "Presidente angolana promovou uma mulher a official general" 13 October 2014. [accessed at dn.pt on 4 June 2018].
[19] Angop, (2012) "Quatro mulheres das FAA promovidas à classe de generais".
http://www.angop.ao/angola/pt_pt/noticias/politica/2012/4/19/Quatro-mulheres-das-FAA-promovidas-classe-generais,9fe7574e-96a7-4737-be23-b0241fcd0555.html (Accessed 28/07/2017).
[20] "First BDF female officers ready for combat" Mmegionline.
[21] "BDF recruits first women privates" Botswana Daily News Feb 1 2015.
[22] "Army women shake-up BDF" Mmegionline 2 September 2016.

sent to Tanzania, recently achieved the rank of a full lieutenant and she is the only woman on the BDF Firing Team.[23]

Women military personnel in DRC serving in Kalemie, Katanga Province. *Photo courtesy of Google images*

The **DRC** has an active military personnel of 144 625. Women comprise a mere 3% of the DRC's Defence Force (FARDC). Girls, however, make up between 30-40% of the child soldiers operative in the many militia groups of this country. The low number of women in FARDC compared to the high numbers in militia groups indicate that the country does not prioritise women in disarmament, demobilisation and reintegration programmes.

About 3100 people serve in the **Lesotho** Defence Force (LDF). This includes 13.6% women, up from 10% in previous years.[24] Lesotho spends around 1.8% of its GDP on the military. Only one woman serves in the role of brigadier general (of nine overall), the highest rank for a woman currently, and only one woman serves as a colonel, out of 11 colonels. Men continue to dominate in the top ranks of the LDF. Women soldiers in Lesotho recently fought against a standing order which stated that women who had served fewer than five years could be discharged from the LDF if they get pregnant.

Female soldiers in Lesotho win court battle against discriminatory practices[25]

Privates Lieketso Mokhele, 'Masaule Letima and 'Masine Ntsoha, three women who the Lesotho defence force dismissed when they fell pregnant, took the military to court in December 2016 and won their case. On 14 February 2018, the Lesotho High Court ruled that it is illegal and invalid for the LDF to demand that women soldiers cannot get pregnant during their first five years in the army. This LDF based the women's dismissals on a standing order it introduced in 2014.[26]

Annette Meerkotter of the South African Litigation Centre, who assisted with the case, noted that it sets an important precedent for the region "that the culture of patriarchy used to justify discriminatory practices against women cannot be upheld by the court."

The judge noted that the standing order had "profound effects on the reproductive rights, freedoms and careers of the female soldiers."

Source: Daily Vox and AfricanLII

The People's Armed Forces and the Gendarmarie make up the military in **Madagascar**. Total military personnel in Madagascar is 21 600 (13 500 active and 8100 reserve) and the country spends about 0.6% of its GDP on the military. Although it has committed to an intake of 10% women in its recruitment drives, it remains unclear how many women now serve in Madagascar's armed forces and Gendermarie.

South Africa has a total military strength of 94 050 (78 050 active and 16 000 reserve personnel).[27] It spends 1.3% of its GDP on defence. The South African National Defence Force (SANDF) is the third strongest force in Africa (after Egypt and Algeria). It has the highest number of women in a defence force in Southern Africa (30%) though women make up only 19% of the combat core. At the end of January 2017, the "department

SA National Defence 3rd strongest force in Africa

---

[23] "From House maid to Botswana's Top ten crack shots" Kutlwano Vol 55 Issue 4 Fberuaru -March 2018.
[24] Matope, T. "Female Officers up to the task of leading army" Lesotho Times October 7, 2017.
[25] https://www.thedailyvox.co.za/three-soldiers-in-the-lesotho-army-are-fighting-their-dismissals-over-pregnancy-fatima-moosa/
[26] https://africanlii.org/content/lesotho-high-court-recognises-sexual-and-reproductive-rights-female-soldiers
[27] GlobalFirePower.com

had 17.78%, or 40 female uniform members in command positions out of 225. The percentage of female generals is gradually increasing from 16% in 2013 to 19% in 2017."[28] The SANDF also promoted another three women to the rank of brigadier general in August 2017.

25%
of
Tanzania
Defence
Force

The rise of women in the South African Defence Force

SANDF has taken great strides since 1994 in recruiting, training and promoting women. Two high ranking women, Major General Ntobeka Mpaxa, chief director of army force preparation, and Lieutenant Colonel Nolubalalo Skritshi, staff Officer 1 Protocol to Chief Army, serve as examples of this.

Mpaxa is a role model to any young aspiring women serving in the South African military. These are huge shoes to fit into as the youth tries to walk in her footsteps for guidance discipline and heroism. Being the first female in the Infantry Formation to command an infantry battalion, the

Major General Ntobeka Mpaxa, one of three major generals in the SANDF. *Photo courtesy of Army Military News SA*

first female commander of the army support base, the first female commandant at the South African Army Combat Training Centre, the first woman to head the South African Army Intelligence Formation - there is much to adore about the former Mkhonto We Sizwe (MK) veteran.

"The empowerment of women in general needs one to be in a position of influence, a position of decision-making and empowering women also does not end with authority, it goes back to the individuals as females. Are they ready to be empowered?" asked Mpaxa.

Mpaxa added that gender equality has improved post democracy "at lower level there is no problem in recruiting as many females as possible." However, "discrimination is visible at the command line, at various boards where decisions are to be made, where males move faster into higher positions than females."

Mpaxa urged women to stop undermining and negatively criticising other female colleagues in higher ranks - "you find that it is growing even among women themselves that they would prefer to be led by a male rather than a female. . . It is a fact that not all men climbing the ladder have been proven in the battlefield, the issue of combat capacity is brought up whenever a female has to rise for instance from a 'One-Star' and so forth. One does not necessarily have to carry a rifle or a machine gun at the highest level, all which is needed is intellectual capital. This cannot go on forever, in whose life time will females be on par with males."

Extract from an article by Themba Katzambe in the SA Army News 2017
[Accessed at http://www.army.mil.za/news/news_2017/aug_17/
womens_month_mpaxa_skritshi_17.htm on 17 June 2018]

 Women constitute 8% of the **Malawi** Defence Force (MDF). In November 2017, the MDF graduated another 1463 soldiers and 14 cadets. Among these recruits, women made up 14% (or 220 women).[29]

Tanzania has an active armed force of about 30 000. Women constitute 25% of Tanzania's Defence Force

(TDF). Zawadi Madawali became the first woman promoted to the rank of lieutenant in the TDF in 1975. She retired at the rank of major general in 2017.

Namibia has made commitments to gender mainstreaming in its defence force though it has an outdated policy for this. Women constitute 23% of the Namibia Defence Force.

---

[28] Parliament. "Spotlight on Ongoing Cuts to Defence and Military Veterans Budget During Budget Vote debate. 26 May 2017.
[29] Malawi Post "Malawi Defence Force Graduates 1463 recruits; urged to desist from Politics" 26 November 2017.

Promotion criteria for the Namibia Defence Force

Namibia has two categories of service people in the military: commissioned and non-commissioned officers. As such, criteria in terms of their promotion differ in some instances. According to the NDF promotion policy, the following criteria govern promotions:

1. *Recommendation:* To qualify for the next rank a commissioned or non-commissioned officer must be recommended in his/her annual confidential report.
2. *Military qualifications:* These will differ between each arm of service and will include passing applicable qualification courses stipulated in the NDF Promotion Policy.
3. *Second lieutenant to lieutenant:* When an officer successfully completes 18 months in the rank of second lieutenant, he or she is automatically promoted to the rank of lieutenant. No officer who fails to meet the necessary standard while in the rank of second lieutenant is to be discharged from service.
4. *Promotions examinations:* Promotions examinations are to be undertaken from the rank of lieutenant to captain and captain to major. Promotion from the rank of major upwards is to be by selection.
5. *Age:* An officer/soldier should be within the stipulated age bracket for promotion.
6. *Selection:* Although qualified and recommended and officer/soldier must be selected for promotion. Selection will depend on the availability of vacant posts. Officers and soldiers have no right to promotion. They are to be promoted by officers'/soldiers' selection/promotion boards.
7. *Other standards:* An officer/soldier to meet the minimum standards in military qualifications, education, medical and personal fitness stipulated in the NDF Promotions Policy.

Source: New Era, Ministry of Defence 20 June 2017 [Accessed at https://www.newera.com.na/2017/06/20/ministry-of-defence-2/ on 17 June 2018]

 The total strength of the **Zambia**n Defence Force is 19 600, (15 100 active). Women make up 10%, and they first entered the force in 1976. In 2009, Fridah Kazembe became the first woman brigadier general. Three women brigadier generals now serve in the ZDF, which also recently promoted the first woman to become a fighter pilot. Although the ZDF has a quota of 30% for women it has made little progress recruiting women and has been unable to meet this target.

 Zimbabwe has a total military strength of 52 000 (30 000 active and 22 000 reserve). The military promoted its first and only woman to brigadier general in 2013. Zimbabwe now also has a woman serving in the position of air commodore. In November 2017, of the 15 officers promoted to be air commodores, none were female and only one woman was among the ten promoted to be wing commanders.[30]

Police services

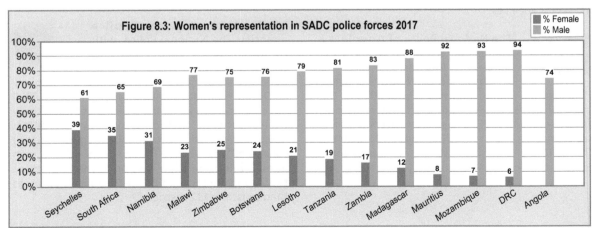

Figure 8.3: Women's representation in SADC police forces 2017

Country	% Female	% Male
Seychelles	39	61
South Africa	35	65
Namibia	31	69
Malawi	23	77
Zimbabwe	25	75
Botswana	24	76
Lesotho	21	79
Tanzania	19	81
Zambia	17	83
Madagascar	12	88
Mauritius	8	92
Mozambique	7	93
DRC	6	94
Angola		74

Source: Cheryl Hendricks compilation of data, 2018.

[30] The Herald. "President promotes 25 Air Force Officers. 30 November 2017.

Zimbabwe promoted 1st & only ♀ to brigadier general in 2013

Figure 8.3 shows that Seychelles, at 39%, records the highest percentage of women in the police services, followed by South Africa at 35%, Namibia at 31%, Angola 26%, Botswana 24% and Malawi has 23% women in the police service. The Tanzania Police Force has 19% women's representation. Nine countries have 20% or more representation of women in their police services. Three - DRC, Mauritius and Mozambique - have fewer than 10%.

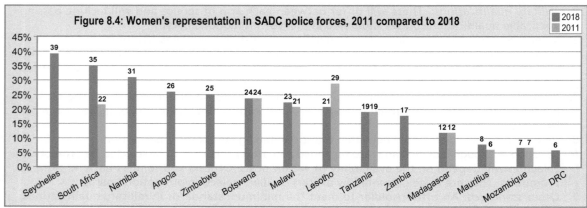

Figure 8.4: Women's representation in SADC police forces, 2011 compared to 2018

Source: Cheryl Hendricks compilation of data, 2010-2018.

Figure 8.4 illustrates that, where data exists it shows women's representation in SADC police forces has remained stagnant. Most countries have seen little increase since 2011, with South Africa as an exception, where women in the police force increased from 22% in 2011 to 35% in 2018.

SADC countries have struggled to provide adequate sex-disaggregated statistics for the security sector, whereas other organisations and countries have provided it for some time. For example, the North Atlantic Treaty Organisation (NATO) website provides pertinent information about various countries. The numbers that do exist indicate that many SADC countries appear to have plateaued in terms of including women into the security services, as well as in the attention that women's participation in the sector receives.

The National Police of **Angola** is a paramilitary force located under the Ministry of Interior. The force has an estimated 6000 patrol officers, 2500 taxation and frontier supervision officers, 182 criminal investigators and 100 financial crimes detectives.[31] In 2017, 6044 police officers took the basic training course, this includes 1595 women. These numbers suggest that Angola's police force consists of about 26% women.[32]

The World Internal Security and Police Index (WISPI) has ranked the **Botswana** police force as the best in Africa.[33] About 8500 officers make up the police force, of which 2000 are women (23.5%).[34] This figure is down from 26%. Botswana recruited its first female police officer, Sylvia Tabitha Muzila, in 1971.

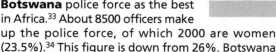

The **Lesotho** Mounted Police Service forms part of the Ministry of Home Affairs and Public Safety. The force has a Child and Gender Protection Unit and it recruited the first cohort of women officers in 1970. In 2017, the government appointed a woman, Mampho Mokhele, as Minister of Police and Public Safety.

Madagascar has two police agencies: The National Police, with responsibility for urban areas, and the Gendermarie, which handles policing outside of urban areas, under the Ministry of Defence. Madagascar has approximately 8000 police officers. In 2018, the police accepted 50 new police officers, including two women (4%). Madagascar's police force (excluding gendermarie) consists of 12% women. The service includes women at all levels of decision-making in the implementation and deployment of the 93 police stations in Madagascar's 112 districts.[35]

[31] Wikipedia, Angola [accessed at en.wikipedia.org on 5 June 2018].
[32] Agencia Angola Press. "Angola: Over 6000 police officers complete training course" 31 July 2017. [accessed at angop.ao on 6 June 2018].
[33] The African Exponent. "Countries with the best police force in Africa" June 6, 2018.
[34] Interpol. "Botswana Police Service".

Angola
police
force
26%

The **Malawi** Police Service dates to 1921. It began recruiting female police officers in 1972. UN Women has worked closely with the Malawi Police Service to strengthen gender mainstreaming within the force.

Namibia has one of the largest percentages of women in its police force at 31%. This also means more Namibian women deploy as part of peace missions in the region and beyond.

 In **Tanzania**, only one woman serves as a police commissioner while nine others serve as deputy commis-

sioners. Women make up 19% of the Tanzania police force. In May 2017, the UN and the Southern African Regional Police Chiefs Cooperation Organisation (SARPCCO), held a conference in Dar es Salaam to share progress on gender equality and on handling cases of sexual and gender-based violence in the region. It called for police forces to employ more women officers in regional police services and to build their capacity.

The **South Africa**n Police Service (SAPS) has a total number of 194 605 employees. Of these about 140 000 would be police officers. It has 35% representation of women in the police services.

31% ♀ in police in Namibia

Activists and police disagree over best way to fight GBV in Tanzania

Tanzanians march to protest the high rates of GBV in the country. *Photo courtesy of The Citizen*

Lack of public awareness on sexual harassment, rape and child abuse hinders police investigations into cases related to GBV. This is bad since it leads to the covering up of crimes, the Tanzania Police Female Network (TPF Net) says.

"Gender-Based Violence is committed within the community. Without cooperation from the victims' close friends and relatives, we cannot make much progress." TPF NET chairperson Tulibake Mkondya said.

In 2013, police in Tanzania established gender and children's desks where survivors could report cases of sexual harassment, rape and child abuse, and other service providers could help survivors and their families.

The "one-stop centre" model includes police and social workers and has helped fast-track cases related to GBV.

But Tanzania police spokesman Barnabas Mwakalukwa said that, while these centres have helped address GBV against women, many men still do not report GBV. He said that society tends to judge men who report GBV harshly due to Tanzanian culture.

Mwakalukwa also noted that, although police receive few cases of violence against men, they exist. In 2016, Iringa and Karagwe recorded the highest number of cases of wives assaulting their husbands. However, activists blame bureaucracy for delays in the processing of GBV cases. They say the justice system drops many cases because women and children cannot travel long distances to hear their cases.

Excerpted from "Why Police Make Little Progress on Gender-Based Violence"
by Helen Nachilongo in The Citizen on 4 November 2017

Correctional and prison services

Data on women in correctional facilities in the region remains scarce. The SADC Women in Correctional Services Network, established in 2015, has not yet created a sex-disaggregated database with this information. However, SADC has deve-

loped a correctional service training manual so that the sector can standardise training across the region. The Barometer will not include further tracking of this sector until reliable data becomes available.

---

[35] Gaby Razafindrokoto, Presentation at the ISS Conference.

must be **included** in negotiation and mediation

Peace processes

Article 28.2: State parties shall, during times of armed and other forms of conflict, take such steps as are necessary to prevent and eliminate incidences of human rights abuses, especially of women and children, and ensure that the perpetrators of such abuses are brought to justice before a court of competent jurisdiction.

Peace negotiations

It is crucially important to include women in negotiation and mediation. However, available data shows that mediation processes seldom involve women and, when they do, women remain underrepresented compared to men. The South African Department of International Relations and Cooperation (DIRCO) runs an annual training for women in mediation. The AU has also started collecting and organising a roster of women who can serve as expert mediators and negotiators in conflict situations across Africa. This is an initiative that SADC could also consider as it builds its mediation capacity.

SADC has established a Mediation Reference Group (MRG). In June 2016, the Africa Centre for the Constructive Resolution of Disputes (ACCORD) held a workshop on conflict management for the MRG

in Durban, South Africa. Despite all the training and roster formations, however, as of early 2018, men still dominate at mediation and negotiation tables in the region.

In June 2016, the SADC Mediation Reference Group (pictured) met in Durban, South Africa, for a conflict management workshop aimed at enhancing SADC's capacity for conflict prevention and resolution. *Photo courtesy of ACCORD*

Peace support operations

Country	Women (%)				
	2013	**2014**	**2015**	**2016**	**2017**
Zimbabwe	35	29	29	35	35
Namibia	21	29	36	26	25
South Africa	15	13	16	18	19
Madagascar	12	17	21	17	13
Zambia	12	16	5	9	9
DRC	8	2	2	3	0
Tanzania	6	6	5	6	5
Malawi	5	3	6	9	9

Table 8.2: Women in peace support operations 2013-2017

Source: Statistics collated by Cheryl Hendricks from 2013 to 2017 using the UNDPKO website detailing monthly mission deployment by country.

Table 8.2 shows that the ratio of women to men deployed as peacekeepers from SADC countries remains relatively stagnant as an overall figure that includes police, troops and experts. Eight SADC countries currently deploy peacekeepers to UN missions: DRC, Madagascar, Malawi, Namibia South

Africa, Tanzania, Zambia and Zimbabwe. Zimbabwe had the most female peacekeepers deployed at 35%. Namibia has shown a steady decline in recent years, from 36% in 2015 to 25% in 2017. Madagascar has also shown a decline, from 21% in 2015 to 13% in 2017, as has the DRC, from 8% in 2013 to zero in 2017. This results in an overall decline in the number of women peacekeepers deployed in the region.

Only South Africa showed a slight improvement in deploying women peacekeepers in 2017 (up one percentage point to 19% in 2017). Overall, Tanzania deploys the highest absolute number of peacekeepers, at 2355, followed by South Africa (1405). In terms of absolute numbers, South Africa led with the average number of women deployed (262) in 2017 followed by Tanzania (121), Zambia (89), Malawi (84), Zimbabwe (31), Namibia (11) and Madagascar (4).

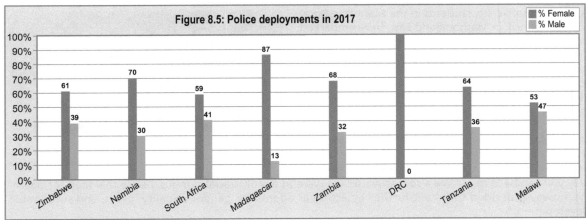

Figure 8.5: Police deployments in 2017

Source: Chery Hendricks compilation of data.

Figure 8.5 illustrates that Malawi (47%), Zimbabwe (44%) and South Africa (41%) have the most women represented in police deployments. DRC only deployed male officers.

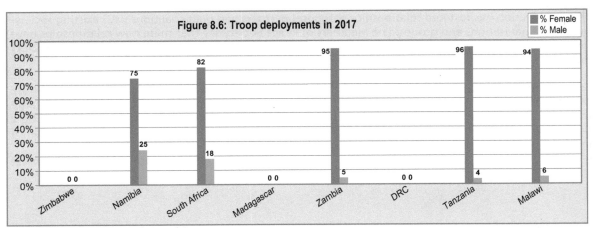

Figure 8.6: Troop deployments in 2017

Source: Chery Hendricks compilation of data.

Figure 8.6 shows that SADC countries sent even fewer women as part of military deployments compared to police deployments. Namibia came in highest, at 25% women troops deployed, followed by South Africa at 18%, then Malawi (6%), Zambia (5%) and Tanzania (4%). Madagascar only deployed police, while Zimbabwe deployed police and experts, but no troops.

Transforming peacebuilding structures
For years, SADC led the African continent in promoting gender equality as well as women's representation in the peace and security sector. For a period, it performed remarkably well, but recent data points to a stagnation in this regard. At the same time, other regions have been moving at a much faster pace in and will soon be on par with SADC, if not surpassing it. Southern Africa also has the hard task of transforming its security sector institutions so that they can tackle civilian women's security issues, such as GBV, alongside equitable gender representation. As conflict and violent extremism continue to threaten the region, it is important that leaders do not use this as an

NEED to FOCUS on GBV & security

excuse to marginalise gender issues. SADC policymakers should instead once again strive to set an example for all of Africa by working together collectively, and engaging SADC citizens, including youth, to tackle chronic challenges in the peace and security sector linked to patriarchal gender relations.

Zimbabwe students build community resilience with a "Peace Society"

A group of university students in the Manyame Rural District Council, in Mashonaland East, have embarked on a community project dubbed the Peace Society. The students have rolled out their initiative on their campus as well as in their communities at large. It forms part of local governance work under the Gender Links Centres of Excellence (COEs) government category.

The Peace Society in 2017.   *Photo: Gender Links*

Nigel Chigumira, a member of the Peace Society, says the project's priority is "to deal with peace, as we are living at a time where violence seems the only way you can be 'a man.' We also discovered we were at a multi-racial campus, hence the need for peace. We however decided to take it further by acting as agents for gender equality, peace and sustainable development."

The intersectional problems youth experienced on their campus inspired the group's main activity. As a multi-racial campus, youth realised that issues of racism and tribalism remain common, so society members decided they wanted to contribute to building a positive and healthy institutional culture. The society has used questionnaires and interviews to garner awareness within their community. Chigumira says other activities include awareness campaigns, outreach and capacity-building programmes.

The organisation has fostered relationships with local partners and built coalitions with existing society-building organisations and groups. The members of Peace Society say that these new relationships have improved the working relationships of individuals in the community. Supporters of the Peace Society include a lecturer and the university's chancellor.

Several female members lead the club and partake in international debate contests. In 2016, Liliosa Mugadza, a graduate, said: "I am proud to win this semester's chairperson post for the society by a large margin. It shows how fast guys can elect on the basis of action as opposed to appearance." The society says men have become more supportive of women empowerment because of their work. The number of incidents of GBV has dropped in the community, too.

Source: Gender Links COE Local Government Summit

Sexual violence during conflict

Article 28.2: State parties shall, during times of armed and other conflict, take steps as are necessary to prevent and eliminate incidences of human rights abuses, especially of women and children, and ensure that the perpetrators are brought to justice before a court of competent jurisdiction.

The world over, women remain at a disproportionately higher risk of becoming victims of conflict-related sexual violence. Armed state and non-state actors frequently commit sexual violence during conflict. These actors also continue to use rape as a strategy or weapon of war, making women's bodies booty during conflict. Indeed, women have accused peacekeepers from SADC countries of sexual violence. Worryingly, military councils have often ignored these accusations or let perpetrators off with a mild reprimand. Activists have called on the UN to employ its zero-tolerance policy more strictly and send troop contingents home when a member is found guilty of such acts.

Another way to address these issues is through the 17 Sustainable Development Goals (SDGs) of the 2030 Agenda for Sustainable Development, which officially came into force on 1 January 2016 with a stronger focus on conflict resolution and GBV than earlier instruments.

sexual violence

in

conflict

Key issues for peace	UNSCRs on women, peace and security	Agenda 2030	Agenda 2063
Reducing violence and making the public feel secure	End of gender-based violence, including sexual violence, and all other forms of violence against women and girls in armed conflict and post conflict situations (see UNSCRs 1325, 1820, 1888, 1960, 2106).	Elimination of all forms of violence against women including trafficking (see target 5.2).	Elimination of all forms of gender-based violence against women and girls (see target 51, 37)
	Integration of a gender perspective into peacekeeping operations and the negotiation and implementation of peace agreements (UNSCRs 1325, 2242).	Significant reduction of all forms of violence and related deaths everywhere (see target 16.1).	Reduction of violent crimes, armed conflict, terrorism, extremism and ensuring prosperity, human security and safety for all citizens (see targets 34, 37 and 36).
	Training of all military and police personnel on sexual and gender based violence (UNSCR 1960).	Education in human rights, gender equality, promotion of a culture of peace and non-violence (see target 4.7).	Elimination of all harmful social practices including female genital mutilation and child marriages (see target 51).
		End of abuse, exploitation trafficking and all forms of violence against children and elimination of all harmful practices such as child, early forced marriage and female genital mutilations (see targets 16.2 and 5.3).	Functional mechanisms for peaceful prevention and resolution of conflict at all levels and a culture of peace and tolerance nurtured in Africa's children through peace education (see target 32).

Table 8.3: Policy frameworks on gender, peace and security

Source: SaferWorld https://www.saferworld.org.uk/resources/publications/1053-gender-peace-and-security-and-the-2030-agenda-a-way-forward-for-south-africa

Table 8.3 shows that the three most relevant regional and international instruments for sustainable and peaceful development have strong provisions on conflict prevention through peace education and eliminating gender-based violence in conflict. Agendas 2030 and 2063 both provides a holistic gendered approach to reduce all forms of violence, as do the combination of UNSCR resolutions on peace.

Next steps

SADC is not immune to the threat of terrorism and cyber insecurity. Regional stakeholders must continue to improve security and take adequate steps to prevent the spread of these threats as they hold particular gendered implications. Next steps over the next year should include:

- Collate sex-disaggregated data across the security sector and publish this on the SADC website to allow easy tracking.
- SADC leaders should adopt and implement strategies to implement the WPS agenda.
- Member states must prioritise gender responsive budgeting and costing for gender mainstreaming, especially in the implementation of NAPs and SDG-5.
- Increase visibility and coverage of women's contributions within the security sector through news article and blogs on the SADC website.

Very few articles exist on the activities of women in defence, police and peacekeeping.
- Improve data collection on women in correctional services.
- Address as a matter of urgency (and as a security issue) the scourge of sexual-related violence in both conflict and non-conflict situations in SADC.
- SADC should utilise its mediation reference group and the women community members it has trained in mediation more effectively.
- Increase the participation of youth, especially young women, in the implementation of UNSCR 1325: a determinant of the successful implementation of the resolution.[36]
- SADC must embark on a more concerted effort to have its member states adopt national action plans on WPS and it must develop tools to be able to track the implementation of its own strategy in this regard.

[36] Ibid.

GREATER
visibility
NEEDED!

CHAPTER 9

Media, Information and Communication

Articles 29-30

Gender Links intern Petronella Ngonyama presents the Gender and Media Progress Study's findings about women in management at the 2017 SADC Gender Protocol Barometer launch in Pretoria, South Africa.   *Photo: Thandokuhle Dlamini*

34%

▲

27%

♀
media managers

KEY POINTS

- The *Gender and Media Progress Study* (GMPS) remains the latest research on women's voices and their role in the media sector. It shows a paltry increase in women sources in the media, from 17% in the 2003 *Gender and Media Baseline Study* (GMBS) to 19% in the 2010 GMPS and 20% in the 2015 GMPS. The proportion of women sources is the single most important measure about giving a voice to women.

- There region has seen an encouraging increase in the proportion of women in media management, from 27% to 34%. Media leadership needs reshaping to cover the differential needs of women working in the media. Industry-oriented solutions need to assist in helping close this gap in media leadership.

- Enrolment of female students into journalism and media studies surpasses that of male students. However, the high proportion of women students is a stark contrast to the low proportion of women in media houses, where men still dominate.

- The sixty-second session of the Commission on the Status of Women review theme focused on women's participation and access to media. It recognised the role the media can play in the achievement of gender equality and the empowerment of women and girls.

- The #Metoo and #TimesUp campaigns have re-energised discussions about gender discrimination and sexual harassment in the media and film industries.

Key trends

Table 9.1: Trends in Media since 2009				
	Target 2030	Baseline 2009	Progress 2018	Variance (Progress minus 2030 target)
WOMEN SOURCES				
% women sources	50%	19%	20%	-30%
Country with highest percentage of women sources	50%	Lesotho (32)	Botswana and Seychelles (28)	-22%
Country with lowest percentage of women sources	50%	Mozambique and Zambia (14)	DRC (6)	-44%
WOMEN IN MANAGEMENT				
% women in management	50%	27%	34%	-16%
Country with the highest percentage of women in management	50%	Lesotho (52)	Lesotho (53)	+3%
Country with the lowest percentage of women in management	50%	DRC (10)	DRC (17)	-23%
WOMEN IN MEDIA IMAGES				
% women in media images	50%	27%	28%	-22%
Country with the highest percentage of women in images	50%		Malawi (74)	-24%
Country with the lowest percentage of women in images	50%		Tanzania (10)	-40%

Source: Gender Links, 2018.

Table 9.1 shows that:
- There has been a mere one percentage point increase in women sources in Southern Africa Development Community (SADC) media (from 19% to 20%) during the tracking period. Botswana and Seychelles recorded the highest proportion of women sources (28%) and DRC has the least (6%). DRC has consistently held the lowest position in this ranking.
- The proportion of women in management has increased from 27% at baseline to 34% in 2018. Lesotho (53%) has the highest proportion of women in decision-making and is the only country in the region to surpass the 50% target. In 2017, gender and media stakeholders in South Africa conducted an in-depth study of women in media, known as the *Glass Ceiling Study*.
- While women comprise only 20% of news sources they account for a much higher proportion of images (28%), suggesting that women remain more likely to be seen than heard. Malawi (74%) has the highest proportion of women in images, while Tanzania (10%) has the lowest.

Background

Despite claims of its waning power in the era of Facebook and Twitter, traditional media remains one of the most powerful agents of change in society. It also remains a sector that has seen limited transformation in terms of gender equality and women's empowerment. This includes in editorial content, where men continue to take up more space, as well as in newsroom policies and practices.

Women and men working in the media should have equal access to professional opportunities, equal pay for work of equal value and equal representation in all echelons of media houses, as well as in the content produced. While progress has occurred in some areas, this chapter highlights that full equality in the sector is still not a reality in the SADC region.

Globally, movements such as the #MeToo and #TimesUp campaigns have refocused attention on the industry and the importance of gender equality in and through the media. Many journalists joined the #MeToo campaign and called for change. Women took to social media to share stories of sexual harassment, unequal pay and workplace discrimination. These movements underscored that sexual harassment remains an enormous problem around the world - and in the SADC region. A recent case of sexual harassment at Primedia Holdings in South Africa, for example, resulted in the resignation of a senior executive. Legislators and media sector stakeholders must take urgent action to address this issue.

It is important to tackle structural issues linked to perceptions and attitudes that centuries of socialisation, and cultural and religious beliefs have reinforced. Another challenge is the lack local role models and mentors for young women who aspire to be journalists, media entrepreneurs or decision makers.

CSW62 focused on ♀ and the media

The 2018 sixty-second session of the Commission on the Status of Women (CSW62) put gender and media on its agenda through its theme:

"Participation in and access of women to the media, and information and communications technologies and their impact on and use as an instrument for the advancement and empowerment of women."

This recognises that the media is a powerful tool and, when used right, it can push the gender equality and women's empowerment agenda forward.

Beijing Declaration and Platform for Action

The Beijing Declaration and Platform for Action (BDPA), an outcome of the 1995 Fourth World Conference on Women, declared the media one of 12 critical areas of concern for the advancement and empowerment of women. The need to advance gender equality in and through the media and Information and Communication Technology (ICT) has been at the core of gender and media advocacy work since the 1995 conference through its two strategic objectives:

- Strategic objective 1: Increase the participation and access of women to expression and decision-making in and through the media and new technologies of communication.
- Strategic objective 2: Promote a balanced and non-stereotypical portrayal of women in the media.

Sustainable Development Goal 5

Targets linked to Sustainable Development Goal (SDG) 5 - "to achieve gender equality and empower all women and girls" - highlight the media's potential to influence the fight for gender equality through encouraging states to enhance the use of enabling technology, in particular ICT, to promote women's empowerment. Although the SDGs do not have a standalone goal on the media, the media is critical to achieving all SDG targets. It plays a vital role in unpacking, packaging and popularising the SDGs in a way that all people can understand and engage with them, even at the grassroots level.

Monitoring women in media

The Global Media Monitoring Project (GMMP) is a one-day voluntary global monitoring project that has taken place every five years since the Fourth World Conference on Women in Beijing in 1995. Working with journalism and media training institutions in the region, GL coordinated the global study in 12 countries. The global coordinator, World Association for Christian Communication (WACC),

launched the GMMP in 2015. The GMMP team will conduct new research in 2020.

Table 9.2: 2015 GMMP research in Africa	
Number of African countries participating	32
Women in the news	22%
Women sources in politics and government	16%
Women sources economy	19%
Women sources sciences and health	37%
Women sources social and legal	26%
Women sources crime and violence	28%
Women sources celebrity, arts, media and sports	15%
Women sources other	22%
Women are reporters	35%
Women as presenters	50%

Source: Global Media Monitoring Project 2015. Who Makes the News?.

The fourth GMMP in 2015 showed that women make up a mere 24% of news sources globally and, as illustrated in Table 9.2, just 22% in Africa.[1] In Africa, women's presence in the news increased from 19% in 2010 to 22% in 2015. In SADC, "there is a one percent increase of women sources in the media from 19% to 20% since 2010."[2]

The International Women's Media Foundation (IWMF) Global Report on the Status of Women in the News Media (2011) had similar findings, revealing that, globally, men hold 73% of top management jobs. Among the ranks of reporters, men hold two-thirds of all jobs. The IWMF report showed that, despite commitments made in Beijing, the glass ceiling is still very much alive in 20 of the 59 nations studied.[3] It will be important to coordinate a follow-up study to track any progress since 2011.

Global efforts for gender equality in and through media

International efforts have reaffirmed the importance of attaining gender equality in and through the media and ICTs. Several legal and normative instruments have stimulated this goal, including:

Global Alliance on Media and Gender

The Global Alliance on Media and Gender (GAMAG) is a "global movement to promote gender equality in and  through media and ICTs in all formats and locations and across different forms of ownership." In 2017, GAMAG released a statement to the CSW to priori-

---

1 http://cdn.agilitycms.com/who-makes-the-news/Imported/reports_2015/global/gmmp_global_report_en.pdf
2 Ndlovu, S and Nyamweda, T. (2015) Gender and Media Progress Study. Johannesburg. Gender Links.
3 https://www.iwmf.org/wp-content/uploads/2013/09/IWMF-Global-Report-Summary.pdf

just
24%
of news
sources
globally!

tise media in advancing women's rights in and through the media and ICTs. GAMAG and its members lead critical discussions on women's participation and access to the media at CSWs. Its members present position papers to assess progress in various dimensions of gender and media, and suggest directions for state, media, research and civil society action. These position papers form the basis of GAMAG-coordinated CSW gender and media sessions

Commission on the Status of Women

The 47th session of the CSW in 2003 underlined the need for media and telecommunications companies to address gender-based discrimination. As a follow up to these discussions, the 62nd session on the CSW in March 2018 presented an important opportunity for international, regional and local-level collaboration to put the media and ICTs at the centre of achieving gender equality. Participants at CSW62 agreed to:

- Develop and implement policies and strategies that promote rural women's and girls' participation in, and access to, media and ICTs, including by increasing their digital literacy and access to information;
- Recognise the important role the media can play in the achievement of gender equality and the empowerment of rural women and girls, including through non-discriminatory and gender-sensitive coverage and by eliminating gender stereotypes, including those perpetuated by commercial advertisements;
- Encourage training for those who work in the media as well as the development and strengthening of self-regulatory mechanisms to promote balanced and non-stereotypical portrayals of women and girls, which contribute to the empowerment of women and girls and the elimination of discrimination against and exploitation of women and girls; and
- Address the digital divide, which disproportionately affects women and girls living in rural areas, by facilitating their access to information and communications technology... in order to promote their empowerment and to develop the skills, information and knowledge that are needed to support their labour market entry, livelihoods, well-being and resilience and expand the scope of information and communications technology-enabled mobile learning and literacy training while promoting a safe and secure cyberspace for women and girls."[4]

The Commission recognised that indigenous women and girls living in rural and remote areas, regardless of age, often have limited access to ICTs. It also recognised that ICTs change the structure of labour markets; they provide new and different employment opportunities that require basic digital fluency. It emphasised the importance of all rural women and girls having the opportunity to acquire such skills as well as the need to invest in gender-responsive ICT infrastructure.

Media Compact

UN Women fostered a partnership with leading media houses for the Step it Up for Gender Equality Media Compact" ("Step it Up") to develop concrete actions for the implementation of the Sustainable Development Agenda and focus on gender equality and women's rights issues on two fronts: 1) in their reporting, disrupting stereotypes and biases and 2) in increasing the number of women in the media, including in leadership and decision-making functions.[5]

The Media Compact encourages media houses, at minimum, to:
- Champion women's rights and gender equality issues through articles, features and news coverage;
- Ensure production of high-quality stories with a focus on gender equality and women's rights, with a minimum of two per month;
- Ensure inclusion of women as sources in stories produced, aiming for gender parity, including across diverse subjects such as business, technology, science and engineering;
- Adopt a gender-sensitive code of conduct on reporting;
- Ensure guidelines for gender-sensitive reporting in orientation and training of staff members;
- Enable equality in the newsrooms through gender-sensitive reporting and by ensuring women journalists receive the same opportunities as their male colleagues and can cover diverse subjects from politics to business, science, sports and technology, while encouraging male journalists to also cover diverse issues, including women's rights and gender equality stories; and
- Ensure women journalists have mentors and guidance for career advancement.

Several SADC media houses, such as Channel Africa, Media 24, City Press and South African Broadcasting Corporation (SABC), have joined the campaign.

UNESCO's Gender Sensitive Indicators for Media

The Gender-Sensitive Indicators for Media (GSIM) project aims to contribute to gender equality and women's empowerment in and through media of all forms, irrespective of the technology.

---

4   Economic and Social Council. Commission on the Status of Women Sixty Second session 2018. Agreed Conclusions.
5   http://www.unwomen.org/en/get-involved/step-it-up/media-compact#sthash.INLxFHhx.dpuf

"Step IT UP"

As noted by UNESCO: "the GSIM is a non-prescriptive set of indicators, designed particularly for media organisations. The purpose is to encourage media organisations to make gender equality issues transparent and comprehensible to the public, as well as to analyse their own internal policies and practices with a view to take necessary actions for change."[6]

UNESCO has trained representatives from 25 French-speaking African national broadcasters on how to apply the GSIM. Through this initiative, UNESCO seeks to strengthen media pluralism and the adoption of gender-sensitive policies in African broadcasting organisations.[7]

Gender and media research in Southern Africa has undertaken some of the most extensive and consistent research on gender equality in and through the media. This research has taken a 360-degree approach to look at the media in depth. It has focused on media education, media content, media composition, media audiences, media regulators and media development organisations. Gender Links has coordinated this research, together with like-minded organisations and journalism and media studies departments across the region.

YEAR	STUDY	WHAT IT COVERED
2003	Gender and Media Baseline	First regional study to monitor news items on gender in the editorial content of Southern African media. It monitored more than 25 000 news items.
2009	Glass Ceilings in Southern African Media Houses	Survey of women and men in a representative sample of media houses - newsrooms, marketing, management, administration.
2010	Gender and Media Progress Study (GMPS)	Monitoring of news items from a representative sample of media outlets over a period of one month. This study followed on from the original 2003 Gender and Media Baseline study.
2010	Gender in Media Education (GIME) study	Staff and student composition, content and practise of media education and training.
2015	Gender and Media Progress Study (GMPS)	A follow-up to the 2010 GMPS research, covering 14 SADC countries.

Table 9.3: Gender and media research in the region

Source: SADC Gender Protocol Barometer 2017.

Table 9.3 shows key gender and media research that has taken place in Southern Africa, culminating in the 2015 Gender and Media Progress Study (GMPS). Covering 27 045 news items, researchers for the 2015 GMPS study monitored news content in 14 SADC countries over one month. This three-part study sought to explore progress made since the 2009 Glass Ceilings study, the 2010 GMPS and the 2010 Gender in Media Education (GIME) audit. Together, the studies analysed women and men in media studies, in media practise, and in media content. The 2015 GMPS represents a culmination of many years of research, advocacy, policy and training.

Tshwaresa Malatji presents some of the GMPS findings at a Barometer launch in Pretoria, South Africa, in 2017.   *Photo: Thandokuhle Dlamini*

---

6 Grizzle, A.(eds). 2012. Gender-Sensitive Indicators for Media. UNESCO. Paris.
7 https://en.unesco.org/training-gender-sensitive-indicators-media

Table 9.4: Summary of key GMPS findings								
AREA	**2003**	**2010**	**2015 OVERALL**	**HIGHEST COUNTRY**	**LOWEST COUNTRY**	**2015 COE**	**2015 NON-COE**	**GLOBAL**
Who speaks in news?	% W	% W	% W	% W	% W	% W	% W	% W
Overall	17%	19%	20%	28%	6%	22%	19%	24%
Private media	N/A	19%	18%	N/A	N/A	N/A	N/A	N/A
Public media	N/A	20%	24%	N/A	N/A	N/A	N/A	N/A
Community	N/A	22%	21%	N/A	N/A	N/A	N/A	N/A
Who is seen?	% W	% W	% W	% W	% W	% W	% W	% W
Images in newspapers	N/A	27%	28%	74%	10%	N/A	N/A	30%
Women in adverts	% W	% W	% W	% W	% W	% W	% W	% W
% women in adverts	41%	N/A	50%	50%	49%	50%	50%	N/A
Who decides?	% W	% W	% W	% W	% W	% W	% W	% W
Women in the media	N/A	41%	40%	55%	26%	40%	37%	N/A
Women in senior management	N/A	28%	34%	67%	0%	34%	39%	N/A
Women in top management	N/A	23%	34%	47%	0%	35%	34%	N/A
Who reports?	% W	% W	% W	% W	% W	% W	% W	% W
All reporters	N/A	27%	34%	69%	0%	34%	34%	37%
TV reporters	38%	N/A	42%	N/A	N/A	50%	49%	38%
TV presenters	45%	46%	61%	68%	30%	47%	55%	57%
Radio reporters	34%	N/A	50%	97%	35%	30%	29%	41%
Print reporters	22%	N/A	39%	100%	31%	33%	31%	35%
Sources and sex of reporter	% W	% W	% W	% W	% W	% W	% W	% W
Female sources/women reporters	N/A	31%	25%	100%	2%	N/A	N/A	16%
Female sources/male reporters	N/A	15%	17%	4%	5%	N/A	N/A	22%
What is reported on?	%	%	%	%	%	%	%	%
Economics	N/A	12%	17%	N/A	N/A	18%	11%	17%
Politics	N/A	19%	21%	N/A	N/A	17%	66%	16%
Sports	N/A	18%	17%	N/A	N/A	18%	19%	N/A
Who speaks on what?	% W	% W	% W	% W	% W	% W	% W	% W
Economics	10%	12%	18%	N/A	N/A	N/A	N/A	21%
Political stories	9%	13%	14%	N/A	N/A	N/A	N/A	18%
Sports	8%	12%	13%	N/A	N/A	N/A	N/A	N/A
Origin of stories	%	%	%	%	%	%	%	%
International	N/A	22%	16%	N/A	N/A	N/A	N/A	26%
SADC	N/A	8%	8%	N/A	N/A	N/A	N/A	N/A
National	N/A	42%	44%	N/A	N/A	N/A	N/A	N/A
Local/community	N/A	18%	28%	N/A	N/A	N/A	N/A	N/A
Gender based violence	%	%	%	%	%	%	%	%
GBV stories compared to total	N/A	4%	1%	1%	0	0.4%	0.4%	N/A
Who speaks on GBV	% W	% W	% W	% W	% W	% W	% W	% W
% women sources	N/A	27%	58%	100%	18%	N/A	N/A	N/A
HIV and AIDS	%	%	%	%	%	%	%	%
HIV and AIDS compared to total	3%	2%	0.2%%	1%	0.1%	N/A	N/A	N/A
Who speaks on HIV and AIDS?	% W	% W	% W	% W	% W	% W	% W	% W
% women sources	39%	20%	30%	100%	23%	N/A	N/A	N/A
Sexual orientation and gender identity	%	%	%	%	%	%	%	%
SOGI stories compared to total	N/A	N/A	0.1%	68%	0	N/A	N/A	N/A
Who speaks on SOGI?	% W	% W	% W	% W	% W	% W	% W	% W
% women sources	N/A	N/A	46%	68%	0	N/A	N/A	N/A
Future of gender and media (GIME)	% W	% W	% W	% W	% W	% W	% W	% W
% female lecturers	N/A	36%	40%	71%	19%	42%	43%	N/A
% female students	N/A	61%	64%	78%	29%	65%	62%	N/A

Source: Gender and Media Progress Study 2015.

Gender and freedom of expression

The year 2017 marked the 26th anniversary of the Windhoek Declaration, which the sector celebrated under the theme "Critical Minds for Critical Times: Media's role in advancing peaceful, just and inclusive societies."

The right to communicate is enshrined as a human right in Article 19 of the Universal Declaration of Human Rights of 1948, which states that "everyone has the right to freedom of opinion and expression; this right includes freedom to hold opinions without interference and to seek, receive and impart information and ideas through any media and regardless of frontiers."

Conversations on freedom of expression or communication often focus on freedom from government interference or the absence of laws that hinder the press and not so much on citizens' freedom to communicate and express themselves in the media. This framing negates discussions on the difficulty of women in reaching certain roles in the media, covering certain topics, or expressing themselves.

Press freedom and gender equality are intertwined: one cannot exist without the other. Gender equality and equality of all voices is implicit in the notion of a pluralistic press, which should reflect the widest possible range of opinions. As noted in a 2018 report from Canada, "Any discussion of freedom of expression must ask, whose freedom, defined by whom? It should not be defined, as it typically has, as men's right to squander the profits of communication companies to secure their own economic and political power or continue to omit and stereotype women in the content of their news and programming."[8]

All SADC countries guarantee the right to freedom of expression. All countries in SADC also have media laws and policies that govern the operations and behaviours of the media. Some countries, however, have embraced stringent media laws that purport to uphold the status quo and which, in many instances, pose a threat to media freedom and democracy. In many ways, freedom of the media continues to decline in the region.

The 2018 *World Press Freedom Index* conducted by Researchers Without Borders revealed that no SADC country ranks among the global top 20. Indeed, Namibia has dropped to 26th place from 24th in 2017. Meanwhile, South Africa's status has improved, moving from 31st to 28th place. Comoros, the new addition to the Southern Africa region, ranks 49th out of 180 countries. eSwatini (152) and DRC (154) remain among the worst in the world for press freedom.[9]

Table 9.5: State of media freedom in SADC	
Country	**Media provisions**
Angola	The constitution protects freedom of speech and of the press, however Angola continues to have a restrictive media environment. Press status for the country is "not free." The only outlets with a truly national reach and most widely accessed - Jornal de Angola, television channel Televisão Publica de Angola (TPA) and Radio Nacional de Angola (RNA) - remain under government's firm grip. Private media is operational; however, it is very limited.[10]
Botswana	The Botswana Constitution enshrines freedom of expression in Chapter 12. On the surface, the country has a free and diverse media environment. However, several laws, like the National Security Act, restrict free access to information. The government has been reluctant to pass the Freedom of Information Act, although several government policies provide for it - including the national strategic vision, Vision 2016.[11]
Comoros	The Comoros Constitution provides for freedom of speech and of the press. However, Reporters Without Borders notes that many journalists self-censor.[12]
DRC	DRC laws and the constitution provide for freedom of speech, information, and the press, but, in practice, these rights remain limited. The government and non-state actors (such as armed groups) often use other regulations and methods to restrict freedom of speech and suppress criticism.[13] The political allegiance found in the stories out of most media outlets in DRC normally reflects that of the owner.
Lesotho	While the Lesotho Constitution does not directly mention press freedom, it guarantees freedom of expression and information exchange. However, multiple laws, including the Sedition Proclamation No. 44 of 1938 and the Internal Security (General) Act of 1984 prohibit criticism of the government, give penalties for seditious libel, and endanger reporters' ability to protect the confidentiality of their sources.[14]
Madagascar	Madagascar enjoys a diverse and pluralised media landscape, which radio has, in recent times, dominated. Madagascar has a liberal policy towards the media, which has fostered the development of media pluralism and diversity.[15]
Malawi	Section 36 of the Malawi Constitution states that the press shall have the right to report and publish freely, within Malawi and abroad, and to be accorded the fullest possible facilities for access to public information. Additionally, Section 35 states that everyone shall have the right to freedom of expression. Radio continues to be the most popular medium of accessing information as it has the widest reach and is available in many languages.[16]

Country	Media provisions
Mauritius	Section 12 of the Constitution of Mauritius has always guaranteed freedom of expression. Within the same section, limitations are possible in the "interests of defence, public safety, public order, public morality or public health." Although Mauritius has not signed the SADC Gender Protocol, its constitution guarantees gender equality across all sectors.
Mozambique	Mozambique's revised 2004 constitution guarantees freedom of the press, explicitly protecting journalists and granting them the right not to reveal their sources. The environment for media freedom worsened in 2013, primarily due to an increase in attacks and detentions of journalists by both security forces and non-state actors, as well as the firing of editors whose coverage politicians deemed overly critical of the government.[17]
Namibia	The constitutional guarantee contained in Article 21.1 (a) of the Namibian Constitution gives all Namibians the right to freedom of expression, including freedom of the press and other media.
Seychelles	Seychelles has very few media outlets. The main outlet is the Seychelles Broadcasting Corporation. The creation of the Seychelles Media Commission sought to provide a platform for adjudication on media issues while ensuring more freedom, and the reduction of television and radio licence fees.
South Africa	In the last couple of years, South Africa has seen the development and establishment of crucial industry bodies in response to the democratic imperative for accountability, including the newly revitalised Press Council and the Broadcast Complaints Commission (BCCSA). However, threats to media freedom from various quarters still exist - some by government and political parties; others from the profit-seeking corporate sector.[18] Conditions for media freedom improved marginally in 2015, with the courts reaffirming journalists' right to access information and further limiting arbitrary restrictions on publishing information in the public interest.[19]
eSwatini	The 2005 Constitution of the Kingdom of eSwatini guarantees freedom of expression. However, subsequent clawback clauses restrict this right, and King Mswati III can suspend the right to freedom of expression at his discretion. There are no laws or parts of laws restricting freedom of expression.
Tanzania	Tanzania has a very vibrant media industry with strong regulatory systems. The new draft constitution makes provisions for media freedom and free media access to all its citizens. Tanzania has many private media houses as well as a strong community media sector. However, human rights groups, media platforms and independent publishers took the government to court in 2018 over the new Electronic and Postal Communications (Online Content) Regulations, which set out a series of prohibited content affecting bloggers, online radio stations, online streaming platforms, online forums, social media users and internet cafes.[20]
Zambia	Article 20 of the Zambian Constitution protects freedom of expression. Regarding media protection in the constitution, Article 20 (2) states that "subject to the provisions of this constitution no law shall make any provision that derogates from freedom of the press." Political issues continue to dominate the mainstream media, and diversity of content in the print media remains limited. Great strides have been made around self-regulation, which has narrowed the divide between state and privately-owned media as they united in the establishment of the self-regulatory body, the Zambia Media Council (ZAMEC). However, citizens often cannot express themselves freely due to the perceived elevated levels of political intolerance.[21]
Zimbabwe	Zimbabwe has repressive media laws which hinder free media practice, including laws around access to information based on the principles of "official secrecy." Its media industry is also highly polarised, with private media aligning itself to civil society and human rights defenders, whilst the public media has been reduced to a government conduit. Persecution of journalists remains common.

Source: Gender and Media Progress Study 2015.

All SADC countries guarantee the **right** to freedom of expression

10 https://freedomhouse.org/report/freedom-press/2015/angola
11 http://downloads.bbc.co.uk/worldservice/trust/pdf/AMDI/botswana/amdi_botswana3_media_health.pdf
12 https://rsf.org/en/comoros
13 http://uncoveringthedrc.blogspot.co.za/2012/01/media-landscape-in-drc.html
14 http://www.mediamonitoringafrica.org/images/uploads/Lesotho_Interim_Report_PrintVersion_2.pdf
15 http://www.unesco-ci.org/ipdcprojects/countries/madagascar
16 http://library.fes.de/pdf-files/bueros/africa-media/09541.pdf
17 https://freedomhouse.org/report/freedom-press/2014/mozambique
18 http://www.gcis.gov.za/sites/www.gcis.gov.za/files/docs/resourcecentre/medialandscape2014_ch5.pdf
19 https://freedomhouse.org/report/freedom-press/2016/south-africa
20 https://edition.cnn.com/2018/04/12/africa/tanzania-blogging-internet-freedoms-africa/index.html
21 http://library.fes.de/pdf-files/bueros/africa-media/10575.pdf

Gender in media laws, policies and training

Article 29.1-3: State parties shall enact legislation and develop national policies and strategies, including professional guidelines and codes of conduct, to prevent and address gender stereotypes and discrimination in the media. parties shall ensure that gender is mainstreamed in all information, communication and media policies, programmes, laws and training in accordance with the Protocol on Culture, Information and Sport. State parties shall encourage the media, and media-related bodies to mainstream gender in their codes of conduct, policies and procedures and adopt and employ gender aware ethical principles, codes of practise and policies, in accordance with the Protocol on Culture, Information and Sports.

Three articles in the SADC Protocol concern the mainstreaming of gender in policies, laws and professional standards in the media. Mindful of constitutional provisions in most SADC countries for freedom of expression, the provisions are not prescriptive.

While governments may have some leverage over the public or state-owned media, the private media guards its independence. Most media stakeholders push for self-regulatory practices. A 2018 research study on the topic notes that "Normative frameworks, national media policies and measures adopted at the level of media organisations are crucial to define principles and goals, reflect normative orientations and develop mechanisms to assess progress and change in response to persisting and plural forms of gender inequality in and through the media."[22]

Gender policies are also important in the institutionalisation of mainstreaming gender equality in and through media. Many media houses lack this instrument and, in places where these exist, questions remain about their effectiveness.

No SADC member states have enacted specific gender and media legislation. However, countries have made progress in other areas, such as in Zimbabwe, where legislators revised the national gender policy in 2017 with the aim of eradicating gender discrimination and inequalities in all spheres, including media and ICTs. Governments must prioritise the enactment of laws to remedy gender gaps and mitigate further misrepresentation in the media.

Gender policies in media houses

In Southern Africa, many countries have national policies that support a gender-sensitive media and prioritise the importance of access and use of media to advance gender equality. The SADC Gender and Development Monitor notes that "Member states have crafted policies to promote the full and equal participation of women in management, programming education training and research through the SADC protocol on gender and development."[23] These assist media leaders in each country to contribute to the push for gender equality.

Yet a 2016 article reminds us that "Training of journalists and media owners or executives is a necessary but not sufficient step to achieving gender equality and women's empowerment in media. Also needed are internal media policies or self-regulation that can enable sustainable changes, as well as national/public policies in support of gender-sensitive media."[24]

Many managers in the sector have expressed contempt for media gender policies at national and institutional levels because they view them as a covert way of pushing unqualified and undeserving women into leadership positions. However, the existence of policies to tackle stereotypes and promote gender equality remains paramount to redressing the rampant sexism and misogyny in the media, which deters women's progress.

Over the years, through the Centres of Excellence (COE) for Gender in Media, Gender Links has

85 media COEs adopted gender policies

---

[22] Padovani, C (2018) Gendering Media Policy Research and Communication Governance, Javnost - The Public, 25:1-2, 256-264, DOI: 10.1080/13183222.2018.1423941.
[23] SARDC, SADC. 2016 SADC Gender and Development Monitor 2016.SADC, SARDC, Gaborone, Harare.
[24] Lourenço, M.E Gender equality in media content and operations: Articulating academic studies and policy presentation https://en.unesco.org/sites/default/files/mas_pub_genderequalitymedia_en_lkd.pdf

worked with media houses across the region to mainstream gender in institutional practices and adopt gender policies. GL has helped more than 85 media houses across the region to draft and develop gender policies and implement action plans.

 In **Zimbabwe**, Gender and Media Connect (GMC) works with media houses to adopt gender-sensitive editorial and administrative policies and practices. The organisation found that ensuring buy-in from key stakeholders is imperative to ensuring the establishment of standards and guidelines for policies. GMC works with mainstream media houses to formulate situational analyses for participating media houses linked to existing gender disparities in the Zimbabwean media.

The existing gaps in media will take longer to close so long as media houses do not have clear gender and media policies or remain unable or unwilling to mainstream gender. There is a need to create mechanisms to ensure implementation of policies and a revision of existing policies to include gender mainstreaming. Close monitoring, evaluation and learning, carried out by media councils' ethical committees, civil society and government departments responsible for communication, must follow this. Women should be able to take part in the development and monitoring of these media polices.

The presence of media self-regulatory bodies, unions and associations can encourage diversity in the media. As the watchdogs of the media, these groups have the responsibility to ensure that media and journalists collectively work towards ethical media environments. Regulatory bodies must also play an active role to in constantly monitoring women's participation in all levels of the media sector. Quota systems should be built into licensing requirements for a media house to be allowed to operate.

Although enacting gender and media policies and laws is one of the most effective ways to achieve gender equality from the top down, stakeholders cannot carry out this approach in isolation. Massive attitude change is needed to alter perceptions and biases that continue to perpetuate gender inequality.

As part of the process for developing newsroom policies, stakeholders must also set specific targets, such as reaching 30% women sources by 2020, and 50% by 2030. Targets help to focus leaders and

mobilise teams behind a goal. They also allow for more effective monitoring and evaluation.

Governments also need to employ progressive policies to shape the agenda of gender in and through the media and ICTs. Legislators must ensure that national gender policies or strategies and action plans make specific reference to the role of media and ICTs in advancing gender equality and the women's empowerment agenda. They must also commit to achieving the targets they set and ensuring a review of media and ICT laws, regulations and policies. It is also increasingly important to ensure laws protect women and girls against online bullying and gender-based violence.

Governments should also lead by example, ensuring gender balance in the appointment of men and women to all regulatory and monitoring bodies, especially of public media, which is usually subsidised by government. It is also important to encourage self-regulatory authorities to use whatever leverage they have at their disposal, especially in relation to publicly-funded media, to ensure accountability. This could include requiring gender balance and sensitivity in institutional structures as well as editorial content through licensing agreements, as well as ensuring annual reports track progress.

Training

Zuhura Selemani Khateeb, a lecturer at the University of Dar es Salaam School of Journalism, talks about her efforts to mainstream gender in curricula.   *Photo: Gender Links*

Training is a critical entry point for mainstreaming gender in the media. Journalism education should be the starting point. By mainstreaming gender in teaching and curricula, training institutions can enable the development of journalism cadres unaffected by a gendered media culture. Therefore, "improved media training is essential to remove gender biases that prevail... The challenge is to integrate gender awareness training into all types and aspects of media training."[25]

---

[25] Lowe Morna, C and Shilongo, P 2004. Mainstreaming gender into media education. Gender Links, Johannesburg.

60%
students
in
media
education

One 2010 study notes that "Teaching gender issues in journalism and communication schools has to do with understanding the construction and impact of the gendered production of media content, and also with the status of women in newsrooms, professional career opportunities, equal payment, and eradication of sexual harassment, among other issues."[26] Unfortunately, many schools still do not view gender as an important part of journalism and media training.

Yet female students form the majority of those studying in many African journalism and media studies departments. In the SADC region, female students make up 60% of those in journalism and media studies. "The high proportion of women students is... a stark contrast to the proportion of women in media houses."[27] Thus, there is a need for empirical data to help us understand why the higher numbers of women studying media is not translating to more women working in the media. Full and accurate data is crucial so that stakeholders throughout the region have baselines they can use to track progress.

As staff in journalism and media studies departments formulate their curricula, course content and assessments they need to be sensitive to the existing inequalities in the media industry and strategise ways to respond existing gaps.

National governments should also support women's education, especially in public institutions of higher learning. Government commitment is necessary to mainstream gender in all publicly-funded media training institutions and encourage private institutions to follow suit. There is also a need to take a fresh look at training curricula offered in institutions teaching journalism and media studies. Women's enrolment and retention in programmes that educators have stereotypically thought of as courses for men could also use a boost.

The GMPS 2015 gender in media education findings covered media departments at 15 tertiary institutions in 11 countries. This is ten fewer institutions than in the 2010 GIME study. These more up to date findings, however, do offer important new information on gender in media education and training.

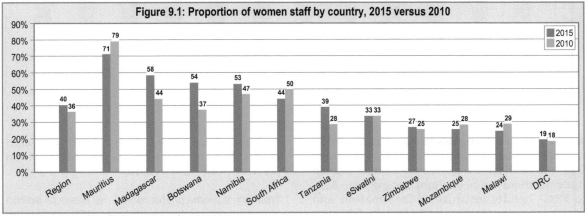

Figure 9.1: Proportion of women staff by country, 2015 versus 2010

Source: Gender and Media Progress Study, 2015.

There has been an increase in the proportion of women trainers: Figure 9.1 shows that the region went from 36% in the 2010 GIME to 40% in the 2015 GMPS. Although change is slow, this is evidence that institutions may have started addressing gender gaps in staff composition.

However, this varies considerably by country: The University of Mauritius continues to lead (71%) although it has declined from 79% in 2010. DRC represents the lowest proportion of female staff (19%). The findings show a steady increase in the proportion of women staff in several countries: from 37% to 58% in Botswana; from 44% to 58% in Madagascar; and from 47% to 53% in Namibia.

25 Lowe Morna, C and Shilongo, P 2004. Mainstreaming gender into media education. Gender Links, Johannesburg.
26 North, L. 2010. The Gender 'Problem' in Australia Journalism Education. Accessed from https://ssrn.com/abstract=2015844 or http://dx.doi.org/10.2139/ssrn.2015844
27 Ibid.

Figure 9.2: Women and men students in media departments - region

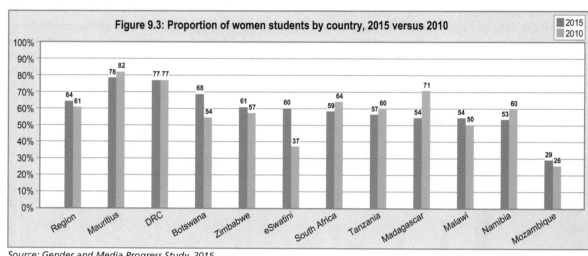

36%

64%

- Women
- Men

Source: Gender and Media Progress Study 2015.

There are more women in journalism and media studies: There has been a steady increase in women students in the region, from 61% in 2010 to 64% in 2015. While men remain in the majority as staff, Figure 9.2 shows that women continue to comprise the majority of students in the departments of media education and journalism training in the 15 tertiary institutions audited.

The high proportion of women students is also higher than the proportion of women working in the media. Newsrooms across the region do not mirror these enrolment figures; women remain underrepresented as staff in media houses.

Figure 9.3: Proportion of women students by country, 2015 versus 2010

■ 2015
■ 2010

	Region	Mauritius	DRC	Botswana	Zimbabwe	eSwatini	South Africa	Tanzania	Madagascar	Malawi	Namibia	Mozambique
2015	64	78	77	68	61	60	59	57	54	54	53	29
2010	61	82	77	54	57	37	64	60	71	50	60	26

Source: Gender and Media Progress Study, 2015.

Women form a large majority of students in several countries: Figure 9.3 shows that, although Mauritius still has the highest proportion of women students, there has been slight decline from 82% to 78%. Faculty Institute of Information and Communication Sciences (IFASIC) in DRC has maintained second position at 77%, the same as in 2010. eSwatini experienced a dramatic increase in women students from 37% to 60%. While in Madagascar and Namibia, the proportion of women

declined. Mozambique is the only country in which women students make up less than half the total (29%, up from 26% in 2010).

Training of media professionals also needs to extend beyond media training institutions. Strengthening the capacity of practicing journalists is important in continuing to put gender on the media agenda.

In **Comoros**, for example, female members of the Association des Femmes Comoriennes de la Presse (AFCP), a local group for journalists, have noted a lack of training as a major issue. Women there join media houses without any basic training or the opportunity for ongoing training. The group says these shortcomings create a barrier for women's development in the sector, preventing them from fully asserting themselves in their jobs. As one of its objectives in 2018, the AFCP will identify the number of women who practice journalism to strengthen their capacity and promote exchanges between Comorian women journalists and those from other countries.

Students from Namibia University of Technology participate in a webinar on the role of media in changing the narrative on women.
Photo: Gender Links

students

▲

than

in

media

Putting gender equality on the front pages in Tanzania

UN Women is working with Gender Links and key media houses in Tanzania to prioritise increased reporting on gender equality. The work includes monitoring and analysing news content in newspapers, radio and television media and engaging and training media personnel through peer learning and sharing by media.

Through this initiative, UN Women hopes to increase prioritisation of gender equality and women's empowerment in news coverage and contribute to an increased understanding of SDG 5 on gender equality.

By providing training and support to Tanzanian media partners through this process, UN Women will arm journalists with knowledge and information about the gender-responsive implementation of the SDGs, and in particular SDG 5, so that they can effectively communicate better on these development priorities and hold all accountable in the achievement of gender equality. Furthermore, UN Women's media monitoring on the coverage of gender equality and women's empowerment will help set targets for gender transformation.

Women and men in media practise

Article 29.4: State parties shall take measures to promote the equal representation of women and men in the ownership and decision-making structures of the media.

Diversity in media workforce composition remains a critical issue in the sector. Having a diverse media workforce will pave the way for an industry that is reflective of the communities it represents. A diverse work force will help shift what the media prioritises as it embodies different perspectives to news coverage on issues.

A simple reflection on media composition reveals that more women have been securing jobs in the media sector. However, an analysis of mere numbers is not enough. We need to assess what women do in the media, what role they play, what kind of stories they tell, how much they earn, etc.

There is limited research on institutional practices, careers and promotion within media industries. One of the latest efforts on this topic globally is the IWMF 2011 report, which shows that women remain grossly under-represented in the media. However, the 2015 GMPS reveals that there is an increasingly critical mass of women entering the industry. But it notes that most women in media have yet to break through the glass ceiling that gives them access to the highest decision-making echelons. Furthermore, the 2017 Barometer noted that "there is presently limited data on ownership of media by women and men in the region - the welcome new parameter introduced in the Post-2015 SADC Gender Protocol. However, the gover-

nance structures of media houses in Southern Africa remain firmly in the hands of men (70%), with women constituting only 30% of those on boards of directors."[28]

Various factors influence the lack of equal representation. Media houses often struggle with a gendered division of labour, which dictates news practices. Women often cover soft news beats compared to the hard news beats covered by men. This affects what journalists report and whose opinions they consult. It also affects the portrayal of women in the media.

Campaigns, like the IWMF-initiated #CheckYour Bylines, act as a conduit to raise awareness about this issue and push media houses to address gaps in news coverage.

But more effort is needed to achieve equal representation. Media owners need to reshape leadership to cover the differential needs of women working in the media and to help propel women up the ranks. Industry-oriented solutions can work alongside activist campaigns to help close the existing gaps in media leadership.

---

28 SADC protocol Barometer 2017.

Women in the media get a leg up from WANIFRA

The World Association of Newspapers and News Publishers (WANIFRA) has initiated the Women in News (WIN) programme, which aims to increase women's leadership and voices in the news. It is equipping women journalists and editors with the skills, strategies, and support networks to take on key decision-making and leadership positions within the media.

In 2018, WANIFRA hosted the Reshaping Media leadership summit in Nairobi. It focused on best practices in mobile storytelling, from newsrooms to audiences; industry solutions to sexual harassment; increasing women leadership in media; and increasing gender balance in news. The project covers more than 80 media houses from 12 countries throughout sub-Saharan Africa and the Middle East, including in Botswana, Kenya, Malawi, Rwanda, Somalia, Tanzania, Zambia, and Zimbabwe.

Amongst other things the project engages women working in the media through hosting roundtable discussions with top management within media to sensitise the industry; creating practical handbooks or online tools on best practices in gender equality; and regional leadership awards to recognise outstanding women editors.

The initiative has already been influential in the careers of many women in the media. Nearly one in five women who participated reported they received a promotion in the six months following their engagement with the programme and 93% of the trained editors and journalists reported an increase in self-confidence.

Source: http://www.womeninnews.org/about

The 2015 GMPS remains the latest regional-wide research covering the status of women in SADC media houses.

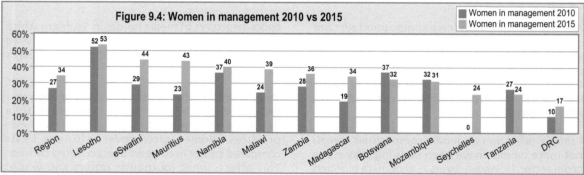

Source: Gender and Media Progress Study, 2015.

Male journalists continue to dominate in the SADC media sector.
Photo: Zotonantenaina Razanadratefa

Figure 9.4 shows that the media remains a largely a male-dominated industry, with men constituting 60% of all employees compared to 40% women. This represents a drop of one percentage point from the 2009 findings.

Considerable variation exists between countries: eSwatini (55%) has the highest proportion of women in the media, while Malawi is lowest at 26%. Of the 12 countries for which researchers could obtain country-level data, ten had fewer than 50% women employees in the media.[29] As only one media house in Zimbabwe responded to the survey, it is one of the countries in which GL does not have country-level results.

---

[29] Insufficient media houses responded in South Africa and Zimbabwe to make country-level conclusions.

However, related work in Zimbabwe reflects the extent to which the media remains a hostile environment for many women. The GMC, through its policy work with four key media houses in Zimbabwe, found a huge imbalance between male and female employees in the media. Of 1266 employees in four major media houses, men held 933 positions, compared to 333 for women. This is even though all media claim they have equal opportunity hiring policies.

 According to the 2017 African Media Barometer, **Zambia** has moved closer to equal representation in the media. The report notes that the Zambia News and Information Services (ZANIS), for example, has all female photographers and a female head of photography. Media houses in Zambia also have female sports photographers covering this male-dominated area. In addition, more females work as journalists in Zambia overall. However, as in other African countries, men still dominate in upper management.

Many policy changes are necessary at the newsroom level, as noted above. There is also a need to deepen engagement with media decision-makers, owners and ministries in charge of media and information communication to establish quotas on the participation of women in the media industry. Quotas will help increase the number of women in the media, including in leadership and decision-making roles and as media owners.

Glass Ceilings Women in South Africa Media houses

Glass ceilings researchers discussing during a project inception meeting.
Photo courtesy of Mauwane Raophala

Gender Links, the South Africa National Editors Forum and the Media Development and Diversity Agency are working in collaboration to assess the glass ceiling in South Africa media houses. The research seeks to assess the numbers of women in the media, the policies in place the effort to empower women and opportunities and safety of women journalists online. This is a follow up research. In 2006, Gender Links (GL) collaborated with the South African National Editors Forum (SANEF) in conducting the first *Glass Ceilings in South African Newsrooms* research studies.

In 2009, GL expanded this research to the SADC region, and conducted a survey of 11 media houses in South Africa. The International Women's Media Foundation (IWMF) incorporated the GL findings from SADC into the Global report on the Status of Women in News Media. The study showed that overall; women constitute 50% of all employees in the South African media. However only 38% of the board of directors, 35% of senior management and 25% of top management. This study will be a follow up to the 2009 Glass Ceiling Research done by GL and borrows from the first Glass Ceiling done in 2006 in collaboration with SANEF. It also builds upon the recently completed Gender and Media Progress Study (GMPS) 2015, which had missing information on the composition of women and men in South African media.

The purpose of this research is to undertake a follow up comprehensive survey on where women and men are in the media industry, especially decision-making and ownership structures, institutional culture and practices. The research also seeks to probe the gendered dimensions of the digital revolution over the last decade.

GL is initiating the research in line with Section J of the 1995 Beijing Platform for Action (BPFA), which identified media as one of the critical areas of concern in achieving gender equality, under two critical areas, women's equal participation in the media and decision-making positions. It also undertakes the research in line with the revised SADC Protocol on Gender and Development that encourages States Parties to promote equal representation of women in the ownership of, and decision-making structures of the media.

Women in media content

Article 29.6: State parties shall encourage the media to give equal voice to women and men in all areas of coverage, including increasing the number of programmes for, by and about women on gender-specific topics that challenge gender stereotypes.

Media **relies** on *(male symbol)* as **experts**

According to Spears (2000), women are generally portrayed in a limited number of roles. Sexualised images of women are rife, and media tends to define women in terms of their physical appearance, not abilities. When it is not portraying women as sex objects, the media most often shows women as victims of violence and homemakers.[30] Although stereotypes of women as caregivers (such as the selfless mother so popular in advertisements) have more positive connotations, they are nevertheless stereotypes, which certainly do not reflect women's complex experiences and aspirations.

In addition to appearing in a limited number of roles, women are often simply missing in the media. Media is much less likely to feature women in news stories and less likely to interview women for their opinions.[31] There is further silencing of women in certain categories, such as rural women, elderly women, young women and women from certain religious groups. Thus, stripping them of their voice, agency and ability to participate in the development of their communities.

When the media does cover issues of concern to women, such as violence, sexual and reproductive health, and women in decision-making, it often confines this coverage to special pages and segments, tagged as "women's issues," rather than leading news.

As the GMMP noted, "Mainstream media coverage continues to rely on men as experts in the fields of business, politics and economics. Women in the news are more likely to be featured in stories about accidents, natural disasters, or domestic violence than in stories about their professional abilities or expertise."[32] Although women desire to contribute to the national discourse and to their local public sphere, media often does not recognise their voices.

The SDGs advocate the imperative of "leaving no one behind," yet that is exactly what is happening when media silences women's voices, experiences and concerns. The underrepresentation and misrepresentation of women can also significantly skew the way women and girls view themselves.

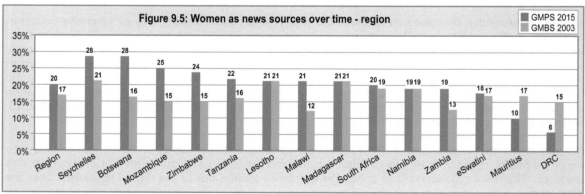

Figure 9.5: Women as news sources over time - region

Source: Gender and Media Progress Study, 2015.

Figure 9.5 shows that there has been a slight increase in the proportion of women sources from 17% in the 2003 GMBS to 20% in this study: journalists still predominantly tell the news from a male perspective.

---

30 Spears, G. and Seydegart, K. 2000. Who Makes the News? Global Media Monitoring Project 2000.
31 Ibid.
32 Ibid.

There is more forward than backward movement at country level: Only two countries (DRC and Mauritius) have slipped backwards on the proportion of women sources. Lesotho, Madagascar and Namibia remained the same over 12 years, while Seychelles has maintained its position at the top (28%). At 28%, Botswana ties with Seychelles and made the most significant improvement, compared to 16% in 2003.

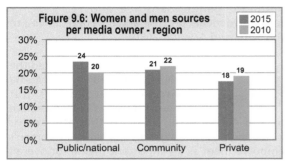

Figure 9.6: Women and men sources per media owner - region

Source: Gender and Media Progress Study, 2015.

Public media leads the way on women's representation: Figure 9.6, which disaggregates women sources according to ownership, shows that journalists working for public media access more women voices (24%) compared to private and community media. Although this number is higher than the privately-owned entities, it remains excessively low considering that public media is funded from public funds. As such, public media has a mandate to represent all constituent voices. Furthermore, even though public media performs better than community and private media, these figures remain very low.

Women make up around a fifth (21%) of sources in community media. As the form of media closest to the people, community media should give access to all segments included ordinary women's voices. It is not. Private media, mostly driven by business imperatives, accesses the lowest proportion of women sources at 18%."

Figure 9.7 below shows that, as noted in the GMPS, "across the region, men's voices continue to dominate in all topic categories. This further emphasises the point that men continue to be voices of authority even on matters that mostly affect women. Gender-based violence and HIV and AIDS represent two of the issues where there is differential impact on women and men, yet men make up the majority of those accessed as sources by journalists."

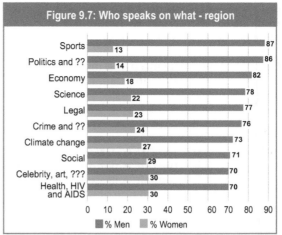

Figure 9.7: Who speaks on what - region

Source: Gender and Media Progress Study, 2015.

In **Tanzania**, UN Women has launched efforts to increase positive coverage of women. This initiative seeks prioritise reporting on gender equality through monitoring and analysing news content in newspapers, radio and television media and engaging and training media personnel through peer learning. The activity, titled *Acceleration of Gender-responsive Sustainable Development Goals localization - Reporting SDGs*, gender equality and empowerment of women in Tanzania, also seeks to support the public awareness and improved coverage and understanding of gender equality and the SDGs, in particular, SDG 5.

In **Zambia**, research conducted monthly by Panos Institute Southern Africa between December 2016 and October 2017 assessed quantity and quality of coverage of women in Zambia's major newspapers. The research also sought to determine the level of participation of women in the media as lead sources and main subjects. Furthermore, it identified the level of play of articles on women.[35] It found that "women are severely marginalised by the media and this undermines public opinion about their abilities and capabilities." Panos is using this information to advocate for better representation and portrayal of women in media coverage.[36] In October 2017, the assessment showed that women's representation in newspapers made up just 10% of total coverage. Given the abovementioned statistic that women make up the majority of journalists in Zambia, this finding shows that even female journalists seek out mostly male voices as sources. This points to a need for further training for both

33 Ndlovu, S and Nyamweda T. (2015) Whose News Whose Views. Southern Africa Gender and Media Progress Study.
34 Ndlovu, S and Nyamweda T. (2015) Whose News Whose Views. Southern Africa Gender and Media Progress Study.
35 How Zambian newspapers report on women covered http://www.panos.org.zm/wp-content/uploads/2017/12/Monthly-report-Oct-2017.pdf
36 Ibid.

Public media leads on ♀

male and female journalists. Gender activists must continue to raise awareness about the importance of diverse voices in media stories.

Gender Links has created a digital media monitoring tool to continue gathering data news sources in Southern Africa.

Gender and media advocacy

 In 2017, GMC **Zimbabwe** hosted a gender and media summit. It presented awards in recognition of good journalistic practices that ensure women's access to expression in the media and flag relevant or topical issues from a gender perspective. Organisers granted awards based on a qualitative and quantitative assessments on the extent journalists and media institutions mainstream gender in their work. The awards recognised gender sensitive content in terms of depth, story angles, language, visuals and placement of stories within a publication or broadcast. In terms of the media institutions, the awards looked at gender sensitive media operations. This includes the adoption and implementation of gender sensitive and aware operational codes, policies and practices.

Tanzania will also host a gender equality and women's empowerment summit in August 2018 to highlight gender sensitive and responsive media practise and coverage, linked to the SDGs and Agenda 2030.

 In 2017, **South Africa** hosted the WANIFRA World News Media Conference. Organizers put Women in News as the centrepiece of the conference, showing that the sector increasingly considers gender equality and women's empowerment as an important theme for overall media development.

Coverage of gender-based violence

 Article 29.7: State parties shall take appropriate measures to encourage the media to play a constructive role in the eradication of GBV by adopting guidelines which ensure gender sensitive coverage.

The SADC Gender Protocol encourages the media to desist from promoting violence against all persons, especially women and children, and from depicting women as helpless victims of abuse and reinforcing gender oppression. It also encourages the media to play a constructive role in the eradication of gender-based violence (GBV) through gender sensitive coverage.

As the #MeToo and #TimesUp campaigns continue to gain momentum, citizens of countries in the global south have found their voices in calling out and reflecting on the sexual harassment in the media and film industry. This has created offshoots to similar campaigns at the local level.

 In **South Africa**, Sisters Working in Film and Television (SWIFT) conducted its first sexual harassment and discrimination survey, which ran from January to April 2017. The study revealed that 67% of women feel unsafe in the workplace, 65% have witnessed sexual harassment, 24% indicated they had been unwillingly touched and 71% felt they did not have a platform or strong

Journalists cover a 16 Days of Activism march in Mozambique in 2012. *Photo: Ruben Covane*

support structure where they could address these issues. Motivated by their research, SWIFT launched the #ThatsNotOK campaign in July, including a series of short films that speak directly to the issue of sexual harassment.

In **Zimbabwe**, sexual harassment in the media is also a cause for concern. GMC started the #GMCShout initiative, which

sees its team working with various media houses to encourage conducive working environments for both male and female journalists. GMC notes that Zimbabwe needs a policy manual or code of conduct for employees that can serve as a guide in finding corrective measures to ending sexual harassment in media houses.

However, as found in the GMPS in 2015:

The media is often part of the problem rather than the solution when it comes to coverage of gender violence: The GMMP 2015 study revealed that "overall, women remain more than twice as likely as men to be portrayed as victims than they were a decade ago, at 16% and 8%, respectively."[37]

GBV is not making the news: The 2015 GMPS found that GBV stories make up a mere 1% of total stories covered in the media, compared to 4% in the 2010 GMPS. This is despite a stern warning from the UN Special Rapporteur on violence against women, Dubravka Šimonovic, who recently called

GBV "an almost acceptable phenomenon" in South Africa, noting that "despite an arsenal of progressive laws and policies to deal with gender-based violence put very ably in place, there has been little implementation, hence impact and gender-based violence continues to be pervasive and at the level of systematic women's human rights violation."[38]

In **South Africa**, recent research undertaken by Media Monitoring Africa following the death of Karabo Mokoena, a young woman whose boyfriend murdered her, shows that media increased its coverage of GBV in May 2017. The research, which focused on 12 media houses, showed most coverage on GBV remains reactionary and coverage is not ongoing or consistent. The research showed that media ran only 10 articles on GBV before Mokoena's death. However, 34 stories on GBV appeared after her story made the news. Articles also focus on the nature of the violence rather than on underlying critical issues that lead to such incidents or that highlight potential solutions.

ICTs and women's empowerment

Article 30: State parties shall put in place information and communication technology policies and laws in the social economic and political development arena for women's empowerment regardless of race, age, religion or class. These policies and laws shall include specific targets developed through an open and participatory process in order to ensure women's and girl's access to ICTs.

Goal 5 of the SDGs highlights the role of media and ICTs in women's advancement, encouraging member states to enhance the use of enabling technology, in particular ICTs, to promote the empowerment of women.[39]

ICTs are an effective tool for women to amplify their voices and mobilise to advance their concerns. However, for women to achieve this, they need to have meaningful access to ICTs, which can be enabled or stunted by several factors, including affordability, relevant content, skills and security. Research on the topic notes that ICTs "allow isolated women to gain access to information that was not previously made available, thus helping them to become better informed members of society and

Emilar Gandhi, Facebook's public policy manager for the SADC region, speaks on a panel about women's safety online during the 2017 Forum on Internet Freedom in South Africa.
Photo courtesy of Petronell Ngonyama

consequently empowering them to speak up."[40] In Lesotho, GL uses ICTs to promote women's awareness on GBV.

---

[37] http://www.unwomen.org/en/news/stories/2015/11/press-release-gmmp#sthash.E8TuFzbf.dpuf
[38] http://www.un.org/sustainabledevelopment/blog/2015/12/despite-progressive-laws-gender-based-violence-pervasive-in-south-africa-un-expert-warns/
[39] SDG (5.b).
[40] Hafkin and Taggart. 2001. Gender, Information Technology and Developing Countries: An Analytic Study. Washington D.C.: USAID, June 2001 http://pdf.usaid.gov/pdf_docs/Pnacm871.pdf

Making ICTs work for gender justice in Lesotho

Gender Links Lesotho, Participatory Initiative for Social Accountability (PISA) and Mainlevel Consulting have piloted an application titled Sedibeng to break silence and promote awareness on GBV.

It seeks to inform women on GBV-related rights and laws in Lesotho and empower them to deal with GBV through knowledge of their rights.

The application also provides a safe online space for women to share experiences and network. It raises awareness on the types of GBV and appropriate reactions and responses.

Participants learn how to use the GBV app in Mafeteng, Lesotho, in 2018.
Photo: Ntolo Lekau

Furthermore, it gives an overview of local GBV-related services. Women GBV survivors involved in the pilot reported that the app served as counselling, encouraging them to share experiences and knowledge. They also appreciated that they can access information on GBV anonymously and felt that *Selibeng* empowered them to become agents of change regarding GBV issues in their communities.

The app is the first of its kind to provide easy access to information on GBV, simplifying the transfer of knowledge - via the app and among women.

Studies show that women journalists benefit from the use of online media platforms. According to the 2015 GMMP, women in Africa report more stories online (41%) than in the traditional media (35%). The study also found more women represented in online stories about politics (32%) and the economy (19%).

Social media has the potential to mobilise attention and accountability for women's rights and challenge discrimination and stereotypes.[41] Women's rights organisations and women of different backgrounds and ages have harnessed the power of social media to bring their concerns to light. "Hashtag activism" has brought women's issues to the forefront of political agendas. Increasingly, efforts across the region use ICTs to increase women's participation, knowledge and voices, as in a case study from Zimbabwe.

Although the proliferation of ICTs provides many possibilities, it adds another dimension to gender inequality, according to research. "New media can also be a double-edged sword for women's rights. Much as women can claim this space to make their voice count, it is also a space that can be used to fuel violence, conflict and misogyny."[42] The struggles that women face offline extend onto digital media platforms. "Barriers faced by women in accessing ICTs, and that may limit their participation in digital life, are exacerbated by offline inequalities."[43]

In 2016, SADC launched an ICT thematic group to facilitate resource mobilisation, planning and monitoring of the implementation of SADC's ICT initiatives. It will also act as a platform for dialogue as well as the interface between SADC and International Cooperating Partners (ICPs) with the main purpose of improving the coordination of all stakeholders in the ICT sector in the region. Unfortunately, the group - so far - has not included strong gender provisions in its priorities.

Data shows there is an increased gender divide in access to ICTs. The International Telecommunication Union (ITU) estimates that the overall gap between men and women concerning access to internet increased from 11% in 2013 to 13% in 2016. Africa has the highest regional gender gap (23%).[44]

---

[41] Loiseau, E and Nowack, K 2014. can social media effectively include women's voices in decision-making processes? OECD Development Centre. Accessed from https://www.oecd.org/dev/development-gender/DEV_socialmedia-issuespaper-March2015.pdf
[42] Ibid.
[43] Promotion, protection and enjoyment of human rights on the Internet: ways to bridge the gender digital divide from a human rights perspective.
[44] International Telecommunication Union. 2016. ICT facts and figures. Accessed from http://www.itu.int/en/ITU-D/Statistics/Documents/facts/ictfactsfigures2016.pdf

266 SADC Gender Protocol 2018 Barometer

Women, especially in rural Africa, remain disproportionately affected by these gaps. Many still do not have access to this technology due to inadequate infrastructure, affordability, availability, language barriers, illiteracy and even discriminatory social norms. Therefore, stepping up efforts in "connecting the unconnected" is important to ensure ICTs continue to contribute effectively to the empowerment of women and girls.

Citizens have been making new calls for leaders in Africa to make universal access to ICTs a reality for women. Governments must recognise that technology is not a luxury but a basic human right that can help women from diverse backgrounds to enhance their freedom of expression and freedom to access information that will improve their lives. Recognising it as such makes it an important conduit for progress on SDG5.

Research notes that "Rapid progress is possible in all countries through simple steps like reducing the cost to connect, introducing digital literacy in schools, and expanding public access facilities."[45] As long as restrictive ICT policies exist, with negligible government efforts to live up to the tenets of universal access to information, the ability of ICTs to aid in the advancement of women and girls' rights will remain limited.

SADC governments need to tap into, and make effective use of, Universal Service Access and Funds to help women increase their access to ICTs and to reduce the cost of using them.[46] Research notes that "USAFs offer a promising path to develop and implement the policies and programmes needed to close the digital divide and, specifically, to tackle barriers to internet access and use for women."[47]

Mobile application amplifies women's voices in Zimbabwe

GMC Zimbabwe has launched a mobile application, called *SpeakZW*, to enable citizens, especially women, to amplify their voices and views on election issues ahead of the 2018 national elections.

GMC notes that Zimbabwe's mainstream media continues to muffle women's voices in the coverage of issues of socio, economic or political importance even though women make up a majority of the country's population of more than 16 million.

This initiative is in responses to the lack of prioritisation of women sources by editors, who often reject articles, asking, "who is she?" The application, which is available in both Shona and IsiNdebele, will give a platform for women to air their views on political issues.

SpeakZW will also help increase the number of women's voices in the monitoring and documentation of issues for a free and fair election.
Users can share the following:
• Registration: share experience of the biometric voter registration process;
• Campaigns: share observations and/or analysis on the campaigning period;
• Voting day: share polling day experience; and
• Results: give an analysis of the outcome of the election.

The organisation is promoting the application among women from different backgrounds, including those in rural Zimbabwe, so that it collates diverse views from people who rarely get the chance to speak out during elections. Although digital barriers remain, especially in terms of digital literacy, access, and affordability, this application will help bridge these challenges and promote equal participation and voice.
Source: http://gmc.org.zw/2018/04/05/interactive-platform-increasing-womens-voices-in-zim-election/

---

[45] World Wide Web Foundation. 2016. Women's Rights online. Accessed from http://webfoundation.org/docs/2016/09/WRO-Gender-Report-Card_Overview.pdf

[46] Universal Service or Access Funds are a mechanism by which a national regulatory authority mandates, oversees and/or coordinates a set of subsidies and fees designed to promote access to telecommunication services for all of a country's population.

[47] https://webfoundation.org/docs/2018/03/Using-USAFs-to-Close-the-Gender-Digital-Divide-in-Africa.pdf

Next steps

Needed: in and through the media

The SADC Protocol on Gender and Development is one of the most comprehensive tools available to help the media promote equal participation and voice. Despite having this instrument, which foregrounds the importance of gender equality in the media, media representations continue to create and recreate discourses that impede processes of gender transformation in and through the sector. Except for the Gender and Media Progress studies carried out every five years, very few other mechanisms exist to comprehensively track the implementation of what member states have agreed to do in the media sector.

As the analysis in this chapter shows, gender disparities remain pervasive in the region's media sector. The region should focus on strengthening various factors to assist in the contribution to gender equality in and through media and ICTs. These include:

Strengthen monitoring: Although the GMPS provides a wealth of data and indicators for holistic reflection of women's representation, it remains one of the only far-reaching media monitoring efforts to track the improvement of gender in the media at a regional level.

Set specific targets: As part of developing newsroom policies, stakeholders need to set specific targets, such as women sources reaching 30% of the total by 2020, and 50% by 2020 (in line with AU targets for women's representation in decision-making). Although targets like this alone are not enough, they help to focus the mind, to mobilise and to conduct more effective monitoring and evaluation.

Improve education and access to it: Stakeholders must pledge to mainstream gender in all publicly-funded media training institutions and encourage privately-funded media training institutions to follow suit. They must also take a fresh look at training curricula through a gender lens and work to improve enrolment of women in media training institutions, especially for programmes that many still see as "men's topics," such as sports, politics, climate change and economy.

Formulate better policies - and ensure their implementation: Governments need to shape the agenda of gender in and through the media and ICTs using progressive policies. They must ensure that national gender policies, strategies and action plans make specific reference to the role of media and ICTs in advancing gender equality and the women's empowerment agenda and commit to achieving their targets. They must also ensure a review of media and ICT laws, regulations and policies to mainstream gender throughout to eliminate gender stereotypes and biases in content. This will also improve access, use, participation and the voices of women in the media. Legislators must also create better laws to protect women and girls against cyber-based GBV.

Improve regulation: Governments should pioneer gender balance in the appointment of men and women to all regulatory and monitoring bodies, especially of government-subsidised public media. Lawmakers should mandate statutory regulatory authorities and encourage self-regulatory authorities, to use whatever leverage they have at their disposal, especially in relation to publicly-funded media, to ensure gender accountability. This could include requiring gender balance and sensitivity in institutional structures as well as editorial content through licensing agreements, as well as annual reports stating progress in this regard.

Expand access to ICTs: Lawmakers must avail resources to ensure that women have greater access to ICTs and relevant content to help enhance their lives and expand their access to economic opportunities.

CHAPTER 10
Gender, climate change and sustainable development

Article 31

Women in Bizana, South Africa, have been making Wonderbags to use for cooking. These environmentally-friendly, non-electric heat-retention cookers use less fuel and water, which minimises deforestation.
Photo: GenderCCSA

own **less** than **10%** of the **land** they manage

KEY POINTS

- Environmental management in the region, land degradation, deforestation, loss of biodiversity, pollution, inadequate access to clean water and sanitation services, and poor urban conditions continue to threaten sustainable development.

- Women can be powerful agents for change in the transition to, and promotion of, sustainable energy.

- Women own less than 10% of the land but they are key managers of the environment.

- Women in the SADC region withstand the worst of natural disasters and climate change yet are not meaningfully engaged in climate justice initiatives.

- Women and girls constitute the majority of those impacted by the effects of climate change and environmental degradation, yet they remain less likely to have access to environmental resources.

- To help mitigate the impact of climate change, women farmers in the Southern Africa Development Community (SADC) region need equal access to environmentally and socially sustainable agricultural inputs, markets, and climate-resilient farming technologies and climate information.

- Many lawmakers have still not mainstreamed gender in SADC sustainable development strategies.

Table 10.1: Trends in Climate change and sustainable development trends since 2012*

	Baseline 2012	Progress 2018	Variance (Progress minus 2030 target)
REPRESENTATION			
50% women in decision-making bodies that address climate change	24%	25% (highest Zimbabwe at 50%, lowest Botswana, DRC and Tanzania at 0%)	-25%
50% women sources on gender and climate change	27%	27% (highest 55% in Seychelles, lowest 7% in Botswana)	-23%
All women in 15 SADC countries have access to electricity	2 countries (Mauritius and Seychelles)	2 countries have hit 100% (Mauritius and Seychelles), followed by eSwatini (97%), South Africa (95%), Botswana (89%), Zimbabwe (62%) and Namibia (62%)	-13 countries
POLICY AND PROGRAMMES			
15 countries have evidence of gender-sensitive climate change policies/strategies linked to the Monitoring, Evaluation and Reporting Framework (MERF)	10 countries (mainly referenced in gender policies)	10 countries (mainly referenced in gender policies)	-5 (data not clear for Angola, DRC, Malawi, eSwatini and Seychelles)
All 15 countries ratify the global climate change treaty (Paris Agreement)	13 countries (Angola, Botswana, DRC, Lesotho, Madagascar, Mauritius, Mozambique, Namibia, Seychelles, South Africa, eSwatini, Zambia and Zimbabwe)	14 countries (Malawi ratified the Paris Agreement in 2017, joining the original 13)	-1 country (Tanzania)
15 countries have existence of gender-sensitive climate change adaptation and mitigation measures (MERF)	Not measured this period	Sporadic evidence	-15 countries
15 countries design gender-responsive capacity building, education and training on environmental management and climate change for sustainable development initiatives	None - capacity building is mostly gender blind	None - this is not systematic and civil society mainly does it	-15 countries
15 countries have inclusive and partici-patory consultations of all stakeholders including women and men in all environmental management, and climate change for sustainable development programmes and initiatives	1 country (Lesotho at 50% women in decision-making)	One country (Zimbabwe has 50% women in climate change decision-making)	-14 countries (Angola, Botswana, DRC, Lesotho, Madagascar, Malawi, Mauritius, Mozambique, Namibia, Seychelles, South Africa, eSwatini, Tanzania, Zambia)
15 countries shall undertake gender analysis and gender mainstreaming of all environmental management, climate change and sustainable development policies, programmes, projects and budgets - from research programmes to mitigation measures and adaptation plans	None - sporadic, no comprehensive analysis	None - sporadic, no comprehensive analysis	-15 countries
15 countries develop gender-sensitive indicators for environmental management for sustainable development		The data available is ad-hoc and cannot be used for comparative purposes	-15 countries; the MERF for the SADC Gender Protocol should include this
Fifteen countries collect and publish gender-disaggregated data on environmental management, climate change and sustainable development, impacts, mitigation and adaptation at every level to guide appropriate planning and programming.	None.	None - data not usually disaggregated.	-15 gender disaggregated data is mainly available only on land ownership.
Fifteen countries ensure sustainable food production systems and implement resilient agricultural practices that increase productivity and production, that help maintain eco-systems, that strengthen capacity for adaptation to climate change, extreme weather, drought, flooding and other disasters and that progressively improve land and soil quality.	None.	No concrete evidence of sustainable food production and resilient agriculture.	-15 countries (some countries such as Botswana, South Africa and Zimbabwe have improved sustainable food production and Zambia has experienced high growth rates in agricultural production).

Source: Gender Links, 2018.

* The Barometer started tracking climate change in 2012.

The updated Protocol on Gender and Development's gender and climate change provisions help close the gender equality gap around climate change. Article 31, 1a, urging states to develop policies, strategies and programmes to address the gender issues in climate change in accordance with the SADC Protocol on Environment and Sustainable Development, will crucially ensure that governments integrate gender into their climate change initiatives.

Governments have often not been keen to hire gender experts when they formulate policies that inform their strategies and programmes in this area. Gender has typically been an afterthought, which makes it difficult to address at a later stage of policy and programme implementation. Legislators have also often seen environmental management and climate change mitigation as a man's job, yet women throughout the region have more and different interactions with the environment due to their multiple roles.

The revised Protocol, which stakeholders amended in 2016, provides for the empowerment of women, elimination of discrimination, and the promotion of gender equality and equity through gender-responsive legislation, policies, programmes and projects.

Table 10.1 shows empirical progress in this sector as well as progress in tracking indicators, including those linked to the SADC Protocol on Environment and Sustainable Development. It highlights advancements over the past year, noting that Malawi ratified the Paris climate treaty in 2017. Additionally, while Tanzania has not formally ratified, its parliament endorsed a plan to ratify in April 2018. There is still a lot of work needed to encourage gender analyses and ensure countries use gender-disaggregated data. Even though many SADC countries have climate change policies and strategies, they do not yet integrate gender.

Climate change poses a challenge for the SADC countries as they work to achieve the SDGs and implement the Protocol on Environment and Sustainable Development. The impacts of climate change and environmental issues, such as floods, deforestation, air pollution, natural disasters, persistent drought, sea-level rise, coastal erosion and ocean acidification continue to disproportionately affect women and girls.

Access to clean energy sources has focused on electrification. However, households within the SADC region have increasingly acquired solar energy. Yet high prices for solar equipment prevent many women from accessing this energy source. Most SADC countries have not achieved universal electricity and clean water supply. This adds to the burdens that women face in their multiple roles.[1]

Background

The impacts of climate change strongly affect the SADC region. Extreme weather events, such as droughts and floods, pose an increasing threat to the population and, according to climate scena-rios, their frequency and intensity will continue to increase. Along with the projected reduction in rainfall and increase in temper-atures across large parts of the region, experts expect climate change will significantly affect productivity in the agricul-tural sector.[2] In SADC, 77% of the population rely on this sector for income and employment. Climate change therefore presents a serious threat to food security and livelihoods, particularly among poor segments of the population in rural areas.

Women smallholder farmers showcasing their gardending project at Nwajaheni primary school in Nwamitwa village in Tzaneen, South Africa.
Photo: Gender CCSA

Climate change **strongly** affects the SADC region

1   Annual Development Effectiveness review (2015) Level 1 Development in Africa, available at
    https://www.afdb.org/fileadmin/uploads/afdb/Documents/Development_Effectiveness_Review_2015/ADER_2015__En__-_Level_1.pdf
2   https://www.giz.de/en/worldwide/53743.html

The projected changes in the earth's climate have severe social and economic implications. It is important to underscore that vulnerability to climate change is not only related to environmental forces, but also to social conditions. Due to their low capacity to adapt, the poor are often the most vulnerable group. Women, making up a disproportionate share of the poor, are therefore among the most vulnerable groups.

In many parts of the SADC region, climate change threatens decades of efforts aimed at improving women's lives and livelihoods.[3] Unfortunately, women in rural areas lack knowledge about the imminent dangers it poses. The frequency and severity of climate extremes often leaves women unable to cope because they often balance their reproductive and productive roles. Women rely on natural resources for their livelihood; climate change threatens these. Some of the factors that influence the higher vulnerability of women to disasters include lack of means and assets to ensure their own safety in situations of flooding, landslides and storms. With changes in the climate, traditional food sources become more unpredictable and scarce. This exposes women to loss of harvests, often their sole sources of food and income.

Women in SADC have already been affected by some of these challenges in various ways.

In **Angola**, metrological data suggests that its coastline has shown an increased variability in rainfall from one year to the next and coastal areas have experienced increasingly variable rainfall and pressure on water supplies and markets. As a result, climate related risks have worsened. To be able to respond to these climate change impacts, it is important for Angola lawmakers to rigorously assess their country's vulnerability in all sectors and come up with adaptation activities that could strategically respond to the areas of greatest need and reduce the magnitude of harmful climate impacts in a cost-effective manner.[4]

In **Botswana**, research shows that climate change is affecting the freshwater supply because ground water comprises 64% of all water consumed in the country, with 80% of the population - and the majority of livestock - depending on boreholes and well fields. Botswana's annual rainfall levels have been declining and, should this

continue, staple crops of maize and sorghum will also decline by around 30%. However, some believe that if rainfall increases, and temperatures become warmer, sorghum production and maize yields may increase slightly. The country's adaptation strategies should focus on creating national food security programmes, early warning systems for droughts, crop shifting, and food aid for rural populations.[5]

The **DRC**, known for its abundance of water, is currently facing a drinking water problem: only around 26% of the population has access to potable water. As a result, the country falls far below the African average of 60%. About 70% of DRC's population is dependent on rain-fed farming. However, climate change, floods and droughts, extreme weather and unpredictable rains, erosion, and an increase in both crop and livestock diseases, means that traditional agricultural practices have become less effective.

Droughts, cause low agricultural yields and declines in livestock, now regularly affect **Lesotho**.[6] On the other hand, heavy snowfalls, strong winds and heavy floods also negatively impact the Basotho people. Lesotho's high vulnerability to climate risks exacerbates this dire and limits its adaptive capacity. The agribusiness sector has been

In 2018, changing weather patterns in Lesotho had a devastating impact on agriculture, including Mathakanye Monyote's maize garden. *Photo courtesy of CRED: Majara Molupe*

Only **26%** of **DRC** people have access to potable water

3 Source: http://www.pambazuka.org/aumonitor/comments/2690/
4 IIEC (2017), Water resource management under a changing climate in Angola's coastal settlements: working paper, available at pubs.iied.org/pdfs/10833IIED.pdf
5 http://www.adaptation-undp.org/explore/southern-africa/botswana
6 http://www.gcca.eu/national-programmes/africa/gcca-lesotho

heavily impacted because it relies heavily on the natural environment and climate conditions.

 Madagascar is battling climate change impacts that mostly affect its agriculture sector.[7] This results in limited productivity and low yields. The country's lack of technical capacity intensifies this problem. Madagascar's rainfall variability and higher temperatures also affect the production of staple rainfed crops such as rice, cassava and maize. Some projections note that the rainfall variability will intensify in some areas of the country, which will result in increased flooding and erosion. In the south, rainfall will become more unpredictable. Because of increased carbon emissions in the atmosphere, sea temperatures and ocean acidity levels continue to rise, and these threaten coral ecosystems and other marine habitats. Madagascar has the longest coastline of any country in Africa and, due to the sea level rise, increased damage from cyclonic and flooding events will affect its population and ecosystems, which will permanently displace many communities from their homes.

Climate change in **Malawi** affects agriculture production, which is a huge challenge because the country remains heavily reliant on it. Researchers have observed intense rainfall, changing rainfall patterns, floods, droughts and prolonged dry spells due to climate change in Malawi. Climate change is already affecting small-scale producers: those who provide more than half the world's food supply and 70% of the food which feeds people in poor countries like Malawi.

 In **Mauritius**, climate change poses risks to the coastline, changing the appearance of parts of the shoreline and threatening the country's tourist industry.[8] Researchers classify Mauritius as the country with the 13th highest disaster risk and it is the seventh most exposed to natural hazards because it is situated in the Indian Ocean's tropical cyclone belt and may suffer more intense cyclones as temperatures rise. Mauritius is setting up an early warning system that will give three days' notice of storm surges and improve its capacity to evacuate people from vulnerable areas. The country is also working hard to reduce its carbon footprint using solar, wind and wave energy, and it has also pledged to cut its own carbon emissions by 30% by 2030.

In **Mozambique**, scientist attribute an increase in the variety of climate-relevant health problems to global warming. A changing climate has multiplied Mozambique's existing health vulnerabilities, including insufficient access to safe water and improved sanitation, food insecurity, and limited access to health care and education. Additionally, the country faces more droughts, floods and tropical cyclones, which will result in devastating consequences for its population and infrastructure. Severe flooding affects the extensive river plains in downstream areas, often claiming lives and destroying livelihoods, particularly among the poorest of the poor. Droughts and flooding can result in crop losses and food shortages.[9]

 **Namibia** has a high variable climate with warmer waters, including the Benguela current, which marine life depend on for survival. Climate change will mean a reduction of fish stocks, which affects the fishing industry. Climate change also affects agricultural productivity and it has already reduced crop productivity. Temperatures are rising, rainfall variability is increasing, and droughts and floods are becoming more frequent in Namibia. It is reported that, by 2050, current methods of rainfed agriculture will be viable only in the Kavango East and Zambezi regions.[10]

Seychelles relies on tourism and fisheries for economic growth, with fish products making up 96% of the total value of domestic exports, according to the World Bank. But in recent years, the nation has battled severe storms and rising sea levels, while warming ocean temperatures have caused a decline in fish stocks. Like many island nations, Seychelles has relied on mangrove forests and coral reefs to fight back against climate change. However, ocean acidification has worn away coral reefs in the area and the country lacks the economic resources to invest in the infrastructure necessary to fight back against the rising sea levels.[11]

 eSwatini faces droughts and erratic rainfall patterns due to climate change that hamper its development efforts. The 2015-2016 El Niño-induced drought affected agricultural production, particularly sugarcane, maize production and livestock, as well as hydropower production.

7 Climatelinks (2017), Climate Risk Profile: Madagascar, available at https://www.climatelinks.org/resources/climate-change-risk-profile-madagascar
8 https://www.ft.com/content/ecaa3e2c-8436-11e7-94e2-c5b903247afd
9 Climatelinks (2017), Climate Change and Health in Mozambique: Impacts on diarrheal disease and Malaria, available at https://www.climatelinks.org/sites/default/files/asset/document/20180226_USAID-ATLAS_Mozambique-Health-and-Climate-Change.pdf
10 https://www.newera.com.na/2018/03/02/namibia-needs-n400bn-for-climate-change/
11 https://qz.com/1216791/seychelles-swaps-debt-for-marine-conservation-climate-change/

Researchers estimate that the country's drought disaster cost it USD $325 billion, which amounted to 7.01% of eSwatini's Gross Domestic Product (GDP).[12]

South Africa has been warming faster than the global average trend. This has resulted in water shortages, including a major water crisis in Cape Town in 2018 that almost resulted in the second most populous city in the country running out of water. The Vaal Dam, one of the largest sources of water supply to Gauteng Province, had also begun to dry up before recent rains. Increases in climate variability and climatic extremes impact both water quality and availability through changes in rainfall patterns, with more intense storms, floods and droughts, changes in soil moisture and runoff, and the resulting effects of increasing evaporation and changing temperatures on aquatic systems.[13] The entire country has been experiencing a serious drought since 2015, with associated crop losses, water restrictions, and impacts on food and water security.

According to the Global Gender and Climate Alliance (GGCA), **Tanzania**'s economy depends on sectors affected by climate change.[14] Climate variability results in significant damage to the country's economy. Studies estimate that climate change will lead to large economic costs, amounting to 1-2% of GDP per year by 2030. Researchers predict that average temperatures in Tanzania will increase to more than 30°C by 2050 (from the current highs of 20-24°C), with significant rainfall variation. Climate change impacts will make large areas of land unsuitable for agricultural production.

Zambia has been facing increased droughts and floods over the last 30 years due to climate change and this has cost the country more than US$13.8 billion according to recent estimates - equivalent to 4% of annual GDP growth. Zambia has also seen many climate change impacts on the health and agricultural sectors. Climate change has resulted in crop failure in some cases, and thus reduced food security in the country.[15]

Zimbabwe has been experiencing much hotter daytime temperatures and the amount of precipitation it receives has frequently deviated from the mean. Climate change has adverse impacts on the lives and wellbeing of Zimbabweans, constraining or reversing progress in social and human development. The impacts of climate change have become more evident with increased incidence of droughts, floods and hailstorms, as well as more hot days and heatwaves. These pose serious problems with far-reaching social, economic, political and environmental consequences. In Zimbabwe, climate change threatens to stall the country's development as well as pose a serious risk to food security and the adaptive capacity of the Zimbabwean population, especially those in vulnerable communities.[16]

Dry riverbeds, like this one in Botswana, are increasingly common sights in SADC.
Photo: Gomolemo Rasesigo

[12] http://www.acclimatise.uk.com/2018/03/14/eSwatini-on-track-to-accessing-the-green-climate-fund/
[13] https://www.traveller24.com/Explore/Green/cop23-climatic-extremes-sas-biggest-climate-change-concern-20171114
[14] http://www.gcca.eu/national-programmes/africa/gcca-tanzania2
[15] https://undp-adaptation.exposure.co/bridging-gaps-in-zambia
[16] UNDP (2017), Zimbabwe Human Development Report, Climate Change and Human Development : Towards Building a Resilient Nation, available at http://hdr.undp.org/sites/default/files/reports/2842/undp_zw_2017zhdr_full.pdf

SA warming faster than the global average

Table 10.2: Gender dimensions of climate change[17][18]	
Area of concern	**Gender implications**
Food security	Most women in the region take part in farming, but women as a group have trouble obtaining education, income, land, livestock, and technology. This means that climate change may negatively impact female farmers more than male farmers by further limiting their resources. Women produced between 60% and 80% of all food in the developing world, yet they own just 10% of all agricultural land and approximately 2% of land rights.
Water	Many countries in the region have been experiencing droughts and water shortages. This has compromised the livelihoods of many communities, particularly of women and young girls whose responsibility, in many countries, is to ensure availability of water. They now must travel long distances to collect water, often exposing themselves to dangerous threats such as human trafficking and sexual violence.
Division of labour	Gender-based prejudices and stereotypes exclude women from areas of the green economy such as transport and energy, wasting human resources to and preventing the SADC region from achieving its full competitive potential.
School drop-out	In many countries, girls and young women have been forced to stay out of school to look for opportunities to generate income for their families as agricultural production in the region declines.
Land	Women, especially single women and widows, still struggle to access land for resettlement and production, including farming to generate income for their families.
Transport	Women depend on access to public transport to a larger degree due to lower levels of car ownership, but also because of their preferences for the use of environmentally-friendly solutions (public transport).
Health	Women are more likely to have a greater awareness of health issues and more highly developed risk perceptions, which often impacts how they perceive health and environmental issues, while men tend to be more strongly oriented towards convenience.
Stress	Stress levels and related diseases may increase for both women and men. Because society expects men to provide for the family, they experience and express stress in different, often more devastating ways than women.
Migration	In many countries, men migrate from rural areas and small towns to move to big cities due to declines of natural resources and agriculture. They often leave women behind to care for the children and the elderly on their own.
Gender violence	Incidents of sexual violence remain frequent in shelters where natural disaster victims take refuge and men and women share limited space with no privacy. These shelter also often lack safe and adequate ablution blocks and often women and girls must walk alone outside at night to relieve themselves, risking sexual abuse.
Energy Poverty	Due to their lower average income, women are at greater risk of energy poverty than men, and have fewer options for investing in low-carbon options such as energy efficiency and renewable energies.
Decision-making	The climate change sector does not equally include men and women at decision-making levels. There is an urgent need to improve gender equality in decision-making in this field, especially the transport and energy sectors, and to increase the number of women with relevant qualifications in scientific and technological areas. as well as the number of women participating in relevant scientific bodies at the highest level.

Source: GenderCCSA 2016.

Table 10.2 illustrates several gender dimensions of climate change. It shows how climate change has become a cause of conflict and how it perpetuates poverty, gender-based violence (GBV) and an increased burden of care work amongst women.

Gender aware climate change policies

Article 31.1a: State parties shall develop policies, strategies, and programmes to address the gender issues in climate change in accordance with the SADC Protocol on Environment and Sustainable Development.
Article 20.2 of the Protocol on Environmental Management for Sustainable Development: State parties shall undertake gender analysis and gender mainstreaming of all environmental management, climate change and sustainable development policies, programmes, projects and budgets.

---

[17] UNESCO (2017), Women underrepresented in decision-making on climate change, available on http://www.unesco.org/new/en/media-services/single-view/news/women_underrepresented_in_decision_making_on_climate_change/ (accessed on 11July 2017).
[18] Wikipedia (2017), Climate Change and Gender, available on https://en.wikipedia.org/wiki/Climate_change_and_gender (accessed 11 July 2017).

produce
60%
to **80%**
of
food
but
own
just
10%
of land
and
2%
land
rights

The United Nations Framework Convention on Climate Change (UNFCCC) is the main international agreement on climate action. It comprises one of three conventions adopted at the Rio Earth Summit in 1992. To date, 195 countries have ratified it. It began as a way for countries to work together to limit global temperature increases and climate change, and to cope with their impacts.

Two of the most prominent issues related to the UNFCCC include:
1. The ratification of the Doha amendment to the Kyoto Protocol, which concerns commitments under the second period, running from 2013-2020; and
2. The Paris Agreement - new global climate change agreement covering all UNFCCC countries, its ratification, implementation and entering into force in 2020.

A woman in Bizana, South Africa, prepares to make a Wonderbag: an environmentally-friendly, non-electric heat-retention cooker.
Photo: GenderCCSA

Kyoto Protocol
In the mid-1990s, the UNFCCC signatories realised that they needed stronger provisions to reduce emissions. In 1997, they agreed on the Kyoto Protocol, which introduced legally binding emission reduction targets for developed countries. The second commitment period of the Kyoto Protocol began on 1 January 2013 and will end in 2020. Thirty-eight developed countries, including the EU and its 28-member states, participate. This second

period is covered by the Doha amendment, under which participating countries have committed to reducing emissions by at least 18% less than 1990 levels. The EU has committed to reducing emissions in this period to 20% less than 1990 levels. As the United States never signed up to the Kyoto Protocol, Canada pulled out before the end of the first commitment period and Russia, Japan and New Zealand are not taking part in the second commitment period, it only now applies to around 14% of the world's emissions. However, more than 70 developing and developed countries have made various non-binding commitments to reduce or limit their greenhouse gas emissions.

The United Nations Framework Convention on Climate Change (UNFCCC)
The UNFCCC is an international environmental treaty adopted on 9 May 1992 and opened for signature at the Earth Summit in Rio de Janeiro from 3-14 June 1992. It then entered into force on 21 March 1994, after enough countries had ratified it. The UNFCCC objective is to "stabilise greenhouse gas concentrations in the atmosphere at a level that would prevent dangerous anthropogenic interference with the climate system." The framework sets non-binding limits on greenhouse gas emissions for individual countries and contains no enforcement mechanisms. Instead, it outlines how specific international treaties (called "protocols" or "agreements") may be negotiated to specify further action towards the UNFCCC objective.

The parties to the convention have met annually since 1995 in Conferences of the Parties (COPs) to assess progress in dealing with climate change. In 1997, they concluded the Kyoto Protocol and established legally binding obligations for developed countries to reduce their greenhouse gas emissions in the period 2008-2012. The 2010 United Nations Climate Change Conference produced an agreement stating that future global warming should be limited to below 2.0 °C (3.6 °F) relative to the pre-industrial level. Signatories amended the Protocol in 2012 to encompass the period 2013-2020 in the Doha Amendment, which, as of 2018, had not entered into force because three quarters of the signatories had not yet deposited their instruments of acceptance. In 2015, world leaders adopted the Paris Agreement, governing emission reductions from 2020 on through commitments of countries in ambitious Nationally Determined Contributions (NDCs). The Paris Agreement entered into force on 4 November 2016.

One of the first tasks set by the UNFCCC was for signatory nations to establish national inventories of greenhouse gas (GHG) emissions and removals, which stakeholders used to create the 1990 benchmark levels for accession of countries to the Kyoto Protocol and for the commitment of those countries to GHG reductions. Countries must submit updated inventories annually.

UNFCCC is also the name of the UN secretariat charged with supporting the operation of the Convention, with offices in Bonn, Germany. From 2010 to 2016, Christiana Figueres served as the head of the secretariat. In July 2016, Patricia Espinosa succeeded Figueres. The secretariat, augmented through the parallel efforts of the IPCC, aims to gain consensus through meetings and the discussion of various strategies.

The Paris Agreement
The Paris Agreement provides nations with an action plan to limit global warming "well below" 2°C covering the period from 2020 onwards.[19]

The main elements of the Paris Agreement:
- *Long-term goal:* governments agreed to keep the increase in global average temperature to less than 2°C above pre-industrial levels and pursue efforts to limit it to 1.5°C;
- *Contributions:* before and during the Paris conference countries submitted comprehensive national climate action plans to reduce their emissions;
- *Ambition:* governments agreed to communicate their contributions every five years to set more ambitious targets;
- *Transparency:* they also accepted to report to each other and the public on how well they do to implement their targets, to ensure transparency and oversight; and
- *Solidarity:* the EU and other developed countries will continue to provide climate finance to assist developing countries, both to reduce emissions and build resilience to climate change impacts.

Under the Paris Agreement (1/CP.21) parties acknowledge that, as climate change is a common concern of humankind:

"Parties should, when taking action to address climate change, respect, promote and consider their respective obligations on human rights, the right to health, the rights of indigenous peoples, local communities, migrants, children, persons with disabilities and people in vulnerable situations and the right to development, as well as gender equality, empowerment of women and intergenerational equity."[20]

Women in South Africa receive farming equipment to help with local agriculture projects. The Paris Agreement allows for assistance to build resilience to climate change in the developing world, including in countries like South Africa.   *Photo: GenderCCSA*

In recognition of the need for women and men to have equal representation in all aspects of the Convention process as well as for climate action to respond to their different needs, experiences, priorities and capacities, signatories focused on two goals under the dedicated gender and climate change agenda item:

1. Improving gender balance and increasing the participation of women in all UNFCCC processes, including in delegations and in bodies constituted under the Convention and its Kyoto Protocol, and
2. Increasing awareness and support for the development and effective implementation of gender-responsive climate policy at the regional, national and local levels.

Two years after the adoption of the Paris Agreement and one year after it entered into force, the main goal of COP-23 in Bonn, Germany, from 6-17 November 2017 revolved around moving forward in defining the guidelines for its implementation. Overall, delegates noted that progress on this critical issue remains too slow and parties left Bonn with a considerable remaining workload if they are serious about finalising the "rulebook" next year at COP-24 in Katowice, Poland. Delegates expressed concerns about the absence of human rights and gender equality in the negotiations on implementation guidelines. In order to be in accordance with the preamble of the Paris Agreement, the guidelines must protect and implement human rights, the rights of indigenous peoples, local communities, migrants, children, persons with disabilities and people in vulnerable situations, and ensure that gender equality, empowerment of women and intergenerational equity remain at

[19] http://www.consilium.europa.eu/en/policies/climate-change/timeline/
[20] https://unfccc.int/topics/gender/the-big.../gender-in-the-intergovernmental-process

Droughts and water shortages

the heart of all climate action by countries under the Paris Agreement. All stakeholders must also sufficiently mainstream these into all workstreams of the Convention. This includes the mainstreaming of gender issues into parties' NDCs - particularly industrialised countries whose NDCs completely lack any references to gender. Gender justice is not only relevant for developing countries.

Gender dimensions of the UNFCCC

The UNFCCC secretariat has been reporting on the composition of national delegations since 2013. Women's participation in national delegations to COP sessions and other meetings under the UNFCCC has varied from a low of 29% attending COP-18 in 2013 to a high of 42% attending the 44th and 46th sessions of the subsidiary bodies in 2016/2017 and 2017/2018. Stakeholders recorded the highest participation of women at a COP after the adoption of decision 23/CP.18 at COP-19: 36%, up from 29% at COP-18. However, at COP-21 and COP-22 the percentage of women fell from the high of 36% to 32%. The highest recorded percentage of female heads of delegation occurred at COP-22, with 27%. This may reflect a lower number of women in senior positions in environment and climate ministries or departments at a national level, from which many parties appoint their delegates to UNFCCC meetings.[21]

There has been gradual but sustained progress in the last decades in recognising and acknowledging the need for equal representation and participation of men and women in decision-making processes to sustainably address climate change. Women bring different perspectives into policymaking processes and programme development. Their participation in every step of the process is essential to ensure the development of sustainable, equitable and inclusive policies and programmes that have long-lasting impact.

This discussion began in 2012, when parties to the UNFCCC considered gender and climate change as a stand-alone agenda item under the COP and the Subsidiary Body for Implementation (SBI). In addition, parties have considered and incorporated gender considerations in many other thematic areas (e.g. finance, technology development and transfer and adaptation) under the Convention and its Kyoto Protocol and Paris Agreement

The government of Fiji presided over the 23rd UNFCCC conference in Bonn, which took place two years after the adoption of the Paris Agreement and one year after it entered into force. While COP-23 represented many missed opportunities and half-hearted commitments it also had two noteworthy success stories: the adoption of the first Gender Action Plan (GAP) to the UNFCCC and the operationalisation of the local communities and indigenous peoples platform.[22]

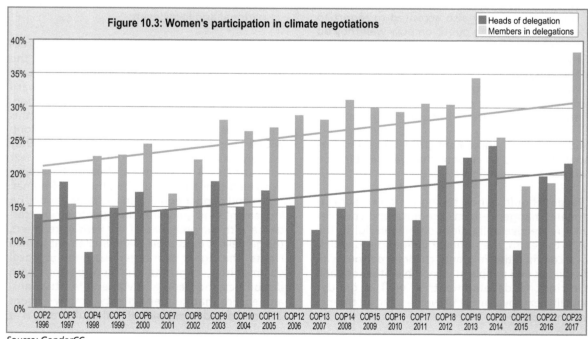

Figure 10.3: Women's participation in climate negotiations

Source: GenderCC.

---

[21] UNFCCC (2017), Achieving the goal of gender balance: Technical paper by the secretariat, available on https://unfccc.int/resource/docs/2017/tp/08.pdf
[22] https://gendercc.net/genderunfccc/unfccc-conferences/bonn-2017.html

278   SADC Gender Protocol 2018 Barometer

Figure 10.1 shows women's participation in COP climate negotiations over time. The head of delegations increased to just less than 25% in 2017 compared to less than 20% in 2016. Additionally, women members of delegations rose dramatically in 2017 compared to 2016.

Women and Gender Constituency of the UNFCCC

The UNFCCC recognises the Women and Gender Constituency (WGC) as one of its nine official observer constituencies. Members of civil society and NGOs make up the constituency groups, which have been broadly grouped into businesses and industry organisations; environmental organisations; local and municipal governments; trade unions; research and independent organisations; and organisations that work for the rights of indigenous people; young people, agricultural workers, and women rights and gender advocacy. Each constituency provides a focal point for easier interaction with the UNFCCC secretariat and individual governments.[23]

The WGC provides several ways for civil society and NGOs working on women's rights and gender justice, environmental protection, or both, to influence the annual conferences and shape the UNFCCC. It provides a platform to exchange information between members and with the UNFCCC secretariat. The constituency also ensures that meetings, workshops and conferences include the participation and representation of women's civil society and NGOs which otherwise would not be able to attend.

Over the past several years of the international climate change negotiations governments across the world, serving as parties to the UNFCCC, have agreed that gender equality and ensuring women's human rights are necessary to climate change mitigation and adaptation. The UN's efforts to reduce greenhouse gas emissions will only succeed through the promotion of rights and justice and the full participation of women. The WGC is working to ensure that women's rights and gender justice remain core elements of the UN Framework Convention on Climate Change. It represents women's and environmental civil society organisations at the annual COPs.

The WGC also fights to ensure that stakeholders embed women's voices and rights in the process and results of the international framework for a sustainable and just future. According to the WGC, the full participation of women and the promotion of rights and justice remains crucial to the success

of any UN efforts to reduce greenhouse gas emissions.[24]

The first Gender Action Plan (GAP) of the UNFCCC

At COP-23, stakeholders reached a decision that marks a milestone in longstanding efforts to integrate gender into international climate policy: the first Gender Action Plan (GAP) under the UNFCCC.[25] It defines five priority areas for action and contains a set of 16 specific activities for the upcoming two years. These include: in-session workshops for delegates on how to develop gender-responsive climate policies, plans and programmes, and the promotion of travel funds to support the participation of women (in particular grassroots, local and indigenous women) from developing countries. Together, these activities aim to advance the implementation of the various gender-related decisions and mandates that already exist but have yet to be sufficiently implemented under the UNFCCC.

A woman in Bizana, South Africa, makes a Wonderbag.
Photo: GenderCCSA

The GAP acknowledges that, so far, the UNFCCC has made little progress towards women's equal participation and developing and implementing gender-just climate policies and actions. It marks a significant step forward in the efforts to advance gender equality in the international climate process.

---

[23] http://womengenderclimate.org/about-us/
[24] http://www.wecf.eu/english/campaigns/2014/Gender-Constituency.php
[25] https://gendercc.net/genderunfccc/unfccc-conferences/bonn-2017.html

SDG13

"UNFCCC is the primary inter-national, inter-govern-mental forum for negoti-ating the global response to climate change"

The test, however, will be in its implementation. For it to live up to its promises, parties must come forward with generous voluntary contributions to supply the necessary funds for each activity.

The GAP also lacks some essential elements. For example, while it includes capacity-building on mechanisms to integrate gender issues into finance, such as gender budgeting, it does not mention the advancement of, and capacity-building on, tools such as Gender Impact Assessments that stake-holders see as crucial for the development of gender-responsive climate adaptation and miti-gation policies. In addition, the UNFCCC has watered down the section on monitoring and reporting on GAP activities, even though stake-holders see it as indispensable to ensure the imple-mentation, and to evaluate the outcomes, of the GAP. Under no circumstance can the GAP turn into yet another hard-won, but vastly ignored, gender-related UNFCCC decision.[26]

Another question remains around the GAP: how will it feed into and inform other negotiation streams crucial for gender mainstreaming progress in the UNFCCC, such as the frameworks and mecha-nisms for finance, technology, and transparency? Climate and gender justice are crucial for the entire process and all countries must integrate human rights and gender equality in their climate plans and formal commitments.

The decisions adopted at COP-23 contain some critical elements. They build on the principles defined by indigenous peoples' organisations, including the need for equal footing with parties in the platform. They also refer to the UN Decla-ration on the Rights of Indigenous Peoples. The platform aims at strengthening the consideration of indigenous peoples' knowledge, technologies, practices and efforts in climate action, enhancing the effective engagement of indigenous peoples in the UNFCCC process, and facilitating the exchange of experience and best practices on mitigation and adaptation.

Yet a tremendous gap continues to exist between the current commitments of countries and the actions needed to keep global warming below 1.5°C. Not even the presidency of the Government of Fiji and the strong presence and leadership of civil society organisations and activists from small island states that carried the stories and the lived realities of people at the frontlines of climate

change moved countries to raise their ambitions. For instance, Germany, the host of this year's COP, will not meet its 2020 targets while it continues to expand coal mining projects and refuses to initiate a phase-out of its fossil fuel production. All economies worldwide must end their dependency on fossil fuels and radically cut greenhouse gas emissions.[27]

The Sustainable Development Goals

The UN Sustainable Development Goals (SDGs) acknowledge the link between the achievement of gender equality and the achievement of all SDGs, including Goal 13 on climate change. Climate change and sustainable development remain inextricably linked. Despite this fact, there is no formal interrelationship between their designated international processes, namely the UNFCCC and the 2030 Agenda for Sustainable Development.

On the one hand, the 2030 Agenda contains an SDG on climate change (SDG-13). SDG 13 acknow-ledges that the "UNFCCC is the primary interna-tional, intergovernmental forum for negotiating the global response to climate change." On the other hand, while the UNFCCC's Subsidiary Body for Scientific and Technological Advice (SBSTA) acknowledges the "importance and interlinkages" of climate and the sustainable development agenda, the reality is that the UNFCCC's secretariat merely "follows the latter, recognising that they are two separate but parallel processes."[28]

It is important to firstly recognise that there are connections. Article 4, paragraph 1(c) of the UNFCCC requires the parties to cooperate to reduce greenhouse gas emissions in the energy, transport, industry, agriculture and forestry sectors. These correspond to SDG-7 (energy), SDG-11 (cities), SDG-9 (industrialisation), SDG-2 (agriculture) and SDG-15 (forests). Further, Article 4, paragraph 1(d) of the UNFCCC requires the parties to cooperate with respect to biomass, forests and oceans, and other terrestrial, coastal and marine ecosystems. These correspond to SDG-14 (oceans, seas and marine resources) and SDG-15 (terrestrial ecosystems, forests, desertification, land degradation and biodiversity).[29]

Secondly, there must be recognition that stake-holders can connect the two overall objectives through the cooperation of international and intergovernmental and non-governmental organisations. Article 7, paragraph 2(l) of the

---

[26] GFDRR (2016) Gender Action Plan : 2016-2021, Fall 2016 Consultative Group Meeting, available at https://www.gfdrr.org/sites/default/files/publication/gender-action-plan-2016-2021.pdf
[27] GenderCC & LIFE (2017) A large step towards gender-just climate policies, but too little overall progress : a joint statement on the outcomes of COP23, available at https://gendercc.net/fileadmin/inhalte/dokumente/6_UNFCCC/COPs/GenderCC_LIFE_Statement_COP23.pdf
[28] http://17goals.org/paris-agreement-sdgs/
[29] Leong, Alvin, Connecting the Dots between the UNFCCC and the SDGs (December 10, 2015). Available at SSRN: https://ssrn.com/abstract=2702831

UNFCCC states that the COP shall: "seek and utilise, where appropriate, the services and cooperation of, and information provided by, competent international organisations and intergovernmental and non-governmental bodies." This is actually a legal mandate - the word "shall" is used.

The UNFCCC contains interrelationships with Agenda 2030 and the SDGs and provides express authority to connect these dots through the facilitation of international and non-governmental organisations. Connecting the dots will require political will, a critical asset at this inflection point when the world moves towards managing the climate crisis while simultaneously implementing a new, ambitious agenda for sustainable development.

Regional frameworks

African Union commitments

The African Union (AU) rallied and coordinated African support for the Paris Agreement. This effort brought the continent of Africa together as one voice to speak on climate change. A common position signalled African countries' commitment to the problem. Some African countries have led climate change mitigation and adaptation policies. These include Ghana, Morocco, Kenya and South Africa. These countries have long integrated climate change issues into their national development planning and implementation across multiple sectors. In addition, Ethiopia came up with its Climate Resilient Green Economy Strategy and a climate finance fund within its ministry of finance for climate compatible investment.[30]

At UN climate conferences, African countries have also been a leading voice in the Group of 77, the coalition of developing countries. Concerns for developing countries, however, remain - particularly around finance, technology transfer and mechanisms for equitable contributions for dealing with climate risk.

At COP-23 in Bonn, attendees celebrated Africa Day on 15 November 2017: a joint initiative of the African Development Bank (AfDB), the African Union Commission (AUC), the United Nations Economic Commission for Africa (ECA) and the New Partnership for Africa's Development (NEPAD). Two years after leaders signed the Paris Agreement at COP-21, African nations continued to consolidate efforts, focusing particularly on partnerships to ensure that developed countries meet their

responsibilities and commitments in terms of funding and encouraging African nations to pursue a low-carbon development path and maintain their nationally-determined contributions. All of this is in line with the UN's SDGs, the AfDB and the AU's Agenda 2063.

A group of South African women harvest produce to sell at Risenga Primary School in Siyandhani, Giyani.   *Photo: GenderCCSA*

The AU adopted this agenda in 2015 with the aim of having a roadmap for strong, peaceful, integrated and prosperous Africa by 2063, 100 years after the establishment of its predecessor, the Organisation for African Unity (OAU).[31] Despite the challenges, African countries remain committed to the agenda. At the 24th Ordinary Assembly of the AU in Addis Ababa in January 2015, members adopted the document Agenda 2063, which could be a game changer for the continent. It is both a vision and an action plan. In the three years since, African nations have made some progress in implementing the vision. Lawmakers have increasingly aligned the new AU development strategies to the Agenda 2063 goals. However, the Agenda is an ambitious project, which needs the political will of all the countries involved and sustained implementation at the levels of state, region, and continent.

At COP-23, the theme for Africa Day, "Partnerships to Implement the Paris Agreement: Africa's Response," accompanied a programme focused on funding, capacity-building, development and technology transfer.[32] Stakeholders also used Africa Day to launch the Africa Nationally Determined Contributions Hub (Africa NDC Hub), a support platform set up by the AfDB and partners: AUC,

> At UN climate conferences, African countries have also been a leading voice in the Group of 77

---

[30] https://www.brookings.edu/blog/africa-in-focus/2017/06/02/even-before-the-u-s-left-the-paris-agreement-africa-stepped-up-to-the-plate-on-climate-change/
[31] Viswanathan, H. H. S (2018) Africa's Agenda 2063: a document of hope, available at https://www.orfonline.org/research/africas-agenda-2063-a-document-of-hope/
[32] https://www.afdb.org/en/news-and-events/africa-day-at-cop23-17551/

UNFCCC, United Nations Development Programme (UNDP), United Nations Environment Programme (UNEP), Food and Agriculture Organisation (FAO), United Nations Economic Commission for Africa (UNECA), NEPAD, Economic Commission for West Africa States (ECOWAS), World Wide Fund for Nature (WWF), and International Institute for Environment and Development (IIED). The Africa NDC works in collaboration with the NDC Partnership to deliver targeted support to African countries as they implement their NDCs.

Meanwhile, the 28th Summit of the Heads of State and Government of the AU, held in February 2017, addressed the alignment between Africa's Agenda 2063, the 2030 Agenda for Sustainable Development and the Paris Agreement on climate change. Reports noted that the AU and the UN will cooperate on implementing and monitoring the SDGs and the Paris Agreement with only one line of reporting. After centuries of marginalisation during the colonial and neo-colonial periods, Africa today has a new resurgence, both politically and economically. The time is ripe for the African people to define and achieve their aspirations for a peaceful and prosperous continent. Leaders have been rekindling the old pan-African spirit, manifested in the ambitious and forward-looking Agenda 2063. Given the seriousness attached to this vision, there is no reason African nations should not achieve most, if not all, targets by 2063.[33]

SADC frameworks for climate change
While the entire world is struggling with the challenges presented by the changing global climate, Southern Africa is uniquely susceptible to the impacts of climate change. In coming decades, experts expect the SADC region to experience higher land and ocean surface temperatures than in the past, which will affect rainfall, winds and the timing and intensity of weather events. As noted earlier in this chapter, climate change poses several risks to SADC goals for regional economic development. Increased frequency of floods, cyclones and droughts may damage infrastructure, destroy agricultural crops, disrupt livelihoods, and cause loss of life.

SADC leaders have committed to several international conventions and programmes on climate change. All SADC Member States have signed on to the following conventions:
• The United Nations Framework Convention on Climate Change, which advocates for reduced emissions toward lowering global temperatures and offers guidance on coping with the impacts of climate change;

• The Ramsar Convention on Wetlands, which specifically targets the preservation of internationally important wetlands and contains a resolution covering climate change impacts, adaptation and mitigation; and
• The Convention on Biological Diversity, which has resulted in numerous decisions and technical papers describing the links between biodiversity and mitigation of climate change effects.

Furthermore, a Memorandum of Understanding between SADC and the World Food Programme highlights adaptation to climate change as one of six principal areas for cooperation. Similarly, stakeholders associated with the African Ministerial Conference on the Environment (AMCEN) and the regional climate change programme have developed a framework of sub-regional climate change programmes.

The SADC Gender and Development Protocol
Stakeholders recently revised the SADC Protocol on Gender and Development so that its objectives align with various global targets and emerging issues. It now covers emerging issues such as climate change. The 36th SADC Summit, held in eSwatini in August 2016, approved the revision and sought to align it with provisions of other instruments relating to sustainable management of the environment as well as the SADC Industrialisation Strategy and Roadmap.

Women learning to use renewable energy and energy effinecent technology in Joubert Park and Alexandra township, South Africa.
Photo: GenderCCSA

SADC **leaders** have committed to **address** climate change

33 http://sdg.iisd.org/news/au-summit-addresses-alignment-between-agenda-2063-paris-agreement-and-2030-agenda/
34 https://www.sadc.int/news-events/news/botswana-signs-revised-sadc-protocol-gender-and-development/

The Protocol now also aligns with the UN SDGs, the African Charter on the Rights of Women in Africa and the AU Agenda 2063. The SADC Gender Protocol Monitoring, Evaluation and Reporting Framework (MERF) and SADC Gender and Development Monitor remain in place to assess progress on the implementation of the instruments and SADC priorities. The SADC region pledged support towards the realisation of Development Agenda 2030 and AU Agenda 2063 in improving the livelihoods of women, especially of women in rural communities, and investing in youth for sustainable development.

The SADC Protocol on Environmental Management for Sustainable Development

The SADC Protocol on Environmental Management for Sustainable Development's main objective is to promote sustainable utilisation and trans-boundary management of the environment. It covers environmental issues such as climate change, waste and pollution, management of chemicals, bio-diversity and natural heritage, sustainable land management, marine and inland resources, as well as cross-cutting issues on gender, science, technology, trade and investment.[35]

The Protocol aims to enhance the protection of the environment; promote equitable and sustainable use of natural resources and the environment; promote shared management of trans-boundary environment and natural resources and promote effective management and response to impacts of climate change and variability. It also facilitates the harmonisation of policies, strategies and legal frameworks to enhance regional coordination of environmental management, as well as regional integration and it provides a legal framework for trans-boundary environment and natural resources.

Adaptation in the water sector

Climate change has already affected water resources in the SADC region and experts predict that access to water will continue to decrease. Thus, the SADC Secretariat has been developing a Climate Change Adaptation (CCA) strategy for the water sector with the goal of lessening impacts of climate change through adaptive water resources development and management in the region. SADC intends to achieve this goal by intervening in all areas of the water sector to decrease climate vulnerability and ensure that water management practices cope with increased climate variability.[36]

The strategy recognises that water issues impact a range of sectors such as energy, health, and agriculture and, as a result, adaptation measures must exist at different levels of governance. Additionally, water administration in the SADC region falls under the Integrated Water Resources Management (IWRM) approach, which offers a goal-oriented system of controlling use of water as a means of slowing the effects of climate change in the region.

The SADC Secretariat, jointly with the Common Market for Eastern and Southern Africa (COMESA) and the East African Community (EAC), facilitates the implementation of a Tripartite Programme on Climate Change that the Norwegian Government, through the Norwegian Ministry of Foreign Affairs, the European Union Commission (EUC) and the UK Department for International Development (DFID) jointly fund. The programme "aims to inject Africa's unified position on climate change into the post-2012 United Nations Framework Convention on Climate Change (UNFCCC) global agreement so as to unlock resources for promoting strategic interventions that sustain productivity and livelihood improvements for millions of climate-vulnerable people in the region."[37]

National strategies

Botswana's Ministry of Environment, Natural Resources Conservation and Tourism is working with Botswana's National Climate Change Committee (NCCC) to develop a climate change policy and strategy: the National Climate Change Policy and Strategy and Action Plan (NCCSAP), which the ministry will implement in cooperation with the UNDP.[38] The NCCSAP has a number of objectives: to develop and implement appropriate adaptation strategies and actions to decrease vulnerability to the impacts of climate change; to develop actions and strategies for climate change mitigation; to integrate climate change effectively into policies and institutional and development frameworks, in recognition of the cross-cutting nature of climate change; and to ensure that Botswana is ready for the post-2015 climate regime when stakeholders will finalise a new Protocol applicable to all parties. Other national initiatives already exist, such as the ongoing Ngamiland Sustainable Land Management Project (NSLMP), designed to enhance resilience and reduce vulnerability of communities to climate change. Botswana submitted its Intended Nationally Determined Contribution (INDC) in 2015, which

---

[35] https://pmg.org.za/committee-meeting/25617/
[36] https://www.sadc.int/themes/meteorology-climate/climate-change-adaptation/
[37] Ibid.
[38] http://southsouthnorth.org/wp-content/uploads/Botswana-diagnostic-2017.05.10.pdf

legislators converted to an NDC in 2016. Botswana intends to reduce overall emissions by 15%, from the base year of 2010, by 2030, at an anticipated cost of US$18.4 billion. The INDC does not specify sources of funding for implementation of mitigation measures or share of government and international contribution to support them, but it identifies the need to clarify these points. Legislators based mitigation estimations on three sectors: energy (mobile and stationary), waste and agriculture. The calculation does not include CH4 emissions from livestock farming - mostly from enteric fermentation - but Botswana plans to implement mitigation measures for this sector (Botswana Government, 2015).

Lesotho's Ministry of Energy and Meteorology submitted its INDC in 2015 (Lesotho Ministry of Energy and Meteorology, 2015). Legislators converted it to an NDC in 2017, which contains greater detail than most other SADC countries, especially on sector specific emissions data.[39] The NDC identifies the need to:

- Build capacity with experts and stakeholders in the preparation and collection of data to enhance information management, ownership, information exchange and dissemination of information sharing within and across sectors;
- Create systemic enabling working environments for the implementation of climate change activities, with regard to institutional arrangements, performance management and reporting to ascertain roles and responsibilities, political will, ownership and empowerment, decision making and service delivery;

Women collect and sort rubbish at the Leribe rubbish dump in Lesotho. The country's climate adaptation strategy includes gender considerations along with measures to reduce women's workload. *Photo: Gender Links*

- Develop a database for reporting raw data, taking into consideration IPCC requirements by carrying out new studies to upgrade the datasets and then making use of remotely sensed data and training on Geographic Information Systems (GIS);
- Obtain data from satellite/remote sensing, including land cover data, and then design consistent reporting formats for the reports;
- Coordinate data pools to establish data archiving and sharing protocols; and
- Support research in climate change.

Unusually, Lesotho's NDC includes gender considerations, noting that women are more vulnerable to climate change because of their relationship with natural resources: women hold responsibility for family food security through food collection, crop production, meal preparation, piggeries, and poultry farming. Household responsibilities - including child-rearing, domestic management and meal preparation - often require women to work longer hours than men. The NDC states that climate change adaptation interventions in Lesotho should include measures to reduce women's workload. Additionally, it states that the formative years of the boy child include herding livestock, to the detriment of their education. Climate change may push good grazing further from villages, thereby affecting boy children negatively. In addition, extreme weather events like heavy snow will increase the risks of herding in remote cattle posts.[40]

Lesotho does not have an official medium- to long-term national climate change adaptation plan. However, it has a formal commitment to developing a new national climate change policy and a sustainable energy policy, with support from the EU.

Madagascar sees a variety of weather and climate phenomena with wide-ranging impacts on human health and safety, natural resource 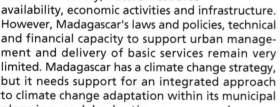 availability, economic activities and infrastructure. However, Madagascar's laws and policies, technical and financial capacity to support urban management and delivery of basic services remain very limited. Madagascar has a climate change strategy, but it needs support for an integrated approach to climate change adaptation within its municipal planning and budgeting processes because lawmakers have drafted local development plans and budgets without robust or comprehensive climate change vulnerability assessments. Participatory budgeting processes could help build

---

[39] http://southsouthnorth.org/wp-content/uploads/Lesotho-diagnostic-2017.05.10.pdf
[40] http://www4.unfccc.int/ndcregistry/PublishedDocuments/Lesotho%20First/Lesotho%27s%20INDC%20Report%20%20-%20September%202015.pdf

capacity and transparency around municipal projects, encouraging greater contribution from taxpayers to fill funding gaps. Madagascar needs multisectoral workshops to ensure participation of regional agents of the national disaster management office, the meteorological agency, and the national climate change office at strategic points within regional and local development planning processes. This would encourage broader buy-in for adaptation objectives.[41]

Mozambique and Madagascar develop mitigation strategies to address disasters

Mozambique and Madagascar are particularly vulnerable to disasters. Thus, both countries have created initiatives to mitigate the impact of disasters.

The Chibuto Municipality in Mozambique faces serious erosion problems caused by landslides in the rainy season. Erosion has caused a lot of damage, the loss of human lives, houses and farms, as well as the deterioration of access roads. The Council initiated an awareness campaign to plant grass and trees to avoid landslides. The municipality, in partnership with the leadership of the neighbourhoods, publicised the campaign.

In addition, to prevent erosion, the community planted 250 different trees at the Samora Machel Primary School and 800 different plants in the 25 de Junho Neighborhood.

The Maxixe municipality in Mozambique is also rebuilding after being devastated by the Cyclone Dineo at the beginning of the 2018. Maxixe is amongst the largest coconut producers in Mozambique. The cyclone severely impacted coconut production. To address this problem, the Council has developed a post-cyclone reconstruction plan. The plan involves the transfer of risk areas (coastal zones) to higher ground. It also identifies safe areas for planting palm.

Meanwhile, bush fires have severely affected the Madagascan landscape. It is difficult to grow anything. Rainfall patterns have been changing and water sources have become increasingly limited. Thus, one local community set up a group to grow young plants and sell them across the island to promote re-forestation. The selling of young trees has become a growing business, especially with bamboo in high demand.

Source: SADC Protocol@Work summits

 With the help of the UNDP, **Malawi** has embarked on a process to establish a national climate change fund to put the country on a green development path.[42] Malawi is recovering from cumulative impacts of 2015 floods followed by severe drought during the 2016-17 cropping season. This calls for a scale-up of household resilience and climate-smart agricultural practices as well as the development of cleaner energy sources. Malawi will find it difficult to achieve the SDGs without action on climate change. Malawi could address climate change and grow its economy by expanding its renewable energy programme, thus creating jobs, while protecting its natural beauty, thus promoting sustainable tourism. Malawi is also creating a national fund by mobilising its domestic revenues, such as mining fees, annual green levies on vehicles and high energy consuming products such as air conditioners. These initiatives both incentivise green behaviour and generate revenue for capitalisation of Malawi's national fund.

---

[41] USAID (2018), Building urban resilience to climate change: A review of Madagascar, available at
https://reliefweb.int/report/madagascar/building-urban-resilience-climate-change-review-madagascar
[42] http://www.mw.undp.org/content/malawi/en/home/presscenter/articles/2017/06/23/establishing-a-national-climate-change-management-fund.html

Lawmakers drafted and adopted **Namibia**'s fifth National Development Plan in May 2017. It includes sectoral programmes that legislators referred to within the NDC. These development plans act as short- to medium-term building blocks to Namibia's Vision 2030. In addition to Namibia's NDC, the 2011 National Policy on Climate Change and National Climate Change Strategy and Action Plan 2013-2020 support the government's climate and development agenda.[43] Namibia aims to reduce greenhouse gas emissions by approximately 89% by 2030. It has a strong focus on adaptation within its NDC and increased adaptive capacities and reduced vulnerabilities remain important for Namibia's natural and human systems. Specific examples of adaptation objectives include climate smart agriculture (CSA); economic and livelihood diversification; smart irrigation and water management systems; and the development of early warning systems and climate data and forecasting.

Seychelles developed its first climate adaptation debt restructuring, which includes a strong marine conservation component, with the support of the Nature Conservancy.[44] It will provide funding to support the country's adaptation to climate change through improved management of coasts, coral reefs and mangroves, resulting in the implementation of the Marine Spatial Plan for the entire Seychelles Exclusive Economic Zone, a territory approximately 3000 times the size of the country's land mass, which Seychelles will manage as marine protected areas (MPAs). The Nature Conservancy will purchase up to $21.6 million of the nation's more than $400 million debt under this scheme, limiting activities such as oil exploration and large-scale development in the most fragile habitat while providing Seychelles with an innovative financial tool to support climate change adaptation, restore coral reef and mangroves nd improve sustainable tourism.[45]

 South Africa is developing a Climate Change Bill to provide a coordinated and integrated response to climate change and its impacts in accordance with the principles of cooperative governance. The bill will also address effective management of inevitable climate change impacts through enhancing adaptive capacity, strengthening resilience and reducing vulnerability to climate change, with a view to building social, economic, and environmental resilience and an adequate national adaptation response. It will

make a fair contribution to the global effort to stabilise greenhouse gas concentrations in the atmosphere at a level that avoids dangerous anthropogenic interference with the climate system within a timeframe and in a manner that enables economic, employment, social and environmental development to proceed in a sustainable manner. The country also continues to reduce carbon emissions while easing the transition to a climate resilient and low carbon economy. Legislators have taken significant actions to respond to, and reduce, emissions and climate impacts, including increasing the inclusiveness of climate action through information sharing.

Zambian legislators launched a National Policy on Climate Change to mitigate the threats posed by climate change to its development process, including attainment of the Vision 2030. This policy provides guidance on how the Zambian economy can grow in a sustainable manner and complement the implementation of the seventh National Development Plan. It will promote coordination of all adaptation and mitigation measures towards combating climate change. Its vision is "A prosperous and climate resilient economy by 2030." Zambia's rationale for formulating the NPCC is to establish a coordinated national response to climate change as it previously addressed climate change issues in a fragmented manner using various sectoral policies, strategies and plans.

 Zimbabwe's first round of consultations in the urban sector on the implementation of a National Adaptation Plan (NAP) to climate change had a smooth start on 23 November 2017 with a call for partnerships to improve the resilience of cities to climate change impacts and support clean and climate smart urban investments. The NAP is a flexible process that builds on the country's existing adaptation activities and helps integrate climate change into national decision-making. It analyses climate risks and adaptation options in the short- and long-term, which helps shape the country's climate policy and implementation of the Climate Change Response Strategy. It also supports the scaling up of climate resilient development initiatives and highlights the benefits to the economy of integrating adaptation to climate change measures in planning, such as in green building investments.[46] More broadly, adaptation investments in urban centres such as those that increase the resilience and reliability of urban infrastructure can improve broader economic

[43] https://ndcpartnership.org/sites/all/themes/ndcp_v2/docs/country-engagement/countries/NCDP_Outlook_Namibia_v1b.pdf
[44] http://destinationreporterindia.com/2018/03/23/seychelles-launches-innovative-climate-adaptation-scheme/
[45] https://www.nature.org/ourinitiatives/regions/africa/seychelles-msp-phase-1-final.pdf

performance by increasing competitiveness and attractiveness for investors and the private sector in general. These also increase resilience in cities, helping basic poverty reduction and attainment of the SDGs. Instead of seeing vulnerability to climate impacts as an additional concern, cities can mainstream resilience into existing efforts.

Capacity

Article 20.3 of the Protocol on Environmental Management for Sustainable Development notes that state parties shall design gender responsive capacity building, education and training on environmental management and climate change for sustainable development initiatives.

Women and men have different capabilities in terms of mitigating and adapting to climate change at the individual and group levels. Education, gender roles, division of labour and income shape the options available to women and men to convert to low-carbon lifestyles and related technologies. Capacity building initiatives on gender and climate change have been attempting to help close the gender gap in climate change mitigation in the region.

Uncovering the dynamics of power relations helps stakeholders understand why some groups contribute differently to greenhouse gas emissions and why climate change affects some differently than others. It also allows for an analysis of the ways in which climate change mitigation and adaptation may lead to different roles and responsibilities in the future. All stakeholders must consider these to identify solutions that draw on the skills, knowledge, resources and experiences of both sexes.

Stakeholder engagement

Protocol on Environmental Management for Sustainable Development Article 20.5: State parties shall employ people-centred, equitable, gender inclusive and participatory consultations of all stakeholders in all environmental management and climate change for sustainable development programmes and initiatives.

The United Nations identifies climate as the defining human development challenge in the 21st century. According to *Climate Risk and Vulnerability, A Handbook for Southern Africa* weather-related disasters between 1980 and 2016 in SADC resulted in damages of $10 billion, left 2.47 million people homeless and affected a further 140 million people.[47]

The post-2015 SADC Protocol on Gender and Development states in **Article 31** in *Part Ten, Gender and Climate Change* that: Develop policies, strategies, and programmes to address gender issues in climate change should be in accordance with the SADC Protocol on Environment and Sustain-

able Development. It also obliges states to conduct research to assess the differential gendered impacts of climate change and put in place effective mitigation and adaptation measures.

Access to clean water is a major challenge across SADC, including in Zimbabwe, where legislators have been trying to adapt to climate change by improving urban infrastructure.
Photo courtesy of Manyame Rural District Council

[46] http://www.zw.undp.org/content/zimbabwe/en/home/presscenter/articles/2017/11/27/climate-change-towards-a-national-adaptation-plan-for-zim.html
[47] Davis-Reddy, C.L. and Vincent, K. 2017: Climate Risk and Vulnerability: A Handbook for Southern Africa (2nd Edition), Council for Scientific and Industrial Research, Pretoria, South Africa.

have *different* **capabilities** mitigating and adapting to climate change

Climate summits promote best practices for mitigating climate change at community level

Gender Links (GL) works with all levels of governments, organisations and communities to implement strategies and programmes to meet the targets set in the Revised SADC Protocol on Gender and Development.

GL gathers good practices and analyses how they contribute to the implementation of the targets set in the Protocol. Participants presented 30 good practices on climate change at summits in 2017 and 2018. They show a growing trend of local, community-based initiatives to address climate change. Summit entries are diverse and there is evidence of targeted strategies that respond to the needs of communities.

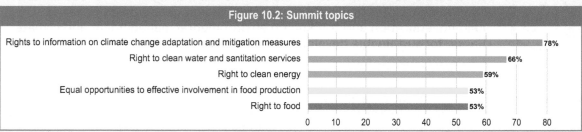

Figure 10.2: Summit topics

Source: Gender Links.

Climate change awareness on the increase: As illustrated in Figure 10.2, more than three quarters of the good practices provided information on adaptation and mitigation measures. A lower number of entries focused on water and sanitation and clean energy.

More work is needed on food rights: Lower proportions of the good practices focused on equal opportunities to effective involvement in food production and food security. This a concern as nutrition is a major challenge in SADC. Experts project that Angola, DRC, Malawi, Tanzania and Zambia will increase their populations at least five-fold by 2100 (UN, 2015). Such growth imposes profound challenges in meeting future food requirements.[48]

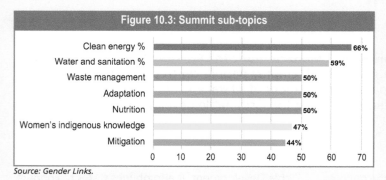

Figure 10.3: Summit sub-topics

Source: Gender Links.

There is little focus on women's indigenous knowledge and mitigation: As illustrated in Figure 10.3, more than half of Summit entries on climate change focused on clean energy and water and sanitation. Meanwhile, half of all the entries focused on waste management, adaptation and nutrition.

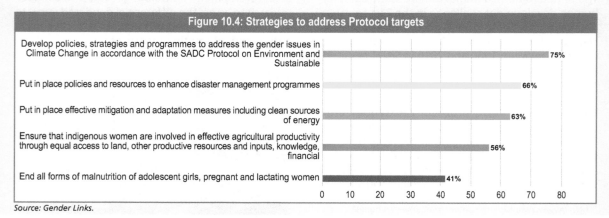

Figure 10.4: Strategies to address Protocol targets

Source: Gender Links.

---

[48] Davis-Reddy, C.L. and Vincent, K. 2017: Climate Risk and Vulnerability: A Handbook for Southern Africa (2nd Edition), Council for Scientific and Industrial Research, Pretoria, South Africa.

Stakeholders prioritise policy while nutrition is low on the agenda: Figure 10.4 shows that, of the total number of climate change entries, 75% contribute to policy development, strategies and programmes. As mentioned previously, nutrition is low on the agenda at 41% and needs urgent attention. Two thirds of the initiatives addressed disaster management policies and resources as well as mitigation and adaptation. About half the entries referred to the involvement of indigenous women in climate change.

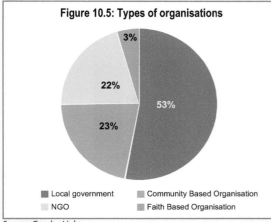

Figure 10.5: Types of organisations

- 3%
- 22%
- 53%
- 23%

■ Local government ■ Community Based Organisation
■ NGO ■ Faith Based Organisation

Source: Gender Links.

Local action to address climate change predominates: The analysis in Figure 10.5 shows that 53% of the case studies on climate change originated from local government. GL works with councils to develop gender action plans that includes climate change as part of the Local Government Centres of Excellence (COE) process. Almost equal numbers of non-governmental and community organisations presented case studies on climate change.

Of the 30 submissions, 13 came from COEs in Zimbabwe. The Zimbabwe councils have been engaged in a diverse set of initiatives to address climate change at the local level.

Table 10.3 provides an overview of the types of

Table 10.3: Types of initiatives implemented by councils	
Council	**Brief description of project**
Right to clean water and sanitation	
Beitbridge Town Council	The Earthworms Waste Water Treatment and Recycling cleans, detoxifies, disinfects and neutralises the waste water from the kitchen, laundry, bath and flush toilet.
Manyame RDC	Three thousand households did not have access to clean water and sanitation. Women and children had to travel long distances in search of water. The Council drills boreholes in all 21 wards every year.
Chegutu Municipality	The Council provides piped water to the residents through a system powered by solar energy.
Right to clean energy	
Murewa Rural Development Council (RDC)	Over the past five years, Council embarked on an ambitious district-wide afforestation and reforestation programme. It established communal woodlots in all the 30 wards. Amongst others, schools participate in tree growing and tree care.
City of Kadoma	The Council targets major events and school programmes to plant "Trees of Memory." At each event people plant a minimum of five trees.
Goromonzi RDC	The Council advocates and educates the community on the importance of tree planting as measure to mitigate climate change. This is important in rural areas where people cut trees down for domestic use.
Waste management	
Municipality of Chinhoyi	There were many illegal dumps in the area increasing the risk of communicable diseases. The Council created a multi-stakeholder committee to raise awareness on waste management and arranged clean-up campaigns.
Chegutu Municipality	Waste recycling reduces illegal dumping and burning of waste. The project also generates money for better livelihoods by creating products from recycled goods.
Gokwe Town Council	The town does not have an approved land fill and the town is currently practicing crude tipping. The community-based health club, Ziso Rehutano, has embarked on a plastic recycling project.
Nyanga RDC	Litter was being thrown everywhere, including in the backyards of residential accommodation, the streets and open spaces. The Council procured bins and established a revolving fund for residents to buy refuse bins at reduced prices; started public education and campaigns; and established a solid waste recycling project.
Municipality of Gwanda	The Council creates self-employment through waste recycling and reuse.
Adaptation	
Manyame RDC	Due to overcrowding and inadequate infrastructure, the Council is re-housing people into planned and environmentally-friendly communal settlements.
Right to information on climate change adaptation and mitigation measures	
Bulawayo City Council	The Council is running education and awareness programmes to promote innovation to overcome climate change in the community.
Right to food	
Umguza RDC	The Council is working with Community Technology Development Organisation (CTDO) to build community resilience from shocks and hazards through crop and livelihood diversification.

Source: Gender Links.

initiatives implemented by the councils and which Protocol targets they address. It shows that councils have been engaging in innovative locally relevant strategies to mitigate and adapt to climate change. Community involvement is central to the initiatives in the councils.

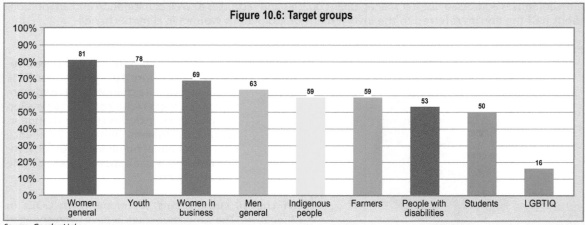

Figure 10.6: Target groups

Source: Gender Links.

Women and youth represent the primary target groups: Figure 10.6 notes that women comprise the primary targets of the climate change good practices (81%) followed by youth (78%). Similar numbers of indigenous people, men, farmers and women in business participate in the good practices. Lesbian, gay, bisexual, trans-sexual, intersex and queer (LGBTIQ) people constitute 16% of the target group.

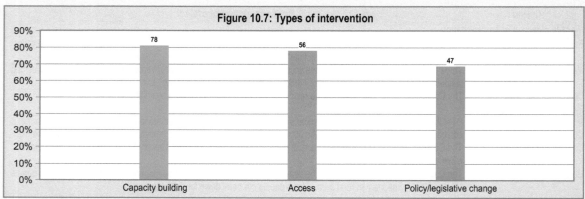

Figure 10.7: Types of intervention

Source: Gender Links.

Capacity-building most common climate change intervention at local level: Figure 10.7 shows that more than three quarters (78%) of the good practices focus on capacity building. Fewer cases focus on access and policy and legislative change. Capacity building is important to promote high levels of ownership within communities to address issues of climate change.

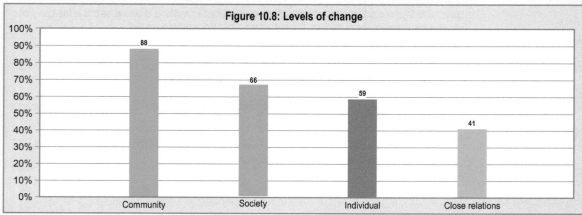

Figure 10.8: Levels of change

Source: Gender Links.

Communities leading the charge: As mentioned earlier and as illustrated in Figure 10.8, communities have been taking ownership of the strategies to address climate change. Similar levels of change occurred in society and amongst individuals.

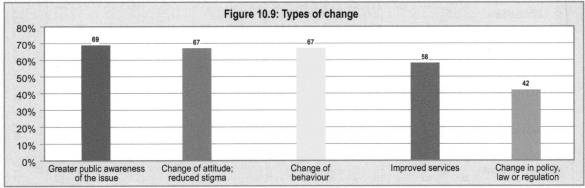

Figure 10.9: Types of change

Source: Gender Links.

Positive change recorded overall: Figure 10.9 shows that, overall, greater public awareness, changes in attitude and behaviour scored at between 69% and 67% when measuring the types of change resulting from the good practices. The low score for changes in policy, law or regulation is a concern. Long term change can only occur if there is an enabling environment guided by a strong policy and legislative framework.

Challenges
The analysis highlights gaps in strategies to address food security and nutrition. With the burgeoning population in SADC, food security will increase in importance. The lack of proper nutrition affects all aspects of people's lives. Children and young people struggle to cope or even attend school because of hunger. Food security needs to move to the top of the climate change agenda.

Lessons learned and next steps
In their submission on using earthworms to recycle water, the Beitbridge Town Council identified the need to embrace scientific research and to demystify the science around climate change. Communities should not be afraid of engaging with scientific innovation and utilising any of the positive outcomes in their own initiatives. GL needs to engage with the local communities on issues of food security and nutrition. The councils and communities also need to prioritise food security in their climate change strategies.

State parties shall utilise local knowledge, particularly women's skills, knowledge and capacities in mitigation and adaptation strategies for environmental management.

Using renewable energy and energy effiency technologies with skills learnt. *Photo: GenderCCSA*

Table 10.4: Representation of women and men in key decision-making positions related to the environment

Source: GenderCCSA 2018.

Sidebar: Climate change decision-making 28% in 2017 ↓ 20% in 2018

All country figures are for the year **2018** (M = Male, F = Female).

Position	Angola M	Angola F	Botswana M	Botswana F	Comoros M	Comoros F	DRC M	DRC F	Lesotho M	Lesotho F	Madagascar M	Madagascar F	Malawi M	Malawi F	Mauritius M	Mauritius F	Mozambique M	Mozambique F	Namibia M	Namibia F	Seychelles M	Seychelles F	South Africa M	South Africa F	eSwatini M	eSwatini F	Tanzania M	Tanzania F	Zambia M	Zambia F	Zimbabwe M	Zimbabwe F	Total Female	Total Male	Overall total	% Female
Minister of Environmental Affairs (Wildlife)	0	1	1	0	1	0	1	0	1	0	1	0	1	0	1	0	1	0	1	0	1	0	0	1	0	1	1	0	1	0	0	1	4	12	16	25
Deputy Minister of Environmental Affairs	0	0	0	0	0	0	0	0	0	0	0	0	0	0	0	0	0	0	1	0	0	0	1	0	1	0	1	0	0	1	0	1	2	4	6	33
Permanent Secretary/DG	0	0	1	0	0	1	0	0	1	0	1	0	0	0	0	1	0	0	1	0	0	0	1	0	0	0	0	0	1	0	0	0	2	6	8	25
Minister of Tourism	1	0	1	0	1	0	1	0	0	1	0	1	1	0	1	0	1	0	1	0	1	0	1	0	1	0	1	0	1	0	1	0	2	14	16	13
Deputy Minister of Tourism	0	0	0	1	0	0	0	0	0	0	0	0	0	0	0	0	0	0	1	0	0	1	0	1	0	0	0	0	0	0	0	0	3	1	4	75
Permanent Secretary/DG	1	0	1	0	1	0	1	0	1	0	1	0	1	0	1	0	1	0	1	0	0	0	1	0	1	0	1	0	1	0	1	0	0	9	9	0
Minister of Fisheries	0	0	1	0	0	0	0	0	1	0	0	0	0	0	1	0	0	0	1	0	0	0	1	0	1	0	0	1	0	1	0	1	3	8	11	27
Deputy Minister of Fisheries	1	0	0	0	0	0	0	0	0	0	0	0	0	0	0	0	0	0	1	0	0	1	1	0	0	0	0	0	1	0	0	0	1	3	4	25
Permanent Secretary/DG	1	0	1	0	0	0	0	0	1	0	0	0	1	0	1	0	0	0	1	0	0	0	1	0	0	0	1	0	1	0	0	0	0	5	5	0
Minister of Water Affairs	0	1	1	0	0	0	0	0	0	0	1	0	0	0	1	0	0	0	0	1	0	0	0	1	0	0	0	0	1	0	0	0	3	10	13	23
Deputy Minister of Water Affairs	1	0	1	0	0	0	0	0	1	0	0	0	0	0	0	0	0	0	1	0	0	0	0	1	0	1	1	0	1	0	0	0	2	5	7	29
Permanent Secretary/DG	0	0	0	0	0	0	0	0	0	0	0	0	0	0	1	0	0	0	0	1	0	0	1	0	0	1	0	0	1	0	0	0	2	7	9	22
Minister of Agriculture	1	0	1	0	1	0	1	0	1	0	1	0	1	0	1	0	1	0	1	0	0	0	0	1	1	0	1	0	1	0	1	0	1	15	16	6
Deputy Minister of Agriculture	0	1	0	0	0	0	0	0	0	0	0	0	0	0	0	0	0	0	0	1	0	0	1	0	0	1	0	0	0	0	0	0	3	6	9	33
Permanent Secretary/DG	1	0	1	0	1	0	0	0	1	0	1	0	1	0	1	0	1	0	1	0	0	0	1	0	1	0	1	0	1	0	1	0	0	8	8	20
Total	7	3	10	1	5	1	4	0	8	1	6	1	6	0	9	1	5	0	12	3	2	2	10	5	6	4	8	1	11	2	4	3	28	113	141	20
Total Composite	10		11		6		4		9		7		6		10		5		15		4		15		10		9		13		7					
Percentage	30%		9%		17%		0%		11%		14%		0%		10%		0%		20%		50%		33%		40%		11%		15%		43%					

Table 10.4 illustrates women's representation in climate change decision-making in the region, which dropped from 28% in 2017 to 20% in 2018. Women have yet to reach one third of those in decision-making positions, nowhere close to 50/50 representation. Seychelles leads the way, increasing from 40% in 2017 to 50% in 2018, followed by Zimbabwe which dropped from 44% in 2017 to 43% in 2018 and eSwatini at 40%. DRC, Malawi and Mozambique have no women in decision-making positions related to climate change.

Research and adaptation measures for climate change

Article 31, 1b: State parties shall conduct research to access the different gendered impacts of climate change and put in place effective mitigation and adaptation measures.
Article 20.6: Protocol on Environmental Management for Sustainable Development: State parties shall, as part of their research agenda, include all aspects of gender in environmental management, risk assessment, emergency and disaster response, and other sustainable development initiatives.

Lack of climate resilience in SADC due to differing economic development, resource availability and infrastructure capacity levels may eventually pose a risk to the entire region. It is important to understand how risks can be shared, for example, through trade, technology transfer and information sharing among SADC countries, and how climate change will exacerbate these risks. The climate across the SADC region is highly diverse and driven by a range of distinct climatic systems. Evidence shows that the SADC region has already experienced an increasing frequency of hot days and decreasing frequency of cold days. Rainfall trends have been variable, but evidence points to an increased inter-annual variability to date, with extremely wet periods and more intense droughts in different countries.

Cyclones in eastern SADC have resulted in extensive flooding, causing economic losses and damage to infrastructure, crops and livelihoods.[49] Droughts in several SADC countries have also changed the length and timing of the growing season and led to a drop in agricultural productivity due to lower crop yields. These impacts have been increasing and becoming persistent, leading to a rise in food insecurity and food prices. This has also affected energy generation at both the smallholder (fuel wood availability) and national scale (loss of hydro-power potential). Additionally, climate-related diseases triggered by heat waves and floods, such as malaria and diarrhoea, have become more prevalent. These current climate-driven impacts mean that people in the SADC region already face many risks.

All countries have been involved in the development of national statements on climate change, notably National Adaptation Plans of Action (NAPAs) and National Adaptation Plans (NAPs). However, although inter-regional opportunities may exist, SADC states have not aligned these plans with those of neighbouring countries. The NAP process has potential to be integrated across the region in a systematic manner through capacity development and knowledge sharing. This, however, is not currently happening.

Several relevant policies and strategies exist at the regional level. These include the SADC Policy Paper on Climate Change, the SADC Water Sector Climate Change Adaptation Strategy and the Regional Climate Change Programme. Several existing sector-specific strategies also support the adaptive capacity of the region, yet legislators have not necessarily built these purposefully for climate change adaptation. These include those focused on shared water, migration and health, fisheries, biodiversity and regional economic integration. Regarding the latter, despite policies promoting integration, the policy environment has generally become more unfavourable to increased regional trade over the past decade.[50]

To adapt to the risks associated with the predicted impacts of climate change, an appropriate response would be for SADC to integrate further. Integration requires adequate infrastructure, not only in terms of transport, but also energy to facilitate economic development in all of the SADC countries. Integration is necessary for the continued growth and

Cyclones led to extensive flooding, economic losses, damage to infra-structure, crops and livelihoods

[49] https://www.sanbi.org/wp-content/uploads/2018/03/ltas-factsheet-1.pdf
[50] https://www.sadc.int/themes/meteorology-climate/climate-change-adaptation/

development of the region, regardless of climate change. However, it is especially pertinent in a drier future.

Countries need to carry out adaptation measures independently. Although integration is required regionally, SADC as an institution is incapable of implementing adaptation measures. It is only with the support of individual nations, implementing a range of changes, that stakeholders can improve the adaptive capacity of the region.[51] However, increased integration comes with risks and complexities. For example, migration between countries that have different development profiles is difficult to control and manage with increased integration.

For the SADC region, it is important to remove disincentives for adaptation to climate change and regional integration. Increased integration should be on the condition that SADC as a whole becomes stronger and better prepared for climate impacts. Lawmakers should catalyse opportunities so that the region develops beyond the current situation, which sees entire communities paralysed by drought or floods year after year. What is especially pertinent is that a resilient country, without a resilient SADC region around it, is in fact not resilient at all. To facilitate this development, all sectors require

better capacity to facilitate increased regional integration.

Countries in the region differ not only economically, but politically, climatically, through capacity, infrastructure, and development too - SADC has numerous asymmetries. Therefore, climate is not the only major consideration. In some sectors, SADC is competent in the development of regional plans. In other sectors, implementation has been inadequate. The challenge for SADC, therefore, is to move beyond planning and into implementation at a regional level. The asymmetries already mentioned make this complicated. Countries are not legally bound, or often do not have the ability to implement. Thus, national sectors within SADC countries should ensure there is adequate support for climate change. Alternatively, a regional hub may support capacity development in order to support implementation.

Aside from the development of capacity, legislators need to re-think funding of initiatives and projects in SADC. Because of the high growth rates of several the SADC countries, there is an opportunity for this to occur. However, without adequate funding to implement, and without integrated planning, there is a risk that some initiatives or infrastructure investments could be maladaptive.

Nutrition innovation in eSwatini

Beekeeping and smart agriculture are creating opportunities for eSwatini communities to increase their food security and providing income generation opportunities.

Climate Smart Agriculture (CSA) includes three innovations: conservation agriculture, permaculture nutrition gardens and ferro-cement water harvesters (tanks). Farmers do not have to buy crops and vegetables but can cultivate them in their own fields even in harsh conditions. The climate smart interventions ensure that every household has at least a meal a day and some income. This innovation is sustainable because it uses local materials.

Youth in eSwatini have also started nursery businesses to supply the farmers with seedlings for permaculture backyard gardens. This also reduces the number of people falling ill as more people have access to a balanced diet that is readily available.

The eSwatini top bar hive way of keeping bees is a simple affordable technique and does not require expensive harvesting machinery for farmers. Training of communities by the Lower Usuthu Sustainable Land management (LUSLM) project aims to eradicate poverty through small stock farming and by increasing the number of climate resilient households.

Beekeeping has been successful in Vikizijula, Mphumakudze and Bulunga. Farmers receive training on beekeeping, its financial implications and the climate change impact. Before the training, farmers cut down trees but now they know they must conserve them. Beekeeping is cost effective because the start-up equipment is affordable. The community has learnt new skills such as hive construction, good hive inspection and management skills.

---

[51] SANBI (2017) Climate Change Adaptation Southern African Development Community : Perspectives for SADC, available on https://www.sanbi.org/wp-content/uploads/2018/04/ltas-factsheet-1.pdf

Access to clean water and energy sources

The interrelationship between water and energy supply, water resources and climate change are particularly relevant to decision-making in Southern Africa, according to a recent World Bank report published as a background paper to support dialogue in the SADC region.[52] The region's water resources are unevenly distributed, both spatially and temporally, leading to significant water scarcity in some parts of the region and relative abundance in others. Leaders also have limited knowledge about the region's overall water resource levels. Experts predict that climate change will reduce rainfall levels, increase rainfall variability, and increase ambient temperatures, but there is little certainty about when and by how much. Consi-dering these spatial differences, the region needs to approach water and energy sector planning in tandem at local, national, river basin, or regional levels, depending on the nature of the issue.

Women walk long distances to collect water in Madagascar, where almost half of the country does not have access to clean water. *Photo: Razanandrateta Zotonantenaina*

The region has uneven distribution of hydrological resources, with southernmost countries like South Africa, Botswana and Namibia receiving much lower levels of rainfall than the northern countries, such as DRC, Angola and Zambia. SADC has 15 major transboundary river basins, with more than 70% of the region's freshwater resources, shared between two or more countries.

Various issues and implications around the energy-water nexus also characterise the region, which has a strong interlinking of energy and water security - something planners, policymakers and investors should recognise. For example, water is crucial for hydropower generation and for cooling in thermal generation plants, while the region needs electricity to advance various stages of the water supply and sanitation value chain.

The SADC region has vast energy resources. Coal has been the source of most power generation activity in the east and northeast regions of South Africa. The region has the potential for 56,000MW of hydropower in DRC and Mozambique alone. A key challenge is accommodating climate change uncertainty when making energy investment decisions. Climate change will continue to have a significant impact on water and energy systems.

 Angola is increasing electric power availability to diversify the economy and meet the increasing energy demand of a growing population. To achieve a targeted 9.9 gigawatt (GW) of installed generation capacity and a 60% electrification rate by 2025, the government has instituted an ambitious infrastructure plan.[53] Legislators have declared that, by the end of 2018, the country's power generation mix will consist of 64% hydropower (4 GW), 12% natural gas (750 MW) and 24% other fossil fuels (1.5 GW). Leaders anticipate this 6.3 GW total once several major projects come online during 2017 and 2018: Soyo (gas) combined cycle plant (750 MW), Cambambe hydroelectric phase 2 (700 MW) and the Lauca hydroelectric project (2.1 GW). For these and future projects, external financing and private project development will be key, especially given the current government budget and economic downturn. Experts estimate current electrification rates at 43% in cities and less than 10% in rural areas. As a result, both businesses and residents rely heavily on diesel generators for power. Given

[52] Water Power Magazine (2017), Addressing the energy-water nexus in Southern Africa, available at http://www.waterpowermagazine.com/opinion/opinionaddressing-the-energy-water-nexus-in-southern-africa-5818909/
[53] https://www.export.gov/article?id=Angola-Electric-Power-Generation

Hydro-logical resources uneven

the four-fold increase in diesel fuel prices during 2015 due to government subsidy cutbacks, many began to explore alternative energy solutions. Angola holds enormous potential for renewable energy production. Mapping studies completed by the Ministry of Energy and Water in June 2014 identified potential for 55 GW solar power, three GW wind power and 18 GW in hydropower throughout the country. To address rural demand, the government is pursuing the development of small-scale off-grid projects leveraging fossil fuels as well as renewable technologies (small hydro, solar, wind and biomass).

Botswana's Department of Energy Affairs (EAD) within the Ministry of Minerals, Energy and Water (MMEWR) leads the country's national energy policy. MMEWR through Botswana Power Corporation (BPC) represents the main decision-maker for the power generation, transmission and distribution. EAD administers the Electricity Supply Act.[54] BPC has an installed capacity of 450 MW from the Morupule B coal-fired power plant. The national demand averages 550 MW, covered by importing up to 150 MW from South Africa that mitigates, but does not prevent, load shedding. In 2013, lawmakers installed two emergency diesel facilities, 70 MW at Matshelagabedi and 90MW at Orapa, to avoid such outages. Morupule A, a 132 MW facility where capacity dropped to 30% in 2012, has been undergoing rehabilitation and upgrading to add capacity. Morupule B also underwent expansion in 2016 to add another 300 MW by 2020. Based on 2013 data, Botswana's national electrification rate reached 66% (54% in rural areas, 65% in urban), but one million people still lack access to electricity.[55]

According to a new study, the **DRC** is in a good position to harness its renewable energy potential to power its electricity needs.[56] According to the report, the country's wind and solar potential, measured at 85GW, could address the country's chronic power shortages and would far surpass the output of the planned 4.8GW Inga 3 Dam on the Congo River. Indeed, the country could install 60GW of that energy at less than $0.07 per kWh, which makes it competitive with conventional power options, notes the report. The DRC has significant renewable energy potential, some of which it could bring online before construction even begins on Inga 3.

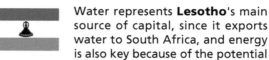

Water represents **Lesotho**'s main source of capital, since it exports water to South Africa, and energy is also key because of the potential that Lesotho's vast water resources offer for renewable energy.[57] Renewable energy output from the Lesotho Highlands Power Project (LHPP) will be 6000 MW from wind and 4000 MW from hydro sources. This is equivalent to about 5% of neighbouring South Africa's electricity needs. Experts estimat Lesotho's hydro generation potential at 450 MW. The Lesotho Solar Energy Society (LESES) has been championing the implementation of solar in the country. Installers and dealers have registered with the LESES and this enables the implementation and enforcement of regulations and standards (REEEP, 2012). Renewables are a priority in the Energy Policy 2015-2025. Specific targets include promoting solar in the design of new buildings and phasing out energy intensive items in old buildings, such as electrical geysers, and replacing them with solar water heating. The Rural Electrification Master Plan aims to increase access to electricity by encouraging the uptake of solar.

Madagascar is the third African country to join the Scaling Solar programme, with a planned 30-40MW solar facility envisaged to help ease daily interruptions of power service.[58] The World Bank highlighted that the island nation suffers from frequent power outages, and fewer than one fifth of the population has access to electricity. The World Bank ranked Madagascar 187 out of 189 countries regarding the difficulty, delay and cost of getting electricity.

The planned Scaling Solar project will provide a reliable alternative to expensive diesel generators, drawing on an abundant source of renewable energy.[59] In September 2017, Siemens signed an MoU with Madagascar to cooperate and identify measures that will fast-track power generation and increase capacity by an additional 300MW by 2019. Other key aspects of the MoU include an assessment of the electrical grid based on the new power generation sources; applying financing concepts that will ensure the long-term sustainability of these infrastructure initiatives; and creating opportunities for local job creation during construction and operation. "The primary goal of this agreement is to increase national power generating capacity and to connect the local

[54] https://www.usaid.gov/powerafrica/botswana
[55] https://www.export.gov/article?id=Angola-Electric-Power-Generation
[56] https://www.esi-africa.com/drc-holds-renewable-energy-potential-reveals-study/
[57] https://wedocs.unep.org/bitstream/handle/20.500.11822/20505/Energy_profile_Lesotho.pdf?sequence=1&isAllowed=y
[58] https://www.esi-africa.com/madagascar-joins-scaling-solar-scheme-with-added-energy-storage/
[59] https://www.esi-africa.com/madagascar-targets-add-300mw-2019/

Vast energy resources

population to the power grid," said Sabine Dall'Omo, Siemens' CEO for Southern and Eastern Africa.

Madagascar has 676MW of installed generation capacity and studies estimate that access to electricity stands at around 20%. Opportunities exist to increase the installed capacity through hydropower and exploring oil reserves to meet the targets set by government, Siemens noted. Improving the country's energy mix will strengthen the well-established agriculture and mining industry and emerging tourism and textile industries.

 In **Malawi**, 90% of people do not have access to electric power and the 10% who do experience frequent power cuts. Blackouts have recently become more frequent because low water levels have affected the country's two hydroelectric power plants. In the past decades, rainfall has declined. As a result, the government is turning to coal to improve the power situation. The energy crisis in Malawi affects almost everyone. Problems exist in the health sector and many have lost jobs because of company closures. Blackouts have even disrupted parliament sessions. Malawi has approached China for funding worth $600 million for a new coal-based power plant in Kammwamba in the south.[60] This is a major concern for environmental experts because coal burning is harmful to the environment. It releases carbon emissions and thus drives climate change. The Paris Climate Agreement is about reducing such emissions and Malawi is a party to the Paris accord. It has committed to mitigating global warming. Building new coal-fired facilities, however, exacerbates the problem. Malawi remains one of the poorest countries in Africa and its current shortage of electricity seems to trump climate commitments in the eyes of its leaders.

Mauritius' Ministry of Energy and Public Utilities has signed an MoU with the Italian Ministry of Environment, Land and Sea for cooperation in renewable energy and energy efficiency.[61] The Italian government will invest two million euros to help the two countries improve scientific research on energy technologies. The agreement will result in the introduction of new smart grid technologies and help improve reliability of grid networks through the expansion of renewable energy portfolios. The two countries will also collaborate to provide energy stakeholders with training and

capacity building in energy efficiency. The first project under the MoU will be a conversion of electrical irrigation pumps into solar pumps. Additionally, an Abu Dhabi Fund for Development (ADFD) loan of $10 million will help the Central Electricity Board install solar PV systems on rooftops of 10 000 households as part of the government's efforts to alleviate poverty while contributing to the national target of achieving 35% of renewable electricity in the energy mix by 2025.[62] This project has the potential to significantly transform the lives of more than 2.5 million people and alleviate poverty by bringing affordable energy to low-income communities.

Community members test a solar powered cooker in South Africa in 2017.
Photo: Gender Links

South Africa's Renewable Energy Independent Power Producer Procurement Programme (REIPPPP) is a collaboration between the public sector and private companies for infrastructure delivery.[63] Experts have hailed the programme as one of the most successful public-private partnerships in Africa in the past 20 years. Its designers created it to kickstart private-sector investment in renewable energy as a response to electricity load shedding. It received the first bids towards the end of 2011 and two years later some of the projects were already up and running. So far, it has awarded more than 6300 megawatts from about 90 renewable energy facilities - mostly wind and solar. The socio-economic effect has also been substantial, with projects required to contri-

[60] https://www.dandc.eu/en/article/order-manage-its-current-energy-crisis-malawi-turns-coal
[61] https://www.esi-africa.com/mauritius-italy-re-energy-efficiency/
[62] http://www.engineeringnews.co.za/article/rwanda-mauritius-get-funding-for-solar-pv-projects-2018-01-15/rep_id:4136
[63] https://mg.co.za/article/2018-02-09-00-water-crisis-look-to-sas-renewable-energy-programme-for-solutions

90%
of
Malawians
no
access
to
electricity

bute a percentage of revenues to ensure local residents benefit directly from the investments attracted into an area.[64]

Renewable, clean energy and gender equality are preconditions for sustainable development and for tackling climate change. Throughout Africa, more than 600 million people (about 50% of the population) do not have access to sustainable, clean energy sources. In Africa, women produce and consume energy in both urban and rural areas.[65] They have responsibility for producing energy through collecting biomass-based fuels and for consuming energy in their household activities, microenterprises and agriculture. Women can be powerful agents for change in the transition to, and promotion of, sustainable energy, through their role as the primary energy managers in households. A gender-responsive energy policy assesses gender gaps, identifies actions to close them and promotes women's engagement in the energy sector, including in decision-making processes.

Integrating gender in energy and water policies

The challenge in many SADC countries is that many stakeholders often place gender in stand-alone chapters of policy documents rather than integrating it across all chapters. In a few instances, some still consider women as vulnerable, rather than recognising them as key agents of change towards sustainable energy solutions. Policies in Kenya and Malawi lump the needs of women, youth and the physically challenged together without referring to the different vulnerabilities - and related root causes - of the three groups. Most seriously, two policies in the region do not include any references to gender, women or men. Moving beyond the policy level, on-the-ground implementation remains challenging and gender gaps abound in the energy sector. Women continue to have less access to efficient energy sources and to meaningful roles in influencing energy policies. Socially-constructed gender roles, identities and underlying power dynamics affect whether (and how) women and men access and use energy and participate in decisions and investments (UN Environment, 2016).

To address implementation challenges, decision-makers need to allocate sufficient budget to implement gender-related energy policy objectives. In addition, they need to implement an appropriate system for measuring progress through key indicators. Except for two policies, the overarching policies and strategies reviewed for this analysis did not include budgets and cost estimates; decision-makers usually specify these in sector implementation and annual work plans.

Leaders must address gender issues and inequalities more comprehensively and consistently in energy policies. Further, such policies must link more closely to programming and budgeting to ensure implementation - and, consequently, meaningful change in the lives of the country's women and men - as envisioned in the SDGs.

There is a need for an initial overview of the regional status of gender integration in overarching national energy policies and strategies. Using this review as a starting point, stakeholder could conduct a more detailed and broader country and regional analysis. It should look at policy development and energy programmes as they relate to women and girls to inform good practices and share experiences for peer learning, replication, scalability and accelerating achievement of results for gender equality and the empowerment of women and girls.

It would be especially useful to conduct further analysis such as gender audits and impact assessments to see how countries implement these policy aspirations on the ground as well as their impacts for citizens. Such analysis could help demonstrate to policymakers the value added to the lives of women and girls, and men and boys. It might also ensure that the narrative depicts women as agents and active participants of change and move beyond an attitude of women as victims and mere recipients of energy solutions and services.

Conclusion

Climate change is a transboundary process that requires a multifaceted response as a basis for entering agreements, joint initiatives and potential solutions. Climate change drivers and impacts remain inherently unequal. Responses to it are difficult to implement due to conflicting decisions and priorities at multiple scales on everything from resource use to the degree and direction of social change - and for whom. This makes it into a

---

[64] Republic of South Africa (2018), Ministry Update for Department of Energy, available at https://www.ipp-projects.co.za/PressCentre/GetPressRelease?fileid...923C...
[65] United Nations Poverty-Environment Initiative (2017) Gender, Energy and Policy : A review of en-ergy policies in East and Southern Africa, available at http://www.unpei.org/sites/default/files/publications/Gender%2C%20Energy%20and%20Policy-%20A%20Review%20of%20Energy%20Policies%20in%20East%20and%20Southern%20Africa-%20Web-%20HR.pdf

phenomenon that influences both existing and future inequalities. Stakeholders need to address not only "who gets what" in terms of resources and services but also who "gets to interpret" and "who gets to represent" the needs and wants of others.

Development has addressed women, gender, nature and environment differently over time and in varied domains and debates. We have learned how the power and dynamics of gender play out in the context of multiple stressors such as food insecurity, ill-health, poverty, inequality and land-use change. By viewing adaptation, development and mitigation as major related processes and with institutional change and technology uptake as part of all three, one can compare preconditions for, and pathways to, gender-informed social change.

Three main finding emerge from a feminist sustainability and science perspective on climate change adaptation through a gender lens. First, the social goal of climate change responses is obviously to respond to impacts, in both a proactive and reactive way. Ideally, responses would mitigate environmental change simultaneously and synergistically while tackling food insecurity, ill-health, inequality and poverty. Second, while doing so, politicians,

policymakers and practitioners would have to continually take gender into consideration as a defining institution in small-scale agriculture regarding both the discursive portrayal of women and the more material distribution of rights, risks and responsibilities. Third, such responses, which would take not only technological solutions but also social relations seriously, should consider structural and institutional change pertaining to norms, rules and values as a way to alleviate the pressure from multiple stressors while also having a synergetic and transformative potential towards increased sustainability.[66]

To conclude, gender is contingent and culturally constructed through norms, rules and values but social relations are also subject to change during major social processes such as those in focus here. Gender is a critical social category and a salient feature of both development and climate change. It has many institutional and structural implications for adaptation and mitigation as well as many practical implications for environmental justice. Beyond that it also enriches the very understanding of climate change impacts and responses - and gender debates provide reasoning and tools for how policy and practice for increased development and sustainability can deal with that.

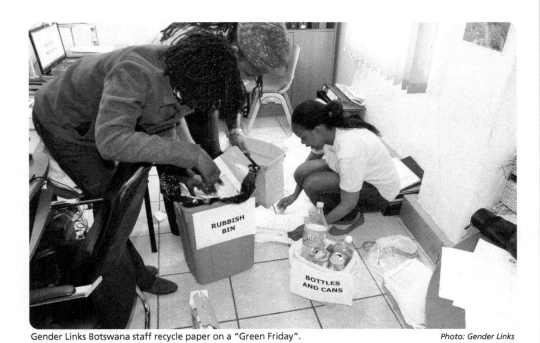

Gender Links Botswana staff recycle paper on a "Green Friday".   Photo: Gender Links

Climate change **drivers** and **impacts**

---

[66] Jerneck, A (2018), What about Gender in Climate Change? Twelve Feminist Lessons from Devel-opment, Lund University Centre for Sustainability Studies, available on www.mdpi.com:8080/2071-1050/10/3/627/pdf

Next steps

- Prepare SADC regional positions to the UNFCC COP-24 Conference in Katowice, Poland.
- Lobby for a direct access mechanism within the Green Climate Fund to enable vulnerable groups within the member states to access the funds for climate change mitigation and adaptation.
- Urge UNFCCC parties, especially the industrial countries to make efforts in cutting emissions and providing financial and non-financial support to countries with fewer capacities. The wide failure of states to reach their emission reduction targets until 2020 proves that current efforts are not ambitious enough.
- Conduct gender audits and impact assessments to see how actors implement climate change and sustainable development policy aspirations on the ground, as well as their impacts for men and women.

- SADC legislators must move beyond planning and into implementation at a regional level.
- National sectors within SADC countries should ensure adequate support for climate change.
- Develop a SADC regional hub to support capacity development in various member countries in order to support implementation of climate change strategies.
- Stakeholders should re-think funding for climate change adaptation and mitigation initiatives and projects in SADC because without adequate funding to implement, and without integrated planning, there is a risk that some initiatives or infrastructure investments could be maladaptive.
- Monitor the implementation of the SDGs and the SADC Protocol to ensure that member states integrate gender in tackling the impacts of climate change.

Malawian farmers say"Adapt to climate change or die.

Photo: Gender Links

CHAPTER 11

Implementation

Articles 32-36

Women demand change in Zimbabwe's democratic processes. Alliance member Women's Coalition is currently leading a campaign to meaningfully include women in political leadership. *Photo courtesy of Women's Coalition*

KEY POINTS

- Comoros, set to become the 16th SADC Member State in August 2018, is a progressive Islamic state, but still facing many gender challenges.

- All of the 15 existing SADC Member States except Mauritius have signed the SADC Protocol on Gender and Development, but only ten have signed the amendment. One more country needs to do so for the amendment to go into force.

- Namibia, the new chair of SADC, received the Gender is My Agenda Campaign (GIMAC) Award in 2017 for its efforts to promote gender equality. Namibia is likely to be next to sign the amended Protocol.

- Only seven SADC countries (Botswana, Madagascar, Mauritius, Mozambique, Namibia, Seychelles and Zimbabwe) submitted their every two year reports in 2018. The Secretariat cited late reports as a "recurring challenge."[1]

- The SADC Non State Engagement Mechanism has gained momentum with a final report to be tabled at the 2018 SADC Heads of State Summit.

- 363 Centres of Excellence for Gender in Local Government councils are championing gender equality at the local level. The 2016 Gender and Local Government Score of 55% rose to 61% in 2017/2018.

- Seven countries held SADC Protocol@Work summits between November 2017 and June 2018, with eSwatini and South Africa holding a joint summit. These yielded 406 best practices on how the SADC Gender Protocol is being applied, especially at the local level.

- The Alliance network spans 136 organisations: 95 NGOS, 35 Community Based Organisations (CBOs) and six Faith Based Organisations (FBOs).

- The Alliance has improved meaningful participation of the Young Women's Alliance through the Community of Practice, blogging and social media.

---

[1] Draft Annotated Agenda Meeting of SADC Ministers Responsible for Gender/Women's Affairs, Johannesburg, South Africa. 3-5 July 2018.

Only **10** SADC countries have signed the amended Protocol

Table 11.1: Trends in Implementation since 2009

Parameter	Target 2030	Baseline 2009	Progress 2018	Variance (Progress 2018-2030 - target)
Number of countries that have signed the Protocol	16	13	14 (Angola, Botswana, Democratic Republic of Congo, Lesotho, Madagascar, Malawi, Mozambique, Namibia , Seychelles eSwatini, South Africa, Tanzania, Zambia and Zimbabwe)	-2(Mauritius and Comoros)
Number of countries that have signed the amended Protocol	14 countries	0 countries	10 (Angola, Botswana, Democratic Republic of Congo, Lesotho, Madagascar, Mozambique, eSwatini, Tanzania, Zambia and Zimbabwe)	-4 (Malawi, Namibia, Seychelles, South Africa)
Gender and Local Government Score	100%	55%	61%	-39%
Number of Alliance country MOU's	16	12	15	-1 (Comoros)
Number of theme MOUs	5	0	1	-4
Knowledge of the Agenda 2030 SADC Gender Protocol	100%	49% (2016)	48%	-1%
Highest	100 %	70% (eSwatini)	58% (eSwatini, Lesotho)	-42%
Lowest	100%	35% (Zimbabwe, Mauritius)	37% (Angola)	-63%
Gender Progress Score	100%	53% (2016)	61%	8%
Highest	100%	Mauritius (65%)	76% (Seychelles)	-24%
Lowest	100%	Mozambique (49%)	51% (Mozambique and Angola)	-49%

Source: Gender Links, 2018.

Table 11.1 shows that:
- Fourteen countries have now signed the SADC Protocol on Gender and Development. Mauritius has still not signed. After Comoros joins SADC, it will also need to sign.
- Ten countries - Angola, Botswana, Democratic Republic of Congo, Lesotho, Madagascar, Mozambique, eSwatini, Tanzania, Zambia and Zimbabwe - have signed and ratified the updated Protocol. Namibia, upcoming chair of SADC is likely to be the next to sign. Three quarters of the 14 signatories have to sign the amended Protocol for it to go into force.
- Gender Links as the coordinating organisation for the Alliance has MOU's with 15 country focal networks. These MOUs now need review in line with the revised Protocol and newly adopted Monitoring, Evaluation and Reporting Framework.
- The Alliance has only one cluster based MOU; these need to be urgently updated.
- The average knowledge score for the Protocol is 48%. eSwatini and Lesotho (58%) had the highest knowledge scores while Angola had the lowest at 37%.
- The average regional Gender Progress Score (GPS) is 61%, eight percentage points higher than the 2016 score of 53%. Seychelles (76%) scored highest while Mozambique and Angola (51%) scored lowest.

Signing of the Protocol

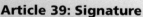

Article 39: Signature
The Protocol shall be signed by the duly authorised representatives of Member States.
Article 40: Ratification
The Protocol shall be ratified by the signatory states in accordance with their constitutional procedures.
Article 41: Entry into force
The Protocol shall enter into force thirty (30) days after the deposit of instruments of Ratification by two-thirds of the Member States.

The average knowledge score for the Protocol is 48%

2018 marks the tenth anniversary of the SADC Gender Protocol. By 2016, all SADC Member States except for Botswana and Mauritius had signed the Protocol. In May 2017, after years of lobbying and advocacy by the Alliance, Botswana signed the amended Protocol which removed specific time frames and aligned the Protocol to the Sustainable Development Goals and the African Union (AU) Agenda 2063.

COUNTRY	SIGNED PROTOCOL	SIGNED the agreement amending the PROTOCOL[2]	RATIFIED PROTOCOL	DEPOSITED INSTRUMENTS
Angola	✓	✓	✓	✓
Botswana	✓	✓	✗	✗
DRC	✓	✓	✗	✗
Lesotho	✓	✓	✓	✓
Madagascar	✓	✓	✗	✗
Malawi	✓	Ready to sign prior to 2018 summit	✓	✓
Mauritius	✗	✗	✗	✗
Mozambique	✓	✓	✓	✓
Namibia	✓	Ready to sign	✓	✓
Seychelles	✓	Committed and preparing to sign	✓	✓
South Africa	✓	Advanced internal consultations	✓	✓
eSwatini	✓	✓	✓	✓
Tanzania	✓	✓	✓	✓
Zambia	✓	✗	✓	✓
Zimbabwe	✓	✓	✓	✓

Table 11.2: Signing and ratification progress of the Protocol by country

Sources: SARDC SANF 17 No 23, June 2017; SADC Gender Monitor 2016; Record of SADC Gender Ministers Meeting 2018.

Table 11. 2 summarises the status of SADC Member States ratification of the Protocol, its amendment, and depositing of instruments with the SADC Secretariat.

At their meeting in Johannesburg in July 2018, SADC Ministers noted that only ten SADC countries had signed the agreement amending the Protocol: They expressed concern that in terms of Article 22 (11) of the SADC Treaty and Article 38 (3) of the SADC Protocol on Gender and Development, an amendment of the Protocol after it has entered into force shall be adopted by a decision of three quarters (11) of the 14 Member States that are parties to the Protocol[3].

Namibia most likely to clinch the deal: The Ministers noted that one more state needed to sign for the amendment to go into force. The ministers noted that Mauritius' position on not signing remained the same; but Seychelles, Namibia, Malawi and South Africa were at various stages of preparing to sign the amendment, with Namibia, the new chair, and host of the 2018 summit, seemingly the likeliest to become the eleventh signatory, allowing the amendment to go into force[4].

2018

marks the

10th

anniversary

of the

SADC

Gender

Protocol

---

[2] SADC (2017) Record: Meeting of Ministers Responsible for Women's Affairs, June 2017; July 2018.
[3] Draft Annotated Agenda Meeting of SADC Ministers Responsible for Gender/Women's Affairs, Johannesburg, South Africa. 3-5 July 2018.
[4] Ibid.

Comoros: What to expect from SADC's latest member[5]

In August this year, SADC will formally welcome Comoros as a new member of the regional group. The Barometer will add Comoros to all its measures in 2019.

A Thomson Reuters Foundation survey has ranked Comoros the best Arab country in the world for women. The survey examined perceptions of gender violence, reproductive rights, the treatment of women within the family, their integration into society and attitudes towards a woman's role in politics and the economy in 22 Arab states.

Comoros, a spice and perfume-producing Indian Ocean archipelago lying between

Comoros women have more rights than women in other Arab countries, reflects a poll in June 2018. *Photo courtesy of Thompson Reuters Foundation*

Mozambique and Madagascar, scored overall best in the poll based on experts' views. It came top for reproductive rights, women in the economy and women in the family. Reasons for Comoros' high ranking in the survey include:

- A Constitution which states that citizens will draw governing principles and rules from Islamic tenets, also refers to citizens' equal rights and duties regardless of sex.
- Comoros has ratified the U.N. Convention on the Elimination of All Forms of Discrimination against Women, sometimes called the world's "bill of rights" for women. It is one of only three Arab League states to do so without any reservations. It has also ratified the Convention on the Rights of the Child and the African Charter on Human and Peoples' Rights.
- Lands and homes are usually awarded to women in case of divorce or separation in Comoros, according to the U.S. State Department.
- Family law states that women may marry and stay in the homes built for them by their parents, over which the husband may not have any right. The furniture remains attached to this home, even if purchased by the husband.
- Half the inmates in Moroni's prisons are being held for sex crimes, a proportion that suggests Comoros has enforced laws against sexual violence.
- More than a third of adult women are in the labour force, U.N. data shows. Women feel equal to their husbands and are mostly in charge about spending household income. Strong matrilineal traditions coexist with a patrilineal system inherited from Islam.
- In the last government, women were installed as minister of telecommunications and labour minister. This represented 20% of Comoros' total ministerial positions, a higher proportion than in any of the other 21 polled Arab states.
- Women are beginning to make their entrance in high, decision-making positions. The state prosecution, the Great Mutual Funds of Comoros, the Postal Bank and the General Planning Commission are all headed by women.
- Women are under no pressure to have boys over girls in Comoros, according to the country's gender experts.
- Comoros' previous president Ahmed Abdallah Mohamed Sambi, a moderate Islamist, was quoted as saying he was not ready to make Comoros an Islamic state and that women would not be forced to wear the veil.

Source: Thomson Reuters Foundation; http://news.trust.org/item/20131111123247-fry3c

---

[3] SADC (2017) Record: Meeting of Ministers Responsible for Women's Affairs, June 2017.
[4] Ibid.
[5] Adapted from information available at http://news.trust.org/item/20131111123247-fry3c

Comoros rated the **best** Arab country in the world for ♀

Gender management systems

Article 33: Financial provisions
1. State parties shall ensure gender sensitive and responsive budgets and planning, including designating the necessary resources towards initiatives aimed at empowering women and girls.
allocate the necessary human, technical
and financial resources for the successful implementation of this Protocol.

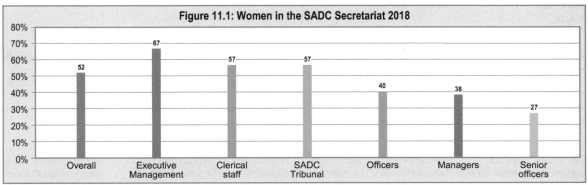

Figure 11.1: Women in the SADC Secretariat 2018

Source: Gender Links, 2018.

SADC Secretariat makes progress in gender mainstreaming: In June 2017, Gender Ministers put in place measures to promote gender parity in the SADC Secretariat. Figure 11.1 shows that as at 11 April 2018, women comprised:
- 52% of all staff.
- 67% of executive management.

- 38% of managers.
- 27% of senior officers.
- 40% of officers.
- 57% of clerical staff.
- 57% of the SADC Tribunal (four out of the seven judges are women).

Table 11.3: Country mapping of National Gender Policies, process and alignment to the Protocol

Country	Gender ministry	Gender integrated in national development plans?	Gender policy (date)	Gender action plan (date)	Aligned to Protocol? If not, how feasible?	In-country Gender Responsive Budgeting (GRB) Process	Upcoming process/entry points
Angola	Ministry for Family and the Promotion of Women.	Yes, The PRRP/ECP have defined objectives targeting women and gender equality. (Post-conflict rehabilitation and National Reconstruction Programme/ Estratégia de Combate à Pobreza).	National Strategy to Promote Gender Equality up to year 2005.	Yes, 2005.	No, not specifically but addresses sectors similarly.	Yes, gender budgeting initiative introduced in 2000. A UNIFEM programme in support of the Ministry of Finance in mainstreaming gender in budgeting processes.	Advocacy on development of aligned policy and implementation plan. Advocacy in women's representation in the upcoming election (August 2017).

Country							
Botswana	No, Gender Affairs Department under the Ministry of Labour and Home Affairs.	Yes.	Yes, draft form 2011.	Yes, based on WID Policy, 1997.	Yes.	UNECA assisting Botswana with gender budgeting process BOCONGO leading civil society leads effort to address GRB.	Baseline implementation of the SADC Gender Protocol and harmonising existing national policies with the Protocol.
Comoros	The government entity in charge of gender is currently the General Commission for Solidarity and Gender Promotion (CGG) housed in the Ministry of Health, Solidarity and Gender.[6]	Gender focal point in each Ministry.	Defined by the Growth and Poverty Reduction Strategy Paper (PRGSP) updated in September 2009, the National Gender Equity and Equality Policy (PNEEG).	Yes adopted in 2008, needs to be reviewed.	Not specifically but country has ratified CEDAW and the Convention on the Rights of the Child and the African Charter on Human and Peoples' Rights.	Through support from the African Development Bank, UN Women and UNICEF.	Comoros participated in the United Nations Human Rights and Gender Thematic Group upstream initiatives.
DRC	Minister of Gender, Women and Children.	Yes.	Yes, adopted 2011.	Yes, adopted 2011.	Yes, costed implementation plan in March 2014.	Implementation of costed plan.	Ongoing backstopping and support from GL and Alliance network.
Lesotho	Ministry of Gender, Youth Sports and Recreation.	Yes.	Yes, 2003 requires review.	Yes, need to review action plan.	In the pipeline led by Alliance focal network, Protocol ratified.	Buy in of GRB.	Hold a GRB workshop.
Madagascar	Ministry of the Population, Social Protection and Promotion of Women.	Yes but hampered by political uncertainty.	Yes, 2004 but requires review.	Yes, 2004 but requires review.	Not fully but aligned to international instruments.	Ad-hoc through UN Agencies and international corporation partners.	Implementation of the reviewed SADC Gender Protocol, review of the gender policy.
Malawi	Yes, Ministry of Gender, Children, Disability and Social Welfare.	Yes, 1996-1999.	Gender Policy 2005 reviewed in 2013 incorporating comments from the Office of President and Cabinet.	Yes, 2005 -2008.	Yes, Gender Equality Act aligned to the Protocol.	Yes, government-driven initiatives with support of SADC Gender Unit.	Alignment of action plan finalised in October 2014. Enforcement of the Gender Equality Act.
Mauritius	Yes, Ministry of Gender Equality, Child Development and Family Welfare.	Yes.	Yes, 8 March 2008.	No, but proposals to formulate may be brought to the Gender Ministry for consideration.	To some extent.	In the process of establishing civil society initiatives around gender budgeting.	Advocacy around signing the Protocol and review of child marriage policies.
Mozambique	Yes, Ministry of Women and Social Action.	Yes.	Yes, March 2006. Requires review.	Yes, addressing gender-based violence.	Yes, finalised in August 2014.	Yes, a joint civil society and government initiative.	Post -2015 implementation of the gender action plan.
Namibia	Yes, Ministry of Gender Equality and Child Welfare.	Yes.	Yes, revised 2010 - 2020 National Gender Policy.	Yes, costed gender action plan developed in 2011.	Yes, thematically incorporates the 28 targets.	Yes, costing of the national gender action plan completed.	Mainstreaming through thematic clusters across government ministries.
Seychelles	Gender Secretariat since 2012 moved to Ministry of Social Affairs, Community Development and Sports.	Yes, but often gender neutral.	Yes, 2012 Draft National Gender Policy.	Yes, still in draft form.	Yes, integrates all 28 targets in the National Gender Policy and costed gender action plan.	Initiatives supported by UNFPA; gender mainstreaming processes supported by the SADC Gender Unit. Follow up workshop scheduled for September 2014.	Finalising the National VAW study, implementation of the gender action plan ongoing.

---

[6] African Development Bank, Gender Profile of Comoros (Accessed 12/06/2018 on https://www.afdb.org/fileadmin/uploads/afdb/Documents/Project-and-Operations/Comoros%20-%20Country%20Gender%20Profile.pdf)

South Africa	Yes, Ministry of Women.	Yes, but not to a large extent.	Yes, adopted 2000.	Yes, plans addressing gender-based violence.	Feasible through advocacy with Alliance focal network.	Yes, gender budgeting initiatives supported by UN Women.	Advocacy and lobbying with Ministry of Women to review Gender policy and Action plan Post - 2015. Lead as SADC chair of Ministries of women in implementing the Post 2-15 Protocol. Engagement mechanism between civil society and Ministry of Women.
eSwatini	No, there is a Gender and Family Unit that has been elevated to the Deputy Prime Minister's office from the Ministry of Home Affairs.	Through the Deputy Prime Minister's office.	Yes, National Gender Policy 2010 to be reviewed and aligned to Protocol.	Yes, plan was developed in 2011 and revised in 2012 to align to Protocol.	Yes.	Has developed gender action Plan aligned to the Protocol. Yes, gender budgeting initiative supported by UNFPA.	Implementation of costed Gender Action Plan Aligned to the Protocol.
Tanzania	Yes. Ministry of Community Development, Gender and Children.	Yes, Mkukuta II and I.	Yes, Gender Policy 2001 which requires review started a review of the policy in 2011.	Yes.	Alignment in tandem with constitution review process; Buy-in of costed implementation plan.	Yes, a strong civil society led process.	Constitutional Review still ongoing. Revision of national gender policy. Advocacy campaign by civil society for the signing of the reviewed Protocol.
Zambia	Ministry of Gender.	Yes, to some extent.	Yes, adopted in 2000.	National Action Plan on Gender-Based Violence (2008-2013).	Has developed costed gender action plan aligned to the Protocol.	Yes, as of the beginning of 2011, the national GRB launched in conjunction with UNIFEM (UN Women).	Constitutional adopted in January 2016, civil society will likely advocate for a review of the Gender Policy following the provision for a gender commission.
Zimbabwe	Yes, Ministry of Women Affairs, Gender and Community Development.	Yes.	Draft Gender Policy reviewed 2013 and is before cabinet	Yes, currently developing one parallel to the national policy review process.	Yes, aligning to Gender Protocol in the revised policy.	Policy reviews, capacity building initiatives, budget analysis processes and feedback sectoral budgeting process.	Implementation of revised National Gender Policy (2017). Alignment of laws to new Constitution.

Source: Gender Links, 2018.

Table 11.3 shows that:
- Fourteen SADC countries have integrated gender in national development plans, with the exception of Madagascar, which is a fragile post-conflict state and has not yet ratified the Protocol.
- Fourteen SADC countries have some sort of gender policy, again with the exception of Madagascar. At least six countries are completing or undertaking reviews after concerns that most policies are dated.

- Eight countries; Namibia, eSwatini, Zambia, DRC, Lesotho, Mozambique, Malawi and Sey-chelles developed costed gender action plans aligned to the Protocol. However, these now need to be aligned to the revised Protocol.
- Nine countries have engaged in GRB initiatives of some kind (Angola, Botswana, Malawi, Mozambique, Namibia, South Africa, Tanzania, Zambia and Zimbabwe). Namibia has achieved continental acclaim in its efforts to mainstream gender.

Namibia wins African Excellence Award on Gender[7]

Namibian President Geingob receiving the African Excellence Gender Awards for 2017 in Windhoek, 6 June 2018.
Photo courtesy of Newera News

Namibian President Geingob received the African Excellence Gender Awards for 2017 in June 2018, taking over from ex-Liberian president Ellen Johnson Sirleaf. A country that has committed to gender equality through creating gender clusters across all line ministries, Namibia has made progress in promoting gender equality and the empowerment of women. The award is given by *Gender Is My Agenda Campaign* (GIMAC) recognising efforts in promoting gender equality through different policy initiatives and interventions.

GIMAC recognised Namibia for its legal and policy frameworks aimed to promote women's rights by the steering committee. Namibia's commitment to gender is demonstrated in the important role women play in politics, including the executive and legislature.The country has seen an increase in women in decision-making positions, following the ruling SWAPO Party's adoption of 50/50 gender representation. This has helped increase women representation in parliament. Namibia aims to fully implement the 50/50 policy in line with the Southern African Development Community Protocol on Gender and Development before the 2030 deadline.

Namibia has mainstreamed the Protocol through the National Gender Policy and Plan of Action. Cabinet has approved the co-ordination mechanism for the implementation of the gender policy. The Cabinet has directed that gender responsive budgeting should be included in all government budget circulars. The Ministry of Finance incorporates gender guidelines into budget call circulars coupled with training of officials on Gender Responsive Budgeting (GRB). Accounting Officers are directed to ensure gender issues are incorporated into all sector policies, programmes, plans, budgets, implementation, monitoring and evaluation[8].

President Geingob committed himself to champion the theme: "Women's Empowerment and Inclusive Governance" during the two-year tenure of the GIMAC Award. Additionally, Namibia is committed to increasing the numbers of women in decision making positions in a meaningful manner.

African leaders that have been rewarded for promoting women rights include Abdoulaye Wade (Senegal), Thabo Mbeki (South Africa), Paul Kagame (Rwanda), Armando Guebuza (Mozambique) and Ellen Johnson-Sirleaf who won it in 2011.

Source: Excerpt from APA News, June 2018
http://apanews.net/en/pays/namibie/news/namibia-gets-african-excellence-award-on-gender

Madagascar's Ministry of the Population, Social Protection and Promotion of Women has taken initiatives such as developing the National Gender and Development Action Plan in an attempt to coordinate gender projects carried out by various actors including civil society, public, or private institutions. Popularisation and monitoring of the Protocol is largely done by civil society. Technical and financial partners, like the U.N. Population Fund, UNICEF, African Union, and UNESCO, have supported the country in the implementation and monitoring of gender commitments[9].

In DRC, the Ministry of Gender, the Family and Child as the focal point for gender issues heavily relies on gender focal persons and international donors to monitor gender equality frameworks. Gender Focal Points exist at each ministry but these resources are underutilised and lack capacity on gender issues. At the provincial level, Gender Focal Points support implementation of The National Gender Policy and represent the Division of Gender at all Levels of the administration. Gender Committees are also in place. Provincial Thematic Groups for Gender serves as a

---

[7] Adapted from information accessed on http://apanews.net/en/pays/namibie/news/namibia-gets-african-excellence-award-on-gender, June 2018.
[8] SADC Gender Monitor (2016)
[9] Gaby Razafindrakoto, World Policy (2016): Gender Equality in Madagascar

mechanism to identify gaps in the sector[10]. However, smooth monitoring of gender equality is hampered by ongoing political unrest in the country.

UCOFEM Director and DRC Alliance focal person, Anna Mayimona Ngemba participates at a media marathon to appeal to all the authorities to get involved in promoting the rights of Congolese women, March 2017.   *Photo courtesy of UCOFEM*

In **Mozambique**, the Ministry of Women and Social Action (MMAS) established a National Directorate of Women (DNM) responsible for advising on gender policies and facilitating gender mainstreaming. The National Council for the Advancement of Women (CNAM) was established as a body to promote and implement gender policies across all the sectors in Mozambique. Both the DNM and CNAM contribute towards regular monitoring and evaluation of the country's gender instruments . The country developed a gender action plan aligned to the Protocol in 2014, although this needs reviewing in light of the revised Protocol.

Gender mainstreaming in local government over the last decade, councils across Southern Africa have worked to localise the SADC Protocol on Gender and Development through their membership of the Centres of Excellence (COE) for Gender in Local Government Programme. The ten-stage COE process involves developing and implementing local level action plans aligned to the Protocol, with flagship projects on local economic development, climate change and ending GBV. Councils share good practices at the annual SADC Protocol @Work summits.

GL is working with

363

COEs in

10

countries

46%

of the total population

Table 11.4: Centres of Excellence for Gender in Local Government[12]				
Country	**No COE Councils**	**Country Population***	**COE Population**	**% Population**
Botswana	32	2 331 390	1 593 140	68%
Lesotho	50	2 173 390	978 757	45%
Madagascar	67	25 254 011	4 800 630	19%
Mozambique	19	29 161 872	5 738 780	20%
Mauritius	3	1 281 103	686 169	54%
Namibia	36	2 574 587	995 989	39%
eSwatini	24	1 328 066	1 162 554	88%
South Africa	20	55 408 513	5 265 062	10%
Zambia	44	17 232 190	9 829 337	57%
Zimbabwe	68	16 111 699	10 275 458	64%
TOTAL	**363**	**152 856 821**	**41 325 876**	**46%**

Source: Gender Links, 2018.

Table 11.4 shows that Gender Links (GL) is working with 363 councils in ten countries that implement the programme. The councils cover a population of over 41 million, or 46% of the total population of the ten countries. Each COE council has Gender Focal Persons (GFP) and Gender Champions (GC) working on the ground to mainstream gender through action plans and gender responsive resource allocations.Key monitoring and evaluation tools and resources have been revised to integrate the SDGs and the Post 2015 SADC Protocol. In 2017/2018, 221 councils from the seven countries that held SADC Protcol@Work summits[13] reported on their progress. The data in this section is derived from these summit entries.

Standard Setting: Each year, the councils score their performance based on a Gender and Local Government Score Card that includes 25 key questions that councils need to answer on women's participation in the councils, its administration; gender mainstreaming policies and processes; how

---

[10] Sida (2016) Democratic Republic of Congo Country Gender Profile.
[11] Japan International Corporation Agency (JICA) - Mozambique Gender Profile (2015).
[12] Adapted from Gender Links Governance COE report, July 2018.

these reflect in gender specific and mainstream programming; and how these are reflected in budgets. In line with the SDG theme, "leave no one behind", the Post 2015 Score Card, now referred to as the Agenda 2030 score card, has a number of new parameters, including youth, disability and other forms of marginalisation. The way the scoring works is that councils score themselves, and then they are independently adjudicated by a panel of experts at the summit. These experts examine portfolios of evidence presented by the councils. Councils are awarded different colour certificates at the summits based on their performance, as a form of motivation.

| Platinum 90% + | Gold 80 -89% | Silver 70-79% | Bronze 61-69% | Green 51-60% | Blue under 50% |

Deepening citizen engagement: An important new innovation in 2017/2018 is citizens contributing to the process through scoring their local authorities. The perception questionnaire involves the same 25 questions that the councils self-score on. 200 women and 200 men in each locality gave their assessment of the gender responsiveness of their councils. Judges assessed the evidence provided by councils, and took into account citizen scoring (similar to 360 degree feedback), in reaching their conclusion. The judges scores are final.

Signs of improvement: In 2016, the average baseline score was 55%. In the 2017/2018 summits, this had risen to 61%. Overall, citizens scored their councils at 59% compared to the 61% score awarded by the judges. The narrow margin between citizen and judges scoring is an important validation of the process. The statistics and examples that follow, drawn from the annual summits, illustrate the impact that the COE's are having on the ground.

50/50 gains momentum: As reflected in Chapter 2 on Gender and Governance, women comprise a mere 23% of elected officials in local government in Southern Africa. This ranges from 6% in the DRC to 48% in Namibia. As various campaigns in Chapter 2 get underway to lobby for women's equal representation in local government, the COE process helps to groom local level leadership through the day-to-day functioning of the councils.

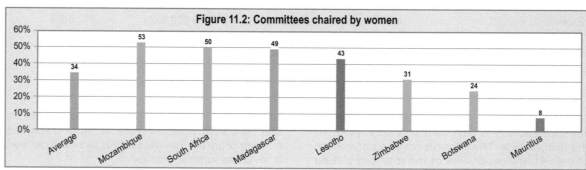

Figure 11.2: Committees chaired by women

Average: 34; Mozambique: 53; South Africa: 50; Madagascar: 49; Lesotho: 43; Zimbabwe: 31; Botswana: 24; Mauritius: 8

Source: Gender Links 2018.

Figure 11.2 shows that on average 34% of COE committees are chaired by women in the seven countries. This ranges from 8% in Mauritius to 53% in Mozambique. Women in COEs in four of the countries have 40% or more women chairing committees. In Zimbabwe and Botswana, the proportion of women chairing COE committees is higher than the proportion of women in councils.

This shows that while the wheels of change turn slowly for women in elected local government, space is being opened for women to exercise leadership through council processes and structures. However, in Mauritius women comprise 26% of councillors, but only 8% of committee chairs. This is a reminder of the underlying patriarchal norms that still need to be challenged.

Citizens scored councils **59%** compared to **61%** score of judges

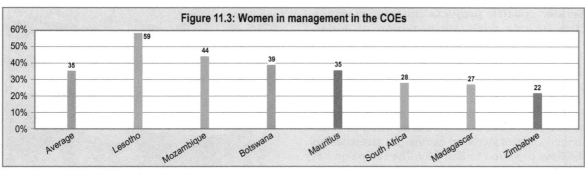

Figure 11.3: Women in management in the COEs

Average	Lesotho	Mozambique	Botswana	Mauritius	South Africa	Madagascar	Zimbabwe
35	59	44	39	35	28	27	22

Source: Gender Links 2018.

Council administration is one area in which more rapid changes to women's representation is possible, as this is based on appointed rather than elective office. Figure 11.3 shows that in all countries, the proportion of women in management in the COEs is higher than councillors. This ranges from 22% in Zimbabwe to 59% in Lesotho, with an overall average of 35%.

Gender management systems in local government: The COEs have set up gender management structures to improve gender mainstreaming in service delivery. These include Gender Focal Persons (GFP - administrative functionaries) and Gender Champions (political leaders), gender committees and service specific sub-committees. The gender management structures have improved documentation of council's records through sex disaggregation as well as training of council staff, community members and councillors on gender equality. These structures will improve implementation of the Post 2015 Protocol.

Getting the gender balance right in Zvimba, Zimbabwe

Located in Mashonaland West Province, Zvimba Rural District Council (RDC) has a gender policy that incorporates the Sustainable Development Goal targets. Of the 35 councillors, about one third (11) are women. The chairperson of council is a woman. Zvimba has eight committees, and four are chaired by women, in line with council policy that for every committee chaired by a woman, the deputy must be male and vice-versa.

In Zvimba young people, people with disabilities and women participate actively in pre-budget consultative, District Aids Action Committee, Water Sanitation and hygiene meetings.

GL-Sida Zvimba field visit.　　　　　*Photo: Tapiwa Zvaraya*

Zvimba has a total workforce of 64 employees, of whom 24 (slightly over one third) are women and 17 are youth. Women constitute 38% of management. Zvimba is breaking new ground with a woman from the council being employed in a non-traditional area of decision-making as the Town Manager of Banket Local Board, a jurisdiction managed by Zvimba RDC.

The council has a sexual harassment policy whose cases are reported to a committee in council through the disciplinary hearing process. The council has ensured that all new buildings and schools and council toilets are disability friendly.

Zvimba RDC is one of the few local authorities in Zimbabwe which boasts of a stand- alone gender committee which sits five times a year. Among its many achievements, the committee has lobbied for a bursary funds for less privileged children to enable them to go to school and the construction of victim friendly units.

Source: Zimbabwe SADC Protocl@Work Summit 2018.

Gender specific projects emerging from the COEs include adequate provision of water, improving health care access to women, reducing GBV through safety and awareness campaigns, climate change mitigation through education and greening projects.

Ending violence, community by community: At least half of the COEs have been involved in the Sixteen Days of Activism campaigns stretched to 365 Days of Action to End GBV. The campaign has become a platform for dialogue between policy makers and the community. IT for advocacy training during the Sixteen Days strengthens networking and accountability. Spanning the period 25 November (International Day of No Violence Against Women) to 10 December (Human Rights Day) with World AIDS Day (1 December) in between, the Sixteen Days rene ws commitment to year-long campaigns to end GBV.

Investing in technologies to end GBV and provide networking platforms: Councils are increasingly working with young women and junior councillors to conduct community GBV awareness campaigns on women's bodily integrity and devise IT tools for tracking delivery, and creating a vibrant Community of Practise. In Lesotho, councils have been involved in developing a GBV application that sets to provide prevention, response and treatment to survivors of GBV.

Strengthening SRHR at the local level: As the custodians of primary health care through local

Participants of the GBV app training in Mohale's Hoek council, Lesotho - March 2018.
Photo: Ntolo Lekau

clinics and in some cases fully fledged health departments, COE councils will in 2018 strengthen work on Sexual Reproductive Health and Rights (SRHR). Councils have started to integrate health, GBV and HIV plans into the broader context of SRHR campaigns, with a strong involvement by young women, emphasising respect for women's bodily integrity and autonomy. These campaigns are largely reflected in council action plans with some going a step further to include them in their integrated development plans.

Gender and local economic development: A key function of local government is to promote local economic development. Councils distribute land and housing; they are responsible for markets and infrastructure; they have access to information on local financing.

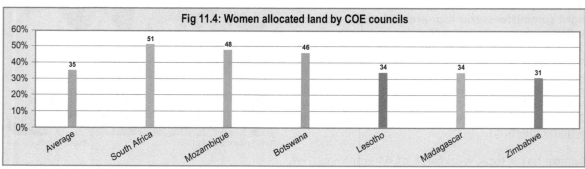
Fig 11.4: Women allocated land by COE councils

	Average	South Africa	Mozambique	Botswana	Lesotho	Madagascar	Zimbabwe
	35	51	48	46	34	34	31

Source: Gender Links 2018.

Madagascar Entrepreneurship training participants, Antananarivo, March 2018.
Photo: Zoto Razanadratefa

Figure 11.4 shows that on average, COE councils allocated 39% of housing to women. This ranged from 33% in Mozambique to 66% in South Africa.

Empowering women, ending gender based violence at the local level - Following a pilot project to link council GBV and Local Economic Development (LED) action plans through entre-preneurship training for survivors of GBV, Gender Focal Persons (GFP) and mentors in 50 councils have been trained to run the Sunrise Campaign themselves[14]. Now including young women with a view to "stopping violence before it starts" as well as working with men's groups in broadening the programme to reach out to households, rather than just individual women, these councils have shown commitment to ending gender violence as per the Agenda 2030 targets.

Botha-Bothe in Lesotho promotes women's empowerment

Botha-Bothe Urban council, the second council to join the Centres of Excellence programme in Lesotho, is an example of a council that is promoting women's empowerment.

The council has arranged for women entrepreneurs in the Sunrise Campaign to form a company to benefit from tenders provided by the council. For example, the women have started supplying the council with toilet paper. Women are encouraged women to register their construction companies and few have been engaged in waste management.

Councillors and council staff of Botha Bothe after receiving a summit award, November 2017. *Photo: Ntolo Lekau*

The council works closely with the representative of district child and gender protection unit which is mandated to deal with gender based violence. Public gatherings ensure citizen participation in council matters in particular job creation.

In line with the principle of "leaving no one behind", people living with disability (PWD) are represented in the council and equally paid. The council employs 56% women, 25% youth and 5% people with disabilities. The council is disability-friendly and accessible for every community member. Strict rules apply to ensure that all council procedures incorporate disability access and opportunities.

The council has a policy of three months provision for maternity leave and flexible nursing hours for three months. The council does not have a sexual harassment policy, but cases of such are reported directly at the nearest police stations.

A number of men are involved in care work supported by the council - the number has increased from eight to 14. The council increased numbers of people who access ARV treatment and this has reduced deaths due to HIV.

Source: Botha-Bothe Institutional Profile submitted at the 2017 Lesotho summit

Gender and climate change: Several councils are implementing gender and climate change projects. For example, Zvimba RDC has a climate change policy which is being implemented. To reduce the effect of deforestation, the council has embarked on a tree planting project. In 2017, the council planted 52400 trees in 32 wards. In 2018 council targeted schools and to date 25000 trees have been planted around schools. Zvimba district is mainly for communal farmers and farm communities who rely on firewood for cooking, with women bearing the major responsibility for gathering firewood. Council in partnership with Environment Africa are constructing biogas digesters that are being used to provide energy for cooking.

Gender Responsive Budgeting (GRB): As councils review their gender and GBV action plans to update these with the new SADC Protocol targets and indicators, an important value-add is the focus on Gender Responsive Budgeting.

---

[14] Gender Links Sunrise Campaign programme (2017 to 2019).

GRB

▲

4%

from

$251mn

in 2016 to

$260mn

in

2017/2018

Table 11.5: Gender budgets in local government

Gender budget type	Amount (US$) 2016/17	Amount (US$) 2016/17	% Increase	% Total 2017/2018
Gender processes in councils				
Promoting gender equality in decision-making and public participation	11 237 338	12 486 758	11%	5%
Promoting employment equity	25 278	263 171	941%	0.1%
Resources allocated for the process around gender mainstreaming 2017	214 675	216 673	1%	0.1%
Amount budgeted for visibility for the Council's Gender Action Plan in 2017	6 337 160	3 273 744	-48%	1.3%
Monitoring, Evaluation and Learning for the Council's Gender Action Plan	1 477 594	1 961 931	33%	0.8%
Sub Total	*19 292 045*	*18 202 277*	*-6%*	*7.0%*
Gender specific initiatives				
Amount for resources budgeted to ending GBV	5 071 261	11 342 850	124%	4.3%
Amount budgeted for promoting gender/youth and disability friendly SRHE, HIV and AIDS programmes	34 222 536	41 907 171	22%	16.1%
Sub total	*39 293 797*	*53 250 021*	*36%*	*20.4%*
Gender mainstream initiatives				
Amount budgeted for gender responsive local economic development	59816 781	68 020 970	14%	26.1%
Amount budgeted for promoting gender/youth/PWD responsive projects on climate change	37 684 748	33 551 234	-11%	12.9%
Amount budgeted for promoting gender/youth and disability friendly infrastructure an social development polices and practices	94 878 840	87 932 764	-7%	33.7%
Sub total	*192 380 369*	*189 504 968*	*-1%*	*72.6%*
Total	**250 966 211**	**260 957 266**	**4%**	**100.0%**

Source: Gender Links Local Government COE report 2018.

Table 11.5 shows that for the 221 COEs that submitted entries to the summits in 2017/2018, GRB rose by 4% from $251mn in 2016 to $260mn in 2017/2018. The table sums up the different categories taken into account in computing GRB figures. These include:

- **Gender mainstreaming processes in councils:** This includes policy formulation; promotion of women's equal representation; the processes around gender mainstreaming; monitoring, evaluation and visibility activities. This is usually a relatively small part of the budget (in this case 7%).
- **Gender specific initiatives:** These include programmes such as GBV and promoting SRHR. For the COE's monitored this constituted one fifth (20%) of the total.
- **Gender in mainstream programming:** This should constituted 73% or the bulk of GRB expenditure as it should. It comprises such mainstream council activities as local economic development, infrastructure, and initiatives related to the environment, such as waste management. Budget allocations counted here are those proven to benefit women, men, boys and girls equally, or affirmatively, for any disadvantaged group. Between 2016/2017 and 2017/

2018, this category of expenditure increased by 36 percentage points, while the other categories of expenditure decreased slightly. This is a positive sign, as mainstream programming constitutes the bulk of council expenditure.

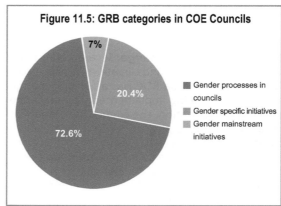

Figure 11.5: GRB categories in COE Councils

- Gender processes in councils
- Gender specific initiatives
- Gender mainstream initiatives

Source: Gender Links, 2017.

Another important feature of GRB is consultations with communities affected about the gender budgeting process. As illustrated in the case study that follows, the process is as important as the product!

Talking budgets enhances gender responsiveness in Chinhoyi, Zimbabwe

Chinhoyi is a Centre of Excellence for Gender in Local Government in Northern Zimbabwe. As part of its gender action plan in 2018, Chinhoyi ensured that women and men, boys and girls were included in community consultations on its 2018 budget. The project is innovative in that by consulting them, stakeholders feel valued and this leads to a gender responsive budget. The council allocated $5000 to this activity. As a result of including the views and voices of women the council has now budgeted $40 000 for gender responsive programming.

Budget consultations with the community in Cooksey Hall, Chinhoyi Zimbabwe. *Photo: Maluwa Mphande*

The Budget is a yearly plan which allocates resources to various Council departments. It helps Council to manage its financial resources wisely and establishes a framework for saving and spending decisions. Early long-term goal setting, saving, investing, education, training, and wise spending decisions are factors that help achieve our goals. We involve stakeholders to enhance transparency. Failure to conduct annual consultations results in complains from stakeholders; poor revenue collection, increased debts, and non- approval of the budget by the Ministry of Local Government due to objections.

We went ward by ward holding meetings with various stakeholders, for example the business community; church fraternity, vulnerable groups; youths; and residents associations. We discussed challenges they are facing as far as council service delivery and operations is concerned. We also assessed our service level benchmark. The community suggested a review of various tariffs.

In 2018 we worked hard to come up with a Gender- Sensitive Budget. We ensured that budget consultations involved men and women, boys and girls and people living with disability. The needs of all these will be incorporated in the budget. Key outcomes include:

• Council has incorporated women as part of the Budget Consultation Committee.

• Council budgeted $40 000 for community projects in which women are the primary beneficiaries.

• Water delivery has been prioritised and stakeholders are now paying their monthly bills due to improved delivery of this core service, resulting in improved revenue collection.

• As a result of water now reaching areas that did not receive it, women have been relieved of ferrying water from long distances.

• Daily working hours of women has been reduced due to reduced distances to fetch water, giving women opportunity to enter labour market and undertake income generating activities.

• Safety and free movement for women in public places has been enhanced through provision of street lights.

Source: Aquilinah Hasha; Municipality of Chinhoyi; SADC Protocol@Work Summit, Zimbabwe, 2018

Regional institutional arrangements

Article 34: Institutional arrangements
1. The institutional mechanisms for the implementation of this Protocol shall comprise the:
(a) Committee of Ministers Responsible for Gender/ Women's Affairs;
(b) Committee of Senior Officials Responsible for Gender/ Women's Affairs; and
(c) SADC Secretariat
2. The Committee of Ministers responsible for Gender/Women's Affairs shall:
(a) ensure the implementation of this Protocol; and
(b) supervise the work of any committee or sub-committee established under this Protocol.
3. The Committee of Senior Officials shall:
(a) report to the Committee of Ministers on matters relating to the implementation of the provisions contained in this Protocol;
(b) supervise the work of the Secretariat;
(c) clear the documents prepared by the Secretariat to be submitted to the Committee of Ministers;
(d) invite the Secretariat to make presentations on gender and development to the Committee of Ministers, as and when necessary; and
(e) liaise closely with both the Committee of Ministers and the Secretariat.
4. The SADC Secretariat shall:
(a) facilitate and monitor reporting by States Parties on the implementation of the Protocol;
(b) coordinate the implementation of this Protocol;
(c) identify research needs and priorities in gender/women's affairs areas; and
(d) provide technical and administrative assistance to the Committee of Ministers and the Committee of Senior Officials.

The Gender Protocol Alliance represents the gender sector in the SADC-CNGO

At their meeting in Ezulwini, eSwatini in June 2017, gender ministers recommended that the Council of Ministers consider rescinding the decision to merge the Gender Unit with the Directorate of Social Human Development and Special Programmes. The Council of Ministers considered and approved the recommendation and maintained the Gender Unit as a stand-alone unit, as reported at the Gender Minister's meeting held in Johannesburg.[15] This is significant as it retains the profiling of the Gender Unit, and ensures that this important cross-cutting function is not relegated to a line function.

The annual meeting of SADC Gender Ministers historically invited member states to include one civil society representative per each delegation of three, ensuring that Women's Rights Organisations (WRO) had a seat at the table of this important meeting. The gender sector was the only one in which civil society had formal representation in this way, making it a best practice for engagement between civil society and the region's inter-governmental body.

The SADC Secretariat discontinued this practise in 2017, stating that all relations with civil society are to be conducted through the SADC Council of NGOs (SADC CNGO) that has formal observer status to the Heads of State Summit. The SADC Gender Protocol Alliance represents the gender sector in the SADC CNGO. This arrangement has limitations in the gender and other sectors as it does not provide direct access to the decision-makers in these sectors. Reflecting the close relationship between WRO and governments at national level, some continue to invite NGO representatives as part of their delegations to the annual gender ministers meetings. However, the bigger issues concerning civil society engagement with governments in the region have led to consultations over the last year on a mechanism for Non State Actor Engagement.

---

[15] Draft Annotated Agenda Meeting of SADC Ministers Responsible for Gender/Women's Affairs, Johannesburg, South Africa. 3-5 July 2018.

Taking SADC to the people: NSA engagement mechanism

Abbie Dithlake, former SADC CNGO Executive Director addressing participants at the 2015 SADC Civil society forum, August 2015.
Photo courtesy of the SADC We Want website

The proposed Non State Actors (NSA) engagement mechanism underscores SADC's desire to have a meaningful engagement with civil society with a view to "taking SADC to the peoples of the region". The Mechanism proposes a two-pronged approach: promoting a two-way communication as well as expanding the range of NSAs that SADC works with in order to enhance community outreach. The guiding principles of the proposed SADC Institutional Mechanism for Engagement with Non State Actors include:

- ***Accessibility and Inclusivity*** - advocated for the development of an appropriate mechanism in which NSAs and SADC Member States can discuss and collaborate on the implementation and monitoring of various regional plans such as the Regional Indicative Strategic Development Plan (RISDP). Such advocacy initiatives have been carried out at regional level through the civil society forums held parallel to formal SADC summits, in consultative meetings with SADC Secretariat and in national policy dialogues. The mechanism calls for access to SADC National Committees and focal points by NSAs. It calls for a reporting relationship to Summit and other SADC Institutions.

- ***Effective participation in formal processes of SADC*** - The consultative role of the SADC-CNGO remains a narrow platform for wider engagement by NSAs. Engagement of SADC by NSA is not formalised and is at the discretion of the Secretariat and Member States. The SADC NSA engagement mechanism calls for real consultation of NSA including observer status.

- ***Accountability and Transparency*** - An analysis of the lack of institutionalised mechanisms shows that NSAs who remain out of the decision-making process of SADC find it difficult to influence the decision-makers. Calls in the NSA engagement mechanism include SADC to take on board the views of NSAs, in particular civil society. Other concerns include need for transparency in SADC decision making processes, especially at ministerial and heads of state level, and poor civil society representation at crucial meetings.

- ***Subsidiarity*** - This principle guides NSA's interaction with SADC for organisations that work at the national and regional level. Applying this principle would support the establishment of an effective engagement mechanism by ensuring that issues, actions and initiatives taken to address them are defined as being either national or regional, and subsequently dealt with through the appropriate institutions and stakeholders at those respective levels. Applying this principle will also ensure that the overlapping of scope and actions is eliminated.

- ***Representativeness*** - The presence of legitimate organisations interacting with mutual respect and recognition is another essential component necessary for the development and establishment of the engagement mechanism.

- ***Working with Umbrella and Apex bodies*** - The engagement with NSAs both at national level and regional levels will be with umbrella and Apex bodies representing the diverse NSA organisations.

- ***Coherence with continental and institutional mandates*** - The proposed mechanism is characterised by regular and structured consultations, accessible and up-to-date information, streamlined coordination and collaboration anchored in SNCs and National Contact Points, publicized communication mechanisms, formal and officially recognised mandates, a code of conduct and formal Accreditation system for NSAs.

Source: Southern Africa Trust - Taking SADC to the People, Final report on the Proposed SADC Non State Actors Engagement Mechanism (June 2016)

Monitoring, Evaluation and Reporting

> **Article 35: Implementation, Monitoring and Evaluation**
> 1. State Parties shall ensure the implementation of this Protocol **in line with the SADC Implementation Action Plan and the SADC Monitoring, Evaluation and Reporting Framework**.
> 2. State Parties shall ensure that national action plans, with measurable timeframes, are implemented, and that national and regional monitoring and evaluation mechanisms are developed and implemented.
> 3. State Parties shall collect data against which progress in achieving targets will be monitored.
> 4. State Parties shall submit reports to the Executive Secretary of SADC once every two years, indicating the progress achieved in the implementation of the measures agreed in the Protocol.
> 5. The Executive Secretary of SADC shall submit the progress reports to Council and Summit for consideration.

In the updated SADC Gender Protocol, SADC Gender Ministers called for regularity in reporting, monitoring and evaluation of the implementation of the Protocol in order to assess progress and challenges, and develop mechanisms for sharing best practices at their June 2016 meeting[16]. The SADC Monitoring, Evaluation and Reporting framework (MERF) aims to improve reporting on gender in the region.

The SADC Gender and Development Monitor is published by SADC with Members States input. Civil Society publishes this annual SADC Gender Protocol Barometer which has tracked progress of implementation of the Protocol since 2009.

The 2018 SADC Gender and Development Monitor will focus on Economic Empowerment. However it appears that publication will be delayed. The SADC Secretariat informed gender ministers at their meeting in Johannesburg in July that the Secretariat sent the MERF tool to Member States in November 2017 for the collection of data, good practices and reporting on the specific articles of the Protocol. However, at the time of the meeting in July 2018, only seven member states (Botswana, Madagascar, Mauritius, Mozambique, Namibia, Seychelles and Zimbabwe) had submitted their reports. The Secretariat noted that "the delayed submission of national progress reports has become a recurring challenge", delaying in this specific instance the production of the 2018 SADC Gender and Development Monitor.[17]

The Southern Africa Gender Protocol Alliance

> ### ALLIANCE ACTIVITY BOX 2017/18
>
> - **August 2017:** The Alliance launches the 2017 SADC Gender Protocol Barometer at the SADC Civil Society Forum and during the annual Alliance meeting
> - **November 2017 to June 2018:** The Alliance holds six national Protocol@work summits showcasing best practices in gender mainstreaming.
> - **December 2017:** The Alliance launches a Community of Practice with resources for implementing the SADC Gender Protocol.
> - **January 2018:** The Alliance hosts an exchange visit with EASSI and the Commonwealth Foundation.
> - **March 2018:** The Alliance holds a first dialogue on its Community of Practice during Women's Day.
> - **March 2018:** The Alliance holds a side event with the Government of Malawi on localising SDGs.
> - **May/June 2018:** The Alliance holds gender and rights scoring meetings assessing governments' performance on gender equality.
> - **May 2018:** The Alliance collaborates with mainstreaming civil society in an inaugural regional civil society meeting exploring common challenges and solutions.
> - **May 2018:** The Alliance contributes to the African Union Gender Strategy (2023).

---

[16] SADC Gender Minister Record (June 2016).
[17] Draft Annotated Agenda Meeting of SADC Ministers Responsible for Gender/Women's Affairs, Johannesburg, South Africa. 3-5 July 2018.

ONLY 7 countries reported in 2018

SADC GENDER PROTOCOL ALLIANCE

Gender Links is the coordinating NGO of the SADC Gender Protocol Alliance, a coalition of 15 national gender networks and five regional NGOs that lead on the various themes of the SADC Gender Protocol. The coalition campaigned for the adoption, implementation and review of the SADC Gender Protocol whic h is now a Southern Africa's roadmap for achieving Sustainable Development Goal (SDG) five - gender equality. The Alliance works with civil society, governments, SADC, Faith based movements, media and local government organisations to hold governments accountable on gender commitments and advocate for gender equality progress.

Table 11.6: Alliance network fact file from mapping	
Total Number of Partners	136
Coverage	
SADC Region	45%
National Level	55%
Type of Organisation	
NGO	95
CBO	35
FBO	6
Areas of Primary Focus	
Women's Rights	88%
Men-for-Change	63%
CSO Mainstreaming Gender	76%
Youth Focus	79%
Youth Integrated into Work	85%
Areas of Work	
Training	79%
Advocacy	73%
Lobbying	55%
Service Delivery	55%
Research	44%
Other	20%

Source: Gender Links.

Taking pride in the Alliance network in Mozambique.
Photo: GL Mozambique

Alliance

WRO

in

SADC

Table 11.6 summarises the latest results of a mapping tool used by the Alliance to track its reach. The table shows that the Alliance network spans 136 organisations. 55% of these are national women's rights and gender organisations. 45% have a regional reach. Of the total, 95 are NGOS, 35 are Community Based Organisations (CBOs) and six are Faith Based Organisations (FBOs). Women's Rights (88%) is the primary focus of these organisations, with 63% also focusing on men; 79% on youth; 85% mainstreaming youth into their work. Training (79%) is a major preoccupation, followed by advocacy (73%); lobbying (55%); service delivery (55%) and research (44%).

At national level, the work of the Alliance is coordinated by focal networks that coordinate WRO within their countries. An example is long standing Alliance partner Forum Mulher in Mozambique.

5

clusters -

VOICE

(Governance,

Constitu-

tional and

Legal Rights;

Media);

CHOICE

(SRHR) and

CONTROL

(Education

and Economic

Justice;

Climate

Change and

Sustainable

Develop-

ment)

Forum Mulher promotes inclusivity through its programmes

Forum Mulher (Women's Forum) is a Women's Network Forum that works for the rights of Mozambican women. The Alliance focal network for Mozambique, Forum Mulher deals with gender and development issues, advocacy and lobby, as well as education and information work.

Through intensive advocacy and lobbying work, Forum Mulher has achieved major influence on the country's new family law, securing the legal position and recognition of women.

Some of its specific areas of work includes strengthening the network of gender trainers and consultants at the provincial

Forum Mulher members march during the International Action Day for Women's Health, 28 May 2018. *Photo courtesy of Forum Mulher*

level, developing policies that include the principles of gender equality and equity, improving knowledge of the rights of women and of the laws defending these rights by disseminating international protocols and national laws; to improve access to justice, especially for victims of gender-based violence, by improving access to legal services, counselling and advocacy on legal instruments.

To improve information dissemination on its work, Forum Mulher, uses its women's related issues through the website, internet, newsletter, radio and television. Forum Mulher focuses on strengthening the institutional capacity of its members, the capacity of provincial women's and gender networks and organisations in four provinces, to support them in working in a co-ordinated manner and advocate for equality of women's rights. Its mission is to boost economic changes and socio-cultural, a feminist perspective, strengthening the actions and the political influence of its members and Mozambican civil society, collaborating with national and international social movements.

Some of Forum Mulher's projects have linked Mozambique to the international community including Latin American countries. Some of the programmes include coordinating the World March of Women, organising marches for approval of the law against domestic violence and family law and influencing gender mainstreaming in the action program for the reduction of absolute poverty (PARPA). The organisation has led advocacy on increasing maternity leave from of 60 to 90 days.

Another famous community outreach programme includes coordinating the feminist caravan in Southern Africa and building capacity of communities on LGBTI issues through training in partnership with Lambda, an LGBTI focus organisation forum and the Commission on the Status of women.

Source: Excerpt from Forum Mulher's institutional profile

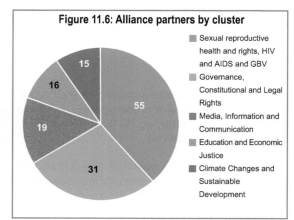

Figure 11.6: Alliance partners by cluster

- Sexual reproductive health and rights, HIV and AIDS and GBV
- Governance, Constitutional and Legal Rights
- Media, Information and Communication
- Education and Economic Justice
- Climate Changes and Sustainable Development

Source: Gender Links, 2018.

The Alliance partners are divided into five clusters - Voice (Governance, Constitutional and Legal Rights; Media); Choice (SRHR) and Control (Education and Economic Justice; Climate Change and Sustainable Development). With 55 organisations, SRHR is the largest cluster; followed by Governance, Constitutional and Legal Rights (31); Media, Information and Communication (19) and Education and Economic Justice (16).

Alliance Community of Practice

The Alliance Community of Practice (CoP) is a virtual platform for all human rights, gender activists and practitioners in the development space, transformational and progressive persons and leaders; to share ideas and engage in a process of collective learning; in a shared domain with other like-minded people with a strong gender equality persuasion. Launched by Alliance partners during the 2017 Sixteen Days of Activism Campaigns period under the banner, end violence, empower women by 2030, the CoP has hosted topical discussions such as Women's Day and gender based violence. The CoP was launched by all 15 SADC countries. The CoP currently has more than 3000 members. The Community features access to all SADC Gender Protocol Barometer data; summit case studies; media clippings and alerts; training materials, forums and dialogues, and many more. The Alliance Community brings together a network of fifteen Southern African countries and all the existing global and continental commitments on gender equality. The Alliance CoP connects the Alliance with the Local Government Community which

Alliance focal points Virginia Muwanigwa and Neesha Ramen discuss the Alliance strategy during the 2017 regional meeting.
Photo: Melody Kandare

brings together local government practitioners in local authorities including Gender Champions and Gender Focal Persons. Alliance community members are also connected to the Media Community-to "connect, collect and coordinate" debate and dialogue, knowledge generation and sharing and capacity building in the media.

Alliance outreach

- *Country level meetings* - The Alliance shares best practices and strategies for gender implementation at the national level through focal network led meetings. The Community of Practice is an online space where the Alliance can dialogue on gender equality issues as well as broader civil society issues.
- *Regional civil society network* - Alliance members have a Memorandum of Understanding with Gender Links. In May, GL and the Southern African Trust convened a workshop on the Sustainability of Southern African regional CSOs.
- *Recognition* - The Alliance was recognised as a SADC gender equality coordinating platform in Southern Africa[18]. Alliance programme staff and members regularly participate in mainstream media interviews and contribute opinion and commentary pieces. The blog site will be used by the Alliance to highlight topical gender issues e.g. when participating in global platforms.
- *New Media* - the Alliance programme has a twitter handle @GenderProtocol managed by the Alliance manager and linked to the Gender Links twitter handle. A number of regional and continental gender movements follow the Alliance on twitter. The Alliance unit is planning to establish an informal community of Practice on Facebook.
- *Website* - the Alliance has a dedicated section on the Gender Links website. Navigation through the website is possible by countries and project. The Alliance blog is embedded on the website.
- *Publications* - A list of stakeholders help with the marketing of all Alliance publications. The publications are also available online for sale for those who want to use them as reference materials. All publications are shared with members for wider distribution.
- *African and global links* - The Alliance is a member of the Women's major group, the Post 2015 Women's coalition and FEMNET. The Alliance also collaborates with mainstream civil society through CIVICUS, the African Civil Society Circle, SADC CNGO and Southern Africa Trust. During this period, the Alliance, through the annual Barometer has spread its wings to East and West Africa, with a Pan African Barometer now being mooted.

---

[18] Regional Organisations Meeting, 29 May 2018 - SADC Presentation.

The
Alliance
is a
member
of the

♀

Major
Group
and
FEMNET

Barometer goes Pan African!

In the year under review, the Alliance strengthened its relations in East Africa, and participated in a ground-breaking meeting in West Africa where participants for the Barometer to go Pan African.

In 2016, the Alliance provided technical support to the Eastern African Sub-regional Support Initiative for the Advancement of Women (EASSI) to produce the first East African Barometer.

In 2017, the Alliance participated at the EASSI two day dialogue that brought together Government representatives, national and regional civil society and women's organisations, the academia and the media to discuss the findings of the East Africa Community (EAC) Gender Barometer. The regional multi-stakeholder dialogue took stock of the achievements of women in the five partner states of East Africa (Uganda, Rwanda, Kenya, Tanzania and Burundi).

Since the Treaty for the EAC came into force in 2000, (17 years to date), there has not been a credible citizen's scorecard to monitor its implementation and especially the promises made in the Treaty through the various Articles that speak to women's rights. This multi-stakeholder dialogue addressed the absence of citizen participation and the need to monitor implementation of the EAC instruments. These include the EAC Treaty Articles on women's rights as well as the regional and international women's rights instruments acceded to by the EAC Partner States, the Beijing Platforms for Action, Convention on the Elimination of all Forms of Discrimination Against Women (CEDAW) and the Maputo Protocol.

In February 2018, EASSI conducted a study visit to the Alliance coordinating NGO, Gender Links to learn about building movements through clusters. The Alliance shared about monitoring evaluation systems, gathering evidence to show progress in implementation and experiences in resource mobilisation.

The West Africa Gender data forum held in Accra in from 10-12 July 2018 called for the production of a Pan African Gender Barometer as a means of amplifying women's voices in the implementation of the 2030 Agenda.

The forum discussions on gender data collection and curation were informed by the gender barometer projects in Southern and East Africa. The forum highlighted the need to track progress towards achieving targets set out in national and regional policies such as the ECOWAS Gender Policy, the Supplementary Act and indicators under the Sustainable Development Goal 5 (Gender Equality).

Presentations made by the different countries showed that most of West African states have developed national gender policies or strategies. At the regional level, bodies such as African Union, Economic Community of West African States (ECOWAS), West African Economic and Monetary Union (UEMOA) have all adopted gender policies and are gradually mainstreaming gender into other policies. ECOWAS has especially been proactive and has taken significant steps towards the promotion of gender equality in the region through the establishment of the ECOWAS Gender Development Centre and the subsequent adoption of its Gender Policy in 2004 as well as the 2015 Supplementary Act relating to Equality of Rights between Women and Men[19].

Despite the existence of these policies, data on the progress made towards eliminating gender inequality within the region is sparse. Gender disparities remain perverse within the economic, social, cultural and political strata of West African States. These factors are even more prevalent in rural communities as negative socio-cultural norms supersede national laws and policies.

Source: Gender Links

[19] Policy for Gender Mainstreaming in Energy https://www.afdb.org/fileadmin/uploads/afdb/Documents/Generic/Documents/ECOWAS Policy for Gender Mainstreaming in Energy Access.pdf

SADC Protocol@Work Summits

Seven countries held SADC Protocol@work summits between November 2017 and June 2018, with eSwatini and South Africa holding a joint summit. These yielded 406 best practices on how the SADC Gender Protocol is being applied, especially at the local level.

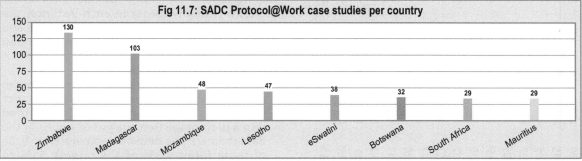

Fig 11.7: SADC Protocol@Work case studies per country

Source: Gender Links Protocol@work data portal (2018).

Figure 11.7 shows the country break down. Zimbabwe gathered the largest number of case studies (132) followed by Madagascar (103). Rural and urban councils are showing improvement in implementing the revised Protocol at the local level through community involvement and targeting key influencers to push for policy change.

Figure 11.8 shows the number of case studies by summit category. Some 159 Centres of Excellence for Gender in Local Government presented institutional case studies. Project based cased studies constituted 181 of the total. Survivors of GBV presented 56 case studies. Fifty four entered the Drivers of Change or leadership category.

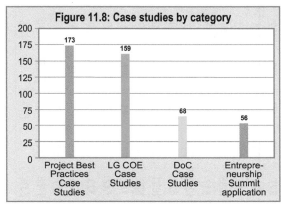

Figure 11.8: Case studies by category

Source: Gender Links Protocol@work data portal (2018).

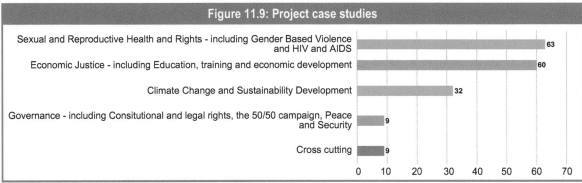

Figure 11.9: Project case studies

Source: Gender Links Protocol@work data portal (2018).

Figure 11.9 shows that the SRHR theme had the highest number of case studies at 63 followed by the economic justice theme at 60 and the climate change theme at 32. The governance theme had the lowest number of case studies presented (9). Nine case studies were cross cutting.

Country	Agenda 2030 SADC Gender Protocol Citizen score card						Agenda 2030 SADC Gender Protocol Quiz						Gender Attitude Survey					
	Women -target	Actual	Men -target	Actual	Total target	Total actual	Women -target	Actual	Men -target	Actual	Total target	Total actual	Women -target	Actual	Men -target	Actual	Total target	Total actual
Botswana	400	448	400	431	800	879	400	426	400	330	800	756	400	424	400	414	800	838
Lesotho	400	404	400	423	800	827	400	387	400	422	800	809	400	340	400	351	800	691
Madagascar	600	498	600	375	1200	873	600	434	600	381	1200	815	600	205	600	172	1200	377
Mauritius	400	141	400	74	800	215	400	326	400	273	800	599	400	110	400	173	800	283
Mozambique	600	564	600	471	1200	1035	600	462	600	374	1200	836	600	543	600	279	1200	822
eSwatini	400	279	400	238	800	517	400	182	400	247	800	429	400	581	400	434	800	1015
Zimbabwe	600	598	600	605	1200	1203	600	564	600	587	1200	1151	600	598	600	614	1200	1212
Angola	500	253	500	376	1000	629	500	300	500	379	1000	679	500	121	500	133	1000	254
DRC	500	501	500	530	1000	1031	500	487	500	500	1000	987	500	209	500	218	1000	427
Malawi	400	279	400	251	800	530	400	278	400	249	800	527	400	256	400	198	800	454
Seychelles	200	70	200	72	400	142	200	93	200	84	400	177	200	63	200	93	400	156
South Africa	700	243	700	299	1400	542	700	500	700	450	1400	950	700	586	700	440	1400	1026
Namibia	400	159	400	164	800	323	400	157	400	156	800	313	400	144	400	153	800	297
Tanzania	600	181	600	94	1200	275	600	184	600	99	1200	283	600	188	600	97	1200	285
Zambia	600	99	600	68	1200	167	600	31	600	9	1200	40	600	343	600	189	1200	532
Sub- total	7300	4717	7300	4471	14600	9188	7300	4811	7300	4540	14600	9351	7300	4711	7300	3958	14600	8669
Percentages		51%		49%		63%		51%		49%		64%		54%		46%		59%

Source: GL Survey Gizmo M and E Data 2018.

Table 11.7 reflects Monitoring and Evaluation forms distributed by Alliance and COE networks during the course of the year to gauge various aspects of progress. In the absence of a substantial research, M and E budget, these forms are distributed at summits, meetings and events. They form part of the learning, popularisation and information sharing at these gatherings. Although the number of forms is below target in each instance, the numbers distributed (ranging between 8000 and 9000 of each) is significant considering the quasi voluntary way in which this "activist research" is conducted. Key facts include:

- *The Citizen Score Card (CSC)*, in which women and men rate their government's performance on a scale of one to ten, and this is computed into a percentage (see analysis of results in the data chapter). The networks administered 9188 of these forms (63% of the target); 51% to women and 49% to men.
- *The Knowledge Quiz* which tests women's and men's knowledge of the SADC Gender Protocol. The networks distributed 9351 of these forms; 64% of target; 51% to women and 49% to men.
- *The Gender Progress Score (GPS)* that measures changes in gender attitudes. Networks distributed 8669 of these forms (59% of target); 54% to women and 46% to men.

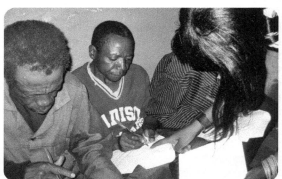

Filling in Alliance M and E Forms in Kapiri Mposhi, Zambia.
Photo: Colleen Lowe Morna

Entries by type of organisation

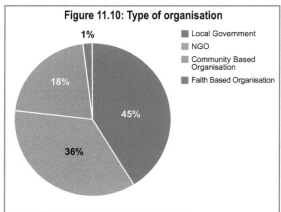

Figure 11.10: Type of organisation

- Local Government
- NGO
- Community Based Organisation
- Faith Based Organisation

1%
18%
45%
36%

Source: Gender Links, 2018.

Figure 11.10 shows that local government made 45% of the summit entries; NGOs contributed 36% of the entries; 18% were made by CBOs and 1% by FBOs.

Summit entries by type of change

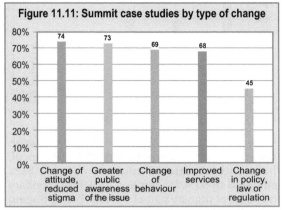

Figure 11.11: Summit case studies by type of change

Source: Gender Links Protocol@work data portal (2018).

When they make their summit entries participants rate the most significant change that occurs as a result of their intervention. Figure 11.11 shows that the main change taking place is changes in attitude (74%) followed by greater awareness of the issue (73%). Change of behaviour (69%) and improved services (68%) rate third and fourth. Change of policies, law or regulation (45%) is the lowest ranked change. The overall findings are encouraging, as the major challenge facing the region is changing attitudes, mindsets and services, rather than more policies or laws.

Knowledge of the Protocol

The SADC Gender Protocol Quiz aims to assess the level of Protocol knowledge amongst SADC citizens. The quiz is administered to an enumerated sample of citizens and data is analysed through Google data studio linked to Survey Gizmo. Gender Links coordinated the data analysis while SADC Gender Protocol members administer the quiz.

The quiz provides multiple choice answers to the following:
1. The Post 2015 SADC Gender Protocol was adopted by Heads of State in:
2. The SADC Gender Protocol was reviewed in line with the:
3. The Post 2015 SADC Gender Protocol (targets):
4. The Post 2015 SADC Gender Protocol declares that (age of marriage):
5. The completely new section in the Post 2015 SADC Gender Protocol is about:
6. The Post 2015 SADC Gender Protocol provision on women in decision-making calls for (women's representation):
7. The new additions on economic empowerment in the SADC Gender Protocol include?
8. SADC member states have made a commitment to (on GBV):
9. The Education Article in the Post 2015 SADC Gender Protocol has been reviewed to include:
10. The Health Article in the SADC Gender Protocol has been expanded to include:

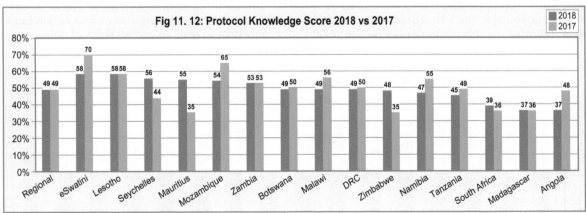

Fig 11. 12: Protocol Knowledge Score 2018 vs 2017

Source: Gender Links Protocol Knowledge survey, 2018.

Figure 11.12 shows that the average regional knowledge score is 48%, a one percentage point decrease from last year's score of 49%. Overall, these scores point to the need for much greater advocacy on the updated Protocol. The Alliance plans to facilitate this process through translating a simplified version of the updated Protocol for all its networks. eSwatini and Lesotho (58%) had the highest scores.

eSwatini chaired SADC in 2016/2017. The SADC Gender Protocol Monitoring and Evaluation Framework (MERF) was adopted at the gender ministers meeting in eSwatini. Mauritius showed the greatest improvement (from 35% to 55%) possibly owing to Alliance advocacy on Mauritius signing the Protocol.

MAIN change = changes in attitude

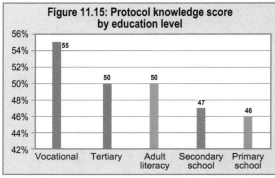

Figure 11.13: Quiz score by sex

Source: Gender Links Protocol Knowledge survey, 2018.

Figure 11.13 shows that 'other sex identities' who include the LGBTI community had the best knowledge of the Protocol at 58% followed by women at 48% and men at 47%.

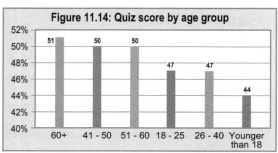

Figure 11.14: Quiz score by age group

Source: Gender Links Protocol Knowledge survey, 2018.

Figure 11.14 shows that the SADC Gender Protocol is best known by older people with 60+ age group scoring 51% followed by 51 to 60 and 41 to 50 at 50% each. Young people (18 to 40) scored 47% and those younger than 18 scored 44%. This is a clear indicator that efforts to popularise the SADC

Gender Protocol with young people need to be redoubled.

Figure 11.15: Protocol knowledge score by education level

Source: Gender Links Protocol Knowledge survey, 2018.

Figure 11.15 shows a clear correlation between education level and knowledge of the Protocol. Those with vocational education scored 55% compared to 50% for tertiary; 47% for secondary and 46% for primary school. An interesting finding is that those with adult literacy scored 50%. This most likely reflects the advocacy work being done at the local level.

Gender Attitudes in the SADC region

The Alliance administers the Gender Progress Score (GPS) which measures the level of gender attitudes in the SADC region across all sexes. The GPS developed by Gender Links, which coordinates the Alliance, includes a standard set of questions to gauge gender attitudes. In 2016 GL added questions on contentious areas such as polygamy; choice of termination of pregnancy; sex work and sexual orientation. The 25 questions are scored on a scale of one equals least progressive to four equals most progressive to give an overall score of 100.

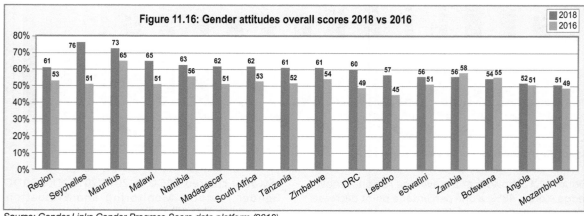

Figure 11.16: Gender attitudes overall scores 2018 vs 2016

Source: Gender Links Gender Progress Score data platform (2018).

Figure 11.16 compares the scores for 2016, the post 2015 baseline with an updated GPS, with the 2017/2018 scores. These are the first two periods

for which a comparison can be done, using the updated GPS. The graph shows that the average regional Gender Progress Score (GPS) is 61%, eight

'other sex identities' who include the **LGBTI** community had the best knowledge of the Protocol

percentage points higher than the 2016 score of 53%. Seychelles is the most gender aware per country at 76% closely followed by Mauritius at 73%, Malawi at 65% and Namibia at 63%. Angola (52%) and Mozambique (51%) have the lowest scores. No country slipped backwards over the period. Seychelles, Malawi, Tanzania and the DRC all showed marked improvement. These overall findings on gender attitudes in the region are encouraging.

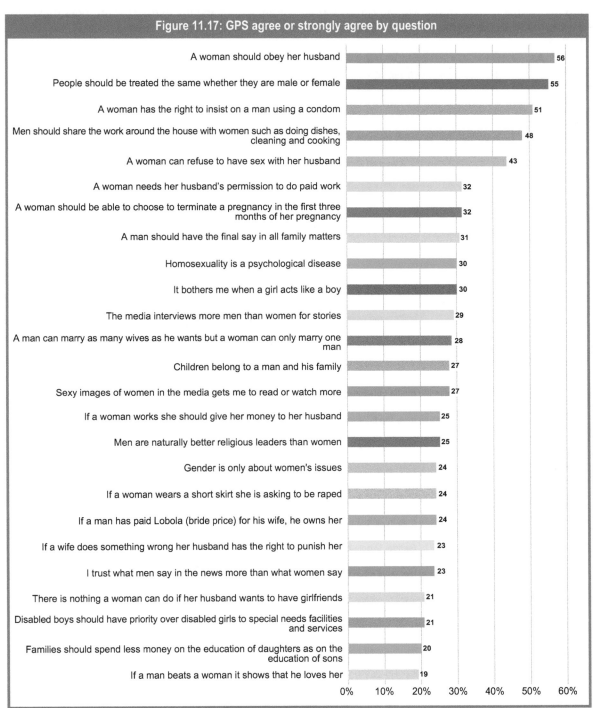

Figure 11.17: GPS agree or strongly agree by question

Question	%
A woman should obey her husband	56
People should be treated the same whether they are male or female	55
A woman has the right to insist on a man using a condom	51
Men should share the work around the house with women such as doing dishes, cleaning and cooking	48
A woman can refuse to have sex with her husband	43
A woman needs her husband's permission to do paid work	32
A woman should be able to choose to terminate a pregnancy in the first three months of her pregnancy	32
A man should have the final say in all family matters	31
Homosexuality is a psychological disease	30
It bothers me when a girl acts like a boy	30
The media interviews more men than women for stories	29
A man can marry as many wives as he wants but a woman can only marry one man	28
Children belong to a man and his family	27
Sexy images of women in the media gets me to read or watch more	27
If a woman works she should give her money to her husband	25
Men are naturally better religious leaders than women	25
Gender is only about women's issues	24
If a woman wears a short skirt she is asking to be raped	24
If a man has paid Lobola (bride price) for his wife, he owns her	24
If a wife does something wrong her husband has the right to punish her	23
I trust what men say in the news more than what women say	23
There is nothing a woman can do if her husband wants to have girlfriends	21
Disabled boys should have priority over disabled girls to special needs facilities and services	21
Families should spend less money on the education of daughters as on the education of sons	20
If a man beats a woman it shows that he loves her	19

Source: Gender Links Gender Progress Score data platform (2018).

Figure 11.17 gives the percentage of those who agreed or strongly agreed on the statements for each of the 25 questions. It reflects the many contradictions that still exist in Southern Africa. For example, 55% of respondents said that people should be treated the same whether they are women or men, yet 56% said that a woman should obey her husband!

Some encouraging results are 48% agreeing or strongly agreeing that men should share household duties; 43% that a woman can refuse to have sex with her husband; 32% that a woman can choose to terminate her pregnancy in the first three months.

While it is heartening that the lowest scores are on issues such as "if a man beats a woman in shows that he loves her" it is sobering that almost one fifth of respondents agreed or strongly agreed with this statement. Overall, the results show that there is still a big lag between normative frameworks and the patriarchal attitudes that drive gender disparities.

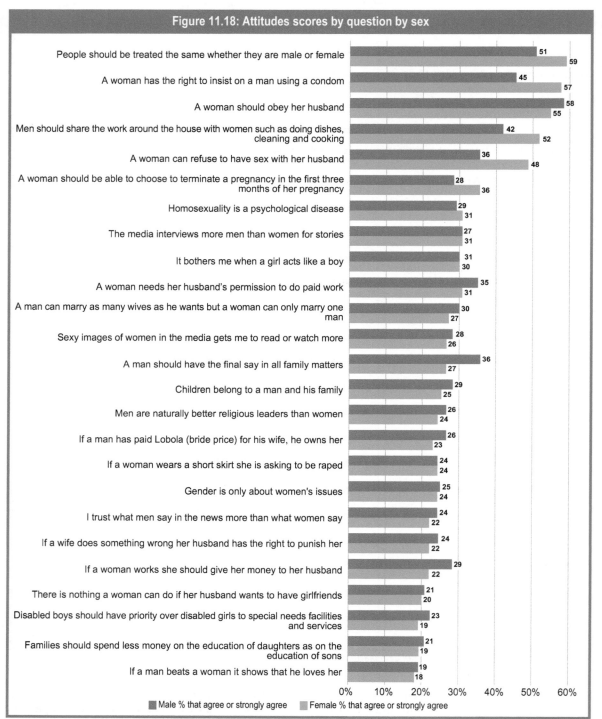

Figure 11.18: Attitudes scores by question by sex

Question	Male % that agree or strongly agree	Female % that agree or strongly agree
People should be treated the same whether they are male or female	51	59
A woman has the right to insist on a man using a condom	45	57
A woman should obey her husband	58	55
Men should share the work around the house with women such as doing dishes, cleaning and cooking	42	52
A woman can refuse to have sex with her husband	36	48
A woman should be able to choose to terminate a pregnancy in the first three months of her pregnancy	28	36
Homosexuality is a psychological disease	29	31
The media interviews more men than women for stories	27	31
It bothers me when a girl acts like a boy	31	30
A woman needs her husband's permission to do paid work	35	31
A man can marry as many wives as he wants but a woman can only marry one man	30	27
Sexy images of women in the media gets me to read or watch more	28	26
A man should have the final say in all family matters	36	27
Children belong to a man and his family	29	25
Men are naturally better religious leaders than women	26	24
If a man has paid Lobola (bride price) for his wife, he owns her	26	23
If a woman wears a short skirt she is asking to be raped	24	24
Gender is only about women's issues	25	24
I trust what men say in the news more than what women say	24	22
If a wife does something wrong her husband has the right to punish her	24	22
If a woman works she should give her money to her husband	29	22
There is nothing a woman can do if her husband wants to have girlfriends	21	20
Disabled boys should have priority over disabled girls to special needs facilities and services	23	19
Families should spend less money on the education of daughters as on the education of sons	21	19
If a man beats a woman it shows that he loves her	19	18

Source: Gender Links Gender Progress Score data platform (2018).

There is still a **big lag** between normative frameworks and the attitudes that drive gender

Figure 11.18 breaks down the responses to questions by sex. It shows similar patterns: a reminder that patriarchal attitudes are not confined to men. 55% women (compared to 58% men) believe that a woman should obey her husband. There are however important differences. For example, 59% women compared to 51% men said that women and men should be treated the same. 57% women compared to 45% men said that a woman has the right to insist on her husband using a condom. 48% women compared to 36% men said a woman can refuse to have sex with her husband. Clearly women are more emphatic about their rights than men. But achieving gender equality in SADC will involve changing the attitudes and mind sets of both women and men.

Next steps

Effective implementation of the revised SADC Gender Protocol requires systemic engagement by SADC, Member States and Non State Actors. Strengthening gender programmes at a local level has the potential to reignite movement building and amplify the voice of women. Collecting the right data to monitor progress is key to sustaining momentum. Key next steps include:

- Advocating for meaningful participation in SADC processes, including observer status through the SADC NSA engagement mechanism.

- Fact finding mission to the Comoros as the newly accepted 16th SADC Member State.
- Strengthening the Alliance through further mapping of NGOs, CBOs and FBOs, and inclusion of marginalised groups.
- Deepening national and regional work on SRHR and connecting efforts between local government and civil society.
- Strengthening the work of the Young Women's Alliance including through use of IT and mobile technologies to build effective gender equality campaigns.
- Alliance regional meeting preceding the SADC Heads of State Summit to be held in Namibia.
- Collaboration with mainstream civil society through the newly established Southern Africa Regional Civil Society platform.
- Holding gender equality dialogues on the Community of Practice including key population groups.

Nikodemus Aoxamub, gay rights activist and spokesperson of Rights Not Rescue Trust (left) addresses participants during a meeting challenging by-laws of sex workers.   *Photo courtesy of The Namibian*

BACKGROUND NOTE ON GENDER AND RELATED INDICATORS

This background note provides information on the various existing indicators considered in developing the new SADC Gender and Development Index (SGDI) aligned to the United Nations Agenda 2030, Africa Union Agenda 2063 and Beijing Plus 20.

The Human Development Index (HDI) - which is not a gender indicator - has four components which are meant to reflect Amartya Sen's "capability" approach to poverty rather than a simple income/expenditure monetary measure of poverty. The HDI components are (a) life expectancy at birth for health, (b) adult (15+ years) literacy rate and (c) combined gross enrolment rate for primary, secondary and tertiary education for education, and (d) gross domestic product (GDP) per capita for income. The four component scores are averaged to get the HDI number. The HDI thus gives a single simple (some would say simplistic) measure of the average achievement of the country in terms of human development. A league table was published in the annual Human Development Reports of the UNDP until 2009, and is widely quoted.

The HDI - like all measures - can be criticised on many grounds. Some of the criticisms are relevant from a gender perspective. Firstly, composite indices are appealing because there is only one number. But having a single number is not useful for policy-making purposes unless one knows WHY the single number is lower than one wants it to be. For example, South Africa's HDI has fallen in recent years. The main reason for this is a significant drop in life expectancy, which is one of the four components. The HDI indicator cannot tell you this. It is only by looking into the components that you can see it.

Secondly, there are data problems. UNDP uses international data-sets in the interests of having a uniform approach. This is probably the only feasible approach for an index covering so many countries and compiled from a single office. However it results in the use of data that are relatively old, and thus indicators that our out-of-date. It also results in individual countries contesting the indicators. The need to have indicators for as many countries as possible can also lead to the use of lowest-common-denominator variables, rather than the variables that would best reflect what the indices aim to measure. Where data are not available, sometimes heroic assumptions have to be made. In the case of the Gender-related Development Index (GDI) (see below), this is especially the case in relation to sex-disaggregation of GDP.

Thirdly, the indicators are all based on averages, and thus do not capture inequalities within a single indicator.

In 1995, at the time of the Beijing Conference, UNDP developed two gender-related indices - the Gender-related Development Index and the Gender Empowerment Measure (GEM) - to complement the HDI.

The GDI uses the same variables as the HDI, but each of the components is adjusted for unequal achievement between women and men. The GDI thus shares all the problems that the HDI has, but also has some further problems.

One problem with the GDI is that it assumes that equality on longevity would mean equal life expectancies for men and women. However, biologically women can expect to live longer than men. So when life expectancies are equal this suggests that women are disadvantaged in some way. This is not reflected in the GDI.

A confusing feature of the GDI is that the method uses only the male-female gap, without considering whether it is males or females who are "doing better". So a country where women outperform men in education will have the same penalty as a country where men outperform women by the same amount. We might think this is not a problem (in that men and boys should not be disadvantaged), but it does complicate how we interpret the GDI if the index combines some components where males are advantaged and others where females are advantaged.

Probably the biggest problem with the GDI is that it is heavily influenced by the income variable, so that wealthier countries will - all other things being equal - be reflected as having less inequality than poorer countries. Analysis has shown that for most countries the earned-income gap is responsible for more than 90% of the gender penalty. Exacerbating this problem is the fact that the income estimates are based on "imputed" rather than real data. Thus for many developing countries the earned income gap is assumed to be 75% because reliable data are not available. The 75% was chosen on the basis of 55 countries (including both developed and developing) for which data are available. Yet another exacerbating feature is that the data for the 55 countries relate only to formal non-agricultural wages. Yet in many African countries only a small proportion of the workforce - and an even smaller proportion of employed women - is employed in the formal non-agricultural sector.

The final problem to be raised here is lack of sex-disaggregated data in some cases. As a result, each year there are fewer countries that have GDI scores than have HDI scores. This means that a higher place in the inter-country ranking for the GDI than the HDI does not necessarily mean that the country is doing relatively well on gender.

The GEM focuses on political, economic and social participation rather than Sen's capabilities. The components are women's representation in parliament, women's share of positions classified as managerial and professional, women's participation in the labour force and their share of national income. Fewer countries have data on all of these elements than on the GDI elements and each year there are therefore fewer countries in the GEM index than in the GDI index.

The GEM measures income in more or less the same way as the GDI, so this component has the problems described above. The influence of the absolute level of income - and thus the bias favouring wealthier countries - is, in fact, stronger for the GEM than the GDI. The political component is problematic in that a parliamentary quota for women will automatically increase the GEM score, but will not necessarily mean that women exercise greater political power in the country.

Development of the Gender Equality Index (GEI) was motivated, at least in part, by the standard measures' lack of attention to issues related to the body and sexuality, religious, cultural and legal issues, ethics, women's rights and care.

The index was called the GEI, rather than the Gender Inequality Index (GII), so as not to focus only on gender imbalances. Instead, the index would measure the extent to which gender equality was achieved in any country.

It was recognised that as a global, comparative measure, the GEI would lose cultural and national specificity and would not capture gender equality in all its dimensions. It was thus proposed that each country also describe the historical and cultural context, and develop country-specific "satellite" indicators to complement the GEI.

The GEI covers eight dimensions, each of which has a number of indicators. The dimensions are:
• Gender identity;
• Autonomy of the body;
• Autonomy within the household;
• Political power;
• Social resources;
• Material resources;
• Employment and income;
• Time use.

The availability and adequacy of the GEI indicators have been tested only in Japan and Indonesia. These tests revealed the especial difficulty of measuring the first two dimensions quantitatively.

In the early 2000s, the United Nations Economic Commission for Africa (UNECA) developed the African Gender Status Index (GSI) and the African Women's Progress Scoreboard (AWPS). The AWPS is based on more qualitative judgments, although these are given numeric scores. The existence of the AWPS along-side the GSI is noteworthy, as it highlights the realisation that some aspects of gender equality cannot be adequately captured by quantitative indicators. The GSI is similar to the GDI and GEM in being computed from quantitative data. A major difference is that there are far more indicators - 43 in all!

The use of 43 indicators has two major drawbacks. Firstly, it means that most countries are likely to lack data on at least one indicator, or be forced to use unreliable data from small samples. Secondly, it means that the meaning of the index - and its direct usefulness for policy-making purposes - is even more obscure than for the HDI, GDI or GEM as one has to examine all the elements in detail to work out why a country is scoring higher or lower. The developers of the GSI acknowledge that there may be too many indicators.

UNECA tested the index in twelve countries (Benin, Burkina Faso, Cameroon, Egypt, Ethiopia, Ghana, Madagascar, Mozambique, South Africa, Tanzania, Tunisia, Uganda). The process took substantially longer than predicted. The delays in part reflected the challenges involved in collecting and checking so many indicators. Even with these delays and despite specifying five-year periods for each indicator, it was not possible to find all the indicators for each country.

The indicators are divided into three blocks, namely social power, economic power, and political power. The indicators all deal with gender issues, understood as the relations between women and men, and thus as needing to compare indicators for men and women. This means that maternal mortality and violence against women are not covered because they only concern women.

Each indicator represents a simple arithmetic comparison of the number of women to the number of men, thus reflecting the gender "gap". (A few of the indicators need a bit of manipulation to be able to get a gap.) Unlike the HDI and GDI, the GSI does not take the overall level of achievement into account. As a result, a good score on the GSI could reflect a high level of equality, but at a level of achievement that is poor for both women and men (girls and boys).

For weighting purposes, each of the three blocks - social, political and economic - has equal weight. Further, within each component of each block, each of the indicators has equal weight. In effect, this means that indicators that are in a component with relatively few indicators "count" more than those in a component with a greater number of indicators. The developers of the GSI suggest that other weighting approaches could be considered, such as:

- Weighting more heavily the components or blocks where there are the biggest gaps.
- Weighting more heavily those that can be changed more easily in the short term so that one can more easily "see" the impact of advocacy and policy changes.
- Giving less weight to the "political power" block because it deals with a small population than the other two blocks.

In the 2010 Human Development Report the GII replaced the GDI. This measure, unlike the GDI, is not influenced by the absolute level of achievement or development. Instead, like the GSI, several of the components focus on the degree of inequality in achievement between males and females on different measures while others focus on levels of women's achievement. The consequence is that a country can score well on this measure even if absolute levels of achievement are low as long as the measures for females and males are equally low.

The three equally weighted dimensions covered by the GII are reproductive health (maternal mortality ratio, adolescent fertility rate), empowerment (share of parliamentary seats held by women and men, attainment at secondary and higher education levels) and labour market participation (labour market participation rate). The rating works in the opposite direction to that of the GDI i.e. a level of 0 indicates no inequality while 1 indicates extreme inequality.

In September 2015, UN Member States adopted the Sustainable Development Goals (SDGs) to be achieved by 2030. Southern African Development Community (SADC) governments joined the rest of the world in adopting these goals.

The SDGs are especially important because they include 17 goals and 169 targets as well as 230 indicators 53 of which relate to gender. Goal five on gender equality has 14 indicators.

The new SGDI on the status of women in SADC countries is based on 36 indicators (compared to 23 in the original SGDI). These are derived from the SDGs, the SADC Protocol on Gender and Development Monitoring, Evaluation and Reporting Framework (MERF), SADC Gender Protocol Attitudes survey, the Gender and Rights Assessment (GRA) and the Media Monitoring (see Executive Summary, and Chapter 11 on Implementation). The new SGDI pushes the envelope in introducing proxy indicators for VAW using the Attitudes Survey; measures of voice using media monitoring; and peer review (the GRA) which is a "qualitative measure with a quantitative value." As explained in the Executive Summary and Chapter 11, this forms part of a continual quest to find more accurate ways of measuring the hard-to-measure aspects of gender equality.

Unlike the original SGDI which measured only six areas, the indicators are grouped under nine categories, namely Constitutional and Legal Rights (1), Governance (7), Education (5), Economy (4), GBV (4), Sexual and Reproductive Health (5), HIV and AIDS (5), Media (3) and Climate Change (2). There are, unfortunately, no indicators for the Protocol Articles on Peace Building and Conflict Resolution. The fact that there are no indicators for this area reflects the difficulty in finding sufficient data across all fifteen countries.

Within some of the categories there are disappointing gaps. Ideally, the SGDI would have included an indicator measuring the disparity in pay between women and men doing paid work. Unfortunately, as discussed in the section on other indicator measures such as the GDI, the available datasets of disaggregated earned income are heavily based on assumptions rather than on empirical data. In respect of the maternity leave indicator, the time given to a woman worker does not necessarily mean that she will receive pay while on leave. In some cases, no pay is guaranteed, in other cases only a proportion of the pay is guaranteed, and in some cases paid leave is only available to certain categories of employees, such as those employed by government.

A criticism of the new SGDI may be the number of indicators and the fact that the gaps in data for one country (Angola) meant that we could not calculate an overall SGDI for this country (this will be rectified in 2018, as the data gaps largely related to media monitoring not conducted in Angola). *However, the SGDI is the most comprehensive gender index for Southern Africa of any of the existing gender indicators, and it overcomes many of the shortfalls identified in this Annex.*

To create the composite index, two challenges needed to be addressed. The first was the differing number of indicators in the various categories and how this should be dealt with in weighting. This was necessary so that, for example, Governance, Education and Training, Health and HIV which all have five or more indicators were not given twice the importance ("weight") of Climate Change and

Constitutional and Legal Rights which have two and one indicators respectively. The second challenge was the difference in the range of "raw scores" that were possible for each indicator and how these could be standardised so that averages were not comparing apples and oranges. If this standardisation were not done, an indicator for which the score could range from 0 to 50 would have only half the weight of another indicator for which the score could range from 0 to 100.

Weighting

Each category is given equal weight by calculating the average score across the indicators in that category. So, for example, for categories with three indicators, the score for that category was the average across the three. This approach also solves the problem of how to deal with countries for which some indicators were missing, as the average was calculated on the available indicators for each country. Nevertheless, while this generated a score for all categories across all countries except for media and climate change in Angola, the averages for countries with missing indicators should be treated with caution as they are not exactly comparable with those of countries for which all indicators were available. The number of missing indicators ranged from zero in Botswana, DRC, Lesotho, Mauritius, Mozambique, Swaziland, Tanzania and Zimbabwe to six in Angola.

Standardisation

Standardisation aimed to convert all "raw scores" into values that range from 0 (for the worst possible performance) to 100 (for the best possible performance).

The indicators consist of several types in terms of what they are measuring:

- Many of the indicators measure the female percentage of people with given characteristics. All the governance, education and media indicators have this form. For these indicators, the raw score could range from 0 to 100. However, if our aim is to ensure that women do not face discrimination, then a raw score of 50 is the target. In standardisation, all scores of more than 50 - of

which several were found, for example, for tertiary education - were therefore changed to 50.

- Several of the indicators measure the percentage of women and girls with a given characteristic. Two examples of such indicators are the percentage of women using contraception and the percentage of women aged 15-24 with comprehensive knowledge on HIV and AIDS. For these indicators, the raw score could range from 0 to 100 and the score therefore did not need further standardisation.

- Several of the indicators measure the female rate for a given characteristic as a percentage of the male rate. Examples here are female and male enrolment in different levels of education. What is being measured here is the gender gap.

- Finally, two of the indicators that relate specifically to gender or women's issues have scores that fall outside the above categories. The first is the number of weeks of maternity leave to which employees are entitled. The second is the maternal mortality rate, which is expressed as the number of deaths for every 100,000 live births. For the first of these indicators, we assumed that the possible range was from 0 to 16 weeks, and calculated the actual number of weeks as a percentage of 16. For the second of these indicators, we set the possible range between 0 and 2000 out of 100,000 (see http://en.wikipedia.org/wiki/ Maternal death), and calculate a score out of 100 by dividing the raw score by 20.

A further challenge in the standardisation process was that while the majority of indicators measure a desirable characteristic, for which a high score indicates good performance, there are a few indicators that measure undesirable characteristic for which higher scores reflected poorer performance. Examples include the female share of people living with HIV, maternal mortality rate and certain of the indicator scores. For these indicators the rate was inverted by subtracting the standardised rate from 100. Detailed workings on the SGDI are available on request from alliance@genderlinks.org.za.

Regional Documents

Africa Economic Outlook 2016, African Development Bank, Organisation for Economic Co-operation and Development, United Nations Development Programme (2016).

Africa regional report on the sustainable development goals, Summary by the Economic Commission for Africa, 2015.

African Economic Outlook 2017 Entrepreneurship and Industrialisation: Entrepreneurship and Industrialisation, African Development Bank, Organisation for Economic Co-operation and Development, United Nations Development Programme (2017).

African Economic Outlook 2017, Entrepreneurship and Industrialisation.

African Leadership (2018), 'Zambia Progresses on ending Child Marriage_ Records 10% Decline' available at: http://africanleadership.co.uk/zambia-progresses-ending-child-marriage%E2%94%80-records-10-decline/ (accessed 12 June 2018).

African Union Roadmap on Harnessing the Demographic Dividend through Investments in Youth in response to AU Assembly decision (assembly/au/dec.601 (xxvi) on the 2017 theme of the year 2017.

African Woman and Child Feature service, 2010. "Beyond Numbers: Narrating the Impact of Women's Leadership in Africa."

Agencia Angola Press. "Angola: Over 6000 police officers complete training course" 31 July 2017. [accessed at angop.ao on 6 June 2018].

Aguayo, F., Kimelman, P., Saavedra, J., Kato-Wallace. (2016). Engaging Men in Public Policies for the Prevention of Violence Against Women and Girls. Santiago: EME/CulturaSalud. Washington, D.C.: Promundo-US. Panama City: UN Women and UNFPA.

AIDS Free. Lessons from GBVI in DRC. available at https://aidsfree.usaid.gov/sites/default/files/aidsfree.usaid.gov/sites/default/files/events/presentations/gbvi_5.10_gennari_moz_0.pdf (Accessed 1 June 2018).

All Africa News (18 February 2018) available http://allafrica.com/stories/201802210524.html (accessed 9 June 2018).

All Africa (2017), 'ESwatini: Kingdom Faces LGBTI Rights Review' available at http://allafrica.com/stories/ 201705010687.html (accessed 11 June 2017).

AllAfrica (2017), 'Lesotho: Ministry Finalises Gender-Based Violence Policy', available at: http://allafrica.com/ stories/201708250190.html (accessed 21 March 2018).

AllAfrica (2018), 'Hundreds of 'abandoned mothers' flock Dar es Salaam RC office for legal assistance,' available at: http://allafrica.com/stories/201804100725.html, (accessed 11 June 2018).

AllAfrica (2018), ESwatini: Parents Want 'Lesbian' Teacher Out' available at: http://allafrica.com/stories/ 201803280593.html (accessed 12 June 2018).

AllAfrica.com, 25 February 2018, Tanzania: Church Wants Girls, Parents Arrested to Curb Teenage Pregnancies.

Amnesty International (2018), Amnesty International 2017/2018 Report, Amnesty International, London.

Amnesty International (2018), Amnesty International Report 2017/2018, Amnesty International, London.

Angola Human Rights Report 2017 https://www.state.gov/documents/organization/265434.pdf.

Angop, (2012) "Quatro mulheres das FAA promovidas à classe de generais" http://www.angop.ao/angola/pt_pt/noticias/politica/2012/4/19/Quatro-mulheres-das-FAA-promovidas-classe-generais,9fe7574e-96a7-4737-be23-b0241fcd0555.html (Accessed 28/07/2017).

Annual Development Effectiveness review (2015) Level 1 Development in Africa, available at https://www.afdb.org/fileadmin/uploads/afdb/Documents/Development_Effectiveness_Review_2015/ADER_2015__En__-_Level_1.pdf

Avert website available at https://www.avert.org/professionals/hiv-around-world/sub-saharan-africa/swaziland.

Batley M, Restorative Justice In The South African Contexthttps://oldsite.issafrica.org/uploads/111CHAP2.PDF.

Britto, Pia Rebello, Stephen J. Lye, Kerrie Proulx, Aisha K. Yousafzai, Stephen G. Matthews, Tyler Vaivada, Rafael Perez-Escamilla, et al. 2016. "Nurturing Care: Promoting Early Childhood Development." Lancet 389 (10064): 91-102.

Byerly, C (2018). Technology and women's empowerment in Media and Gender a holistic Agenda, WACC Canada.

Centres for Disease Control and Prevention. (2004). Sexual Violence Prevention: Beginning the Dialogue. Atlanta, GA p. 3.

Chiramba, K, Musariri, L. and Rasesigo, G. (unpublished). Botswana Relationship Study. Gender Links.

Chiramba, K. Musariri, L and Rasesigo G, (2018-unpublished). Botswana Relationship Study. Gender Links.

Chronic Poverty Research Centre (2011).

Cited in Piers Pigou "The Zimbabwe Defense Forces have taken control of the country. What exactly happened? [Accessed at crisisgroup.org on the 4 June 2018].

Climate links (2017), Climate Change and Health in Mozambique: Impacts on diarrheal disease and Ma-laria, available at https://www.climatelinks.org/sites/default/files/asset/document/20180226_USAID-ATLAS_Mozambique-Health-and-Climate-Change.pdf.

Climatelinks (2017), Climate Risk Profile: Madagascar, available at https://www.climatelinks.org/resources/climate-change-risk-profile-madagascar

CNBC Africa (2018), 'Committee on the Rights of Persons with Disabilities Reviews the Initial Report of the Seychelles' available at: http://www.cnbcafrica.com/apo/2018/02/28/committee-on-the-rights-of-persons-with-disabilities-reviews-the-initial-report-of-the-seychelles/ (accessed 12 June 2018).

CNBCAFRICA, 24 October 2017, "Human Rights Committee Considers the Report of Mauritius".

Commission for Gender Equality (2017), 'Gender Commission Supports COSATU and SACCAWU Strike at Shoprite' available at: http://www.cge.org.za/category/press-statement/page/2/ (accessed 18 April 2018).

Commonwealth Compendium of Good Election Management Practice.

Commonwealth Secretariat (2016) Election Management: A Compendium, of Commonwealth Good Practice.

Davis-Reddy, C.L. and Vincent, K. 2017: Climate Risk and Vulnerability: A Handbook for Southern Africa (2nd Edition), Council for Scientific and Industrial Research, Pretoria, South Africa.

Davis-Reddy, C.L. and Vincent, K. 2017: Climate Risk and Vulnerability: A Handbook for Southern Africa (2nd Edition), Council for Scientific and Industrial Research, Pretoria, South Africa.

Department of State, USA. (2016). Trafficking in persons 2016 report. (0nline) available at https://www.state.gov/documents/organization/258876.pdf (accessed 14 July 2017).

Department of State, USA. Trafficking in persons 2017 report. Available at https://www.state.gov/documents/organization/271345.pdf (accessed 25 May 2018).

DHS website available at http://dhsprogram.com/Where-We-Work/Country-Main.cfm?ctry_id=39&c=Tanzania&r=1 (cited in SADC Barometer 2017).

Diala, A, (2018), "Legal integration of state laws and customary laws is inevitable" available at http://nai.uu.se/news/articles/2018/04/18/162652/index.xml (accessed 22 May 2018).

Dullah Omar Website available at https://dullahomarinstitute.org.za/women-and-democracy/notourleaders accessed 30 May 2018.

End VAW Now website http://www.endvawnow.org/en/articles/1564-one-stop-centres-osc.html accessed 2 June 2018).

Eye Witness News (2008), 'Afriforum: Presidency Files Notice to Appeal SADC Tribunal Ruling', available at: http://ewn.co.za/2018/03/23/afriforum-presidency-files-notice-to-appeal-sadc-tribunal-ruling (accessed 12 June 2018).

FHI 360. Mozambique GBV integration available at https://www.fhi360.org/sites/default/files/media/documents/resource-spt-cap-mozambique-gbv-integration.pdf (Accessed 1 June 2018).

Formalisation of informal trade in Africa: Trends, experiences and socioeconomic impacts, FAO, 2017.

Gaby Razafindrokoto, Presentation at the ISS Conference on Gender and Security, June 2015.

Gender Links, (2011). Zero tolerance to female genital mutilation (FGM).

GenderCC & LIFE (2017) A large step towards gender-just climate policies, but too little overall pro-gress: a joint statement on the outcomes of COP23, available at https://gendercc.net/fileadmin/inhalte/dokumente/6_UNFCCC/COPs/GenderCC_LIFE_Statement_COP23.pdf.

GFDRR (2016) Gender Action Plan: 2016-2021, Fall 2016 Consultative Group Meeting, available at https://www.gfdrr.org/sites/default/files/publication/gender-action-plan-2016-2021.pdf.

Ghorbani, M. (2015) Witchcraft Accusations Perpetuate Women's Oppression in Sub-Saharan Africa available at https://www.awid.org/news-and-analysis/witchcraft-accusations-perpetuate-womens-oppression-sub-saharan-africa (accessed 29 May 2018).

Girls not Brides website available at https://www.girlsnotbrides.org/kenya-becomes-19th-country-launch-african-union-campaign-end-child-marriage/ (accessed 10 June 2018).

Globo "Presidente Angolan promovou uma mulher a official general" 13 October 2014. [Accessed at dn.pt on 4 June 2018].

Govender, K et al. HIV Prevention in Adolescents and Young People in the Eastern and Southern African Region: A Review of Key Challenges Impeding Actions for an Effective Response. The Open AIDS Journal, 2018, 12, 3-00.

Government of Botswana. 2018. Country Progress Report - Botswana http://www.unaids.org/sites/default/files/country/documents/BWA_2018_countryreport.pdf accessed 10 July, 2018.

Government of the Republic of Zambia. 2018. Country Progress Report -Zambia. http://www.unaids.org/sites/default/files/country/documents/ZMB_2018_countryreport.pdf accessed 10 July, 2018.

Green, A (2017), In an apparent crackdown, Tanzania government raids NGO meeting on reproductive rights', available at: https://www.devex.com/news/in-an-apparent-crackdown-tanzania-government-raids-ngo-meeting-on-reproductive-rights-89394, (accessed 11 June 2018).

Grizzle, A. (eds). 2012. Gender-Sensitive Indicators for Media. UNESCO. Paris.

Hafkin and Taggart. 2001. Gender, Information Technology and Developing Countries: An Analytic Study. Washington D.C.: USAID, June 2001 http://pdf.usaid.gov/pdf_docs/Pnacm871.pdf.

Head of Department: Western Cape Education Department & another v S (Women's Legal Centre as Amicus Curiae) (1209/2016) [2017] ZASCA 187 (13 December 2017).

Hinde, 2017. #MeToo: All Sexual Harassment Experiences Are Worth Reporting, But Don't Feel Pressured To Share Opinion piece https://www.huffingtonpost.co.uk/entry/sexual-harassment-experiences-me-too-hashtag-pressure-to-share-stories_uk_59e5dbf1e4b0a2324d1d825e (accessed 1 June 2018).

How Zambian newspapers report on women covered http://www.panos.org.zm/wp-content/uploads/2017/12/Monthly-report-Oct-2017.pdf.

Human Rights Watch (2017), 'South Africa Events of 2017' available at https://www.hrw.org/world-report/2018/country-chapters/south-africa (accessed 10 June 2018).

Human Rights Watch (2017), You will get Nothing: Violation of Property and Inheritance Rights of Widows in Zimbabwe, Human Rights Watch, New York.

Human Rights Watch (2018), 'Malawi: Letter to Human Rights Commission re Public Inquiry into LGBTI Rights' available at: https://www.hrw.org/news/2017/08/21/malawi-letter-human-rights-commission-re-public-inquiry-lgbti-rights (accessed 1 April 2018)

Human Rights Watch (2018), World Report 2018, Human Rights Watch, New York.

Human Rights Watch, 2018, https://www.hrw.org/sites/default/files/swaziland_1.pdf.

IAS Webinar, 25 Jan 2017. The Double Burden; HIV and Cervical Cancer.

IIEC (2017), Water resource management under a changing climate in Angola's coastal.

International Campaign for Women's Right to safe Abortion (2018), 'MADAGASCAR - Attempt to legalise therapeutic abortion sabotaged' available at: http://www.safeabortionwomensright.org/madagascar-attempt-to-legalise-therapeutic-abortion-sabotaged/ (accessed 11 April 2018).

International Crisis Group. "Zimbabwe's Military-Assisted Transition and Prospects for Recovery" Briefing No.134 December 2017.

International Telecommunication Union. 2016. ICT facts and figures. Accessed from http://www.itu.int/en/ITU-D/Statistics/Documents/facts/ictfactsfigures2016.pdf.

Inter-Parliamentary Union (2016). Sexism, harassment and violence against women parliamentarians.

ISSC, IDS and UNESCO (2016), World Social Science Report 2016, Challenging Inequalities: Pathways to a Just World, UNESCO Publishing, Paris.

Jerneck, A (2018), What about Gender in Climate Change? Twelve Feminist Lessons from Development, Lund University Centre for Sustainability Studies, available on www.mdpi.com:8080/2071-1050/10/3/627/pdf.

Jewkes, R., Dunkle, K., Nduna, M., Shai, N. 2010. Intimate partner violence, relationship power inequity, and incidence of HIV infection in young women in South Africa: a cohort study. Lancet 376(9734):41-8.

Johnson, Rucker C., and C. Kirabo Jackson. 2017. "Reducing Inequality through Dynamic Complementarity: Evidence from Head Start and Public-School Spending." NBER Working Paper 23489, National Bureau of Economic Research, Cambridge, MA.

Klees, Steven J. 2017. "Will We Achieve Education for All and the Education Sustainable Development Goal?" Comparative Education Review 61 (2): 425-40.

Laura Robinson, Shelia R. Cotten, Hiroshi Ono, Anabel Quan-Haase, Gustavo Mesch, Wenhong Chen, Jeremy Schulz, Timothy M. Hale & Michael J. Stern (2015) Digital inequalities and why they matter, Information, Communication & Society, 18:5, 569-582,DOI:10.1080/1369118X.2015.1012532.

Laurent, C. (2013), The Killing of Women and Girls Around the World. Academic Council on the United Nations System (ACUNS) Vienna Liaison Office. Available at http://acuns.org/wp-content/uploads/2013/05/Claire-Laurent.pdf (accessed 3 August 2017).

Laurent, C. (2013), The Killing of Women and Girls Around the World. Academic Council on the United Nations System (ACUNS) Vienna Liaison Office. Available at http://acuns.org/wp-content/uploads/2013/05/Claire-Laurent.pdf (accessed 3 August 2017).

Leigh Johnson, 17 December, 2017. South Africa's HIV treatment programme: a phoenix rising from the ashes? https://www.groundup.org.za/article/south-africas-hiv-treatment-programme-phoenix-rising-ashes/ Accessed 5 July, 2018.

Leong, Alvin, Connecting the Dots between the UNFCCC and the SDGs (December 10, 2015). Availa-ble at SSRN: https://ssrn.com/abstract=2702831.

Lesotho Defence Force (Regular Force) (Discharge Regulations 1998).

Lesotho Population Based HIV Impact Assessment. 2017. Summary Sheet Preliminary Results.

Loiseau, E and Nowack, K 2014. Can social media effectively include women's voices in decision-making processes? OECD Development Centre. Accessed from https://www.oecd.org/dev/development-gender/DEV_socialmedia-issuespaper-March2015.pdf.

Loswick, A., Naidoo T., Smith R., Dhlamini M. and Mawowa S. (2016) "Gender, Peace and Security and the 2030 Agenda: A way forward for South Africa."

Lourenço, M.E Gender equality in media content and operations: Articulating academic studies and policy presentation https://en.unesco.org/ sites/default/files/mas_pub_genderequalitymedia_en_lkd.pdf

Lovenduski,J. and Karam,A. (1998) "Women in parliament: Making a Difference" in "Beyond Numbers: Women in Parliament." International IDEAS: p 136.

Lowe Morna, C and Shilongo, P 2004. Mainstreaming gender into media education. Gender Links, Johannesburg.

Lowe Morna, C. Dube S and Makamure, L (2017). SADC Gender Protocol Barometer 2017.

Lowe Morna, C. Makamure, L, Dube S. (2016). SADC Gender Protocol Barometer 2016. SADC Gender Protocol Alliance (cited in SADC Barometer 2017).

Lowe-Morna, 1996.

Lowe-Morna, C and Walter, D. (2009). SADC Gender Protocol Barometer, Gender Links website, available at http://genderlinks.org.za/shop/sadc-gender-protocol-baseline-barometer-2009/ (accessed 12 June 2016).

Lowe-Morna, C, 50/50 by 2030: A Handbook for Gender Inclusive Elections in Commonwealth Africa; Commonwealth Secretariat (2017).

Lowe-Morna, C., Dube, S. Makamure, L.(2017) SADC Gender Protocol Barometer (online) available at http://genderlinks.org.za/shop/sadc-gender-protocol-barometer-2017/ (accessed 20 May 2018).

Lowe-Morna, C., Dube, S. Makamure, L., Robinson, K, (2014) SADC Gender Protocol Barometer (online) available at http://genderlinks.org.za/shop/sadc-gender-protocol-barometer-2016/ (accessed 12 July 2017).

Mabetha (2018) GL News Service http://genderlinks.org.za/news/lesotho-domestic-violence-bill-2018-beacon-hope-ending-gbv/ (accessed 25 May 2018).

Machisa, M, T. and. Musariri L. (2013). Peace Begins at Home, the Gender Based Violence Indicators Study, Limpopo Province of South Africa. Gender Links.

Malawi Post "Malawi Defence Force Graduates 1463 recruits; urged to desist from Politics" 26 November 2017.

Matope, T. "Female Officers up to the task of leading army" Lesotho Times October 7, 2017.

Melton, CL. How HIV affects cervical cancer risks and outcomes. https://www.infectiousdiseaseadvisor.com/hivaids/hiv-and-cervical-cancer-risk-outcomes/article/713414/ accessed 2 July, 2018.

Michael Aeby. 2018. Peace and Security Challenges in Southern Africa: Governance Deficits and Lacklustre Regional Conflict Management. Policy Note No.4. Nordiska Africa Institute.

Minerson, Todd, H. Carolo, T. Dinner, C. Jones. (2011). Issue Brief: Engaging Men and Boys to Reduce and Prevent Gender-Based Violence. Status of Women Canada. Available at http://whiteribbon.ca/wp-content/uploads/2012/12/wrc_swc_issuebrief.pdf (accessed 29 July 2017).

Motivations for Voluntary Medical Male Circumcision Among Adolescents in South Africa, Tanzania, and Zimbabwe. https://www.hivsharespace.net/resource/age-differences-perceptions-and-motivations-voluntary-medical-male-circumcision-among accessed July 5, 2018.

Mucuta, D. (2017) "Bravura das Mulheres nas fileiras das FAA" http://jornaldeangola.sapo.ao/reportagem/bravura_das_mulheres__nas_fileiras_das_faa (Accessed 28/07/2017).

Musariri L., Nyambo, V., Machisa, M, T., Chiramba, K. (2014). The Gender Based Violence Indicators Study, Western Cape. Gender Links. Available at http://genderlinks.org.za/wpcontent/uploads/imported/articles/attachments/19466_chp6_gbv_wc_pg89-pg108lr.pdf#page/10 (accessed 1 August 2017).

Musariri L., Nyambo, V., Machisa, M, T., Chiramba, K. (2015). The Gender Based Violence Indicators Study, Lesotho. Gender Links.

Musariri, L. and. Chiramba K, Dimensions of VAW in selected areas of Zambia, unpublished.

Musariri, L. Nyambo, V. Machisa, MT, and Chiramba, K. (2014) Lesotho GGBV Baseline Study. Gender Links.

Musariri, L., Machisa M, T,. Nyambo, V. and Chiramba, K. (2014) The Gender based violence Indicators Study: Lesotho. Gender Links. available at http://genderlinks.org.za/programme-web-menu/publications/gender-based-violence-indicators-study-lesotho-2015-02-27/

Musariri, L (2018) Field notes: Masculinities and violence research project, Johannesburg. (Unpublished).

Namibian Broadcasting Corporation (2017), 'Commonwealth impressed with Namibia's Gender Equality in Decision-Making Structures' available at: https://www.nbc.na/news/commonwealth-impressed-namibias-gender-equality-decision-making-structures.10097 (accessed 27 March 2018). Ndlovu, S and Nyamweda T. (2015) Whose News Whose Views. Southern Africa Gender and Media Progress Study.

Newsday (2018), 'Speaker blasts Tsvangirai family', available at: https://www.newsday.co.zw/2018/03/speaker-blasts-tsvangirai-family/ (accessed 11 June 2018).

NewsDeeply (2017), 'Drought Threatens to Undo Mozambique's Gender Equality Progress' available at: https://www.newsdeeply.com/womenandgirls/articles/2017/01/19/drought-threatens-undo-mozambiques-gender-equality-progress (accessed 18 April 2018).

Njeuhmeli, E. et al. Scaling Up Voluntary Medical Male Circumcision for Human Immunodeficiency Virus Prevention for Adolescents and Young Adult Men: A Modeling Analysis of Implementation and Impact in Selected Countries. https://www.hivsharespace.net/resource/scaling-voluntary-medical-male-circumcision-human-immunodeficiency-virus-prevention accessed July 5, 2018.

North, L. 2010. The Gender 'Problem' in Australia Journalism Education. Accessed from https://ssrn.com/abstract=2015844 or http://dx.doi.org/10.2139/ssrn.2015844.

Observer website. Available at http://www.observer.org.sz/news/74803-cops-trained-on-gbv.html (accessed 1 August 2017).

OECD Gender Index, 2014.

Oregon Violence Against Women Prevention Plan; Oregon Department of Human Services; Office of Disease Prevention Epidemiology.

OSISA (2013), 'Tough times for LGBTI in Namibia too' available at: http://www.osisa.org/lgbti/blog/tough-times-lgbti-namibia-too (accessed on 17 March 2018).

OSISA: Women and the Extractive Industry in Southern Africa.

OSISA: Women working in the informal economy: Challenges and Policy Considerations, 2015.

Padovani, C (2018) Gendering Media Policy Research and Communication Governance, Javnost - The Public, 25:1-2, 256-264, DOI: 10.1080/13183222.2018.1423941.

Parliament. "Spotlight on Ongoing Cuts to Defence and Military Veterans Budget During Budget Vote debate. 26 May 2017. Peacewomen.org [accessed on 20 May 2018].

PEPFAR. 2018. PEPFAR 2018 Report to Congress. Washington, DC. https://www.pepfar.gov/documents/organization/279889.pdf Accessed 9 July, 2018.

Peter Fabricus. 2018. "Is another Boko Haram or al Shabaab erupting in Mozambique?" ISS Today 14 June.

Pincock K, (2018), 'Punishment won't stop teenage pregnancies in Tanzania because 'bad behaviour' isn't the cause', available at: https://theconversation.com/punishment-wont-stop-teenage-pregnancies-in-tanzania-because-bad-behaviour-isnt-the-cause-90187, (accessed on 9 June 2018).

Pindula (2018), 'Mudede sued for not allowing men to acquire birth certificates for their children' available at: https://news.pindula.co.zw/2018/04/05/mudede-sued-for-not-allowing-men-to-acquire-birth-certificates-for-their-children/ (accessed 10 June 2018),

Pindula News (2018), 'Updated: Tsvangirai Family Disowns Elizabeth, Planning To Grab Entire Inheritance', available at: https://news.pindula.co.zw/2018/02/19/tsvangirai-family-disowns-elizabeth-planning-grab-entire-inheritance/ (accessed 11 June 2018).

Population Council (2017), 'Child Marriage in Zambia' available at: http://www.popcouncil.org/uploads/pdfs/2017RH_ChildMarriageZambia_brief.pdf (accessed 15 April 2018).

Powell, A. (2015). Seeking rape justice: Formal and informal responses to sexual violence through technosocial counter-publics. Theoretical Criminology.

Priest from the Roman Catholic Church, Rev Father Leonard Kasimila.

Private Lieketso Mokhele and Ors v The Commander of the Lesotho Defence Force and Ors, CIV/APN/442/16.

Promise. Washington, DC: World Bank. doi: 10.1596/978-1-4648-1096-1. License: Creative Commons Attribution CC BY 3.0 IGO.

Promotion, protection and enjoyment of human rights on the Internet: ways to bridge the gender digital divide from a human rights perspective.

Pseudonym used in the "I' story collected by GL as part of the GBV Relationship Study.

Quote by Tarcila Rivera, Indigenous Rights Activist from Peru, Spotlight Initiative CSW 2018 http://www.unwomen.org/en/news/stories/2018/3/news-coverage-csw62-side-event-on-the-eu-un-spotlight-initiative (accessed 2 June 2018).

Ramuhovhi and Others v President of the Republic of South Africa and Others (CCT194/16) [2017] ZACC 41; 2018 (2) BCLR 217 (CC); 2018 (2) SA 1 (CC) (30 November 2017).

Reporters Without Borders https://rsf.org/en/ranking.

Republic of Mauritius Statistics on HIV/AIDS (as at end of June 2016). http://health.govmu.org/English/Documents/HIVJun%20web2016.pdf. Last accessed 8 July, 2017.

Republic of South Africa (2018), Ministry Update for Department of Energy, available at https://www.ipp-projects.co.za/PressCentre/GetPressRelease?fileid...923C...

Research and Advocacy Unit available at http://researchandadvocacyunit.org/blog/2017/07/07/politically-motivated-violence-against-women-zimbabwe (accessed 2 June 2018).

RiseUp (Undated), 'Ending Child Marriage in Malawi' available at: http://www.riseuptogether.org/wp-content/uploads/2016/09/Malawi-Case-Study-FINAL.pdf (accessed 18 April 2018).

SADC Gender and Development Monitor 2016.

SADC Industrialisation strategy and roadmap 2015-2063,http://www.ilo.org/wcmsp5/groups/public/---africa/---ro-addis_ababa/---ilo-pretoria/documents/meetingdocument/wcms_391013.pdf.

SADC Protocol on Employment and Labour.

SADC Protocol on Gender and Development Article 29 (1-7).

SANBI (2017) Climate Change Adaptation Southern African Development Community : Perspectives for SADC, available on https://www.sanbi.org/wp-content/uploads/2018/04/ltas-factsheet-1.pdf.

SARDC, SADC. 2016 SADC Gender and Development Monitor 2016.SADC, SARDC, Gaborone, Harare.

SHIMS2. 2017. Swaziland HIV incidence measurement survey2. A population based HIV Impact Assessment. Summary sheet.

Sida (2015). Preventing and Responding to Gender-Based Violence: Expressions and Strategies available at http://www.sida.se/contentassets/3a820dbd152f4fca98bacde8a8101e15/preventing-and-responding-to-gender-based-violence.pdf (accessed 3 July 2017).

Skosana, I (2017), 'Less than 7% of health facilities nationwide offer abortions - Amnesty International', available at: http://bhekisisa.org/article/2017-02-14-00-only-260-health-facilities-nationwide-offer-abortions-amnesty-international/ (accessed 11 June 2018).

South Africa Department of Justice available at http://www.justice.gov.za/rj/rj.html (accessed 27 May 2018).

South Africa Violence Prevention Model and Action Plan developed by Gender Links, UNICEF (2008). Available at https://www.unicef.org/southafrica/SAF_resources_violenceprevmodel.pdf.

South African Government website www.dac.gov.za/content/mrm-arts-and-culture-hosts-imbizo-anti-femicide-soweto (accessed 21 May 2018).

Spears, G. and Seydegart, K. 2000. Who Makes the News? Global Media Monitoring Project 2000.

Swazi Observer (2018), 'FODSWA President calls for Tertiary Education for the Disabled' available at https://www.pressreader.com/eSwatini/swazi-observer/20180329/281719795135548 (accessed 10 June 2018).

Swaziland Joint Civil Society. (2017). Civil Society report on the Implementation of the Covenant on Civil and Political Rights 120th session of the Human Rights Committee.

Swaziland Joint Civil Society. (2017). Civil Society report on the Implementation of the Covenant on Civil and Political Rights 120th session of the Human Rights Committee.

The 2016 Africa regional report on the sustainable development goals, United Nations Economic Commission for Africa, 2015 Addis Ababa, Ethiopia.

The African Exponent. "Countries with the best police force in Africa" June 6, 2018.

The Citizen (2017), 'Angola Backs Down on Total Abortion Ban' available at https://citizen.co.za/news/news-africa/1542075/angola-backs-total-abortion-ban/ (accessed 1 April 2018).

The Citizen (2018), 'King Mswati's 8th wife commits suicide following 'abuse', available at: https://citizen.co.za/news/news-africa/1880787/2king-mswatis-8th-wife-commits-suicide/ (accessed 10 June 2018).

The Herald. "President promotes 25 Air Force Officers. 30 November 2017.

The Maravi Post (2017), 'Malawi female judges commit on women rights protection; sign MoU, to provide legal clinics,' available at: http://www.maravipost.com/malawi-female-judges-commit-women-rights-protection-sign-mou-provide-legal-clinics/ (accessed 30 March 2018).

Thompson, C. (2017). A Life of Its Own: An Assessment of the 16 Days of Activism Against Gender-Based Violence Campaign, Center for Women's Global Leadership, New Jersey available at http://16dayscwgl.rutgers.edu/downloads/16-days-documents-general/1500-16-days-campaign-assessment-report/file (quoted in Barometer 2017).

Thompson, C. (2017). A Life of Its Own: An Assessment of the 16 Days of Activism Against Gender-Based Violence Campaign, Center for Women's Global Leadership, New Jersey available at http://16dayscwgl.rutgers.edu/downloads/16-days-documents-general/1500-16-days-campaign-assessment-report/file (cited in Barometer 2017).

Twaweza (2017), Unfinished Business: Tanzanians' Views on the Stalled Constitutional Review Process, Sauti za Wananchi. Brief No. 44.

UIS Fact sheet 39, The world needs almost 69 million new teachers to reach the 2030 education goals, UNESCO, October 2016.

UN Expert Group (2007) available at http://www.un.org/womenwatch/daw/egm/IndicatorsVAW/IndicatorsVAW_EGM_report.pdf (accessed 10 June 2018).

UN Women website available on http://www.unwomen.org/en/news/stories/2018/3/press-release---eu-un-spotlight-initiative-urges-action-on-vaw (accessed 29 May 2018).

UNAIDS RSA ESA. April 2018. Presentation to SADC meeting on Prevention. "Reinvigorating prevention in SADC Region Are we on track ".

UNAIDS. 2017. Blind Spot. Geneva, Switzerland.

UNAIDS/UNICEF (2016) 'All in to end adolescent AIDS: A progress report' [pdf.

UNDP (2017), Zimbabwe Human Development Report, Climate Change and Human Development: Towards Building a Resilient Nation, available at http://hdr.undp.org/sites/default/files/reports/2842/undp_zw_2017zhdr_full.pdf.

UNDP: Social Protection in Africa, A Review of Potential Contribution and Impact on Poverty Reduction, March 2014.

UNESCO (2017), Women underrepresented in decision-making on climate change, available on http://www.unesco.org/new/en/media-services/single-view/news/women_underrepresented_in_decision_making_on_climate_change/ (accessed on 11July 2017).

UNFCCC (2017), Achieving the goal of gender balance: Technical paper by the secretariat, available on https://unfccc.int/resource/docs/2017/tp/08.pdf.

UNFPA ESA. 2017. Menstrual Health Management in East and Southern Africa: a Review Paper. Johannesburg, South Africa.

UNHCR Congolese Situation: Responding to the Needs of Displaced Congolese and Refugees. Supplementary appeal January to December 2018. [Accessed at reporting.unhcr.org on 19 May 2018].

UNHCR, 2018. The Democratic Republic of the Congo: Regional Refugee Response Plan, January - December 2018.

UNICEF (2018) 'Child Marriage' available at: http://www.unicef.org/search/search.php?q_en=child+marriage&go.x=0&go.y=0 (accessed 12 June 2018).

UNICEF Zimbabwe Media Centre. Cervical Cancer Vaccine Introduced in Zimbabwe. https://www.unicef.org/zimbabwe/media_21520.html accessed 5 July, 2018.

United Kingdom Government (2018), 'PM speaks at the Commonwealth Joint Forum Plenary: 17 April 2018', available at: https://www.gov.uk/government/speeches/pm-speaks-at-the-commonwealth-joint-forum-plenary-17-april-2018 (accessed 11 June 2018).

United Nations Children's Fund, Child Marriage: Latest trends and future prospects, UNICEF, New York, 2018. https://data.unicef.org/wp-content/uploads/2018/06/Child-Marriage-data-brief.pdf Last accessed 29 June, 2018.

United Nations Children's Fund (UNICEF) and the World Health Organization (WHO), 2017. Tracking Progress towards Universal Coverage for Reproductive, Newborn and Child Health: The 2017 Report. Washington, DC: https://data.unicef.org/wp-content/uploads/2018/01/ Countdown-2030.pdf   Accessed 17 June, 2018.

United Nations Poverty-Environment Initiative (2017) Gender, Energy and Policy : A review of energy policies in East and Southern Africa, available at http://www.unpei.org/sites/default/files/publications/Gender%2C%20Energy%20and%20Policy-%20A%20Review%20of%20Energy%20Policies%20in%20East%20and%20Southern%20Africa-%20Web-%20HR.pdf.

United Nations website available at http://www.un.org/en/spotlight-initiative/index.shtml (accessed 23 May 2018).

United Nations. (2007). Indicators to measure violence against women: Expert Group Meeting Report, United Nations, available at http://www.un.org/womenwatch/daw/egm/IndicatorsVAW/IndicatorsVAW_EGM_report.pdf (accessed June 2016).

United Nations. 2013. Statement by Malawi Minister available at http://www.un.org/womenwatch/daw/csw/csw57/generaldiscussion/memberstates/malawi.pdf (accessed 1 August 2017).

University of Pretoria (2015), African Disability Rights Year Book (2015) Volume 3, Pretoria.

UNODC Global Study available at https://www.unodc.org/gsh/ (accessed 3 June 2018).

UNODC Report (2016) available https://www.unodc.org/documents/justice-and-prison-reform/LegalAid/Global_Study_on_Legal_Aid_-_FINAL.pdf (cited in SADC Barometer 2017).

UNODC Website at http://www.unodc.org/southernafrica/en/stories/unodc-continues-to-combat-gender-based-violence--meets-sadc-to-strengthen-cooperation-on-criminal-justice.html (accessed 1 June 2018).

UNWOMEN Thematic Brief on Women's Leadership and Political Participation. See http://www.unwomen.org/-/media/headquarters/attachments/sections/library/publications/2013/12/un%20womenlgthembriefuswebrev2%20pdf.pdf. Retrieved 28 July 2017.

USAID (2018), Building urban resilience to climate change: A review of Madagascar, available at https://reliefweb.int/report/madagascar/building-urban-resilience-climate-change-review-madagascar.

USAID. (2016). Angola Human Rights Practices Report. Available at https://www.state.gov/documents/organization/265434.pdf (accessed 29 May 2018).

USAID. 2017. Police Action Planning Report available at https://aidsfree.usaid.gov/sites/default/files/2017.1.4_police-action-planning-report_v2.pdf (accessed 1 August 2017).

Viswanathan, H. H. S (2018) Africa's Agenda 2063: a document of hope, available at https://www.orfonline.org/research/africas-agenda-2063-a-document-of-hope/.

VOA, 17 February 2017, 'Tanzania Stops Private Health Centers From Offering AIDS Services'.

Vukuzenzele (2014), 'Women, people with disabilities empowered' available at https://www.vukuzenzele.gov.za/women-people-disabilities-empowered (accessed 10 June 2018).

Warren S (2018), 'In Lesotho, Women say they are Finding their Abortion on Facebook' available at: https://edition.cnn.com/2018/03/07/health/lesotho-abortions-asequals-intl/index.html, accessed 12 June 2018.

Water Power Magazine (2017), Addressing the energy-water nexus in Southern Africa, available at http://www.waterpowermagazine.com/opinion/opinionaddressing-the-energy-water-nexus-in-southern-africa-5818909/.

WHO, 2017. Leading the realization of human rights to health and through health: report of the High-Level Working Group on the Health and Human Rights of Women, Children and Adolescents: Report of the High-Level Working Group on the Health and Human Rights of Women, Children and Adolescents. http://apps.who.int/iris/bitstream/handle/10665/255540/9789241512459-eng.pdf;j Accessed 16 June, 2017.

Wikipedia (2017), Climate Change and Gender, available on https://en.wikipedia.org/wiki/Climate_change_and_gender (accessed 11 July 2017).

Wikipedia, Angola [accessed at en.wikipedia.org on 5 June 2018].

World Bank. 2018. The Economic Impacts of Child Marriage: Women's Health Brief. http://documents.worldbank.org/curated/en/794581498512672050/pdf/116834-BRI-P151842-PUBLIC-EICM-Brief-WomensHealth-PrintReady.pdf Accessed 26 June, 2018.

World Bank. 2018. World Development Report 2018: Learning to Realize Education's.

World Health Organisation (2002). The world health report 2002 Reducing risks, promoting healthy life, World Health Organisation.

World Health Organization (WHO) and the United Nations Children's Fund (UNICEF), 2017. Progress on drinking water, sanitation and hygiene: 2017 update and SDG baselines. Geneva: Switzerland.

World Resources Institute (2018), 'Making Women's Voices Count in Community Decision-Making on Land Investments' available at: https://www.business-humanrights.org/en/tanzania-mozambique-poor-rural-women-discriminated-in-compensation-after-displacement-to-pave-way-for-agribusiness-says-report (accessed 11 June 2018).

World Wide Web Foundation. 2016. Women's Rights online. Accessed from http://webfoundation.org/docs/2016/09/WRO-Gender-Report-Card_Overview.pd.

www.sadc.int.

Young women and the demographic dividend, African Women's Development and Communication Network (FEMNET), June 2017.

Websites

http://allafrica.com/stories/201805250765.html

http://blogs.lse.ac.uk/europpblog/2017/08/12/violence-against-women-in-politics-is-rising-and-its-a-clear-threat-to-democracy/ (accessed 2 June 2018).

http://cdn.agilitycms.com/who-makes-the-news/Imported/reports_2015/global/gmmp_global_report_en.pdf

http://cyber.law.harvard.edu/population/abortion/Zimbabwe.abo.html

http://databank.worldbank.org/data/reports.aspx?source=Education%20Statistics#

http://destinationreporterindia.com/2018/03/23/seychelles-launches-innovative-climate-adaptation-scheme/

http://dhsprogram.com/topics/gender-Corner/index.cfm (cited in SADC Barometer 2017)

http://documents.worldbank.org/curated/en/481341525730456994/pdf/Project-Information-Document-Integrated-Safeguards-Data-Sheet-DRC-Gender-Based-Violence-Prevention-and-Response-Project-P166763.pdf

http://documents.worldbank.org/curated/en/481341525730456994/pdf/Project-Information-Document-Integrated-Safeguards-Data-Sheet-DRC-Gender-Based-Violence-Prevention-and-Response-Project-P166763.pdf

http://downloads.bbc.co.uk/worldservice/trust/pdf/AMDI/botswana/amdi_botswana3_media_health.pdf

http://eduictseychelles.blogspot.ca/

http://genderlinks.org.za/barometer-newsletter/zero-tolerance-to-female-genital-mutilation-fgm-2011-02-01/ (accessed 30 July 2017)

http://library.fes.de/pdf-files/bueros/africa-media/09541.pdf

http://library.fes.de/pdf-files/bueros/africa-media/10575.pdf

http://mwnation.com/female-engineers-want-girls-field/

http://sdg.iisd.org/news/au-summit-addresses-alignment-between-agenda-2063-paris-agreement-and-2030-agenda/

http://sheconquerssa.co.za/ and http://www.kznhealth.gov.za/mediarelease/2018/KZN-health-MEC-excited-about-the-impact-of%20%E2%80%93she-conquers-campaign-at-umgungundlovu27022018.htm   accessed July 15, 2018.

http://southsouthnorth.org/wp-content/uploads/Botswana-diagnostic-2017.05.10.pdf

http://southsouthnorth.org/wp-content/uploads/Lesotho-diagnostic-2017.05.10.pdf

http://srhr.org/abortion-policies/country/swaziland/

http://srhr.org/abortion-policies/documents/countries/01-Angola-Penal-Code-2014.pdf

http://uncoveringthedrc.blogspot.co.za/2012/01/media-landscape-in-drc.html

http://womengenderclimate.org/about-us/

http://www.unaids.org/en/resources/presscentre/featurestories/2018/june/transgender- dignity-key-to-health-and-well-being Accessed 10 July, 2018.

http://www.unesco.org/new/en/brasilia/about-this-office/single-view/news/education_2030_incheon_declaration_and_and_framework_for_ac/

http://www.unesco.org/new/en/education/themes/leading-the-international-agenda/efareport/

http://www.unesco-ci.org/ipdcprojects/countries/madagascar

http://www.unwomen.org/en/get-involved/step-it-up/media-compact#sthash.INLxFHhx.dpuf

http://www.unwomen.org/en/news/stories/2015/11/press-release-gmmp#sthash.E8TuFzbf.dpuf

http://www.wecf.eu/english/campaigns/2014/Gender-Constituency.php

http://www.who.int/news-room/fact-sheets/detail/maternal-mortality Accessed June 17, 2018.

http://www.who.int/whosis/whostat2006ContraceptivePrevalenceRate.pdf

http://www.worldbank.org/en/publication/wdr2018

http://www.worldbank.org/en/publication/wdr2018

http://www.zw.undp.org/content/zimbabwe/en/home/presscenter/articles/2017/11/27/climate-change-towards-a-national-adaptation-plan-for-zim.htm

http://www4.unfccc.int/ndcregistry/PublishedDocuments/Lesotho%20First/Lesotho%27s%20INDC%20Report%20%20-%20September%202015.pdf

https://africanlii.org/content/lesotho-high-court-recognises-sexual-and-reproductive-rights-female-soldiers

https://edition.cnn.com/2018/04/12/africa/tanzania-blogging-internet-freedoms-africa/index.html

https://en.unesco.org/gem-report/report/2015/education-all-2000-2015-achievements-and-challenges

https://en.unesco.org/training-gender-sensitive-indicators-media

https://freedomhouse.org/report/freedom-press/2014/mozambique

https://freedomhouse.org/report/freedom-press/2015/angola

https://freedomhouse.org/report/freedom-press/2016/south-africa

https://gendercc.net/genderunfccc/unfccc-conferences/bonn-2017.html

https://gendercc.net/genderunfccc/unfccc-conferences/bonn-2017.html

https://laws.parliament.na/cms_documents/abortion-and-sterilization-c5c7b99b28.pdf

https://lesotholii.org/ls/legislation/num-act/6

https://medium.com/@FP2020Global_20685/madagascar-enacts-historic-family-planning-law-8ac7ab62e0ad. Accessed June 20, 2018

https://mg.co.za/article/2018-02-09-00-water-crisis-look-to-sas-renewable-energy-programme-for-solutions

https://ndcpartnership.org/sites/all/themes/ndcp_v2/docs/country-engagement/countries/NCDP_Outlook_Namibia_v1b.pdf

 https://partneraid.ch/en/about-us/

https://pmg.org.za/committee-meeting/25617/

https://qz.com/1216791/seychelles-swaps-debt-for-marine-conservation-climate-change/

https://rsf.org/en/comoros

https://southerntimesafrica.com/site/news/africa-grapples-with-huge-disparities-in-education-higher-enrolment-numbers-mask-exclusion-and-inefficiencies

https://srhr.org/abortion-policies/documents/countries/01-Seychelles-Termination-of-Pregnancy-Act-2012.pdf

https://srhr.org/abortion-policies/documents/countries/02-Mauritius-Criminal-Code-Amendment-Act-2012.pdf
https://sz.usembassy.gov/remarks-ambassador-lisa-peterson-sadc-charter-women-science-engineering-technology-national-archives-lobamba/
https://sz.usembassy.gov/remarks-ambassador-lisa-peterson-sadc-charter-women-science-engineering-technology-national-archives-lobamba/
https://tradingeconomics.com/angola/public-spending-on-education-total-percent-of-government-expenditure-wb-data.html
https://undp-adaptation.exposure.co/bridging-gaps-in-zambia
https://unfccc.int/topics/gender/the-big.../gender-in-the-intergovernmental-process
https://webfoundation.org/docs/2018/03/Using-USAFs-to-Close-the-Gender-Digital-Divide-in-Africa.pdf
https://wedocs.unep.org/bitstream/handle/20.500.11822/20505/Energy_profile_Lesotho.pdf?sequence=1&isAllowed=y
https://womeninleadership.hivos.org/an-analysis-of-zambias-sixteen-councillor-by-elections-in-2018/
https://www.afdb.org/en/news-and-events/africa-day-at-cop23-17551/
https://www.avert.org/professionals/hiv-programming/prevention/pre-exposure-prophylaxis accessed 10 July, 2018.
https://www.avert.org/professionals/hiv-programming/prevention/preventionmothertochildtransmission Last accessed 3 July, 2018.
https://www.avert.org/professionals/hiv-programming/prevention/voluntary male medical circumcision. Last accessed 3 July, 2018.
https://www.awid.org/news-and-analysis/witchcraft-accusations-perpetuate-womens-oppression-sub-saharan-africa (accessed 29 May 2018).
https://www.brookings.edu/blog/africa-in-focus/2017/06/02/even-before-the-u-s-left-the-paris-agreement-africa-stepped-up-to-the-plate-on-climate-change/
https://www.brookings.edu/blog/africa-in-focus/2018/04/02/a-house-of-justice-for-africa-resurrecting-the-sadc-tribunal/
https://www.ced.org/blog/entry/the-economic-impact-of-early-exposure-to-stem-education
https://www.dandc.eu/en/article/order-manage-its-current-energy-crisis-malawi-turns-coal
https://www.dropbox.com/home/Harmonizing%20on%20GBV%20statistics_workshop?preview=GBV+Workshop+Outcome+Statement+-+09+March+2018.pdf
https://www.esi-africa.com/drc-holds-renewable-energy-potential-reveals-study/
https://www.esi-africa.com/madagascar-joins-scaling-solar-scheme-with-added-energy-storage/
https://www.esi-africa.com/madagascar-targets-add-300mw-2019/
https://www.esi-africa.com/mauritius-italy-re-energy-efficiency/
https://www.export.gov/article?id=Angola-Electric-Power-Generation
https://www.export.gov/article?id=Angola-Electric-Power-Generation
https://www.ft.com/content/ecaa3e2c-8436-11e7-94e2-c5b903247afd
https://www.girlsnotbrides.org/child-marriage/tanzania/ (accessed 10 June 2018).
https://www.girlsnotbrides.org/kenya-becomes-19th-country-launch-african-union-campaign-end-child-marriage/
https://www.giz.de/en/worldwide/53743.html
https://www.globalfinancingfacility.org/sites/gff_new/files/Tanzania_One_Plan_II.pdf
https://www.globalpartnership.org/blog/can-pre-primary-education-help-solve-learning-crisis-africa
https://www.globalpartnership.org/country/democratic-republic-congo
https://www.google.co.za/#safe=off&q=abortion+bill+1991+democratic+republic+of+Congo (UN Publication)
https://www.hivsharespace.net/resource/females-peer-influence-and-support-adolescent-males-receiving-voluntary-medical-male .accessed July 5, 2018.
https://www.hivsharespace.net/resource/parental-communication-engagement-and-support-during-adolescent-voluntary-medical-male .accessed July 5, 2018.
https://www.hrw.org/report/2017/02/14/i-had-dream-finish-school/barriers-secondary-education-tanzania
https://www.hrw.org/report/2018/04/05/bitter-harvest/child-labor-and-human-rights-abuses-tobacco-farms-zimbabwe
https://www.hrw.org/world-report/2018/country-chapters/angola Accessed 15 June, 2018.
https://www.hsph.harvard.edu/population/abortion/ZAMBIA.abo.htm
https://www.ipu.org/resources/publications/reports/2018-03/women-in-parliament-in-2017-year-in-review
https://www.ipu.org/resources/publications/reports/2018-03/women-in-parliament-in-2017-year-in-review
https://www.iwmf.org/wp-content/uploads/2013/09/IWMF-Global-Report-Summary.pdf
https://www.nature.org/ourinitiatives/regions/africa/seychelles-msp-phase-1-final.pdf
https://www.ncbi.nlm.nih.gov/pmc/articles/PMC1461415/
https://www.newera.com.na/2018/03/02/namibia-needs-n400bn-for-climate-change/
https://www.news24.com/Africa/News/drc-conflict-weak-education-leave-millions-out-of-school-20170911
https://www.news24.com/SouthAfrica/News/girls-pit-toilet-death-reveals-sad-state-of-school-sanitation-ngos-20180316
https://www.newsday.co.zw/2018/06/making-a-case-for-25-young-womens-quota-in-zimbabwe/
https://www.parliament.gov.za/storage/app/media/Docs/bill/9febb155-8582-4a15-bf12-5961db2828c2.pdf
https://www.sadc.int/about-sadc/sadc-institutions/org/
https://www.sadc.int/news-events/news/botswana-signs-revised-sadc-protocol-gender-and-development/
https://www.sadc.int/themes/meteorology-climate/climate-change-adaptation/
https://www.sadc.int/themes/meteorology-climate/climate-change-adaptation/
https://www.sanbi.org/wp-content/uploads/2018/03/ltas-factsheet-1.pdf
https://www.shedecides.com accessed June 27, 2018.
https://www.sida.se/English/press/current-topics-archive/2016/african-network-uses-information-to-fight-gender-based-violence/
https://www.thedailyvox.co.za/three-soldiers-in-the-lesotho-army-are-fighting-their-dismissals-over-pregnancy-fatima-moosa/
https://www.timeslive.co.za/news/africa/2018-05-24-analysis-witch-prostitute-women-to-face-sexism-in-zimbabwe-elections/
https://www.traveller24.com/Explore/Green/cop23-climatic-extremes-sas-biggest-climate-change-concern-20171114
https://www.unesco.org.ls/single-post/2017/11/13/Lesotho-National-Commission-hosts-Intergenerational-Dialogue-of-women-in-STEM-on-the-11th-October-2017
https://www.unicef.org/media/media_53234.html
https://www.unicef.org/publications/files/SWCR2013_ENG_Lo_res_24_Apr_2013.pdf
https://www.unicef.org/violencestudy/reports.html
https://www.usaid.gov/powerafrica/botswana
https://www.weforum.org/reports/the-global-gender-gap-report-2017 ; http://uis.unesco.org/country/ZA Accessed April 2018.
https://www.womenonwaves.org/en/page/5009/abortion-law-mozambique
https://zimbabwe.unfpa.org/en/news/zimbabwe-school-health-policy-promote-sexual-and-reproductive-health-schools. Accessed June 30, 2018.

The SADC Protocol on Gender and Development

Encompasses

commitments made in all regional, global and continental instruments for achieving gender equality.

Enhances

these instruments through a Monitoring, Evaluation and Reporting Framework.

Advances

gender equality by ensuring accountability by all SADC Member States, as well as providing a form for the sharing of best practices, peer support and review.

SADC GENDER PROTOCOL ALLIANCE

Lightning Source UK Ltd.
Milton Keynes UK
UKHW05f1627181018

330749UK00005B/22/P